William Richards

A pocket dictionary, Welsh-English = Geiriadur llogell, cymraeg a saesoneg

William Richards

A pocket dictionary, Welsh-English = Geiriadur llogell, cymraeg a saesoneg

ISBN/EAN: 9783744738729

Printed in Europe, USA, Canada, Australia, Japan

Cover: Foto ©Paul-Georg Meister /pixelio.de

More available books at **www.hansebooks.com**

A POCKET DICTIONARY,
WELSH—ENGLISH.

GEIRIADUR LLOGELL
CYMRAEG A SAESONEG,

WEDI EI

ADOLYGU, EI DDIWYGIO, A'I HELAETHU,

GAN

W. RICHARDS, LL.D.

WREXHAM:

ARGRAFFWYD A CHYHOEDDWYD GAN R. HUGHES AND SON.
LONDON: SIMPKIN, MARSHALL, AND CO.

RHAGYMADRODD.

Mae yr awyddfryd cynyddol sydd yn mhlith y Cymry i ymgydnabod yn fwy â'r iaith Saesoneg yn un o arwyddion gobeithiol yr amserau. Am bob un o'n cydgenedl ag oedd yn deall Saesoneg yn nechreuad y ganrif hon, mae yn debyg na fethem wrth ddyweud fod ugeiniau os nad canoedd yn ei deall yn awr. O'r ochor arall, y mae rhifedi mwy nag a feddylid o'r Saeson sy'n ymweled a'n gwlad yn ystod misoedd yr haf yn gwneuthur ymdrech nid bychan i ddysgu Cymraeg.

Ond mae yn eglur nas gall neb feistroli iaith estronol heb gymorth geiriaduron. Nis gellir dyweud fod y gwahanol Eiriaduron sydd yn awr ar y maes yn rhai *ymarferol* o herwydd y mae ynddynt filoedd o eiriau nad arferwyd erioed, ac ond odid nad arferir byth; ac y mae hyny, wrth reswm, yn chwyddo y gwaith, nes peri ei fod allan o gyraedd y dosparth iselradd. *Geiriadur rhâd ymarferol* yw hwn i'r lluaws nad allant hyfforddio i gael rhai mwy.

Ond er fod llawer o'r geiriau anarferedig wedi eu gadael allan, eto y mae yn cynwys pob gair sydd mewn arferiad gyffredin wrth siarad ac ysgrifenu.

Cymerwyd gofal mawr yn narlleniad y tafleni, fel yr hyderir nad oes ynddo un gwall gwerth ei nodi.

Rhagfyr 14, 1861.

ABREVIATIONS USED IN THE WORK.
BYRIADAU ARFEREDIG YN Y GWAITH.

a. or adj.	adjective	enw gwan
ad. or adv.	adverb.	rhagferf
con. or conj.	conjunction	cysylltiad
int. inter. or interj.	interjection	cyfryngiad
n.	noun	enw cadain
pre. or prep.	preposition	arddodiad
pref.	prefix	blaenddodiad
pr. or pro.	pronoun	rhagenw
v.	verb	parwyddiad

GEIRIADUR CYMRAEG A SAESONEG.

A WELSH-ENGLISH DICTIONARY.

A	ACH
A, an interrogative adverb, "A ddaw efe?" An affirmative adv. "Efe a ddaw."	Absen, n. f. slander, detraction
	Absenol, a. absent
	Absenu, v. to slander, to backbite; to speak ill of any one
A, ac, con. and, as	
A, ag, prep. with	Absenwr, n. m. backbiter; absentee; slanderer
A, pron. who, which, that	
A, int. oh	Abwy, n. m. a carcase, a carrion
A, prefix, as, athref from tref	Abwyd, n. m. a bait; fodder
Ab, or ap, n. m. a son	Abwydiad, n. m. a baiting, a foddering
Ab, Epa, n. m. ape, monkey	
Abad, n. m. an abbot	Abwydo, v. to bait, to feed
Abadaeth, n. f. abbacy,	Abwydwr, n. m. one who baits
Aber, n. m. the fall of one river into another, or into the sea, a confluence of water	Abwydyn, n. m. a bait; a worm
	Abwydyn y cefn, the spinal cord
	Ac, see A.
Aberth, n. m. oblation, sacrifice	Acan, n. f. a saying; accent
Aberthiad, n. m. a sacrificing	Acen, n. f. accent
Aberthu, v. to sacrifice	Acenawl, a. enunciative
Aberthwr, n. m. sacrificer	Aceniad, n. m. accentuation
Aberu, v. to disembogue	Acenu, v. to accent, to sound
Abl, a. able, powerful, wealthy	Atw, ad. there, hence
Abledd, n. m. ability, power	Ach. n. f. a fluid liquid; a stem
Abrediad, n. m. transmigration	Achles, n. f. succour, refuge, defence; manure
Abredu, v. to transmigrate	
Abrwysg, a. unwieldy; heavy	Achlesawl, a. succouring
Abrwysgaw, v. to inebriate	Achlesiad, n. m. a succouring
Abrwysgl, a. huge, vast, immense	Achlesu, v. to succour, to cherish
	Achleswr, n. m. succourer [ish

| ACH | 6 | ADA |

Achlesydd, n. m. succourer
Achlud, n. m. covert, obscurity
Achlwm, v. to knot, to tie
Achlysur, n. m. cause, motive; occasion, opportunity
Achlysuro, v. to occasion
Achlysurol, a. occasional
Achlyw, n. m. a hearing
Achos, n. m. cause
Achosadwy, a. effectible [cause
Achosedig, a. endued with a
Achosedigol, a. effectuative
Achosi, v. to cause, to occasion
Achosiad, n. m. a causing
Achosol, a. efficient: effectual
Achosoldeb, n. m. effectiveness
Achref, a. suppliant, craving
Achres, n. f. a row, a rank
Achretawr, n. m. a creditor
Achreth, n. m. a trembling
Achrwm, a. crooked or bent
Achrwym, n. m. a restraint
Achryf, a. strong, potent, powerful, able
Achub, v. to save, to secure
Achubadwy, a. salvable
Achubiad, n. m. a saving
Achubiaeth, n. m. a securing
Achubol, a. saving; delivering
Achubwr, n. m. a saviour
Achudd, n. m. seclusion
Achul, a. narrow; lean; squalid
Achwaith, n. m. sourness
Achwaneg, a. more, additional
Achwanegiad, n. m. augmentation, addition
Achwanegol, a. augmentative
Achwanegu, v. to increase
Achwlwm, n. m. a tie
Achwr, n. m. genealogist
Achwre, n. m. a shelter, a skreen
Achwy, a. tending to be foremost, busy-body
Achwyn, n. m. complaint: v. to complain [ed
Achwynedig, a. being complain-
Achwynedigaeth, n. m. accusation, charge

Achwynedigol, a. accusatory
Achwynol, a. plaintive
Achwyngar, a. querulous
Achwyngarwch, n. m. querulousness
Achwyniad, n. m. a complaining
Achwyniaeth, n. m. accusation
Achwynwr, n. m. a complainer
Ad, a. a going on, over, or to. It is a general prefix to words, answering to RE [ain
Adaddawiad, n. a promising ag-
Adaddewid, n. a second promise
Adaddo, v. to promise again
Adaerwch, n. importunity
Adafael, n. a distraint
Adafaeliad, n. a distraining
Adafaelu, v. to attach, to seize
Adail, n. a building
Adain, n. a wing; a bird
Adalw, v. to recall; to revoke
Adalwad, n. a recalling
Adan, n. a fin; a spoke
Adanadl, n. respiration
Adanadliad, n. a respiring
Adanadlu, v. to respire
Adanerch, n. second greeting
Adanerchiad, n. a resaluting
Adanerchu, v. to resalute
Adanfon, v. to send again
Adanfoniad, n. a sending again
Adanfonol, a. sending again
Adar, n. p. birds, fowls
Adara, v. to fowl
Adarol, a. relating to birds
Adardy, n. an aviary, a cage
Adarddelw, v. to reassert
Adarddelwad, n. reassertion
Adaren, n. a female bird
Adargi, n. a setting dog
Adargoel, n. augury
Adargoelio, v. augurize
Adargop, n. a spider
Adargopwe, n. a spider's web
Adarwr, n. a fowler [fowling
Adarwriaeth, n. the practice of
Adaw, v. to glide off; to fly
Adawr, n. chewing the cud

ADB	7	ADF

Adbeniad, n. re-assignment
Adbenodi, v. to subdivide
Adbenod, n. subdivision
Adbenu, v. to re-assign
Adblan, n. a second setting
Adblaniad, n. a transplanting
Adblanu, v. to transplant
Adblyg, n. a second fold
Adblygadwy, a. reduplicable
Adblygedd, n. recurvity
Adblygiad, n. a recurvation
Adblygol, a. reduplicate
Adblygu, v. to fold back
Adborion, n. p. leavings, refuse
Adbrawf, n. re-tasting
Adbrofi, v. to taste again
Adbrynadwy, a. redeemable
Adbrynedigaeth, n. redemption
Adbrynedig, a. redeemed
Adbryniad, n. a ransom
Adbrynol, a. redeeming
Adbrynu, v. to repurchase
Adbrynwr, n. re-purchaser
Adchwanegol, a. additional
Adchwanegu, v. to re-augment
Adchwedl, n. a rumour
Adchwilio, v. to research
Adchwiliedig, a. researched
Adchwiliwr, n. a researcher
Adchwilio, v. to revolve
Adchwyl, n. a circumvolution
Adchwyladwy, a. revolvable
Adchwyliad, n. a revolving
Adeg, n. opportunity, season
Adeginad n. the second budding
Adegino, v. to bud again
Adeilad, n. a building
Adeiladaeth, n. architecture
Adeiladol, a. edifying architect-
Adeiladu, v. to build [ural
Adelledydd, n. architect
Adeiladedig, a. built
Adeilo, v. to build or construct
Adeilwr, n. architect, builder
Adeiniad, n. a winging
Adeinio, v. to fly, to wing
Adeiniog, a. winged, pinioned
Adeinol, a. relating to wings

Adeiriad, n. tautology
Adeirio, v. repeating of words
Adeiriog, a. tautological
Aden, n. a wing, a pinion
Adenedig, a. regenerated
Adenedigaeth, n. regeneration
Adeni, v. to regenerate
Adennill, v. to regain
Adennilliad, n. a thing regained
Adennillwr, n. regainer
Adenw, n. a second name
Adenwi, v. to name again
Aderbyniad, n. a receiving back
Aderyn, n. bird, a fowl
Adethol, v. to reselect
Adfach, n. the beard of a dart
Adfachiad, n. a re-hooking
Adfachog, a. barbed, bearded
Adfachu, v. to barb, to re-hook
Adfail, n. a ruin
Adfarn, n. reversed judgement
Adfarnedig, a. rejudged [ment
Adfarniad, n. reversion of judge-
Adfarnu, v. to rejudge
Adfath, n. a recoinage
Adfathiad, n. a recoining
Adfathu, v. to recoin
Adfedyddio, v. to rebaptize
Adfeddianu, v. to repossess
Adfeddianol, a. repossessive
Adfeddiant, n. re-possession
Adfeddianwr, n. m. repossessor
Adfeddwl, n. second thought
Adfeddyliad, n. recollection
Adfeddylied, v. to recollect
Adfeiliad, n. a decaying
Adfeiliedig, a. decayed, in ruin
Adfeilio, v to decay, to moulder
Adfeiliog, a. decaying; ruinous
Adfeïo, v. to recriminate
Adfer, n. what is restored
Adferadwy, a. restorable
Adferedig, a. restorable
Adferedigaeth, n. restoration
Adferiad, n. a restoring
Adferol, a. restorative
Adferth, n. comfort
Adferthiad, n. a comforting

| ADF | 8 | ADG |

Adferthol, a. comforting [create
Adferthu, v. to comfort, to re-
Adferwi, v. to boil again
Adferwr, n. restorer
Adferyd, v. to make restitution
Adfesur, n. a second measure: v. to measure a second time
Adflagur, n. a second bud
Adflaguro, v. to bud again
Adflas, n. insipidity of taste
Adflin, a. fatigue over again
Adflinder, n. irritation
Adflino, v. to irritate
Adflith, n. a second milk
Adflitho, v. to yield second milk
Adflodau, n.m. second blossoms
Adflodeuad, n. m. refloration
Adflodeuo, v. to reflourish
Adflodeuog, a. reflorescent
Adfraenar, n. m. second fallow
Adfrawd, n.f. a reversed or second judgment
Adfryd, n.m. a second intention
Adfwriad, n. m. a recasting
Adfwrw, v. to recast
Adfwynhau, v. to re-enjoy
Adfydiog, a. in adversity; miserable, wretched
Adfydig, a. distressed, wretched
Adfyd, ad. perhaps, it may be
Adfyddin, n.f. a corps of reserve
Adfyfyrdod, n. m. reconsideration, reflection
Adfyfyriad, n. m. reconsidering
Adfyfyrio, v. to reconsider
Adfynegiad, n.m. a redeclaring
Adfynegu, v. to declare again
Adfyw, n.m. lack of life; fallow a. revived, alive again
Adfywhau, v. to reanimate
Adfywiad, n. m. a revival
Adfywiant, n.m. reanimation
Adfywio, v. to revive
Adfywiocau, v. to reinvigorate
Adfywiogi, v. to reanimate
Adffugio, v. to disguise anew
Adffurfio, v. to reform; to repair
Adffurfiwr, n. m. a reformer

Adffynu, v. n. to prosper again
Adgadarnhau, v. to re-fortify
Adgadw, v. to keep again
Adgais, n. m. a second attempt
Adgam, a. recurvous
Adgan, n. f. an episode
Adganu, v. to describe
Adgas, a. odious, disagreeable
Adgasglu, v. to collect again
Adgasrwydd, n. m. odiousness
Adgasu, v. to act disagreeable
Adgeisio, v. to seek again
Adgenedledig, a. regenerated
Adgenedliad, n.m. regeneration
Adgenedlu, v. to regenerate
Adgerydd, n. m. a reprimand
Adgeryddadwy, a. reprehensible
Adgeryddiad, n.m. a reprimand
Adgeryddol, a. reprehensive
Adgeryddu, v. to reprimand
Adgip, n. m. a resnatch; a reprise
Adglaf, a. relapsed to sickness
Adglefychu, v. to relapse
Adglwyfo, v. to wound again
Adglymiad, n. m. renodation
Adglymu, v. to tie again
Adgnithio, v. to retouch
Adgno, n. m. second chewing.
Adgno, cydwybod, remorse
Adgnoi, v. to chew the cud
Adgodi, v. to raise again
Adgof, n. m. remembrance
Adgofio, v. to recollet
Adgofiol, a. recollective [mind
Adgoffa, n. m. a recalling to
Adgoffau, v. to recall to mind
Adgryfhau, v. to reinvigorate
Adgrynhoi, v. to collect again
Adguddio, v. to reconceal, to hide again
Adgur, n. m. a repulse, a rebut
Adguriad, a. repulsion
Adguro, v. to repel, re-conquer
Adgwymp, n. m. a fall back
Adgwympo, v. to relapse
Adgydiedig, a. rejoined
Adgydio, v. to rejoin

Adgyfansoddi, v. to recompose
Adgyfanu, v. to reintegrate
Adgyfarch, v. to resalute ' [ain
Adgyfhau, v. to make whole ag-
Adgyflawni, v. to complete anew.
Adgyfleu, v. to replace
Adgyfnerthu, v. to reinforce
Adgyfodi, v. to rise again
Adgyfodiad, n. m. resurrection
Adgyffroad, n. m. resuscitation
Adgyffroi, v. to resuscitate
Adgylchiad, n. m. revolution
Adgymeriad, n.m.reassumption
Adgymodi, v. to reconciliate
Adgyneu, v. to rekindle
Adgynrychioli, v. to represent another
Adgynrychu, v. to represent
Adgynull, v. to collect again
Adgynulledig, v. a. recollected
Adgynull, v. to collect again
Adgynulledig, v. a. recollected
Adgynulliad, n. a reassembling
Adgynyrchiad, n. reproduction
Adgyrch, n. m. a recourse
Adgyswllt, n. m. rejunction
Adgysylltu, v. to reunite
Adgywain, v. to carry back
Adgyweirio, v. to refit
Adgyweiriol, a. reparative
Adgyweiriolion, n. restoratives
Adgyweiriwr, n. m. a repairer
Adgywreinio,v.to make exact a-
Adhaeriad, n. reassertion (gain
Adheddychu v. to repacify
Adholi, v. to re-examine, to question again
Adhoni, v. to reassert
Adladd, n. m. second crop: v. to kill again
Adlaes, a. trailing, draggling
Adlais,n.m.reverberation; echo
Adlam, n. a back step; a home
Adlamiad, n. m. a stepping back
Adlamu, v. to step back; to rebound
Adlef, n. m. resonance, echo
Adlefariad, n. m. peroration

Adlefaru,v.to perorate, to speak again, to recite
Adleau, v. to replace
Adleisio, v. to resound
Adlenwi, v. to fill again
Adles, n.m. that is not a benefit
Adlif, n. m. ebb tide, a reflux
Adlifeiriant, n. m. refluence
Adlifeirio, v. to reflow
Adlifiant, n. m. a reflowing
Adlifo, v. to flow back
Adlithrad, n. m. a sliding back
Adlithro, v. to slide back
Adliw, n. m. a varnish, a retint
Adliwio, v. to recolour
Adloddi, v. to grow after cutting
Adloes, n. m. a reiterated pang
Adloewi, v. to brighten again
Adlog, n. m. compound interest
Adloni, v. to cherish again
Adlonyddu, v. to assuage or quiet again
Adlosgi, v. to burn again
Adlunio, v. to reform, to copy
Adlusgo, v. to drag back
Adlyfnhau v. to repolish
Adlythyr, n. m. a rescript
Adnabod, n. m. recognition: v. to recognize, to know, to be acquainted with
Adnabyddedig, a. acquainted
Adnabyddiad, n.m. recognition
Adnabyddiaeth, n.f.knowledge, cognizance
Adnabyddol, a. recognizing
Adnabyddus,a.knowing,known
Adnabyddwr, n.m. a recognizer
Adnaid, n. f. a rebound
Adnawdd, n. m. a resource
Adnawf, n.m. a swimming back
Adne,n.m.custody, safe keeping
Adnerth, n. m. a second power
Adnerthedig, a. reinforced
Adnerthu, v. to reinforce
Adneu, n.m. a deposit, a pledge
Adneuad, n. m. a pledging
Adnewid, v. to rechange
Adnewyddiad, n.m. renovation

Adnewyddu, v. to renovate, to renew
Adnewyddwr, n. m. a renovator
Adnod, n. f. a sentence, a verse
Adnodi, v. to divide into verses
Adnofiad, n. a swimming back
Adnofio, v. to swim back
Adnydd, n. m. a gate post
Adoew, n. m. a spur
Adofidio, v. to grieve again
Adofidiol, a. reafflicting
Adofwyad, n. m. a revisiting
Adofwywr, n. m. a revisitor
Adofyn, v. to ask again, to reclaim
Adohebu, v. to recommunicate, to respond
Adolrhain, v. to follow after, to retrace
Adolwch, n. m. intreaty, prayer
Adolwg, n. retrospect
Adolygu, v. to review
Adolygwr, n. m. a reviewer
Adran, n. f. a subdivision
Adraniad, n. m. a subdivision
Adranu, v. subdivide
Adranwr, n. m. a subdivider
Adranydd, n. m. a subdivider
Adredeg, v. to run again, to run back
Adrediad, n. m. a recurrence
Adref, ad. home, homewards
Adrefu, v. to return home
Adrif, n.m. second reckoning
Adrifiad, n.m. a counting again
Adrifo, v. to recount
Adrifwr, n. m. a recounter
Adrodd, v. to relate
Adroddi, v. to return a gift
Adroddiad, n. m. a narration
Adroddol, a. declaratory
Adroddwr, n. m. a relater
Adrwym, n. m. a restringent
Adrwymiad, a. rebinding [ing
Adrybudd, n.m. a second warning
Adrybuddio, v. to warn again
Adrysedd, n.m. a second excess
Adryw, n. m. secondary species

Adrywiad, n.m. degeneration
Adrywio, v. to degenerate
Adrywiol, v. degenerating
Adsaf, n. f. a second standing
Adsain, n. f. echo
Adsefydlu, v. to re-establish
Adseilfanu, v. to found anew
Adseiniedig, a. echoed
Adseinio, v. to resound, to echo
Adseiniol, a. resounding
Adson, v. to rumour again
Adsylw, n. m. a second observation
Adsylwi, v. to view again
Adsyllu, v. to glance at again
Aduno, v. to agree again
Adunedig, a. reunited, rejoined
Adurddedig, a. reordained
Adurddiad, n. m. reordination
Adurddo, v. to honour again; to re-ordain
Adurddol, a. reordinative
Adwaen, v. to recognize
Adwaeniad, n. recognition
Adwair, n. aftermath
Adwanychiad, n. a relapsing
Adwanychu, v. to enfeeble again
Adwedyd, v. to say again, to re-
Adwedd, n. a renewed state [peat
Adweinig, a. recognisable; known
Adweirio, v. to repair
Adweled, v. to recover sight
Adweliad, n. a recovering of sight
Adwerth, n. undervalue
Adwerthwr, n. depreciator
Adwerydd, n. second spring
Adwirio, v. to recertify
Adwisg, n. an undress
Adwisgo, v. to disarray; to undress
Adwledd, n. a slender feast
Adwneyd, v. to undo
Adwneuthur, v. to repair
Adwnio, v. to double-stitch
Adwy, n. a gap; a pass
Adwyo, v. to make gaps
Adwyog, v. having gaps

Adwydd, n. fallow ground
Adwyn, n. a metal
Adwynol, a. metalic
Adwynig, a. glittering
Adwyr, a. recurvous, bent back
Adwyro, v. to recline back
Adwyriad, n. recurvation
Adwyrni, n. a recurviture
Adwys, n. second summons
Adwysio, v. to summon again
Adwyth, n. a hurt; a blast
Adwythol, a. blasting; hurting
Adymgasgliad, n. a reassembling
Adymgasglu, v. to re-assemble
Adymgyfarch, v. to re-salute
Adymgymeriad, n. a mutual reassumption [mutually
Adymgymmodi, v. to reconcile
Adymgynnull, v. to re-assemble
Adymrithio, v. to re-appear
Adymweled, v. see ad. and ymweled, and the same with all words, prefixed with ad. not mentioned here
Adyn, n. a fribble, a wretch
Adyru, v. to drive back
Adysgrif, n. a transcript
Adysgrifenu, v. to transcribe
Adysgrifenwr, n. a transcriber
Adystwytho, v. to make pliant again
Adystyried, n. re-consideration; v. to reflect, to re-consider
Add, n. impulse. A prefix to enhance the sense of words
Addangc, n. a crocodile
Addas, a. meet, suitable, proper
Addasiad, n. a suiting, a fitting
Addasol, a. befitting; convenient
Addasrwydd, n. suitableness
Addasu, v. to suit, to adapt
Addaw, n. a promise
Addawd, n. a repository
Addawedig, a. promised
Addawiad, n. a promising
Addawl, n. worship
Addawydd, n. a promiser

Addef, v. to acknowledge, to own
Addefedig, a. confessed
Addefiad, n. confession
Addefol, a. confessing
Addefwr, n. a confessor
Addewid, n. a promise
Addewidiol, a. promissory
Addfed, a. ripe, mature
Addfediad, n. a ripening
Addfedrwydd, n. ripeness
Addfedu, v. to ripen
Addfwyn, a. gentle, meek, mild
Addfwynder, n. gentleness
Addoed, n. an appointed time
Addoedi, v. to set a time; to defer [respiting
Addoediad, n. prorogation, a
Addoer, a. frigid; chilly
Addoeredig, a. chilled
Addoeri, v. to chill
Addocriad, n. refrigeration
Addoladwy, a. adorable; divine
Addoledig, a. praised; worshipped
Addoli, v. to worship, to adore
Addoliad, n. a worshipping
Addoliadol, a. devotional
Addoliant, n. worship, adoration
Addolwr, n. worshipper
Addon, n. fruit; offspring
Addu, v. to go, to proceed
Adduned, n. a vow; a desire
Addunedu, v. to make a vow
Addunedwr, n. vower
Adduniad, n. a vowing
Addunwr, n. one that makes a
Addurn, n. an ornament [vow
Addurnedig, a. ornamented
Addurniad, n. adornment
Addurniaeth, n. ornature
Addurno, v. to ornament
Addurnol, a. ornamental
Addurnwr, n. a decorator
Addfwynfryd, n. a virtuous mind
Addysg, n. instruction
Addysgedig, a. instructed
Addysgiad, n. an instructing
Addysgu, v. to instruct, to teach

Addysgiadol, a. dictatic
Addysgwr, n. an instructor
Aed, n. a going; a proceeding
Aeg, n. faculty of utterance
Ael, n. a jut out; a brow
Aeldrem, n. a leering
Aeldrwm, a. stern, frowning
Aele, a. woeful, sad, piteous
Aeled, n. an ailment
Aelfawr, a. big browed
Aelgerth, n. the check bone
Aeliog, a. browed; full browed
Aelod, n. a limb, a number
Aelodi, v. to form a member
Aelodiad, n. forming a member
Aelodog, a. limbed
Aelwyd, n. a hearth; family
Aelwydiad, n. a hearth-full
Aelwyd, a. prosperous
er, n. slaughter; battle; heir
Aerfan, n. a field of battle
Aeron, n. fruits of trees
Aerwy. n. a collar; torques
Aes, n. a flat body; a target
esel, n. verjuice; vinegar
Aeserw, n. plank
Aeth, n. a point, a furse: v. he went; he has gone
Aethawl, a. pungent, poignant
Aethiad, n. a smarting
Aethnen, n. an aspen, a poplar
Aethwelit, n. latter-math
Aethwydd, n. aspen wood
Af, n. progress, a going on; a prefix to words, answering to un
Afach, n. a grapple, a holdfast
Afaeth, n. blandishment
Afal, n. an apple
Afaleua, v. to gather apples
Afall, n. an apple tree
Afallach, n. an orchard
Afallen, n. an apple tree
Afallwydd, n. apple trees
Afan, n. raspberries: a. high, loud
Afanc, n. a crocodile
Afanen, n. a raspberry

Afanwydd, n. a raspberry-brake
Aflach, a. unwell, unhealthy
Aflacth, n. blandishment
Aflechyd, n. indisposition
Aflafar, n. loss of speach; dumb
Aflafarwch, n. lack of utterance
Aflan, a. unclean, poluted
Aflanhad, n. a polluting
Aflanhau, v. to pollute
Aflariaidd, a. ungentle
Aflathr, a. without polish
Aflathraidd, a. unpollished
Aflawen, a. not merry
Afleferydd, n. dumbness
Aflendid, n. uncleanness
Aflerw, a. slovenly, untidy
Afles, n. disadvantage; hurt
Aflesol, a. disadvantageous
Aflesrwydd, n. disadvantage
Aflesu, v. to damage, to hurt
Aflonder, n. uncheerfulness
Aflonydd, a. unquiet, restless
Aflonyddiad, n. molestation
Aflonyddu, v. to disquiet
Aflonyddwch, n. disquietude
Aflonyddwr, n. a molester
Afloyw, a. not clear, muddy
Afloywder, n. muddiness
Aflun, a. void of form
Afluniad, n. deforming
Afluniaidd, a. deformed
Aflunieiddio, v. to disfigure
Aflwfr, a. uncowardly; daring
Aflwydd, n. misfortune
Aflwyddianus, a. unprosperous
Aflwyddiant, n. misfortune, want of prosperity
Aflwyddo, v. to miscarry, to fail
Aflwyddol, a. unprosperous
Aflyfnder, n. ruggedness
Aflym, a. blunt; not sharp
Aflymder, n. want of sharpness
Aflywodraeth, n. misrule
Aflywodraethus, a. ungovernable
Afon, n. a river
Afonig, n. a brook, rivulet, a rill
Afonol, a. like a river
Afr, n. a flowing principle

Afrad, n. waste
Afradiad, n. a lavashing
Afradlawn, a. extravagant
Afradlondeb, n. prodigality
Afradloni, v. to waste, to lavish
Afradloniad, n. lavishing
Afradlourwydd, n. prodigality
Afradu, v. to squander, to lavish
Afraid, a. needless, unnecessary
Afreol, n. disorder, misrule
Afreolaidd, a. irregular
Afreolaeth, n. irregularity
Afrif, a. numberless
Afrifad, n. innumerableness
Afrifed, a. innumerable
Afrifo, v. to miscount
Afrllad, n. consecrated wafers
Afrlladen, n. a cake, a wafer
Afrugl, a. faultering, hesitating
Afrwydd, n. difficulty: a. unprosperous [ness
Afrwydd-deb, n. unpropitious-
Afrwyddiad, n. a retarding
Afrwyddo, v. to retard, to hinder
Afrwyddol, a. unpropitious
Afrwym, a. unbound, untied
Afrywiaeth, n. degeneracy
Afrywiedig, a. degenerated
Afrywio, v. to degenerate
Afrywiog, a. harsh, degenerate
Afrywiogi, v. to grow rough
Afrywiogrwydd, n. degeneracy, rigour; harshness
Afu, n. the liver
Afuad, n. the rot
Afuol, a. hepatical
Affwys, n. a precipice: a. steep
Ag, n. f. an opening, a cleft: prep. with
Agen, n. a cleft, a chop, a chink
Agendor, n. a yawning gulf
Agenig, n. a small cleft
Ageniad, n. a rifting, a cleaving
Agenog, a. leaky; full of clefts
Agenu, v. to crack, to cleave
Ager, n. vapour; steam, reek
Agerfd, n. steam; vapour
Ager ldol, a. steaming; reeking

Agerfa, n. air vent
Ageru, v. to cast a steam
Agorad, n. an opening
Agored, a. open, expanded
Agor, Agori, Agoryd, v. to open, to expand
Agoriad, n. what opens; a key
Agoriadol, a. aperient
Agorol, a. opening, expanding
Agorwr, n. an opener
Agos, a. proximate; near; nigh
Agosiad, n. approximation
Agosrwydd, n. nearness
Agro, a. very heavy; pensive, sad
Agwedd, n. condition; form
Agweddiad, n. modification
Agweddol, a. habitual
Agweddu, v. to modify; to form
Aha, interj. ha, ha
Ai, ad. is it: conj. comp. or, either
A'i, pron. comp. that, her, him
Aidd, n. zeal, ardency
Ail, a. second; like. A prefix answering to RE. See Ad
Ailachosi, v. act as second cause
Ailadeiladu, see Ail and Adeiladu, and the same with all other words not mentioned here, prefixed with Ail
Alaeth, n. grief, sorrow, wailing
Alaethu, v. to grieve, to wail
Alaethus, a. mornful, doleful
Alar, n. loathing, surfeit
Alarch, n. a swan
Alarchen, n. a cygnet
Alariad, n. a surfeiting
Alarllyd, a. loathsome, surfeiting
Alarm, n. a mighty shout
Alarmu, v. to call to arms; to shout, or surprise
Alaru, v. to loath or surfeit
Alaw, n. chief of the waters; instrumental music
Alawr, n. a plate, receptacle
Alban, n. upper part. Scotland
Albrys, n. cross bow
Alcan, n. white metal; tin
Alch, n. grate, gridiron

Alfarch, n. stitch, spasm
Algar, n. reindeer
Alis, n. hell ; the lowest point
Aliw, n. saliva, spittle
Almaen, n. Germany
Alon, n. music, harmony
Alp, n. precipice, craggy rock
Alsawdd, n. algebra
Alwar, n. purse
Allair, n. paraphrase
Allan, a. out, without: off
Allanol, a. outward, exterior
Allog, n. alum
Alleg, n. fable, allegory
Allegiad, n. allegorizing
Allegu, v. allegorize
Alleiriad, n. a paraphrasing
Alleirio, v. to paraphrase
Allor, n. altar
Allt, n. cliff
Alltrem, n. a wild stare
Alltremiad, n. a wild gazing
Alltrodiaeth, n. estrangement
Alltud, n. alien, another land
Alltudaeth, n. banishment
Alltudedd, n. a state of exile
Alltudes, n. female exile
Alltudo, v. to banish
Alltudol, a. banishing
Alltudwr, n. exiler
Allwedd, n. key
Am, prep. about, round : conj. for, because. A prefix answering to Circum
Amaethiad, n. husbandry
Amaethiaeth, n. tillage
Amaethol, a. husbandry
Amaethu, v. to husband
Amaethwriaeth, n. husbandry
Amaethwr, Amaethydd, n. cultivator, agriculturist
Amaethyddol, a. agricultural
Amaethyddiaeth, n. agriculture
Ambell, a. scarce, few
Amcan, n. intent, a purpose
Amcaniad, n. intention
Amcaniaeth, n. conjecture
Amcanol, a. intentional

Amcansail, n. hypothesis
Amcanu, v. to guess, to design, to purpose
Amcanus, a. inventive
Amcanwr, n. inventor
Amchwyl, n. circumvolution
Amdan, n. a trevet
Amdo, n. a shroud [oped
Amdoedig, a. shrouded ; envel-
Amdoi, v. to enwrap, to shroud
Amdorch, n. encircling wreath
Amdori, v. to amputate, to cut
Amdorchi, v. to clasp [about
Amdraill, n. circumvolution
Amdramwy, v. to wander about
Amdraul, n. corrosion
Amddifad, a. orphan, destitute
Amddifadu, v. to render destitude [defend
Amddiffyn, n. defence: v. to
Amddiffynedig, a. defended
Amddiffynfa, n. a strong hold
Amddiffyniad, n. a defending
Amddiffynwr, n. a defender
Amddiiladu v.to clothe all round
Amedrych, a. chewy on all sides
Amfordwyad, n. circumnavigation [ing
Amforddwyol, a. circumnavigat-
Amfrwys, a. branching about
Amfylchu, v. to notch again
Amgadarnhau, v. to strengthen round
Amgaer, n. a fortification
Amgaeru, v. to immure on every side
Amgall, a. circumspect, wary
Amgan, n. minstrelsy
Amgau, v. to shut round
Amgauad, n. a hemming in
Amgauedig, a. hemmed in
Amgeiniad, n. minstrel
Amgeledd, n. solicitude ; care
Amgeleddiad, n. a succouring
Amgeleddol, a. succouring
Amgeleddu, v. to cherish, to succour [tering
Amgeleddus, a. succouring, fos-

Amgeleddwr, n. a cherisher
Amgelog, a. circumspect
Amgelwch, n. solicitude
Amgen, ad. also; but; otherwise
Amgenach, ad. better; rather
Amgenaeth, n. difference
Amgeneirio, v. to paraphrase
Amgenu, v. to differ, to alter
Amglawdd, n. an entrenchment
Amgloddiad, n. entrenchment
Amgledru, v. to rail round
Amgludo, v. to carry about
Amglwm, n. a clasper
Amglywed, v. to apprehend
Amgneifio, v. to clip round
Amgnoi, v. to bite round, to corrode
Amgreinio, v. to roll about
Amgrom, a. convex
Amgron, a. globular
Amgud, n. a curly lock
Amgudyn, n. a ringlet of hair
Amgudd, n. treasure: a. hidden on all sides
Amguddio, v. to inwrap
Amgudd, n. a choice rarity
Amguddfa, n. a museum
Amgyff, n. support on every side
Amgyffrawd, n. immagination
Amgyffred, n. comprehension
Amgyffrediad, n. comprehending
Amgyffredol, a. comprehensible
Amgyffredu, v. to comprehend
Amgyffroad, thorough agitation
Amgyffroi, v. to agitate all round
Amgylch, n. a circuit; an environ; a. round about
Amgylchedd, n. circumference
Amgylchiad, n. a surrounding
Amgylchiadol, a. circumscribing
Amgylchu, v. to surround
Amgylchyn, n. circumferentor
Amgylchyniad, n. encompassing
Amgylchynu, v. to surround
Amgylchynol, a. encompassing
Amgylchynwr, n. circumscriber
Amgynniwair, v. to hover round
Amgynull, v. to collect again

Amgynnulliad, sub. a collection from all sides
Amgyrhaeddu, v. to extend
Amgywain, v. to carry round
Amhad, n. mixed seed
Amhafal; a. parallel
Amherawdr, n. an emperor
Amhir, a. lengthened round
Amhwedd, sub. intreaty: v. to crave
Amias, n. a sensation round
Amig, n. greediness
Aml, a. often; plentiful
Amlhâd, n. an increasing
Amlhau, v. to multiply
Amlbrïod, n. a polygamist
Amlbriodas, n. polygamy
Amlder, n. frequency
Amldroed, n. polypus
Amlddull, a. multiform
Amldduw, n. polytheist
Amlediad, n. expansion
Amledd, n. abundance; store
Amleglwys, n. pluralist
Amleiriog, a. loquacious
Amlenw, a. multinomial
Amlenwi, v. to fill around
Amlew, a. devouring on all sides
Amlewyrchiad, n. a shining on every side
Amlgell, a. having many cells
Amliaith, a. polyglot [es
Amlieithog, a. of many languag-
Amlifeiriant, n. circumfluence
Amlifiad, n. circulation
Amlifo v. to flow about
Amlinell, n. surrounding line
Amliw, n. a stain: a. stained
Amliwiad, n. discolouring
Amliwiog, a. motley, coloured
Amlochrog, a. multilateral
Amlosgi, v. to burn round
Amlran, n. many shares
Amlryw, n. miscellany: multi-
Amlsill, a. polysyllabical [farious
Amlwedd, a. of divers forms
Amlwg, a. apparent, evident
Amlygder, n. conspicuousness

Amlygedig, a. manifested
Amlygedd, n. apparentness
Amlygiad, n. manifestation
Amlygiadol, a. explanatory
Amlygol, a. demonstrative
Amlygrwydd, n. obviousness
Amlygu, v. to manifest
Amlynu, v. to adhere around
Ammaeth, n. dainty
Ammau, Ammheu, v. to doubt
Ammawr, n. placidity
Ammeuthu, v. to make dainty
Ammeuthyn, a. rare, dainty
Ammheuad, n. a doubting
Ammheuaeth, n. doubt
Ammheugar, a. hesitating
Ammheüus, a. doubting
Amheuol, a. doubtful
Amheuwr, n. a sceptic
Ammod, n. a contract
Ammodi, v. to covenant
Ammodiad, n. a contracting
Ammodol, a. conditional
Ammodwr, n. a contractor
Ammwyth, n. a carousal
Amnaid, n. a beck
Amneidiad, n. a beckoning
Amner, n. a purse
Amnerydd, n. a purser
Amorchudd, n. a cover around
Amrafael, n. contention
Amrafaelgar, a. contentious
Amrafaeliad, n. a bickering
Amrafaelio, v. to contend
Amrafaelus, a. contentious
Amran, n. circular division
Amraniad, n. division round
Amrant, n. the eye-lid
Amrant-hun, n. a short nap
Amrantu, v. to wink, to blink
Amranu, v. to divide round
Amrentyn, n. close of the eye
Amrith, a. of various aspects
Amrosgo, a. vast, unwieldy
Amrwygiad, n. dilapidation
Amrwym, n. a bandage round
Amrwymo, v. to bind round about
Amryallu, v. multipotent

Amrydwll, a. full of holes, porous
Amrydyb, n. a paradox
Amryddarn, a. of various pieces
Amryddull, a. multiform
Amryfal, a. divers, sundry
Amrafaeledd, n. diversity
Amryfaliad, n. diversifying
Amryfalu, v. to diversify
Amryfath, a. miscellaneous
Amryfawl, a. arrogant, haughty
Amryfeiliad, n. variation
Amryfiad, n. excessiveness
Amryfodd, a. of various modes
Amryfoldeb, n. arrogance
Amryfu, v. to commit excess
Amryfus, a. faulty; excessive
Amryfusedd, n. excess; oversight; a falling out
Amryfuseddu, v. to fall out
Amryfwyd, n. variety of viands
Amrygant, n. a circling rim
Amrygar, a. loved on all sides
Amrygasgliad, n. a complex
Amrygoll, n. loss every way
Amrygur, n. plain in every way
Amrygwyn, n. great tribulation
Amryhollt, a. having many clefts
Amrylais, a. of divers sounds
Amrylaw, a. of various hands
Amrylawr, a. of several floors
Amrylef, a. of many tones
Amryliw, a. of various colours
Amrylon, a. pleased various ways
Amrylun, a. of divers forms
Amrylys, n. mixt herbage
Amrynerth, a. multipotent
Amrysedd, n. excess on all sides
Amryson, n. contention, v. content, to debate
Amrysongar, a. contentious
Amrysongarwch, n. contentiousness
Amrysoniad, n. a contending
Amrysonol, a. contending [ious
Amryw, a. sundry, divers, various
Amrywaith, n. variegated work
Amrywedd, a. of various aspects
Amrywellt, n. variety of grass

Amrywiad, n. diversification
Amrywiaeth, n. variety
Amrywiaethu, v. to diversify
Amrywiaeth, n. a dialect
Amrywiedig, a. diversified
Amrywio, v. diversify
Amrywiog, a. various
Amrywiogaeth, n. intermixture
Amrywiol, a. miscelaneous
Amsang, n. a treading about
Amsathr, n. a trembling about
Amsathru, v. to tread about
Amseinio, v. to reverberate
Amser, n. season; time: a. timely
Amserol, a. timely, seasonable
Amseroldeb, n. seasonableness
Amseru, v. to time, to fix a time
Amwasgu, v. to compress
Amwe, n. a selvage
Amwedd, n. style; conformity
Amweddu, v. to make conform-
Amwel, circumspect, wary [able
Amweled, v. to be circumspect
Amwes, n. enjoyment
Amwisg, n. a covering
Amwisgo, v. to shroud, to inwrap
Amwiw, a. excellent every way
Amwniad, n. a stiching all reund
Amwnio, v. to stitch round
Amwresygu, v. to begirt
Amwys, a. equivocal: witty
Amwysiad, n. a punning
Amwyth, n. wrath; ferocity
Amyd, n. mixt corn
Amygiad, n. giving refuge
Amyn, conj. except; unless; but
Amynedd, n. patience [ing
Amyneddgar, a. patient, forbear-
Amyneddgarwch, n. forbearance
Amyneddus, patient
Amyriad, n. an intermeddling
Amyru, v. io intermeddle
Amysgar, n. bowels, entrails
An, n. an element, principle. privative particle equal to un
Anad, a. peculiar, especial
Anadl, n. the breath
Anadlfyr, a. short breathed

Anadliad, n breath, respiration
Anadlog, a. breathing
Anadlu, v. to breath
Anadlyn, n. m. a single breath
Anadnabyddiaeth, n. want of acquaintance
Anadnabyddus, a. unknown
Anaddas, a. improper, unmeet
Anaddasiad, n. disqualification
Anaddasu, v. to disqualify
Anaddfed, a. unripe
Anaddurno, v. to disarray
Anaele, a. awful, terrific
Anaf, n. m. a wound, blemish
Anafaelgar, a. void of hold
Anafiad n. m. blemish
Anafod, n. sore, ailment
Anafu, v. to maim or hurt
Anafus, a. blemished
Anagweddiad, n. disfiguring
Anagweddus, a. unseemly
Anair, n. infamy, ill report
Analwedig, a. uncalled
Anallu, n. inability
Analluoedd, n. impotency
Analluogi, a. to disenable
Analluog, a. unable
Analluogrwydd, n. impotence
Anamgyffred, n. incomprehsion
    a. inconceiveable
Anamgyffredol, a. inconceivable
Anaml, a. rare, infrequent
Anaml, n. scarcity, fewness
Anamlwg, a. indistinct
Anamlygawl, a. unmanifesting
Anamlygiad, n. indistinction
Anamyneddgar, a. impatient
Anamyneddrwydd, n. impatience
Anamryfused, n. unerringness
Anamserol, a. untimely
Anamseru, v. to render untimely
Ananwyl, a. unendearing
Ananghofus, a. unforgetting
Anaradwy, a. unarable
Anarlliad, n. inalienation
Anaraul, a. not calm, ruffled
Anarbed, a. unsparing
Anarbedrwydd, unsparingness

| ANA | 18 | ANF |

Anarcholladwy, a. invulnerable
Anardymmer, n. indisposition
Anarferol, a. unaccustomed
Anarferu, v. to disuse
Anarfog, a. unarmed
Anarwyddocâd n. insignificance
Anattaliadwy, a. unrestrainable
Anattebol, a. unanswerable
Anchwiliadwy, a. unsearchable
Andras, n. an enemy; Satan
Andwyo, v. to ruin; to disorder
Andwyol, a. ruining
Anëang, unspacious, unample
Anebrwydd, a. not quick
Anedifarus, a. unrelenting
Anedifeiriol, a. impenitent
Anedifeirwch, n. impenitence
Anedmygedd, n. irreverence
Aneffeithiol, a. ineffectual
Aneffeithioldeb, n. inefficacy
Aneglur, a. not clear, indistinct
Aneglurdeb, n. indistinctness
Anegwan, a. potent, unfeeble,
Aneiddil, a. unslender
Aneirif, a. innumerable
Aneirifedd, n. innumerableness
Anelwig, n. shapeless
Anennill, a. without gain
Anenwog, a. unrenowned
Anenwogi, v. to make ignoble
Anenwogrwydd, n. ignobleness
Anerch, n. a salute, a greeting; v. to salute, to greet
Anerchiad, n. a salutation
Anerchol, a. gratulatory
Anerchwr, n. complimenter
Anermygawl, a. inorganical
Anesgariad, n. inseperability
Anesgor, a. without deliverance
Anesgud, a. not quick, slow
Anesmwyth, a. uneasy, painful
Anesmwythder, n. uneasiness
Anesmwytho, v. to make uneasy
Anewyllysgarwch, n. unwilling-
Anfad, a. naughty [ness
Anfadu, v. to become naughty
Anfadrwydd, n. impiousness
Anfaddeuant, n. unforgiveness

Anfalch, a. humble
Anfanwl, a. inaccurate
Anfanylrwydd, n. inacuracy
Anfarwol, a. immortal
Anfarwoldeb, n. immortality
Anfas, a. not shallow; deep
Anfawl, v. void of praise
Anfedrus, a. unskilful, bungling
Anfedrusedd, n. unskilfulness
Anfedrusrwydd, n. unskilfulness
Anfeddygol, a. incurable
Anfeddylgar, a. incogitative
Anfeidredd, n. infinity
Anfeidrol, a. infinite; immense
Anfelus, a. not sweet; insipid
Anfelusder, n. lack of sweetness
Anferth, a. without beauty
Anferthedd, n. unsightliness
Anfesurol, a immeasureable
Anfethiant, n. infalability
Anfodd, n. displeasure
Anfoddgar, a. displeasing
Anfoddhad, n. a displeasing
Anfoddhau, v. to displease
Anfoddiad, n. disobliging
Anfoddio, v. to displease
Anfoddlawn, a. discontented
Anfoddlondeb, n. discontented-
Anfoddloni, v. to discontent [ness
Anfoddog, a. dissatisfied, implacable [ness
Anfoddogrwydd, n. implacable-
Anfoddogi, v. to discontent
Anfoes, n. immorality, rudeness
Anfocsgar, a. unmannerly
Anfoesol, a. immoral
Anfoesoldeb, n. immorality
Anfoethus, a. not dainty
Anfon, a. sending; v. to send
Anfonadwy, a. that may be sent
Anfonedd, a. without nobility
Anfoneddig, a. ungenteel
Anfoneddigaidd, a. ungentle
Anfoniad, n. a mission
Anfonol, a. missive; missionary
Anfri, n. disrespect, disesteem
Anfucheddol, a. of ill habit
Anfudd, a. lack of profit

| ANF | 19 | ANG |

Anfuddiol, a. unprofitable
Anfwyn. a. unkind, uncivil
Anfwynhau, v. to cease enjoying
Anfwynder, n. unkindness
Anfyfyrdod, n. unstudiousness
Anfyfyriol, a. inconsiderate
Anfynegol, a. undeclared
Anfynych, a. unfrequent, seldom
Anfywiog, a. inactive
Anfywiogrwydd, n. inanimation
Anffawd, n. misfortune
Anffel, a. not cunning, unwily
Anffodiog, a. unfortunate
Anffodrwydd, n. miscarriage
Anffrwynol, a. unbridled
Anffrwythlawn, a. unfruitful
Anffurfiol, a. deformed
Anffyddlawn, a. unfaithful
Anffyddlondeb, n. unfaithfulness
Anffyniant, n. improsperity
Angad, n. grasp of the hand
Angar, n. receptacle of heat
Angeu, n. death
Angawl, a. capacious
Angder, n. capaciousness
Angel, n. an angel
Angell, n. a pinion; an arm
Angen, n. necessity; need; fate or destiny
Angerdd, n. hot steam; heat; strength, force
Angerddol, a. vehement; intense
Angerddoldeb, n. vehemency
Angeuo, v. to render deadly
Angeuol, a. deadly; mortal
Angeuoldeb, n. mortality
Anghadarn, a. unpowerful
Anghaead, a. unshut
Anghacriad, n. a dismantling
Anghaeth, a. unconfined
Anghaffaeliad, n. non-attainment
Anghaledu, to make inobdurate
Anghaloni, v. to dishearten
Anghall, a. indiscreet
Anghallineb, n. indiscretion
Anghar, n. unloveliness
Anghariad, n. disaffection
Anghariadus, a. unamiable

Angharu, v. to cease to love
Angharuaidd, a. unlovely
Anghefnogi, v. to discourage
Angheinder, n. inaccuracy
Anghel, a. uncovered; unveiled
Angheledig, a. unconceiled
Anghelfydd, a. unskilful
Anghelfyddyd, n. unskilfulness
Anghelu, v. to reveal
Anghen, n. a destitude state
Anghenfil, n. a monster
Angheniad, n. necessitating
Angheniatâu, v. to disallow
Anghenus, a. necessitious
Anghenoctyd, n. necessitude
Angenrhaid, n. necessity
Anghladd, a. uninterred
Anghlaer, a. not bright; not clear
Anghlod, n. dishonour; dispraise
Anghlodfawr, a. dishonourable
Anghlyd, a. uncomfortable
Anghoel, n. disbelief
Anghoelgar, a. disbelieving
Anghoelio, v. to disbelieve
Anghoeth, a. impure
Anghof, n. forgetfulness
Anghofio, v. to forget
Anghofus, a. forgetful, oblivious
Anghorfful, a. incorporeal
Anghosp, a. without punishment
Anghraff, a. void of sharpness
Anghrafft, n. a pattern
Anghred, n. unbelief
Anghredadwy, a. incredible
Anghredadyn, n. an infidel
Anghrediniaeth, n. unbelief
Anghrediniol, n. incredulous
Anghredu, v. to disbelieve
Anghrefydd, n. impiety
Anghrefyddol, a. irreligious
Anghrist, n. antichrist
Anghroesaw, n. inhospitability
Anghroesawgar, a. inhospitable
Anghroesawu, v. to treat inhospitably
Anghroyw, a. inarticulate
Angrhwn, a. not round
Anghryno, a. incompact

Anghrynodeb, n. incompactness
Anghudd, a. unobscured
Anghwaneg, a. additional [ion
Anghwanegiad, n. augmentat-
Anghwanegol, a. augmentative
Anghwanegu, v. to augment
Anghybyddlyd, a. uncovetious
Anghydbwys, a. not equipollent
Anghydfod, n. disagreement
Anghydfodol, a. disagreeing [ity
Anghydffurfiad, n. nonconform-
Anghydffurfiol, nonconforming
Anghydgerdd, n. discordance
Anghydnabyddus, unacquainted
Anghydnaws, a. unsocial
Anghydsafedd, n. disagreement
Anghydsail, a. incompatible
Anghydsain, a. discordant
Anghydsyniad, n. incompliance
Anghydsynio, v. to disagree
Anghydsyniol, a. dissentaneous
Anghydweddol, a. inconsistent
Anghydwybod, a. unconscionable
Anghyfaddas, a. inconvenient
Anghyfaddasol, a. incongruous
Anghyfaddasu, v. to render inconvenient
Anghyfaddef, a. unconfessed
Anghyfagos, a. incontiguous
Anghyfamserol, a. unseasonable
Anghyfan, a. incomplete
Anghyfander, n. discontinuity
Anghyfanedd, a. uninhabited
Anghyfanedd-dra, n. desolation
Anghyfaneddol, uninhabitable
Anghyfaneddu, v. to desolate
Anghyfansawdd, n. decomposite
Anghyfansoddi, v. to decompound
Anghyfartal, a. disproportional
Anghyfartaledd, n. disproportion
Anghyfartalu, v. to disproportion
Anghyfarwydd, a. unacquainted
Anghyfatebol, a. unanswerable
Anghyfathrach, without kindred
Anghyfeiliorn, a. unerring
Angby feillgar, unfriendly [ness
Anghyfeillgarwch, n. unfriendli-
Anghyfeiriad, n. indirectness
Anghyfwrdd, a. incontiguous
Anghyfyrddol, a. unopposing
Anghyfiaith, a. of different language
Anghyfiawn, a. unrighteous
Anghyfiawnder, n. unjustice
Anghyfiawnhaol, a. unjustifying
Anghyfieithu, v. to mistranslate
Anghyfieuad, n. disjunction
Anghyfing, a. unconfined
Anghyflawn, a. uncomplete
Anghyflawnder, n. incompletion
Anghyfle, n. lack of opportunity
Anghyfleu, v. to displace
Anghyfleus, a. inconvenient
Anghyfleusdra, n. inconveniency
Anghyflo, a. not with calf
Anghyfluniad, n. disconformity
Anghyflym, a. not quick
Anghyfnewidiad, immutability
Anghyfnewidiol, a. immutable
Anghyfnewid, a. void of change
Anghyfnod, a. inopportune
Anghyfochrol, a. not parallel
Anghyfodol, a. not rising
Anghyfoed, a. of unequal age
Anghyfoen, a. not big with lamb
Anghyfoes, a. not contemporary
Anghyfraith, n. illegality
Anghyfranol, incommunicative
Anghyfidro, a. imperfect
Anghyfrdwyth, a. unelastic
Anghyfredol, a. inconcurrent
Anghyfreidiol, a. unnecessary
Anghyfreithgar, a. unlitigious
Anghyfreithiol, a. illegal
Anghyfreithlawn, a. unlawful
Anghyfreithlondeb, n. unlawfulness
Anghyfraith, a. without semblance
Anghyfrodeddu, v. to untwine
Anghyfroddol, a. uncontributive
Anghyfrwydd, a. unexpeditious
Anghyfrwys, a. uncunning [tion
Anghyfryngiad, n. unintervention
Anghyfrysedd, a. unexcessive

Anghyfundod, n. disagreement
Anghyfundeb, n. disunion
Anghyfuwch, unequal in height
Anghyfwedd, a. incompatible
Anghyfwerth, a. unequivalent
Anghyfwng, a. void of space
Anghyfystyr, a. of different im-
Anghyffelyb, a. dissimilar [port
Anghyffelybrwydd, n. dissimilarity
Anghyffred, a. uncomprehended
Anghyffredin, a. uncommon
Anghyffröad, n. want of motion
Anghyhoedd, a. not public
Anghyhuddol, a. unnaccused
Anghyhyd. a. unequable
Anghyhyrol, a. unmusculous
Anghymal. a. jointless
Anghymath, a. dissimilar
Anghymdeithasol, a. unsociable
Anghymedrol, a. immoderate
Anghymeradwy, a. unacceptable
Anghymeradwyaeth, n. unacceptableness
Anghymeriad n. inacceptation
Anghymesur, a. unproportioned
Anghymar, a. matchless
Anghymariaeth, n. disparity
Anghymelliad, n. incompulsion
Anghymen, a. inelegant
Anghymbleth, a. uncomplicated
Anghymhwys, a. unqualified; improper
Anghymhwysder, n. unfitness
Anghymodiad, n. disagreeing
Anghymodlonedd, n. irrasibility
Anghymwl, a. cloudless
Anghymwynas, n. unkindness
Anghymydogol, a. unneighbour-
Anghymyn, a. intestate [ly
Anghymysg, a. unmingled
Anghyndyn, a inobstinate
Anghynes, a. not warm; uncheerful
Anghynyrfol, a. undisturbing
Anghynnar, a. not early; unforward
Anghynnefin, a. unusual

Anghynnefod, a. uncustomary
Anghynneuol, a. uncontending
Anghynnil, a. unfrugal [ting
Anghynniweiriol, a. unfrequen-
Anghynnrychol, a. not present
Anghynnull, a. uncollective
Anghynnwys, n. incontinence
Anghynyrch, a. void of increase
Anghynnysgaeth, a. unendowed
Anghynghanedd, inconsonancy
Anghyrbwyll, a. without a hint
Anghyrchedig, a. unapproached
Anghyrchol, a. unrecurrent
Anghyrhaeddiad, n. non-attainment
Anghysain, a. dissonant
Anghysbell, a. not adjoining
Anghystadledd, n. disproportion
Anghystal, a. unequivalent
Anghysefin, a. unprimitive
Anghysgodi, v. to unshelter
Anghyson, a. discordant
Anghysondeb, n. disagreement
Anghystlynol, a. unallied
Anghystuddiol, a. unafflicting
Anghystwyol, a. unchastising
Anghysur, a. comfortless
Anghysurus, a. disconsolate
Anghysylltiad, n. disjunction
Anghyttal, a. without contribution
Anghytoni, v. to discord
Anghyttras, a. void of kindred
Anghyttundeb, n. disagreement
Anghyttuniad, a. inconcurrence
Anghyttuno, v. to disagree
Anghythruddol, unperturbated
Anghywair, a. innaccurate; discordant
Anghyweithas, a. untoward
Anghywerth, a. unequivalent
Anghywilydd, a. shameless
Anghywilydd-dra, n. impudence
Anghywir, inaccurate; faithless
Anghywirdeb, n. inaccuracy
Anghywlad, n. an absentee
Anghywraint, a. unskilful [ness
Anghywreinrwydd, n. unskilf'l-

Angladd, n. a burial, a funeral
Anglawdd, n. a cemetry
Anglef, n. a hollow noise
Angor, n. an anchor
Angordreth, n. anchorage duty
Angoredig, a. anchored
Angori, v. to anchor
Angoriad, n. an anchoring
Angraddol, a. ungraduated
Angraifft, n. correction; example
Angreddfol, a. degenerative
Angreiddiol, a. unscorching
Angylaidd, a. angelical
Angyles, n. a female angel
Angyliaeth, n. angelic state
Anhad, a. fretful; seedless
Anhaeddiant, n. demerit
Anhaeddol, a. undeserving
Anhael, a. illiberal; mean
Anhaelioni, n. illiberality
Anhaerllugrwydd, n. unfrowardness
Anhalogrwydd, n. undefiledness
Anhallt, a. unsaline, unsalted
Anhanesol, a. unhistorical
Anhanfod, a. non-existent
Anhap, n. mischance, mishap
Anhapus, unfortunate, unhappy
Anhardd, a. unseemly indecent
Anhatru, v. to disarray
Anhawdd, a. uneasy: difficult
Anhawddgar, a. unamiable
Anhawl, n. nonsuit
Anhawsder. n. difficulty
Anhebgor, n. indispensableness
Anheddychol, a. unpacificatory
Anheddychlawn, a. unpeaceful
Anheinyf, not nimble; sluggish
Anhelaeth, a. inextensive
Anheulog, a. not sunny; obscure
Anhidlaid, a. unstrained
Anhiliog, a. destitute of progeny
Anhocedus, a. undeceitful
Anhoddiad, n. indefeasibility
Anhoenus, a. unlively; sluggish
Anhoff, unamiable; undesirable
Anholiadol, a. uninterrogatory
Anholltog, a. uncleft, unsplit

Anhonedig, a. unasserted
Anhoriant, n. want of indulgence
Anhoywder, n. unsprightliness
Anhualu, v. to unfetter
Anhudoliaeth, n. unallurement
Anhuddol, a. unobscured
Anhulio, v. to divest of covering
Anhunanedd, disinterestedness
Anhunedd, n. sleeplessness
Anhwyl, n. indisposition
Anhwylio, v. to distract
Anhwylus, a. out of order
Anhwylusdod, n. obstruction
Anhŷ, a. not bold, bashful
Anhyalledd, n. impossibility
Anhyar, a. not easily ploughed
Anhyawdledd, n. ineloquency
Anhyballedd, n. infallibility
Anhybarch, unworthy of respect
Anhybarthedd, n. indivisibility
Anhyblygrwydd, n. inflexibility
Anhybwylledd, n. imprudence
Anhydawdd, a. undissolvable
Anhyder, n. distrust
Anhyderus, a. distrustful
Anhydòr, a. infrangable
Anhydraeth, a. unuterable
Anhydraidd, a. impenetrable
Anhydraigl, a. undeclinable
Anhydraul, a. indigestible
Anhydrefn, not easily arranged
Anhydrig, a. uninhabitable
Anhydrinedd, n. untractability
Anhydro, a. unconvertible
Anhydwyll, a. undeceivable
Anhydyn, a. obstinate [ness
Anhydynrwydd, n. untractable-
Anhyddadledd, indisputability
Anhyfder, a. inexperienced
Anhyfedrwydd, n. unskilfulness
Anhyfryd, a. unpleasant
Anhyffordd, a. impassable
Anhyfrwyn, a. not easily bridled
Anhygael, a. unattainable
Anhygall, a. not apt to be wary
Anhygar, a. unamiable [noxious
Anhygas, a. not execrable, inob-
Anhyglod, a. disreputable

Anhyglud, a. not easy to carry
Anhyglyw, a. inaudible
Anhygoel, a. incredible
Anhygof, a. immemorable
Anhygoll, a. inadmissable
Anhygosp, a. incorrigible
Anhygred, a. incredible
Anhygryn, a. not apt to tremble
Anhygudd, a. not easily hidden
Anhygwymp, a. unapt to fall
Anhygwyn, a. unapt to complain
Anhygyrch, a. unfrequented
Anhyladd, a. not easily cut off
Anhylanw, a. unsatiable
Anhyḷaw, a. unhandy, inexpert
Anhyled, a. inexpansible
Anhylosg, a. incombustible
Anhynaws, a. inaffable; untoward
Anhynod, a unnotable
Anhysbys, a. not manifest
Anhysbysrwydd, n. uncertainty
Anhysbydd, a. exhaustless
Anhywaith, a. untractable
Anial, n. a desert: a. uncleared
Anialog, a. desert, savage
Anialfan, n. a savage scene
Anialu, v. to desolate
Anialwch, n. a wilderness
Anian, n. a nature; instinct
Anianawd, n. temperament
Aniander, n. naturalness [ology
Aniandduwiaeth, n. physic-the-
Anianddysg, n. physiology
Anianol, a. natural
Anianolder, n. natural right
Anianydd, n. naturalist
Anianyddiaeth, n. physics
Anianyddol, a. physiological
Anifeilaidd, a. brutish, brutal
Anifeilcidd-dra, n. brutality
Anifeilciddio, v. to imbrute
Anifeilhau, v. to brutalize
Anifeilig, a. brutal, beastial
Anifel, n. animal
Anlanwaith, a. uncleanly
Anlanweithdra, n. uncleanliness
Anlew, a. not brave; not clever

Anlewder, n. uncourageousness
Anlewdid, n. dastardliness
Anloyw, a. not bright, not lucid
Anllad, a. wanton, lascivious
Anlladaidd, a. apt to be wanton
Anlladedd, n. wantonness
Anlladfab, n. a wanton man
Anlladferch, n. a wanton woman
Anlladu, v. to grow wanton
Anllarialdd, a. ungentle
Anllathraidd, a. unresplendent
Anllathrudd, a. void of fornication
Anllesol, a. disadvantageous
Anllettygar, a. inhospitable
Anlliosog, a. unfrequent
Anlliosogrwydd, n. infrequence
Anlliw, a. colourless: n. a stain
Anllosgadwy, a. incombustible
Anllosgedig, a. unignited
Anllostog, a. without a tail
Anlluddedig, a. unfatigued
Anllwybraidd, not easily passed
Anllygredd, n. incorruption
Anllygredigaeth, n. incorruptive
Anllwythedig, a. imburdened
Anllygradwy, a. incorruptible
Anllythyrenog, a. illiterate
Anllythyrog, a. illiterate
Anllywodraeth, n. anarchy
Anmhar, a. out of repair
Anmharch, n. disrespect
Anmharod, a. unprepared [ory
Anmharattoawl, a. unpreparat-
Anmhendod, n. indecision
Anmhenodol, a. indefinitive
Anmherchenogi, v. to unappropriate [ning
Anmherthynasol, a. unappertai-
Anmherthynu, v. to make irrele-
Anmhetrus, a. indubious [vant
Anmhlantadwy, a. barren
Anmhlcidiol, a. impartial
Anmhlethol, a. uncomplicated
Anmhlygu, v. to undouble
Anmhrawf, a. without proof
Anmhreswyl. a. without a home
Anmhridwerth, without ransom

Anmhriodolrwydd, n. disappropriateness
Anmhrydferthedd, n. inelegancy
Anmhreiddiog, a. undepredatory
Anmhriod. a. unmarried
Anmhriodol, a. unappropriated
Anmhrofiadol, a. unpropationary
Anmhrudd, a. insedate
Anmhryderus, a. unanxioust
Anmhrydferth, a. inelegant
Anmhrydlon, a. unseasonable
Anmhrysur, a. undiligent
Anmhuredd, n. impurity
Anmhwyll, n. indiscretion
Anmhwylledd, n. irrationality
Anmhwyllog, a. irrational
Anmhybur, a. impotent, infirm
Anmlasus, insipid, tasteless
Anmraint, n. dishonour
Anmri, a. void of privilege
Anmrwd, a. unheated, unboiled
Annadleuadwy, a. incontestable
Annadleuol, a. undisputative
Annair, n. reproach, disgrace
Annarbobaeth, n. improvidence
Annarpwylliad, n. impersuasion
Annarfod, a. endless; infinite
Annarllenol, a. unlegible
Annarostyngiad, n. insubjection
Annarpar, a. unprepared
Annattodol, a. inexplicable
Annatoddiad, n. indissolvability
Anneallus, a. unintelligent
Annechreuol, a. uncomencing
Annedwydd, a. nnhappy
Annedwyddwch, n. unhappiness
Annedd, n. a dwelling
Anneddfa, n. a dwelling place
Anneddfolder, n. immorality
Anneddiad n. residing
Anneddl, n. a dwelling place
Ann ddu, v. to dwell
Annefnyddiol, a. unsubstantial
Annefod, n. lack of ceremony
Annefodol, a. unceremonial
Anneffro, a. unwake
Annegyddol, a. unnegative
Annehender, n. indexteriety

Anneilio, v. to drop leaves
Anneillledig. a. underived
Anneilltuoldeb, inseparability
Anneirfuwch, n. a young cow
Anneiryd, a. irrelevant
Annesyfol, a. unrequesting
Annelog, a. on the bend; aiming
Anneliad, a stretching; aiming
Annelu, v. to stretch; to aim
Anner, n. a heifer [ableness
Annerbynioldeb, n. unaccept-
Annerth, n. impotence
Annestledd, n. indelicacy
Annewisiol, a. ineligible
Annewr, a. irresolute
Annhaeniad, n. inexpansion
Annhaerni, n. uninportunity
Annhananadwy, a. unignitable
Annhaw, a. unsilent, untacit
Annhawel, a. unsilent
Annhebyg, a. dissimilar
Annhegwch, n. unfairness
Annheilwng, a. unworthy
Annheilyngdod, n. unworthiness
Annhelmlad, n. apathy
Annhelediw, a. ungraceful
Annheredd, n. impurity
Annherfyn, a. boundless
Annherfynol, a. infinite
Annherfysgol, a. untumultuous
Annhesog, a. void of sun heat
Annheuluog, a. undomestical
Annhiriog, a. void of land
Annhirion, a. unpleasant
Annhlysni, n. inelegance
Annhô, a. void of covering
Annhoddadwy, a. indissolvable
Annholiant, n. undimunition
Annholladwy, a. undeductable
Annhoradwy. a. irrefragable
Annhorneth, a. void of p oduce
Annhostedd, n. inseverity
Annhosturi, n. ruthlessness
Annhosturiol, a. unpitying
Annrhachwantus, a. uncovetous
Annrhaethadwy, inexpressible
Annrhafodol, a. unbustling
Annhrallodus. a. unafflicting

Annhrancedig, a. unannihilated
Annhrafferthus, a. unassiduous
Annhras, a. void of kindred
Annhrefig, a. nonresident
Annhrefnu, v. to disorder
Annhrefnus, a. disorderly
Annhreiddiol, a. unpenetrating
Annhremygol, a. undespising
Annhrethadwy a. untaxable
Annhreilledig, a. unconsumed
Annhrigiant, n. nonresidence
Annhroseddus, intransgressive
Annhrugarog, a. unmerciful
Annhruthrol, a. unfulsome
Annhrwsiadus, a. unarrayed
Annbrwydded, n. unlicensed
Annhrybelid, a. inelegant
Annhryloyw, a. untransparent
Annhrywanadwy, impenetrable
Aunhuddo, v. to uncover
Annhueddol, a. impartial
Annhwng, a. nonjuring
Annhwyllo, v. to uudeceive
Annhwyllodrus,a. unfraudulent
Annhycianus, a. unsuccessful
Annhyciant, n. improsperity
Annhymig, a. unseasonable
Annhymoraidd, a. unseasonable; uncomfortable
Annhyner, a. unkindly, harsh
Annhynged, n. misfortune
Annhyngedfenol, a. unfated
Annhywyll a. inobscure
Annialedig, a. unrevenged
Anniarhebus. a. unproverbial
Anniog, a. unslothful, not idle
Annibech, a. not sinless
Anniben, a. infinite
Anniblog, a. unbedaggled
Annibynol, a. independent
Annichell, a. without guile
Annichlyn, a. incircumspect
Anniddan, a. comfortless
Anniddig, a. unappeased
Anniddigrwydd, n. peevishness
Anniddos, a. not secured from
Anniddymol, undefeasible [wet
Annifaol, a. unconsuming

Annifianadwy, a. unfading
Annifrif, a. unsedate
Annifrodol, a. undilapidating
Anniffoddadwy,a.unquenchable
Annigiol, a. unoffending
Annigonedd, n. unsufficiency
Annigrifol, a. unamusing
Annileadwy, a. indelible
Annilys, a. uncertain, not sure
Annillynu, v. to make ugly
Anniofal, a. not careless
Anniogel, a. not secure
Annioledig, a. unobliterated
Annirgel, a. unconcealed
Annirmygol, a. undespicable
Annirnadiad, n.inapprehension
Annirprwyol, a. unsupplying
Annirwestwch, n. inabstinency
Annirwyol, not liable to penalty
Anniryw, a. undegenerate
Annisberod, a. undispersed
Annisgynol, a. undescending
Annistrywiol, a. undestructive
Anniwair, a. unclean, unchaste
Anniwallus, a, unsatiating
Anniweirdeb, n. incontinence
Anniwyd, a. indolent
Anniwygiol, a. unreforming
Anniwylledig, a. uncultivated
Annodi, v. to suspend
Annoeth, a. unwise, imprudent
Annoethineb, n. indiscretion
Annofi, v. to become refractory
Annog, n. incitement; v. to indite; to exhort
Annogaeth, n. admonition
Annogedig, a. incited; admonished
Annogiad, n. an inciting
Annogol, a. inciting
Annolurus, a. unpainful
Annoniog, a. giftless, unskilful
Annos, n. a driving; v. to drive to chase
Annuw, a. atheistic; faithless
Annuwiaeth, n. atheism
Annuwiol, a. ungodly, wicked
Annuwioldeb, n. ungodliness

Annwfn, n. the great deep
Annwyd, n. a cold, a chillness
　Cael yr annwyd, to catch cold
Annwydaidd, a. chilly, cold
Annwydedd, n. chilliness
Annwydog, a. cold, chilly
Annyben, a. void of purpose; endless [iousness
Annybendod,n.endlessness; ted-
Annybenol, a. inconclusive
Annyblyg, a. unfolded
Annychweladwy, a. irreversible
Annychymygol, a. unimaginary
Annyddan, a. comfortless
Annyfal, a. lazy, heedless
Annyfodadwy, a. inaccessable
Annyfrol, a. not watery
Annyffygadwy, a. indefectible
Annygymodol, a. unconciliatory
Annyledus, a. unincumbent
Annylyedog, a. not having claim
Annylynol, a. inconsequent
Annymchweladwy, a. not returnable
Annymunol, a. undesirable
Annynsoddol, a. impersonal
Annynwaredol, a. unimitative
Annyoddefadwy, a. unsufferable
Annyolchgar, a. unthankful
Annyrchafedig, a. unexalted
Annysbeidiol, a. unintermitting
Annysbendawd, n. inconclusive
Annysgedig, a. unlearned [ness
Annysglaer, a. not bright
Annysgwyliad, n. inexpectation
Annystaw, a. not silent
Annyundeb, n. disagreement
Annyunol, a. disagreeable
Annywedadwy, a. unspeakable
Annyweddog, a. unconjugal
Annywyllyniog, a. uncultivated
Anobaith, n. hopelessness
Anobeithiad, n. desperation
Anobeithio, v. to despair
Anobeithlon, a. unhopeful
Anobrwy, a. unrequited
Anobryn, a. void of reward
Anocheladwy, a. unavoidable

Anodidog, a. unexcelling
Anodinebus, a. unadulterous
Anoddefadwy, a. insufferable
Anoeth, n. incomprehensibility
Anofal, a. careless; imprudent
Anofidiol, a. untroubled
Anofnog, Anofnus, a. fearless
Anofwyedig, a. unvisited
Anofynol, a. uninquisitive
Anogonol, a. inglorious
Anohebol, a. uncorresponding
Anolau, a. indistinct; dark
Anolrhain, a. trackless
Anoludog, a. poor, not rich
Anoluddiol, a. unobstructed
Anolygiadol, a. unspeculative
Anolygus, a. unsightly, ugly
Anollyngedig, a. unloosened
Anorbwyllig, a. not frantic
Anorchestol, a. unexcelling
Anorchfygedig, a. unvanquished
Anorchuddio, v. to uncover
Anoresgynadwy, unconquerable
Anorfod, a. unsurmounted
Anoriog, a. unfickle; sedate
Anormesol, a. unmolesting
Anorphen, a. endless, infinite
Anorphwyllog, a. undistracted
Anorphwys, a. restless, unquiet
Anorsafol, a. unstationary
Anorthrechol, a. unsubduing
Anorweddol, a. unrecumbent
Anosodedig, a. undeposited
Anosteg, a. unsilent, noisy
Anostyngol, a. unsubjected
Anrhadlon, a. ungracious
Anrhagddarbodus, unforeseeing
Anrhagfarnedig, a. unprejudicated
Anrhagflaenol,a.unanticipating
Anrhaghanfodol, a. not preexistent [vidential
Anrhagluniaethol, a. not pro-
Anrhagorol, a. not excelling
Anrhagrithiol, a. not hypocritial
Anrhaith, n. pillage; distress
Anrhanog, a. unparticipating
Anrheg, n. a present, a gift

Anrhegedig, a. presented, gifted
Anrhegiad, n. a presenting
Anrhegol, a. presenting, giving
Anrhegu, v. to present, to give
Anrheidiol, a. not necessitating
Anrheidus, a. not necessitious
Anrheithgar, a. depredatory
Anrheithiad, n. depredation
Anrheithiedig, a. desolate
Anrheithio, v. to prey, to spoil
Anrheithiol, a. depredating
Anrheithiwr, n. a desolater
Anrhiniol, a. unmysterious
Anrhinwedd, n. want of virtue
Anrhithio, v. to disappear
Anrhodresol, a. unostentatious
Anrhoddedig, a. unbestowed
Anrhwydd, a. not free, difficult
Anrhwym, a. unbound, untied
Anrhwystrus, a. unobstructive
Anrhybyddiedig, unforewarned
Anrhydedd, a. honour
Anrhydeddol, a. honouring
Anrhydeddiad, n. honouring
Anrhydeddu, v. to honour
Anrhydeddus, a. honourable
Anrhyddiad, a. void of liberty
Anrhyfygus, a. unpresuming
Anrhythedig, a. undistended
Ansadrwydd, n. instability
Ansafadwy, a. unstable
Ansangedig, a. untrampled
Ansalw, a. not vile or mean
Ansail, a. baseless, vileness
Ansarhaus, a. uninsulting
Ansarig, a. not froward
Ansathredig, a. untrodden
Ansawdd, n. a being, a person; a state; a quality
Ansawdd-air, an adjective
Ansefydlog, a, unstationary
Anseibiant. n. want of leisure
Anseiliedig, a. unfounded
Anseiniol, a. unresounding
Ansenol, a. unrebuked
Anserchog, a. void of love
Anserchiad, n. a ceasing to love
Anserchogi, to become loveless

Anserchu, v. to cease loving
Ansiaradus a. not loquacious
Ansigladwy, a. firm, stable
Ansodi, v. to personify
Ansodol, a. personal
Ansodoldeb, n. personality
Ansoddadwy, a. that may blend
Ansoddi, to endow with quality
Ansoddiad, n. constituting
Ansoddol, a. component
Ansomgar, a. undeceiving
Ansoniarus, a. not sonorous
Ansyberwyd, n. incivility
Ansylweddol, a. unsubstantial
Ansymudoldeb, n. immobility
Ansyniad, n. inadvertency
Ansynwyr, a. senseless, witless
Ansyrthiol, a. not apt to fall
Antur, n. an attempt, venture
 ad. scarcely, hardly
Anturiedig, a. adventured
Anturiad, n. a venturing
Anturiaeth, n. an enterprize
Anturio, v. to venture
Anturiol, a. adventurous, bold
Anu, v. to contain, to hold
Anudon, n. false oath, perjury
Anudonol, a. falsely swearing
Anudoniaeth, n. perjury
Anufudd, a. disobedient
Anufuddhau, v. to disobey
Anufudd-dod, n. disobedience
Anundeb, a. disunion
Anunion, a. indirect, crooked
Anuniondeb, n. indirectness
Anuno, v. to disunite
Anunol, a. disagreeing
Anurddas, n. dishonour
Anurddasol, a. dishonourable
Anurddasu, v. to dishonour
Anurddo, to deprive of orders
Anwadal, a. unsteady
Anwadalder, n. unsteadiness
Anwadalu, v. to act inconstantly
Anwadalwch, n. fickleness
Anwaddol, a. dowerless
Anwaeredd, n. incontinency
Anwahaniad, indiscrimination

| ANW | 28 | ANY |

Anwahanred, uncharacteristic; indiscriminate
Anwaharddus, a. unprohibitory
Anwahoddedig, a. uninvited
Anwaith, n. inaction
Anwar, a. ungentle, arrogant
Anwaradwyddus, not disgrace-
Anwaredol, not delivering [ful
Anwaredd, n. ungentleness
Anwarth, a. shameless [ious
Anwarthruddol, a. unignomin-
Anwasanaethol,a. unserviceable
Anwasgar, a. unscattered
Anwasgodol, a. unsheltered
Anwastad, a. uneven, unsteady
Anwe, n. a woof
Anweddaidd,a.unseemly [ried
Anweddog, a. unyoked, unmar-
Anweddol, a. immoderate
Anweddus, a. unbeseeming
Anweinyddiol, a. unconducive
Anweladwy, a. invisible
Anwelladwy, a. incurable
Anwenwynig, a. unpoisonous
Anwes, n. indulgence
Anwesog, a. indulgent; peevish
Anwir, a. untrue; wicked
Anwiredd, n. untruth, iniquity
Anwireddol, a. iniquitous
Anwirio. v. to falsify, to lie
Anwirion, a. not innocent
Anwisgiedig, a. unclothed
Anwiw, a. unworthy, useless
Anwladaidd, a. not rustic
Anwledychiad, misgovernment
Anwneuthuradwy,a. impractic-
Anwresog, a. unfervid [able
Anwrhydri, n. unmanliness
Anwrol, a unmanly, cowardly
Anwroldeb, n. invirility
Anwrolder, n. unmanliness
Anwrteithiol, a. uncultivated
Anwrthblaid, a. unopposed
Anwrthbrawf, a. unrefuted
Anwrthdro, a. unrecurrent
Anwrthebol, a. unreplying
Anwrthnysig, a. unrefractory
Anwrthodadwy, a. unrejectable

Anwrthredol, a. unretrograde
Anwrthsafiad, n. inopposition
Anwrthun, a. undeformed
Anwrthwynebol, a. unopposing
Anwybod, a. ignorant, dull
Anwybodaeth, n. ignorance
Anwybyddiaeth, inconsiousness
Anwych, a. not brave, infirm
Anwyd, n. temper, cold [ing
Anwydaidd, a. affecting, dispos-
Anwydiad, n. disposition
Anwydol, a. temperamental
Anwyl, a. unbashful; beloved, dear. O'r anwyl, dear me
Anwylad, n. an endearing
Anwylaeth, n. endearment
Anwylaidd, a. endearing, lovely
Anwylhau, v. to endear, to love
Anwylo, v. to become lovely
Anwylder n. unbashfulness
Anwylddyn, n. a sweatheart
Anwyledd, n belovedness
Anwylyd, n. a loved one
Anwyllt, a.unwild, not furious
Anwyn, a. unimpassioned
Anŵyr, a. unoblique
Anwyrthiol, a. not miraculous
Anwysedig, a. unsummoned
Anwystledig, a. unpledged
Anwywder, n. unfadingness
Anymadroddus, a. untalkative
Anymaros, a. unforbearing
Anymarfer, a. unaccustomed
Anymarhous, a. impatient
Anymbleidiol, a. impartial
Anymchweladwy,a. irreversible
Anymdaenol, a. inexpansive
Anymdrechol, a. uncontentious
Anymddibynol, a. independent
Anymddiriad, n. diffidence; v. to mistrust
Anymddygiad, n. misdemeanor
Anymgeledd, a. uncherished
Anymgyffred, a. incomprehensi-
Anymgynal,a.incontinent [ble
Anymgyrchol, a. incongressive
Anymladdgar, a.not apt to fight
Anymofynol, a. uninquisitive

ANY 29 ARCH

Anymogel, incautious [emulate
Anymorchestiad, n. a ceasing to
Anymranol, a. unschismatic
Anymrithiol, a. undisguising
Anymroad, n. non-resignation
Anymroddiad, n. inapplication
Anymrysonol, a. incontentious
Anymsyniad, n. inconsideration
Anymuniad, n. disunion
Anymwad, a. unrenounced
Anymwthgar, a. inobtrusive
Anymyrus, a. unimportunate
Anynad, a. peevish, petulent
Anynadrwydd, n. petulence
Anyni, a. without energy
Anysplenydd, a. unresplendent
Anysgogol, a. unmoveable
Anysgrifenedig, a. unwritten
Anysgrythyrol, a. unscriptural
Anysgymod, n. dissention
Anysprydol, a. unspiritual
Anystig, a. unassiduous
Anystumiad, n. inflexibility
Anystwyth, a. unpliable, stiff
Anystwytho, v. to grow stiff
Anystyniad, n. inextension [ness
Anystyriaeth, n. inconsiderate-
Anystyrio, v. to be inconsiderate
Anystywallt, a. untoward
 Any other word not mentioned here commencing with AN, see AN, then the remaining part of the word.
Ar, n. the faculty of speech: n. surface, ploughed land, prep. on, upon. Ar i fyny, upwards ar i waered, downwards, pref. gives intensity to the signification of words; as arch in English.
Arab, a. joyous, merry, pleasant
Arabawl, a. yielding, merrriness
Arabedd, n. jocundity, drollery
Arabeddu, v. to create mirth
Arabeddus, a. facetious
Arabwr, n. a jester, a buffoon
Arad, n. a plough
Aradiad, n. tillage

Aradol, a. ploughing; arable
Aradu, v. to plough, to till
Aradwr, n. a ploughman
Aradwy, n. ploughing: a. arable
Araeth, n. speech, oration
Araf, a. slow, soft, mild, still
Arafaidd, a. rather slow; gentle
Arafedd, n. slowness
Arafeiddio, v. to slacken pace
Arafu, v. to go slower
Arafwch, n. slowness, mildness
Arall, a. another, other
Arallair, n. a paraphrase
Aralledig, a. diversified
Aralleg, n. an allegory
Arallegol, a. allegorical
Arallegiad, n. an allegorizing
Arallegu, v. to allegorize
Arallegwr, n. an allegorizer
Aralliad, n. alteration
Arallrwydd, n. alternity
Arallu, v. to alter; to invert
Aramred, n. perambulation
Aran, n. high place, or alp
Araul, a. serene; pleasant
Arbed, n. a sparing, a saving: v. to spare, to save.
Arbediad, n. a sparing a saving
Arbedol, a. saving, sparing
Arbedwr, n. a sparer [peculiar
Arbenig, principal; excellent;
Arbenigol, a. superior, excell-
Arbenigrwydd, n. supremacy [ing
Arbenog, a. principal, supreme
Arbenol, a. sovereign, supreme
Arberyglu, v. to endanger
Arbetrus, a. very dubious
Arbetruso, v. to doubt much
Arbrinder, n. great scarcity
Arbwyll, n. reason, intellect
Arbwylleb, Arbwylleg, n. logic
Arbylu, v. to blunt greatly
Arch, n. a request, a petition, a demand: n. a trunk, or chest: a. chief, topmost, prin-
Archangel, n. archangel [cipal
Archdeyrn, n. a monarch
Archdeyrnaeth, n. monarchy

| ARCH | 30 | ARDD |

Archdeyrnol, a. monarchial
Archddug, n. an archduke
Archddugiaeth, n. archdukedom
Archdduges, n. archduchess
Archddugol, a. archducal
Archedig, a. demanded, required
Archedigaeth, n. requisition
Archedigol, a. imperative
Archen, n. a shoe, sandal
Archenad, n. apparel, clothing
Archenu, v. to put on shoes
Archesgob, n. archbishop
Archesgobaeth, n. archbishopric
Archesgobawd, n. archiepiscop-
Archiad, n. a demanding [acy
Archlen, n. the loin, or waist
Archoll, n. a wound, a cut
Archolladwy, a. vulnerable
Archolledig, a. wounded, cut
Archolli, v. to wound, to cut
Archolliad, n. a wounding
Archwaeth, n. savour, taste
Archwaethiad, n. a savouring
Archwaethu, v. to savour
Archwaethus, a. savoury
Ardal, n. a region, a province
Ardalaeth, n. a marquisate
Ardalwr, n. a marquis; a borderer, a countryman
Ardalydd, n. a marcher
Ardant, a. clamorous, noisy
Ardawch, a. hazy and sultry
Ardebed, n. the face, feature
Ardeml, n. a spread out
Ardochi, v. to become hazy
Ardraws, a. transverse, cross
Ardrem, n. prospect, view
Ardremu, v. to survey, to behold
Ardreth, n. a tax, a rate
Ardrethiad, n. a rating
Ardrethol, a. rated, taxed
Ardrethu, v. to rate or tax
Ardymmher, n. temperature
Ardymmherol, a. temperamental
Ardymmheru, v. to temper
Ardyst, n. an open witness
Ardystio, v. to certify
Ardd, n. ploughed land

Arddadgan, v. to denounce
Arddangos, to indicate, to shew
Arddangosiad, n. indication
Arddangosol, a. indicative
Arddal, n. support, a bearing
Arddansawdd, n. ontology, the science of entities.
Arddansodol, a. metaphysical
Arddant, n. a gag-tooth
Arddawd, n. a prefix, an adjunct
Arddawn, n. a talent
Arddedig, a. tilled, ploughed
Arddedfol, a. institutional
Arddeddf, n. an institute
Arddefod, n. a ceremony
Arddefodol, a. ceremonial
Arddelw, n. a claim, a challenge; an assertion, v. to claim; to assert
Arddelwad, n. an averment
Ardderchafad, Ardderchafiad, n. advancement
Ardderchafu, to elevate highly
Ardderchedd, n. excellence
Ardderchog, a. excellent, exal-
Ardderchogi, v. to dignify [ted
Arddiad, n. a ploughing
Arddigon, n. superfluity
Arddigoni, v. to make an excess
Arddigonol, a. superabundant
Arddisgyn, v. to befall, to hap-
Arddisum, a. diminutive [pen
Arddodi, v. to prefix, to annex
Arddodiad, n. a preposition, a prefix. Arddodiad dwylaw, the imposition of hands.
Arddodol, a. prepositive
Arddoniant, n. great endowment
Arddosbarth, n. indiscretion
Arddrych, n. a prospect; view
Arddu, a. very black, or dark: v. to plough, to till
Arddull, n. form, image
Ardduniant, n. sublimity
Arddunol, a. unique; majestic
Ardduo, v. to blacken over
Arddwr, n. a ploughman
Arddwriaeth, n. agriculture

Arddwrn, n. a wrist
Arddwyo, v. to manage
Arddygraff, n. orthography
Arddyled, n. obligation, duty
Arddyledog, a. under obligation
Arddyledus, a. highly incumbent
Arddymchwelyd, v. to overwhelm
Arddyrch, a. uplifted, exalted
Arddyrchafiaeth, n. superemin-
  ence, exaltation
Arddyrchafu, v. to highly exalt
Arddysbaid, n. discontinuity
Arddysg, n. classical learning
Arddysglaer, a. resplendent
Arddysgwyl, v. to be in expect-
Arddystaw, a. very silent [ation
Arddystyru, v. to contemplate
Areb, n. faculty of speaking
Arebol, a. fluent, witty, smart
Arebu, v. to talk wittily
Arebydd, n. a witty person
Aredig, n. ploughing, tillage
  v. to plough, to till
Areiliad, n. what guards
Areilio, v. to attend
Areithfa, n. an oratory
Areithiad, n. an haranguing
Areithio, v. to harangue, to make
Areithiol, a. oratorial [a speech
Areithydd, n. an orator
Aren, n. a kidney
Areiniol, a. tending to be witty
Areuledd, n. serenity
Arf, n. a weapon, tool
Arfaeth, n. design, intent
Arfaethiad, n. a purposing
Arfaethol, a. intentional
Arfaethu, to design, to purpose
Arfaethus, a. designing
Arfaethwr, n. a designer
Arfanwl, a. very accurate
Arfdy, n. an armoury
Arfedig, a. armed
Arfeichio, v. to give bail
Arfeiddio, v. to adventure
Arfeilio, v. to decay [the ankle
Arfeilyn, n. a leather band round
Arfel, n. a design

Arfelu, v. to draw a likeness
Arfelydd, n. a delineator
Arfer, n. use, custom: v. to use
  to accustom
Arferiad, n. an accustoming
Arferol, a. customary, usual
Arferoldeb, n. usage, custom
Arferu, v. to use, to inure
Arfgell, n. an armoury
Arfiad, n. an arming
Arflodeuad, n. reflorescence
Arfod, n. opportunity, season
Arfodig, a. convenient, timely
Arfodog, a. having opportunity
Arfodol, a. opportune
Arfoel, a. bald-pated
Arfoelaidd, a. tending to baldness
Arfoeledd, n. baldness
Arfoeli, v. to grow bald
Arfoelni, n. baldness
Arfog, a. armed, bearing arms
Arfogaeth, n. armour
Arfogai, n. m. one armed at all
  points; the palmer
Arfogi, v. to put in arms
Arfogwl, n. a dried skin on a post
  with pebbles in it
Arfoledd, n. exultation
Arfoliant, n. enconium
Arfoll, n. reception, welcome;
  contract; promise
Arfor, n. the seaside: a. maritime
Arfordir, n. maritime land
Arfordref, n. a sea-port town
Arfordwy, n. maritime region
Arforol, a. maritime. seafaring
Arfraint, n. prerogative
Arfri, n. high privelege
Arfu, v. to arm
Arffed, n. a lap, a forepart
Arffedaid, n. lapful
Arffedog, n. fosterer
Arffedogaeth, n. fosterage
Arffordd, n. the high road
Arfforddi, v. to direct the way
Arfforddol, a. wayfaring
Argae, n. a stoppage, a dam
Argaead, n. a shutting in

Argaëedigaeth, n. obstruction
Argaeol, a. astringent
Argaeth, a. unslaved, captive
Argaledu, v. to make obdurate
Argan, a. very bright
Arganfod, n. perception; v. to perceive, to fascinate
Arganlyn, v. to follow
Arganu, v. to elucidate
Ar au, v. to inclose
Argeisio, v. to endeavour
Argelu, v to seclude, to secrete
Arglawdd, n. an embankment
Argledriad, n. a protector
Arglod, n. fame, renown
Argludiad, n. deportation
Arglwydd, n. one having domin-
Arglwyddes, n. a lady [ion, a lord
Arglwyddiaeth, n. a dominion; a lordship
Arglwyddiaethu, v. to govern
Arglwyddo, v. to domineer
Arglybod, v. to get notice
Arglyw, n. the sense of hearing
Arglywed, v. to hear of
Argnoi, v. to chew
Argoch, a. reddening, blushing
Argochedd, n. ruddiness
Argochi, v. to redden, to blush
Argoed, n. a shelter of wood
Argoel, n. an omen, a token
Argoeliad, n. a betokening
Argoelio, v. to portend [ing
Argoelus, a. ominous, portend
Argof, n. remembrance
Argofio, v. to call to memory
Argoll, n. perdition, total loss
Argolli, v. to lose; to condemn
Argor, n. a high circle
Argospi, v. to punish openly
Argraff, n. an impression; print, or stamp; an inscription
Argraffadwy, a. impressible
Argraffdy, n. printing office
Argraffedig, impressed, printed
Argraffiad, n. an impression
Argraffol, a. impressive;
Argraffu, v. to imprint, to print

Argraffwasg, n. printing-press
Argraffwr, n. printer
Argraffydd, n. printer
Argraffyddiaeth, n. printer's art
Argrap, n. slight touch
Argre, n. origin
Argreol, a. incipient, primeval
Argrëu, v. to inchoate, to origin-
Argrwm, a. protuberant [ate
Argrwn, a. outwardly round
Argrych, a. ruffled over
Argryn, a. tremulous, shivering
Argu, a. very precious; lovely
Argudd, n. a covering
Argurio, v. to pain greatly
Argyfenw, n. paronomisia
Argyfio, v. to equalize
Argyflëad, n. location
Argyfludd, n. an impediment
Argyfnerth, n. a corroborative
Argyfnod, n. a conjuncture
Argyfran, n. an allotment
Argyhoeddadwy, a. reprehensible
Argyhoeddi, v. to reprimand
Argyhoeddiad, n. reprehension
Argyhoeddol, a. reprehensive
Argyhoeddwr, n. admonisher
Argyhuddiad, n. impeachment
Argyhuddo, v. to impeach
Argylchedd, n. alternity
Argylchol, a. alternate
Argyllaeth, n. ardent desire
Argymhelliad, n. impulsion
Argymhenu, v. to debate
Argymhwyso, v. to make equable
Argynal, v. to uphold
Argynelwi, v. to characterize
Argynil, a. very saving
Argynyddu, v. to increase greatly
Argynygiad, n. a venturing
Argysgodi, v. to overshadow
Argywain, v. to carry upon
Argyweddiad, n. a detrimenting
Argyweithas, n. intercourse
Arhawl, n. interrogatory
Arhoew, a. very sprightly
Arholi, v. to interrogate
Arhudo, v. to fascinate

| ARH | 33 | ARN |

Arhudd, n. an over-shadow
Arhwyliad, n. progression
Ariad, n. a ploughing, aration
Arial, n. vigour, wantonness
Arian, n. silver; money
Ariana, v. to save money
Arianaid, a. silvery [bribery
Ariandag, n. silver quinsy; a
Ariandal, n. payment in money
Arianigar, a. loving money; covetous
Arian-glawdd, n. silver mine
Ariantlu, v. mercenary host
Ariantlys, n. rue
Arianof, n. silversmith
Arianog, a. monied, wealthy
Arianol, a. of a silver quality
Arianrod, n. the constellation called corona septentrionalis
Ariant, n. silver; money
Arianu, v. to silver
Arianydd, n. money-changer
Arianwaith, n. silverwork
Arien, n. hoarfrost, dew
Aries, n. an omen, a foreboding
Arlachar, a. very glittering
Arlafar, n. faculty of speech
Arlafariad, n. enunciation
Arlain, n. a foremost rank
Arlais, n. the temple
Arlamu, v. to bound up
Arlanw, n. an overflowing
Arlas, a. tipped with blue
Arlathru, v. to polish highly
Arlaw, a. contiguous
Arlechu, to seclude, to skulk
Arlechwedd, n. slope of a hill
Arlediad, n. extension
Arlef, n. an exclamation
Arlefariad, n. enunciation
Arlen, n. an envelopement
Arlenwi, v. to overflow
Arlesgu, v. to enfeeble
Arlesiant, n. great advantage
Arlethu, v. to overlay
Arlithio, v. to allure, to entice
Arlliw, n. a glazing, a varnish
Arlochi, v. to protect safely

Arloesi, v. to empty, to evacuate
Arlog, n. compound interest
Arloni, v. to please highly
Arlosgiad, n. a singing
Arlost, n. a stock, shaft, or butt
Arluched, n. radiation
Arlud, a. oppressed with anxiety
Arluddiad, n. interception
Arluddias, v. to intercept, to hinder
Arluddiol, a. intercipient
Arlun, n. a portrait, a likeness
Arluniaeth, n. prefiguration
Arluniaethu, v. to prefigure
Arlunio, v. to delineate
Arluo, v. to obstruct, to hinder
Arlwm, a. very bare, or exposed
Arlwnc, n. a great indraught
Arlwrw, n. a deposit; ad. forward towards
Arlwy, n. a provision; a mess
Arlwyad, n. preparation of food, a cooking
Arlwyant, n. preparation of food
Arlwybr, n. a track, a foot step, a path-way
Arlwydd, n. a lord; a master
Arlwyddes, n. a lady; a mistress
Arlwyddiaeth, n. dominion
Arlwyddo, v. to bring, to yield
Arlwyo v. to prepare food to cook
Arlwyso, v. to purge, to cleanse
Arlwythiad, n. a burdening
Arlwywr, n. a caterer; a cook
Arlydan, a. superficial
Arlyfasu, v. to adventure [ing
Arlym, a. very pungent or pierc-
Arlyriad, n. prostration
Arlys, n. a supreme court
Arlythyriad, n. superscription
Arlyw, n. a supreme director
Arlywodraeth, supreme govern-
Arlywydd, n. a president [ment
Arllwys, v. to pour out to empty
Armerth, n. a providing; baking
Armerthiad, n. preparation
Arnes, n. a presage, an omen
Arnaf, prep. upon, on; upon me

Arnod, n. a mark, a character
Arnodi, v. to mark, to note
Arnodiad, n. annotation
Arnodydd, n. an annotator
Arnoethu, v. to denudate
Aro, int. I pray
Arobaith, n. earnest expectation
Arobrid, n. desert, merit
Arobrwyo, v. to reward
Arobryn, n. desert, merit
Arodawr, n. a rhetorician
Aroddefiad, a. passiveness
Aroediad, n. assignation
Arofni, v. to overawe
Arofydd, n. an upper graduate
Arofyn, n. intent, design; v. to intend, to design
Arogl, Arogledd, n. scent, smell
Aroglber, a. odoriferous
Arogldarthu, v. to burn incense
Arogliad, n. a scenting
Arolygu, v. to survey
Arolli, v. to split, to lay open
Aros, Arosi, v. to stay, to wait
Arosiad, n. a tarrying
Arosol, a. tarrying, lingering
Arsangiad, n. a treading upon
Arsangu, to tread upon, to press
Arsarig, a. very perverse
Arsathru, v. to trample upon
Arsawr, n. savour, or scent
Arseddiad, n. a sitting upon
Arsefydliad, n. a stationing
Arseibiant, n. leisure
Arseiniad, n. a resounding
Arswyd, n. dread, terror
Arswydiad, n. a dreading
Arswydo, v. to dread, to be afraid
Arswydol, Arswydus, a. terrible
Arsylw, n. a keen look, a stare
Arsylwedd, n. substance
Arsylliad, a. gazing earnestly
Arsyllu, v. to gaze
Arsyn, n. astonished; stupified
Arsyth, a. upright; rigid
Artaith, n. torment, torture
Arteithfa, n. a place of torture
Arteithiad, n. a tormenting

Arteithio, v. to torture
Arteithiol, a. torturing
Arteithydd, n. a torturer
Arth, n. a bear
Arthaidd, a. bear-like
Arthes, n. a she bear
Arthiad, n. a barking
Arthiaw, v. to bark, to growl
Arthog, a. bearish, gruff
Aru, v. to plough, to till
Aruchaf, a. upmost, topmost
Aruchel, a. very high, lofty
Aruthredd, n. amazement
Aruthriad, n. a wondering
Aruthro, v. to wonder
Aruthrol, a. amazing [to guide
Arwain, v. to conduct, to lead,
Arwasgodi, v. to overshadow
Arwasgu, v, to overpress
Arwawdio, v. to laud, to praise
Arwawl, n. a luminary
Arwe, n. tecture; a woof
Arwedd, n. a carriage
Arweddawd, n. a conveyance
Arweddiad, n. a conveying
Arweddu, v. to convey, to bear
Arweiniad, n. a conducting
Arweiniol, a. leading
Arweithiad, n. superstruction
Arwel, a. conspicuous, manifest
Arweled, v. to perceive
Arwenu, v. to simper
Arwep, n. the visage
Arwerth, n. public sale
Arwerthu, v. to sell by auction
Arwest, n. vocality; vocal music
Arwisg, n. an upper garment
Arwisgo, v. to enrobe, to array
Arwniad, n. a quilting
Arwr, n. a hero, a worthy; a ploughman
Arwraig, n. a heroine
Arwredd, n. heroism, bravery
Arwron, n. a hero, a worthy
Arwydd, n. a sign, a banner
Arwyddair, n. a motto
Arwyddfardd n. herald bard
Arwyddfarddoniaeth, n. heraldry

| ARW | 35 | ATT |

Arwyddiad, n. signification
Arwyddlun, n. an emblem
Arwyddo, v. to signify, to imply
Arwyddol, a. signifying, imply-
Arwyddocau, v. to signify [ing
Arwyddyd, n. direction
Arwyl, n. funeral solemnity
Arwyliant, n. obsequies
Arwylo, to mourn over the dead
Arwylwisg, n. mourning dress
Arwymp, a. supremely fair
Arwyn, n. bliss; adj: happy; very white
Arwyneb, n. a surface
Arwynebedd, n. a superficies
Arwynebol, a. superficial
Arwyntio, v. to scent, to smell
Arwystl, n. a test; a pledge
Arwystlo, v. to mortgage
Arwystrolaeth, n. a mortgaging
Arymchwelyd, v. to revert
Arymdaith, n. a sojouring
Arymddwyn, n. a deportment
Aryrngais, n. an effort
Arymgyrch, n. a recurrence
Arymledu, v. to expand over
Arysgrif, n. indorsement
   Any other word not mention-ed here, commencing with AR, see AB, pref. then the remaining part of the word.
Asbri, n. skill; trick; mischief
Asbriol, a. full of tricks
Asdell, n. a plank; a shingle
Asdelliad, n. a planking
Asdyllen, n. a plank, a board
Asdyllodi, v. to plank, to board
Asen, n. a rib; a she ass. Asen y frân, spare rib of pork
Asgell, n. a wing
Asgellhaid, n. wing-swarm
Asgellog, a. winged
Asgellu, v. to wing; to fly
Asgellwrych, n. spray
Asgellwynt, n. side-wind
Asgen, n. harm, damage
Asgethru, v. to splinter
Asglinen, n. a stem, a lineage

Asglod, n. a chip
Asgre, n. the heart; the bosom
Asgri, n. a tremour
Asgwn, a. depressed, debased
Asgwrn, n. a bone
Asgyrneiddio, v. to become bone
Asgyrniad, n. ossification
Asgyrnig, a. bony, large boned
Asgyrnog, a. bony, full of bone
Asgyrnu, v. to ossify
Asiad, n. a joining, a soldering; or cementing
Asio, v. to join, to solder
Astrus, a. perplexed
Astrusi, n. perplexity, trouble
Asur, n. the blue sky, azure
Aswy, n. the left, the sinister
Aswyniad, n. a craving
Asyn, n. a male ass
At, prep. to, toward, so far as
At, a. prefix, synonymous with RE
Atafael, n. distraint, seizure
Atafaelu, v. to destrain, to seize
Atbarotôi, v. to reprepare
Atberchenogaeth, repossession
Atblygiad, n. reduplication
Atborion, n. leavings; scraps
Atborioni, v. to make leavings
Atchwedlu, v. to report
Atchwel, n. a return
Atddodiad, n. opposition
Ateb, n. an answer, a reply: v. to answer, to reply
Atebiad, n. an answering [ble
Atebol, a. responsible, answera-
Atfod, v. to be again; to be
Atgor, n. a team
Atgrymu, v. to incurvate
Atil, n. second conception
Atre, a. jocund, playful, funny
Attaeniad, n. respersion
Attal, n. a stop, a hindrance; v. to stop, to detain
Attalfa, n. an impediment
Attalgar, a. retentive
Attaliad, n. a stoppage
Attaliaeth, n. aposiopesis; defect of speech

| ATT | 36 | AWD |

Attaliedydd, n. restrainer
Attaliwr, n. restrainer
Attalmu, v. to act upon again
Attarddiad, n. renascence
Attaro, v. to strike again
Atteg, n. a prop, or stay
Attegiad, n. a propping
Attegu, v. to stay, to uphold
Attill, n. reduplication
Attoi, v. to come on again
Attolwg, n. importunity
Attolygu, v. to importune
Attorchi, v. to fold back
Attori, v. to refract
Attrais, n. reprisal
Attraws, a. crossing back
Attref, n. deserted place
Attrefiad, n. depopulation
Attrefnu, v. to arrange anew
Attreg, n. delay; demur
Attreiddio, v. to penetrate again
Attre glo, v. to roll again
Attreisio, v. to make reprisal
Attrethu, v. to tax again
Attro, n. a recurrence
Attrosi, v. to pass over again
Attrwch, n. recision
Attwf, n. a second growth
Attwg, n. a prospering
Attwyn, v. to bring back, return
Attybiad, n reconsideration
Attyblygu, v. to reduplicate
Attychwel, v. to return again; n. a fallen back
Attyfiant, n. regermination
Attymp, n. second season
Attynu, v. to pull, or draw back
Attywallt, v. to regurgitate
Athlygu, v. to glance over
Athost, a. pungent, severe
Athrai, n. a falling away
Athrais, n. violence, force
Athraw, n. a teacher, a master
Athrawd, n. calumny
Athrawedig, a. instructed
Athrawiaeth, n. instruction
Athrawiaethu, to indoctrinate, to instruct

Athrawu, n. ontology, v. to in-
Athrawus, a. instructive [struct
Athrechu, v. to vanquish
Athref, n. a domain, a mansion
Athrefiad, n. domestication
Athrefig, a. domestic, homely
Athrefniad, n. regulation
Athreio, v. to diminish
Athreiddio, v. to penetrate
Athreigliad, n. revolution
Athrem, n. a glance, a look
Athrig, n. a stay, a delay
Athrin, n. a conflict
Athrist, a. very sad, pensive
Athrodi, v. to calumniate, to slander
Athrodiad, n. caluminiating
Athrofa, n. an academy
Athroniaeth, n. philosophy
Athru, a. very pitiful, or vile
Athrugar, a. pitiful; vast
Athrwch, n. a cut through
Athrwm, a. very heavy
Athrwst, n. a great noise
Athrwydd, a. very fluent
Athrylith, n. intuition; genius
Athrylithgar, a. intuitive
Athrywyn, n. happiness, pacifi-
Athu, v. to go, to proceed [cation
Athyn, a. very tenacious
Athywyll, a. tenebrous
Athywys, v. to conduct
Au, n. the liver: v. to go, to proceed
Auad, n. affection of a liver
Aul, n. dung, manure, soil
Auon, a currency; a halfpenny a scruple
Aur, n. gold; a golden
Aw, n. a fluid; a flowing
Awch, n. edge; ardency
Awchiad, n. acuteness
Awchlym, a. sharp-edged
Awchlymu, to sharpen, to point
Awchu, v. to sharpen
Awchus, a. keen; greedy
Awd, n. season, opportunity
Awdl, n. an ode; rhyme

Awdwr, n. an author
Awdurdod, n. authority
Awdurdodi, v. authorize
Awduriaeth, n. authorship
Awdwl, Awdlau, n. opportunity
Awel, n. a gale, a breeze, wind
Awelaidd, a. like a soft gale
Awelan, n. a gale, a breeze
Awelog, a. breezy, windy
Awelu, v. to blow a soft gale
Awen, n. genious; fancy; taste
Awenol, a. poetical
Awenu, v. to smile; to simper
Awenydd, n. a poet, a genius
Awenyddiaeth, n. poetry
Awenyddol, a. poetical
Awg, n. keenness; eagerness
Awgrym, n. a sign; a beckoning
Awgrymu, v. to make signs
Awl, n. primeval light; praise
Awn, n. a flowing together of atoms, or particles
Awr, n. an hour. Yn awr, now
Awrgylch, n. horary circle
Awrhon, ad. at present, now
Awrol, a. horary; hourly
Awrlais, n. a clock
Awrwydr, n. an hour-glass
Aws, n. defiance, challenge
Awsaidd, a. ripe; tender, soft
Awst, n. the month of August
Awydd, n. ardent desire; avidity
Awyddfryd, n. zeal
Awyddo, v. to desire earnestly
Awyddol, a. desirous; zealous
Awyddu, v. to be anxious for
Awyddus, a. desirous, eager
Awyn, n. rein of a bridle
Awyr, n. the air, the sky
Awyraidd, a. aërial, airy

Awyrogaeth, n. pneumatics
Awyrolaeth, n. pneumatics
Awyroldeb, a. airiness
Awyroli, v. to become airy
Awyrydd, n. an aërostatist
Awyryddiaeth, n. aërostation
Awys, n. general invitation; marriage rites

B

Ba, n. a being in; immersion
Baban, n. a babe, baby
Bacon, n. berries
Bacwn, n. bacon
Bacsau, n. stockings without feet
Bach, n. a hook; a grapple: a. little, small, minute
Bachell, n. a grapple; a hook
Bachellu, v. to grapple; to snare
Bachgen, n. a boy, a child
Bachgenaidd, a. boyish, childish
Bachgenos, n. little youngsters
Bachgenyn, n. dim, a little boy
Bachiad, n. a hooking, a grappling: a bending, like a hook
Bachig, a. smallish, diminutive
Bachigyn, n. a very little thing
Bachog, a. hooked; crooked
Bachol, a. hooking; grappling
Bachu, v. to hook, to hitch; to grapple: to go into nooks
Bâd, n. a boat; a ship's boat
Badaid, n. a boatful
Badwr, n. a boatman
Badd, n. a bath
Baddon, n. a bathing place
Baedd, n. a boar
Baeddaidd, a. boarish
Baeddgig, n. boar's flesh [dirty

Baglu, v. to hold with a crook
Bagwn, n. strength, potency
Bagwy, n. a cluster, bunch
Bai, n. a fault, a vice
Baich, n. a burden, a load
Baich, n. an outcry
Baid, n. briskness
Baidd, n. a daring
Bais, n. flats, shallows; ford
Bal, n. a prominence; a bud
Bala, n. a shoot out; efflux
Balalwyf, n. a palm-tree
Balanu, v, to shoot, to bud
Balant, n. a shooting, a sprouting, a budding
Balasar, n. azure, sky-blue
Balasarn, n. a ballast
Balc, n. a break in furrow land
Balcio, v. to break furrows
Balciog, a. having irregular furrows
Balch, a. proud; towering
Balciwr, n. breaker of furrows
Balchder, n. pomp; pride
Balchedd, n. pomp; pride
Balchïo, v. to grow proud
Balchineb, n. arrogance; pomp
Baldardd, n. a budding
Baldarddu, v. to bud
Baldog, n. a punch, a squab
Baldordd, n. a babbling
Baldorddi, v. to babble, to tattle
Baldorddus, a. babbling
Baldorfi, v. to mutter
Balennyn, n. a bud
Balgur, n. a springing out
Balog, n. a jut; a pinacle; a fidula, a valve; a flab; a jetting, flapped, valved
Balwyf, n. palm wood
Balwyfen, n. a palm tree
Ball, n. erruption; plague
Ballasg, n. shell: porcupine
Ballasgu, v. to busk
Ballaw, v. to shout, to scream
Ballawg, n. a hedgehog
Balleg, n. a bow net; a purse
Ballegrwyd, n. a wear net

Bàn, n. a prominence; a peak; a branch; a. lofty, high, loud
Banc, n. a platform, a table
Baner, n. a banner, a flag
Banffaglu, v. to light a bonfire
Bangaw, n. the bandage of honour: a. compact
Bangeibr, n. a minister
Bangor, n. upper row, a compacture, a high circle; a college, seminary
Bangori, v. to cope or bind together, to wattle the binding row of a fence
Bannwch, n. a wild sow
Baniar, n. a banner
Banierog, a. bearing ensign
Banierydd, n. standard-bearer
Banllef, n. a loud shout
Banllefain, v. to shout
Bannas, n. a mat
Bannod, n. article; clause
Bannodi, v. to make clauses
Banon, n. an exalted person, a queen, empress
Bant, n. a high place; a. prominent, high, lofty
Banu, v. to raise, to erect
Banw, n. a swine, a farrow pig
Banwel, n. upward look; sky
Banwes, n. a sow, a farrow sow the fish called gilt head
Bâr, n. a top, a summit, a tuft; agitation; impulse; ire, fury, wrath: a bar, a bolt, a rail
Bara, n. bread; sustenance
Baran, n. a wren
Baranres, n. a front rank
Baranu, v. to front; to present
Baranwg, n. a presence
Barcer, n. a tanner
Barcud, n. a kite; a buttock
Barcutan, n. a kite, a glead
Bardysen, n. a shrimp
Bardd, n. a bard
Barddacth, n. bardism
Barddair, n. the bard's word
Barddas, n. bardism; lore

Barddol, a. bardic
Barddawr, n. bardic genius
Barddes, n. a female bard
Barddonol, a. poetical
Barddoneg, n. bardic lore
Barddoniaeth, bardism, poetry, the science of poetry
Barddoniaidd, a. that is after the bardic manner
Barf, n. a beard; whiskers
Barfiad, n. a bearding
Barfle, n. crest of a helmet
Barfog, a. bearded: the fin fish; the lesser wood-chat, a bird.
Barfogyn, n. a barbel
Barfu, v. to beard, to grow into a beard
Barfwr, a. barber, a shaver
Bargod, n. jut; skirt; eaves
Bargodi, v. to overhang
Bariaeth, n. viciousness
Baril, n. a barrel, a cask
Barilaid, n. a barrelful
Bar.lan, n. a small barrel
Barilo, v to barrel
Barlen, n. the lap
Barn, n. judgment
Barnedig, a judged; condemned; sen'enced
Barnedigaeth, n. judgment
Barniad, n. a judging [castingr
Barnol, a. that is judging, o
Barnu, v. to judge, to condemn
Barnwr, n. a judge
Barnydd, n. a judge
Baron, n. a chief, a baron
Baroniaeth, n. a barony
Barog, a. ireful : n. a spur
Barth, n. ground floor : floor
Barug, n. a rime, hoar
Barugiad, n. casting a rime
Barugo, v. to cast a hoar
Barus, v. vicious, mischievous
Bâs, n. a shallow, a shoal : a. shallow; low, flat
Basaidd, a. shallowish
Basdardd, n. a bastard
Basdarddes, n. female bastard

Basdarddiad, n. bastardising
Basdarddiaeth, n. bastardy
Basdarddio, v. to bastardise
Basdarddu, v. to spring from a base origin
Basder, n. shallowness
Basg, n. plaiting, basket-work
Basged, n. a basket
Basgedaid, n. a basketful
Basgedog, a. having a basket
Basgedol, a. basketted
Basgedwr, n. a basket maker
Basiad, n. a shallowing
Basu, v. to make shallow
Batel, drawing a bow; battle; combat, a fight
Batelu, v. to draw a bow; to battle, to war, to fight
Bath, n. a likeness or emblem; a copy; a coin
Bathdy, n. a mint
Bathedig, a. coined; stamped
Batheinio, to stamp effigies
Bathell, n. a small coin
Bathiad, n. coining; coinage
Bathodyn, n. a medal
Bathog, a. having coin; monied
Bathol, a. that is coined
Bathor, n. a dormouse
Bau, n. boof
Bauad, n. bearer of a saw-pit
Baw, n. dirt, mire; excrement
Bawaidd, a. dirty, vile; sordid
Bawd, n. a thumb, a toe
Bawdŷ, n. necessary-house
Bawdd, n. a drowning
Bawddyn, n. a dirty fellow
Bawlyd, a. dirty, miry, nasty
Be, conj. mutation of Pe
Bechan, n. a little female a. little, small
Bechgynos, n. little boys
Bechyn, n. a small hook
Bed, n. a state of inaptness
Bedlemod, n. strollers
Bedw, n. the birch
Bedwen, n. a birchen
Bederw, n. a birch grove

| BED | 40 | BER |

Bedwlwyn, d. a birch grove
Bedydd, a. baptizm
Bedyddfa, n. a baptistry
Bedyddfaen, n. baptismal font
Bedyddfan, n. baptistry
Bedyddio, v. to baptize
Bedyddiol, a. baptismal
Bedd, n. a grave, sepulchre
Beddfaen, n. a tombstone
Beddgor, n. mausoleum
Beddlech, n. a gravestone
Beddol, a. sepulchral
Beddrod, n. burial place
Beddrodol, a. sepulchral
Beiad, n. a blaming
Beiadwy, a. blamable (ing
Beichiad, n. a bawling; a load-
Beichio, v. to bowl; to load
Be.chiog,a.burdened; pregnant
Beichiogi, v.to become burdened; to conceive
Beiddgar, a. presumptious
Beiddiad, n. a daring
Beiddio, v. to presume, to dare
Beiddiol, a. presuming, daring
Beiedig, a. blamed, cencured
Beili, n. an outlet; a court, or yard; a mound
Beio, v. to blame, to censure
Beiol, a. blaming, censuring
Beiri, n. a kite, a glead
Beirniad, n. a judge
Beirniadaeth, n. jurisdiction
Beirniadu, v. to judge
Beirniadol, a. critical
Beisdon, n. sea-brink
Beisfa, n. a shallow place
Beisfan, n. a shallow place
Beisfor, n. a shallow sea
Beisgawn, n. a stack, a mow
Beisgawniad, n. a stacking
Beisgawnu, v. to stack corn
Beisiad, n, a shallowing
Beisiaw, v. to grove shallow
Beisiawl, a. shallowing
Beisle, n. shallow place
Beius, a. faulty, blameable
Beiusrwydd, n. blameableness

Beiwr, n. a blamer; censor
Bel, n. tumult; havoc; war
Bela, n. a wolf; the henbane
v. to wrangle; to war
Belach, n. trouble, molestation
Bele, n. the marten
Belg, n. a ravage
Belgiad, n. ravager; a Belgian
Bellach, ad. at length; now
Bendigaid, a. blessed
Benyw, n. female; a woman
Benywaidd, a. feminine
Benywol, a. female
Ber. n. a lance, a pike; a spit
n. a shank; a leg
a. short; brief; scanty
Bera, n. pyramid; a stack
Beraes, n. a short shield
Berai, n. a turn-spit, a jack
Beran, n. a little spit; a broach
Berasgell, n. the penguin
Berdroell, n. a jack wheel
Berdas, n. a shrimp
Berfa, n. a barrow
Berfain, a. slender-shanked
Berfaydd, n. a barrow man
Bergam, a. bow-legged
Beri, n. a kite, a glead
Beriau, n. a short yoke
Berllysg, n, a truncheon
Bernais, n. a varnish; a cover
Beroes, n. short life
Berrwy, n a. fetter
Berth, n. perfection, beauty: a. fair, pleasant; rich
Berthiad, n. a beautifying
Berthog, a. endowed, wealthy
Berthogi, v. to endow
Berthu, v. to beautify
Berthyd, n. ornament, jewel
Beru, v. to pike, to spit
Berw, n, boiling, ebullition
Berwad, n. boiling, decoction
Berwadwy, a. decoctible
Berwedig, a. boiled, decocted
Berwedydd, n. a boiler
Berwedd, n. a boiling state
Berweddu, v. to brew, to decoct

Berwi, v. to boil; to bubble
Berwol, a. boiling; bubbling
Berwr, n. cresses
Berwydd, n. a boiler; brewer
Berwydda, v. to brew
Berwyddfa, n. a brewery
Bery, n. a kite, a glead
Berysgrifen, n. brachygraphy
Beth, pron. MUTATION OF PETH what
Beudail, n. cow dung
Beudy, n. cow house
Beunydd, a. daily
Bid, v. let it be, be it; n. a quickset hedge
Bidan, n. twig; a fribble
Bidio, v. to set a hedge
Bidog, n. a hanger; a short sword
Bidogan, n. a dagger
Bidogi, v. to poniard, to stab
Bidogyn, n. a poniard
Bidwal, n. an encampment
Biswail, n. a drain in a cow house; cow dung
Bisweliad, n. a dunging
Biswelio, v. to drop dung
Blaen, n. a point; a top
Blaenafiaeth, n. primacy
Blaenanedig, a. first born
Blaendardd, n. a first building
Blaendocio, v. to beard wool
Blaendori, v. to cut the end
Blaendrwch, n. apheresis
Blaendrwyth, n. prime solvent
Blaenddod, n. a prefix
Blaenddodi, v. to prefix
Blaenddodiad, n. a prefixing
Blaeneudir, n. bordering land
Blaenfain, a. sharp-pointed
Blaenfed, a. antecedent
Blaenffrwyth, n. first-fruit
Blaengnwd, n. first crop.
Blaenhogi, v. to sharpen point
Blaeniad, n. a pointing
Blaenio, v. to form into a point
Blaenlaeth, n. first milk
Blaenllaw, n. first hand: yn mlaen llaw, before hand

Blaenllym, a. sharp pointed
Blaenllymu, v. to sharpen a point
Blaennewydd, n. new moon
Blaenol, a. foremost, primary
Blaenor, n. a leader
Blaenori, v. to precede
Blaenoriad, n. a preceding
Blaenoriaeth, n. antecedence
Blaenorol, a. antecedent, leading
Blaenred, n. the foremost
Blaenredol, a. precurrent
Blaenredu, v. to forerun
Blaenu, v. to point; to precede
Blagur, n. a sprout, a bud
Blaguriad, n. a sprouting
Blaguro, v. to sprout, to bud
Blagurol, a. sprouting, budding
Blaguryn, n. a sprout, a bud
Blaidd, n. the visage; a wolf
Blan, n. splendour; light
Blanc, n. a young horse
Blanu, v. to cast a splendour
Blas, n. taste, savour, relish
Blasaidd, a. having some taste
Blaseiddio, v. to give a taste
Blasiad, n. a tasting
Blasu, v. to taste; to relish
Blasus, a. relishing, savoury
Blasuso, v. to give a relish
Blaw, n. effusion; a flow
Blawd, n. meal, flour
Bleiddiadwy, a. ravening
Bleiddag, n. wolf bane
Bleiddgi, n. a wolf dog
Bleiddig, a. like a wolf
Bleiniad, n. leader; ear of corn
Blew, n. hairs, hair
Blewio, v. to grow to hair
Blewog, a. shaggy, hairy
Blewogi, v. to grow hairy
Blewogrwydd, n. hairiness
Blewyn, n. hair
Blewynog, n. alfine
Bliant, n. fine linen, cambric
Blif, n. catapulta
Blifai, n. a projectile
Blifio, v. to bow from an engine

Blifyn, n. a ball, a bullet
Blin, a. tired; troublesome
Blinder, n. fatigue; trouble
Blinderog, a. fatigued
Blinderus, a. tiresome, tired
Blinedig, a. troubled; disturbed; wearied
Blinfyd, n. tribulation
Bling, n. flaying, a strip
Blingiad, n. a flaying
Blingo, v. to excoriate, to flay
Blingwr, n. flayer
Blino, v. to trouble; to tire
Blinwr, n. disturber
Blisg, n. shells, husks
Blisgiad, n. a shelling
Blisgo, v. to shell, to husk
Blisgyn, n. shell, husk
Blith, n. milk: a. milch
Blithog, a. giving milk
Blodau, n. blossoms, flowers
Bloden, n. floweret
Blodeuad, n. flowering
Blodeulyd, a. flowered, mothery
Blodeuo, v. to flourish; to flour
Blodeuog, a. bloomy, flowery
Blodeuogrwydd, n. floweriness
Blodeuol, a. flowering
Blodeuwr, n. a florist
Blodeuwydd, n. flowering trees
Blodeuyn, n. a flower
Blodio, v. to make meal
Blodiog, a. farinaceous
Blodiwr, n. a mealman
Blodwaith, n. meal dust
Blodwraig, n. meal woman
Blodwy, a. mellow
Blodyn, n. floweret, flower
Bloddest, n. a rejoicing
Bloddestu, v. to make rejoicing
Bloedd, n. a shout
Bloeddfawr, a. vociferous
Bloeddgar, a. apt to vociferate
Bloeddian, v. to keep shouting
Bloeddio, v. to shout
Bloeddiol, a. shouting, bawling
Bloeddiwr, n. shouter
Bloen, n. a floweret

Bloesg, n. a broken noise: a. lisping, faltering
Bloesgedd, n. a lisping
Blocsgi, v. to falter, to lisp
Bloesgni, n. a lisping
Bloesgwr, n. a lisper
Bloffi, v. to mingle, to jumble
Bloneg, n. lard, grease
Blonegen, n. the leaf, or caul that covers the stomach
Blota, v. to meal; to beg meal
Blotai, n. a begger of meal
Bloteiaeth, n. a mealing
Blotty, n. meal house
Blöyn, n. blossom
Blwch, n. box
Blwng, n. angry look: a. surly
Blwth, n. a blast, a puff
Blwydd, n. a year; a budding
Blwyddiad, n. a yearling
Blwyddol, a. yearly, annual
Blwyddyn, n. a year
Blychaid, n. a box full
Blychu, v. to put in a box
Blychyn, n. a small box
Blydd, a. soft, tender; sappy
Blyddiad, n. a rising of sap
Blynedd, n. a year
Blyneddol, a. yearly, annual
Blyngu, v. to grow angry
Blingder, n. a ruffled temper
Blyngu, v. to frown; to ruffle
Blys, n. a longing, a craving
Blysgar, a craving
Blysiad, n. a longing
Blysig, a. voluptuous
Blysigrwydd, n. voluptuousness
Blysion, n. dainties
Blysio, v. to lust, to long
Blythar, n. a belch
Blytheiriwr, n. a belcher
Bo, v. may be: interj. bo: n. a bugbear, a scarecrow
Bocsach, n. vaunting
Bocsachu, v. to vaunt
Bocsachwr, n. bragger
Boch, n. chop, cheek
Bochaid, n. a chop full

Bochdew, a. fat-cheeked
Bochgern, n. a jole
Bochgernaid, n. a chop-full
Bochlug, a. blub-cheeked
Bochiad, n. a munching
Bochio, v. to munch
Bochlaes, a. flabby-cheeked
Bochlwyd, a. pale-cheeked
Bochlwyth, n. chop-full
Bochlwytho, v. to stuff greedily
Bochog, a. blub-cheeked
Bod, n. being, exsitence : v. to be, to exist
Bòd, n. mountain kite
Bodlon, a. contented, pleased
Bodlondeb, n. contentedness
Bodloni, v. to satisfy, to please
Bodolaeth, n. existence
Bodrwy, n. a ring
Bodd, n. will, consent
Bodda, n. the red shrank, a bud, TROEDGOCH
Boddgar, a. easily pleased
Boddgarwch, n. contentedness
Boddhâd, n. pleasing, satisfying
Boddhau, v. to please
Boddi, v. to drown, to immerse
Boddiad, n. a drowning
Boddineb, n. contentment
Boddiwr, n. satisfier
Boddlon, a. willing : contended
Boddlondeb, n. satisfaction
Boddlonedig, a. satisfied
Boddlongar, a. satisfactory
Boddloni, v. to please, to satisfy
Boddloniad, n. a satisfying
Boddlonol, a. tending to please
Boddlonrwydd, n. contentedness
Boddlonwr, n. a satisfier
Boddog, a. pleased
Boddol, a. contented, willing
Boddoldeb, n. contentment
Boddus, a. agreeable, pleasing
Boddwr, n. drowner
Bog, n. a rising up, swell
Bogeilchwydd, n. swelling of the navel
Bogeilglwm, n. boss of the navel

Bogeiliaidd, a. umbilical
Bogel, n. navel ; a nave
Boglwm, n. a boss, knob
Boglyniad, n. bossing
Boglynu, v. to boss ; to bubble
Boglynwaith, n. embossment
Bol, n. belly
Bolaid, n. belly-full
Bolchwydd, n. tympany, swell
Bolchwyddo, v. to swell the belly ; to swagger
Boldyn, a. tight-bellied
Bolera, v. to spunge ; to guzzle
Bolerai, n. a guzzler
Bolgan, n. a pouch ; a budget
Bolglwm, n. boss ; tuft
Bolgwd, n. paunch-belly
Bolheulo, v. to bask in the sun
Boliad, n. a bellying
Bolio, v. to belly, to gorge
Boliog, a. big-bellied
Bolol, n. goblin, ghost, bugbear
Bolrwth, a. gluttonous
Bolrwym, a. bound, costive
Bolrwymedd, n. costiveness
Bolrwymo, v. to make costive
Bolrwymyn, n. belly-band
Bolrythi, n. greediness
Bolrythiad, n. gormandizing
Bolrythu, v. to gormandize
Bolwag, a. empty bellied
Bolwst, n. a hernia ; a cholic
Bolystog, a. hernious
Bolystyn, n. hernia
Bollt, n. bolt, spar, dart
Bolltad, n. bolting, stalk
Bolltedig, a. bolted, darted
Bon, n. stock, stem, base
Bonad, n. basement
Bonbren, n. harness stretcher
Boncaeth, n. a mass, a whole
Bonclust, n. root of the ear ; a box on the ear
Bonclustio, v. to box the ear
Boncyff, n. stump, stock
Bondew, a. thick-legged
Bondid, n. plough-chain
Bondo, n. eaves, first thatch

Bonedd, n. stock, pedigree
Boneddig, adj. having a stock; noble, genteel.—Gwr boneddig, a gentleman
Boneddigaidd, a. genteel, noble
Boneddigeiddrwydd, n. gentility
Bonffaglu, v. to burn all round
Bongam, a. bandy-legged
Bonglwm, n. knob on the end
Boniad, n. the aft ox in a team
Bonllost, n. the tail end
Bonog, adj. stemmed, stalked, thick-shanked
Bonsang, n. base, ayer
Bontin, n. a buttock; rump
Bor, n. centre, focus
Bore, n. the dawn, morning: a. early; morning
Boreddydd, n. a day spring
Borefwyd, n. breakfast
Boregwaith, n. morning
Boreu, n. dawning, morning
Boreuedd, n. earliness
Boreuo, v. to become day
Boreuol, a. dawning, morning
Boreuwisg, n. morning dress
Bost, n. bragging, boast
Bostiad, n. boasting
Bostio, v. to brag, to boast
Bostiwr, n. a boaster
Bot, n. a round body
Botas, n. buskin; boot
Botaswr, n. boot-maker
Botwm, n. button; boss
Botymog, a. buttoned; bossed
Botymu, v. to button, to boss
Both, n. stock or nave; a boss
Bothog, a. stocked, shanked
Bothell, n. bottle; blister
Brac, a. free, frank, open
Brad, n. perfidy; a break off
Bradbwll, n. trap-pit
Bradfwriad, n. sedition
Bradfwriadu, v. to plot sedition
Bradiad, n. a doing treachery
Bradus, a. treacherous
Bradwr, n. traitor
Bradwriaeth, n. treason

Bradwrus, a. traitorous
Bradwy, n. a break off, blemish
Bradwyad, n. a crumbling off
Bradwyo, v. to crumble away
Bradychiad, n. a betraying
Bradychol, a. betraying
Bradychu, v. to betray
Bradychus, a. betraying
Brae, n. a cutting off
Braen, n. rot, corruption: adj. rotten, corrupt
Braenar, n. fallow
Braenariad, n. fallowing
Braenaru, v. to fallow
Braenedig, a. putrified
Braenedigol, a. putrefactive
Braenedd, n. putridity
Braeniad, n. a rottening
Braenllyd, a. putrid; sinewy
Braenllydedd, n. mouldiness
Braenu, v. to rot, to putrify
Brâg, n. malt; a. sprouting
Bragaldian, v. to babble
Bragaldio, v. to gabble
Bragawd, n. m. a sprouting; a compound; bragget, a liquor
Bragdy, n. a malt house
Bragio, v. to branch, to issue
Bragoelyn, n. braggett liquor
Bragodyn, n. a sprout, a germ
Bragu, v. to malt
Bragwair, n. marsh-bent
Bragwr, n. a maltster
Braich, n. arm, branch [hardly
Braidd, a. ultimate: ad. just;
Braint, n. privilege
Braisg, a. gross; large, thick
Braith, a. motley, variegated
Bral, n. hairbrained one
Bram, n. fart, short puff
Bramu, v. to fart
Brân, n. a crow
Branaidd, a. like a crow
Branes, n. flight of crows
Branos, n. young crows
Bras, n. cross bow
Brâs, a. thick, fat; large; gross
Brasâd, n. growing fa:

Brasâu, v. to grow fat
Brasbwyth, n. basting-stitch
Brasbwythwr, n. a baster
Brasder, n. fatness, grossness
Braslïain, n. coarse linen
Braslun, n. a rough-cast
Brasnaddu, v. to rough hew
Brasu, to make gross or rough
Brasweithio, v. to rough work
Brat, n. a piece, clout, rag
Bratiog, n. clouted, ragged
Bráth, n. a bite, stab, sting
Brathedig, a. bitten; wounded
Brathiad, n. a stabbing, biting
Brathol, a. stabbing, biting
Brathu, v. to sting, to bite
Brau, a. brittle, frail; frank
Braw, n. terror, fright
Brawd, n. a fellow, brother
Brawd, n. judgment, sentence
Brawdfaeth, n. a fostering
Brawdgarwch, n. brotherly love
Brawdio, v. to give a verdict
Brawdladdiad, n. fratricide
Brawdle, n. judgment seat
Brawdol, a. brotherly
Brawdoliaeth, n. fraternity
Brawdoldeb, n. brotherliness
Brawdwr, n. a judge, a judger
Brawddeg, n. a sentence
Brawddegol, a. sentential
Brawl, n. a swell out, a boast
Brawn, n. a fatness, richness
Brawychiad, n. a terrifying
Brawychu, v. to terrify
Brawychus, a. terrific
Brawychwr, n. a terrifier
Breccini, n. despumation
Breci, n. wort, sweet wort
Brech, n. an eruption, a pox; a. brindled, freckled
Brechdan, n. bread and butter
Brechlyd, a. pocky; measly
Brechog, a. pocky; measled
Bredych, n. prodition
Bref. n. a lowing; a bleat
Brefai, n. pennyroyal
Brefan, n. a lump of butter

Brefant, n. a windpipe
Breferad, n. a bellowing
Brefiad, n. a lowing; a bleating
Brefu, v. to low; to bleat
Breg, n. a rupture, a fissure
Bregedd, n. fragrility, frailty
Bregol, a. fragile, brittle
Bregu, v. to become fragile
Bregus, a. broken; fractious
Bregyn, n. a grain of malt
Breiad, n. a topping; a rippling
Breichiad, n. an arm-full
Breichdlws, n. a bracelet
Breichell, n. a sleeve
Breichiad, n. using of the arms
Breichiol, a. brachial
Breichled, n. a bracelet
Breichrwy, n. a bracelet
Breila, n. a rose; a wild rose
Breilw, n. a rose
Breiniad, n. enfranchisement
Breinio, v. to give privilege
Breiniog, a. privileged: free
Breiniol, a. privileged; free
Breiniolaeth, enfranchisement
Breinioli, v. to enfranchise
Breiniolwr, n. a dignifier
Breintlys, n. privilege court
Breintlythyr, n. letters-patent
Breing, n. the commonalty
Breisgiad, n. a growing bulky
Breisgion, n. hurds, refuse
Breithell, n. what is of varied texture; a cawl; a conflict
Breithred, n. a conflict
Bremian, a. puffing, farting v. to puff; to fart
Brenig, n. limpets
Brenin, n. a sovereign; a king
Breninbysg, n. king fish
Brenindod, n. royalty
Brenindy, n. a king's house
Brenines, n. a queen
Breninesol, a. queenly
Breninfraint, n. royal privilege or prerogative
Breniniaeth, n. a kingdom
Breninlys, n. a king's court

Breninol, a. kingly, royal
Breninoli, v. to royalise
Breninwisg, n. a king's robe
Breninwr, n. a royalist
Bres, a. having a bunchy top
Bretyn, n. a little rag
Brethyn, n. cloth, woollen cloth
Brethyniaeth. n. woollen drapery
Brethynol, a. made of cloth
Brethynwr, n. a woollen draper
Brëu, v. to low; to bleat
Breuad, n. a cannibal, a slaughterer; a grave-worm
Breuan, n. a hand-mill
Breuandy, n. a mill-house
Breuaniad, n. a grinding
Breuanllif, n. a grindstone
Breuant, n. a windpipe
Breuanu, v. to bray, to brake
Breubys, n. a bit, a crumb
Breuder, n. brittleness
Breuddil, n. a grinder
Breuddilad, n. a grinding
Breuddilo, v. to grind, to consume
Breuddwyd, n. a dream
Breuddwydiad, n. a dreaming
Breuddwydio, v. to dream
Breuddwydiol, a. dreaming
Breuddwydiwr, n. a dreamer
Breufer, a. sonorous; lowing
Breulif, a. brittle-edged
Breuo, v. to grow brittle
Breuod, n. brittleness; frail
Breuol, a. brittle, frail
Breuolaeth, n. brittleness
Breuolder, n. brittleness
Brëyr, n. a baron
Brëyrol, a. baronial
Bri, n. dignity; rank; honour
Brïaidd, a. honorary
Brid, n. erruption; the scab
Brido, v. to break out
Bridol, a. errup'ive; scabby
Briduw, n. warranty; earnest
Bridd, n. a springing forward
Brig, n. a top, a summit; a branch or top of a tree [lander
Brigant, n. a summit; high-
Brigantiad, n. a highlander
Brigbori, v. to browse, to nibble
Brigdori, v. to top, to prune
Brigddyrnu, v. to top thresh
Briger, n. a tuft; head of hair
Brigfain, a. cuspated, pointed
Brigladd, v. to lop the tops
Briglwyd, a. hoary-headed
Briglwydo, v. to grow hoary
Brigo, v. to top
Brigog, a. having tops; branchy
Brigol, shooting up; branching
Brigwn. n. andirons
Brigwyn, a. white-topped
Brigyn, n. a top branch, a twig
Brigynol, a. branching out
Brïo, v. to dignify
Brïol, a. dignified; honorary
Brisgiad, n. a leaving a trace
Brisgo, v. to track, to trace
Brith, a. mixed, motley, pied
Brithad, n. a variega'ing
Brithdwym, n. sort of candle
Brithedd, n. variegation
Brithgi, n. a mongrel dog
Brithgoch, a. variegated with red
Brithlas, a. dappled grey
Brithlen, n. arras
Britho, v. to variegate
Brithodi, v. to use mixed rhyme
Brithog, a. variegated, dappled
Brithol, a. variegating
Brithryw, a. heterogeneous
Brithwlaw, n. drizzling rain
Brithwyn, a. motley white
Bri hyd, n. mixed corn
Brithyll, n. a trout
Brithyn, n. a beau
Briw, n. a wound, a cut
Briwant, n. a broken state
Briwddail, n. herbage
Briwedig, a. broken; wounded
Briweg, n. stone-crop
Briwfara, n. broken bread
Briwiaith, n. a jargon
Briwion, n. fragments
Briwioni, v. to crumble
Briwionyn, n. a crumb

Briwio, v. to break; to crumble; to cut; to wound; to hurt
Briwysioni, v. to crumble
Briwysionyn, n. a small crumb
Brewwlaw, n. drizzling rain
Briwwydd, n. dry brush wood
Bro, n. inhabited land, a country
Broaidd, a. rural, country-like
Broawl, a. like cultivated land
Brocen, n. the breast, the bosom
Broch, n. din, tumult; froth, foam; wrath
Brochell, n. a tempest
Brochi, v. to chafe, to fume
Brochiad, n. a chafing, a fuming
Brochus, a. fuming; blustering
Brodawr, n. a member of society
Brodedd, n. a concurrence [ing
Brodiad, n. embroidering, darn-
Brodio, v. to embroider, to darn
Brodiog, a. embroidered, darned
Brodir, n. cultivated land
Brodordy, n. a collegiate house
Brodoriad, n. fraternisation
Brodoriaeth, n. fraternity
Brodoriol, a. federative
Brolio, v. to brag, to vaunt
Brolwydd, n. patriotism
Bron, n. a breast, a pap, a breast of a hill. Ger bron, in presence of, before; Yn mron, almost
Brona, v. to give the breast
Bronaidd, a. swelling as a breast
Bronallt, n. a smooth declivity
Bronawg, a. full-breasted
Brondor, n. breast-plate
Bronddu, a. black-breasted
Broneg, n. breast-plate
Bronfraith, a. mottled-breasted; n. a thrush
Bron-gengl, n. a breast-leather
Bron-glwm, n. a breast-knot
Bron-gul, a. narrow-chested
Bronisel, a. low-chested
Bronllain, n. breast-cloth
Bronlydan, a. broad-chested
Bronrain, a. high-breasted
Bronrhuddyn, n. the redbreast
Bront, a. filthy; surly
Bronten, n. a dirty wench
Bronuchel, a. high-chested
Bronwen, a. white-breasted
Bronwst, n. pain of the breast
Bronwyn, a. white-breasted; n. the small celandine
Broth, n. a stir, a tumult
Bru, n. the womb, the belly
Bruawl, belonging to the womb
Brud, n. a chronicle; a surmise
Brudai, n. a chronicler
Brudiaeth, n. chronology
Brudio, v. to record; to surmise
Brudiol, a. chronological
Brwchan, n. caudle, flummery
Brwd, a. hot, acrid, warm
Brwnt, a. foul, nasty, dirty; surly
Brwyd, n. a brooch, a braid; a. full of holes
Brwyden, n. the reeds of a loom
Brwydo, v. to make interstices; to embroider
Brwydrad, n. a battling
Brwydrin, n. a combating
Brwydro, v. to battle, or to fight
Brwydrol, a. battling [in war
Brwydwaith, n. embroidery
Brwydweithydd, an embroiderer
Brwydydd, n. an embroiderer
Brwydr, n. a battle, a conflict
Brwyn, n. a pricking; a smarting rushes; a. pricking, smarting
Brwynad, n. a pricking
Brwyneg, n. a place where rushes grow
Brwynen, n. a rush; a track
Bywyniad, n. a smelt
Brwyno, v. to prick; to throb
Brwynog, a. having rushes
Brwys, a. luxuriant, fertile
Brwysg, a. unwieldy; drunk
Brwysgedd, n. inebriety
Brwysgo, v. to become drunk
Brwysgol, a. unwieldy; drunk
Brwyso, v. to grow luxuriantly
Bry, a. high : ad. upwards, above
Brycan, n. a rug

Brych, n. a rough covering; the afterbirth of a cow; a. brindled freckled
Brychau, n. motes, flue
Brychell, n. a trout
Brychen, n. a bubbling, a spring
Brycheuad, n. a gathering of flue
Brycheulyd, a. full of dirty spots
Brycheuo, to pick; to maculate
Brycheuog, a. full of dirt
Brycheuyn, n. a mote, a hair
Brychiad, n. a salmon trout
Brychni, n. freckliness
Brychog, a. brindled, freckled
Brychu, v. to brindle, to freckle
Brychwyn, a. of a brindled white
Brychyn, n. a speckled one
Brychynu, v. to speckle
Bryd, n. impulse; mind, thought
Brydai, n. a heating iron, a heater
Brydain, a. of a heating quality
Brydaint, n. inflamation
Brydaniaeth, n. inflamation
Brydian, v. to inflame; to throb
Brydiannol, a. simmering
Brydiannu, to simmer; to throb
Brydiannus, a. heating
Brydiant, n. a heating
Brydio, v. to heat; to throb
Brydiog, a. heated; throbbing
Brydiol, a. of a heating quality
Brydiolrwydd, n. inflamatoriness
Brydlon, a. resolute, intent
Brydlonedd, n. resoluteness
Brydd, a. feeble, weak, sickly
Brygawthan, v. to babble, or
Brygawthwr, n. a babbler [prate
Brygu, to grow out, to overspread
Bryn, n. a hill, a mount
Brŷn, n. grudge, malice
Brynar, n. ploughed land
Bryncyn, n. a clod
Bryncynog, a. full of clods
Bryncynu, v. to break clods
Brynial, v. to be heaping
Bryniog, a. full of hills, hilly
Brynti, n. filthiness, nastiness; a filthy animal

Brys, n. quickness, haste; a. hasty quick, speedy
Brysg, n. a track, or mark
Brysgar, a. quickening; hasty
Brysgyll, n. a truncheon
Brysiad, n. a hastening
Brysio, v. to hasten
Brysiol, a. hastening, hurrying
Bryste, Caerodor, n. Bristol
Brysyll, n. a truncheon
Brythai, n. a rioter
Brytheirio, v. to belch
Brython, n. tumultuous ones; one of three primitive tribes of the Cymry
Brythoneg, n. the Brython speech
Brythonig, a. relating to the tribe of Brython
Brythu, v. to quarrel, to brawl
Brywes, n. bread steeped in broth or pot liquor
Brywio, v. to invigorate
Brywiog, a. vigorous, lively
Brywusder, n. wantonness
Bu, n. a being; a cow; v. was, it came to pass
Buach, n. a churl, a clown
Bual, n. a buffalo, a bison; a
Bualgen, n. buff-leather [bugle
Bualgorn, n. a bugle horn
Buan, n. that is quick; a hare; a. swift, nimble, fast
Buanog, a. full of swiftness
Buanol, a. accelerative
Buander, n. swiftness, speed
Buandroed, a. swift-footed
Buanedd, n. fleetness, velocity
Buarth, n. a cattle yard, a fold
Buarthfa, n. a folding place
Buarthiad, n. a folding
Buarthog, a. folded, penned
Buarthu, v. to shut in a fold
Buch, n. life; cattle, kine
Buchedd, n. course of life
Bucheddiad, n. a leading, a life
Bucheddol, a. living; moral
Bucheddoldeb, n. morality
Bucheddu, v. to lead a life

Buches, n. a milking fold
Budr a. dirty, nasty, vile
Budrâd, n. defilement
Budredd, n. filthiness, dirt
Budreddi, n. nastiness, filth
Budreddu, v. to defile
Budriaith, n. obscene speech
Budro, v. to dirty, to soil
Budrog, a. abounding with dirt
Budrogen, n. a filthy wench
Budrol, a. dirtying, soiling
Budd, n. profit, gain
Buddai, n. a churn ; a bittern
Buddeilw, n. cowhouse posts
Buddfawr, a. advantageous
Buddiant, n. advantage, gain
Buddio, v. to profit, to avail
Buddiol, a. profitable
Buddioldeb, a. profitableness
Buddioli, v. to make profitable
Buddugol, a. victorious, trium-
Buddugoliaeth, n. victory [phant
Buelin, a. of horn : n. a bugle
Bugad, n. a confused noise
Bugadu, v. to threaten, to vaunt
Bugail, Bugeiliwr, Bugeilydd, n. a shepherd, a herdsman
Bugeilio, v. to tend a flock
Bugeiliad, n. a tending of flock
Bugeileg, n. a bucolic
Bugeilffon, n. a shepherd's crook
Bugeilgan, n. a pastoral song
Bugeilgi, n. a shepherd's dog
Bugeiliaeth, n. pastoral care
Bugeiliaidd, a. pastoral
Bugloddi, to turn up the ground
Bugunad, n. a belowing
Buguned, v. to bellow, to roar
Buguno, v. to bellow, to roar
Bugunwr, n. one who roars
Bul, n. a seed-vessel, hull
Buladd, n. the herb cameleon
Bulwg, n. cockle weed, corn-rose
Bumustl, n. the ox-bane
Bun, n. a woman, a maiden
Buna, a. ten hundred thousand
Bur, n. violence, rage
Burgun, n. a carcase
Burgunio, v. to mangle to death
Burguniol, a. cadaverous
Buria, n. a carcase
Burth, n. a violent thrust
Burthiad, n. a driving off
Burwy, n. a cow fetter
Bury, n. a carnivorous bird
Burym, n. barm, yeast, froth
Bus, n. the human lip
Bustach, n. a steer, a bullock
Bustachu, v. to buffet about
Bustl, n. gall, bile, choler
Bustlaidd, a. like gall
Bustlo, v. to yield gall
Buwch, n. a cow
Büyn, n. a bullock
Bw, n. a threat; terror; bugbear interj. of threatening
Bwa, n. a bow, an arch
Bwâd, n. bowing, a bowering
Bwâu, v. to bend like a bow
Bwbach, n. a bugbear, a goblin
Bwbachog, a. abounding with hobgoblins ; terrifying
Bwbachu, v. to scare ; to buffet
Bwbachus, a. easily scared
Bwbechni, n. bastiality
Bwcai, n. a maggot
Bwcled, n. a buckler
Bwch, n. a buck
Bwgan, n. a bugbear
Bwgwth, n. a threat, a menace
Bwgwth, v. to threaten ; to scare
Bwhwman, n. a fluctuation ; v. to waver (corn ; a budget
Bwlan, n. a straw vessel to hold
Bwlch, n. a gap, a defile ; a. broken, notched
Bwmp, n. hollow sound; Aderyn y bwn, a bittern
Bwn, n. a spear head
Bwng, n. an orifice, a bung
Bwrdais, n. a burges
Bwrdeisdref, n. a borough town
Bwrdd, n. a table ; a board
Bwriad, n. a casting, a design
Bwriadol, a. purposing or intending

Bwriadu, v. to purpose, intend or design; to resolve; to devise
Bwrlymiad, n. a gurgling
Bwrlymol, a. gurgling
Bwrlymu, v. to gurgle
Bwrn, n. a truss, a heap, a load
Bwrnel, n. a bundle, a pack
Bwrw, n. a cast, a throw; a tally; v. to cast, to throw; to imagine. Bwrw ewyn, v. to foam. Bwrw gwlaw neu eira, to rain or snow
Bwsg, n. a grafting tool
Bwt, n. a hole; a button hole; a dung cart; a basket placed in a stream to catch fish.
Bwtias n. a pair of boots
Bwth, n. a hut, a booth
Bwthyn, n. a small cabin or hut
Bwyd, n. meat, food, victuals
Bwydiar, n. a voider
Bwydiog, a. gluttonous
Bwydlys, n. salad
Bwydo, v. to feed, to give food
Bwydwr, n. a feeder
Bwyell, n. an axe, a hatchet
Bwyellan, n. a little hatchet
Bwyellgaib, n. a pick-axe
Bwyellig, n. a small hatchet
Bwys:fil, n. a wild beast
Bwys'filaidd, a. brutish, beastly
Bwyta, v. to take food, to eat
Bwytâd, n. an eating
Bwytadwy, a. eatable, edible
Bwytai, n. a greedy eater
Bwytal, n. victuals, viands
Bwytaol, a. eating
Bwytawr, n. an eater
Bwytëig, n. given to eating
Bwytty, n. a pantry, buttery
By, conj. mutation of ry, if
Bychaidd, a. like a buck
Bychan, a. little, small
Bychander, n. littleness
Bychanedd, n. smallness
Bychaniad, n. a making little
Bychanig, a. dimminutive
Bychanigo, v. to disparage

Bychanigyn, n. a very little, small, or minute thing
Bychanu, v. to lessen; to slight
Bychod, n. a small matter
Bychygyr, n. a drone, a wasp
Byd, n. a world, or universe; gwyn fyd, happiness
Bydol, a. worldly, secular
Bydoldeb, n. worldliness
Bydolddyn, n. a worldling
Bydwraig, n. a midwife
Bydyssod, n. the universe
Bydd, a tie, a keeping together
Byddag, n. a snare, a spring
Byddagliad, n. a taking in a snare
Byddar, a. deaf
Byddardra, n. deafness
Byddariad, n. a deafening
Byddarlys, n. the house-leek
Byddaru, v. to deafen, to stun
Byddarwch, n. deafness
Byddin, n. a snare, an ambush, a band, or troop, an army
Bydd niad, n. an embattling
Byddino, v. to embattle
Byddinol, a. embattling
Byddu, v. to be, to endure
Bygegyr, n. a drone bee
Bygwth, v. to threaten
Bygylu, v. to intimidate
Bygythiad, n. a threatening
Bygythio, v. to threaten
Bygythiol, a. threatening
Bylchog, a. breached, notchy
Bylchiad, n. a breaching
Bylchu, v. to make a notch
Bynag, a. soever
Byr, a. short, brief; abrupt
Byrâd, n. a shortening
Byrâu, v. to shorten
Byrbryd, n. a luncheon
Byrbwyll, a. thoughtless, giddy
Byrbwylldra, n. thoughtlessness
Byrder, n. shortness
Byrdon, n. bass in music
Byrdra, n. shortness, brevity
Byrddiad, n. a boarding
Byrddio, v. to board

Byrddwn, n. bass in music
Byrfys, n. the little finger
Byrhoedledd, n. shortness of life
Byriad, n. a breviat, an arm
Byriau, a short plough yoke
Byrllysg, n. a truncheon
Byrnaid, n. a truss, a bundle
Byrniad, n. a trussing, a bundling
Byrniaw, v. to truss, to bundle
Bys, n. a finger
Bysiad, n. a fingering
Bysio, v. to finger
Bysle, n. a finger-stall
Byson, n. a finger ring, a ring
Bystwn, n. a whitlow
Byswain, n. a thimble
Byth, n. eternity: adv. for ever
Bytheuad, n. a hound
Bytheuadgi, n. a hound dog
Bythfyw, a ever-living
Bythol, a. eternal, perpetual
Bytholrwydd, n. everlastingness
Byw, v. to live, to exist; a. alive living, quick.
Bywâu, to animate, to enliven
Bywâus, a. animating
Bywed, n. a core of fruit; pith
Byweiddio, v. to animate
Bywfyth, a. everliving
Bywi, n. earth-nuts, orchis
Bywiad, n. vivification [mate
Bywiocâu, v. to vivify, to animate
Bywiog, a. lively, vigorous
Bywiogi, to animate, to revive
Bywiol, a. living, animate
Bywiolaeth, n. livelihood
Bywion, n. emmets, ants
Bywionyn, n. an emmet
Bywlys, n. the house-leek
Bywull, n. buds, grafts, scions
Bywullu, v. to bud, to graft
Bywyd, n. life, existence
Bywydol, a. relating to life
Bywyn, n. pulp of fruit
Bywynaidd, a. like a pulp [pulp
Bywyneiddio, v. to grow to a
Bywynog, a. having pulp

C

CA, n. a keep, a hold; a shutting on; a holding, v. he will have
Cäad, n. a getting, having
Caban, n. a booth, a cabin
Cabl, n. blasphemy, curse
Cablaidd, a. blasphemous
Cablair, n. calumny
Cablawd, n. blasphemy
Cabledig, a. blasphemed
Cabledd, n. blasphemy
Cabliad, n. a blaspheming
Cablu, v. to blaspheme
Cablwr, n. a blasphemer
Cabol, a. polished, bright
Cabolfaen, n. a polishing stone
Caboli, v. to polish
Caboliad, n. a polishing
Cabrawd, n. rusticity
Cacamwci, n. the great burdock
Cacynen, n. a hornet, a wasp
Cach, n. ordure, dung, soil
Cachad, n. a dirty sloven
Cachgi, n. a coward
Cad, n. a striving; a battle
Cadach, n. a kerchief, a clout
Cadair, n. a seat of presidency
Cadar, n. a defence, a shield
Cadarn, a. compact, powerful
Cadarnâd, n. strengthening
Cadarnâu, v. to strengthen, to
Cadarnder, n. potency [fortify
Cadas, n. brocade
Cadawl, a. relating to war
Cadbais, n. coat of mail
Cadben, n. a captain
Cadbenaeth, n. captainship
Cadechyn, n. a clout, a rag
Cadeirfardd, n. graduated bard
Cadeiriad, n. a chairing
Cadeirio, v. to chair
Cadeiriol, a. chaired; cathedral
Cader, n. a hill-fort; a chair.
 Cader buwch, cow's udder
Cadernid, n. strength
Cadfarch, n. a war horse

| ANW | 52 | ANY |

Cadfiled, n. the march of battle
Cadfiliad, n. a general
Cadflaen, n. the van of an army
Cadfridog, n. a general
Cadganu, v. to forswear
Cadgorn, n. a horn of battle
Cadlan, n. a field of battle
Cadlas, n. a close, a croft, a yard
Cadlys, n. an intrenchment
Cadnaw, Cadno, n. a fox
Cadnoes, n. a she fox
Cadraith, n. military discipline
Cadrawd, n. rage of battle
Cadres, n. a line of battle
Cadseirch, n. war-harness
Cadu, v. to battle, to conflict
Cadw, n. a keeping; a flock, a herd; v. to keep, to preserve
Cadwad, n. a keeping
Cadwadog, n. a preservative
Cadwadol, a. preservative
Cadwadwy, a. preservable
Cadwaith, n. action, battle
Cadwedig, preserved, guarded, kept, saved
Cadwedigaeth, n. preservation
Cadwedigol, a. preservative
Cadweidiaeth, n. preservation
Cadweini, n. knight-service
Cadwen, n. a bandage, a chain
Cadwent, n. a field of battle
Cadwfa, n. a reservoir
Cadwr, n. a warrior
Cadwraeth, n. preservation
Cadwraidd, n. radiation of sin-
Cadwy, n. a covering a rug [ews
Cadwyd, v. to keep, to preserve
Cadwydd, n. a brake
Cadwyn, n. a bond, a chain
Cadwynad, n. a chaining
Cadwynedigaeth, n. catenation
Cadwyno, v. to chain
Cadwynodi, v. to rhyme altern-
Cadwynog, a. chained [ately
Cadwynol, a. chaining
Cadwynor, n. a binder in chains
Caddug, n. an obscurity; an eclipse

Caddugo, to obscure, to darken
Caddugol, a. gloomy, obscure
Cae, n. an inclosure, a hedge, a field; a. inclosed, shut, close
Caead, n. a cover, a lid; a. inclosed, shut, closed
Caeadlen, n. a curtain
Caeadrwydd, n. inclosed state
Caeadu, v. to inclose, to close
Cael, v. to get, to have
Caenen, n. a covering; a layer
Caenenu, v. to incrustate
Caeniad, n. a coating over
Caenu, v. to incrust
Caeog, a. inclosed, wreathed
Caeol, a. tending to close
Caeor, n. a sheep fold
Caer, n. a fort; a wall; a city
Caerog, a. fortified, fenced
Caeru, v. to wall, to fortify
Caerwaith, n. fortification
Caeth, n. a bondman, a slave
Caeth, a. bound, straight
Caethder, n. restriction
Caethedig, a. restricted
Caethes, n. a female slave
Caethforwyn, n. a bondwoman
Caethfyd, n. a state of slavery
Caethglud, n. a captive [tive
Caethgludiad, n. a carrying cap-
Caethgludo, v. to carry captive
Caethaid, n. a straitening
Caethiant, n. confinement
Caethiw, a. confined, servile
Caethiwed, n. slavery, bondage
Caethiwedig, a. confined
Caethiwo, v. to confine, to en-
Caethiwol, a. confining [slave
Caethlwnc, difficult swallowing
Caethnawd, n. a slavish state
Caethrawd, n. bondage
Caethu, v. to confine, to enslave
Caethwas, n. a bondman
Caf, n. a void, a hold, a cave
Cafall, n. a cell, a chancel
Cafn, n. a trough, a canoe
Cafniad, n. a scooping
Cafnu, v. to scoop, to hollow out

Caffad, n. attainment
Caffael, v. to get, to ob'ain
Caffaeliad, n. a getting hold of
Caffawd, n. acquirement
Caffell, n. a grasper, a valve
Caffiad, n. grasping; a throwing about the arms, to seize
Cagl, n. sheep dung; mire
Caglog, a. bedaggled, daggled
Caglu, v. to bedaggle
Cangen, n. a nymph; a branch
Cangenog, a. having branches
Cangeniad, n. a branching
Cangenu, v. to branch out
Canghell, n. a chancel
Canghellog, a. having a chancel
Canghellor, n. a chancellor [ship
Canghelloriaeth, n. chancellor-
Canghellydd, n. a chancellor
Caib, n. a mattock, a hoe
Cainc, n. a branch, a bough
Cail, n. a fold, a sheep-fold
Caill, n. a testicle
Cain, clear, bright, fair, beauti-
Cair, n. berries [ful
Cais, n. an effort; a getting
Cala, n. a stem, a stalk
Calaf, n. a reed, a stalk
Calafog, a. having a reed
Calan, first day of every month
Calch, n. lime, enamel
Calchiaid, n. a coat of enamel
Calchaidd, a. calcareous
Calchdo, n. enamel covering
Calchedig, a. covered with lime
Calchiad, n. a liming
Calchog, a. calcareous, limed
Calchwr, n. a lime burner
Caled, n. hardness, hardship; a. hard, hardy; severe
Calededd, n. hardness, obduracy
Caledi, n. hardness; hardship
Calediad, n. a hardening
Caledrwydd, n. hardness
Caledu, v. to harden
Caledwch, n. hardness
Calen, n. a whetstone
Calon, n. a heart; a centre

Calondid, n. heartiness
Calonog, hearty, valiant [courage
Calonogi, to hearten up, to en-
Calonogrwydd, n. heartiness
Call, n. what starts out
Call, a. wise, prudent
Callaidd, a. somewhat cunning
Callawr, n. a cauldron
Callder, n. circumspection
Called, n. stalks of pulse, thistles, and the like
Calledd, n. discreetness
Callestr, n. pyrites; flint
Callestrol, a. flinty, of flint
Callineb, n. circumspection
Callod, n. fungi; agaric
Callodryn, n. a knotted stalk
Calloraid, n. a chaldron-ful
Cam, n. circumvention; a step, stride, or pace; a. crooked;
Camarfer, n. misusage
Camder, n. crookedness
Camdriniaeth, n. mismanage-
Camdroi, v. to pervert [ment
Camdybiad, n. misconception
Camddeall, v. to misunderstand
Camddirnad, v. to misappre-
Camddodi, v. to misplace [hend
Camedd, n. a bending
Cameg, n. felly of a wheel
Camen, n. a whirl, a curve
Camenw, n. misnomer
Camenwad, n. misnaming
Camfa, n. stile or step
Camfarnu, v. to misjudge
Camfeddiant, n. usurpation
Camfeddylio, v. to misconceive
Camgred, n. heresy
Camgyfrifiad, n. a misreckoning, a miscounting
Camgymmeriad, n. a mistake
Camgymmeryd, v. to mistake
Camlas, n. a trench, a ditch
Camlwrw, n. a fine for injury
Camlywodraeth, n. misgovern-
Camosod, v. to misplace [ment
Camosodiad, n. a misplacing
Camp, n. a feat; a game

| CAM | 54 | CAN |

Campfa, n. a place for games
Campio, v. to strive at games
Campus, a. excellent, masterly
Campwri, n. masterpiece
Camraw, n. a shovel
Camre, n. a pace, a step
Camreoli, v. to misgovern
Camrifo, v. to miscount
Camsyniad, n. misconception
Camsynied, v. to misconceive
Camwedd, n. iniquity, injustice
Camweddog, a. iniquitious
Camweddu, v. to transgress
Camweddus, a. iniquitious
Camweithred, n. a misdeed
Camwri, n. perversion, abuse
Camymddwyn, v. to misconduct
Camymddygiad, misconducting
Camystum, n. distortion
Camystyr, n. a wrong sense [ion
Camystyriaeth, n. misconstruct-
Camystyried, v. to misapprehend
Cân, n. a descant, a song
Càn, n. sight; brightness; whiteness, flour: a. white
Canad, n. a bleaching
Canaid, n. a luminary
Canawd, n. a descanting
Canbost, n. a prop, a baluster
Candryll, a. all to pieces
Canedig, a. blanched, whitened
Canfed, a. hundredth
Canfod, v. to behold, to perceive
Canfodadwy, a. perceptible
Canfodiad, n. a perceiving
Canfys, n. the ring-finger
Canhauol, n. pellitory
Caniad, n. license, consent: n. a song, music
Caniadaeth, n. science of song
Caniatâd, n. permission
Caniatâol, a. permissive
Caniatâu v. to permit, to consent
Canlyn, v. to follow, to pursue
Canlyniad, n. a following
Canlyniadol, a. consequential
Canlynol, a. following
Canlynwr, n. a follower

Canllaw, support; ballustrade
Canllawiaeth, n. supportation
Canmol, v. to commend
Canmoladwy, a. commendable
Canmoliad, n. commendation
Canmoliaeth, n. commendation
Canmoliaethol, commendatory
Canmoliant, n. commendation
Cannu, v. to contain
Cannwynol, a. congenial
Canol, n. a middle, a centre
Canolaidd, a. middling; central
Canolberth, n. a middle point
Canoldir, n. an inland region
Canoli, v. to centre
Canoliad, n. what is central
Canolig, a. middling, ordinary
Canolog, a. middlemost, central
Canolydd, n. a middle man
Canon, a song; a canon, a rule
Canonwr, n. a canonist
Canplyg, a. hundredfold
Canryg, n. rye-flour
Cant, n. an orb, rim, or verge of a circle; a hundred
Cantel, n. a rim of a circle
Cantell, n. a rim or verge
Cantor, n. a singer
Cantores, n. a songstress
Cantref, n. a canton, a hundred
Cantro, a. centuple
Cantroed, a. centipede
Cantwr, n. a singer
Cantwraig, n. a songstress
Cànu, v. to bleach, to whiten
Canu, v. to sing; to play music
Canwaith, a hundred times
Canwelw, a. of a bluish white
Cànwr, n. a bleacher
Canwr, n. a singer
Canwraidd, a. hundred-rooted
Canwraig, n. a songstress
Canwriad, n. a centurion
Canwyl, n. a horse-mask
Canwyll, n. a candle
Canwyllbren, n. a candlestick
Canwyllwr, a dealer in candles
Canwyllydd, n. a chandler

Canwyllyr, n. a chandelier
Canwyr, n. a plane
Canwyro, v. to plane; also to mark beasts by cutting the ear
Canwyrydd, n. a planer
Canyddiaeth, n. the art of singing
Canys, conj. because, for
Cap, n. a cap, a hood
Capan, n. a cap, a lintel
Capel, n. a chapel; a place of divine worship
Car, n. a raft, a frame, a drag
Câr, n. a friend, a relation; a. near, prep. on, by, at
Carad, n. endearment
Caradwy, a. amiable, lovely
Carai, n. a lace, a thong
Caraid, n. a drag-full
Caran, n. crown of the head
Carbwl, a. clumsy, awkward
Carchar, n. a prison
Carchariad, n. imprisonment
Carcharor, n. a prisoner
Carcharu, v. to imprison
Cardod, n. charity, alms
Cardodi, v. to give charity
Cardodol, a. charitable
Cardota, v. to go a begging
Cardotëiaeth, n. mendicity
Cardotty, n. an almshouse
Cardotyn, n. a beggar
Caredig, a. beloved, loving
Caredigo, v. to caress
Caredigol, a. caressing
Caredigrwydd, n. kindness
Careg, n. a stone
Caregiad, n. petrifaction
Caregog, a. full of stones, stony
Caregol, a. petrifactive
Caregos, n. pebbles
Carennydd, kindness; kindred
Cares, n. a kinswoman
Carfagl, n. a trap
Carfan, n. a binder, a stead, a beam, a rail, a row, a ridge
Cariad, n. love; a lover
Cariadaidd, a. lovely, amiable
Cariadol, a. loving, endearing

Cariadus, a. loving, beloved
Cario, v. to carry, to bear
Carlam, n. a prance, a gallop
Carlamog, a. galloping
Carlamiad, n. a galloping
Carlamu, v. to prance
Carn, n. a heap; a hoof; a hilt, haft, handle: a. notorious
Carnaflog, a. cloven-footed
Carnbwl, a. clumsy, bungling
Carnedd, n. heap of stones
Carneddog, having stone heaps
Carneddu, v. to heap up stones
Carnen, n. a heap; a wild sow
Carnog, a. having a hoof
Carnol, a. hoofed
Carnu, v. to heap, to pile
Carol, n. love song, carol
Caroli, v. to carol
Carp, n. clout, rag
Carpio, v. to tear to rags
Carpiog, a. ragged, tattered
Cartref, n. a home, an abode
Cartrefiad, n. an abiding at home
Cartrefol, a. homely, domestic
Cartrefu, v. to stay at home
Carth, n. that which is peeled or scoured off; hemp; rind
Carthai, n. a cathartic
Carthbren, n. plough-staff
Carthedig, a cleansed
Carthen, n. a sheet or cloth
Carthglwyd, n. dung barrow
Carthiad, n. a cleansing
Carthlyn, n. an emetic
Carthol, a. scouring; rinded
Carthu, v. to scour, to cleanse
Caru, v. to court, to love
Caruaidd, a. endearing, loving
Caruciddio, v. to endear
Carw, n. stag, hart
Carwiwrch, n. roebuck
Carwr, n. a lover
Cas, n. separated state; castle; hatred: a. hateful
Casid, n. hating, enmity
Casâu, v. to hate, to be disgusted
Casâwr, n. a hater

| CAS | 56 | CED |

Casedd, n. hatred, enmity
Caseg, n. mare
Casgl, n. a heap, collection
Casgledig, a. gathered, collected
Casgledigol, a. collective
Casgliad, n. a collection
Casgliadol, a. collective
Casglu, v. to collect, to gather
Casglwr, n. collector
Casineb, n. hatred, enmity
Casnach, n. nap of cloth
Cost, n. a trick
Castan, n. a chesnut
Castanwydd, n. chesnut trees
Castell, n. a fortress, castle
Castelliad, n. a fortifying
Castellu, v. to fortify
Castio, v. to play tricks
Castiog, a. full of tricks
Castyr, n. rod of a horse
Catau, v. to combat, to bicker
Cateri, n. spreading oaks
Catrwd, n. regiment
Catrodawl, a. regimental
Catrodi, v. to form into battalion
Cath, n. cat
Cathaidd, a. feline, like a cat
Cathdericai, n. caterwauler
Cathl, n. melody, hymn
Cathliad, n. hymning
Cathlu, v. to hymn, to sing
Cau, v. to shut, to inclose: n. a hollow, vacuum: a. shut
Cauad, n. a shutting
Caued, a. inclose, shut, close
Cauedig, a. shut, close
Cauedigeeth, n. a shutting
Caul, n. a maw; rennet; curd
Caw, n. band, wrapper
Cawci, n. a jackdaw
Cawd, n. what incloses
Cawdd, n. a darkening; displeasure; offence; vexation
Cawell, n. a hamper, a basket
Cawellaid, n. a hamper-full
Cawellan, n. a small hamper
Cawellu, v. to hamper
Cawellyn, n. a small hamper

Cawg, n. a basin, a bowl
Cawgaid, n. a basin-full
Cawgyn, n. a small basin
Cawiad, n. a binding round
Cawl, n. cabbage; broth, gruel; pottage
Cawlai, n. a feeder on pottage
Cawlaid, n. making hodgepodge
Cawlio, v. to mix disorderly
Cawn, n. reeds, stalks; reed grass
Cawna, v. to gather reeds
Cawnen, n. a straw vessel
Cawod, n. shower
Cawodi, v. to shower
Cawr, n. a giant
Cawraidd, a. gigantic
Cawrchwil, n. a bull-chaffer
Cawredd, n. might, puissance
Cawres, n. a female giant
Cawrfil, n. an elephant
Caws, n. cheese; curd
Cawsa, v. to gather cheese
Cawsaidd, a. cheese-like; curdled
Cawsdŷ, n. a cheese-house
Cawsellt, n. a cheese-vat
Cawselltu, to put cheese in a vat
Cawsiad, n. a curdling
Cawsio, v. to turn to cheese
Cawsion, n. curds
Cawslestr, n. a cheese-mould
Cawswasg, n. a cheese-press
Cawswr, n. a cheesemonger
Cebr, n. a rafter
Cebystr, n. a tether, a halter
Cecr, n. a brawl
Cecraeth, n. a wrangling
Cecraidd, a. apt to wrangle
Cecren, n. a shrew, a scold
Cecri, n. snappishness
Cecru, v. to wrangle
Cecrus, a. snapish, quarrelsome
Cecryn, n. a wrangler, a brawler
Cecys, n. hollow stalks; hemlock
Ced, n. a favour, a gift, relief
Cedafien, n. a napkin
Ceden, n. shaggy hair, nap
Cedenog, a. shaggy
Cedenu, v. to make shaggy

Cedor, n. hair of pubescence
Cedorfa, the bottom of the belly
Cedorwydd, n. giant fennel
Cedu, v. to confer or gift
Cedwid, n. custody, possession
Cedys, n. faggots, bundles
Ceddw, n. mustard
Cefn, n. a back; a ridge
Cefnaint, n. a middle part
Cefnant, n. support; a great-grandchild
Cefnbant, a. saddle-backed
Cefnder, Cefnderw, dyrw, n. first cousin
Cefndwn, a. broken backed
Cefnddryll, n. a chine
Cefnen, n. a gently rising hill
Cefnfor, n. the main sea
Cefn-grwba, a. hunch-backed
Cefn-grwca, a. crook-backed
Cefn-grwm, a. hump-backed
Cefn-hwrwg, a. hunch-backed
Cefnllif, n. a high flood
Cefnog, a. backed, courageous
Cefnogaeth, n. backing
Cefnogi, v. to back, to encourage
Cefnogiad, n. a a backing
Cefnu, v. to back; to turn a back
Ceffyl, n. a horse
Ceg, n. a mouth, an opening
Cegaid, n. a mouthful
Cegddu, n. the hake fish
Cegiad, n. a mouthing
Cegid, n. the hemlock
Cegin, n. a kitchen
Ceginiaeth, n. cookery
Ceginwr, n. a cook, a kitchener
Cegio, v. to mouth; to choke
Cegol, a. of a mouth, mouthed
Cegrwth, a. wide-mouthed
Cegrythiad, n. a mouthing
Cegrythu, v. to open the mouth
Cegu, to mouth; to glut [widely
Cengl, n. a band; a hank
Cengliad, n. a winding
Cengliadur, n. a winding reel
Cengliedydd, n. a reeler
Cenglog, a. reeled in hanks
Cenglu, v. to hank, to girth
Cenglyn, n. a bandage
Ceibiad, n. a hoeing
Ceibio, v. to use a hoe or mattock, to hoe
Ceibren, n. a rafter
Ceidwad, n. a keeper, preserver, saviour
Ceidwadaeth, n. preservation
Ceidwadol, a. preservative
Ceidwadwy, a. preservable
Ceingel, n. a hank; a girth
Ceingell, n. twisting reel
Ceinglo, v. to hank; to girth
Ceingliad, n. hanking
Ceingliadur, n. winding wheel
Ceingyll, n. a reel to twist ropes
Ceilio, v. to fold cattle
Ceiliog, n. a cock; a male bird
Ceiliogwr, n. a cock-master
Ceiliogwydd, n. a gander
Ceiliogyn, n. cockerel
Ceilysyn, n. a nine-pin
Ceimwch, n. a lobster
Ceinach, n. a hare
Ceinad, n. circumspection
Ceinciad, n. a branching out
Ceincio, to branch out, to ramify
Ceinciog, a. full of branches
Ceinciol, a. branching
Ceinder, n. elegance; beauty
Ceinedd, n. elegance
Ceinfalch, a. ostentatious
Ceinioca, v. to collect money, as by brief; to gather pence
Ceiniog, stamped coin; a penny
Ceiniogwerth, n. a penny-worth
Ceinion, n. ornaments, jewels
Ceinionydd, n. a jeweller
Ceinwen, a. splendidly white
Ceirch, n. oats, oat
Ceirchen, n. a grain of oats
Ceiriad, n. a bearer
Ceirios, n. cherries
Ceiriosen, n. a single cherry
Ceirniad, n. a hoofed animal
Ceisbwl, n. a blunt churl, a catchpoll

Ceis.au, n. an extortioner; a bailiff; a tax-gatherer
Ceisid, n. a seeking, a trying
Ceisiedydd, n. one who seeks
Ceisio, v. to seek, to attempt
Ceiswr, n. one who seeks
Ceithiwed, n. bondage
Cel. n. a shelter, a hiding
Celadwy, a. apt to hide, hiding
Celain, a. involved in shades; n. a carcase
Celan, n. a dead body
Celanedd, n. a heap of carcases
Celaneddog, a. strewed with dead
Celaneddu, v. to make carnage
Celc, n. concealment; a wile
Celcadwy, a. concealable
Celclad, n. a concealing
Celcyn, n. dissembler
Celcyniaeth, n. dissimulation
Celdy, n. arbour
Celedig, a. hidden, concealed
Celedigaeth, n. concealment
Celfan, n. place of retreat
Celf, n. art, craft, mystery
Celfi, n. instruments, tools
Celfydd, a. skilful, artful
Celfyddgar, a. scientific
Celfyddus, a. technical
Celfyddyd, n. art, craft
Celfyddydol, a. artificial
Celi, n. the Deity
Celt, n. shelter, covert
Celu, v. to conceal, to hide
Celwrn, n. tub, piece
Celwydd, n a lie, falsehood
Celwyddo, v. to lie
Celwyddog, a. false, lying
Celwyddus, a. lying
Celwyddwr, n. liar
Celydd, n. sheltered place
Celyn, n. holly wood
Celyneg, n. holly grove
Celynog, a. having holly
Celyrnaid, n. tub-full
Cell, n. cell; seclusion; grove
Cellaig, n. hart, stag
Cellawg, a. abounding with cells

Celli, n. grove; bower
Cellt, n. flint stone
Cellwair, n. a joke; v. to joke
Cellweirgar, a. jocular
Cellweiriad, n. a joking
Cellweirio, v. to joke; to hint
Cellweiriol, a. joking
Cellweirus, a. jocular, jesting
Cemi, n. crookedness
Cemmaes, n. a circle for games
Cemyw, n. a male salmon
Cèn, n. a skin, a peel, scales
Cenad, n. messenger, permission
Cenadiaeth, n. an embassy
Cenadol. a. missive, missionary
Cenadu, v. to permit, to send
Cenadwr, n. a messenger
Cenadwri, n. mission, embassy
Cenau, n. a cub, a whelp
Cenaw, n. offspring; a cub, a whelp, a scion
Cenawes, n. a she cub
Cenawg, a. scaly, scurfy
Cenedl, n kindred, tribe, nation
Cenedlaeth, n. a generation
Cenedlaethol, a. generating
Cenedlawr, n. a progenitor
Cenedlog, a. having a family
Cenedlol, a. of a family
Cenedledig, a. begotten, gener-
Cenedledigol, a. generative [ated
Cenedliad, n. procreation
Cenedlig, a. national; gentile
Cenedlu, to beget, to generate
Cenfaint, n. a progeny; a herd
Cenfigen, n. envy, malice
Cenfigeniad, n. an envying
Cenfigenol, a. envying, envious
Cenfigenu, v. to grudge, to envy
Cenfigenus, a. envious, spiteful
Cenin, n. leeks
Ceninen, n. a single leek
Cenllysg, n. a stormy shower; hail stones
Cenu, v. to scale, to scurf
Cêr, n. tools, furniture
Ceraint, n. relatives, kindred
Cerbyd, n. a chariot, a coach

| CER | 59 | CEU |

Cerdd, art, craft art of poetry; a piece of poetry, a song
Cerddawr, n. an artist; a singer, a musician
Cerdded, v. to walk, to travel
Cerddediad, n. a walking
Cerddedrwydd, n. peregrination
Cerddedwr, n. a walker
Cerddgar, a. harmonious, musical
Cerddores, a female artist
Cerddoriaeth, n. the science of singing
Cerf, n. method; art; trade
Cerfiad, n. figuring; sculpture
Cerfio, v. to model, to form, to carve
Cerfyll, n. sculpture; a statute
Ceriach, n. small tools; trifles
Cerien, n. a medlar
Cerlyn, n. a miser
Cern, side of the head; the jaw
Cerniad, n. a turning the side of the head; a jawing
Cernial, n. to go cheek by jawl
Cernio, v. to turn the jaw
Cernod, n. a blow on the cheek
Cernodiad, n. a buffetting
Cernodio, v. to buffet, or beat the head
Cerpyn, n. a clout, a rag
Cert, n. cart
Certaid, n. a cart load
Certiad, n. a carting
Certwyn, n. a cart, a wain
Certh, a. evident; imminent
Certhedd, n. imminence
Cerwydd, n. a stag, a hart
Cerwyn, n. a mashing tub
Cerwynaid, n. a tub-full
Cerydd, n. chastisement
Ceryddadwy, a. corrigible
Ceryddedigaeth, n. chastisement
Ceryddiad, n. correction
Ceryddol, a. castigatory
Ceryddu, v. to correct, to chastise
Ceryddus, a. reproving
Ceryddwr, n. a chastiser
Ceryn, n. a tool; a surly chap

Ces, n. a point of divergency
Cesail, n. arm pit; bosom
Cesair, n. hailstones
Cesciliad, n. arm full; taking in arms
Cescirio, v. to shower hail
Ceseiryn, n. a hailstone
Cest, n. a receptacle; narrow-mouthed basket
Cestawg, a. round-bellied
Cetawg, n. a satchel, a bag
Ceten, n. a little cabinet
Cetyn, n. a piece; a pipe
Cethern, n. furies, fiends
Cethin, a. dun, dusky; ugly
Cethinen, n. a swarthy one
Cethino, v. to make dusky; to make ugly; to become ugly
Cethledd, n. melody, singing
Cethlydd, n. the cuckoo
Cethr, n. spike, a nail
Cethrawl, a. pricking
Cethrawr, n. a pike
Cethren, n. a spike, a nail
Cethrin, a. piercing; horrid
Cethru, v. to drive; to pierce
Cethrwr, n. one who drives
Cethw, n. mustard
Ceuad, n. an excavation
Ceubal, n. a ferry boat
Ceubelfa, n. ferrying place
Ceubren, n. a hollow tree
Ceudod, n. the bosom
Ceuedig, a. inclosed; hallowed
Ceuedd, n. hallowness
Ceufa, n. a gulf, an abyss
Ceufawr, a. yawning
Ceugant, n. vacuity; infiinity a. certain, sure
Ceulad, n. coagulation
Ceulaidd, a. chylacerous
Ceulan, n. a hollow bank
Ceulaw, Ceulo, v. to coagulate
Ceulawr, n. a curdling tray
Ceuled, n. rennet
Ceuleden, n. a curd
Ceuledig, a. curdled
Ceulfraen, n. crumbly curds

Ceulfraenu, v. to make cheese
Ceunant, n. a ravine, a brook
Ceulon, n. cheese rennet
Ceuo, v. to excavate
Ceuol, a. inclosing
Ci, n. a dog; a holdfast
Ciaidd, a. dog-like, dogged
Cib, n. a cup; a seed-vessel
Cibaid, n. a cup-full
Cibaw, v. to raise a rim; to knit the brow
Cibawg, a. having a cup or shell
Cibddall, a. purblind
Cibddalledd, n. purblindness
Cibddu, a. swarthy, dusky
Cibedrych, v. to glance over
Cibglawr, n. a trap door
Cibied, a. of expanding rim
Cibli, n. a favourite thing
Cibwst, n. chilblains, kibes
Cibyn, n. a cup, a follicle; a shell: half a bushel
Cibynaid, n. half a bushel
Cibynog, a. having a skell
Cic, n. a foot, a kick
Cicio, v. to kick
Cidwm, n. a voracious beast
Cidws, n. a greedy one
Cidysen, n. a goat; a faggot
Cleidd-dra n. doggedness, savageness
Cieiddio, v. to grow dogged
Cieiddrwydd, a doggedness
Cig, n. flesh; flesh-meat
Cigaidd, a. carneous, like flesh
Cigdy, n. shamble
Cigddysgl, n a meat dish
Cgfa, n. a shamble
Cigfach, n. a flesh hook
Cigfwyd, n. flesh meat
Cigfran, n. a raven
Ciglyd, a. like flesh, carneous
Cignoeth, a. grinning, snaaling
Cigo, v. to grow fleshy
Cigog, a. full of flesh
Cigol, a. of flesh; sarcotic
Cigwain, n. a flesh fork; a spear
Cigweiniad, n. a clutching

Cigwr, Cigydd, n. a butcher
Cigyddiaeth, n. a butcher's trade
Cgydd.o, v. to butcher
Cil, n. a back; a recess; a corner; a retreat, a flight
Cilc, n. a fragment, a corner
Cilchweryn, n. a gland
Cildant, n. alto harp-string
Cildrem, n. a leering look
Cildremio, v. to leer
Cildremydd, n. a leerer
Cildro, n. a turn back
Cildroi, v. to turn backward
Cildyn, a. obstinate, stubborn
Cildynog, a. apt to pull back
Cildynu, v. to pull back
Cilddant, n. a back tooth
Ciledrych, v. to look aside
Cilegored a. half-open a-jar
Cilegori, v. to half-open
Ciler, n a butter tray
Cilfach, n. a nook; a creek
Cilgi, n. a cowardly dog
Cilgwthio, v. to drive back
Ciliedig a. driven back
Cilio, v. to retreat, to withdraw, to go out of the way
Cilolwg, n. a sly look, a leer
Cilolygu, v. to leer aside
Cilwen, n. a half smile
Cilwenu, v. to simper
Cilwg, n. frown of contempt
Cinio, n. a meal; a dinner
Cniawa, v. to eat a meal; to dine
Cingroen, n. stinking mushroom
Cip, n. a quick pull or snatch
Cipdrem, n. a quick glance
Cipen, n. a grapple, a grapnel
Cipgais, n. a scrambling
Cipgar, a. snatching; captious
Cipio, v. to snatch; to whisk
Cipiol, a. snatching; whisking
Cipiwr, n. a snatcher
Cipyll, n. a dry stump
Ciprys, n. a scramble, a brawl
Ciprysgar, a. brawling
Ciprysu, v. to scramble
Cist, n. a chest, a coffer

Cistan, n. a small chest
Cistbridd, n. potter's clay
Cistfaen, n. a stone chest
Cistwely, n. a press-bed
Ciw, a. clever, trim, neat
Ciwdawd, n. a tribe, clan
Ciwed, n. a rabble, a mob
Cladd, n. a trench, a pit
Cladde, n. a chimney piece
Claddedig, a. intrenched, buried
Claddedigaeth, n. burying
Claddfa, n. a burying place
Claddiad, a. burial
Claddu, v. to dig a pit; to bury
Claer, a. clear, bright, shining
Claerder, n. clearness
Claerwen, a. bright shining
Claf, n. a sick person; a. sick, ill, diseased
Clafaidd, a. sickly, indisposed
Clafr, n. scurf, leprosy
Clafdŷ, n. an infirmary
Clafrdŷ, n. lazaretto
Clafrlyd, a. leprous; mangy
Clafru, v. to grow leprous
Clafu, v. to sicken, to full ill
Clafus, a. sickly, indisposed
Clai, n. clay; marl
Clain, n. prostrate state
Clais, n. a stripe; a mark a bruise; a rivulet
Clamp, n. a mass; a lump
Clap, n. a lump; a knob
Clapio, v. to make a lump, to
Claplog a. lumpy [grow lumpy
Clasdir, n. glebe-land
Clasg, n. a heap, a pile
Clasordŷ, n. a cloister-house
Clau, a. incessant, even; temperate; sincere
Clauar, a. temperate, mild; lukewarm; indifferent, not ardent
Clauarder, n. temperateness; indifference; lukewarmness
Clauaredd, n. temperature
Clauarineb, n. temperateness
Clauarwch, n. temperateness
Clauaru, v. to make mild

Clawdd, n. dike, ditch, pit; fence or hedge, wall
Clawr, n. a surface, a cover
Claws, n. a close; yard
Cleb, n. driveller
Clebar, n. clack, silly talk
Clebarddus, a. babbling
Clebren, n. a prating, gossip
Clec, n. crack, smack
Cleca, v. to clack, to gossip
Clecai, n. a clacker
Cleciad, n. a cracking
Clecian, v. to crack to smack
Cledr, n. a flat body; a shingle
Cledren, n. a shingle; a stave
Cledriad, n. a railing, a pailing
Cledrog, a. shingled
Cledru, v. to pail, to rail
Cledrwy, n. lattice-work
Cledd, n. rest; the left; sword; north
Cleddeu, n. a blade; a sword
Cleddiwig, n. a delf; a quarry
Cleddof, n. a sword cutler
Cleddog, a. bearing a sword
Cleddyf, n. a blade; a sword
Cleddyfwr, n. swordsman [ship
Cleddyfyddiaeth, n. swordsman-
Clefri, n. the leprosy
Clefryd, n. erruptive disease
Clefwch, n. disease, ailment
Clefychlyd, a. sickly
Clefychu, v. to fall sick
Clefyd, n. fever, sickness
Clefydog, a. liable to sickness
Clegyr, n. cliff, rock
Clegyrog, a. rugged, rocky
Cleiad, n. casing; a peat
Cleiawg, a. clayey
Cleibwll, n. clay pit
Cleidir, n. clay land
Cleien, n. rotten stone
Cleigio, v. to dip, to immerge
Cleilyd, a. clayey, clayish
Cleiniad, n. a lying prostrate
Cleinio, v. to lie prostrate
Cleio, v. to become clay
Cleisio, v. to bruise, to mark

Cleisiog, a. streaked; bruised
Clem, n. slive, slice
Clemio, v. to slice, to slive
Clep, n. clap, clack
Clepai, n. babbling gossip
Clepian, v. to babble, to clack
Clepio, v. to clack, to prate
Clêr, n. minstrels; gad flies
Clera, v. to stroll as minstrels
Cleren, n. a gad-fly; the rattles in the throat
Clerwriaeth, n. minstrelsy
Cleudaer, a. incessant
Cleuder, n. sincerity
Cleufryd, a. honest, sincere
Cleufrydedd, n. equanimity
Clewt, n, a clatter; a scolding
Clewtian, n. to clatter
Clicied, n. latch, catch
Cliciedu, v. to fasten with latch
Cliciedyn, n. a latch
Clin, n. a spark, sparkle
Clindarddach, n crackling noise: v. to crackle
Clip, n. precipice, crag
Clô, n. lock, close; knob
Clöad, n. a closing; a locking
Clob, n. a knob; a boss
Cloben, n. a large bouncer
Clobyn, n. a large lump
Clocian, v. to cluck as a hen
Cloch, n. a bell, a bubble
Clochaidd, a. sonorous, noisy
Clochdardd, n. a clucking
Clochdŷ, n. a steeple; a belfry
Clochiad, n. a bubbling
Clochydd, n. a bellman, a sexton, a parish clerk
Clôd, n. praise; fame
Clodadwy, a. commendable
Clodfawr, a. celebrated; famous
Clodforedd, n. celebrity
Clodfori, v. to celebrate, to extol
Clodforiad, n. a celebrating
Clodforus, a. commendable
Clodforwr, n. a praiser
Clodiad, n. a praising
Clodus, a. extolling, praising

Clodwiw, a. commendable
Clodymgais, v. to seek fame
Cloddfa, n. a quarry
Cloddiad, n. a trenching
Cloddio, v. to trench, to embank, to dig, to quarry
Cloddiog, a. trenched, embanked
Cloddiwr, n. a ditcher, a quarryman; a maker of fences
Clöedig, a. closed; locked
Clöedigaeth, n. a locking; a conclusion
Clöen, n. a boss, a stud
Cloer, n. a locker; a closet
Cloeren, n. a small window
Clofen, n. a knot, or point of ramnification in trees
Clofenog, a. branchy, spriggy
Clofenu, v. to branch, to sprig
Cloff, n. a lame person: a. lame, limping, halting
Cloffni, n. lameness
Cloffi, v. to lame; to grow lame
Cloffiad, n. a laming
Cloffrwym, n. a fetter
Cloffrwymol, a. fettered
Cloffrwymo, v. to fetter
Clog, n. a detached stone
Clogan, n. a large stone
Clogwrn, n. a crag; a rock
Clogwyn, n. precipi
Clogwynog, a. full of precipices
Clogyrnog, a. craggy, rocky
Cloi, v. to close, to lock
Cloig, n. a hasp; a hitch; helm for thatching
Cloigen, n. what is tied at the end; a hitch, a whisk of straw
Cloigyn, n. a hasp; a hitch
Cloigynu, v. to hasp; to hitch
Clòl, n. a pate, a skull
Clopa, n. a noddle; a knob; a thick head; a club
Clopen, n. a noddle, a jolthead
Cloren, n. a rump, a tail
Cloriad, n. a closing with a lid
Clorian, n. scales; balance
Clorianu, v. to balance, to weigh

Clorianwr, n. a weigher
Clorio, v. to put on a cover
Cloriog, a. having a lid or cover
Cloryn, n. a small lid or cover
Clos, n. a pair of breeches
Clôs, a. compact, neat, tidy
Closyn, n. a pair of breeches
Clöyn, n. a boss, the eye-ball
Clöynu, v. to emboss, to stud
Clud, n. any sort of carriage
Cludadwy, a. portable
Cludai, n. a carriage
Cludeiriad, n. a forming a heap
Cludeirio, v. to heap, to pile
Cluder, n. a heap, a pile
Cludfa, n. a carrying place
Cludiad, n. a bearing
Cludo, v. to carry, to heap
Cludydd, n. a porter, a bearer
Cludd, n. an overwhelming
Clug, n. a mass; the mumps
Clugiar, n. a partridge
Clugio, v. to squat; to perch
Clun, n. a hip, a haunch
Clunhecian, v. to limp
Clunlaes, a. a hipshot, limping
Clunwst, n. the sciatica
Clust, n. an ear; a handle
Clust-dlws, n. an ear-ring
Clusten, n. an auricle
Clustfeiniad, n. a pricking the ears; a listening
Clustfeinio, v. to prick up the ears; to listen closely
Clustfyddar, a. deaf-eared
Clustgyfaddef, n. auricular confession
Clustiog, a. having ears
Clustiol, a. auricular
Clustlipa, a. flap-eared
Clustog, n. a cushion, a pillow
Clustogan, n. a cushionet
Clustogi, v. to cushion
Clwc, n. a clucking: a. tender, soft to the touch
Clwcian, v. to cluck
Clwm, n. a knot, a tie
Clwpa, n. a knob, a club

Clws, a. compact, neat, trim
Clwt, n. a piece; a patch
Clwtyn, n. a small patch; a rag; a clout
Clwyd, n. plaited work, a hurdle; a roost
Clwyden, n. a hurdle; a flake
Clwydedig, a. hurdled, wattled
Clwydo, v. to wattle, to hurdle
Clwyf, n. a disease; a wound
Clwyfiad, n. to a sickening; a wounding
Clwyfo, v. to sicken; to wound
Clwyfol, a. sickening, wounding
Clwyfus, a. sickly; wounded
Clwys, n. a close, an inclosure
Clwys-dŷ, n. a cloister house
Clybod, n. the hearing
Clyd, a. sheltering, comfortable
Clydach, n. a sheltered glade
Clydo, v. to render comfortable
Clydrwydd, n. comfortableness; a sheltered state
Clydwr, n. shelter; refuge
Clymiad, n. a knotting, a tying
Clymog, a. knotty; entangled
Clymu, v. to knot, to tie
Clyryn, n. a hornet, a gad-fly
Clysu, v. to make compact
Clytiad, n. a patching
Clytio, v. to patch, to piece
Clytiog, a. patched; ragged
Clytwaith, n. patch-work
Clyw, n. the sense of hearing
Clywed, v. to hear
Clywedig, a. audible
Clywedigaeth, n. the hearing
Clywedog, a. sonorous
Clywiadur, n. a hearer
Cna, n. a knob, a door-button
Cnaif, n. a crop, a shearing
Cnap, n. a knob; a button
Cnapen, n. a knob; a bowl
Cnapio, v. to form knobs
Cnapiog, a. knobbed, knappy
Cnapiogrwydd, a. ruggedness
Cnawd, n. human flesh
Cnawdio, v. to incarnate

Cnawdol, a. carnal, fleshly
Cnawdoli, v. to incarnate
Cnawdoliad, n. incarnation
Cnawdoliaeth, n. incarnation
Cnawdolrwydd, n. carnality
Cnec, n. a crash, a snap, a jar
Cnecian, v. to crash; to jar
Cneccus, a. jarring; wrangling
Cneifdy, n. a shearing house
Cneifiad, n. a shearing
Cneifiedig, a. shorn, fleeced
Cneifio, v. to shear, to clip
Cneifion, n. clippings, flocks
Cneifiwr, n. a shearer
Cnes, n. a deposit; prey
Cneua, v. to get a nutting
Cneuen, n. a nut
Cneuo, v. to become a nut
Cneullu, v. to become a kernel
Cneullyn, n. a kernel
Cnic, n. a slight rap, a snap
Cnif, n. toil, pain, trouble
Cnifflad, n. a skirmishing
Cnith, n. a soft touch or tap
Cnithio, v. to tap, to twitch
Cno, n. a bite; a chewing
Cnöad, n. a bi'ing; a chewing
Cnöawl, a. biting; a chewing
Cnoc, n. a rap, a knock
Cnocell, n. a raper; a pecker
Cnocellu, v. to rap; to peck
Cnocio, v. to knock, to beat
Cnociwr, n. one that knocks
Cnod, n. a crop; a bunch
Cnofa, n. a gnawning, a griping
Cnoi, v. to gnaw, to chew
Cnöwr, n. a chewer; a biter
Cnu, n. a bundle; a fleece
Cnuch, n. a junction; a joint
Cnud, n. a proup; a pack
Cnul, n. a passing bell, a knell
Cnüog, a. fleecy
Cnwb, n. a bunch, a knob
Cnwc, n. a bump, a lump
Cnwd, n. a crop; a covering
Cnwff, n. a lump; a lunch
Cnwpa, n. a knob; a club
Cnwyf, n. a mash, a crush

Cnydfawr, a. fructiferous
Cnydiad, n. a producing, a crop
Cnydio, v. to fruitify, to crop
Cnydiol, a. fructiferous, fruitful
Co, n. rotundity; concavity
Còb, n. a tuft; a thump
Côb, n. a cloak; a top coat
Coban, n. a mantle; a coat
Cobiad, n. a thumping
Cobio, v. to tuft; to thump
Cobyn, n. a tuft, a bunch
Coblyn, a thumper; a pecker; a goblin
Cocos, n. cockles; cogs of a wheel
Cocraeth, n. fondling
Coch, n. a red colour: a. red
Cochder, n. redness
Cochddu, a. of a reddish black
Cochfelyn, a. copper-coloured
Cochgangen, n. a chub fish
Cochi, v. to redden; to blush
Cochiad, n. grouse, red game
Cochl, n. a mantle, a cloak
Cochlas, a. of red blue; purple
Cochrydd, a. crimson, ruddy
Cochwydd, n. ruddy appearance
Cochwyn, a. of a reddish white
Côd, n. a bag, a pouch, a budget
Codaid, n, a bag-full
Coden, n. a bag, a pouch
Codenog, a. having bags
Codenu, v. to bag; to blister
Codi, v. to rise; to swell up
Codiad, n. a rising; a raising
Codog, a. having bag; rich
Codwm, n. a fall, a tumble
Codymiad, n. a tumbling
Codymu, v. to fall, to tumble
Codymwr, a tumbler; a wrestler
Coed, n. wood, trees, timber
Coeda, v. to gather wood
Coeden, n. a tree, a standing tree
Coedog, a. having trees, woody
Coedol, a. of the wood; wooden
Coedwal, n. a wood covert
Coedwig, n. wood; forest
Coedwr, n. a woodman
Coedwrych, n. a quickset

Coeg, a. empty; vain; saucy
Coegaidd, spiteful, saucy; vain
Coegchwedl, n. an empty state
Coegdyb, n. an idle whim
Coegddall, a. half blind
Coegddellni, n. purblindness
Coegedd, n. silliness
Coegen, n. saucy wench
Coegenadd, a. coquettish
Coegfalch, a. conceitedly proud
Coegfalchedd, n. conceitedness
Coegfeddyg, n. a quack doctor
Coegfeddiginiaeth, n. quackery, empyrsm
Coegfolach, n. vain boasting
Coegfran, n. a jackdaw
Coegfrwnt, a. obscene; vile
Coegio, v. to make void; to trick
Coegni, n. sauciness
Coegsiarad, n. empty talk
Coegsiared, v. to talk foolishly
Coegwr, n. a vain person
Coegymddangosiad, n. a false appearance
Coegymffrost, n. vain boasting
Coegyn, n. conceited fellow
Coegynaidd, a. coxcomical
Coel, n, an omen; belief, trust
Coelbren, n. a record or letter, stick; a ballot stick; a lot
Coelcerth, n. a bonfire
Coeledig, a. credited, believed
Coeledigaeth, n. credibility
Coeledd, n. credibility; belief
Coelgar, credulous, apt to believe
Coelgarwch, n. credulousness
Coelgrefydd, n. superstition
Coelgrefyddol, a. superstitious
Coelgyf redd, n. a curing of disorders by charms
Coeliadwy, a. credible; authentic
Coelio, v. to believe, to credit
Coeliwr, n. a believer; a creditor
Coes, n. a leg; a shank
Coesgain, a. bandy-legged
Coeshir, a. long-legged
Coesnoeth, a. bare legged
Coesog, a. legged; shanked

Coesol, a. belonging to the leg
Coeswisg, covering for the leg
Coeta, v. to gather wood
Coettrych, n. a grafting stock
Coeth, a. ardent; pure, purified
Coethaidd, a. tending to be pure
Coethi, v. to stimulate, to purify
Coethiad, n. stimulation; a refining
Coethiedydd, n. a purifier
Coethol, stimulating; refining
Coethwr, n. a purifier
Côf, n. memory; record
Cofel, n. a memorial
Cofiad, n. a remembering
Cofiadur, n. a remembrancer, a recorder, a secretary
Cofiadwy, a. memorable
Cofiant, n. memoir, record
Cofiedydd, n. remembrancer
Cofio, v. to remember, to recollect
Cofl, n. the embrace; the bosom; the folding of the arms
Coflaid, n. what is embraced; a bosom friend; a darling
Cofleidiad, n. an embracing
Cofleidio, v. to fold in the arms
Cofleidwr, n. an embracer
Coflyfr, n. a memorandum book
Coflys, n. a court of record
Cofnod, n. a memorandum[ister
Cofrestr, n. a catalogue, a register
Cofrestriad, n. a registering
Cofrestru, v. to register
Cofrestrwr, n. registrar
Cofus, a. memorable; mindful
Cofweinydd, n. prompter
Cofwyl, n. memorable festival
Coffa, v. to remember
Coffadwriaeth, n. remembrance
Coff dwriaethol, com'emorative
Coffâu, v to remember, to record
Coffawr, n. remembrancer
Coffâd, n. remembering
Coffor, n chest, coffer
Coffio, v. to gorge, to quaff
Cog, n. cook; cuckoo; lump
Cogan, n. cup, bowl

Cogeilliaid, n. distaff full
Cogel, n. distaff, truncheon
Cogl, n. club, cudgel
Cogor, n. a chatter, trackling
Cogwrn, n. knob, crab
Còl, n. a peak; a sting; beard of corn; embryo
Colacth, n. a nursing
Coledd, n. cherishing
Coleddiad, n. a cherishing
Coleddwr, n. cherisher
Coleddu, v. to cherish
Colfen, n. a bough, branch
Collog, a. having a sting
Colof, n. a stem, prop
Colofn, n. pillar, column
Colofnaidd, a. having pillars
Colomen, n. pigeon, dove
Colomendy, n. pigeon-house
Coludd, n. the bowels
Coluddyn, n. a gut
Colwydd, n. neck bones
Colwynydd, n. acchoucheur
Colwynyddes, n. midwife
Colyn, n. sting: pivot
Coll, n. loss, damage; hazle-
Colled, n. loss, damage [wood
Collediad, n. a losing
Colledig, a. lost; condemned
Colledigaeth, n. perdition, ruin
Colledu, v. to damage, to injure
Colledus, a. damaging, losing
Collen, n. hazel; sapling
Collfarn, n. condemning sen-
Collfarnu, to condemn [tence
Colli, v. to lose; to be lost
Colliad, n. a losing; spilling
Compawd, n. compass
Conglfaen, n. corner stone
Conglog, a. angular, cornered
Congl, n. corner, angle
Copa, n. a top; tuft; crest
Copog, a. tufted; crested
Copyn, n. spider; a tuft
Côr, n. circle; close; crib; college; choir
Côrach, n. a dwarf, pigmy
Côraidd, a. dwarfish

Corbed, n. corbel; a jutting
Corbedwyn, n. a darling
Corbwll, n. a plash, buddle
Corbwyo, v. to domineer
Corbwyll, n. a slight hint
Corcen, n. a spruce girl
Cord, n. twist, cord
Corden, n. rope, string
Cordedd, n. a twisted state
Cordeddiad, n. a twisting
Cordeddu, v. to twist
Cordd, n. a circle; tribe
Cordderw, n. dwarf oak
Corddi, v. to turn, to churn
Corddiad, n. a churning
Cored, n. a wear or dam
Coredu, v. to form a dam
Coreddu, v. to circulate
Coreddus, a. circling, rotatory
Corelw, n a reel, dance
Coren, n. female dwarf
Corfan, n. metrical foot
Corfinydd, n. architect
Corfran, n. a jackdaw
Corfryn, n. a hillock
Corff or Corph, a body, a corpse
Corffol, a. bodied; corporeal
Corffi, v. to body; to take in the
Corffilyn n. a small thing [body
Corffolaeth, n. a personality, a whole
Corffolaethu, v. to personify
Corfforaeth, n. corporation
Corffori, v. to form into body
Corfforol, a. corporeal, personal
Corgeimwch, n. a prawn
Corgi, n. a curdog
Corhwyad, n. a teal
Corlar, n. a partridge
Còrig, n. a little dwarf
Corlan, n. a sheepfold, a pen
Corlaniad, n. a folding
Corlanu, v. to fold, to pen
Còrlong, n. a small pool
Corlyn, n. a small ship
Corn, n. a horn; a corn; a top; a top of a chimney; roll
Cornaid, n. a horn-ful

Cornant, n. a brook, a rill
Cornbig, n. a sea pike
Cornboer, n. phlegm
Cornchwigl, n. a lapwing
Cornchwiglen, n. a lapwing
Cornel, n. a corner, an angle
Cornelog, a. angular
Cornelu, v. to make a corner
Corni, v. to grow horny
Corniad, n. a horning
Cornicell, n. a reed pipe
Cornig, n. a horn; a whirl
Cornio, v. to horn; to butt
Corniog, a. horned; turreted
Cornwyd, n. a pestilence
Cornwydol, a. pestilential
Coron, n. a crown, a diadem
Coronog, a. having a crown, regal
Coronedigaeth, n. coronation
Coroni, v. to crown
Coroniad, n. a crowning
Coronig, n. a coronet
Cors, n. a bog, a quag; a fen
Corsen, n. a bog plant; a reed
Corseniad, n. a reeding
Corsenog, a. full of reeds
Corsenu, v. to reed, to boll
Corsfrwyn, n, bulrushes
Corshwyad, n. a fen duck
Corslwyn, n. a reed bog
Corsog, a. boggy; fenny
Corswig, n. a gelder rose
Cort, n. a cord, a rope
Cordyn, n. a cord, a string
Corwalch, n. a sparrow-hawk
Corwgl, n. a coracle
Corwynt, n. a whirlwind
Coryn, n. crown of the head
Corynrwy, n. a diadem
Corynu, v. to shave the crown
Corysgwr, n. a radiation
Cos, n. an itching
Cosgordd, n. a retinue
Cosi, v. to assuage itching
Cosiad, n. a scratching
Cosp, n. chastisement
Cospad, n. a chastising
Cospadwy, a. punishable

Cospedig, a. chastised
Cospedigaeth, n. punishment
Cospedigol, a. castigatory
Cospi, v. to chastise, to punish
Cospiad, n. a punishing
Cospol, a. castigatory [isher
Cospwr, n. a chastiser; a pun-
Cost, n. a coast; cost, charge
Costio, v. to expend; to cost
Costiol, a. relating to cost
Costog, a. sluggish; morose
Costogi, v. to grow surly
Costrel, n. a flaggon; a jar
Costrelaid, n. a jar-full
Costrelan, n. a phial; a jar
Costrelig, n. a small jar
Costrelu, v. to put in a jar
Costrelwr, one that puts in a jar
Costus, a. chargeable, dear
Coswr, n. a scratcher
Cosyn, n. a single cheese
Cot, n. a short tail or crop
Coten, n. a little dag or tail
Cotwm, n. a dag-wool; cotton
Cotymog, a. dagged, ermined
Cothi, v. to squirt, to eject
Cothwr, n. an ejector
Cowyllu, v. to envelop
Cowyn, n. the plague
Cowynog, a. full of biles
Crab, n. a crinkle, a shrink
Crach, n. scabs; itch; maneg
Crachen, n. a scab; a crust
Crachenu, v. to form a scab
Crachfeddw, a. half drunk
Crachfeddyg, n. a quack
Crachlyd, a. apt to be scabby
Crachog, a. full of scabs
Craf, n. cloves; claws; garlic
Crafangiad, n. gripe; handful
Crafange, n. a claw, a crab fish
Crafangiad, a clawing, a griping
Crafangio, v. to claw, to gripe
Crafangwr, n. a clawer, a griper
Crafell, n. a scraper
Crafellu, to use a slice; to scrape
Crafen, n. a flake; a crust
Crafiad, n. a scraping

Crafu, v. to scrape, to scratch
Crafwr, n. a scratcher
Craff, n. a clasp; a cramp: a. securing, sure; keen
Craffder, n. keeness; skill
Craffiad, n. a securing
Craffiniad, n. scarification
Craffinio, v. to scarify
Craffu, v. to secure hold; to ken
Craffus, a. penetrating, piercing
Craffwr, n. perceiver
Crag, n. a hard crust
Cragen, n. a shell
Cragenaidd, a. crustaceous
Cragenog, a. having a shell
Crai, n. heat; potency; the heart; the eye of a needle a. vivid: fervid; fresh
Craid, n. vehemency; force
Craidd, n. a centre; the heart
Craig, n. a crag; a rock
Crair, n. a token; a relic
Craith, n. a scar; a cicatrice
Cram, n. an incrustation
Cramen, n. a scab over a sore
Crameniad, n. scabbing
Cramenog, a. covered with scab
Cranenu, v. to scab over
Crammwyth, n. a pancake
Crammwythen, n. a fritter
Crange, n. a crab; a cancer
Crangen, n. a wen
Crangenog, a. full of wens
Crap, n. a grapple, a catch
Crapiad, n. a grappling
Crapio, v. to grapple; to snatch
Crapiog, a. grappling, snatching
Crapiwr, n. a grappler
Crâs what is parched; a toast: a. parched, acrid; saucy
Crasaidd, a. of a parching nature; acrid
Crasair, n. sauciness
Crasboeth, a. acrid, pungent
Crasboethi, v. to parch with heat
Crasboethiad, n. a parching, or a drying with heat
Crasdant, n. a sharp note

Crasder, n. aridity; sauciness
Crasdir, n. parched ground
Crasedig, a. parched; toasted
Craselriog, a. malepert
Crasgalaf, n. the herb flavin
Crasgnoi, v. to scranch [ing
Crasiad, n. a parching; a roast-
Crasiedydd, n. a roaster
Crasol, a. parching, drying
Crasu, v. to parch, to roast
Craswr, n. a parchet; a dryer
Crasyd, n. parched corn
Crawen, n. a crust
Craweniad, n. incrustation
Crawenog, a. crusted, crusty
Crawenol, a. incrustating
Crawenu, v. to become crusty
Crawn, n. a collection; pus
Crawni, v. to collect; to form
Crawnllyd, a. purulent
Crawnol, a. collecting
Crëad, n. a creation
Crëadol, a. creating, plastic
Crëadur, n. a creature
Crëaduriaeth, n. creation
Crëawd, n. formation, creation
Crëawdwr, n. a creator
Crebach, n. what is shrunk: a shrunk, withered
Crebachiad, a. shrinking
Crebachlyd, a. apt to contract, or shrink
Crebachu, v. to shrink
Crebachwr, n. one that shrinks
Crebog, a. shrunk, withered
Crebwyll, n. fancy, invention
Crebwyllo, v. to imagine
Crebwylliad, n. an imagining
Creciad, n. a chirping
Crecian, v. to chirp, to chatter
Creciar, n. the darker hen
Crech, n. a shriek, a scream; a. rough, rugged, curled
Crechiad, n. a shrieking out
Crechian, v. to shriek, to crash
Crechol, a. screaming
Crechwen, n. a shrill laugh
Crechwenu, v. to laugh out

Cred, n. belief; faith; religion
Credad, n. a believing
Credadwy, a. credible
Credadyn, n. a believer
Crededd, n. belief, credibility
Credin, a. believing, credulous
Crediniaeth, n. a belief
Credo, n. a belief, a creed
Credol, a. believing, crediting
Credu, v. to believe, to credit
Credus, a. inducing belief
Credwr, n. a believer
Creddiad, n. temperament
Creddu, v. to dispose
Creedig, a. created, formed
Creadigaeth, n. creation
Cref, a cry, a scream: a. strong, powerful
Crefiad, n. a craving; a suing
Crefiant, n. a craving
Crefol, a. craving, imploring
Crefu, v. to cry, to crave
Crefydd, n. devotion; religion
Crefyddol, a. devout, religious
Crefyddoldeb, n. religiousness
Crefyddu, v. to act religiously
Crefyddwr, n. a religionist
Crefft, n. a handy-craft; a trade
Crefftwr n. a handy-craftsman, a mechanic; a tradesman
Creffyn, n. a brace, a clasper
Creffyniad, n. a bracing
Creffynu, v. to brace, to plate
Creg, a. hoarse, of rough voice
Cregen, n. an earthen vessel
Cregenu, v. to make pottery
Cregenydd, n. a potter
Creglais, n. a hoarse voice
Creglyd, a. apt to hoarse
Cregu, v. to become hoarse
Cregyna, v. to gather shells
Cregynog, a. having shells
Cregynol, a. testaceous
Cregyr, n. a screamer, heron
Creiad, n. a freshening
Creider, n. freshness; purity
Creiddiad, n. pervasion
Creiddiol, a. pervasive

Creiddyn, n. what juts into
Creifion, n. scrapings
Creigiaidd, a. rocky
Creigio, v. to grow rocky
Creiglog, a. rocky, craggy
Creigiogrwydd, n. rockiness
Creigiol, a. apt to be rocky
Creilwg, n. charred furse
Creiniad, n. a wallowing
Creinio, v. to wallow
Creiniol, a. wallowing, rolling
Creiniwr, n. a wallower
Creio, v. to freshen, to brisken
Creirfau, v. to swear by the relics
Creirdŷ, n. a house for relics
Creirfa, n. a reliquary
Creiries, n. a jewel, a beauty
Creisier, n. a calcinatory
Creision, n. calcined matter; dross of anything burnt
Creisioni, v. to calcine
Creithen, n. a cicatrice, a scar
Creithiad, n. cicatrization
Creithio, v. to cicatrize
Creithiog, a. full of scars
Creithiol, a. cicatrisive
Cremog, n. a pancake
Crencyn, n. a small crab
Crepa, n. a crabbed dwarf
Crepian, v. to creep, to hobble
Crepaniog, a. creeping
Crepog, a. shrunk; withered
Cres, n. a hardening by heat
Cresiad, n. inflamation
Crest, n. scum, dregs; scurf
Cresten, n. a crusted surface
Crestenu, v. to gather scurf
Crestiad, n. incrustation
Crestog, a. being crusted over
Crestol, a. apt to incrustate
Crestu, v. to incrustate
Cresu, v. to parch, to scorch
Creth, n. disposition, purpose
Creu, v. to create
Creuan, n. the cranium
Creuled, a. drenched in gore
Creulon, a. bloody, cruel
Creulonacth, n. cruelty

Creuloni, v. to wax cruel
Creulonrwydd, n. cruelty
Creulys, n. groundsel
Creuol, a. gory, bloody
Crew, n. a shout, an outcry
Crëwr, n. a creator, a former
Crewt, n. a faint cry
Crewtian, v. to whine, to pule
Cri, n. a cry, a clamour: a. rough, rude; raw, fresh
Criad, n. a crying, a bawling
Crib, n. a comb; a crest, a top
Cribach, n. a hay-hook
Cribarth, n. a ridged hill
Cribddail, n. extortion; pillage
Cribddeilio, v. to extort
Cribddeiliwr, n. an extortioner
Cribell, n. a cock's comb
Cribiad, n. a combing
Cribin, n. a hay-rake
Cribiniad, n. a raking
Cribinio, v. to rake
Cribiniwr, n. a raker
Cribion, n. combings
Cribo, v. to comb, to card
Cribog, a. indented; crested
Cribwr, n. a comber, a carder
Cricell, n. a cricket
Cricellu, v. to chirp, to chatter
Criciad, n. a cricket
Criciedydd, n. a creaker
Crif, n. a row of notches
Crifellu, v. to notch, to grave
Crifiad, n. a notching
Crig, n. a crick
Criglyn, n. a faint trace
Crigyll, n. ravine; creek
Crimmell, n. a sharp ridge
Crimmog, n. a shin, a greave
Crimmogiad, n. a shinning; a kick on the shin
Crimmogio, v. to shin
Crimp, n. a sharp ridge
Crimpiad, n. a crimping
Crimpio, v. to crimp
Crin, a. brittle, fragile; niggard
Crinad, n. a growing brittle
Crinder, n. brittleness

Crinell, n. what is clung
Crinelliad, n. crepitation
Crinellu, v. to cling; to cracle
Crinlys, n. the violet
Crino, v. to wax brittle, to clung
Crintach, a. niggardly
Crintachrwydd, n. niggardliness
Crintachu, v. to grow niggardly
Crintachwr, n. a niggard
Crinwydd, n. dry brushwood
Crio, v. to cry, to clamour
Crip, n. a scratch; a notch
Cripiad, n. a scratching
Cripio, v. to scratch, to claw
Cripiog, a. having scratches
Cripiol, a. scratching, clawing
Cripiwr, n. a scratcher
Cris, n. a scale, a hard crust
Crisb, n. a crisp coating
Crisbin, a. crumbling, crisp
Crisbinio, v. to crisp, to dry
Crisial, n. crystal
Crisialad, n. crystalization
Crisialaidd, a. crystaline
Crisialu, v. to crystalize
CRIST, n. Christ, Messiah
Cristion, n. a christian
Cristionogaeth, n. christianity
Cristionogaidd, a. christianly
Cristionogol, a, christianly
Croca, a. crooked, tortuous
Croch, a. rough, forcible; eager
Crochan, n. a boiler, a pot
Crochanaid, n. a pot-full
Crochenu, v. to make pottery
Crochenydd, n. a potter
Crochenyddiaeth, n. pottery
Crochenyn, n. a little pot
Crochlais, n. a rough voice
Crochlef, n. a shrill shout
Crochlefain, n. a scream
Crochlefwr, n. a great shouter
Crochleisio, v. to vociferate
Croen, n. a skin, a hide
Croendew, n. thick-skinned
Croenog, a. having skin
Croenol, a. cutaneous
Croenen, n. a cuticle

Croengyrchu, v. to wrinkle a skin
Croeni, v. to skin, to skin over
Croeniad, n. a skinning
Croes, n. a cross; a crucifix: a. cross, transverse
Croesaw, n. a welcome
Croesawgar, a. hospitable
Croesawiad, n. a welcoming
Croesawl, a. transversial
Croesawu, v. to welcome
Croesawus, a. hospitable
Coesdroi, v. to contort
Croesdynu, v. to contend
Croesen, n. a coquette; a jilt
Croesffon, n, a cross staff
Croesffordd, n. a cross road
Croesgynghanedd, n. alliterative consonancy
Croeshoeliad, n. crucifixion
Croeshoelio, v. to crucify
Croesi, v. to cross, to put across
Croesiad, n. a crossing
Croesineb, n. crossness
Croeslath, n. a purlin
Crog, n. a cross, a crucifix; a. hanging, over-hanging
Crogadwy, a. that may be hung
Crogbren, n. a gallows
Crogedyf, n. a dropwort
Crogell, n. a place to hang meat
Crogen; n. a gill; a jaw
Crogi, v. to hang, to suspend
Crogiad, n. a hanging
Croglath, n a springe
Croglen, n. a hanging; a curtain
Croglith, n. the mass of the cross
Crogwr, n. a hangman
Crom. a. bending, boughed
Cromen, n. a dome, a cupola
Cromglwyd, n. a thatch hurdle
Crombill, n. the craw, crop or gorge of a bird
Cromllaid, n. a crop full
Cromlech, n. an incumbent flag, a stone of covenant
Cron, a. round, circular
Cronbleth, n. a bobbin
Cronell, n. a globule; a globe

Cronellog, a. globular
Cronellu, v. to glomerate
Cronen, n. a globe, a sphere
Cronfa, n. a receptacle; a dam
Cronglwyd, n. a roof hurdle
Croni, v. to board, to dam
Croniad, n. a damming
Cropa, n. a crop, or a craw
Cropiad, n. a creeping
Cropian, v. to creep, to crawl
Cropiedydd, n. a creeper
Crotawg, a. plump, round
Croten, n. a little plump girl
Croth, n. a bulge; a womb
Crothawg gibbous; big-bellied
Crothell, n. a bulge; a bansticle
Crothi, v. to bulge, to swell
Croyw, a. clear; brisk; fresh
Croywder, n. freshness
Croywi, v. to freshen; to brisk
Cru, n. a hollow rotundity
Crub, n. a swelling out
Crud, n. a cover, a case
Crug, n. a heap, a tump
Crugo, v. to heap, to swell
Crugog, a. having heaps
Crugdardd, n. a pustule
Crugdarddu, v. to imposthumate
Crugiad, n. a heaping up
Crugyll, n. a place of tumps
Crugyn, n. a small heap
Crygynu, v. to pile, to heap
Crygynog, a. full of tumps
Crwb, n. a round hunch
Crwbach, n. a hook, a crook
Crwban, n. a tortoise
Crwc, n. a bucket a pail
Crwca, a. crooked, bowed, bent
Crwcau, v. to bow, to curve
Crwcwd, n. a round squat
Crwm, a. bending, concave
Crwmach, n. convexity
Crwn, a. round, circular
Crwt, n. a crust; a dumpy one
Crwtyn, n. a little dumpy one
Crwth, n. a bulge, a trunk; a belly; a violin
Crwybr, n. a scum; honeycomb

Crwydr, n. a wandering
Crwydrai, n. a wanderer
Crwydrol, a. wandering
Crwydredigaeth, a. vagrancy
Crwydriad, n. a vagabond
Crwynllys, n. the gentian
Crwynwr, n. the skinner
Crybwyll, n. a hint; an idea
Crybwylliad, n. a hinting
Crybwyllo, v. to intimate
Crybychawl, a. crinkling
Crybychiad, n. a crinkling
Crybychu, v. to crinkle
Crycydu, v. to squat down
Crŷch, n. a wrinkle; a ripple a. wrinkled; rippling
Crychedd, n. roughness
Crychiad, n. a wrinkling, crepature; a shake in music
Crychiant, n. curliness
Crychias, n. a rough boiling
Crychlais, n. a broken voice
Crychlam, n. a caper
Crychlamiad, n. a capering
Crychnaid, n. a skip, a frisk
Crychneidio, v. to skip
Crychni, n. curliness
Crychrawn, a. frizzly, haired
Crychu, v. to ruffle; to ripple
Crychydd, n. a ruffler; a heron;
Cryd, n. a quake; a fever [a crane
Crydiad, n. a shivering
Crydian, v. to keep shivering
Crydio, v. to shiver, to quake
Crydiol, a. shivering, quaking
Crydu, v. to tremble, to shudder
Crydus, a. shivering, trembling
Crydwst, n. a shivering fit
Crydd, n. a shoemaker
Cryddiaeth, n. shoemaking
Cryddu, v. to stretch round
Cryf, a. compact; strong, mighty
Cryfder, n. strength, might
Cryfhâd, n. a strengthening
Cryfhau, v. to strengthen
Cryfhaus, a. strengthening
Cryg, n. hoarseness: a. rough, harsh, hoarse

Crygeldwen, n. the galaxy
Crygen, n. a fit of hoarseness
Crygi, n. hoarseness
Crygiad, n. a making hoarse
Cryglus, n. cramberries
Cryglyd, a. apt to be hoarse
Crygni, n. hoarseness
Crygyn, n. a fit of hoarseness
Crymain, a. flexuous, flexile
Crymaint, n. a flexion
Crymai, n. a puttock
Cryman, n. a reaping hook
Crymaniad, n. falcation
Crymanu, v. to use a sickle
Crymder, n. a bend, a curve
Crymanwr, n. reaper
Crymdwyn, n. a tumulous
Crymedd, n. deflexure
Crymfach, n. a crochet
Crymol, a. bowing, curving
Crymu, v. to bow; to curve
Cryn, n. a shake, a quake: a. shaking, quaking; middling
Crynâad, n. a rounding
Crynach, n. a shiver, a shudder
Crynachol, a. shuddering
Crynachu, v. to shudder
Crynâu, v. to conglomerate
Crynder, n. rotundity
Crynedigaeth, n. tremulation
Crynfa, n. a shivering fit
Crynfaen, n. a pebble
Cryniad, n. a trembling
Cryniog, n. a ten bushel measure
Cryno, a. compact, trim, tidy
Crynöad, n. a summary; a making tidy
Crynöawl, a. gathering together
Crynodeb, n. compactness
Crynoi, v. to collect together
Crynol, a. shaking, trembling
Crynswth, n. a mass, a whole
Crynsypio, v. to conglomerate
Crynu, v. to tremble, to quake
Crynwr, n. a trembler, a quaker
Crynwraidd, n. bulbous roots
Crynyn, n. a globule
Crys, n. haste, velocity; a shirt,

Crysbais, n. a waistcoat [ation
Crysfad, n. a bishop's confirm-
Cryslain, a. a shirt bosom
Crytiad, n. a plumping
Crythog, a. gibbous; bulky
Crythor, n. a fiddler
Crythu, v. to swell out
Crythyn, n. a small pox; a kit or small fiddle
Cryw, n. a slice, a slicer
Cu, n. approximation; a. amiable, beloved
Cuch, n. a knit of the brow
Cuchiad, n. a frowning
Cochio, v. to knit the brow
Cuchiog, a. frowning; angry
Cuchiol, a. frowning
Cud, n. celerity; flight
Cudeb, n. affection, amity
Cudyll, n. a kestril; a falcon
Cudyn, n. a lock, as of hair
Cudynog, a. having flowing locks
Cudd, n. a gloom; a hide
Cuddan, n. a wood pigeon
Cuddfa, n. a hiding place
Cuddiad, n. a concealing
Cuddiedig, a. hidden, concealed
Cuddiedigaeth, n. concealment
Cuddio, v. to hide, to conceal
Cuddiol, a. hiding, concealing
Cuedd, n. affectionate, loving
Cueddu, v. to render loving
Cufydd, n. half a yard; a cubit
Cul, n. narrowness; the lean: a. narrow, strait; lean
Culhâu, v. to narrow
Culder, n. narrowness
Culiad, n. a narrowing
Culni, n. narrowness; leaness
Cun, n. a leader, a chief: a. attractive; lovely
Cunell, n. a phalanx
Cuniad, n. a leader, a chief
Cunnellt, n. weapons of war
Cunnog, n. a milk pail
Cunnogaid, n. a pail-full
Cunogi, v. to put in a pail
Cunnogyn, n. a piggin

Cuol, a. loving, affectionate
Cûr, n. a beat, a throb; care
Curedig, a. beaten, knocked
Curfa, n. a beating; a throb
Curiad, n. a pining, a vexing
Curio, v. to pine, to vex
Curiol, a. pining, vexing
Curioldeb, n. piningness
Curo, v. to beat, to throb
Curwlaw, n. a heavy rain
Curyll, n. a sparrow hawk
Cus, n. a kiss; a salute
Cusaniad, n. a kissing
Cusanu, v. to kiss; to salute
Cusanwr, n. a kisser
Cut, v. a hovel, shed, or stye
Cuwch, n. knit of the brow
Cuwr, n. a wooer, a lover
Cw, n. concavity; lettuce; ad. wherefrom, whence
Cwb, n. a concavity; a cote
Cwbl, n. a whole, a total
Cwblhâd, n. fulfilling
Cwblhâu, v. to fulfill, to finish
Cwbledd, n. entireness
Cwblhawr, n. finisher
Cwcwll, n. a hood, a cowl
Cwch, n. a boat, a hive
Cwd, n. an injection or throw: n. a bag or pouch
Cweryl, n. strife, quarrel
Cweryliad, n. a quarelling
Cwerylu, v. to quarrel
Cwestiwn, n. a question
Cwfl, n. a hood, a cowl
Cwg, n. a rise; a jet; a knob
Cwgyn, n. a bnot; a knuckle
Cwhwfan, n. a waving; a. waving; panting
Cwhwfanu, v. to wave: to pant
Cwl, n. a flagging; a fault; a box for raising couls
Cwla, a. faulting; languid
Cwlas, n. an apartment
Cwlbren, n. a bludgeon
Cwliaw, v. to make faulty
Cwlwm, n. a knot, a tie
Cwlltr, n. a coulter

Cwm, n. a hollow, a dingle
Cwman, n. a kive; a rump
Cwmarch, n. a deep dingle
Cwmwd, n. a wapentake
Cwmpas, n. a compass
Cwmpasol, a. compassing
Cwmpasu, v. to compass
Cwmwl, n. a cloud
Cwn, n. a top, a summit
Cŵn, n. dogs
Cwnawl, a. rising, elevating
Cwningen, n. a rabbit
Cwnu, v. to arise; to support
Cwpan, n. a cup, a bowl
Cwpanaid, n. a cup-full
Cwpl, n. a coupling, a couple
Cwr, n. a limit; a corner; a circle, a skin [ting
Crwcwd, n. a stooping; a squat-
Cwrn, n. a spire; a pile
Cwrnaid, n. a curveting
Cwrt, n. a mound; a court
Cwrw, n. ale, strong beer
Cwrwgl, n. a coracle; a boat
Cwsg, n. sleep
Cwsgbar, a. causing sleep
Cwt, n. a roundness; a cot; a stye; a rump, a skirt
Cwta, a. short; abrupt
Cwtâu, v. to shorten, to curtail
Cwtiad, n. a plover; a coot
Cwtiar, n. a coot, a water rail
Cwtog, a. bob-tailed, squabby; n. a squab, a scut
Cwtoges, n. a short squab
Cwtogi, v. to shorten, to curtail
Cwtogiad, n. a curtailing
Cwtws, n. a lot; a scut
Cwtyn, n. a bob-tail; a plover
Cwtysyn, n. a lot, a ticket
Cwthr, n. the rectum
Cwyd, n. a stir, an agitation
Cwymp, n. a fall, a tumble
Cwympiad, n. a falling
Cwympo, v. to fall; to cast down
Cwympol, a. falling; declining
Cwympwr, n. one that falls
Cwyn, n. plaint, complaint

Cwynfan, n. lamentation; v. to complain
Cwynfanus, a. complaining
Cwyniad, n. a complaining
Cwyno, v. to complain
Cwynofain, v. to bewail
Cwynofaint, n. a wailing
Cwynol, a. complaining
Cwynos, n. a supper
Cwynosa, v. to eat supper
Cwynwr, n. a complainer
Cwŷr, n. wax, gum
Cwyreli, n. cerat; salve
Cwyren, n. a cake of wax
Cwyriad, n. a waxing
Cwyro, v. to cover with wax
Cwyros, a. of waxy quality
Cwyrol, n. a cornel tree
Cwys, n. a furrow
Cwysed, n. a gore, a gusset
Cwysiad, n. a furrowing
Cwysig, n. a small furrow
Cwyso, v. to furrow
Cwysol, a. furrowing
Cy, a. prefix used to denote a mutual act or effect
Cybol, a. holding, grasping
Cyboli, v. to blend, to mix
Cyboliad, n. a blending
Cybolwr, n. a mingler
Cybydd, n. a miser, a niggard
Cybyddol, a. coveting, greedy
Cybydd-dod, n. avarice
Cybyddes, n. a female miser
Cybyddiad, n. a coveting
Cybyddiaeth, n. covetousness
Cybyddu, v. to act miserly
Cycyllog, a. hooded, cowled
Cycyllu, v. to wear a hood
Cychaid, n. a boat-full a hive-full
Cychawl, a. boat-like; hive-like
Cychedd, n. a concavity
Cychiad, n. a covering; a hiving
Cychu, v. to cover; to hive
Cydfradu, v. to conspire
Cydfradwr, n. a conspirator
Cydfradwriaeth, n. a conspiracy

Cydfwriad, n. combination
Cydfwyta, v. to eat together
Cychwyfan, v. to hover; to rock
Cychwyn, n. stir, a move
Cychwyniad, n. a commencement; a setting off
Cyd, n. a junction; a coupling, used as a prefix to denote a mutual act
Cyd, a. joint, united, common : ad. whilst, as long as: conj. forasmuch, since
Cydaddoli, v. to worship together
Cydaid, n. a bag-full
Cydair, a. unanimous
Cydan, n. a small bag
Cydbechu, v. to sin together
Cydbell, a, equidstant
Cydblaid, n. a confederate
Cydbwys, a. of equal weight
Cydbwyso, v. to equipoise
Cyd-ddwyn, v. to concur
Cyd-dynu, v. to concur [gether
Cyd-ddyoddef, v. to endure together
Cyd-ddyrchafu, to exalt together
Cydeffeithiad, n. connutrition
Cydenw, n. namesake
Cydenwad, n. agnomination
Cydestyniad, n. co-extention
Cydetifedd, n. a co-heir
Cydetifeddu, v. to inherit jointly
Cydetifeddwr, n. a joint inheritor
Cydfa, n. a convention
Cydfaethiad, n. connutrition
Cydfantoli, v. to equilibrate
Cydfloedd, n. conclamation
Cydfod, n. co-existence; concord, or agreement
Cydfodd, n. concord, agreement
Cydfrad, n. conspiracy, plot
Cydfynediad, n. con-comitancy
Cydffrydiad, n. a confluence
Cydffurfiad, n. a conformation
Cydffurfio, v. to conform
Cydgais, n. a competition
Cydgam, n. dalliance; delay
Cydganu, v. to sing in concert
Cydgar, n. a correlative

Cydgarenydd, n. consanguinity
Cydgerdd, n. a symphony
Cydgerddediad, n. concomitancy
Cydglymiad, n. alligation
Cydgnawd, n. carnal copulation
Cydgor, n. united choir
Cydgorffoli, v. to concorporate
Cydgorffori, v. to consubstantiate
Cydgwyniad, n. condolence
Cydgyfaneddu, v. to occupy together
Cydgyfaneddwr, a joint occupier
Cydgyfarch, v. to congratulate
Cydgyfarfod, n. coincidency
Cydgyfartaledd, n. co-equalty
Cydgyfathrach, n. con-sociation
Cydgyfranogi, v. to intercommunicate
Cydgylchiad, n. convolution
Cydgyrchu, v. to assemble together
Cydgyrhaeddiad, co-existension
Cydhanfod, n. co-existence
Cydiad, n. a joining; a coupling; a biting; a laying hold
Cydiaith, a. of one language
Cydiaw, v. to join; to couple; to bite, to take hold
Cydieuad, n. conjugation
Cydieuo, v. to yoke together
Cydlais, n. consonance
Cydlawenhau, v. to congratulate
Cydlef, n. a joint shout
Cydlefaru, v. to speak together
Cydles, n. mutual advantage
Cydlif, n. a conflux
Cydlyniad, n. a cohesion
Cydnabod, n. aquaintance recognition
Cydnabyddiaeth, n. aquaintance
Cydnabyddus, a. aquainted together; expert
Cydnad, n. conclamation
Cydnaid, n. a joint leap
Cydnaws, a. connatural
Cydnerth, n. equipollence
Cydnesu, to approach mutually
Cydnewid, v. to interchange

Cydoddef, n. sympathy
Cydoed, n. a contemporary
Cydoes, a. coeval, coevous
Cydoesi, v. to contemporise
Cydofal, n. a mutual care
Cydol, a. complete, whole
Cydolrwydd, n. continuity
Cydradd, a. of equal degree
Cydraid, n. mutual want
Cydraith, n. mutual rule
Cydran, n. a joint share
Cydranu, v. to share mutually
Cydranwr, n. a joint sharer
Cydrawd, n. concurrence
Cydred, a. concurrent
Cydroddi, v. to give mutually
Cydrwymo, v. to bind together
Cydryddid, n. mutual liberty
Cydryw, n. hermaphrodite: a homogeneous
Cydrywineth, n. homogeneity
Cydsain, n. a consonant
Cydseinio, v. to agree in sound
Cydsiarad, n. confabulation
Cydsisial, v. to whisper together
Cydsoriant, n. mutual offence
Cydsylweddiad, consubstantiat-
Cydsylltiad, n conjunction [ion
Cydsyniad, n. unanimity
Cydsynio, v. to consent
Cydu, v. to bag, to pouch
Cydundeb, n. unity, union
Cyduniad, n. a consenting
Cydwaed, a. to the same blood
Cydwaeddiad, n. conclamation
Cydwas, n. a fellow servant
Cydwe, n. a contexture
Cydwedd, n. a yoke fellow
Cydweddu, v. to accord
Cydweinidog, n. a fellow servant
Cydweitho, v. to co-operate
Cydweithiwr, n. a fellow labourer
Cydweithredu, v. to co-operate
Cydwelydd, n. a consociate
Cydwerth, n. an equivalent
Cydweu, v. to interweave
Cydwybod, n. conscience
Cydwybodol, a. conscientious
Cydwybodolrwydd, n. conscientiousness
Cydwyneblad, n. confrontation
Cydwysiad, n. convocation
Cydyfed, v. to drink together
Cydymattal, to abstain mutually
Cydymaith, n. a companion; v. to accompany [pathy
Cydymdeimlad, n. mutual sym-
Cydymdeithas, n. company
Cydymdeithasu, v. mutually to asscociate [tually
Cydymdrafodi, v. to strive mu-
Cydymddiried, n. mutual trust
Cydymddwyn, to bear mutually
Cydymgais, n. competition
Cydymgilio, to recede mutually
Cydymgyrch, n. concurrence
Cydymholi, v. enquire mutually
Cydymlid, n. mutual pursuit
Cydymliw, n. mutual reproach
Cydymaith, n. companion
Cydymeithasu, v. to consociate
Cydymoddef, v. to bear mutually
Cydymranu, v. to secede together
Cydymrodd, v. to yield mutually
Cydymroi, v. to resign mutually
Cydymryson, n. mutual strife
Cydymuniad, n. mutual union
Cydymweddu, v. to conform mu-
Cydyn, n. a little bag [tually
Cydyru, v. to drive together
Cyf, a. prefix of general use, denoting a mutual act or effect
Cyfab, a. with foal
Cyfaddas, a. convenient, meet
Cyfaddasu, v. to render meet
Cyfaddef, v. to confess
Cyfaddefiad, n. confession
Cyfagos, a. near, contiguous
Cyfagu, v. to nurse together
Cyfagwedd, n. conformity
Cyfagweddu, v. to conform
Cyfaill, n. a friend
Cyfammod, n. covenant
Cyfammodi, v. to covenant
Cyfamser, n. mean time

Cyfamseru, to make opportune
Cyfan, a. entire, whole, total
Cyfanol, a. entire, integral
Cyfander, n. entireness
Cyfandroed,a. web-footed
Cyfanedd, n. integrality
Cyfaniad, n. a making whole
Cyfannedd, n. inhabited place: adj. inhabited; domestic
Cyfanneddiad, n. inhabitation
Cyfanneddle, n. habitation
Cyfanneddol, a. habitable
Cyfaneddu, v. to inhabit
Cyfaneddwr, n. inhabitant
Cyfanrif, n. total number
Cyfanrwydd, n. entireness
Cyfansawdd, a composite
Cyfansoddi, v. to compose; to arrange the letters
Cyfansoddiad, n. composition
Cyfansoddol, a. compositive
Cyfansoddwr, n. composer
Cyfanu, v. to make whole
Cyfanwerth, n. wholesale
Cyfar, n. a front, facing; joint ploughing; acre
Cyfarch, n. address, greeting: v. to greet, to salute
Cyfarchedigol, v. congratulatory
Cafarchiad, n. a greeting
Cyfarchol, a. complimentary
Cyfarchwel, n. reproach
Cyfarchwr, n. congratulator
Cyfarchwyl, n. a survey
Cyfaredd, n. a charm
Cyfareddu, v. to cure by charm
Cyfarfod, an assembly, a meet-
Cyfartal, a. proportional [ing
Cyfartalai, n. a standard
Cyfartaledd, n. poportionate-
Cyfartaliad, n. an equation [ness
Cyfartalu, v. to proportonate
Cyfarth, n. a barking, a yelp: v. to bark, to yelp
Cyfarthiad, n. a barking
Cyfarthfa, n. a baiting with dogs n. junction of hills
Cyfarthiad, n. a barking

Cyfaru, v. to plough together
Cyfarwydd, n. a wizard: a. guiding; skilful
Cyfarwyddiad, n. direction
Cyfarwyddo, v. to direct
Cyfarwyddol, v. directing
Cyfarwyddwr, n. director
Cyfarwyddyd, n. experience
Cyfarwynebu, v. to comfort
Cyfatteb, v. to correspond
Cyfattebiad, n. a corresponding
Cyfattebiaeth, n. correspondence
Cyfattebol, a. corresponding
Cyfategu, v. to uphold jointly
Cyfathrach, n. affinity, kind
Cyfathrachu, v. to join alliance, to join in matrimony
Cyfhâu, v. make whole
Cyfddydd, n. the day-spring
Cyfebol, a. big with foal
Cyfebr, v. going with foal
Cyfebriad, n. gestation
Cyfebru, v. to gestate
Cyfebrwydd, n. foal in embryo
Cyfechni, n. joint security
Cyfechwyn, n. joint loan
Cyfedliw, n. mutual reproach
Cyfeddach, n. a banquet, a festivity
Cyfeiliorn, n. deviation
Cyfeiliornad, n. a deviating
Cyfeiliorni, v. to deviate
Cyfeiliornus, a. devious, erring
Cyfeiliornwr, n. a wanderer
Cyfeilw, a. of the same colour
Cyfeillgar, a. friendly, sociable
Cyfeillgarwch, n. sociableness
Cyfeilachu, v. to associate
Cyfeillach, n. friendship
Cyfeilio, v. to associate
Cyfeiriad, n. direction
Cyfeirio, v. to direct; to guide, to make towards
Cyfeiriol, a. directing, leading
Cyfeirnod, n. note of reference
Cyfeiryd, v. to direct, to lead
Cyfeisiau, n. a mutual want
Cyfeisteddiad, a jointly sitting
Cyfeithrin, v. to nurse together

Cyfelin, n. a cubit, a measure of 18 inches
Cyfelinaid, n. a cubit length
Cyfenw, n. a surname
Cyfenwi, v. to give a surname
Cyfer, n. opposite situation
Cyferbyn, a. opposite, fronting
Cyferbyniad, n. contraposition
Cyferbynied, v. to counteract
Cyferbynu, v. to set in opposition, to contrast; to counteract
Cyferbynwr, n, contraster
Cyfergyd, n. a concussion
Cyferlyn, v. to pursue together
Cyferthiad, n. sanctification
Cyferwenu, v. to flatter
Cyferyd, n. opposite place
Cyfhogi, v. to sharpen together
Cyfiach, n. etymology
Cyfiachydd, n. etymologist
Cyfiachyddol, a. etymological
Cyfiaith, n. vernacular speech: a. of the same language
Cyfiaw, v. to make equable
Cyfiawn, a. just, righteous
Cyfiawnder, n. justice, equity
Cyfiawnedd, n. justness
Cyfiawnhâd, n. justification
Cyfiawnhâu, v. to justify
Cyfiawniad, n. a rectifying
Cyfieithiad, n. translation
Cyfieithu, v. to translate
Cyfieithydd, n. a translator
Cyfieuo, v. to conjugate
Cyfing, a. distressed; restricted
Cyfladd, v. to coincide, to match
Cyflaeth, n. a confection a mixture
Cyflafan, n. a massacre
Cyflafanu, v. to murder
Cyflafar, a. mutually speaking
Cyflafaredd, n. a parley
Cyflafaru, v. to parley, to confer
Cyflaid, n. the arms full
Cyflam, a. regular
Cyflanw, n. a complement
Cyflawn, a. complete, full
Cyflawnder, n. completeness [fil
Cyflawni, v. to complete, to ful-

Cyfle, n. opportunity, place
Cyfleâad, n. collocation
Cyfleâu, v. to collocate
Cyfled, a. of equal breadth
Cyfledu, v. to co-extend
Cyflef, a. of united voice
Cyflegr, n. a gun, a cannon
Cyflegriad, n. a firing, ; a gun
Cyflegru, v. to fire a gun
Cyflenwad, n. a repletion
Cyflenwi, v. to fulfil, to replenish
Cyfles, n. mutual benifit
Cyfleu, v. to collocate; to deposit
Cyfleus, a. convenient, suitable
Cyfleusdra, n. convenience
Cyflewyrch, n. equable light
Cyflino, v. to contort
Cyfliwio, v. to tint alike
Cyflo, a. big with calf
Cyfloca, v. to take hire
Cyflochi v. to harbour equally
Coflog, n. salary, wages
Cyflogedig, a. that is hired
Cyflogi, v. to hire, to bind
Cyflogiad, n. a hiring
Cyflogwas, n. hired servant
Cyflun, a. of the same form
Cyflunedd, n. equiformity
Cyfluniad, n. conformation
Cyfluniaeth, n. ratio of food
Cyflunio, v. to configure; to model, to organize, to construct
Cyflwngc, n. an abstinence
Cyflwng, a. swallowing up
Cyflwr, n. condition, state, disposition, temper; property
Cyflwyniad, n, presentation
Cyflwyno, v. to send; to address to dedicate; to present
Cyflym, a. nimble, keen
Cyflymder, n. quickness
Cyflymiad, n. acceleration
Cyflymu, v to accelerate
Cyflyn, a. mutually adhering
Cyflyniad, n. cohesion
Cyflys, a. courtly, courtlike
Cyfnai, n. a third cousin
Cyfnaid, a. of mutual leap

Cyfnaith, n. pledge
Cyfnaws, n. a common nature; of the same quality
Cyfneithio, v. to betrothe
Cyfnerth, n. support, firmness
Cyfnerthedigion, n. restoratives
Cyfnerthedd, n. compactness
Cyfnerthi, n. steadiness
Cyfnerthiad, n. confirmation
Cyfnerthu, v. to strengthen
Cyfnesaf, next, nearest in place
Cyfnesafedd, n. contiguity
Cyfnesafiad, n. a next of kin
Cyfnesâu, v. to approximate
Cyfnesiad, n. approximation
Cyfnesu, v. to approximate
Cyfnewid, n. commerce, barter
Cyfnewid, v. to exchange
Cyfnewidiad, n. alteration
Cyfnewidiaeth, n. exchange
Cyfnewidio, v. to commutate
Cyfnewidiog, a. alternate
Cyfnewidiol, a. changeable [ity
Cyfnewidioldeb, n. commutabil-
Cyfnewidiwr, n. a chapman
Cyfnifer, n. an even number
Cyfnither, n. a female cousin
Cyfnod, n. season
Cyfnodol, a. periodical
Cyfnodiad, n. connotation
Cyfnodiedydd, n. commentator
Cyfnos, n. evening twilight
Cyfnosi, v. to become night
Cyfnyddu, v. to twine together
Cyfochr, a. parallel
Cyfochredd, n. a paralellism
Cyfochrog, a. collateral [up
Cyfod, n. a tarrying: v. arise, get
Cyfodi, v. to rise, to get up
Cyfodiad, n. a rising up
Cyfoed, a. coetaneous, coeval
Cyfoedydd, n. a contemporary
Cyfoen, a. big with lamb
Cyfoes, a. coetaneous, coeval
Cyfoesi, v. to contemporise
Cyfoeth, n. opulence, wealth
Cyfoethog, a. opulent, rich [rich
Cyfoethogi, v. to enrich, to grow

Cyfog, n. a vomit, an emetic
Cyfogi, v. to vomit, to cast up
Cyfogiad, n. a vomiting
Cyfoglyn, n. an emetic
Cyfogwydd, n. convergency
Cyfoli, v. to praise together
Cyfoll, a. integral; complete
Cyfongl, n. a right angle: a. of even angles
Cyfor, n. a confine, a border: a. even with the edge
Cyforio, v. to fill up
Cyfosod, v. to place together
Cyfosodiad, n. a synthesis
Cyfrad, a conspiracy [possession
Cyfraid, n. competency, needful
Cyfraith, n. mutual right; law, judicial process
Cyfran, n. portion, share, rate
Cyfranai, n. a participle
Cyfrandal, n. an instalment
Cyfranedigol, a. contributive
Cyfraniad, n. contribution
Cyfranog, a. participant
Cyfranogi, v. to participate
Cyfranol, a. participating
Cyfranu, v. to contribute; to impart; to partake
Cyfrangu, v. to come in contact, to meet together
Cyfrben, a. complete, perfect
Cyfrdal, n. equivalence, value
Cyfreidiol, a. necessary
Cyfreithgar, a. litigious; quarrelsome
Cyfreithiad, n. litigation
Cyfreithio, v. to litigate; to go to law
Cyfreithiol, a. legal, lawful
Cyfreithiwr, n. a lawyer, attorney; a litigant
Cyfreithlon, a. lawful
Cyfreithlondeb, n. legality
Cyfreithloni, v. to legalize
Cyfrenin, a. mutually sharing
Cyfres, n. a contecture
Cyfrestru, v. to interweave
Cyfrgoll, n. perdition, loss

| CYF | 80 | CYF |

Cyfrgolli, v. to lose utterly
Cyfrgolledig, a. being lost
Cyfrif, n. account, reckoning: v. to count, to reckon
Cyfrifadwy, a. accountable
Cyfrifedig, a. being reckoned or esteemed
Cyfrifiad, n. a counting
Cyfrifol, a. accounted; reputed
Cyfrin, a. privy; conscious
Cyfrinach, n. a secret
Cyfrinachu, v. to talk secrets
Cyfriniad, n. a making mystic
Cyfriniaeth, n. a mystery
Cyfrinio, v. to mysterize
Cyfriniol, a. mysterious
Cyfrodedd, n. concurrent state: a. combined, twisted together
Cyfrodeddiad, n. a twining
Cyfrodeddu, v. to twine together
Cyfrodol, a. concurrent
Cyfroddiad, n. contribution
Cyfrugliad, n. confrication
Cyfrwch, n. a conjunction
Cyfrwng, n. an interval: prep. [between
Cyfrwy, n. a saddle
Cyfrwydd, a. expeditious
Cyfrwymiad, n. construction
Cyfrwymo, v. to bind together
Cyfrwymyn, n. a bracer
Cyfrwyo, v. to saddle
Cyfrwys, a. cunning, subtle
Crfrwysdra, n. craftiness
Cyfryngol, a. intermediate
Cyfryngdod, n. mediation
Cyfryngiad, n. a mediating
Cyfryngu, v. to intercede
Cyfryngwr, n. a mediator, an intercessor, an umpire
Cyfryw, a. homogeneous; like
Cyfuno, v. to accord, to unite
Cyfundeb, n. concord
Cyfuniad, n. an according
Cyfuwch, a. of equal height
Cyfwasgu, v. to compress
Cyfweddu, v. to resemble
Cyfwng, n. an intervention
Cyfyl, n. contiguity: a. nigh

Cyfyng, a. narrow, strait, close
Cyfyngder, n. narrowness, strait-
Cyfyngiad, n. a narrowing [ness
Cyfyngu, v. to narrow, to close
Cyfyrder, n. second cousin
Cyfystyr, a. synonymous
Cyff, n. a stock, a stump, a stem, a block
Cyffaith, n. confection
Cyffawd, n. mutual pleasure
Cyffeithiad, n. a confecting
Cyffeithio, v. to confect
Cyffelyb, n. likeness: a. like
Cyffelybiad, n. comparison
Cyffelybiaeth, n. similitude
Cyffelybiaethu, v. to make a simile
Cyffelybu, v. to compare
Cyfferi, n. confects, nostrums
Cyfferiaeth, n. pharmacopœa
Cyffes, n. a confession
Cyffesiad, n. a confessing
Cyffesu, v. to confess, to own
Cyffiad, n. a becoming stiff
Cyffiaw, v. to benumb
Cyffin, n. a confine, a limit
Cyffinid, n. an abutment
Cyffiniden, n. a spider
Cyffinio, v. to bind
Cyffoden, n. a concubine
Cyffodiad, a. jointly prospering
Cyffrawd, n. an impulse
Cyffre, n, pervasion, mixture
Cyffred, n. comprehension; a whole: v. to comprehend: a. universal; whole
Cyffrediad, n. comprehension
Cyffredin, a. common; univers- al; impartial
Cyffrediniaeth, n. generality
Cyffredinol, a. universal
Cyffredinoli, v. to generalize
Cyffreuad, n. communication
Cyffro, n. concussion; agitat- ion; motion, stir
Cyffröad, n. a concussing; a moving or agitating
Cyffröawl, a. impulsive, moving

Cyffroedigaeth, n. agitation	Cylchyniad, n. a surrounding
Cyffröi, v. to concuss, to move	Cylchynu, v. to encircle
Cyffwrdd, v. to meet, to touch	Cylion, n. flies; gnats; wasps
Cyffyrddiad, n. contact, touch	Cylionen, n. a fly; a wasp
Cyffylog, n. a woodcock	Cylmu, Cylymu, v. to tie
Cyffyr, n. substance, matter	Cylor, n. earth-nuts
Cyhoedd, a. public; notorious	Cylla, n. a maw, stomach
Cyhoeddi, v. to publish	Cyllaeth, n. sorrow, grief
Cyhoeddiad, n. publication	Cyllaig, n. a stag in season
Cyhudded, n. accusation	Cyllell, n. a cutter, a knife
Cyhuddiad, n. impeachment	Cyllellu, v. to cut with a knife
Cyhuddo, v. to impeach	Cyllen, n. cutter, chopper
Cyhuddol, a. impeaching	Cyllid, n. revenue, tax
Cyhyd, so long, of equal length	Cyllido, v. to pay a tax
Cyhydedd, co-extension; equation; the equator	Cyllidydd, n. tax-gatherer
	Cylltawr, n. ploughshare
Cyhydeddu, v. to co-extend	Cyllu, v. to make a parting
Cyhydiad, n. co-extension	Cymdeithas, n. a society
Cyhydiaeth, n. a parolomolon	Cymdeithasgar, a. sociable
Cyhydreg, n. mutual strife	Cymdeithasiad, n. association
Cyhyr, n. a muscle	Cymdeithasol, a. sociable
Cyhyraeth, n. mutual system	Cymdeithasrwydd, n. sociableness
Cyhyrawg, a. musculous	Cymdeithasu, v. to associate [ness
Cyhyredd, n. muscularity	Cymdeithiad, n. consociation
Cyhyrwch, n. brawniness	Cymdeithiogi, v. to associate
Cyhyryn, n. a piece of flesh	Cymdeithio, v. to consociate
Cyl, n. concavity; a kiln	Cymdeithydd, n. a companion
Cylafaredd, n. conciliation	Cymhar, n. partner
Cylafareddu, v. to conciliate	Cymhares, n. a partner
Cylafareddus, a. conciliatory	Cymhariad, n. comparing
Cylch, n. a circle; zone, a round; circuit; a hoop: prep. about	Cymhariaeth, n. comparison
	Cymharol, a. paired, coupled
Cylchog, circled; hooped [round	Cymharu, v. to pair; to compare
Cylchol, a. circular; periodical; surrounding	Cymharwr, n. comparer
	Cymheri, n. pertubation
Cylchdroi, v. to circumvolve	Cymhell, n. compulsion: v. to compel; to instigate; to offer
Cylchedd, n. circumference	
Cylchedlen, n. a curtain	Cymhellai, n. spur
Cylchen, n. circuit, compass	Cymhelliad, n. compulsion
Cylchfrith, a. ring streaked	Cymhen, a. eloquent; pert
Cylchig, n. a circlet	Cymhendod, n. eloquence
Cylchlifiant, n. circumfluency	Cymheniad, n. adornment
Cylchrediad, n. circumambiency, cylchrediad	Cymhenu, v. to set off
	Cymhercyn, a. tottering
Cylchu, v. to encircle, to hoop	Cymherchen, a. jointly owned
Cylchwy, n. a circle; a shield	Cymherfedd, n. centre
Cylchwyl, n. an aniversary	Cymhibau, n. the wind pipe and liver; a hemhorrhage
Cylchynawl, a. circling	

CYM 82 CYM

Cymhleth, a. twisted together
Cymhlethiad, n. intertexture
Cymhlethu, v. to interweave
Cymhlith, a. blended together
Cymhlithiad, n. commixion
Cymhlitho, v. to blend
Cymhlyg, a. complex
Cymhlygiad, n. complication
Cymhlygu, v. to complicate
Cymhorth, n. assistance, aid: v. to assist, to aid
Cymhorthfa, v. to seek aid
Cymhorthiad, n. a succouring
Cymhorthol, a. succouring
Cymhraff, a. of equal thickness
Cymhwys, a. of equal weight; suitable, proper, convenient
Cynhwyso, v. to adapt
Cymhwysiad, n. adjustment
Cymmaint, a. of equal bigness, quantity or number; as much
Cymmal, n. a joint: articulation of limbs
Cymmaliad, n. a jointing
Cymmalog, a. jointed; knotty
Cymmalu, v. to form joints
Cymmalwst, n. rheumatism
Cymman, a. complete, perfect
Cymmanfa, n. an assembly
Cymmathiad, n. an assortment
Cymmathu, v. to assort
Cymmaws, a. complacent
Cymmed, n. a hedge stile
Cymmedliw, n. compliment
Cymmedr, n. proportion [ness
Cymmedredd, n. proportionate-
Cymmedriad, n. proportioning
Cymmedrol, a. proportionable; moderate [ality
Cymmedrolaeth, n. proportion-
Cymmedroldeb, n. moderation
Cymmedroli, v. to proportion
Cymmedrolwr, n. moderator
Cymmeintioli, n. equal bulk
Cymmer, n. a confluence
Cymmeradwy, a. acceptable
Cymmeradwyad, n. acceptation
Cymmeradwyedig, a. qualified

Cymmeradwyo, v. to make acceptable or suitable
Cymmeradwyoldeb, n. acceptableness
Cymmeriad, n. acceptation
Cymmerwi, v. to concoct
Cymmeryd, v. to accept, to take
Cymmesur, a. suitable, proper
Cymmesuriad, commensuration
Cymmesuro, v. to proportion; to render meet or proper
Cymmesurol, a. commensurate
Cymmod, n. concord, peace
Cymmodi, v. to reconcile
Cymmodiad, n, conciliation
Cymmodol, a. reconciling
Cymmodroddi, v. to appease
Cymmrwd, n. mortar, plaster
Cymmrydu, v. to plaster
Cymmrys, a. altogether hasty
Cymraeg, n. Welsh
Cymraes, n. Welsh woman
Cymreigiad, n. a Wallicising
Cymreigiaeth, n. Wallicism
Cymreigiaidd, a. Welshified
Cymreigeiddio, v. to become Welshified
Cymreigio, v. to Wallicise
Cymreigiol, a. Welshified
Cymreigydd, n. a Welsh critic
Cymro, n. Welshman
Cymröaidd, a. relating to Wales
Cymru, n. Wales; Cambria
Cymu, v. to close together
Cymun, n. a communion
Cymuno, v. to take the sacrament
Cymuniad, n. a communion
Cymunwr, n. communicant
Cymwd, n. a township
Cymwedd, n. connection
Cymwynas, n. kindness
Cymwynasgar, a. natured, kind, courteous, good
Cymwynasu, v. to act kindly
Cymydog, n. neighbour
Cymydogaeth, n. neighbourhood
Cymydoges, n. neighbour
Cymydogol, a. neighbourly

Cymyllad, n. clouding
Cymylog, a. cloudy, gloomy
Cymylu, v. to become cloudy
Cymyn, n. bequest; an excision
Cymynaeth, n. bequeathing
Cymynai, n. testator: n. felling hatchet
Cymynedd, n. an excision
Cymyniad, n. bequeathing: a hewing off
Cymynu, v. to bequeath: v. to hew, to to fell timber
Cymynwr, n. bequeather; a woodcutter [pound
Cymysg, n. mixture: a. com-
Cymysgedd, n. commixture
Cymysgfa, n. chaos
Cymysgiad, n. mixing
Cymysgu, to compound; to mix
Cyn, n. foremost part, or chief; a first chief; prep. before: ad. before: conj. sooner than; a. prefix denoting priority: n. wedge; chisel
Cyna, v. to follow dogs
Cynaber, n. head of a stream
Cynach, n. seeding plant
Cynâig, a. apt to follow dogs
Cynallu, n. first power
Cynamser, n. antiquity
Cynamserol, a. primitive
Cynan, n. faculty of speech
Cynaniad, n. enunciation
Cynanu, v. to prelate
Cynarch, n. primary request
Cynarchwaeth, n. foretaste
Cynarddelwi, v. to affirm beforehand
Cynarfaeth, n. permeditation
Cynarfaethu, v. to premeditate
Cynarfer, n. original usuage
Cynarparu, v. to predispose
Cynauaf, n. autumn, harvest
Cynauafa, v. to harvest
Cynauafu, v. to gather a harvest
Cynbechod, n. original sin
Cynblant, n. first born
Cynbrawf, n. rudiment

Cynbryd, n. prototype
Cynbwyll, n. forethought
Cyndad, n. patriarch
Cyndardd, n. first issue
Cyndawd, n. antecedence
Cyndeyrn, n. chief
Cyndwf, n. first growth
Cyndy, n. dog house
Cyndyn, a. stubborn, perverse
Cyndynrwydd, n. stubborness
Cynddail, n. the first leaves [ing
Cynddangosiad, n. premonstrait-
Cynddarbodi v. to pre-conceive
Cynddarbodaeth, n. preconcept-
Cynddaredd, n. madness [ion
Cynddawd, n. pre-position
Cynddeall, v. to pre-conceive
Cynddeddf n. instinct
Cynddefawd, n. precept
Cynddefnydd, n. original matter
Cynddeiriog, a. mad; furious
Cynddeiriogi, v. to madden
Cynddelw, n. archetype
Cynddethol, v. to pre-elect
Cynddirnad, n. pre-surmise
Cynddodiad, n. preposition
Cynddosbarth, n. premonstration
Cynddrych, n. object
Cynddrychiolydd, n. a represent-
Cynddyrchiol, a. present [ative
Cynddrygedd, n. mischief
Cynddull, n. first form
Cynddulliad, n. prefiguration
Cynddydd, n. break of day
Cynêica. v. to go after dogs
Cynell, n. dog kennel
Cynenid, a. primogeneal
Cynenidedd, n. primogeniture
Cynenw, n. christian name
Cynenwad, n. prenomination
Cynesgor, n. first delivery
Cynethol, v. to pre-elect
Cynfab, n. first born, male
Cynfam n. first mother
Cynfardd. n. primitive bard
Cynfas, n. sheet of cloth, to bed sheet
Cynfebyd, n, early infancy

Cynfedydd, n. first baptism
Cynfedd, n. original bias
Cynfeddiant, n. pre-occupation
Cynflas, n. foretaste
Cynflith, n. first milk
Cynfod, n. pre-existence
Cynfodol, a. pre-existent
Cynfraint, n. prerogative
Cynfrith, a. of variegated front
Cynfro, n. a first country
Cynfrodor, n. an aborigine
Cynfrwydr, n. front of battle
Cynfyd, n. antidiluvian world
Cynfyl, n. native place
Cynffon, n. tail, rump
Cynffonog, a. having a tail
Cynffoni, to form a tail, to cringe
Cynffrwyth, n. first fruit
Cynhaid, n. first swarm
Cynhanfod, n. pre-existence
Cynhasedd, n. a mutual bond
Cynhebrwng, n. funeral
Cynhebyg, a. alike, similar
Cynhebygol, a. comparative
Cynhebygu, v. to compare
Cynhefyg, n. principal
Cynhefin, n. growth of a year
Cynhen, n. contention, strife
Cynhenid, a. inbred, natural
Cynhenllyd, a. quarrelsome
Cynhenhol, a., contentions [rel
Cynhenu, v. to contend, to quar-
Cynhenus, a. contentious [rel
Cynhes, a. warm; cheering
Cynhesiad, n. a warming
Cynhesrwydd, n. warmth
Cynhesu, v. to warm
Cynhordy, n. court house
Cynbwrf, n. commotion: trou-
ble; disturbance
Cynhyrfiad, n. an agitating
Cynhyrfu, to move, to convulse
Cynhyrfwr, n. an agitator
Cyni, n. anguish, anxiety
Cyniad, n. principal
Cyniant, n. priority
Cynio, v. to wedge; to chizel
Cynllaeth, n. first milk

Cynllaith, n. humidity
Cynlliw, n. first colour
Cynllog, n. common interest
Cynllun, n. pattern, model
Cynllunio, v. to model
Cynlluniwr, n. a modeller
Cynllwyn, n. waylaying
Cynllwyno, v. to waylay
Cynllwynwr, n. lurker
Cynnadledd, n. colloquy
Cynnadliad, n. a conversing
Cynnadl, n. intercourse
Cynnadlu, v. to intercourse
Cynnal, v. to sustain, to bear
Cynnaliad, n. support
Cynnaliaeth, n. maintenance
Cynnaliwr, n. supporter
Cynnar, a. early, timely, soon
Cynnaru, v. to be early
Cynnarwch, n. earliness
Cynau, ad. ere, now; a while
  ago, lately
Cynnawn, n. leading strait
Cynne, n. ignition, burning
Cynneall, n. pre-conception
Cynnechre, n. first origin
Cyneddfol, a. habitual
Cyneddfu, v. to habituate
Cynneddf, n. disposition
Cynneddwd, n. custom, usage
Cynnefin, a. accustomed
Cynnefiniad, n. accustoming
Cynnefindra, n. inurement
Cynnefino, v. to accustom
Cynnefnydd, n. first matter
Cynnefodi, v. to habituate
Cynnelw, n. pattern
Cynnerth, n. first power
Cynnethol, v. to pre-elect
Cynneu, v. to kindle to fire
Cynneuad, n. a kindling
Cynnewis, n. pre-election
Cynhefig, a. principal
Cynnhwf, n. first growth
Cynnifer, a. of equal number
Cynniferedd, n. even number
Cynniferydd, n. a quotient
Cynnifind, n. conflictor

Cynnil, a. skilful; thrifty, saving
Cynniliad, n. a saving
Cynnildeb, n. frugality
Cynnilledd, n. savingness
Cynnilio, v. to use skill; to save
Cynniwair, n. hovering about
Cynniweirfa, n. place of resort
Cynniweirio, v. to hover about
Cynniweiriol, a. hovering
Cyniweiriwr, n. hoverer
Cynnod, n. prime mark
Cynnodiad, n. prime mark
Cynorthwy, n. succour, aid
Cynorthwyad, n. assisting
Cynorthwyo, v. to support; to maintain; to succour
Cynnorthwywr, n. succourer
Cynnrych, n. an example
Cynnrychiad, n. exhibition
Cynnrychiol, a. presential
Cynnrychioldeb, n. presentness
Cynnrychioli, v. to represent
Cynnrychiolwr, representative
Cynnud, n. fire wood, fuel
Cynnulliad, n. a collection
Cynnull, v. to collect
Cynnulleidfa, n. assembly
Cynnuta, v. to gather fuel
Cynnutai, n. gatherer of fuel
Cynnwynol, a. natural
Cynnwys, n. admission, leave: a. compact, close: v. to contain: to harbour
Cynnwysder, n. compactness
Cynnwysedig, a. comprehended
Cynnwysfawr, a. comprehensive
Cynnwysiad, n. making compact; inclusion; epitome
Cynnydd, n. increase, growth
Cynnydd ad, n. an increasing
Cynnyddol, a. increasing
Cynnyddu, v. to increase
Cynnyg, n. proffer, offer; v. to offer; to tender
Cynnygiad, n. a proposition
Cynnygiol, a. tendering
Cynnygwr, Cynnygydd, n. a proposer

Cynnyrch, n. produce
Cynnyrchiad, n. production
Cynnyrchiol, a. productive
Cynnyrchioldeb, n. productiveness
Cynnyrchioli, v. to make productive; to become productive
Cynnyrchu, v. to increase [tive
Cynnysgaeth, n portion, fortune
Cynnysgaethiad, n. endowment, a settling a fortune
Cynnysgaethu, v. to endow
Cynoes, n. first age, antiquity
Cynoesol, a. primevous
Cynosod, v. to prepose
Cynron, n. maggots, worms
Cynronllyd, a. maggotty
Cynronyn, n. a maggot
Cynryw, n. essence; purity
Cynrywiad, n. origination
Cynsail, n. a rudiment; a proposition; a sublinth
Cynsefydlu, v. to predetermine
Cynseilo, v. to premise
Cynsylwi, v. to foresee
Cynsymudiad, n. first motion
Cynsyniad, n. pre-surmise
Cynt, a. first, earliest, prime: ad. formerly, before
Cyntaf, a. first chief, earliest
Cyntafanedig, a. first-born
Cyntedd, n. entry, porch
Cyntefig, a. primary, primitive
Cyntefigiad, n. origination
Cyntefigiaeth, n. primitive, state
Cyntefin, n. the first of May: a. amphibious
Cynteig, a. prime, or primal
Cyntenid, a. primogenial
Cyn hun, n. first sleep, a nap
Cynwas, n. a chief minister
Cynwawl, n. primeval light
Cynwawr. n. a first dawn
Cynwe, n. end of a web
Cynwedd, n. first appearance
Cynweled, n. a foresight
Cynwelediad, n. foreseeing
Cynwyd, n. mischief; a evil

Cynwyl, a. bashful, modest
Cynwyre, v. to ascend up
Cynyd, v. to rise, to arise
Cyngan, n. speech, discourse
Cynghad, n. a concourse
Cynghan, a. consonant
Cynghanedd, n. consonancy
Cynghaneddol, a. harmonious
Cynghaneddu, v. to harmonize
Cynghanu, v. to love mutually
Cynghas, n. mutual hate
Cynghau, v. to close together
Cynghawg, n. complicate metre, so called
Cynghaws, n. issue at law, a suit; an advocate or council
Cynghawsaeth, n. pleadings
Cynghawsedd, n. law process
Cynghel, n. privacy: ad. private or concealed
Cynghelu, v. to conceal
Cynghloi, v. to lock together
Cynghlwm, n. a connection
Cynghlwyf, n. a contagion
Cynghlymu, v. to tie together
Cynghogi, v. to complicate
Cyngholli, v. to cast to perdition
Cynghor, n. a coucil, advice, recipe
Cynghori, v. to counsel; to advise
Cynghoriad, n. advising
Cynghorol, a. counselling
Cynghorus, a. considerable
Cynghorwr, n. a councellor
Cynghrair, n. treaty
Cynghreirio, to enter into treaty
Cynghreiriol, a. confederate
Cynghreiriwr, n. a sworn confed-
Cynghroes, a. intersecant [erate
Cynghroesi, v. to intersect
Cynghrhon, a, spheric
Cynghrwm, a. of convex form
Cynghryn, mutually trembling
Cyngwerth, n. equivalence
Cynghwys, n. mutual citation
Cyngwysl, n. mutual pledge
Cyrafol, n. service berries
Cyraith, n. law of fate

Cyrawol, n. berries
Cyrbibion, n. dribblets
Cyrcydu, v. to squat, to cower
Cyrch, n, a centre, gravity; an inroad; an attack
Cyrchadwy, a. approachable
Cyrchafael, n. an uplifting
Cyrchell, n. what surrounds
Cyrchfa, n. a resort
Cyrchiad, n. a coming to
Cyrchle, n. a place of resort
Cyrchnaid, n. a bound upon
Cyrchu, v. to gravitate to approach; to set on; to fetch
Cyrchwr, n. a fetcher
Cyrfaidd, a. rotund, circling
Cyrfawd, n. curvetting
Cyfrdŷ, n. an alehouse
Cyrfydd, n. ale-brewer
Cyrfyll, n. a trunk, a case
Cyrhaedd, n. reach, extent: v. to attain; to reach
Cyrhaeddadwy, a. attainable
Cyrhaeddiad, n. a reaching
Cyrhaeddol, a. within reach
Cyrhaeddu, v. to attain, to reach
Cyrhaeddyd, v. to reach, to attain
Cyriad, n. a skirting round
Cyrid, n. carnal copulation
Cyrio, v. to skirt, to rim
Cyriogi, v. to set a border
Cyrnad, n. a blowing a horn
Cyrnaid, n. a prance, a bound
Cyrncidio, v. to prance
Cyrnen, n. a cone; a stack
Cyrnenaidd, a. conical
Cyrnenu, v. to pile up
Cyrniad, n. a projecting as a horn; to pile up, to stack
Cyrnig, a. corneous; horned
Cyrnio, v. to pile, to stack
Cyrniog, a. cornigerous, horned
Cyrniogyn, n. a piggin
Cyryglwr, n. a coracle-man
Cys, a prefix denoting mutuality of effect or action, of the same force as cyd and cyf
Cysail, n. constituent part

Cysain, n. consonancy
Cysawd, n. an affix, a suffix
Cysawdd, n. a compound
Cysdadl, a. disputable; equal
Cysdadlaeth, n. competition
Cysdadliad, mutually disputing
Cysdadlu, v. to vie; to debate
Cystadlwr, n. a competition
Cysdawd, n. a butting together
Cysdedlydd, n. a competitor
Cysdodi, v. to place in custody
Cysefin, a. primary, primitive
Cysefino, v. to originate
Cysefiniad, n. originality
Cysegr, n. a sanctuary
Cysegriad, n. consecration
Cysegredig, a. consecrated
Cysegrol, a. consecrate
Cysegr-ladrad, n. sacrilege
Cysegrlan, a. sonsecrate, sacred
Cysegru, v. to consecrate
Cysegrydd, n. a consecrator
Cyseiliad, n. constitution
Cysciniad, n. a consonant
Cyseinio, v. to sound together
Cysellt, n. an opportunity
Cysgfa, n. numbness
Cysgiad, n. a sleeping
Cysgiadol, a. soporific, soniferous
Cysgiadur, n. a sleeper; a sluggard; a dormant animal
Cysgladyr, n. an opiate
Cysglyd, a. sleepy, drowsy
Cysgod, n. a shadow, a shade; a shelter
Cysgodfa, n. a shady place
Cysgodi, v. to shadow; to shelter
Cysgodiad, n. a shadowing
Cysgodog, a. sheltering
Cysgodol, a. shadowy, sheltering
Cysgrwydd, n. sleepiness
Cysgu, v. to sleep; to benumb
Cysgwr, n. a sleeper
Cysgwal, n. a dormitory
Cysiad, n. somnolence
Cysni, n. drowsiness
Cysodi, v. to compose
Cysodiad, n. a composing

Cysodol, a. compositive
Cysodoldeb, n. compositiveness
Cysodwr, n. a composer
Cysodydd, n. a compositor
Cysodyr, n. a composing-stick
Cysoddi, v. to combine, to blend
Cysoddiad, n. a combining
Cysoddol, a. combining
Cyson, a. concordant, harmonious; constant
Cysondeb, n. concordance
Cysoni, v. to make consonant, to harmonize
Cysoniad, n. harmonics
Cyspell, n. propinquity: a. close together, compact
Cysail, n. a constituent part
Cyswllt, n. a conjunction
Cyswr, n. contempt: a. glum
Cysylltiad, n. a conjoining
Cysylltu, v. to conjoin
Cystal, a. equivalent, equal: ad. so good, as good
Cystawci, n. a mastiff
Cystig, a. severe, austere, harsh
Cystled, ad. so good, as good
Cystlwn, n. kindred, affinity
Cystlynan, n. a family stock
Cystlyned, n. kindred, alliance
Cystlynu, v. to form connection
Cystogi, v. to toil, to drudge
Cystraw, n. concord rule
Cystrawen, n. syntax
Cystrawenol, a. syntactical
Cystrawenu, v. to construct
Cystrawenydd, n. a grammarian
Cystrawiad, n. construction
Cystrawiaeth, n. constructure
Cystrawu, v. to construct
Cystudd, n. affliction, grief
Cystuddiad, n. an afflicting
Cystuddio, v. to afflict
Cystuddiedig, a. afflicted
Cystuddiol, a. afflicting
Cystuddiwr, n. an afflictor
Cystwy, n. chastisement
Cystwyad, n. a chastising
Cystwyo, v. to chastise

Cystwyol, a. castigatory
Cysur, n. comfort, consolation
Cysuriad, n. a comforting
Cysuro, v. to comfort, to console
Cysurol, a. comforting
Cysurus, a. comforting, cheering
Cysurwr, n. comforter
Cytiad, n. abbreviation
Cytio, v. to abbreviate
Cythlwng, n. a fasting, a fast
Cythraul, n. the devil, satan
Cythrawl, a. adverse
Cythreuliaeth, n. demonolotry
Cythreulig, a. devilish
Cythriad, n. an excretion
Cythru, v. to eject, to cast off
Cythrudd, n. perturbation
Cythruddedigaeth, n. perturbated state [a ruffling
Cythruddiad, n. a purturbating,
Cythruddus, a. provoking
Cythruddwr, n. a vexer
Cythrwfl, n. trouble, motion
Cyw, n. young bird, a chick
Cywain, v. to convey, to carry
Cywair, n. connexion, order; a key in music; accordant, or-
Cywarch, n. hemp, flax [derly
Cywarchlen, n. a canvass
Cywarsang, n. a tread over
Cyweddol, a. conformable
Cyweirdant, n. a key string
Cyweirdeb, n. correctness
Cyweirgorn, n. a turning key
Cyweiriad, n. correction
Cyweirio, v. to correct, to rectify; to dress; to tune
Cyweiriol, a. corrective
Cyweiriwr, n. a repairer
Cyweithas, n. a society; commerce; intercourse
Cyweithasiad, n. association
Cyweithasol, a. social [plaisance
Cyweithasrwydd, courtesy, com-
Cyweithasu, v. to have intercourse; to be social together
Cyweithio, v. to co-operate
Cyweithydd, n. a co-efficient;
an auxiliary; a multitude
Cywely, n. a bedfellow
Cywelyes, n. a concubine
Cywelyog, a. having a bedfellow
Cywelogaeth, n. concubinage
Cywen, n. a young hen
Cywenig, n. a little pullet
Cywer, n. a curdler; a rennet
Cywerth, n. equivalence
Cywerthol, a. equivalent
Cywerthu v. to bargain
Cywerthyddu, v. to estimate
Cywilydd, n. shame, disgrace
Cywilyddgar, a. shameful
Cywilyddiad, n. a shaming
Cywilyddio, v. to shame
Cywilyddus, a. shameful
Cywir, a. correct, sincere
Cywirdeb, n. correctness
Cywiriad, n. a loyalist
Cywirio, v. to perfect; to fulfil; to be sincere
Cywrain, a. skilful; accurate
Cywraint, n. a skilful one
Cywreindeb, n. accuracy
Cywreiniad, a making accurate
Cywreinio, v. to make exact
Cywreiniwr, n. one who makes perfect
Cywreinrwydd, n. skilfulness
Cywreinwaith, n. curious work-
Cywres n. a concubine [manship
Cywydd, n. a kind of metre; perception; conscience
Cywyddiaeth, n. rationality
Cywyddol, a. conscious
Cywyll, n. culture, tillage
Cywyllu, v. to culture
Cywyn, n. a rise, a swell

CH

CHWA, n. a blast, a puff
Chwad, n. a gust, a jerk
Chwaer, Chwiorydd, n a sister
Chwaerol, a. like a sister
Chwaroliaeth, n. a sisterhood

Chwaeth, n. savour, taste
Chwaethiad, n. a tasting
Chwaethu, v. to savour
Chwaethus, a. sapid, gustful
Chwaf, n. a strong gust: adv. instantly
Chwai, a. active, brisk, alert
Chwaith, adv. neither
Chwaithach, adv. much less
Chwal, n. a spreading
Chwaladwy, a. dissipatable
Chwaliad, n. a scattering
Chwalu, v. to strew, to spread
Chwaneg, a. more: n. a greater
Chwanegiad, addition [quantity
Chwanegol, a. additional
Chwanen, n. a flea
Chwannog, a. desirous, greedy
Chwannogi, v. to grow greedy
Chwant, n. appetite, lust
Chwanta, v. to lust, to covet
Chwantach, n. desire, lust
Chwantu, v. to lust, to covet
Chwantus, a. lustful, lusting
Chwap, n. a sudden stroke: adv.
Chwapiad, a slapping [instantly
Chwapio, v. to strike, to slap
Chwardd, n. a laugh, laughter
Chwarddiad, n. a laughing
Chwarddol, a. laughing
Chwarddu, v. to laugh
Chwarddus, a. apt to laugh
Chware, n. play: v. to play
Chwarëad, n. a playing
Chwarel, dart; a lump, as from milk curdling in the breast
Chwarellad, a darting; a kern-
Chwarefu, to dart; a kern [ing
Chwaren, n. a gland; a blotch
Chwarenaidd, a. like a gland
Chwareniad, n. a kerning
Chwarenog, a. full of glands
Chwarenol, glandulous [blotches
Chwarenu, v. to kern; to form
Chwarëol, a. playing, sportive
Chwareu, n. play: v. to play
Chwareuad, n. a playing
Chwareuaeth, n. diversion

Chwareudŷ, n. a theatre
Chwareufa, n. a theatre
Chwereugar, a. playful
Chwareuol, a. playful
Chwarëydd, n. a player
Chwarëyddes, n. a female player
Chwarëyddiaeth, n. play
Chwarf, n. a whirl; a fusee
Chwarwriaeth, n. player s art
Chwarwy, n. disport play
Chwarwyad, n. a disporting
Chwarwyo, v. to disport
Chwarydd, n. a player
Chwaryddes, n. a player
Chwaryddiad, n. a playing
Chwaryddiaeth, n. a play
Chwaw, n. a blast, a breeze
Chweban, n. a sextain
Chweblwydd, a. sexennial
Chwech, a. six
Chweched, a. sixth
Chwechedran, n. sixth part
Chwechedwaith, n, sixth time
Chwedeg, a. sixty
Chwedegfed, a. sixtieth
Chwedi, adv. then: prep. after
Chwedl, n. a saying. a fable, a
Chwedla, to gossip [story, a tale
Chwedlai, n. a gossip
Chwedlëig, a. gossiping
Chwedleua, v. to gossip
Chwedleuaeth, n. a colloquy
Chwedleugar, a. fond of talk
Chwedleuo, v. to discourse
Chwedleuog, a. talkative
Chwedleuol, a. colloquial
Chwedleuydd, n. a discourser
Chwedlgar, a. loquacious
Chwedliad, n. a fabling
Chwedlu, v. to fable
Chwedlydd, n. a fabulist
Chwefr, n. violence, rage
Chwefrol, a. violent, severe
Chwefror, n. February
Chwefru, v. to act violently
Chweg, a. dulcet, luscious
Chwegiad, n. dulcification
Chwegr, n mother-in law

Chwegrwn, n. father-in-law
Chwegu, v. to dulcify
Chweiad, n. a moving briskly
Chweider, n. agility
Chweina, v. to catch fleas
Chweinial, v. to hop as fleas
Chweiniog, a. full of fleas
Chweinllyd, a. breeding fleas
Chweinllys, n. fleabane
Chweio, v. to move briskly
Chweiol, a. full of agility
Chweledig, a. being revolved
Chweledigaeth, n. revolution
Chweliad, n. rotation
Chweliedydd, n. a disperser [over
Chwelyd, n. a detour: v. to turn
Chwelydr, n. a chip of a plough
Chwennych, v. to covet
Chwennychiad, n. a desiring
Chwennychol, a. desirous
Chwennycholdeb, n. the quality of being desirable [desire
Chwennychu, v. to covet or
Chweochrol, a. sex-angular, six-
Chwepyn, n. an instant [sided
Chwerfan, n. a whirl; a fusee
Chwerfiad, n. a whirling
Chwerfu, v. to whirl
Chweriad, n. a playing about
Chwerig, a. indecent; sportive
Chwern, a. rapid, violent [laugh
Chwerthin, n. laughter; v. to
Chwerthinedd, n. laughableness
Chwerthingar, Chwerthinog, a. apt to laugh
Chwerthiniad, n. a laughing
Chwerthiniol, a. laughable
Chwerthinus, a. laughable
Chwerw, a. bitter; sharp: severe

Chwesill, a. of six syllables
Chwetheg, n. sixteen
Chwetho, a. sextuple, sixfold
Chwëu, v. to grow sharp
Chwi, n. a swift turn: pron. you
Chwib, n. a pipe, a tube
Chwiban, n. a whistle
Chwibaniad, n, a whistling
Chwibanllyd, a. apt to whistle
Chwibanogl, n. a flageolet
Chwibanol, a. whistling
Chwibanu, v. to whistle
Chwibanydd, n. a whistler
Chwibiad, n. a trilling
Chwibio, v. to quaver
Chwibiol, a. trilling
Chwibl, a. tart, sour, acid
Chwiblad, n. a souring
Chwiblaidd, a. somewhat sour
Chwibledd, n. sourness
Chwibleian, n. a nymph
Chwiblni, n. acerbity
Chwibol, n. a tube, a pipe
Chwibolog, a. tubular
Chwibon, n. a whistler; a stork
Chibwrn, n. giddiness: a. giddy,
Chwid, n. a quick turn [dizzy
Chwido, v. to quirk, to juggle; to make a quick move
Chwidog, a. full of quirks
Chwifio, v. to fly around
Chwifiol, a. whirling; vagrant
Chwiff, n. a hiss, a whiff
Chwiffiad, n. a hissing
Chwifflo, v. to hiss, to whiff: a. sibilant; whiffling
Chwig, n. whey fermented; a. fermented; sour
Chwiglen, n. a sharp stone

Chwildroi, v. to turn dizzily
Chwilen, n. a beetle, a chafer
Chwilena, v. to pry; to pick
Chwilenai, n. a pilferer
Chwilfa, n. a research
Chwilfriw, a. all to pieces
Chwilfriwiad, n. a shattering
Chwilfriwio, v. to shatter
Chwilfynwg, n. the neck joint
Chwilgi, n. a prying dog
Chwilgorn, n. a pivot, a reeling
Chwiliach, v. to pry; to pilfer
Chwiliad, n. scrutiny, search
Chwiliadol, a. searching
Chwiliadwy, a. searchable
Chwilied, to search, to examine
Chwiliedydd, n. a searcher
Chwilio, v. to search, to seek, to look for
Chwiliogaeth, n. sorcery
Chwilloges, n. a sorceress
Chwiliores, n. a hornet
Chwilioryn, n. a maggot
Chwilog, a. whirling: n. the lesser guillemot
Chwilota, v. to catch beetles
Chwilotai, n. a pryer about
Chwim, Chwimiad, n. motion
Chwimio, v. to move briskly
Chwimiol, a. full of motion
Chwimp, n. a turn; a hap
Chwimwth, a. nimble, speedy
Chwimythder, n. nimbleness
Chwip, n. a quick turn: a. quick, swift
Chwipiad, n. a whipping
Chwipio, v. to whip, to slap
Chwipyn, n. a quick turn: a. quick, instantly
Chwistrell, n. a syringe
Chwistrelliad, n. a squirting
Chwistrellu, to syringe; to squirt
Chwitchwat, n. a sly pilferer
Chwith, a. sinister untoward
Chwithig, a. sinister, left
Chwithigrwydd, n. corruptness
Chwithio, v. to feel awkward
Chwithol, a. sinister

Chwithrwd, n. a rustling
Chwithrwd, v. to rustle
Chwiw, n. a whirl; an attack or fit of disccase
Chwiwbigo, v. to pilfer
Chwiwdwll, n. a lurking hole
Chwiwell, n. a whirler; the widgeon; the female salmon
Chwiwgi, n. a sculking dog; a thief, a rogue
Chwiwiad, n. turning round
Chwiwian, v. to hunt about
Chwiwio, v. to fly about; to pry, to pilfer
Chwiwladrad, n. a pilfering
Chwiwladrata, v. to pilfer
Chwiwleidr, n. a pilferer
Chwiws, n. widgeons
Chwychwi, pron. yourselves
Chwyd, n. ejection, vomit
Chwydalen, n. a blister
Chwydalu, v. to blister
Chwydaliaeth, n. gesticulation
Chwydawydd, n. a bufoon
Chwydawyr, n. viscous matter, said to drop from meteors
Chwydiad, n. a vomiting
Chwydo, v. to gesticulate
Chwydr, n. ejected matter
Chwydredd, n. ejected matter
Chwydu, v. to vomit
Chwydus, a. apt to vomit
Chwydd, n. a swelling
Chwyddiad, n. a swelling
Chwyddo, v. to swell out
Chwyddol, a. apt to swell
Chwyf, n. motion or stir
Chwyfain, v. fluctating
Chwyfiad, n. a stirring
Chwyfo, v. to stir, to waver
Chwyl, n. a turn; a course; a while; an event: ad. while, as long as
Chwyldro, n. a turn; a vortex
Chwyldroi, v. to whirl round
Chwylfa, n. an orbit, a course
Chwyliad, n. a rotation
Chywlo, v. to turn, to revolve

Chwyn, n. a stir, weeds
Chwynan, n. a fly wheel
Chwyniad, n. a weeding
Chwyno, v. to stir about
Chwynog, a. full of weeds
Chwynogl, n. a hoe
Chwynogli, v. to grub up weeds
Chwyrn, n. a whirl; a snarl: a. rapid; active
Chwyrnad, n. whirling; snoring
Chwyrndra, n. rapidness
Chwyrnell, n. a whirligig
Chwrnelliad, n. a whirling
Chwyrnellu, v. to whirl, to whiz
Chwyrnfor, n. a strong eddy
Chwyrniad, n. a snarler
Chwyrnog, a. whirling; snarling
Chwyrnogl, n. a rattle
Chwyrnogli v. to rattle, to whiz
Chwyrnogliad, n. a rattling
Chwyrnolad, v. to snort: n. a snorting
Chwyrnes, n. a hornet
Chwyrnu, v. to hum; to whiz; to snort; to snarl; to snore
Chwys, n. perspiration, sweat
Chwysbair, a. sudorific
Chwysdwll, n. sweat pore
Chwysfa, n. a sudatory
Chwysiad, n. a sweating
Chwysig, a. apt to sweat
Chwysigen, n. a bladder
Chwysigeniad, n. a blistering
Chwysigenog, a. blistered
Chwysigenu, v. to blister
Chwysigl, n. a blister
Chwysiglen, n. a blister
Chwyslyd, a. apt to perspire
Chwysog, a. full of sweat
Chwysoglen, n. the sharp dock
Chwysol, a. sweating
Chwysu, v. to sweat, to perspire
Chwyth, n. a blast; breath
Chwythad, n. a blasting, a breathing
Chwythaint, n. respiration
Chwythbren, n. a blowpipe
Chwythedd, n. act of blowing

Chwythell, n, a whistle
Chwytheliiad, n. a whistling
Chwythgorn, n. a cornet
Chwythiad, n. a blowing
Chwythiedydd, n. a blower
Chwythig, a. windy; inflated
Chwythigell, n. what is inflated
Chwythigen, n. a bettle
Chwythlyd, a. blowing, puffing
Chwythol, a. blowing; breathing
Chwythu, v. to blow, to blast
Chwythyn, n. a puff, a blast

D

Da, n. what is had; goods, chattels, stock, cattle: a. good, well: adv. well, good
Dacw, adv. there is, yonder is
Dad, a. prefix equivalent to RE, UN, and DIS in English
Dadadeilio, v. to unbuild
Dadafaelu, v. to relax
Dadangori, v. to disanchor
Dadanelu, v. to unstretch
Dadansoddi, v. to unqualify
Dadarfogi, v. to disarm
Dadblanu, v. to displant
Dadblygu, v. to unfold
Dadboeni, v. to divest of pain
Dadbrofi, v. to disprove
Dadbrynu, v. to repurchase
Dadbwytho, v. to unstitch
Dadbynio, v. to disburden
Dadchwerwi, v. to disimbitter
Dadchwiliad, n. a researching
Dadchwilio, v. to search again
Dadebru, v. to resusciate
Dadechwyno, v. to return a loan
Dadedfryd, v. to restore
Dadegnio, v. to cease toiling
Dadegru, v. to make brisk what is flat, or stale
Dadenhudd, n. disclosure
Dadeni, n. a second birth
Dadenyn, v. to extinguish
Daderbyn, v. to receive back

Dadergyd, n. a repulsion
Dadergyriad, n. a retorting
Dadesmwytho, to divest of ease
Dadeuogi, v. to clear of guilt
Dadfachellu, v. to ungrapple
Dadfachu, v. to unhook
Dadfaglu, v. to disentangle
Dadfalchio, v. to cure of pride
Dadfarnu, to revoke judgement
Dadfarwâu, v to resuscitate
Dadfawdd, n. emersion
Dadfechnïo, v. to exonerate bail
Dadfeddiant, n. dispossession
Dadfeddwi, v. to soberize
Dadfeichio, v. to disburden
Dadfeilio, v. to fall, to ruin
Dadfeio, v. to clear of fault
Dadferiad, n. restoration
Dadferthu, v. to revive
Dadferu, v. to revolve to dissolve
Dadflaenu, v. to blunt a point
Dadflasu, v. to divest of taste
Dadflino, v. to rid of fatigue to refresh
Dadflisgo, v. to cast off a shell
Dadflodeuo, v. to drop blossoms
Dadflysio, v. to divest of longing
Dadfoddloni, v. to dissatisfy
Dadfraenu, v. to rid of putridity
Dadfreinio, v. to disfranchise
Dadfriad, n. a dishonouring
Dadfrochi, v. to unruffle
Dadfrythu, v. to quell a tumult
Dadfyddaru, v. to cure of deafness
Dadffrydiant, n. a reflux [ness
Dadffrydio, v. to flow back
Dadgadwyno, v. to unchain
Dadgaenu, to take off a surface
Dadgaeru, v. to dismantle or to reduce a fortification
Dadgaethu, v. to disenthral
Dadgan, n. a recital ; repetition
Dadganiad, n. a reciting
Dadganu, v. to recite, to say
Dadgaregu, v. to unpetrify
Dadgeiniad, n. a reciter
Dadgladdu, v. to disinter
Dadglöi, v. to unlock

Dadgroeni, v. to remove the skin or bark
Dadgroni, v. to undam
Dadgrychu, v. to unwrinkle
Dadgrymu, v. to unbend
Dadguddiad, n. revelation
Dadguddio, v. to reveal
Dadgydiad, n. disjunction
Dadgyfaniad, n. disruption
Dadgyfaneddu, v. to leave of inhabiting
Dadgyfartalu, to disproportion
Dadgyfluniad, n. a divesting o conformation
Dadgyfrodeddu, v. to untwine
Dadgylchu, v. to uncircle
Dadgymalu, v. to disjoint
Dadgymysgu, v. to unmingle
Dadgysodi, v. to unshelter, to distribute type
Dadgysoni, v. to make discord
Dadgysylltu, v. to disjoin
Dadgyweirio, v. to disorganise
Dadhalogi, v. to rid of polution
Dadhalltu, v. to rid of saltness
Dadhanfodiad, n. annihilation
Dadholi, v. to re-examine
Dadhualu, v. to unfetter
Dadhuddo, v. to uncover
Dadhulio, v. to uncover
Dadhuno, v. to awake
Dadieuo, v. to unyoke
Dadl, n. dispute, debate, plea
Dadlaesu, v. to tuck up
Dadlam, n. a rebound
Dadleâu, v. to displace
Dadlenwad, n. depletion
Dadleu, v. to dispute, to argue
Dadleuad, n. disputation
Dadleuwr, n. disputer
Dadlewygu, v. to revive
Dadlidio, v. to rid of anger
Dadlif, n. an ebb, reflux
Dadliwio v. to discolour
Dadlu, v. to depate, to argue
Dadlunio, v. to divest of form
Dadlwytho, v. to unload
Dadlygru, v. to rid of corruption

Dadlythyru, v. to obliterae
Dadnaid, n. a rebounding
l'adnaws, n. indisposition
Dadnerthu, v. to rid of strength
Dadnewid, v. to re-exchange
Dadnoddi, v. to divest of refuge
Dadnwyfo, v. to enervate
Dadnychu, v. to rid of agony
Dadnyddu, v. to untwist
Dadobeithio, v. to rid of hope
Dadoeri, v. to divest of cold
Dadofalu, v. to divest of care
Dadofidio, v. to rid of grief
Dadofni, v. to rid of fear
Dadoleuo, v. to relume
Dadolrain, v. to retrace
Dadorbwyllo, v. to rid of madness; to recover one's senses
Dadorchuddio, v. to develope
Dadoresgyn, v. to reconquer
Dadorfod, v. to overcome again
Dadormesu, v. to cease troubling
Dadorthrechu, v. to rid of op; res-
Dadosodi, v. to displace [sion
Dadosgli, v. to strip branches
Dadostegu, v. to break silence
Dadranu, v. to subdivide
Dadredeg, v. to run back
Dadreibio, v. to disenchant
Dadreiddio, v. to repenetrate
Dadreithio, v. to divest of law
Dadrestru, v. to disarrange
Dadrin, v. to rid of mystery
Dadrisgio, v. to strip off the bark
Dadrithio, v. to disappear
Dadroddi, v. to give back
Dadrwyddo, v. to disentangle
Dadrwymo, v. to unbind
Dadrwystro, v. to disencumber
Dadryddâu, v. to free again
Dadrywio, v. to degenerate
Dadsaethu, v. to shoot back
Dadsafiad, n. reposition
Dadsangu, v. to tread back
Dadsarfiu, v. to rid of offence
Dadsathru. v. to tread again
Dadsefydlu, v. to rid of stability
Dadseinio, v. to reverberate

Dadseirchio, v. to unharness
Dadserchu, v. to divest of love
Dadsideru, v. to unfringe
Dadsori, v. to divest of anger
Dadswyno, v. to disenchant
Daduno, v. to disunite
Dadurddo, v. to degrade
Dadwarchâu, v. to raise a siege
Dadwasgodi, v. to unshelter
Dadwasgu, v to unpress
Dadweinio, v. to unsheath
Dadweithio, v. to unwork
Dadwersyllu, v. to strike tents
Dadweu, v. to unweave
Dadwibio, v. to reel back
Dadwiriaw, v. to divest of truth
Dadwisgaw, v. to disarray
Dadwlitho, v. to dry up dew
Dadwneud, Dadwneuthur, v. to
Dadwnio, v. to unsew [undo
Dadwrdd, v. to make a noise
Dadwregysu, v. to ungird
Dadwreiddio, v. to eradicate
Dadwridio v. to cease blushing
Dadwynebu to rid of surface
Dadwyrain, v. to resurge
Dadwyre, v. to reascend
Dadwystlo, v. to unpledge
Dadymattal, v. to cease restraining one's self
Dadymbleidio, v. to divest one's self of reason
Dadymchwel, v. to overturn
Dadymorchi, v. to become unfolded [one's self of trouble
Dadymdrafferthu, v. to divest
Dadymdrefnu, v. to disorder one's self [self of partiality
Dadymdueddu, v. to divest one's
Dadymdyru, v. to become dispersed [gling
Dadymdderu, v. to cease wran-
Dadymddieithrio, v. to divest one's self of strangeness
Dadymddilladu, v. to undress one's self [self
Dadymglymu, v. to untie one's
Dadymgreuloni, v. to divest

one's self of cruelty [one's self
Dadymguddio, v. to cease hiding
Dadymgysylltu, v. to disconnect one's self [self
Dadymlëu, v. to displace one's
Dadymloni, v. to cease cheering one's self
Dadymnyddu, v. to become untwisted
Dadymorchuddio, v. to divest one's self of covering
Dadymrwymo, v. to disengage one's self
Dadymylu, v. to emarginate
Dadysgrif, n. a transcript shape
Dadystumio, v. to divest of land,
Daear, n. earth, globe, soil, ground
Daearaidd, a. terreous, earthy
Daearblant, n. mortals
Daeardy, n. dungeon
Daearen, n. the earth
Daearfochyn, n. badger
Daearfyd, n. terrestial world
Dacargi, n. terrier
Daeargoel, n. geomancy
Daeargryn, n. earthquake
Daeargyrch, a. earth-seeking
Daearhwch, n. female badger
Daeariad, n. grounding
Daearlawr, n. ground-floor
Daearllyd, a. earthy
Daearllys, n. the peony
Daearod, n. interment
Daearog, a. terrestrious
Daearogan, n. geomancy
Daearol, a. terrestial
Daearoldeb, n. terrestrialness
Daearoli, v. to terrestrify
Daearollad, n. terrestrification
Dacaru, v. to inter; to earth
Daed, ad. as good, so good
Daer, n. fixed state : a. slow
Daearawd, n. a claiming; a fixing [tuary
Daered, n. appurtenance; mor-
Daeargri, n. a doleful cry
Daeriad, n. a fixing, setting

Daerodi, v. to decree
Daeru, v. to fix, to decree
Dafad, n. a sheep, ewe
Dafaden, n. wart, schirrus
Dafadenog, a. full of warts
Dafadenu, v. to grow warty
Dafates, n. flock of sheep
Dafniad, n. a dropping
Dafnog, a. having drops
Dafnol, a. trickling, dropping
Dafnu, v. to trickle, to drop
Dafyn, n. a drop
Dagr, n. a tear, a drop; knife
Dagreuo, v. to lachrymate
Dagreuol, a. lachrymal
Dagru, v. to shed tears
Dai, n. that causes, the Deity
Daiar, n. the earth; earth
Daiawn, n. good: a. good
Daif, n. singe, blast
Daig, n. what is effused
Dail, n. leaves; foilage
Daill, n. product, issue
Dain, a. pure; fine; delicate
Daioni, n. goodness; good
Daionus, a. beneficial, good
Dair, n. an effusion, a song
Dais, n. a wish, a desire
Daith, n. flash, blaze
Dal, n. a hold, catch; a stop: v. to hold; to bear, to catch, to detain, to arrest
Dâl, n. a leaf, a lamina
Dala, v. to hold, to bear, catch
Dalbren, n. holdfast
Dalen, n. a leaf, a lobe
Dalenog, a, foliacious, leaved
Daleniad, n. foliation
Dalenu, v. to foliate
Dalfa, n. a capture, a hold
Daliad, n. holding
Daliaden, n. support, prop
Dalledydd, n. detainer
Daliwr, n. holder
Dall, n. blind one: a. blind
Dalliad, n. a blinding
Dallineb, n. blindness
Dallineb, n. blind worm

| DAL | 96 | DAM |

Dallt, n. the understanding: v. to understand
Dallu, v. to grow blind
Dam, a prefix to denote being about, or circumscribe
Damaethu, v. to be husbanding or cultivating
Damblygu, v. to fold round
Damborthi, v. to be upholding
Dambrynu, v. to be purchasing
Dambwyo, v. to beat about
Damcanu, v. to be contriving
Damchwa, n. an over-turn
Damchwaen, n. an accident
Damchweiniad, n. a chancing
Damchweinio, v. to happen
Damdeithio, v. to perambulate
Damdoi, v. to cover about
Damdorchi, v. to wreath about
Damdori, v. to cover about
Damdramwy, v. to travel about
Damdreiglo, v. to circumvolve
Damdreimio, v. to look about
Damdroi, v. to turn round
Damdrosi, v. to drive about
Damdrychu, v. to be amputating
Damdwrdd, n. a confused stir
Damdwyo, v. to be castigating
Damdyfu, v. to grow about
Damdyngu, v. to appraise
Damdyru, v. to heap about
Damdywys, v. to lead about
Damddal, v. to hold in [about
Damddyblygu, v. to be folding
Damfachu, v. to grapple about
Damfwrw, v. to cast about
Damffrydio, v. to flow about
Damgaeru, v. to fortify about
Damgludo, v. to carry about
Damglymu, v. to be tying about
Damlewyrchu, v. to illumine
Damlifo, v. to flow round
Damlunio, v. to be forming
Damlygu, v. to be elucidating
Damlynu, v. to adhere about
Dammeg, n. a parable
Dammegol, a. allegorical
Dammegu, v. to allegorize
Damnoddi, v. to be protecting
Damnoethi, v. to expose
Damnyddu, v. to twist about
Damranu, v. to be separating
Damred, n. circulation
Damredu, v. to circulate
Damrithio, v. to be seeming
Damrodi, v. to wheel round
Damrwymo, v. to be tying round
Damryson, v. to be disputing
Damrywio, v. to be varrying
Damsangu, v. to dance round
Damsathru, v. to tread round
Damwain, n. accident, chance
Damweiniad, n. a chancing
Damweiniaeth, n. a chance
Damweinio, v. to happen
Damwyn, n. fortune, hap
Dân, n. a lure, a charm
Danadl, n. the nettles
Danadlen, n. a nettle
Danas, n. deer; venison
Danfon, v. to send, to convey
Danfoniad, n. a sending
Danfonol, a. missionary
Danheddian, n. dentition
Danheddog, a. toothed
Danheddu, v. to teeth; to bite
Dannod, v. to reproach; to upbraid; to twit
Dannodiad, n. a reproaching
Dannodwr, n. upbraider

Daneiddiol, a. dainty
Daneithion, n. dainties
Danteithrwydd n. deliciousness
Dangos, v. to show, to disclose, or make known
Dangosadwy, a. ostensible
Dangosedigol, a. demonstrative
Dangoseg, n. an index
Dangosiad, n. a shewing
Dangosiadol, a. demonstrative
Dangosiadus, a. showy
Dangosol, n. indicative, shewing
Dangoswr, n. one who shews
Dar, a. prefix that implies before, upon, or about to be, anologous to PRE : n. a noise or din
Darammhau, v. to hesitate
Daramred, n. circulation : to go about
Daramrediad, n. a circulating
Darbenu, v. to raise upright ; to form a perpendicular
Darblygu, v. to double over
Darbod, n. a preparation : v. to prepare, to provide
Darbodaeth, n. forecast
Darbodiad, n. a preparing
Darbodol, a. precautious [ness
Darbodoldeb, n. precautious
Darbodus, a. provident
Darborthi, v. to sustain to main
Darbwyo, v. to verberate [tain
Darbwyll, n. persuasion
Darbwyllo, v. persuade
Darbwyso, v. to preponderate
Darchwantu, v. to covet
Darchwhareu, v. to sport about
Darchwennych, to covet greatly
Darchwilio, v. to pry about
Darchwyddo, v. to swell up
Darddiffynu, v. to protect
Darddodi, v. to prefix
Darddonio, v. to endow
Darddosbarthu, v. to elucidate
Darddringo, v. to climb up
Darddullio, v. to describe
Darddwyrain, v. to soar aloft

Darddwyso, v. to make dense
Darddychrynu, v. to intimidate
Darddychwel, v. to recur back
Darddyfod, v. to come to pass
Dareb, n. a proverb, an adage
Darebu, v. to use a proverb
Daredrych, v. to observe
Daredd, n. tumultuous din
Daregnïo, v. to use exertion
Daren, n. a noise, or din
Darestyn, v. to extend over
Darfachu, v. to grapple over
Darfaddeu, v. to be remitting
Darfalanu, v. to bud out
Darfathru, v. to trample over
Darfeilo, v. to pile up
Darfelyddu, v. to imagine
Darferu, v. to accustom
Darfaethu, v. to miscarry, to fail
Darfinio, v. to acuate, to edge
Darfod, n. a finish : v. to finish ; to be ended
Darfodadwy, a. perishable
Darfodedig, a. evanescent
Darfodedigaeth, n. consumption
Darfodiad, n. a finishing
Darfodoldeb, n. transientness
Darfodol, a. finishing, ending
Darfoddio, v. to please
Darfoethu, v. to nourish tenderly
Darfoli, v. to be celebrated
Darfolli, v. to receive kindly
Darfradu, v. to act treachery
Darfrathu, v. to vulnerate
Darfreinio, v. to dignify
Darfritho, v. to variegate
Darfriwio, v. to be fracting
Darfrochi, v. to be ruffling
Darfrodiad, n. embroidery
Darfrudio, v. to prognosticate
Darfrydio, v. to be throbbing
Darfrysio, v. to be speeding
Darfrywio, v. to make brisk
Darfrwytho, v. to blandish
Darfrydiol, a. residing, abiding
Dargadw, v. to be securing
Dargaenu, v. to stratify
Dargraethu, v. to restrict

DAR 98 DAR

Dargamu, v. to be bending
Dargantu, v. to form a rim
Darganu, v. to blanch
Dargasglu, v. to heap
Dargau, v. to envelope
Dargeisio, v. to persevere
Dargelu, v. to over-veil
Dargilio, v. to recede
Dargipio, v. to snatch
Dargipiwr, n. a snatcher
Dargledru, v. to lattice over
Dargleinio, v. to crawl
Dargleisio, v. to make weals
Darglodi, v. to extol
Dargludo v. to transport
Dargluddio, v. to overwhelm
Darglymu, v. to knot
Dargnifio, v. to toil
Dargnithio, v. to pat upon
Dargnoi, v. to keep gnawing
Dargochi, v. to redden
Dargodi, v. to rise over
Dargoddi, v. to oversway
Dargoelio, v. to credit partly
Dargoethi, v. to purify
Dargofio, v. to call to mind
Dargoffa, v. to memorize
Dargolledu, v. to cause a loss
Dargolli, v. to lose
Dargospi, v. to castigate
Dargrafu, v. to scrape
Dargraffu, v. to cause a mark
Dargrasu, v. to parch slightly
Dargredu, v. to half credit
Dargroni, v. to collect
Dargrothi, v. to bulge, or swell
Dargrwydro, v. to peregrinate
Dargrybwyllo, v. to intimate
Dargrychu, v. to ruffle [slightly
Dargrynu, v. to conglomerate
Dargrysio, v. to accelerate
Darguchio, v. to frown
Darguddio, v. to seclude
Dargulo, v. to narrow
Darguro, v. to reverberate
Dargwympo, v. to fall
Dargydio, v. to join
Dargyfaddo, v. to menace

Dargyfaddef, v. to own partly
Dargyhoeddi, v. to expose
Dargylchynu, to circumference
Dargynnullo, v. to heap
Dargynnwys, v. to make compact
Dargynnyg, to attempt or offer
Dargynyddu, v. to augment
Dargynu, v. to elevate
Dargyrchu, v. to resort [tend
Dargyrhaedd, v. to reach or ex-
Dargysdadlu, v. to proportion
Dargysgodi, v. to adumbrate
Dargysgu, v. to fall asleep
Dargysodi, v. to combine
Dargysoni, v. to harmonize
Dargystuddio, v. to excruciate
Dargysylltu, v. to conjoin
Dargywain, v. to convey
Darhedeg, v. to hover
Darheidio, v. to swarm
Darhonni, v. to assert
Darhuno, v. to doze
Dariad, n. a making a din
Dariasu, v. to pervade
Darladu, v. to be benevolent
Darlafaru, v. to enunicate
Darlamu, v. to hop
Darlechu, v. to skulk
Darledu, v. to expand
Darleddfu, v. to slant
Darleisio, v. to resound
Darleisiwr, n. reverberator
Darleithio, v. to make humid
Darlenwi, v. to superabound
Darlesu, v. to cause benefit
Dar'ethru, v. to slope
Darlethu, v. to overlay
Darleu, v. to lecture, to read
Darlewyrchu, v. to shine
Darlidio, v. to inflame
Darlifo, v. to flow
Darlith, n. a sermon, a lecture
Darlithio, v. to initiate
Darlithiwr, n. a lecturer
Darliwio, v. to give a tint
Darlochi, v. to give a refuge
Darloesi, v. to perfuse
Darloni, v. to gladden

| DAR | 99 | DAS |

Darlosgi, v. to singe
Darluchio, v. to sprinkle [ing
Darluniodraeth, the art of draw-
Darluddio, v. to obstruct
Darlunien, n. a map
Darlunio, v. to portray, to delineate, to represent
Darluniwr, n. an artist, drawer
Darlwybro, v. to tract [pering
Darlwyddo, v. to cause pros-
Darlwythiad, n. a loading
Darlwytho, v. to load
Dalyfnu, v. to polish
Darlyngcu, v. to eructate
Darlynu, v. to adhere
Darlythyru, v. to superscribe
Darlywio, v. to superintend
Darllain, Darllen, v. to read
Darllaw, n. a brewing: v. to pour, to brew
Darllen, v. to read, to peruse
Darllewyrchu, v. to illumine
Darmain, n. a prognostication v. to prognosticate
Darmerth, n. a preparation
Darmerthiad, n. a preparing
Darmerthu, v. to prepare
Darn, n. a piece, a patch
Darneidio, v. to hop
Darniad, n. a piecing
Darnio, v. to piece, a patch
Darnod, n. distinction
Darnodi, v. to distinguish
Darnofio, v. to swim
Daroddef, v. to suffer
Darofyn, v. to intimate
Darogan, n. prediction; to pre-
Daroganiad, n. predicting [dict
Daroganu, v. to predict
Daroganwr, n. a foreteller
Darogwyddo, v. to incline
Daron, n. the thunderer
Darostwng, n. debasement: v. to subdue .
Darostyngiad, n. subjection
Darostyngu, vo be subject
Darpar, n. preparation
Darpariaeth, n. a preparing

Darparu, v. to prepare
Darre, v. to effuse; to blush
Darstain, n. tinkle, a clang; v. to tinkle, to clang
Darsteinio, v. to tinkle
Darswydo, v. to intimidate
Darswyddo, v. to superintend
Darswyno, v. to enchant
Darsylw, n. an observation
Darsylwad, n. observation
Darsylwedd, n. an essence
Darsylweddu, v. to element
Darsylwi, v. to observe
Darsyllu, v. to stare, to gaze
Daru, v. to finish, to end; to tinkle, to clank
Darwain, n. ministration: v. to administer
Darwareu, v. to disport
Darwedd, n. compliancy
Darweddu, v. to direct
Darweiniwr, v. director, leader
Darweithio, v. to supererogate
Darwel, n. perspicacity
Darwcled, v. to perceive
Darwellad, n. perception
Darwenu, v. to smile
Darwib, n. a hovering
Darwibio, v. to hover
Darwirio, v. to assert
Darwystlo, v. to pledge
Darymchwelyd, v. to revert
Darymdeithio, v. to sojourn
Darymgeisio, v. to make effort
Darymranu, v. to divide
Darymred, n. an excursion: a colliquation; a diarhœa; v. to run; to move about; to run ont
Darymrithio, v. to seem to be
Darymroi, v. to resign
Darymsangu, v. to trample
Darymsathru, v. to tread
Darymsawdd, n. adjunct
Darystain, n. a tinkle a peal
Darysteinio, v. to tinkle,
Dâs, n. a heap; a stack
Dasedig, a. ricked, stacked

Dasgwrn, n. a cone, a rick
Dasgyrn, n. a stacking
Dasiad, n. a ricking, stacking
Dasmal, n. a gentle touch
Dasmalu, v. to touch gently
Dasol, a. cumulated; stacked
Dasu, v. to stack, to rick
Daswl, n. a pile; a stack
Daswrn. n. a cone; a pile
Dasyliad, n. a piling up
Dasylu, v. to pile, to rick
Dasyrnu, v. to heap, to rick
Dathliad, n. celebration
Dathlu, v, to celebrate
Dau, n. two, a. two
Daw, n. a boon; a son-in-law a coming onward
Dawd, n. a deposit; a giving
Dawes, n. a daughter-in-law
Dawg, n. a portion, or share
Dawn, n. gift; virtue; grace
Dawni, v. to gift, to endow
Dawnus, a, gifted, virtuous
Dawr, v. to care, to regard
De, n. activity; a parting, right, right side; the south : v. to part; to right; a. separate right; south
Dead, n. a parting; separation
Deadell. n. a flock, a herd
Deadellog, a. gregarious
Deadelliad, n. a herding
Deadellu, v. to form a herd
Deaeth, n. separation
Deall, n. intellect; understanding: v. to understand
Deallol, a. intellectual
Dealladwy, a. apprehensible
Dealledig. a. gifted with reason
Dealledigaeth, n. understanding, comprehension
Dealledigol: a. intellective
Deallgar, a. intelligent, wise
Deallgarwch, n. intelligence
Dealliad, n. intellection
Deallol, a. intellective
Deailt, n. understanding
Deailltiad. n. intellection

Dealltwr, n. intellectualist
Dealltwriaeth, n. understanding comprehension
Dealltwrus, a. intelligent
Deallu, v. to understand
Deallus, a. intelligent, knowing
Deau, n. the right; the south a. right, dexterous
Deawl, v. tending to separate
Debed, v. to go, to depart
Dechre, n. beginning, origin
Dechreuad, n. origination
Dechreuol, a. original, initial
Dechreu, v. to begin
Dechreuad, n. a beginning
Dechreuedig, a. begun
Dechreuol, a. initial primitive
Dechreuwr, n. a beginner
Dedfryd. n. restoration; verdict, adjudicant
Dedfrydiad, n. adjudication
Dedfrydol, a. adjudicating
Dedlidio, v. to be angry ag in
Dedwinedd, n. evanescence
Dedwino, v. to fade away
Dedwinoldeb, n. evanidness
Dedwydd, n. a state of bliss; a. of renewed intelligence; discreet; happy
Dedwyddiad, n. beatification
Dedwyddo, v. to beatify
Dedwyddol, a. beatific
Dedwyddus, a. beatific; blessed
Dedwyddwch, n. happiness
Dedwyn, a. calmed of passion
Dedylliad, n. a sucking
Dedyllio, v. to suckle
Dedd, n. an order, rule
Deddf, n. statute, law, ordinance
Deddfiad, n. ordination
Deddfol, a. ceremonial
Deddfolder, n. ordinateness
Deddfoli, v. to make ordinal
Deddfolrwydd, n. ceremonialness
Deddfu, v. to institute
Deddfwr, n. a legislator
Deëuad, n. rightly; southing

Deëuo, v. to use dexterity; to tend to the south
Def, n. use, one's own [sheep
Defeidiog, a. abounding with
Defeidydd, n. a shepherd
Defeita, v. to hunt after sheep
Defiad, n. a bringing
Defni, n. droppings, drops
Defniad, n. a trickling
Defnio, v. to drop, to trickle
Defnydd, n. element, matter
Defnyddgar, a. useful
Defnyddiad, n. materialation
Defnyddiadau, v. to materialize
Defnyddiodraeth, materialism
Defnyddio, v. to prepare matter to make use of
Defnyddiol, a. material; useful
Defnyddioldeb, n. materiality
Defnyddiwr, n. one who forms
Defnyn, n. a drop, a particle
Defnyniad, n. a dropping
Defnynu, v. to drop, to trickle
Defod, n. usuage, custom
Defodedig, a. iustituted
Defodi, v. to fix a custom
Defodiad, n. institution
Defodol, a. accustomed
Defodolder, n. customariness
Defodwr, n. an institutor
Defyn, n. matter or stuff
Deffro, a. moving awake: v. to rouse; to awake
Deffroad, n. a rousing; a waking
Deffrol, v. to rouse; to wake
Defröol, a. tending to awake
Deffrous a. wakeful
Deffrousrwydd, n. wakefulness
Deffrowr, n. an awaker
Deg, n. ten: a. ten
Degaid, n. a decade
Degban, a. having ten parts
Degeidio, v. to form decades
Degfed, n. a tenth: a. tenth
Degiad, n. a decimal
Degol, a. decadary; decimal
Degoli, v. to decimate
Degoliad, n. decimation

Degoliaeth, n. tithing
Degplyg, n. a decuple
Degryn, n. a single drop
Degryniad, n. a dropping
Degrynu, v. to fall in drops
Degsill, a. often syllables
Degtro, a. of ten turns
Degu, v. to decimate
Degwm, n. a tenth; a tithe
Degymiad, n. a tithing
Degymol, n. relating to tithe
Deheu, n. dexterity; south
Deheubarth, n. south region
Deheuder, n. dexterity
Deheudra, n. dexterousness
Deheuedd, n. dextrality
Deheuig, a. dexterous, dexter
Deheulaw, n. a right hand
Deheuol, a. dexter; southern
Dehongli, v. to interpret
Dehongliad, n. interpretation
Dehonglwr, n. expounder
Dehonglydd, n. expounder
Deifiad, n. a singeing, blasting
Deifio, v. to singe; to blast
Deifiol, a. singeing; blasting
Deifniad, n. nurturing
Deifriad, n. a setting in order
Deifriad, v. to put in regimen
Deifyr, n, a regimen; verse
Deigr, n. a drop; a tear
Deigriad, n. lachrymation
Deigrio, v. to shed tears; to
Deigrol, a. lachrymal [trickle
Deigryn, n. tear, drop
Deigrynol, a. falling in drops
Deigryniad, n. a trickling
Deigrynu, v. to fall in drops
Deigyniad, n. emanation
Deigynu, v. to emanate
Deilen, n. a leaf, foil
Deiliach, n. mixed leaves
Deiliad, n. folliatfon; subject, tenant
Deiliadaeth, n. foliage
Deiliant, n. foliation, foliage
Deiliar, a. foliacious, leafy
Deilio. v. to put out leaves

Deiliog, a. bearing leaves
Deilw, n. small of the leg
Deilliad, n. an issuing, a proceeding
Deillio, v. to derive, to proceed
Deilliol, a. proceeding, deriving
Deincod, n. teeth an edge
Deincodyn, n. apple seed
Deinio, v. to charm, to allure
Deintgraff, n. tooth drawer
Deintgryd, n. gnashing of teeth
Deintiad, n. dentition
Deintio, v. to teeth, to bite
Deintiol, a. dental
Deintlwch, n. tooth powder
Deintrod, n. cog wheel
Deintur, n. tenter frame
Deintws. n. little tooth
Deintwst, n. tooth-ache
Deintydd, n. dentist
Deiriad, n. a dinning
Deiryd, v. to belong, to pertain, to be related
Deisiad, n. a ricking, a piling
Deisio, v. to stack, to pile
Deisyf, n. request, intreaty: v. to request, to desire
Deisyfiad, n. a requesting
Deisyfol, a. beseeching
Deisyfu, v. to beseech, to crave
Deisyfwr, n. beseecher
Deisyn, n. hank, skein
Dêl, n. approach: v. will come; a hard or rigid state
Del, a. stiff; pert, saucy; smart
Delaidd, a. stiffish, smart
Delbren, n. log; cudgel
Delder, n. stiffness; pertness
Delfaen, n. delvin, kellus
Delf, n. a numskull; a churl
Delffaidd, a. oafish; stupid
Delffeiddio, v. to stupify
Delid, n. metal, mineral
Delor, n. wood-pecker
Delw, n. an image, idol, form, manner, semblance
Delwad, n. a formation, a forming. n. a statue

Delwadol, a. formative
Delwaddoli v. to idolatrize
Delwaddoliad, n. an idolling
Delwaddoliaeth, n. idolatry
Delwaddolwr, n. idolater
Delwant, n. imagery
Delwedd, n. resemblance
Delweddu, v. to describe, to portray, to make like a statue
Delwi, v. to give a form; to become as a statue; to wax pale, to be confounded
Dell, n. rift, slit or cleft
Delli, n. blindness
Dellni, n. blind state
Dellten, Delit, n. lath, splint
Delltenïad, n. splintering
Delltenog, a. splintered, latticed
Delltenu. v. to splinter to lattice
Delltwr, n. lattice maker
Deniad, n. an alluring
Denol, v. alluring, enticing
Denwr, n. enticer, seducer
Denu, v. to entice, to allure
Dengwaith, a. ten times
Dengyn, a. clownish, rustic
Deodi, v. to extract; to put off
Deol, n. exile, banishment: v. to banish, to separate
Deoladwy, a. separable, banish-
Deolawd, n. separation [able
Deoledig, a. exiled, separated
Deoliad, n. separation; a banishing   [giver; dean
Deon, n. the distributor; the
Deon, n. strangers, visitors
Deor, n. a hatching, a taking out of the shell: v. to brood to hatch
Deoriaid n. a hatched brood
Deorain, v. to brood, to hatch
Deoriad, n. a hatching
Deorllyd, a. in a state to hatch
Der, a. hard, stubborn
Dera, n. a fury, fiend, devil; the staggers
Deraidd, a. apt to be stubborn
Derbi, v. will come to pass

DER 103 DEW

Derbyn, n. a receipt; v. to admit, to receive
Derbynadwy, a. receivable
Derbynfa, n. receptacle
Derbyniad, n. reception
Derbyniol, a. admissible
Derbynioldeb, n. acceptableness
Derbyniwr, n. receiver
Derch, a. elevated, exalted
Derchafael, n. ascension
Derchafawl, a. elevating
Derchafiad, n. exaltation
Derchafiaeth, n. elevation
Derchafu, v. to elevate
Derchawl, a. elevating, exalting
Derchiad, n. an elevating
Derchu, v. to elevate, to exalt
Derdri, n. obduracy
Dere, v. come thou
Deriad, n. a frowardly acting
Deriaw, v. to act frowardly
Derlin, n. the heart of oak
Derlwyn, n. an oak grove
Derllydd, a. poured, effused
Derllyddiad, n. depletion
Derllyddu, v. to pour out
Dernyn, n. a piece, a patch
Derwin, a. oaken, made of oak
Derwydd, n. a druid
Derwyddol, a. druidic, druidical
Derwyddoni n. druidism
Deryw, v. it is done
Dês, n. system, order, rule
Desgyn, to ascend, to mount
Desgyneb, n. a climax (in rhe
Desgyniad, n. ascension (toric)
Desgynol, a. ascending
Dest, n. order, or trim
Destl, a. neat, trim; delicate
Destlaidd, a. apt to be trim
Destliad, n. a putting in trim
Destlu, v. to make neat
Destlus, a. nice, neat trim
Destlusrwydd, n. neatness
Dethol, v. to pick, to select
Detholedig, a. chosen, picked
Detholiad, n. a selecting
Deu, v. to come, to arrive

Deuad, n. coming, arrival
Deuarddeg, n. twelve
Deuawl, a. future, coming
Deubarth, a. of two parts
Deubarthiad, n. bisection
Deubarthu, v. to bisect
Deuben, n. a pair, two heads
Deubenog, a. two headed
Deublyg, a. double
Deublygiad, n. duplication
Deublygiaeth, n. duplicature
Deublygu, v. to duplicate
Deudro, n. two turns: a. twice
Deudroed, n. two feet
Deudroediog, a. bipedal
Deuddaint, a. bidental
Deuddeg, a. twelve
Deuddegfed, a. twelfth
Deuddyblyg, a. two-fold, duplicate
Deueiriog, a. equivocal
Deuenwol, a. binomial
Deufed, a. second
Deufin, of two edges, two-edged
Deugain, a. forty
Deugeinfed, a. fortieth
Deulais, a. of two sounds
Deuleisiad, n. diphthong
Deulin, n. the two knees
Deuliw n. two colours
Deulun, u. two forms; a pair
Deulygeidiog, a. binocular
Deunaw, a. eighteen
Deuochrog, a. of two sides
Deuodd, n. the twain, the two
Deuol, a. future, coming
Deurydd, n. the cheeks
Deuryw, n. two sorts or kind
Deutu, n. two sides; about
Deuwedd, n. two form
Deuwynebog, a. having two face
Dewin, n. a diviner, a wizard a. divine, theological
Dewines, n. a witch
Dewiniad, n. a divining
Dewiniaeth, n. divination
Dewinio, v. to divine
Dewis, n. choice
Dewisiad, n. a choosing

Dewiso, v. to choose [ect]
Dewisol, a. choice, desirable, sel
Dewr, n. a brave one, a hero: a. brave, bold; stout
Dewrâu, v. to grow bold
Dewrder, n. bravery, valour
Dewredd, n, bravery, prowess
Dewryn, n. a pert one
Di, a. privative pref., syn. with DIS, IN, IR, UN, LESS
Diarbed, a. unprogressive
Diach, a. void of origin
Diachles, a. unsuccoured
Diachludd, a. unobscured
Diachos, a. without cause
Diachub, a. not to be saved
Diachudd, a. unsecluded
Diachwyn, a. uncomplaining
Diadbryn, a. without redemption
Diadchwaeth, a. void of relish
Diadeg, a. inopportune
Diadflas, a. without relish
Diadfyd, a. unafflicted, unvexed
Diadgas, a. not disagreeable
Diadgof, a. void of recollection
Diadlais, a. void of resonance
Diadlam, a. not to be repassed
Diadlif, a. without a reflux
Diadnabod, a. unrecognized
Diadnair, a. reproachless
Diadran, a. undivided
Diadred, a. void of recurrence
Diadrwym, a. unrestricted
Diadwedd, a. void of retrospect
Diadwerth, a. undepreciated
Diadwyth, a. innoxious
Diaddurn, a. unadorned
Diadwyn, a. unkind; indecent
Diaddysg, a. learned
D.ael, a. without a brow
Diaelod, a. without a limb
Diaeth, a. without pain
Diafael a. without a hold
Diafiach, a. undiseased
Diafl, n. the devil
Diafles, a. void of advantage
Diaflwydd, a. void of misfortune
Diaflym, a. not blunt

Diafrad, a. without waste
Diafrwydd, a. unobstructed
Diagor, a. without opening
Diagwedd, a. void of method
Diangeu, a. deathless
Dianglad, n. an escape
Diangol, a. escaping
Dianc, n. escape, retreat; v. to escape, to avoid
Diaid, a. void of zeal
Diail, a. unequalled
Diailenedig, a. unregenerated
Dial, n. vengeance, revenge: v. to avenge; to revenge
Dialaeth, a. void of sorrow
Dialar, a. not mourning
Dialbren, n. a gallows
Dialedd, n. vengeance
Dialeddgar, a. vengeful, vindict-
Dialeddiad, n. an avenging [ive
Dialeddol, a. avenging
Dialeddu, v. to avenge
Dialfawr, Dialgar, a. revengeful
Dialiad, n. a revenging
Dialu, v. to revenge
Dialw, a. uncalled, unnamed
Dialydd, n. an avenger
Dialyddiaeth. n. vengeance
Diallu, a. unable, impotent
Diamcan, a. void of design
Diamdlawd, a. not necessitous
Diamddiffyn, a. defenceless
Diamgeledd, a. succourless
Diamgelog, a. uncircumspect
Diamgen, a. not otherwise
Diamgudd, a. not enveloped
Diamgyffred, void of comprehen-
Diamgylch, unsurrounded [sion
Diamhafal, a. incomparable
Diaml, a. unfrequent
Diamlwg, a. obscure
Diammhau, a. doubtless
Diammheuaeth, n. certainty
Diammhëus, a. unsuspecting
Diammod, a. unconditional
Diammynedd, a. impatient
Diamrafael, a. uncontentious
Diamrosgo, a. not unwieldy

Diamryfus, a. not excessive
Diamryson, a. void of strife
Diamwedd, a. incongruous
Diamwel, a. uncircumspect
Diamwes, a. void of enjoyment
Diamwys, a. unequivocal
Dianadl, a. breathless
Dianaf, a. without defect
Dianair, a. reproachless
Dianerch, a. ungreeted
Dianfodd, a. not unwilling
Dianfon, a. without mission
Dianfwyn, a. not unkind
Dianffawd, without misfortune
Dianhap, a. without mischance
Dianhardd, a. not unlovely
Dianhwyl, a. undisordered
Dianial, a. not overgrown
Dianian, a. unnatural
Diannedd, a. without dwelling
Diannel, a. aimless
Diannod, a. instantaneous
Diannog, a. unexited
Diannwyd, a. unchilled
Dianrheg, a. giftless
Dianrhydedd, without honour
Diantur, a. without enterprise
Dianudon, a. not perjured
Dianwadal, a. unwavering
Diaraf, a. not dilatory or slow
Diaraul, a. inclement
Diarbed, a. unsparing
Diarchenad, a. unclothed
Diarcholl, a. without wound
Diarchwaeth, a. tasteless
D.arddel, v. to expel: a. claim-
Diareb, a. proverb   [less
Diarebol, a. proverbial
Diarebu, v. to use adages
Diarebydd, n. proverbialist
Diarf, a. unarmed
Diarfaeth, a. void of purpose
Diarfer, a. unusual
Diarfod, a, inopportune
Diarffordd, a. out of the way
Diargae, a. without obstacle
Diargel, a. undisguised
D'argraff, a. unprinted

Diarlocs, a. exhaustless
Diarludd, a. unobstructed
Diarlwy, a. unprovided
Diarmerth, a. without provision
Diarobryn, a. unmerited
Diarofyn, a. unintentional
Diarogl, a. without scent
Diaros, a. without delay
Diarswyd, a. dauntless
Diartaith, a. without torture
Diarw, a. not rough
Diarwybod, a. unknowing
Diarwydd, a. without token
Diarymchwel, a. unreverting
Dias, n. a din, a clamour
Diasbri, a. without wiles
Diasgell, a. wingless
Diasgen, a. unblemished
Diasgloff, a. without lameness
Diasgwrn, a. without bone
Diaspad, n. a clangor, a cry
Diasped, v. to clang
Diaspedain, v. to resound
Diastrus, a. unperplexed
Diasu, v. to cling, to clamour
Diasw, a. not left or awkward
Diateb, a. unanswered
Diattal, a. unimpeded
Diattreg, a. undelayed, direct
Diattro, a. without reversion
Diathraw, a. without a teacher
Diathrawd, a. uncensured
Diathrin, a. unused to labour
Diau, a. true, surely
Diawch, a. unapt, not keen
Diawdlyn, n. beverage
Diawdwydd, n. bay-trees
Diawgrym, a. unskilful
Diawl, n. devil, one destitude of light
Diawlaidd, a. devilish; hellish
Diawledig, a. possessed of a de-
Diawles, n. a she devil   [vil
Diawlig, a. of devilish nature
Diawllo, v. to call the devil
Diaws, a. unapt
Diawydd, a. without avidity
Dib, n. a fall, a depth

Dibaid, a. unceasing, incessant
Dibaith, a. indistinct
Diball, a. sure, infallible
Dibara, a. not durable, short
Dibarod, a. unprepared
Dibarch, a. void ef respect
Dibech, a. without sin, sinless
Diben, a. headless, endless
Dibenaeth, a. without a chief
Diberchen, a. unpossessed
Diberfedd, a. without entrails
Diberthynas, a. irrelevent
Diberygl, a. without danger
Dibetrus, a. unhesitating
Dibil, a. having no peel
Dibl, n. a skirt; a daggle
Diblaid, a. without party
Diblant, a. childless
Dible, n. skirts; daggles
Dibleth, a. unplaited
Diblaid, n. bedaggling
Diblysg, a. without shell or husk
Diblo, v. to daggle, to draggle
Diblog, a. bedaggled
Diblu, a. featherless, unfledged
Diblwyf, a. having no parish
Diblydd, a. not mellow or soft
Diblyg, a. without a fold
Dibobl, a. without people
Diboen, a. painless; unwearied
Diboeth, a. without heat
Diborth, a. helpless, unaided
Dibr, n. a saddle
Dibra, v. to put on a saddle
Dibraidd, a. without flocks
Dibrawf, a. witbout proof
Dibres, a. without copper
Dibreswyl, a. having no abode
Dibrid, a. priceless
Dibridd, a. without earth
Dibryn, a. unscanty, unscarce
Dibriod, a. unmarried
Dibrudd, a. indiscreet
Dibrwy, a. improvident
Dibryd, a. inopportune
Dibryder, a. without anxiety
Dibryn, a. without purchase
Dibrysur, a. not diligent

Dibur, a. impure
Dibwyll, a. senseless, witless
Dibwys, a. not heavy, light
Dibybyr, a. void of energy
Dibyn, n. a steep, a hanging
Dibynai, n. a pendulum
Dibynaidd, a. pendulous
Dibyniad, n. an impending
Dibynog, a. appendant
Dibynol, a. impending
Dibynu, v. to hang, to depend
Dibynydd, n. dependent
Dicen, n. a hen, female bird
Dichell, n trick
Dichellgar, a. wily, crafty
Dichelliad, n. a devising
Dichellu, v. to use craft
Dichellus, a. crafty, inventive
Dichlyn, a. assidious
Dichlynder, n. assiduity
Dichlynedd, n. assiduity
Dichlynu, v. to act assiduously
Dichon, v. to be able
Dichoni, v. to be effectual
Dichoniad, n. effectuation
Dichwant, a. without desire
Dichwerw, a. not bitter
Dichwith, a. not awkard
Dichwyn, a. without weeds
Did, n. a teat; fluency
Didad, a. fatherless
Didaen, a. without expansion
Didaer, a. not importunate
Didal, a. without pay, unpaid
Didalch, a. unfractured
Didalm, a. incessant
Didanc, a. not tranquil
Didardd, a. uneffusive
Didarf a. unchased, a unscared
Didaro, a. unaffected
Didarth, a. without vapour
Didasg, a. without task or job
Didaw, a. not silent, or tacit
Didawel, a. not calm
Didawl, a. incessant, unabated
Didech, a. without skulking
Dideimlad, a. unfeeling
Dideithi, a. imperfect

Diden, n. teat, nipple
Didenog, a. having teats
Diderfyn, a. endless, boundless
Diderfysg, a. undisturbed
Didi, n. nipple, pap
Didlawd, a. not poor
Didlos, a. unhandsome
Didoi, v. to uncover
Didolc, a. without dent
Didoll, a. free of toll
Didonfryd, a. unfroward
Didoni, v. to pare, to peel
Didor, a. uninterupted
Didoraeth, a. unprofitable
Didorch, a. unwreathed
Didoriad, a. unbroken
Didost, a. unsevere
Didosturi, a. pitiless
Didrachwant, a. without lust
Didrafn, a. without change
Didrafferth, a. without bustle
Didraha, a. without haughti-
Didrai, a. undiminished [ness
Didraigl, a. without turning
Didraill, a. unrevolving
Didrais, a. without oppression
Didrallod, a. without distress
Didramgwydd, a. unstumbling
Didramwy, a. unfrequented
Didranc, a. endless; incessant
Didras, a. without kindred
Didraserch, a. without doating
Didraul, a. wasteless; inexpen-
  sive; without dimunition
Didraw, n. a stray
Didrawd, a. without currency
Didrawiad, a. unimpelled
Didraws, a. not cross
Didref a. without a dwelling
Didrefn, a. disordered
Didreftad, without inheritance
Didremyg, a. without contempt
Didres, a. without labour
Didreth, a. free of tribute
Didri, n. trouble
Didrist, a. undejected: n. the
  plant borage [ing
Didro, a. direct, without turn-
Didroed, a. footless
Didrosedd, a. without transgres-
Didru, a. without misery [sion
Didrugar, a. unpitying
Didrugaredd, a. merciless
Didrwch, a. not fractious
Didrwm, a. not heavy
Didrwst, a. noiseless
Didrwydded, a. unlicensed
Didrydar, a. without clamour
Didryf, n. solitary spot
Didrythyll, a. not wanton
Didrywedd, a. without instinct
Diduchan, a. without grumbling
Didudd, a. without sovering
Diduedd, a. impartial
Didwf, a. without growth
Didwg, a. unprosperous
Didwll, a. without hole
Didwn, a. whole, unfractured
Didwrf, a. without tumult
Didwy, a. unarranged
Didwyll, a. undeceitful
Didwyth, a. without elasticity
Didŷ, a. houseless
Didyb, a. unsuspected
Didymhestl, a. untempestuous
Didyner, a. not mild
Didyr, n. sadness, sorrow
Didywyll, a. not dark
Didywyn, without resplendence
Didda, a. without goodness
Diddannod, a. reproachless
Diddarbod, a. improvident
Diddarfod, a. endless
Diddawn, a. ungifted, graceless
Diddawr, a. unconcerned
Diddeall, a. irrational
Diddefnydd, a. unsubstantial;
  useless
Didderbyn, a. unreceiving
Diddestl, a. untidy
Diddewis, a. without choice
Diddial, a, without revenge
Diddichell, a. undesigning
Diddiflan, a. not evanescent
Diddiffodd, a. unquenchable
Diddig, a. appeased

Diddiglad, n. an appeasing
Diddillad, a. without clothes
Diddim, n. nothing: a. being nothing; worthless
Diddiogl, a. not lazy
Diddioich, a. unthankful
Diddirnad, a. not comprehended
Diddiwedd, a endless, infinite
Diddiwyll, a. uncultivated
Diddolur, a. painless. unailing
Diddori, v. to be unconcerned
Diddos, n. dry shelter: a. without drops
Diddosbarth, a. unclassified
Diddrwg, a. void of evil
Didduw, a. godless, atheistical
Diddwyn, a. being weaned
Diddyblyg, a. undoubled
Diddychryn, a. fearless
Diddyfniad, n. a weaning
Diddyfnu, v. to wean
Diddyled, a. out of debt
Diddym, a. destitute; void
Diddymadwy, a. defeasible
Diddymder, n. nothingness
Diddymedig, a. annulled
Diddymedigaeth, n. abrogation
Diddymiad, n. annihilation
Diddymol, a. annihilating
Diddymu, v. to annihilate; to annul; to depreciate
Diddyrus, a. not intricate
Diddysg, a. unlearned, illiterate
Diebrydol, a. obstructive
Diebrydu, v. to frustrate
Diebyd, n. onset, assault
Dieching, a. unstraitened
Diechrys, a. not alarming
Diechwith, a. not awkward
Diechyr, a. sturdy; inflexible
Diedfydd. a. certain, doubtless
Diedifar, a. impenitent
Dieding, a. unrestrained
Diedlaes, a. without drooping
Diedlid, a. without anger
Diedliw, a. reproachless
Diedlym, a. without pungency
Diedmyg, a. without reverence

Diedrin, a. without bustle
Diedrysedd, a. unsuperfluous
Diedw, a. unfaded
Dieddaint, a. incompact
Dieddrin, a. not mysterious
Dieddyl, a. not inherent
Dieflyn, n. a little devil
Diefras, a. not slender
Diefrydd, a. unmaimed
Dieffaith, a. ineffectual
Diegin, a. having no germ
Dieglur, a. indistinct
Dieglyd, a. unwavering
Diegni, a. without exertion
Diegryn, a. untrembling
Diegwan, a. not feeble
Diegweddi, a. dowerless
Diegwyl, a. inopportune
Diengyd, v. to flee, to escape
Dieiddil, a. not feeble
Dieiddo, a. without property
Dieilig, a. unharmonious
Dieinig, a. without agitation
Dieiriach, a. without dispute
Dieiriol, a. without intercession
Dieisiau, a. unnecessary
Dieisor, a. matchless
Dieithr, a. without exception
Dielusen, a. without charity
Dielw, a. worthless; ignoble
Diell, a. unblemished, perfect
Diemyg, a. not overthrown
Diemyth, a. infallible
Dien, n. extinction, death: a. calm, without motion
Dienaid, a. inanimate
Dienbyd, a. without peril
Diencil, a. not receding
Dienig, a. sad; without activity
Dienllib, a. irreproachable
Diennill, a. unprofitable
Dienw, a. anonymous
Dienwaededig, a. uncircumcised
Dienwaediad, a. uncircumcision
Dienydd, n. violent death
Dienyddiad, n. a putting to death
Dienyddol, a. life-divesting
Dienyddu, v. to put to death

Dienyddwr, n. an executioner
Dieppil a. having no issue
Dierbyn, a. without reception
Diergryd, a. without trembling
Diergryn, a. unshaken; fearless
Dierlyd, a. unpursued
Dierwin, a. not rough or harsh
Diesgeulus, a. not intelligent
Diesgud, a. not nimble
Diesmwyth, a. uneasy
Dietifedd, a. childish
Dieuog, a. guiltless
Dieurwydd, n. certainty
Diewyllys, a. intestate
Dif, n. a cast off, ejection
Difa, n. extermination
Difâd, n. an exterminating: a. destitute of good
Difaddeu, a. without remission
Difael, a. profitless
Difaeth, a. without nourishment
Difai, a. blameless, faultless
Difalch, a. void of pride
Difam, a. motherless
Difan, a. spotless, unspotted
Difancoll, a. total loss
Difaniad, n. a vanishing
Difant, n. a vanished state
Difanu, v. to vanish
Difanw, a. evanescent
Difanwl, a. not exact
Difar, a. without wrath
Difarf, a. beardless, shaved
Difariaeth, a. without mischief
Difarn, a. void of judgement
Difarw, a. deathless, immortal
Difas, a. not shallow
Difaswedd, a. without levity
Difechni, a. not having bail
Difedydd, a. unbaptized
Difeddiant, a. unpossessed
Difeddw, a. sober
Difefl, a. void of reproach
Difelo, v. to exculpate
Difeiriad, n. a repenting
Difenwad, n. a contemning
Difenwi, v. to contemn
Difenwyd, a. unblest; joyless

Difesur, a. immeasurable
Difeth, a. infallible, certain
Difiad, n. annoyance
Difilain, a. not ferocious
Difin, a. edgeless
Difio, v. to fling; to annoy
Difiog, a. annoying; wild
Diflaen, a. without point
Diflaen, n. beard of a dart: a. without a point
Diflan, a. without lusture; fading
Diflanedigaeth, n. disappearance
Diflaniad, n. a vanishing
Diflanol, a. evanescent
Diflant, n. evanescence
Diflanu, v. to vanish away
Diflas, a. tasteless; disgusting
Diflasdod, n. disgust, insipidity
Diflaslad, n. a disgusting
Diflasu, v. to disgust; to become disgusted
Diflin, a. not tired, unwearied
Diflisg, without shell; unpeeled
Diflodau, a. destitute of flowers
Diflwng, a. not sullen
Difoes, a. void of manners
Diforwyno, v. to constuperate
Difr, n. a cast; a metre
Difrad, a. not treacherous
Difradw, a. not defective
Difraint, a. not privileged
Difraisg, a. not bulky or large
Difrau, a. not fragile or brittle
Difraw, a. fearless; careless
Difrawd, n. dispersion; waste; devastation
Difrawu, v. to grow careless
Difrawwch, n. unconcern
Difreg, a. of frailty
Defreinio, v. to disfranchise
Difri, a. undignified, ignoble
Difrif, a. serious, sedate
Difrig, a. not having tops
Difrisg, a. trackless
Difro, a. exile: n. an exile
Difrodaeth, n. extravagance
Difrodi, v. to make havoc
Difrodiad, n. a wasting

Difrwysg, a. not inebriated
Difrycheulyd, a. immaculate
Difryd, having no mind; listless
Difrydaeth, n. inattention
Difrys, a. not in haste
Dif ryw, a. not luxuriant
Difuchedd, a. immoral
Difudd, a gainless not profitable
Difurn, a. free from evil design
Difwng, a. unwavering
Difwlch, a. breachless
Difwriad, a. undesigned
Difwrw, a. improvident
Difwyn, a. unenjoyed
Difydr, a. without meter
Difyfyr, a. uncontemplated
Difygwth, a. void of threatening
Difyngiad, a. void of stammering
Difyn, n. a fragment
Difyniad, n. a cutting to pieces
Difynio, v. to carve, to mince
Difyr, a. diverting, amusing
Difyredigaeth, n. amusement
Difyrgar, a. tending to divert
Difyriad, n. a diverting
Difyru, v. to divert, to amuse
Difyrus, a. divertive ; amusing
Difyrwch, n. diversion, play
Difysgu, v. to unmix, to separate
Difvw, a. lifeless, inanimate
Diffaeth, n. a wilderness ; an outcast ; a waif: a. unfruitful, barren, foul
Diffawd, n. a misfortune: a. unfortunate, luckless
Diffeithder, n. foulness
Diffeithfa, n. foul ground
Diffeithiad, n. a laying waste
Diffeithio, v. to lay waste
Diffeithwch, n. a wilderness
Differ, n. defence, guard
Differiol, a. defensive
Differu, v. to defend, to guard
Differyd, v. to defend, to ward
Difflais, a. not ravaged
Diffodd, n. what is extinct ; v. to extinguish
Diffoddi, v. to extinguish

Diffoddiad, n. extinction
Diffordd, a. pathless
Diffred, v. to protect
Diffrediad, n. protection
Diffreidiad, n. a protector
Diffreidio, v. to protect
Diffreidiog, n. a guardian
Diffrwyn, a. unbridled
Diffrwyth, a. fruitless ; feeble
Diffrwytho, v. to make abortive
Diffryd, v. to protect
Diffuant, a. unfeigned
Diffur, a. without perception
Diffwyn, n. defence, guard
Diffwys, n. a precipice
Diffydd, a. faithless, infidel
Diffyg, n. defect, failure. Diffyg yr haul, an eclipse of the sun. Diffyg anadl, shortness of breath
Diffygiad, n. defection
Diffygio, v. to be defective
Diffygiol, a. defective, weary
Diffyn, n. defence, guard
Diffynadwy, a. defensible
Diffynol, a. defensive
Diffyniad, n. a defending
Diffyniant, a. unprosperous
Diffynu, v. to defend ; to guard
Dîg, n. passion ; anger; ire : a. angry, displeased
Digabl, a. uncalumniated
Digadarn, a. not powerful
Digae, a. unenclosed, unfenced
Digaer, a. unwalled; unfortified
Digaeth, a. unconfined
Digaethiwed, a. unconfined
Digainc, a. not having branches
Digais, a. not seeking; negligent
Digaled, a. not obdurate
Digalon, a. heartless, dispirited
Digalondid, n. heartlessness
Digaloni, v. to dishearten
Digaloniad, a. disheartening
Digam, a. not bent
Digamwedd, a. faultess
Digamwri, a. void of iniquity
Digar, a. not loved ; forlorn

Digarad, a. disregarded; forlorn
Digarc, a. careless; unanxious
Digarchar, a. unimprisoned
Digardd, a. unstigmatised
Digariad, a. unbeloved, forlorn
Digaru, v. to cease loving
Digas, a. without hatred, unhated
Digaer, n. anger, displeasure
Diged, a. without treasure
Digedenu, v. to remove nap
Digeintach, a. without bickering
Digel, a. not hidden, not secret
Digelwydd, a. free from falsehood
Digellwair, a. not joking
Digen, a. without scales, or scurf
Digenedl, a. without a family
Digenfigen, a. without envy
Digeraint, a. without kindred
Digerdd, a. artless; songless
Digerth, a. not imminent
Digerydd, a. without rebuke
Digiad, n. an angering
Digib, a. having no husk
Digig, a. without flesh, fleshless
Digil, a. unreceding; firm
Digilwg, a. without frown
Digio, v. to offend, to anger
Diglefyd, a. free from disease
Digliw, a. incompact, deformed
Diglod, a. without fame
Digloff, a. not lame or halt
Diglwyf, a. uninfected; sane
Digllon, a. angry, wrathful
Digllonder, n. wrathfulness
Digllonedd, n. displeasure
Diglloni, v. to be displeased
Digoed, a. without wood
Digofaint, n. anger, displeasure
Digoll, a. without loss or lapse
Digolled, a. free of loss, safe
Digollediad, n. indemnification
Digolledu, v. make good a loss
Digon, a. & ad. enough
Digonedd, n. abundance
Digoni, v. to suffice, to satisfy
Digoniant, n. prevalency
Digonoi, a. sufficient; sated
Digonoldeb, n. abundance

Digonoli, v. to satiate
Digor, n. habit; passion
Digorffori, v. to disembody
Digosp, a. unpunished
Digost, a. without expense
Digraff, a. not keen
Digraid, a. impassionate
Digrain, n. error: a wandering
Digrawn, a. unaccumulated
Digred, a. unbelieving, infidel
Digreulon, a. not cruel
Digribddail, a. without extortion
Digrif, a. amusing, jocose
Digrifâu, v. to amuse, to please
Digrifedd, n. pleasantry
Digrifwch, n. amusement
Digrintach, a. not miserly
Digroen, a. having no skin
Digroniad, a. unbounded
Digrybwyll, a. not alluded to
Digrych, a. unwrinkled
Digryn, a. without trembling
Digryno, a. incompact, untidy
Digu, a. not affectionate
Digudd, a. unconcealed
Digus, a. displeasing
Digwl, a. blameless, faultless
Digwsg, a. sleepless
Digwydd, a. without lapse
Digydwybod, a. unconscionable
Digyfaill, a. friendless
Digyfanedd, a. not domestic
Digyfarwydd, a. uninformed
Digyfieuo, v. to disjoin
Digyfludd, a. unimpeded
Digyfnerth, a. helpless
Digyfnewid, a. unchangeable
Digyfoeth, a. without wealth
Digyfraid, wanting necessaries
Digyfraith, a. lawless
Digyfran, a. unparticipated
Digyfrif, a. of no account
Digyfrwng, a. not intervening
Digyfrwydd, a. unpropitious
Digyfwng, a. close, immediate
Digyfyng, a. unconfined
Digyffelyb, a. dissimilar, unparalleled

Digyffro, a. undisturbed
Digyngor, a. void of council
Digyngwedd, a. unassimilating
Digyngyd, a. inconsiderate
Digymal, a. jointless
Digymeriad, a. of no estimation
Digymhar, a. matchless
Digymhell, a. unconstrained
Digymhorth, a. helpless
Digymhwyll, a. irrational
Digymwl, a. cloudless
Digymysg, a. uncompounded
Digynaliaeth, a. without support or maintenance
Digynedd, a. without virtue
Digynhen, a. not discordant
Digynhwrf, a. unagitated
Digyniwair, a. unfrequented
Digynorthwy, a. helpless
Digynydd, a. without increase
Digynyrch, a. unproductive
Digynyred, a. unfrequented
Digynysgaeth, a. unendowed
Digyrith, a. not mean
Digysdadliad, a. incomparable
D'gysellt, a. unadapted
Digyswllt, a. disjunctive
Digywair, a. without order
Digywilydd, a. shameless
Dihaeddiant, a. unmerited
Dihafarch, a. not listless; energetic, courageous
Dihaint, a. without infection
Dihalen, a. without salt
Dihalog, a. unpolluted
Dihallt, a. not saline
Dihamdden, a. without leisure
Dihanfod, a. without existence
Dihap, a. luckless, unfortunate
Dihatriad, a. denudation
Dihawdd, a. not easy
Dihawl, a. without claim
Dihawnt, a. without alacrity
Dihedd, a. peaceless
Dihenydd, n. he that is without origin. Yr hen Ddihenydd, the ancient of Days
Diheurad, n. an apology

Diheured, n. adage
Diheuro, v. to apologise
Dihewyd, a. without zeal
Dihil, a. without progeny
Dihinedd, n. foul weather
Dihoced, a. fraudless, sincere
Dihoen, a. dispirited, cheerless
Dihocni, v. to grow languid
Dihoff, a. unamiable, unloved
Diholedig, a. undemanded
Dihort, a. without rebuke
Dihudd, a. without covering
Dihufen, a. having no cream
Dihul, a. without covering
Dihun, a sleepless
Dihwyl, a. disorderly
Dihyder, a. without reliance
Dihyfryd, a. unpleasant
Dil, n. structure; texture. Diliau, mêl, honeycomb
Diladrad, a. without theft
Dilaes, a. without trailing
Dilaeth, a. without milk
Dilafar, a. not loquacious
Dilain, a. worked upon; wasted
Dilaith, a. not moist or damp
Dilawch, a. without refuge
Dile, a. extinct; without place
Dilead, n. abolition
Dilech, a. not apt to sculk
Diled, a. without breadth
Diledach, a. not of base origin
Diledfryd, a. not listless
Dilediaith, adj. free from provincialisms
Diledief, a. of unbroken accent
Diledlyth, a. undejected
Diledrith, a. void of delusion
Diledryw, a. undegenerate
Dileddyf, a. unbiassed; direct
Dilëedigaeth, n. extinction
Diler, n. instrument
Dilerbren, n, meting rod
Diles, a. profitless, useless
Dilesg, a. unfeeble
Dilëu, v. to raze; to blot out
Dilew, a. not clever or skilful
Dilewych, a. unilluminated

Diliad, n. operation
Dilid, a. not wrathful
Dilin, a. wrought, beaten
Dilio, v. to make accurate
Diliw, a. colourless: n. phantom
Dilon, a. not pleased
Diludd, a. unobstructed
Diluddedu, v. to rid of fatigue
Dilun, a. awkward; formless
Dilwch, a. undusty
Dilwgr, undefiled, unpolluted
Dilwrf, a. uncowardly
Dilwybr, a. pathless, trackless
Dilwydd, n. the celandine
Dilŵydd, a. unprosperous
Dilwyn, v. to shed, to cast off
Dilwyth, a. not having a burden
Dilyd, Dilyn, v. to follow
Dilyfyn, a. not smooth
Dilygad, a. sightless, eyeless
Dilyniad, n. a following
Dilyniaeth, n. a following
Dilynol, following; consequent
Dilys, a. unavoidable; certain
Dilysdod, n. certainty
Dilysiad, n, a making certain
Dilysiant, n. unavoidableness
Dilysol, a. unacceptionable
Dilysioldeb, n. unavoidableness; inseparability
Dilysrwydd, n. certitude
Dilysu, v. to make unavoidable; to certify
Dilywodraeth, a. anarchial
Dill, n. a plait, a fold
Dillad. n. apparel, clothes
Dilladiad, n. a clothing
Dilladu, v. to clothe, to dress
Dilladwr, n. a clothier; a tailor, habit-maker
Dilliad, n. a folding
Dillni, n. smartness; elegance
Dillyn, n. an ornament: a. smart, trim, spruce
Dillynder, n. smartness, gaiety
Dillynes, n. a smart female
Dim, n. nothing; anything; something; everything; tri-
fle: a. no; any: adv. in no degree, not at all
Dimai, n. a halfpenny
Dimedd, n. nothingness
Dimeiwerth. a halfpenny worth
Din, n. a hill, fort, fortress
Dinag, a. without exception
Dinam, a. unexceptionable
Dinas, n. a city; a fortress
Dinasol, a. belonging to a city
Dinawdd, a. without perception
Dincod, n. teeth, an edge; apple seed
Dinerth, a. impotent; feeble
Dinerthedd, n. impotence
Dinesig, a. belonging to a city
Dinesydd, n. a citizen
Dinesyddiaeth, n. muncipality
Dinesyddio, v. to denizen
Dinewid, a. without change
Dinidr, a. without hindrance
Diniwed, a. harmless, innocent
Dinod, a. of no note or mark
Dinodd, a. without juice or sap
Dinodded, a. defenceless
Dinoeth, a. not naked or bare
Dinwych, a. not languishing
Dinwyf, a. without liveliness
Dinwyth, a. inoxious
Dinystr, n. destruction
Dinystriad, n. a destroying
Dinystrio, v. to destroy
Dinystriol, a. destructive
Diobaith, a. without hope
Diober, a. worthless, useless
Diochel a. unavoidable
Diod, n. drink, beverage
Diodgar, a. given to drinking
Diodi, v. to give drink
Diodid, a. not dubious
Diodlestr, n. a drinking cup
Diodr, a. uninterrupted
Diodrig, a. without delay
Diodrydd, a. given to drinking
Dioddef, a. without suffering
Dioed, a. without delay
Dioedran, a. not of age
Dioer, a. doubtless; verily

Diofal, a. careless; secure
Diofaledd, n. carelessness
Diofalu, v. to become careless; to make secure
Diofalus, a. negligent
Diofalwch, n. negligence
Diofer, a. not vain or useless
Diofid, a. without affliction
Diofryd, n. vow; decision
Diofrydiad, n. a vowing
Diofrydog, a. vowed; devoted
Diofyn, a. undaunted, fearless
Diog, a. slothful, sluggish, slow,
Diogan, a. reproachless [lazy
Diogel, a. unexposed; secure
Diogeledd, n. safety, security
Diogeliad, n. a securing
Diogelu, v. to secure, to guard
Diogelwch, n. safety, security
Diogelwr, n. a securer
Diogi, n. idleness, laziness
Diogi, v. to grow idle or lazy
Diogwydd, a. uninclined
Diogyn, n. idler, sluggard
Dioheb, a. unanswerable
Diohir, a. without delay
Diol, a. having no marks
Diolch, n. thanks; praise: v. to give thanks
Diolchgar, a. thankful; obliged
Diolchgarwch, n. thanksgiving
Diolchiad, n. a thanking
Dioledig, a. blotted out
Dioli, v. to blot out
Dioliad, n. obliteration
Diolo, v. to deveolpe
Diolrain, a. uninvestigated
Diolud, a. without wealth
Dioludd, a. unobstructed
Diolwch, v. to show gratitude
Diolwg, a. sightless, blind
Diommedd, a. without refusal
Diorchudd, a. undisguised
Diorchwyl, a. unemployed
Diorfod, a. unconstrained
Dioriog, a. unfickle; steady
Diormes, a. unmolested
Diorphen, a. without end

Diorphwys, a. restless
Diorsaf, a. unstationery
Diorseddiad, n. a dethroning
Diorseddu, v, to dethrone
Diorwag, a. not trifling
Diorwan, a. without feebleness
Dios, a. unmoved; doubtless
Diosg, v. to undress
Diosgryn, a. unagitated
Diota, v. to tipple
Diotach, n. a tippling
Diotty, a. tippling house
Diotwr, n. a tippler, a sot
Dir, n. force; certainty: a. of force; certain, sure: pref. denoting vehemence or excess
Diradd, a. without rank
Diragfarn, a. without prejudice
Diragfwriad, a. improvident; without predetermination
Diragfyfyr, a. unpremediated
Diragofal, a. improvident
Diragor, a. without excellence
Diragrith, a. without hypocrisy
Diragwel, a. without foresight
Diraid, a. unnecessary, useless
Diran, a. without division
Dirboen, n. extreme pain
Dirboeni, v. to excruciate
Dirchwant, n. ardent desire
Dirchwant, profuse perspiration
Dirdan, a. extremely distended
Dirdra, n. an outrage
Dirdynu, v. to pull extremely
Dirddwys, extremely condensed
Direb, n. a trite saying
Direidi, n. mischievousness
Direswm, a. irrational
Dirfaint n. extreme bulk
Dirfarn, n. a harsh sentence
Dirfawr, a. extremely large
Dirfod, v. to be of necessity
Dirganfod, v. to look earnestly
Dirgariad, n. extreme love
Dirgel, n. a secret place: a. secret, occult
Dirgeledig, a. secreted, hidden
Dirgeledigaeth, n. a mystery

Dirgeledd, n. secrecy
Dirgelfa, n. a secret place
Dirgelgynghor, n. privy-council
Dirgeli, n. secrecy, privacy
Dirgeliad, n. a secreting
Dirgelu, v. to secrete
Dirgelwch, n. a secrecy
Dirglwyf, n. extreme aching
Dirglymu, v. to tie tightly
Dirgrynu, v. to convulse
Dirgwyn, n. exteme complaint
Diriad, n. iteration; impulse
Diraiad, a. mischievous
Diried, a. unlucky; mischievous
Diriedo, v. to become unlucky
Dirinwedd, a. without virtue
Dirio, v. to iterate; to urge
Diriol, a. iterating; urgent
Dirlais, n, an emphasis
Dirmyg, n. irony; contempt
Dirmygiad, n. a slighting
Dirmygol, a. contemptuous
Dirmygu, v. to contemn
Dirmygus, a. contemptuous
Dirnad, surmise, discernment; v. to surmise; to discern
Dirnadiad, n. supposition
Dirni, n. extremity, vivacity
Dirnwyf, n. extreme vivacity
Dirodres, a. without pomp
Diroddef, v. to suffer greatly
Dironi, v. to shed grain
Dirperiad, n. a meriting
Dirperu, v. to deserve
Dirprwy, n. a supply
Dirprwyad, n. a supplying
Dirprwo, v. to supply
Dirprwywr, n. one who supplies; an agent; an attorney
Dirus, a. without starting
Dirwaedd, n. an outcry
Dirwaenu, v. to dissever
Dirwan, a. extremely weak
Dirwarthu v. to cover
Dirwasg, v. to press extremely
Dirwen, n. a broad smile
Dirwenu, v. to smile, to laugh
Dirwest, n. abstinence, fast

Dirwestfa. n. a fasting, a fast
Dirwestu, v. to abstain, to fast
Dirwgnach, a, without grumbling or murmuring
Dirwy, n. penalty, a fine
Dirwyad, n. a fining
Dirwym, a. without restriction
Dirwyn, n. violent passion
Dirwyo, v. to fine
Dirwyol a. finable, penal
Dirwystr, a. unobstructed
Dirybudd, a. having no notice
Diryfedd, a. not marvellous
Diryfyg, a. unpresumptuous
Dirym, a. without power; feeble
Diryw, a. debased, degenerate
Dis, a prefix synon. with un
Disail, a. without foundation
Disalw, a. not vile, undebased
Disar, a. without offence
Disathr, v. untrodden
Discar, a. unloved, inamiable
Discloff, a. not lame
Discudd, a. uncovered
Discyfrith, a. uncongenial
Discyn, v. to descend, to alight
Discynfa, n. place of descent
Discyniad, n. a descending
Discynol, a. descending
Disefyd, a. sudden
Disefydlog, a. unstationary
Disefydlu, a. to rid of stability
Disegur, a. without leisure
Disciblaut, a. unindulged
Discrch, a. without fondness
Diserfyll, a. not tottering
Diserth, a. not declivous
Diseuthyg, a. not abortive
Disgwall, a. without defection
Disgwrth, a. without resistance
Disgyr, a. without impulse
Disiarad, a. tacit, without talk
Disigl, a. firm, unshaken
Disiomi, v. to undeceive
Disiomant, n. indeception
Disliw, a. colourless; pale
Diso, adv. beneath, below
Disodli, v. to trip heels

Disoddi, v. to cease sinking
Dison, a. without noise, silent
Disoniarus, a. unsonorous
Disorod, a. pure
Disorodi, v. to clear of dross
Disothach, a. clear of refuse
Dispar, a. without parity; odd
Disporth, a. without support
Disprofi, v. to disprove
Dispur, a. impure, unclean
Dispwyll, a. crazy, distracted
Dist, n. joist in a floor
Distadl, a. object, worthless
Distadledd, n. worthlessness
Disudd, a. juiceless, sapless
Disug, a. juiceless
Disut, a. out of order; unwell
Diswn, a. without noise
Diswrth, a. not sluggish
Diswta, a. not sudden
Diswydd, a. without office
Diswyn, a. without charm
Disyched, a. without thirst
Disychedu, v. to allay thirst
Disyflyd, a. without motion
Disyfyd, a. unstaying: sudden
Disylw, a. heedless, inadvertent
Disylwedd, a. unsubstantial
Disylweddu, v. to unsubtiantiate
Disymud, a. immoveable
Disymudedd, n. immobility
Disymwth, a. sudden, abrupt
Disyndod, a. without surprise
Disynwyr, a. foolish, senseless
Ditiad, n. an uttering
Ditian, v. to speak, to say
Ditio, v. to utter or express
Diunion, a. undoubted
Diurddas, a. without dignity
Diurddiad, n. degradation
Diw, n. entireness: a. total
Diwad, a. without denial
Diwadnu, v. to trip up heels
Diwaddod, a. without dregs
Diwaddodi, v. to defecate
Diwaddoli, v. to disendow
Diwael, a. not vile or base
Diwaelod, a. bottomless

Diwaelodi, v. to clear of lees
Diwag, a. not empty or vague
Diwagedd, a. without vanity
Diwahan, a. indiscriminate
Diwahardd, a. unforbidden
Diwahodd, a. uninvited
Diwair, a. unimparting; continent, chaste; faithful
Diwaith, a. without work
Diwala, a. unsatisfied, not full
Diwall, a. not lacking
Diwalliad, n. a satiating
Diwallt, a. hairless, bald
Diwallu, v. to provide; to satiate; to divest of want
Diwarafun, a. unbegrudged
Diware, a. without play
Diwarogaeth, n. emancipation
Diwarogi, v. to emancipate
Diwarth, a. reproachless
Diwarthaf, a. without superior
Diwarthâu, v. to uncover
Diwarthrudd, a. reproachless
Diwarthu, v. to clear of reproach
Diwarthus, a. unreproachful
Diwasanaeth, a. unserviceable
Diwasgar, a. undispersed
Diwasgod, a. without shelter
Diwasgodi, v. to unshelter
Diwatwar, a. without mockery
Diwedydd, n. the evening; the end of the day
Diwedd, n. end conclusion
Diweddaf, a. last, latest
Diweddar, a. tardy, slow; late
Diweddarâu, v. to make late
Diweddaru, v. to become late
Diweddarwch, n. lateness
Diweddglo, n. conclusion
Diweddiad, n. ending
Diweddol a. conclusive
Diweddu, v. to end, to conclude
Diweddwr, n. a finisher
Diwegi, a. without vanity
Diweirdeb, n. continence
Diweirin, a. continent, chaset
Diweithred, a. without deeds
Diwellâu, v, to cease mending

Diwellig, a. not apt to fail
Diwellt, a. without grass
Diwen, a. without smiling
Diweniaeth, a. without flat'ery
Diwenwyn, a. not venomous
Diwerth, a. worthless
Diwes, a. immediate
Diwest, a. visitless, unvisited
Diwestl, a. without confusion
Diwesu, v. to approximate
Diwg, a. not frowning
Diwir, a. without truth
Diwisg, a. without covering
Diwladaidd, a. not rustic
Diwlith, a. dewless
Diwlydd, a. without vegetation
Diwni, a. seamless
Diwobrwg, a. rewardless
Diwosgo, a. without flinching
Diwosgryn, a. without trembling
Diwraidd, a. without root
Diwregysu, v. to ungirdle
Diwreiddiad, n. eradication
Diwreiddio, v. to eradicate
Diwres, a. without heat
Diwrnod, n. a day
Diwrnodol, a. diurnal
Diwrnodio, v. to do a day's work
Diwrtaith, a. unameliorated
Diwrth, a. without opposition
Diwrthdro, a. without reverting
Diwrthdyn, without contention
Diwrthddadl, a. without controversy or dispute
Diwrtheb, a. uncontradicted
Diwrthladd, a. unrepugnant
Diwrthlam, without recurrence
Diwrthryn, a. without resistance
Diwrthwyneb, a. unopposed
Diwrthymdrech, a. irresistible
Diwryg, a. feeble, infirm
Diwrym, a. seamless
Diwybod, a. unknowing
Diwyd, a. adherence; assiduous, diligent
Diwydiaeth, n. assiduity
Diwydio, v. to be diligent
Diwydrwydd, n. diligence

Diwyg, n. a repaired state; a not vitiated
Diwygiad, n. reformation
Dwygiadwy, a. reformable
Diwygio, to amend, to reform
Diwygol, a. corrective
Diwygiwr, n. reformer
Diwyl, a. unbashful, impuden
Diwyledd, n. impudence
Diwyll, n. clearance; culture
Diwylliad, n. cultivation
Diwylliant, n. culture, worship
Diwyllio, v. to cultivate
Diwyliodraeth, n. cultivation
Diwyn, a. not white or fair
Diwyniad, n. a dirtying
Diwyno, v. to dirty
Diwyr, a. not oblique, straight
Diwyth, a. without wrath
Diymadferth, a. inactive
Diymanerch, a. ungreeted
Diymarbed, a. unabstemious
Diymarbod, a. unprepared
Diymarfer, a. unaccustomed
Diymattal, a. unrestrained
Diymchwiliad, a. uninquisitive
Diymdaro, a. unable to strive
Diymdro, a. inflexible
Diymddiffyn, a. defenceless
Diymddiried, a. unconfiding
Diymgais, a. void of exertion
Diymgel, a. unsecluding
Diymgeledd, a. uncherished
Diymgudd, a. unsecluded
Diymgyrch, a. unapproached
Diymmod, a. steadfast
Diymogel, a. unguarded
Diymoralw, a. uninquisitive
Diymosgryn, a. unable to crawl
Diymryson, a. without dispute
Diymroad, a. unresolved
Diymsyniad, a. insensible
Diymwad, a. undeniable
Diymwared, a. irremediable
Diymwasg, a. uncompressed
Diymwel, a. unvisiting
Diymwrthladd, a. unopposing
Diymwrthryn, a. unresisting

Diyni, n. without vigour
Diysbryd, a. lifeless, spiritless
Diysig, a. unconsuming
Diysgog, a. immovable
Diystryw, a. void of tricks
Diystwng, a. unsubjected
Diys'yr, a. inconsiderate
Diystyriaeth, inconsiderateness
Diystyru, v. to despise
Do, adv. yes, yea
Dobrwy, n. a bribe; a fee
Dobrwyo, v. to bribe; to fee
Dobry, adv. underneath, below
Doco, adv. yonder
Dodi, v. to put, to lay, to deposit, to place, to give
Dodiad, n. a laying; a giving
Dodiadol, a. positional
Dodol, a. posited, set, laid
Dodrefn, n. furniture
Dodrefniad, n. a furnishing
Dodrefnu, v. to furnish
Dodrefnyn, a piece of furniture
Dodw, n. a laying, a setting
Dodwy, v. to lay, to deposit
Doddi, v. to come
Doe, n. yesterday
Doedyd, v. to say, to speak
Doeth, a. wise
Doethder, n. wisdom
Doethi, v. to show wisdom
Doethineb, n. wisdom
Doethyn, n. wiseacre
Dof, n utensil: a. tame, gentle
Dofaeth, n. domesticity
Dofawd, n. training
Dofedig, a. trained, tamed
Dofiad, n. a taming
Dofr, n. trained state
Dofraeth, n. usage; domesticity, lodging, quarters
Dofredig, a. domiciliated
Dofreithiad, n. domiciliation
Dofreithio, v. to domiciliate
Dofriad, n, domiciliation
Dofrol, a. domiciliating
Dofydd, n. one who forms or trains, tamer: the Lord

Dofyddiad, n. organiser
Dog, n. share, dividend
Dogn, n. due quantity, share
Dognedd, n. quantity; enough
Dogni, v. to proportion
Dogniad, n. proportioning
Dognol, a. proportional
Dôl, n. a winding; bow; dale; ring; noose, loop
Dolog, a. having windings
Dolef, n. shout
Dolefain, v. to shout
Dolen, n. loop, ring, bow
Doleniad, a. a forming a bow, ring or loop
Dolenu, v. to form a ring
Dolff, n. curve or bow
Dolffyn, n. dolphin
Doli, v. to form a ring or loop
Doloch, n. moan, wailing
Dolur, n. ache, pain, soar
Dolurio, v. to pain, to ache
Dolurus, a. sore, painful
Dolwch, n. adoration
Dolystain, n. trembling noise
Dolysteinio, v. to quiver
Dolystum, n. curved form
Dolystumiad, n. a. curving
Dolystumio, v. to curve
Don, a. that overspreads
Dondiad, n. a taunting
Dondio, v. to taunt
Doniad, n. an endowing
Donio, v. to endow, to gift
Doniog, a. endowed, gifted
Doniol, a. endowing, giving
Dôr, n. a clausure; door
Dorfod, v. to be concerned
Dorglwyd, n. covering hurdle
Dori, v. to be concerned
Doriad, n. a being concerned
Dorlawd, n. a fondling
Dorlota, v. to fondle
Dorth, n. covering; limit
Dos, n. drop, particle: v. go, do thou go [ion
Dosbarth, n. class, discriminat-
Dosbarthedig, a. classified, dis-

tinguished; discriminated
Dosbarthedigaeth, n. classification, distinction
Dosbarthiad, n. distinguishing
Dosbarthol, a distributive
Dosbarthu, v. to distribute, to distinguish, to determine
Dosbarthus, a. discretive
Dosbarthwr, n. distributer, an analyser
Dosben, n. a particular
Dosbeniad, n. a particularising
Dosi, v. to trickle, to drop
Dosiad, n. a trickling, dropping
Dosog, a. having drops
Dosol, a. dropping
Dosraniad, n. an analysing
Dotiad, n. a confusing
Dotian, v. to confuse
Dotio, v. to confuse, to puzzle
Dra, n. produce, essence
Draen, n. prickle, thorn
Draenog, n. hedgehog: a. full of prickles
Draenblu, n. down feathers
Draened, n. urchin, hedgehog
Draenen, n. thorn, thornbush
Draeneta, v. to hunt urchins
Draenglwyd, n. thorn hurdle
Draenllwyn, n. thorny brake
Drag, n. fragment, piece
Dragiad, n. tearing in pieces
Dragio, v. to tear in pieces
Dragiog, a. having rents
Dragon, n. leader in war
Dragwm, n. scaly coat
Draig, n. dragon; lightning
Drain, n. thorns, prickles
Draw, ad. yonder, at a distance

Dreiniog, a. thorny
Dreinllyd, a. thorny, prickly
Dreinios, n. small prickles
Drel, n. clown
Drelaidd, a. churlish, boorish
Drelgi, n. churlish dog
Dreliad, n. a scolding
Drelio, v. to use low abuse
Drelyn, n. a churlish one
Drem, n. sight, look, aspect
Drew, n. stench, stink
Drewbryf, n. bug
Drewedig, a. stinking
Drewg, n. the darnel
Drewgoed, n. bean trefoil
Drewi, n. stench, stink
Drewiant, n. a stinking
Drewsawr, n. fetid smell
Dring, n. a flight of steps
Dringediad, n. escalade
Dringfa, n. a place to climb
Dringiad, n. a climbing
Dringiedydd, n. a climber
Dringlyn, n. a pendulum
Dringo, v. to climb
Drud, n. a daring one, a hero: a. daring; dear, costly
Drudaniaeth, n. a dearth
Drudiant, n. forwardness
Drudwen, n. a starling
Drudws, n. the starlings
Drudwst, n. a chattering
Drudwy, n. chatter; starling
Drwg, n. evil mischief: a. evil, bad, naughty
Drws, n. a doorway, a door
Dry, a. forward, foremost
Drych, n. aspect; mirror
Drychiannog, a. sightly

Drydol, a. economical
Drygair, n. an ill report
Dryganedd, n. evil disposition
Dryganiaeth, n. mischief, malignity
Dryganian, n. malignity
Dryganianu, v. to fly in passion
Drygarfer, n. bad custom
Drygbwyll, a. irrational
Drygdyb, n. bad opinion
Drygdybio, v. to think evil of
Drygdybus, apt to think evil
Drygddamwain, n. mischance
Drygddyn, n. mischievous person, wicked fellow
Drygedd, n. malignity
Drygewyllys, n. ill will
Drygfoes, n. ill manners
Drygfwriad, n. evil intention
Drygfyd, n. adversity
Dryghin, n. badly inclined
Drygioni, n. badness, mischief
Drygionus, n. vicious, wicked
Dryglam, n. a mischance
Drygnaws, n. peevishnes
Drygsawr, n. bad smell
Drygu, v. to harm, to hurt
Drygus, a. tending to evil
Drygweithred, n. evil deed
Drygweithredwr, n. an evil doer; culprit, felon
Drygyrferth, n. a wailing
Dryll, n. a piece, a fragment a [gun
Drylliach, n. dribbets, snips
Drylliad, n. a breaking in pieces
Dryllio, v. to break in pieces
Drylliog, a. shattered, broken
Dryllyn, n. small piece
Dryllyniach, n. dribblets
Dryntol, Dyrnddol, n. the handle, of a cup pot or jug
Dryon, n. the supreme one
Drysawr, n. a door-keeper
Drysores, n. a door-keeper
Drysu, n. briar brambles
Dryw, n. a druid; a wren
Drywol, a. druidical, druidic
Du, n. ink; adj. black, sable; gloomy

Duad, n. a blacking; a bay in a building; length of plough
Duch, n. a sigh; a groan [land
Duchan, n. a lampoon; a jeer
Duchaniad, n. a lampooning
Duchanol, a. lampooning
Duchanu, v. to lampoon
Duder, n. darkness; gloom
Dudew, a. thick black
Duedd, n. blackness gloom
Dueg, n. melancholy
Dug, n. that is over; a duke
Duges, n. a duches
Dugiaeth, n. a dukedom
Dugiol, a. belonging to a duke
Duglais, n. a black stripe
Duglwyd, n. the restharrow
Dul, n. bang, thump
Dulaid, n. a thumping
Dulas, a. blackish blue
Dulio, v. to bang, to thump
Duloew, a. of shining black
Dulwyd, n. dusky colour
Dulyn, n. black water; melancholy; Dublin
Dulys, n. lovage, an herb
Dull, n. figure, shape, farm, manner; pattern
Dulliad, n. formation
Dulliedig, a. formed, modified
Dullio, v. to form, to shape
Dullnewid, v. to transfigure
Dullnewidiad, transfiguration
Dullwedd, n. style
Duo, v. to blacken; to darken
Dur, n. hard matter; steel
Duraidd, a. of steely nature
Durdeb, n. steeliness; solidity
Duren, n. a steel to strike fire
Durew, n. a black frost
Durf, n. what is dense
Durfin, a. dense, close hard
Durfing, a. dense,; austere
Duriad, n. a steeling
Durio, v. to steel; to edge
Duro, a. of steel; solid, a dense
Duryn, n. a beak, a snout
Durynog, a. beaked, snouted

Duw, n. God, the Deity
Duwdeb, n. divinity
Duwdod, n. Godhead
Duwiaeth, n, deism, Godhead
Duwies, n. a goddess
Duwin, a. of divine nature
Duwindeb, n. divine nature
Duwineb, n. divinity
Duwinydd. n. a theologian, a
Duwinyddiaeth,theology [divine
Duwiol, a. godly, pious
Duwiolaeth, n. theocracy
Duwioldeb, n. godliness, piety
Duwioli, v. to deify
Duwioliad, n. deification
Dwb, n. mortar, cement
Dwbiad, n. a daubing
Dwbio, v. to daub, to plaster
Dwbiwr, n. plasterer
Dwbl, a. twofold, double
Dwf, n. what glides ; a glider
Dwfn, a. deep
Dwfr, n. water
Dwg, n. a bearing a carrying
Dwgan, n. a trull, a trab
Dŵl, n. reason. judgement
Dwlw, n. action of the mind
Dwll, n. an overspread
Dwn, n. a murmur; bass: a. dun, swarthy, dusky
Dwnad, n. report, rumour
Dwndriad, n. a prating
Dwndro, v. to prate, to chat
Dwndwr, n. prating, tattle
Dwned, v. to express, to say
Dwr, n. a fluid ; water
Dwrd, n. a threat; a chiding
Dwrdiad, n. a chiding
Dwrdio, v. to chide; to threaten
Dwrdiol, a. chiding
Dwrdd, n. a rustle, a stir
Dwrn, n. a fist ; a hand
Dws, n, what oozes out
Dwsel, n. a faucet, a tap
Dwthwn, n. a juncture; day
Dwy, n. a cause ; rule, order : two [wings
Dwyadeinio, a. having two

Dwyar. n. stirrups
Dwydon, n. a dipthoug
Dwydalenog, a. bipetalous
Dwyeg, n. a milt. a spleen
Dwyen, n. the gills
Dwyf, n. the self-existent
Dwyfasglog, a. bivalve
Dwyfawg, n. tne betany
Dwyfed, a. second
Dwyfol, a. divine, godly
Dwyfolaeth, n. deification
Dwyfolder, n. godliness
Dwyfoli, v. to deify
Dwyfron, n. the breasts
Dwyfroneg, n. the breast-plate
Dwylaw, n. the two hand
Dwyliw, n. two female parties
Dwylofaid, the full of both hands
Dwylofi, v. to stroke with hands
Dwyn, a. agreeaable : v. to bear, to carry; to carry away ; to
Dwyndeb, n. pleasantness [steal
Dwynol, a. pleasing, agreeable
Dwyr, n. the dawn ; orient
Dwyrain, n. the east : a. abounding with dawnings
Dwyran, n. two shores
Dwyre, n. a bursting to light : v. to rise, to view
Dwyread, n. a rising up
Dwyreain, v. to rise, to view
Dwyreiniol, a. oriental
Dwyreinwynt n. east wind
Dwyreol, a. ortive, surgent
Dwys, a. dense, heavy, grave
Dwysder, n. density, gravity
Dwysiad, n. condensation
Dwysill, n. dissyllable
Dwyso, v. to condense
Dwysogaeth, n. condensation
Dwysol, n. condensing
Dwyw, n. producing cause
Dwywaith, adv. twice
Dy, a pref. denoting, force and iteration : pron. thy, or thine
Dyad, n. effect, efficacy
Dyadel, v. to leave, to suffer
Dyall, n. the understanding ; v.

to understand, to comprehend
Dyalladwy, a. comprehensible
Dyar, n. a din, noise: v. to make a tumult
Dyarchiad, n. a demanding
Dyaros, v. to be tarrying
Dyban, n. an ant, emmet
Dybarthu, v. to be separating
Dyben, n. conclusion, end
Dybendod, n. conclusion
Dybeniad, n. a concluding
Dybenol, a. concluding
Dybenrwydd, n. conclusiveness
Dybenu, v. to conclude
Dybleidio, v. to take a part
Dyblisgo, v. to strip off shells
Dyblyg, n. a double, a fold: a. double folded
Dyblygiad, n. a doubling
Dyblygol, a. duplicative
Dyblygu. v. to double, to fold
Dyboeri, v. to spit about
Dybori, v. to browse
Dyborth, n a support
Dyborthi, v. to support
Dyborthiad, n. a supporting
Dybreiddio, v. to be depredating
Dybry, n. the sea-hen
Dybryd, a. sad; ugly; horrid
Dybryder, n. pensiveness
Dybryderu, v. to be sadly musing
Dybryn, n. purchase: merit
Dybrynol, a. meritorious
Dybrynu, v. to get esteem
Dyburo, v. to purify
Dybwyllo, v. to persuade
Dybyr, a. pensive, or sad
Dybyrdod, n. a melancholy
Dybyrio, v. to depress
Dych, n. a groan, sigh
Dychan, n. groan
Dychiad, Dychiant, n. a sigh
Dychio, v. to sigh, to groan
Dychiori, v. to utter sighs
Dychlaig, n. a drooping
Dychlais, n. a breaking out
Dychlam, n. a fluttering
Dychlamiad, n. a fluttering

Dychlamol, a. fluttering
Dychlamu, v. to flutter
Dychlyd, n. what is carried
Dychludo, v. to carry
Dychluddo, v. to inclose
Dychrain, n. a crawling
Dychre, n. a croaking
Dychreu, v. to croak
Dychrymu, v. to how
Dychryn, n. terror, frigh
Dychrynadwy, a. terrible
Dychryndod, n. terror [ened
Dychrynedig, a. terrified, fright-
Dychryniad, n. a a frightening
Dychrynllyd, a. fearful terrible
Dychrynol, a. terrifying
Dychrynu, v. to frighten
Dychrynwr, n. a trembler, frigt
Dychrys, n. haste, hurry [ener
Dychrysiad, n. a hurrying
Dychrysio, v. to hurry
Dychurio, v. to be afflicted
Dychwaen, n. chance, event
Dychwaeth, n. relish
Dychwant, n. appetite
Dychwardd, n. laughter
Dychwedlu, v. to discourse
Dychwel, n. a turn, course
Dychweladwy, a. revertible
Dychweledig, a. reversed
Dychwelfa, recurrence; return
Dychweliad, n. a recurring; a returning; a conversion
Dychwelwr, n. one who turns, or returns; a convert
Dychwelyd, v. to return
Dychwydd, n. a heaving
Dychwyl, a. revolution
Dychwysu, v. to sweat
Dychyfaer, n. recounter
Dychyfalûu, v. to assimilate
Dychyfarfod, v. to meet
Dychyfcirio, v. to come in contact
Dychyfiad, n. equalisation
Dychyfuno, v. to agree
Dychyffröi, v. to agitate
Dychymyg, n. invention; a riddle or enigma

Dychymygiad, n. a devising
Dychymygol, a. imaginary
Dychymygu, v. to devise
Dychymygwr, n. a deviser
Dychymysg, n. commixion
Dychyrchu, to come on, to resort
Dyd, interj. hold, avast
Dydach, v. to skulk, to lurk
Dydanio, v. to take fire, to ignite
Dydarddu, v. to break out, to
Dydechu, v. to skulk [spring forth
Dydi, pron. thou, thee [divided
Dydoledig, segregated; parted or
Dydoleg, n. a diæresis
Dydoli, v. to segregate
Dydoli, v. to segregate
Dydoliad, n. a segregating
Dydoliaeth, n. segregation
Dydolwr, n. separator, a divider
Dydoni, v. to pare a surface
Dydori, v. to break
Dydreiddio, v. to penetrate
Dydrëu, v. to bore, to pierce
Dydrwyno, v. to follow a scent
Dydwyllo, v. to deceive
Dydwytho, v. to make elastic
Dydynu, v. to attract
Dydd, n. a day; day-time, Four divisions: bore, morning; anterth, forenoon; nawn, noon; echŵydd, evening
Dyddad, n. a becoming day
Dyddamwain; n. a casualty
Dyddan, a. alluring, amusing
Dyddan-gar, a. diverting
Dyddaniad, n. a diverting
Dyddanol, a. tending to allure
Dyddanu, v. to divert, to amuse
Dyddanwch, n. diversion; pleasantness; comfort
Dyddanwr, Dyddanydd, a comforter, a consoler; a diverter
Dyddarbod, n. providence
Dyddarfod, v. not to be ending
Dyddarnu, v. to cut in pieces
Dyddâu, v. to become day
Dyddawed, v. to come
Dyddawr, n. a being concerted

Dyddeisyf, v. to implore
Dyddelu v. to come
Dyddelwi, v. to be as an image
Dyddenu, v. to entice
Dyddestlu, v. to decorate
Dyddfiad, n. a growing pale
Dyddfu v. to grow pale
Dyddiad n. a dating, a date
Dyddiadur, n. diary, journal
Dyddiant, n. fixing a day
Dyddio, v. to become day; to [date
Dyddigio, v. to irritate
Dyddiol, a. daily, diurnal
Dyddlyfr, n. an almanac
Dyddisgyn, v. to descend
Dyddiwr, days-man
Dyddolwch, n. worship
Dyddon, n. a blank: a. blank
Dyddonio, v. to endow
Dyddordeb, n. concern
Dyddori, v. to be concerned
Dyddoriad, n. a caring for
Dyddoriant, n. concern, care
Dyddosbarthu, v. to analyse
Dyddwyn, v. to bear; to convey
Dyddwyrain, v. to rise
Dyddwyre, v. to ascend
Dyddwyso, v, to condense
Dyddyfnu, v. to absorb
Dyddyfru, v. to water
Dyddygyd, v. to convey, to bear
Dyddym, n. a mere nothing
Dyddamgyrchu, v. to congregate
Dyddymant, n. annihilation
Dyddymol, a. annihilating
Dyddymu, v. to annihilate
Dyddyrchafu, v. to elevate
Dyddyrchu, v. to rise
Dycithrad, n. estrangement
Dyeithr, n. a stranger: a. excepted; strange: conj. except
Dyeithriad, n. s ranger
Dyeithro, v. to estrange
Dyelw, n. a right
Dyen, a. brisk, active
Dyenig, a. frank; generous
Dyerbyn, v. to receive
Dyerchi, v. to demand

Dyethol, v. to select
Dyfachu, v. to grapple
Dyfais, n. device, invention
Dyfal, n. simile, riddle :a. incessant; tedious; diligent; industrious
Dyfalâd, n. a going on
Dyfalâu, v. to be going on
Dyfalder, n. diligence
Dyfalgerdd, n. descriptive song
Dyfaliad, n. making a simile
Dyfalu, v. to make a simile to liken; to guess to describe
Dyfarnu, v. to pass sentence
Dyfeirio, v. to grow furious
Dyfeisiad, n. invention
Dyfeisio, v. to devise; to guess
Dyfeithrin, v. to be nursing
Dyfelu, v. to bicker, to brawl
Dyfeiriad, n. a dropping
Dyferiog, n. dropping; leaky
Dyferu, v. to drop, to drizzle
Dyferwad, n. ebullition
Dyferwi, v. to boil
Dyferyn, n. a single drop
Dyferynu, v. to drizzle
Dyfeth. n. failing; nullity
Dyfetha, v. to destroy
Dyfethiad, n. a destroying
Dyfethlu, v. to entangle
Dyfethwr, n. a destroyer
Dyfian, v. to move slowly
Dyfinio, v. to set an edge
Dyflaenu, v. to sharpen
Dyflanu, v. to illumine
Dyflisgo, v. to strip of shells
Dyfloen, n. a splinter
Dyfnâd, n. a deepening
Dyfnad, n. what is inured
Dyfnawd, n. profundity
Dyfnder, n. deepness
Dyfnu, v. to suck; to be used
Dyfod, v. to come; to be; to come to pass
Dyfodiad, n. a coming
Dyfodiant, n. futurity
Dyfodol, a. adventitious, coming [future
Dyfolio, v. to guzzle

Dyfrâd, n. irrigation
Dyfrâu v. to irrigate
Dyfrbwysiant, n. hydrostatics
Dyfrefu, v. to bleat
Dyfrfydrai, n. hydrometer
Dyfrgi, n. an otter
Dyfrglwyf. n. the dropsy
Dyfrhynt. n. water-course
Dyfriad, n. watering; irrigation
Dyfriar, n. water-hen, coot
Dyfrbigo, v. to top, to prune
Dyfrio, v. to dignify
Dyfritho, v. to variegate
Dyfriwo, v. to crumble
Dyfrlan, n. water brink
Dyfrle, n. bed of a river
Dyfrllyd, a. waterish, watery
Dyfrogan, n. l ydromancy
Dyfrol, a. watery, aqueous
Dyfru, v. to water
Dyfrwraint, n. a tetter
Dyfry, adv. upward; aloft
Dvfryd, n. a longing: a. longing
Dyfrydaeth, n. a longing
Dyfrydio, v. to heat
Dyfrydol, a. longing
Dyfrydu, v. to muse; to long
Dyfrys, n. haste, speed
Dyfrysiad, n. a hastening
Dvfrysio, v. to hasten
Dyfu, v. to move on; to come
Dyfustlo, v. to embitter
Dyfwrw, v. to cast out
Dyfwyn, n satisfaction
Dyfwynâd, n. a satisfying
Dyfwyni, n. satisfaction
Dyfwyno, v. to satisfy
Dyfwyta, v. to eat often
Dyfyn, n. a citation
Dyfyniad, n. a citation
Dyfynol, a. citatory
Dyfynu, v. to draw to; to cite
Dyfwyo, v. to augment
Dyfyru, v. to curtail
Dyfysgu, v. to make confusion
Dyffrydio, v. to stream
Dyffryn n. valley, dale, vale
Dyffugliad, n. ventilation

| DYF | 125 | DYH |

Dyffustol, v. to beat
Dyffysgo, v. to hurry
Dygadwy, a. portable
Dygamu, v. to bend
Dyganre, n. concomitance
Dyganu, v. to chant
Dygas, n. hatred; a. hated
Dygasedd, n. enmity, hatred
Dygegu, v. to gargle, to mouth
Dygelu, v. to conceal
Dygen, n. malice, grudge
Dygiad, n. a bearing, a carrying
Dygiadus, a. decorous, trained
Dygiannus, a. conductory
Dygiant, n. deportment
Dygleigio, v. to sink
Dygleisio, v. to make weals
Dyglist, n. slime, bitumen
Dyg udo, v. to waft
Dygluddo, v. to hem in
Dyglyw, n. a hearing
Dyglywed, v. to hear, to listen
Dygnod, n. a toiling
Dygnol, a. striving, toiling
Dygnedd, n. trouble
Dygniad, n. toiling
Dygnoad, n. mastication
Dygnoi, v. to masticate
Dygnu, v. to toil hard
Dygnudo, v. to flock together
Dygochi, v. to blush, to redden
Dygoddi, v. to aggrieve
Dygofio, v. to call to mind
Dygolli, v. to lose
Dygospi, v. to punish
Dygraffu, v. to impress
Dygredu, v. to believe
Dygreidio, v. to impassion
Dygreinio, v. to crawl
Dygrenu, v. to grasp
Dygrëu, v. to create
Dygroni, v. to accumulate
Dygrychu, v. to rumple
Dygrymu, v. to bow
Dygrynu, v. to quake
Dygrysio, v. to speed
Dyguddio, v. to hide
Dyguro, v. to reverberate

Dygwydd, n. lapse; hap
Dygwyddiad, n. a befalling
Dygwyddo, to befall, to happen
Dygwyddol, a. accidental
Dygwympo, v. to fall
Dygychwyn, v. to set off
Dygyd, v. to bear, to convey, to carry, to take away
Dygydfod, n. accordance
Dygyfalâu, v. to assimilate
Dygyfarfod, v. to meet
Dygyfarth, v. to bark
Dygyfarwyddo, v. to direct
Dygyfeirio, v. to meet together
Dygyflwyn, v. to approach
Dygyfodi, v. to rise
Dygyfor, v. to cause tumult
Dygyfranc, v. to deal together
Dygyfwrw, v. to cast
Dygyfysgi, n. a confusion
Dygyffroi, v. to agitate
Dygynweddu, v. to comply
Dygyhoeddi, v. to publish
Dygylchu, v. to encompass
Dygylchynu, v. to circumscribe
Dygyllaeth, n. a longing
Dygymell, v. to instigate
Dygymeryd, v. to accept
Dygymod, v. to agree
Dygymrodedd, n. congeniality
Dygymyredd, n. estimation
Dygymysgu, v. to mix
Dygymynu, v. to hew
Dygyn, a. severe, painful, hard
Dygynal, v. to uphold
Dygynull, v. to collect
Dygynwys, n. continence
Dygynu, v. to rise over
Dygyrchu, v. to assail
Dygyrhaedd, v. to attain
Dygysgodi, v. to adumbrate
Dygysgu, v. to slumber
Dygystuddio, v. to afflict
Dygythruddo, v. to agitate
Dygywain, v. to carry
Dyhaeddu, v. to merit
Dyhaenu, v. to spread over
Dyhaeru, v. to affirm, to assert

Dyhaith, v. to merit
Dyhead, n. a panting
Dyhebgor, v. to dispense
Dyhebu, v. to respond
Dyhedeg, v. to hover
Dyheddu, v. to respond
Dyhedeg, v. to hover
Dyheddu, v. to tranquilise
Dyheiddio, v. to merit
Dyhenydd, n. giver of life
Dyheu, v. to pant, to puff
Dyheuad, n. a panting
Dyheuddyd, v. to explore
Dyheued, v. to pant, to puff
Dyheueg, n. a wish; sigh
Dyheuro, v. to assert
Dyhewyd, n. resolution
Dyhewydd, n. maturity
Dyhewyn, n. what is matured
Dyhidlo, v. to distil
Dyhir, a. loitering; worthless
Dyhiriad, n. a loitering
Dyhriant, n. prolongation
Dyhirio, v. to loiter
Dyhiro, v. to trifle
Dyhirwch, n. worthlessness
Dyhiryn, n. worthless one
Dyhoddio, v. to faciliate
Dyholi, v. to investigate
Dyhoryd, v. to frustrate
Dyhudded, n. consolation
Dyhuddiad, n. an appeasing
Dyhuddiant, n. consolation
Dyhuddo, v. to appease
Dyhynt, n. a. journey
Dyhyntio, v. to take a course
Dyhysbyddu, v. to drain
D.l, n. due, debt or right
Dylad, n fluxion, a flowing
Dyladwy, a. suitable, meet
Dylafwch, n. scratching, itch
Dylaith, n. dissolution; corps
Dylamu, v. to skip
Dylan, n. a fluid; the ocean
Dylanwad, n. influence
Dylathru, v. to a polish
Dylawch, n. protection
Dylechu, v. to skulk

Dyled, n. due right, debt
Dyledgar, a. dutiful
Dyledog, a. having due; noble
Dyledswydd, n. duty, obligation
Dyledu, v. to make due
Dyledus, a. due, obligatory
Dyledwr, n. debtor
Dylefain, v. to clamour
Dylenwi, v. to fill
Dyleu, v. to be obliged
Dyli n. temper, habit
Dylid, n. obligation, duty
Dylif, n. flood; warp
Dylifad, n. flowing, warping
Dyliflannu, v to flow
Dylifiant, n. defluxion
Dylifo, v. to flow; to warp
Dylinio, v. to kneel
Dyliw, n. shadow, hue
Dylochi, v. to protect
Dylod, n. shrillness; key of D
Dylofi, verb. to stroke with the hand; to allay
Dylofyn, n. a handful
Dylor, n. a shrill utterance
Dylosg, n. coke, charcoal
Dylosgi, v. to calcine, to char
Dylu, v. to be obliged, to owe.
Dylwn, I ought, I should
Dyluchio, v. to be throwing
Dyludo, v. to adhere
Dylunio, v. to delineate
Dylusg, n. what is drifted on shore, by floods
Dylysgo, v. to hale, to drag
Dylw, n. obligation, duty
Dylwch, n. a fluid; a deluge
Dylwf, n. a bundle, a whisp
Dylwr, n the hind part
Dylwyf, n. re-wood, fuel
Dyly, v, to be due, to claim
Dylyed, n. obligation, debt
Dylyedogi, v, to render entitled
Dylyfu, v. to lick
Dylymu, v. to sharpen
Dylynu, v. to adhere
Dylyu, v. to be a duty
Dylliad, n. an overshadowing

Dyllu, v. to overshadow
Dylluan, n. an owl
Dyllwng, v. to let go
Dyllyr, n. the abyss
Dynia, adv. here, lo here
Dymborthi, v. to be mutualy aiding; to support one's self
Dymchwelyd, v. to overturn
Dymchweliad, n. subversion
Dymchweldir, the earth-board of a plough
Dymchwydd, n. a swelling
Dymdanu, v. to spread
Dymddadlu, to dispute together
Dymddenu, v. to allure
Dymddwyn, v. to bear
Dymestyn, v. to extend
Dymfoddio, v. to please one's self
Dymgadw, v. to abstain
Dymgaru, to be mutually loving
Dymgeio, v. v. to exert
Dymgelu, v. to conceal
Dymgilio, v. to recede
Dymgodi, v. to lift one's self
Dymgofio, v. to remember
Dymgredu, v. to trust mutually
Dymguro, v. to beat mutually
Dymgyfarch, v. to greet
Dymgyrchu, v. to resort together
Dymheddu, v. to pacify
Dymhuno, v. to doze
Dymnoddi, v. to take refuge
Dymoddeu, v. to suffer
Dymranu, v. to divide
Dymreddi, v. to resign
Dymuno, v. to desire
Dymunol, a. desirable
Dymuniad, n. a desiring
Dymwadu, v. to deny one's self
Dymwared, v. to deliver
Dymweled, v. to visit
Dyn, n. a person, a man
Dyna, adv. there, lo there
Dynan, n. a little woman, a lass
Dynuod, n. humanity
Dyndeb, n. manhood
Dyndid, n. manhood, manliness
Dyne, n. effusion; panting

Dynead, n. an effusing
Dyneol, a. effusive; shedding
Dynes, n. a woman, a female
Dynesâu, v. to approximate
Dynesiad, n. accession
Dynesu, v. to draw near
Dynĕu, v. to effuse; to shed
Dyngarwch, n. philanthropy
Dyniad, n. human being
Dyniadu, v. to humanise
Dyniawed, n. a steer, a heifer
Dyniolaeth, n. humanity
Dynionach, n. frail men
Dyno, n. a little person
Dynodi, v. to discriminate
Dynoethi, v. to denudate
Dynol, a. human, of man
Dynoli, v. to make human
Dynoliaeth, n. humanity
Dynos, n. little people
Dynsawdd, n. a person
Dynsodi, v. to personify
Dynsodiant, n. personification
Dynwared, v. to imitate
Dynwarediad, n. imitation
Dynwaredolder, n. imitability
Dynyddu, v. to twist
Dynygu, v. to thrive
Dynyn, n. a little man
Dyochri, v. to square
Dyodi, v. to put off, to strip
Dyodwf, n. augmentation
Dyoddef, v. to suffer, to abide
Dyoddefadwy, a. sufferable
Dyoddefaint n. suffering
Dyoddefgar, a. patient, passive
Dyoddefiad, n. a suffering
Dyoddefant, n. passion
Dyoddefus, a. patient, passive
Dyoddefwr, n. a sufferer
Dyoedi, v. to delay
Dyoerain, v. to cool
Dyofalu, v. to care for
Dyoganu, v. to predict
Dyogwyddo, v. to incline
Dyol, n. a track; a footstep
Dyolaeth, n. a tracing
Dyolaith, n. dissolution

Dyoli, v. to follow a track
Dyolwch, n. gratitude; worhsip
Dyollwng, v. to let loose
Dyoresgynu, v. to subjugate
Dyorfod, v. to conquer, to over-
Dyorladu, v. to bless [come
Dyormesu, v. to molest
Dyosgi, v. to put off, to put
Dyrag, n. progress: prep. before
Dyragu, v. to precede to go be-
Dyrain, v. to frisk about [fore
  n. friskness
Dyranu, v. to divide
Dyrathu, v. to rub, to chafe
Dyrawr, n. impulse: a. urgent
Dyrch, n. a rising; an assault
Dyrchaf, n. an assault
Dyrchafael, n. ascension
Dyrchafiad, n. exhaltation
Dyrchafiaeth, n. promotion
Dyrchafol, a. elevating
Dyrchafu, v. to elevate, exalt;
  to advance; to ascend
Dyrchiad, n. exhaltation
Dyrchu, v. to exalt, to rise
Dyre, n. wantoness, lust
Dyred, v. to move on; to come
Dyredi, v. to run to and fro
Dyreidio, v. to necessitate
Dyres, n. stairs
Dyrewi, v. to freeze
Dyri, n. a kind of metre
Dyrifiad, n. numeration
Dyrnaid, n. a handful
Dyrnchwith, a. left-handed
Dyrnddol, n. handle of a cup
Dyrnfedd, n. hand-breadth
Dyrnfiaidd, n. a battle-axe
Dyrnfol, n. a gauntlet
Dyrniad, n. a threshing
Dyrnod, n. a box, a blow
Dyrnu, v. to box, to thresh
Dyrnwr, n. a thresher
Dyroddi, v. to give, to bestow
Dyröi, v. to give, to yield
Dyrraith, n. fate; jeopardy
Dyru, v. to impel to drive
Dyrwn, n. a hollow noise

Dyrwyddo, v. to accelerate
Dyrwyn, v. to wind, to twist
Dyrwyniad, n. a winding
Dyrwynwr, n. one who winds
  yarn, a winder
Dyrynu, v. to wind round
Dyrys, a. intricate, entangled
Dyrysi, n. intricacy; a brake
Drysiad, n. an entangling
Dyrysien, n. a briar
Dyryslwyn, n. bramble brake
Dyrysni, n. intricacy
Dyrysu, v. to entangle
Dyrywio, v. to assimilate
Dysail, n. a foundation
Dysathru, v. to tread, to tramp-
Dyscarthu, v. to cleanse [le
Dysceulad, n. coagulation
Dysclaer, a. glittering, bright.
Dyscleirdeb, n. a splendour
Dyscleiriad, n. a glittering
Dyscleirio, v. to glitter, to shine
Dyscloffi, v. to make lame
Dyscor, n. a tabernacle
Dyscori, v. to shut round
Dyscrio, n. clamour
Dyscyfrith, n. congenial form
Dyscymod, n. agreement
Dyscymodi, v. to concur
Dyscyrchu, v. to gravitate
Dysdyll, n. a dropping
Dysdylliad, n. distillation
Dysdyllu, v. to distil
Dyseiliad, n. a founding
Dysenu, v, to vituperate
Dyserenu, v. to sparkle
Dyseuthu, v. to shoot
Dysg, n. learning, erudition
Dysgad, n. instruction
Dysgadur, n. one instructed
Dysgadwr, n. instructor
Dysgedig, a. learned, instructed
Dysgedigol a. instructive
Dysgiad, n. tuition, teaching
Dysgliad, n. a dishful
Disgl, n. a dish, platter
Dysgleini n. a glare
Dysgloen, n. a splinter

Dysglu, v. to put in a dish
Dysgodres, n. tutoress
Dysgogan, n. a prediction
Dysgoganu, v. to predict
Dysgogi, v. to agitate, to stir
Dysgol. a. instructive
Dysgori, v. to clamour
Dysgu, v. to teach, to learn
Dysgubell, n. besom, slut
Dysgwedyd, v. to recite
Dysgweini, v. to minister
Dysgwr, n. a learner
Dysgwyl, n. watch: expectation
Dysgwyl, v. to expect
Dysgwylgar, a. watchful
Dysgwyliad, n. expectation
Dysgybl, n. a disciple
Dysgyblaeth, n. discipline
Dysgymon, n. combustible
Dysgyr, n. a scream
Dysgyrio, v. to scream, a cry
Dysgyrnu, v. to grin, to snarl
Dysgywen, a. splendid, bright
Dyslyncu, v. to gulp up
Dysmythu, v. to vanish
Dyspaddu, v. to castrate, to geld
Dyspeidio, v. to desist
Dyspeillo, v. to unsheath
Dyspeinio, v. to divest of
Dyspenu, v. to determine
Dysplcidio, v. to take part
Dysplcinio, v. to radiate
Dysporthi, v. to support
Dyspwyll, n. discretion
Dyspwyllo, v. to reason
Dyspwyo, v. to verberate
Dyspyddu, v. to drain; to bale
Dystain, n. one who lays things
Dystaw, a. silent calm [in order
Dystawiad, n. a silencing
Dystewi, v. to silence
Dystraw, n. a sneeze
Dystreulio, v. to rinse
Dystrewi, v. to sneeze
Dystrewiad, n. a sneezing
Dyströl, v. to whirl
Dystrych, n. spume, froth
Dystrychu, v. to spume

Dystryw, n. destruction
Dystrywiad, n. a destroying
Dystrywio, v. to destroy
Dystrywiwr, n. a destroyer
Dysuddo, v to sink
Dysychu, to dry
Dysylu, v. to make compact
Dysyllu, v. to gaze, to stare
Dyt, inter. hold, avast, stop
Dyuno, to unite, to agree
Dyw, n. that is; a day
Dywadnu, v. to take to the heels
Dywadu, v to renounce
Dywaesu, v. to warrant
Dywal, a. fierce, furious
Dywalâu, v. to grow fierce
Dywalder, n. fierceness
Dywallo, v. to pour, to shed
Dywalltrain, v. to lavish
Dywanu, v, to digress
Dywasgaru, v. to scatter
Dywasgodi, v. to shelter
Dywasgu, v. to constrict
Dywawd, v. to utter, to speak
Dywededig, a. said, spoken
Dywediad, n. a saying
Dywedwst, n, the mumps
Dywedyd, v. to speak, to say
Dyweddi, n. an espousal
Dyweddiad, n. an espousal
Dyweddio, v. to espouse, to wed
Dyweinio, v. to convey
Dywellygio, v. to fail
Dywenu, v. to smile
Dywenydd, n. pleasure, bliss
Dywirio, v. to verify
Dywisgo, v. to dress
Dywrthebu, v. to respond
Dywrthredu, v. to go adversely
Dywthio, v. to protrude
Dywy, n. vapour; fog
Dywydd,§ n. a swelling with milk in the udder
Dywyllu, v. to darken over
Dywyn, v. to make fair or white;
Dywyndeb, blessedness [to bless
Dywyni, n. a blessing
Dywystlo, v. to pledge

E

E. pron. he, his; it
Eang, a. ample, large, free
Eangder, n. amplitude
Eangiad, n. an amplifying
Eangol, a. spacious
Eangu, v. to make ample
Eb, n. issuing out; utterance v to go; to send from; to say
Ebach, n. a nook, a corner
Ebaeth, n. a nook, a corner
Eban, n. a pass by or through
Ebargofio v. to forget
Ebargofiad, n. a forgetting
Ebiaith, n. part or division of a sentence
Ebill, n. an auger; a peg
Ebilldaradr, n. a small auger
Ebilled, n. a gimblet; a peg
Ebilliad, n. a boring; pegging
Ebillio, v. to bore; to peg
Ebod, n. dung, ordure
Ebodni, v to void dung, as a
Ebol, n a colt, a foal [horse
Eboles, n. a shew colt, a filly
Eboli, v. to become a colt
Eboliog, a. being with foal
Ebolydd, adv. without delay
Ebran, n. provender, fodder
Ebraniad, n. a foddering
Ebranu, v. to bait, to fodder
Ebreidiad, n. a passing onward
Ebri, n. egress; a pass word
Ebrifed, a. numberless
Ebrill, n. April
Ebrilliaidd, a. like April
Ebru, v. to pass out; to utter
Ebrwydd, a. quick, hasty; soon
Ebrwyddiad, n. acceleration
Ebrwyddo, v. to accelerate
Ebrwyddol, a. accelerating
Ebrydu, v. to pass onward
Ebryfygiad, n. a neglecting
Ebryfygu, v. to neglect
Ebwch, n. a gasp, a sigh
Ebychiad, n. a sighing
Ebychu, v. to gasp; to sigh
Ebyd, n. a pass off, or by
Ebyri, n. that causes dread
Ebyrn, n. a brook bank
Ecraidd, a. of harsh nature
Ecriad, n. a becoming harsh
Ecrwr, n. a sharp dealing person, an extortioner
Ech, n. that yields, or pervades
Echaeth, n. seclusion rest
Echain, to be secluded: to rest
Echdoe, n. the day before yesterday: adv. on the day before yesterday
Echdywyn, n. splendour
Echdywyniad, n. a glittering
Echdywynu, v. to glitter
Echeiniad, n. a giving origin to
Echel, n. axis, axle-tree
Echen, n. source, origin; stock, tribe, family, or nation
Eching, n. a strait; restraint
Echlur, n. what causes paleness; a. of a pale hue, livid
Echlys, n. motive; occasion
Echlysu, v. to cause, to render
Echlysur, n. cause, motive
Echlysuro, n. to be a cause
Echlysurol, a. occasional
Echnos, n. night before last
Echre, adv. rather, more so
Echrestr, n. a register
Echrestriad, n. a registering
Echrestru, v. to register
Echryd, n. abashment
Echrydiad, n. a shivering
Echrydu, v. to quake, to shiver
Echrydus, a. shocking, horrid
Echryni n. a quake; horror
Echryniad, n. trepidation
Echrynol, a. quaking, shivering
Echrynu, v. to quake, to tremble
Echrys, n. shocking
Echrysder, n. direfulness
Echrysiad, n. shock of horror
Echrysiant, n. a malignant dis-
Echryslawn, a. horrible [temper

Echrysder, n. direfulness
Echrysioni, v. to be direful
Echryslonrwydd, n. direfulness
Echrysol, a. shocking, horrid
Echu, v. to go aside, to retire
Echudd, n. a seclusion
Echuddio, v. to seclude
Echur, n. anguish, pain [horse
Echw, n. what has a motion;
Echwa, v. to be on a horse-back
Echwaint, n. a being riding
Echweg, a. lusciosu to the taste
Echwith, a adverse; awkward
Echwng, a. contiguous: v. to envelope
Echwraint, n. a state of rest
Echwydd, n. cessation; autumn; eve
Echwyddo, v. to be still
Echwyn, n. a loan, or hire
Echwyna, v. to borrow; to lend
Echwyniad n. a borrowing
Echwynwr, n. a lender, or giver upon trust; creditor
Echwynydd, n. a creditor
Echwyrth, a. sottish, dull
Echyngu, v. to approximate
Echyr, n a reach
Ed, n. aptitude; velocity
Edaf, n. thread, or yarn
Edafeddog, a. full of thread
Edafeddu, v. to form into thread
Edau n. thread, or yarn
Edeyn, n. dim, single thread
Edeifniad, n. one that is trained up, educated, or civilised
Edfryd, n. restoration: v. to restore, to return
Edfrydiad, n. restoration
Edfrydol, a. tending to restore
Edfrydydd, n. a restorer
Edfudd, n. interest, profit
Edfyn, n. cast off; departure
Edfyn, v. to go off; to depart
Edfynt, n. cast off; departure
Edgyllaeth, n. dejection, separ-
Edifar, a. penitent, sorry [ion
Edifarhâd, n. a repenting

Edifarhau, v. to repent
Edifaru, v. to repent
Edifarus, a. penitent, contrite
Edifarhawr, n. a repenter
Edifeiriol, a. repenting, penitent
Edifeirwch, n. repentance
Edlaes, a. slack, trailing
Edlid, n. vexation; irritation
Edlin, n. heir apparent
Edliw, n. reproach, upbraiding: v. to upbraid, to reproach
Edliwiad, n. an upbraiding
Edliwiant, n. a reproach
Edliwied, v. to reproach
Edliwiwr, n. an upbraider
Edlwg, n. a review, a view
Edlygiad, n. a reviewing
Edlygu, v. to review, to view
Edlym, a. pungent, piercing
Edlymiad, n. a making acute
Edlymu, v. to make acute
Edlyniad, n. a smearing
Edlynu, v. to smear, to daub
Edmyg, n. reverence, honour: a. reverent; honoured
Edmygedd, n. reverent
Edlymgiad, n. reverencing
Edlymygu, v. to revere
Edn, n. a fowl, a bird
Ednain, n. the winged
Ednan, n. a bird
Ednarmes, n. augury
Ednarmu, v. to augurise
Ednawg, a. having wings
Ednawl, a. relating to birds
Ednid, n. entanglement
Ednogaeth. n. ornithology
Ednogyn, n. a fly; a gnat
Ednydd, n. a writhe
Ednyddu, v. to writhe back
Ednyfedd, n. that is refined
Ednyw, n. essence: spirit
Edrif, n. recounting
Edrifo, v. to recount
Edrin, n. a murmuring noise
Edrinaw, v. to reverberate
Edriniad, n. a remurmuring
Edring, n. a lease, or holding

Edrath, n. a simulation
Edrwyth, n. a resolvent
Edrych, n. appearance; v. to look, to behold
Edrychedigaeth, n. appearance
Edrychiad, n. a looking
Edryd, n. a resource; a stock: v. to restore, to renew
Edrydiad, n. a restoration
Edrydd, n. a teller
Edryf, n. a resource, origin
Edryfiad, n. a reassuming
Edryfu, v. to reasume
Edrysedd, n. superfluity
Edryw, n. instinct; scent
Edrywant, n. a trace by scent
Edrywedd, n. instinct: scent
Edryweddu, v. to trace by scent
Edw, a. fady, faded, withered
Edwad, n. fading, away
Edwaint, n. a fading, a decay
Edwedd, n. a state of decay
Edwi, v. to decay, to fade
Edwica, v. to extort, to forestal
Edwin, a. fading, withering
Edwinaw, v. to fade, to decay
Edwiniad, n. a withering
Edyn, n. a winged one, a fowl
Edyrn, n. sovereignty
Edd, n. an instant, a gliding
Eddain, n. a move, or glide: v. to pass on; to glide
Eddestl, n. a fleet one, a steed
Eddestr, n. a chariot horse
Eddeu, v. to give impulse
Eddi, n. thrums; fringe
Eddrin, n. a whispering: v. to whisper
Eddrith, n. varied appearance
Eddu, v. to press on, to go
Eddwll, a. covered; submissive
Eddyl, n. relation; attribute
Eddyllder, n. submission
Eddyllu, v. to be humble
Ef, pron. it; he, or him
Efa, v. to agitate, to move
Efain, v. to be moving
Efan, n. motion; course

Efe, pron. he, or him
Efel, a. being like, similar
Efelwch, n. similitude
Efelychu, v. to resemble
Efelly, ad. in that way, so
Efengyl, n. the gospel
Efengylaidd, a. evangelical
Efengyles, n. female evangelist
Efengyliaeth, n. evangelism
Efengylu, v. to evangelize
Efnys, n. enemies, foes
Efo, pron. he, him: conj. with, along with
Eforu, ad. to-morrow
Efrad, n. treachery; crime
Efras, n. plumpness
Efre, n. tare, weed
Efrefiad, n. a lowing
Efrefu, v. to low, to bleat
Efrllid, n. merit, desert
Efryd, n. study, meditation
Efrydio, v. to meditate
Efrydd, a. maimed, disabled
Efryddiad, n. a maiming
Efryddu, v. to maim, to disable
Efwyr, n. hog parsnip
Efydd, n. copper; brass
Efydden, n. a copper pan
Efyddiad, n. a coppering
Efyddu, v. to copper
Efyddwaith, n. copper work
Efyntau, pron. he or him, also
Efyrnig, n. a yearling goat
Effaith, n. an effect
Efleithiad, n. effectuation
Effeithio, v. to effectuate
Effeithiol, a. effectual
Effeithiolaeth, n. effectuation
Effeithioldeb, n. efficaciousness
Effeithioli, v. to effectuate
Effro, a. agitated; awake
Effroad, n. rousing, waking
Effroi, v. to rouse; ro wake
Effrom, a. haughty, stubborn
Eg, n. that is open; acre
Egalen, n. whetstone
Egawr, n. an opening
Egfaen, n. a haw a berry

Egin, n. germ, shoots, blades
Eginad, n. a germination
Egino, v. to germinate
Eginol, a. germinant, shooting
Eginyn, n. a germ, a shoot
Eglau, n. a bank; a gulf
Eglog, a. gaping, yawning
Eglur, a. bright, clear, plain
Egluraad, n. explanation
Egluradwy, a. demonstrable
Egluraint, n. splendour
Egluráu, v. to explain
Eglurdeb, n. clearness
Egluredig, a. exemplified
Egluriad, n. explanation
Egluriadol, a. explanatory
Egluro, v. to manifest
Eglurwr, n. an explainer
Egluryn, n. an exampler
Eglwg, a. manifest, lucid
Eglwys, n. a church
Eglwysiad, n. a churching
Eglwysig, a. of the church
Eglwyso, v. to church
Eglyd, a. hovering; weavering
Eglyn, n. the saxifrage
Egni. n. effort, endeavour
Egniad, n. a making effort
Egnio, v. to endeavour
Egniol, a. vigorous, forcible
Egnius, a. impeteous, forcible
Egored, a. open, expanded
Egoredigaeth, n. an opening
Egori, v. to open, to disclose
Egoriad, n. that opens; the key
Egoriadol, a. opening
Egredd, n. staleness, acidity
Egriad, n. a growing stale
Egrifft, n. spawn of frogs
Egroes, n. eglantine berries
Egroesen, n. eglantine berry
Egru, v. to grow stale, or acid
Egryd, Egryn. n. a tremble
Egrygi, n. hoarseness
Egrynedig, a. trembling
Egwal, n. a cot, a hut
Egwan, a. feeble, dropping
Egwanaeth, n. imbecility

Egwander, n. feebleness
Egweddi, n. dowery
Egwy, n. a plague, a pest
Egwya. v. to break in blotches
Egwyd, n. the fetlock
Egwydled, n. a small of the leg
Egwyddor, n. rudiment
Egwyddori, v. to initiate
Egwyddoriad, n. initiation
Egwyddorol, a. rudimental
Egwl, n. opportunity
Egyr, a. sharp, tart, eager
Ehagru, v. to make ugly
Ehed, n. a flight: a. flying
Ehedeg, v. to fly, to skim
Ehedfaen, n. a loadstone
Ehedfan, v. to hover
Ehediad, n. a flight
Ehedion, n. refuse of corn
Ehedog, a. having flight
Ehedol, a. relating to flight
Ehedydd, n. a flyer; a lark
Ehedyn, n. a winged creature
Ehegr, n. the stagger of a horse
Ehegru, v. to move rapidly
Ehegyr, a. abrupt: ad. quickly
Ehelaeth, a. extensive, wide
Ehelaethiad, n. an enlarging
Ehelaethu, v. to amplify
Ehoeg, n. green : a. green
Ehofnedd, n. intrepidity
Ehofni, v. to act daring
Ehofnol, a. daring, bold
Ehud, a. flighty, rash, heedless
Ei, pron. his, her; its
Eich, pron. your
Eichiad, n. a crying out
Eichio, v. to sound; to cry
Eidiaw, v. to frisk, to enliven
Eidiawl, a. vigorous, lively
Eidiogi, v. to invigorate
Eidion, n. a beast, steer
Eidral, n. ground-ivy
Eiddew, n. the ivy
Eiddiad, n. a possessing
Eiddior, n. hether or ling
Eiddiaw, v. to possess
Eiddiawg, a. owned: n. slave

EID	EIL
Eiddig, a. jealous: n. a jealous one; a zealot	plait, to construct
Eiddigedd, n. zeal, jealousy	Eilir, n. regeneration; spring
Eiddigeddu, v. to grow jealous	Eiliw, n. aspect, figure, hue
Eiddigio, v. to grow jealous	Eiliwed, n. reproach, shame
Eiddigor, n. superior	Eiloes, n. second age
Eiddigus, a. jealous; zealous	Eilon, n. music, melody: n. a hart, a roebuck
Eiddil, a. slender, small	Eilun, n. a copy; a resemblance; an image: an idol
Eiddilnâd, n. extenuation	
Eiddilâu, v. to grow slender	Eilunaddolgar, a. idoaltrous
Eiddilliad, n. extenuation	Eilunaddoli, v. to worship idols
Eiddilo, v. to extenuate	Eilunaddoliad, n. idolatry
Eiddilwch, n. slenderness	Eilunaddolwr, n. an idolater, a worshipper of images
Eiddion, n. personal property	
Eiddiorwg, n. the ivy	Eiluniad, n. an imitation
Eiddo, n. property; chattels	Eiluniaeth, n. an imitating
Eiddun, a. desirous, fond	Eiluniant, n. portaiture
Eidduneb, n. desire, choice	Eilunio, v to imitate
Eiddunedu, v. to desire	Eilw, n. music, melody
Eidduno, v. to desire, to wish, to pray; to vow	Eilwaith, n. second time or turn
	Eilwy, n. tha tmakes melody
Eiddunol, a. delectable	Eilwydd, n. love meeting
Eiddwg, a. contiguous, near	Eilydd, n. a musician
Eiddwng, a. contiguous	Eilyg, n. melody; delight
Eiddyganu, v. to approximate	Eiiyw, n. music, melody
Eiglad, n. a bringing forth	Eilywiant, n. minstrelsy
Eiglaeth, n. a teeming estate	Eill, pron. they or those
Eigian. n. centre; origin: v. to bring forth; to sob	Eilldu, n. outward side [ing
	Eilliad, n. a cutting close or shav-
Eiglaw, v. to generate	Eilliedydd, n. a cutter, a shaver
Eigiawl, a. teeming, prolific	Eillio, v. to cut off; to shave
Eigion, n. a source; a middle the abyss, or ocean	Eilliwr, n. a shaver, a barber
	Ein, n. property: pron. our
Eigraeth, n. virgin state	Einawr, ad. now, at present
Eigrau, n. stockings without feet	Einioes, n. course of life, life
Eigyr, n. a virgin, a maid	Eingio, v. to expand or dilate
Eilar, n. second ploughing	Eingion, n. an anvil
Eilchwyl, ad. once more	Eira, n. snow
Eilewydd, n. a musician	Eiras, n. that glows, a cinder
Eilfaint, n. second rate	Eirchiad, n. one who demands
Eilfam, n. second mother	Eirchiol, a. mandatory
Eilfydd, a. being second or like	Eirfydd, n. blazoner of arms
Eilfyddu, v to imitate	Eirlach, v. to deprecate
Eiliad, n. a constructing	Eirlachiad; n. a deprecating
Eilliant, n. a consrtucture	Eiriachus, a. deprecating
Eilier, n. the butterfly	Eirtan. a. splendid, bright fair
Eilig, a. apt to glide	Eirianawl, v. tending to make
Eilio, v. to place alternately, to	Eirianedd, n. splendour [fair

Eirianrodd, n. the galaxy
Eirianu, v. to make splendid
Eirias, n. a glowing; a cinder
Eiriasedd, n. glowingness
Eiriasu, v. to burn fiercely
Eiriesyn, n. a glowing cinder
Eirif, n. a number; a counting
Eirifaw, v. to enumerate
Eirifiad, n. enumeration
Eirig, a. splendid, shining, gay
Eirio, v. to brighten
Eirioes, n. purity of life
Eiriol, v. to intercede
Eiriolad, n. an interceding
Eiriolaeth, n. intercession
Eirioli, v. to entreat; to pray
Eiriolus, a. persuasive
Eiriolwch, n. intercession
Eiriolwr, n. intercessor
Eirion, n. ornaments, jewels
Eirioni, v. to adorn with jewels
Eirionyn, n. a border; a ruffle
Eirionynu, v. to fringe; to ruffle
Eirllyd, a. apt to be snowing
Eirthiaw, v. to growl; to bait
Eirwlaw, n. a sleeting rain
Eiry, n. snow
Eiryaidd, a. like snow, snowy
Eiryog, a. having snow
Eiryn, n. plums
Eirynllys, n. St. John's-wort
Eirynwydd, n. plum-trees
Eisen, n. a rib; a lath
Eisglwyf, n. pleurisy
Eisiaw, v. to lathe; to lattice
Eisieu, n. want, need, lack
Eisicuedig, a. necessitated
Eisiwyd, n. indigence
Eisoes, ad. likewise; already
Eisor, a. equal, similar, like
Eisorawd, n. counterpart
Eisori, v. to make similar
Eisilled, n. offspring, issue
Eiste, n. the act of sitting
Eiste, v. to sit, to be seated
Eistedd, n. a sitting, a sit: v. to sit; to be seated
Eisteddfod, n. a sitting, a session

Eisteddiad, n. a sitting, a seating
Eisteddial, v. to sit often
Eisteddig, a. sedentary, sitting
Eisteddol, a. sitting, sedentary
Eiswng, n. a sob; a sigh
Esyddynt, n. a tenement
Eithaf, n. extremity, farthest; a. extreme, farthest
Eithafed, n. an extremity
Eithafig, a. extreme, ultimate
Eithen, n. a prickle, or point
Eithin, n. furze, whin, gorse: a. full of prickles
Eithinen, n. a furze bush
Eithinfyw, n. the savine
Eithinog, a. full of furze
Eithiw, a. full of prickles
Eithr, a. except; besides
Eithriad, n. an exception
Eithraw, v. to except, to exclude
Eithrawl, exceptive, exclusive
El, n. inteligence, spirit
Elach, n. a little sorry fellow
Elaeth, n. spiritual being
Elaig, n. a minstrel
Elain n. a hind, a fawn
Elanedd, n. intestines
Elawch, n. indulgence
Elcys, n. ganzas, wild geese
Elech, n. a slate, a flag
Eleni, n. this year: ad this year
Elest, n. flags, or sedges
Elestr, n. flag; fleus de lys
Elestren, n. flag; fluer de lys
Elf, n. elementary principle
Elfaeth, n. elementation
Elfed, a. autumn
Elfen, n. particle; element
Elfeniad, n. elementation
Elfenol, elemental, elementary
Elfenu, v. to element
Elfod, n. intellectual existence
Elfyd, intellectual world
Elfydd, n. elementary principle earth, land
Elfyddan, n. the earthly globe
Elfydden, n. earth: region
Elfyddu, v. to element

Eiff, n. pure state ; a demon
Elgain, a. supremely fair
Elgeth, n. the chin, the jaw
Eli, n. a salve, a plaister
Eliad, n. a doing with salve
Eliaw, v. to apply a salve
Elin, n. angle; an elbow
Elinad, n. a making an angle
Elinaw, v. to angle; to elbow
Elinawg, a. angular; jointly
Elindys, n. caterpillars
Elor, n. a bier; a hearse
Elu, v. to move on: to go
Elus, a. bounteous, charitable
Elusen, n. bounty. alms [turn
Elusenaidd, a. of a charitable
Elusendod, n. alms-giving
Elusendy, n. alms-house
Elusengar, a. charitable
Elusengarwch, charitableness
Elusoni, n. bounty, charity
Elusenwr, n. an almoner
Elw, n. goods; profit, gain
Elwa, v. to get wealth ; to trade
Elwant, n. profit ; lucre
Elwch, n. shout of joy; joy
Elwi, v. to turn to profit
Elwig, a. tending to produce
Elwl, n. the reins
Elwlen, n. a kidney
Elyd, n. what is fused
Elydn, n. brass
Elydraidd, a. like brass, brassy
Elvdyr, n. brass, bell-metal
Elyf, n. that glides : a. gliding
Elyw, n. aloes, juice of aloes
Ell, n. that is divided or outward ; a. outward extreme
Ellael, n. an eyebrow
Ellaig, n. a pear
Ellain, a. radiant, splendid
Ellast, n. thistle
Ellbwyd, n. famine; hunger
Ellmyn, n. foreigners; Germans
Elltrewen, n. gossip; stepmother
Ellt, n. that is parted off
Ellwedd, n. outward aspect
Ellydd, n. a cutting off

Ellyll, n. an elf or goblin
Ellylldan, n. ignis fatuus
Ellylles, n. a she goblin
Ellyllyn, n. a little imp
Ellyn, n. a cutter, a razor
Ellynedd, n. the last year
Em, n. a jewel, or gem
Emano, ad three days since
Emenydd, n. the brain
Emig, n. a little jewel
Eminiog, n. a door-post
Emyl, n. a border or edge
Emyn, n. a hymn, a chaunt
En, n. a living principle; a being; a spirit: a. essential
Enad, n. animation
Enaid, n. a soul; life
Enain, a. essential, pure
Enaint, n. an ointment
Enawel, n. a hurricane
Enawr, n. an intelligence
Enbyd, a. dangerous, perilous
Enbydiad, n. an endangering
Enbydrwydd, n. perilousness
Enbydu, v. to endanger
Enbydus, perilousness, danger- [ous
Encil, n. retreat, flight
Enciliad, n. a retreating
Encilio, v. to retreat
Enciliwr, n. retreater
Encudd, n. a concealment
Encuddio, v. to conceal
Encyd, n. a space, a while
Enchwardd, n. loud laughter
Enderig, n. a steer; an ox
Enddawd, n. a setting mark
Enddodiant, n. distinction
Enddwl, n. the affection
Eneidfaddeu a. cast for death
Eneidio, v. to endue with soul
Eneidiog, a. having a soul
Eneidiol, a. animated
Eneidioli, v. to animate
Eneidrwydd, n. the temples
Eneiniad, n. an annointing
Eneini, v. to annoint
Eneiniog, a. annointed
Eneiniwr, n. annointer

Eneirchio, v. to put in armour
Ener, n. an intelligence
Enfawr, a. very great, huge
Enfil, n. an animal, a beast
Enfyged, n. worship, aspect
Enfysg, n. rainbow
Enhuddaw, v. to envelope
Enhuddawl, a. envelope
Enhudded, n. envelopment
Enhuddiad, n. an enveloping
Enhued, n. follower of the chase
Eni, v. to exert the soul
Eniain, a. temperature; a. very clear; intense
Enid, n. wood lark; chaffinch
Enig, a. full of spirits
Eniwaid, n. damage, harm
Eniwaw, v. to endamage
Eniwawl, a. hurtful, noxious
Eniwed, n. damage, harm
Eniwedu, v. to damage
Eniweidiad, n. a damaging
Eniweidio, v. to endamage
Enllib, n. slander, calumny
Enllibiad, n. a slandering
Enllibio, v. to slander
Enllibiol, a. calumnious
Enllibiwr, n. a slanderer, a de-
Enllibus, a. contumelious [famer
Enllyn, n. victuals, meat
Enllynu, v. to moisten food
Ennill, n. advantage, gain: v. to get advantage
Ennillgar, a. advantageous
Ennilliad, n. a gaining
Ennyd, n. a while, a space leisure; spare time
Ennyn, n. a kindling: v. fo kindle, to burn
Ennyniad, n. a kindling
Ennynol, a. tending to kindle
Ennynu, v. to kindle, to inflame
Enrhy, n. abundance, much
Enrhyal, n. breed, increase
Enrhyfedd, a. wonderful, strange
Enrhyfeddu, v. to marvel
Enserth, n. a slip: a. slippery
Entraw, n. a teacher, a master

Entrew, n. sneeze: a snort
Entrewi, v. to sternutate
Entrewiad, n. sternutation
Entrych, n. the firmament
Enw, n. name, appellation
Enwad, n. a naming
Enwadol, a. denominative
Enwaered, a. very low; prone
Enwai, n. nominative case
Enwaid, a. having a name
Enwaidedig, a. circumsised
Enwaidiad, n. circumcision
Enwaidio, v. to circumcise
Enwaidiwr, n. a circumsiser
Enwair, a. full of energy
Enwaisg, a. very brisk or gay
Enwawd, n. nomination
Enwedig, a. specified, especial
Enwedigaeth, n, specification
Enwedigo, v. to specify
Enwedigol, a. especial
Enweirus, a. energetic
Enwi, v. to name, to enitle
Enwir, a. very true; perfect
Enwog, a, renowned, famous
Enwogi, v. to make renowned
Enwogrwydd, n. renownedness
Enwol, a. nominal, naming
Enwyll n. very wild
Enwyn, a. very white also buttermilk
Enycha, interj. behold, lo
Enyd, n. while, time, space
Enydd, n. seat of intellect
Enyfed, n. energy, vigour
Eng, n. space: a ample
Engherdded, n. a sojourning
Engi, v. to set at large, to free
Englyn, n. a metre so called
Engu, v. to set at large, to free
Engur, a. marvellous, amazing
Engurio, v. to marvel
Engwarth, n. a beach
Engwth, n. a push: a. sudden
Engyl, n. expanding principle fire; angels
Engyn, n. an outcast, a wretch
Engyrth, a. awful, direful

Eoca, v. to catch salmon
Eofnder, n. confidence, boldness
Eofneg, n. the parrhesia
Eofni, v. to make bold
Eofniad, n. a growing bold
Eog, n. a salmon
Eogyn, n. a samlet
Eon, a. bold, daring, forward
Eondra, n. boldness, daringness
Eoni, v. to grow daring
Eorth, a. diligent, assiduous
Eos, n. a nightingale
Eosaidd, a. like a nightingale
Epa, n. an ape, a monkey
Epples, n. leaven: ferment
Eppil, n. offspring, issue
Eppiledd, n. offspring
Eppilgar, a. prolific, teeming
Eppiliad, n. bringing forth
Eppilio, v. to generate, to multiply
Eppiliwr, n. one who generates
Epynt, n. an ascent, a slope
Er, n. impulse forward: prep. for, because of, in the place of, in order; towards: to; for the sake of, though; from, since
Erain, a. having impulse
Eraint, n. a ball; a cup; a pear
Erbarch, n. respect, deference
Erbin, n. the calamint
Erbwl, a. tending to blunt
Erbyliad, n. a blunting
Erbyn, n. contrast, opposition: prep. against, opposite
Erbyniad, n. a receiving
Erbyniwr, n. a receiver
Erch. n. dark brown, or dun: a. dusky, dun: dismal
Erchi, to ask, to demand
Erchlais, n. a dismal noise
Erchlias, n. raven grey
Erchliw, n. a dun colour
Erchryn, a. agitating, quaking
Erchryniad, n. agitating
Erchrynu, v. to agitate
Erchwyn, n. a side or stead
Erchwynedig, a. transitive
Erchwyniad, n. transition
Erchwynio, v. to make a transit
Erchwys, n. a pack of hounds
Erchyll, a. ghastly, horrible
Erchylldod, n. ghastliness
Erchyllrwydd, n. frightfulness
Erchyllu, v. to make gashtly
Erchynu, v. to uplift
Erchywynu, v. to transmigrate
Erdolygu, v. to beseech
Erdd, n. impulse, forward: prep. for the sake of, for
Erddrwng, a. confused
Erddrym, a. potent, robust
Erddrymedd, n. potency
Erddwyn, v. to bear away
Erddygan, n. euphony
Erddyganu, v. to produce melody
Erddygniad, n. a toiling hard
Erddygnu, v. to toil hard
Ereill, n. others: pron. others
Ereinnwg, n. pear orchard
Eres, a. marvelous strange
Eresi, n. amazement, wonder
Eresu, v. to marvel
Erf, n. briskness: a. brisk
Erfai, a. brisk, gay, lively
Erfawr, a. very great, vast
Erfid, n. junction; conflict: v. to come in contact
Erflawdd, a. tumultuous
Erfyn, n. dim, a weapon; a tool: n. petition, prayer
Erfyniad, n. a petition
Erfyniaw, v. to petiton
Erfyniol, a. supplicatory
Erfyniedydd, n. a beseecher
Erfyniwr, n. one who solicits, or begs, an implorer
Erganiad, n. celebrating
Erganu, v. to sing, to celebrate
Erglyw, n. listening, attention
Erglywed, v. to listen, to hear
Erglywiad, n. a listening
Ergryd, n. a trembling, dread: v. to tremble; to terrify
Ergrydiad, n. tremulousness

Ergrydio, v. to cause, to quake
Ergrydiol, a. tending to agitate
Ergryf, a. endowed with strength
Ergryn, n. terror, horror, dread
Ergrynawd, n. trepidation
Ergrynedig, a. made to tremble
Ergryniad, n. tremulation
Ergrynig, a. apt to tremble
Ergrynol, a. terrifying
Ergrynu, v. to tremble
Ergwydd, n. a tumble, a fall
Ergwyn, n. cause of complaint
Ergwyno, to make to complain
Ergyd, n. a propulsion, throw, cast; shot; stroke
Ergydiad, n. a striking
Ergydio, v. to propel, to throw, to cast; to shoot; to charge
Ergydiol, a. propulsive
Ergydiwr, n. thrower, shooter
Ergyr, n. impulse, thrust
Ergyrch, n. an onset, an attack
Ergyrchiad, n. an attacking
Ergyrchu, v. to make an onset
Ergyriad, n. an impulsion
Ergyrio, v. to impel, to thrust
Ergyriol, a. impulsive
Erhelfa, n. a hunting party
Eriaw, v. to make progress
Erin, a. moving, progressive
Erioed, adv. from the beginning; ever the past; never the past
Eriw, n. progress, course
Erlewyn, n. a meteor
Erlid, n. a pursuit, a chase: v. to pursue; to persecute
Erlidedig, a. persecuted
Erlidedigaeth, n. persecution
Erlidfa, n. a pursuit, a chase
Erlidiad, n. a pursuing
Erlidigaeth, n. persecution
Erlidfa, n. a pursuit, a chase
Erlidiol, a. pursuing, chasing
Erlidiwr, n. pursuer; persecutor
Erlif, n. a great torrent; flood
Erlifiad, n. a deluging an overflowing
Erlifo, v. to flow in a torrent

Erlyn, n. pursuit, chase: v. to pursue, to follow
Erlyniad, n. a pursuer [ing
Erlyniaeth, n. the act of persu-
Erlyniedydd, n. pursuer
Erlynol, a. persuing, chasing
Erllen, n. a lamp
Erllyfasu, v. to adventure
Erllynedd, adv. since last year
Ermaes, a. external, outward
Ermid, n. a junction; conflict
Ermig, n. instrument, tool
Ermilus, a. prowling about
Ermoed, adv. in all my life
Ermyg, n. what claims respect
Ermygu, v. to adore, to revere
Ern, n. earnest, pledge
Ernes, n. earnest, pledge
Erniw, n. harm, hurt
Erniwed, detrement, hurt
Erniwiad, n. a doing harm
Erniwiant, n. detriment, hurt
Erniwio, v. to harm, to hurt
Erniwiol, a. detrimental, hurtful
Erno, v. to give earnest money
Ernwy, n. briskness, vivacity
Ernych, n. that gives anguish
Ernychiad, n. a tormenting
Ernychol, a. tormenting
Ernychu, v. to torment, to vex
Ernyd, n. a precipice, a slope
Ertrai, n. ebb, ebb tide
Erth, n. an effort, a push
Erthiad, n. a making effort
Erthrwch, n. a tear, anguish
Erthu, v. to make effort
Erthwch, n. a puffing
Erthychain, v. to puff; to groan
Erthrychiad, n. a puffing
Erthrychu, v. to mangle
Erthyl, n. an abortion, untimely birth
Erthyliad, n. abortion
Erthylog, a. miscarrying
Erthylu, v. to miscarry
Erw, n. a slang of land; an acre
Erwan, n. a stab, a sting
Erwaniad, n. a stabbing

Erwanu, v. to stab, to sting
Erwawd, n. a panegyric
Erwch, n. impulse, a drive
Erwig, n. dim, plot of land
Erwyd, n. a pole, a perch
Erwydd, n. coopers' staves
Erwydden, n. dim, stave
Erwyll, a. gloomy, dusky
Erwyn, a. very white splendid
Erwyr, a. oblique, or wry
Erydd, n. an eagle
Eryf, n. impulsion, a push
Eryfed, n. quaffing
Eryl, n. a watch, a look
Eryr, n. an eagle; the shingles
Eryral, n. the eagle stone
Eryran, n. a young eagle
Eryrol, a. aquiline, like an eagle
Eryres, n. a female eagle
Eryri, n. the shingles: Snowdon
Erysdyddiau, adv. days ago
Erysgwyddiad, n. a shouldering a jutting out
Erysi, n. amazement, wonder
Es, n. separation; a shoot. It is used as a prefix, of a similar signification to ex; and also, as a termination of feminine personal nouns, and of the third person of verbs
Esbyd, n. guests, strangers
Esg, n. what shoots out
Esgaeth, a. void of restraint
Esgaidd, a. nimble, brisk
Esgair, n. a shank, a leg
Esgar, n. separation; a foe
Esgarant, n. adversary
Esgardio, v. to make chaps
Esgardd, n. rupture, ruption
Esgardde, n. a dispersion
Esgaredd, n. separation
Esgariad, n. a separating
Esgario v. to separate, to part
Esgeiddig, a. moving gracefully
Esgeirca, v. to move the shanks
Esgeiriog, a. having shanks
Esgemydd, n. a bench
Esgeulus a. negligent, heedless

Esgeulusdod, n. disregard
Esgeulusdra, n. negligence
Esgeulusiad, n. a neglecting
Esgeuluso, v. to disregard, to neglect
Esgeuluswr, n. a neglecter
Esgid, n. a shoe
Esglyw, n. defence, shelter
Eglwyn, v. to defend, to protect
Esgob, n. a bishop, a diocesan
Esgobaeth, n. bishopric
Esgobawd, n. diocese
Esgobdy, n. a bishop's house
Esgobol, a. episcopal
Esgor, n, partage; parturition: v. to separate; to bring forth
Esgorol, a. parturient
Esgordd, n. strangers
Esgoredig, a. delivered
Esgoredigol, a. parturent [ance
Esgoreddfa, n. place of deliver-
Esgori, v. to get over; to bring
Esgoriad, n. parturition [forth
Esgorwraig, n. midwife
Esgoryd, to part from, to deliver
Esgorydd, n. an accoucheur
Esgud, a. nimble; flippant
Esgudogyll, n. wood lark
Esgus, n. apology; excuse
Esgusodiad, n. excusation
Esgusodol, a. excusing
Esgusodydd, n. an excuser
Esgusol, a. excusatory
Esgymol, a. unassociating
Esgymun, a. excommunicate
Esgymu, v. to dissolve society
Esgyn, v. to ascend, to rise
Esgynedigaeth, n. ascension
Esgynol, a. ascending, rising
Esgynfa, n. an ascend, a rise
Esgynfaen, n. horse-block
Esgyniad, n. ascension
Esgyniaith, n. a climax
Esgynlawr, n. scafold; platform
Esgyr, n. a day's ploughing
Esgyrndy, n. a bone house
Esgyrniad, n. ossification
Esgyrniog, a. bony, having bones

Esgyrnol, a. ossific, bony
Esgyrnygu, v. to grin
Esill, n. offspring progeny
Esilling, n. origin, source
Esillydd, n. offspring, issue
Esing, n. act of bursting out
Esiw, a. in a state of want
Esiwydd, n. a state of want
Esiwyddu, v. to feel want
Esmwyth, a. soft, smooth; easy
Esmwythâad, n. softening; a mollifying, an asuaging
Esmwythâu, v. to soften, to ease
Esmwythder, n. easiness, quietness, tranquility, rest
Esmwythiad, n. a quieting
Esmwythid, n. state of ease
Esmwytho, v. to smooth, to ease
Esgoryn, n. the mumps
Esplydd, a. delicate, tender
Esplydden, n. a pippin
Est, n. a state of separation
Estriciad, n. a bustling
Estrico, v. to bustle, to haste
Estrig, a. apt to dart away
Estron, n. a stranger, foreigner
Estroneiddio, v. to estrange
Estrones, n. the stranger
Estroniad, n. estrangement
Estronol, a. strange, foreign
Estl, n what ranges
Estyll, n. staves, shingle
Estyllen, n. a shingle, a board
Estyllodi, v. to slit into boards
Estyllu, v. to do with shingles
Estyn, n. an extent, a grant
Estyn, v. to extend, to reach
Estynedig, a. extended, stretched
Estyniad, n. a reaching out
Estynol, a. extending
Estynwr, n. an extender
Estyr, n. that darts away
Esu, v. to push away
Eswrn, n. a fetlock joint
Esyddyn, n. a mansion
Esyllt, n. that is fair, or open
Esyth, n. sharp sticks, waggets
Esythu, v. to drive a stake

Etewyn, n. a firebrand
Etifaw, v. to inherit; to own
Etifedd, n. heir, an infant
Etifeddes, n. an heiress
Etifeddiad, n. an inheriting
Etifeddiaeth, n. an inheritance
Etifeddog, a. having a child
Etifeddol, a. hereditary
Etifeddu, v. to inherit
Etifiant, n. an heirship
Eto, con. yet, still, also: adv. yet, again, still
Etwa, con. yet, still: adv. yet
Eth, n. that is in motion
Ethais, n. that spreads out
Ethol, v. to select, to choose: n. selection, choice: a select
Etholedig, a. choosen, the elect
Etholedigaeth, n. the act of electing, selection
Etholiad, n. an election
Etholydd, n. an elector
Etholwr, n. an elector
Etholyddiaeth, n. electorship
Ethrefiad, n. domestication
Ethrefig, a. domestical, homely
Ethrefu, v. to domesticate
Ethrewyn, v. to conciliate
Ethrin, n. conflict, toil
Ethrinio, v. to conflict
Ethriniol, a. conflicting, toiling
E'hryb, n. cause, occasion
Ethrychwil, n. a lizard
Ethrylith, n. intuition
Ethrywyllt, a. ferocious, furious
Ethrywyn, v. to conciliate
Ethu, v. to proceed, to go
Ethw, a. of pervading quality
Ethy, n. a spur
Eu, pro. their, them
Euain, v. to be moving
Euddon, n. mites, acarus
Euddoni, v. to breed mites
Eugi, v. to bawl, to shriek
Eulon, n. excrements, dung
Euocâu, v. to make guilty
Euod, n. worms in sheep's liver
Euog, a. guilty; false

Euon, n. bots in horses
Euraid, a. golden, of gold
Euraidd, a. golden
Euraint, n. that is of gold
Eurben, n. the gilt head
Eurdalaeth, n. golden coronet
Eurdorch, n. a wreath of gold
Eurdde, a. covered with gold
Eurem, n. golden jewel
Eurfaen n. a chrysolite
Eurfail, n. a golden goblet
Eurfrodiad, n. golden brocade
Eurgain, a. of golden brightness
Eurgalch, n. gold enamel
Eurgrawn, n. collection of gold; a golden treasure
Euriad, n. a gilding
Eurian, a. of gold, golden
Eurlen, n. arras, gold leaf
Eurliw, n. a gold colour
Eurwedd, a. of golden hue
Eurych, n. goldsmith; tinker
Eurychaeth, n. goldsmith's art; tinker's trade
Eurydd, n. a goldfiner
Euryll, n. a jewel of gold
Euryn, n. a golden trinket
Ew, n. that glides; that is sleek or smooth
Ewa, n. an uncle
Ewach, n. a weakling, a fribble
Ewaint, n. young people
Ewerddon, n. a green spot of land, Ireland
Ewi, v. to listen, to attend
Ewiar, a. smooth; clear; sleek
Ewig, n. a hind; a deer, a doe
Ewin, n. a nail; a talon, a claw
Ewinallt, n. a steep cliff
Ewinbren, n. a guide, in carpentry
Ewinfedd, n. a nail measure
Ewingraff, a. sharp-clawed
Ewingrwn, a. turned as a nail
Ewino, v. to use the nails
Ewinog, a. having nails, clawed
Ewinor, n. a whitlow
Ewinrew, n. nipping frost

Ewinwasg, n. an agnail
Ewn, a. daring, bold, brave
Ewybr, a. quick, nimble, fleet
Ewybraidd, a. of swift nature
Ewybraw, v. to glance, to dart
Ewybredd, n. velocity
Ewybren, n. the firmament
Ewybriad, n. a glancing
Ewydn, a. tuff, clammy, viscous
Ewydnaw, v. to grow viscous
Ewyll, n. will, action of mind
Ewylliad, n. a volition
Ewyllio, v. to exert the will
Ewyllys, n. will or desire
Ewyllysgar, a. willing, desirous
Ewyllysgarwch, n. willingness
Ewyllysiwr, n. willer, desirer
Ewyn, n foam, spume, froth
Ewynedd, n. foaminess
Ewyngant, n. a surge
Fwyniad, n. a foaming
Ewynog, a. foamy, frothy
Ewynu, v. to foam, to froth
Ewythr, n. an uncle

F

Is of a similar sound to the English V; and is used as a mutation of m. and B. It is not a radical letter in the welsh language, but the following words are commonly used with it:—

Fal, Fel, con. similar, like: adv. as if, so
Felly, adv. in that way, so
Fy, pro. my

FF

Has the sound of English F.
Ffa. n. what is enveloped
Ffaced, n. a curd, a curdle
Ffad, n. a disguise, a mask
Ffadu, v. to mask, to feign
Ffadw, a. of a dark bay colour
Ffael, n. a failing, a fault
Ffaeliad, n. a failing

Ffaelu, v. to fail, to miss
Ffaeth, a. luxuriant. rich, ripe
Ffaethder, n. luxuriancy
Ffaethedig, a. fecundated
Ffaethiad, n. fecundation [low
Ffaethol, a. tending to make mel-
Ffacthu, v. to make luxuriant
Ffaethus, a. luxuriant, mellow
Ffaethuso, v. to fecundate
Ffaethusrwydd, n. mellowness
Ffag, n. what tends to unite
Ffagl, n. a blaze, a flame
Ffagliad, n. a blazing
Ffaglog, a. blazing, flaming
Ffaglu, v. to blaze, to flame, to conflagrate
Ffaglwr, n. a blazer, one who bears a blaze; an incendiary
Ffaglydd, n. a blazer
Ffagod, n. a faggott, a bundle
Ffagoden, n. a faggot
Ffagodi, v. to faggot, to bundle
Ffai, n. cessation; forgetting
Ffaig, n. extremity; a stop; a turn; an embarassment
Ffain, n. what is conical
Ffair, n. eminence, a fair
Ffaith, n. a fact; an act
Ffal, n. closure; heel of shoe
Ffald, n. a fold; a pinfold
Ffaling, n. a mantle, a cloak
Ffalingaw, v. to cloak, to robe
Ffalingiad, n. a cloaking, a rob-
Ffalm, a. whirling, twirling [ing
Ffals, a. masket; deceitful, false
Ffalsder, n. deceitfulness, false-
Ffalsedd, n. deceitfulness [ness
Ffalstedd, n. dissimulation, fal-
sity [elve
Ffalsu, v. to use falsity, to dec-
Ffall, n. a squab: a. squabby
Ffallach, n. a squabby one
Ffallachog, a. of a squabby form
Ffan, n. a surface, a covering
Ffaner, n. a supreme, a sover-
Ffanwg, n. a covered state [eign
Ffangyl, n. what covereth; safe-
Ffar, n. that extends out [ty

Ffaraon, n. the high powers
Ffargod, n. a big paunch
Ffas, n. a ligature, a band
Ffasg, n. a tie, a bundle
Ffasgell, n. a bundle, a whisp
Ffasgelliad, n. a bundling
Ffasgellu, v. to tie in bundles
Ffasgiad, n. ligation
Ffasgu, v. to bind, to tie
Ffat, n. a pat, a smart blow
Ffatiad, n. a giving a pat
Ffatio, v. to part, to strike light-
Ffatiwr, n. a patter. [ly
Ffau, n. a den, a cave
Ffaw, n. radiancy; glory: rad-
iant; glorious; fair
Ffawd, n. fortune, luck; fate; prosperity; happiness
Ffawdd, n. radiation, splendour
Ffawg, n. delight: a. pleasing
Ffawr, n. a course
Ffawydd, n. pine, fir, deal; beech
Ffe, n. what is outward
Ffed, n. an outside; presence; demeanour: a. outward
Ffedawnen, n. neckloth, cravet
Ffedel, n. the front or lap
Ffedog, n. an apron
Ffedogaid, n. an apronful
Ffedogi, v. to put in an apron
Ffedon, what screens; a screen
Ffedonas, n. a screen; a fan
Ffedu, v. to place outward; to expose
Ffedus, a. exposed; manifest
Ffei, int. begone! off! shame! fie
Ffeiad, n. a shaming away
Ffeigiad, n. a driving; to ex-
tremity
Ffeigiol, a. ultimate; puzzling
Ffeinid, n. a rising into a point
Ffeinidwydd, n. pine trees
Ffeio, v. to put to shame
Ffeiriad, n. a bartering
Ffeirio, v. to barter, to change
Ffeiriwr, n. a chapman
Ffeithiant, n. effectuation, op-
Ffeithio, v. to effectuate [eration

Ffeithiol, a. effectuating; operative [wily
Ffêl, a. subtile, fine; cunning
Ffelaidd, a. of a subtile nature; sly [a chief
Ffelaig, n. perceptive source;
Ffelder, n. subtilty, slyness
Ffelrwydd, n. craftiness
Ffelu, v. to act subtilely
Ffen, n. a flowing principle; air
Ffenestr, n. air hole; window. it is used figuratively for the vagina
Ffenestrog, a. having windows
Ffenestrol, fenestral, windowed
Ffenestru, v. to make windows
Ffer, a. what is solid; a severe cold; a concrete; the ankle: a. dense; fixed; solid; strong with cold
Fferadwy, a. congealable [ness
Fferod, n. congealation; numb-
Fferder, n. congealedness
Fferdd, a. solid; firm; thick
Fferedig, a. congealed, fixed
Fferedigaeth, n. congealment
Fferiad, n. congelation
Fferis, n. steel; a fire steel
Fferllyd, a. congealing; chilling
Ffern, n. the ankle bone
Fferu, v. to concrete; to freeze
Fferyll, n. chymist; metalurgist
Fferylliad, n. a chymist
Fferyllaeth, n. chymistry
Fferyllt, n. metalist; artisan
Fferylltaeth, n. mechanical art
Fferylltiad, n. a metalist
Ffes, n. subtilty; knowledge
Ffesawd, n, craft, subtilty
Ffesawl, a. of a subtle nature
Ffesig, a, clever, cunning
Ffêst, a. fast, speedy, quick
Ffestin, a. of active nature
Ffestiniad, n. hastening
Ffestinio, v. to festinate, to hast-
Ffesu, v. to make haste [en
Ffesu, v. to penetrate, to ken
Ffetan, n. budget, a saucy girl
Ffetanu, v. to budget, to bag
Ffetanwr, n. a bagman
Ffetur, n. wild oats
Ffetus, a. subtle, sly, wily
Ffi, n. a loath: inter. fie
Ffiaidd, a. loathsome, detestable
Ffieidd-dra, n. abomination, dis-
Ffieiddiad, n. abhorence [gust
Ffieiddio, v. to loath, to abominate [able
Ffieiddiol, a. abhorent, abomin-
Ffieiddiwr, n. an abhorrer
Ffieiddrwydd, n. abhorrence
Ffil, n. a scud, a quick dart
Ffilcas, n. offcasts, old rags
Ffilog, n. a wing; a filly, a wanton girl: a. that scuds or darts
Ffiloges, n. flirting girl
Ffilor, n. a minstrel, a fiddler
Ffiloreg, n. vain babbling, idle
Ffilores, n. a female fiddler [talk
Ffill, n. a writhe, a twist
Ffilliad, n. a writhing about
Ffillio, v. to writhe, to twist
Ffin. n. a boundary, a limit
Ffinedd, n. a boundary
Ffinfa, n. a boundary
Ffinfaen, n. a boundary stone
Ffiniad, n. a bounding
Ffinio, v. to bound, to limit
Ffiniol, a. bounding, limiting
Ffiogen, n. a coney, a rabbit
Ffion, n. a crimson hue: a. crimson
Ffith, n. a gliding motion
Ffithell, n. a young salmon
Ffithelliad, n. a platting the upper row of rods in hedging
Ffithellu, v. to plat the top row in hedging
Ffithlen, n. a glider, a writher
Ffithliad, n. a gliding
Ffithlio, v. to glide, to dart
Ffla, n. a parting off, or from
Fflaced, n. a flock, a bunch
Ffladr, a. doting; oafish; flattering
Ffladraidd, a. oafish; fondling

Ffladriad, n. doting
Ffladru, v. to dote, to fondle
Fflag, n. what parts from, or rifted
Fflaim, n. a lancet
Fflair, n. a feist; a puff
Fflais, n. a break, a rent
Fflam, n. a flame, a blaze [ing
Fflamaidd, a. like a flame, flam-
Fflameg, n. inflamation, blearedness
Fflamiad, n. a flaming
Fflamio, v. to inflame, to blaze
Fflamiol, a. flaming, blazing
Fflamllyd, a. flammeous, flamy
Fflamwch, n. a flaming state
Fflamychu, v. to emit flame
Fflask, n. a basket: a flask
Fflasgaid, n. a flaskful
Fflasged, n. a straw vessel
Fflau, n. a spread out, radiation
Fflaw, n. a ray, a dart
Ffle, n. a hem round, a closure
Fflech, n. a squeak, a squeal
Ffled, n. restraint; refusal, a. restricted; scarce
Ffleg, n. a squeak, a squeal
Fflegam, squeaking; chuckling
Ffleimio, v. to lance, to use a
Ffleiriad, n. a feisting [fleam
Ffleirio, v. to feist; to stink
Ffleiryn, n, a stinkard
Ffles, n. lees, or dregs
Fflew, n. that keeps in; a guard
Ffliclad, n. a darkening over
Fflicio, v. to be overcast
Fflich, n. a squeak, a squeal
Fflichio, v. to squeak out
Fflöad, n. a darting, radiation
Ffloch, a. rise, abrupt; quick
Fflochen, n. a splinter; a rift
Fflochenu, v. to splinter
Fflochi, v. to dart suddenly
Fflochiad, n. a darting out
Fflöew, radiant, lucid, dazzling
Ffloi, v. to radiate, to diverge
Fflöyn, n. a shiver; a shred
Fflu, n. a breaking out

Fflur, n. bright hue; bloom
Fflureg, n. a ship's prowl forecastle
Ffluro, v. bloom, to seem bright
Ffluwch, n. a bushy hair
Fflw, n. tendency, to spread out
Fflwch, a. rife, full, brisk
Fflychio, v to break out suddenly [flee
Ffo, n. a flight, to retreat: v. to
Ffoad, n. a running away, a fleeing
Ffoadur, n. a fugitive [ing
Ffoaduriad, n. a fugitive
Ffoadures, a. fugitive, fugacious
Ffoawd, n. the act of retreating
Ffoawdr, n. a fugitive
Ffoawl, a. fugitive, fleeing
Ffoc, n. fire place, furnace
Ffod, n. a shank, a leg
Ffodog, a. thick-shanked
Ffodio, v. to prosper, to be lucky
Ffodiog, a. prosperous
Ffodus, a. fortunate, lucky
Ffoddi, v. to cast a splendour
Ffoddiain, a. phosphoric
Ffoddiaint n. phosphorus
Ffoedig, a. fugitive, retreating
Ffoedigaeth, n. fugation
Ffoedigrwydd, n. fugacity
Ffoi, v. to retreat, to run away, to flee
Ffol, round; silly, foolish; vain
Ffoledd, n. foolishness, folly
Ffolen, n. buttoc, haunch
Ffolenig, n. a little buttock
Ffolenog, a. of large buttock
Ffolenu, v. to become round
Ffoles, n. a silly female
Ffoli, v. to delude; to deride
Ffolineb, n. foolishness, folly
Ffoll, n. a broad squab
Ffollach, n. a squab, a waddler
Ffon, n. a staff; a cudgel
Ffondoriad, n. a striking with a stick, a breaking a stick on one [to cudgel
Ffondorio, v. to beat with a stick,
Ffonodio, v. to cudgel

Ffonwaew, n. javelin
Ffor, n. an opening, a pass
Fforch, n. a fork; a prong
Fforchaid, n. what is taken up on a fork [a. bisulcous
Fforchdroed, n. a cloven foot
Fforchi, v. to fork; to furcate
Fforchiad, n. furcation, a forking
Fforchog, a. forked; straddling
Fforchogi, v. to divaricate, to straddle
Fforchogiad, n. a forking
Fforchol, a. forking, forked
Fforchwain, n. a rustic cart
Ffordd, n. a way, a passage, highway
Fforddiad, n. a directing a way. a finding out a way
Fforddio, v. to explore a way, to direct a way
Fforddol, a. wayfaring
Fforddoli, v. to direct a way
Fforddrych, a. wayfaring
Forddwr, n. a traveller
Fforddrwydd, n. a wayfare
Fforest, n. a forest; a park
Fforestu, v. to forest
Fforfed, n. a forfeit
Fforiad, n. an exploration
Fforio, v. to explore a way
Fforiol, a. exploratory
Ffos, n. a ditch, a trench
Ffosawd, n. a gash, a cut
Ffosi, v. to trench, to ditch
Ffosiad, n. a trenching
Fosp, n. breach, a gap
Ffoswn, n. a gasher; a sword
Ffothell, n. a blister, a wheal
Ffothelliad, n. a blistering
Ffothellu, v. to blister
Ffraeth, a. prompt, fluent
Ffraethaidd, of fluent utterance
Ffraethder, n. fluency
Ffraetheb, n. oratory
Ffraethebu, v. to harangue
Ffraethineb, n. eloquence
Ffraethoneg, n. elocution

Ffral, n. a crazy fellow
Ffranc, n. a youth, a freeman a frenchman
Ffranc, a. prompt; free, frank
Ffrancon, n. a beaver
Ffrau, n. a flux, a torrent: a. streaming, gushing
Ffraul, n. a rippling
Ffraw, n state of motion, bustle: a. full of motion, alert
Ffrawd, n. commotion, bustle
Ffrawdd, n. stir or tumult: a. agitated; prompt
Ffrawdden, n. humour, fancy
Ffrawddenus, a. humoursome
Ffrawddiain, a. full of motion
Frawddu, v. to be full of bustle
Ffawddun, n. a commotion
Ffrawddus, a. agitated, bustling
Ffrec, n. chatter, gibberish
Ffregod, n. a preachment
Ffregodi, v. to chatter
Ffreinig, a. free; of free growth
Ffrcs, a. active, pure, fresh
Ffresgaidd, a. of a fresh nature
Ffresgiad, n. freshness
Ffresgu, v. to grow fresh
Ffreuad, n, a gushing out
Ffreulad, n. a purling; a rippling
Ffreulo, v. to purl; to ripple
Ffreuo, v. to gush, to spurt
Ffreuol, a. gushing, spouting
Ffrew, n. a state of stillness
Ffrewi, v. to quell, to pacify
Ffrewyll, n. a scourge, whisp, whip
Ffrewylliad, n. a scourging
Ffrewyllio, v. to whip to scourge
Ffrewylliwr, n. a scourger
Ffrewyllydd, n. a scourger
Ffrewyn, n. a quelled state
Ffrewynu, v. to stop a quarrel
Ffrewynydd, n. a pacifier
Ffrid, n. sudden start
Ffridd, n. a forest; a park
Ffril, n. a trifling thing
Ffrill, n. a twiter, a chatter

Ffrin, n. the brow of a cliff
Ffring, n. a brow, a ledge
Ffris, n. a nap, a frieze
Ffrist, n. a cube; a dice
Ffristial, n. a dice-box
Ffrit, n. a quick start or jerk
Ffritten, n. a flighty female; a little girl
Ffrittyn, n. a flighty fellow
Ffriw, n. mien, aspect
Ffroch, n. fury, rage: a. raging
Ffroell, n. inflammation
Ffroen, n. a nostril, a nose
Ffroeni, v. to snort, to snuff
Ffroeniad, n. a snorting
Ffroeniol, a. of the nostril
Ffroenllym, a. sharp of scent
Ffroenllymder, n. keenness of scent
Ffroenuchel, a. of high gait
Ffroenydd, n a snorter
Ffroes, n. an omelet
Ffrom, a. fuming; testy, touchy
Ffromder, n. testiness
Ffromi, v. to fume; to be testy
Ffromiad, n. a taking a pet
Ffronc, n. a cage; a hut
Ffros, n. a quick rise, a toss
Ffrost, n. a vaunt; ostentation
Ffrostiad, n. a vaunting
Ffrostio, v to vaunt, to boast
Ffrostiwr, a bragger, a boaster
Ffrowyll, n. outrage, tumult
Ffrowyllu, v. to do outrage
Ffrowys, a. turbulent; terrible
Ffrwch, n. violent ruption
Ffrwd, n. a stream, a torrent
Ffrwg, n. violence, outrage
Ffrwgwd, n. squabble, brawl
Ffrwm, a. luxuriant, rank
Ffrws, n sudden motion
Ffrwst n. hurry, bustle
Ffrwt, n. jet, a toss; a frisk
Ffrwyd, n. pulsion, impulse
Ffrwydro, v. to explore
Ffrwydrol, a. exploding
Ffrwyl, n. drizzle, mist
Ffrwylo, v. to drizzle

Ffrwyn, n. a bridle; restraint
Ffrwyno, v. to bridle
Ffrwynol, a. bridling
Ffrwys, n. vehemency
Ffrwys, a. vehement, violent
Ffrwyso, v. to act violently
Ffrwyth, n. fruit; strength
Ffrwythiad, n. fructification
Ffrwythiannu, v. to fructify
Ffrwythiant, n. fructification
Ffrwythineb, n. fructuosity
Ffrwythlon, fruitful: luxuriant
Ffrwythlondeb, n. fruitfulness
Ffrwythloni, v. to be fruitful
Ffrwytho, v. to frutcify, to bear
Ffrydan, n. a stream, et [fruit
Ffrydiad, n. a flowing
Ffrydio, v. to stream
Ffrydiol, a. streaming
Ffrydiolrwydd, n. fluidity
Ffrymiaw, v. to grow luxuriant
Ffryn, n. a quiver, a shudder
Ffrysiad, n. a bustling
Ffrysio, v. to bustle
Ffrystell, n. a hurly-burly
Ffrystellu, v. to bustle
Ffrystiad, n. festination
Ffrystio, v. to hurry off
Ffrystiol, a. full of bustle
Ffrystiwr, n. a bustler
Ffu, n. fleeting state; a. passing
Ffuanniad, n. a feigning
Ffuannol, feigning, dissembling
Ffuanu, v. to feign, to dissemble
Ffuant, n. a feint, a pretence
Ffuantu, v. to counterfeit
Ffuantwr, n. a hipocrite
Ffug n. feint, disguise
Ffugiad, n. a disguising
Ffugio, v. to disguise
Ffugiwr, n. a deceiver
Ffugliad, n. an inflation
Ffugllaw, v. to inflate
Ffugyr, n. a type, a figure
Ffull, n. haste; celerity
Ffulliad, n. a hastening
Ffullio, v. to hasten, to bustle
Ffulliog, a. full of bustle

Ffumer, n. a chimney
Ffun, n. a bundle, a bind
Ffunell, n. a small bundle
Ffunen, n. a lace, a fillet
Ffuneniad, n. a filleting
Ffunenu, v. to bind, to lace
Ffunud, n. figure, manner
Ffur, a. wary, wily, wise
Ffured, n. a wily one, a ferret
Ffuredu, v. to ferret out
Efurf, n. shape; form; order
Ffurfafen, n. a firmament
Ffurfeiddio, v. to frame
Ffurfiad, n. a shaping
Ffust, n. a flail, a thrasher
Ffustiad, n. a thrashing
Ffusto, v. to beat, to bang
Ffwdan, n. bustle, hurry
Ffwdanu, v. to be in a hurry
Ffwdanus, a. fidgetty, hurried
Ffwg, n. what is volatile
Ffwgws, n. dry leaves; tobacco
Ffwl, n. a blunt one; a fool
Ffwlach, n. refuse; light-corn
Ffwn, n. a pwff; a sigh
Ffwrch, n. a furcation
Ffwrdd, n. a going off, : prep off, from : ad. away
Ffwrn, n. a furnace, an oven
Ffwrw, n. soft hair: fur
Ffwtiar, n. a squab, a paunch
Ffwtog, n. a short tail, a scut
Ffwyl, n. a stroke; a foil
Ffwyn, n. hay newly cut
Ffwynen, n. a hay bandage
Ffwynog, n. a meadow
Ffwyr, n. a drive: an onset
Ffwyriad, n. an impulsion
Ffwyro, v. to impel
Ffyd, n. garments, robes
Ffydd, n. faith, reliance
Ffyddio, v. to have faith
Ffyddiol, a. relating to faith
Ffyddlon, a. faithful
Ffyddlondeb, n. faithfulness
Ffydloniad, n. a faithful one
Ffylor, n. dust, powder
Ffyll, a. overgrown; gloomy

Ffyllio, v. to overshade
Ffynadwy, a. fortunate
Ffyned, n. a respiration
Ffynegl, n. a furrow
Ffyneglu, v. to furrow
Ffynel, n. an air-hole, a vent
Efyniant, n. prosperity
Ffyniannus, a. prospering
Ffynnon, n. a fountain, a well,
Ffynnonell, n. an issue [a spring
Ffynnoni, v. to rise in springs
Fynnu, v. to prosper
Ffyr, n. a solid body
Ffyrf, a. thick; firm, steady
Ffyrfau, v. to become thick
Ffyrfder, n. thickness firmness
Ffyrfeiddio, v. to become firm; to make firm
Ffyrfiant, n. thickness
Ffyrnig, a. fierce
Ffyrnigo, v. to grow fierce
Ffyrnigrwydd, n. fierceness
Ffysg, n. impetuosity: a. hasty, impetuous
Ffysgiad, n. a hastening
Ffysgio, v. to hasten
Ffysgiol, a. impetuous

G

GAD, n. a parting; leave
Gadael, v. to quit, to leave
Gadaw, v. to quit, to leave
Gadawedigaeth, n. act of leaving
Gadawiad, n. a leaving
Gadawedig, a. relinquished permitted
Gafael, n. a hold, a grasp
Gafaelfach, n. grappling-hook
Gafaelgar a. apt to hold
Gafaelgarwch, n. tenaciousness
Gafaelgi n. mastiff dog
Gafaeliad, n. a hold; a caption
Gafaeliog, a. having hold
Gafaelu, v. to hold, to grasp
Gafaelus, a. apt to lay hold
Gafaelwr, n. a distrainer
Gafl. n. a fork: the stride

Gaflach. n. a fork; the stride an angle; a dart
Gaflachiad, n. a forking
Gaflachu, v. to furcate
Gaflaw, n. a salmon peel
Gaflaweg, n. a salmon-net
Gafr n. a goat, a she-goat
Gafraidd, a. like a goat
Gafren, n. a little goat
Gafriad, n. a stacking of corn
Gafriaw, v. to stack corn
Gafrlam, n. a capriole
Gag, n. an aperture, a cleft
Gagen, n. a cleft, a chink
Gagendor, n. yawning gulf
Gageniad, n, a rifting
Gai, n. foam, spray, froth
Gail, n. the eyelid
Gaing, n. a wedge
Gair, n. word; a saying
Gaith, n. utterance: a. open
Gâl, n. a plain; a gaol; a foe a. spread out; clear, fair
Galaeth, n. the galaxy
Galan, n. dead body, corpse
Galanas, n. murder
Galanastra, n a massacre
Galanasol, a. murderous
Galanasu, v. to murder
Galar, n. mourning, grief
Galareb, n. threnody
Calargân, n. a monody
Galariad, n. a mourning
Galarloes. n. pang of grief
Galarnad, n. lamentation
Galarnadu, v. to utter moans
Galarnwyf, n. passion of grief
Galaru, v. to lament
Galarus, a. mournful, sad
Galarwisg, a. mourning dress
Galarwr, n. a mourner
Galawnt, a. fair, brave, gallant
Galeg, n. Gaulish tongue
Galiod, n. people of Gaul
Galofydd, n. an architect
Galofyddiaeth, n. architecture
Galon, n. hostile ones, foes
Galw, n. a call; a vocation

Galwad, n. calling: vocation
Galwai, n. vocative case
Galwedig. a. called, named
Galwedigaeth, n. a calling
Galwedigol, a. denominative
Galwyn, n. a gallon, eight pints
Gall, n. energy; ability
Gallad, n. a being able
Galldwymyn, n. tertian ague
Galldwyn, n. the plague
Galledig, a. potential
Galledigaeth n. possibility
Galled, v. to be possible, to be able
Gallt n. an ascent, a cliff
Galltofydd, n. a mechanic
Gallu, n. power, ability: v. to be able, may or can
Galluad, n. a making able
Galluadwy, a. possible
Galluedigaeth, n. a making able
Galluedd, n. puissance
Galluog. a powerful, mighty
Galluogrwydd, n. potentiality
Galluogi, v. to empower
Galluol, a. energetic, potent
Gân, n. a birth; the thrush: n. capacity; a mortice
Gan, prep. with, in connection: conj. because; whereas
Ganiad, n. a containing
Gânu, v. to contain, to hold
Gâr, n. the ham; the shank
Gar, prep. at, by, near
Garan, n. a shank; a crane
Garanu, v. to shank, to shaft
Gardys, n. a garter
Gardd. n. a close; a garden
Garddiad, n. a gardening
Garddu, v. to make a garden
Garddwr, n. a gardener
Garddy, n. the seed caraway
Gargam, a. knock-kneed
Garhir, a. long-shanked
Garllaes, a. limping, halting
Garlleg, n the garlick
Garllegan, n the head of garlick
Garm, n. a shout, an outcry
Garmiad, n. a shouting

| GAR | 150 | GEN |

Garmio, v. to set up a cry
Garmiol, a. shouting, bawling
Garsyth, a. stiff in a ham
Garth, n. a buttress; a ridge; enclosure
Garthan, n. an encampment
Garthan, v. to fortify, to defend
Garthon, n. an ox-goad
Garw, n. a rough; a torrent; the after-birth: a. rough
Garwâad, n. a roughening
Garwâu, v. to roughen
Garwedd, n. a roughness
Garwen, n. a virago
Gâst, n. a bitch
Gâu, n. a falsehood, a lie: a. masked, false
Gauaf, n. the winter
Gauafdy, n. a winter-house
Gauafle, n. winter quarters
Gauafnos, n. winter night
Gauafol, a. wintry, brumal
Gauafu, v. to pass a winter
Gaugrefydd, n. heresy
Gaw, n. a sinew, a tendon
Gawl, n. a dawn: a. holy
Gawr, n. shout; a grey colour
Gawri, v. to bawl
Gawriad, n. a shouting
Gawy, a. sinewy; nervous
Gefail, n. tongs, pincers; smithy
Gefeiliad, n. a nipping
Gefeilio, v. to hold with tongs
Gefell, n. a twin
Gefyn, n. a fetter
Gefyniad, n. a fettering
Gefynog, a. fettered, sheckled
Gefynu, v. to fetter
Gefynwr, a. fetterer
Geian, a. spray, foam
Geifawr, a. greatly foaming
Geilig, a. hunting, exploring
Geilwad, n. a caller; a driver
Geingiad, n. a wedging
Geingio, v. to drive a wedge
Geida, n. good report, fame
Geirdardd, n. etymology
Geirdarddawg, a. etymological

Geirdro, n. pun, quibble
Geirdroi, v. to pun, to quibble
Geirddadlu, v. to cavil
Geirddoeth, a. of discreet words
Geirgar, a. verbose, wordy
Geiriad, n. a wording
Geiriadur, n. a dictionary
Geirio, v. to word, to phrase
Geiriog, a. abounding in words
Geiriol, a. verbal, verbose
Geiriolaeth, n. phraseology
Geirwir, a. of true words
Geirydd, n. a worder: a speaker
Gel, n. aptness to glide; a leech
Gelach, n. a sorry fribble
Gele, n. a leech
Gelen, n. that glides; leech
Geleurudd, a. crimson stained
Geleuruddio, to stain with blood
Gelin, n. a shoot, a sprig
Gelwain, v. to be crying out
Gelwig, n. brushwood
Gelyn, n. a foe, an enemy
Gelynes, n. a female foe
Gelyniaeth, n. hostility
Gelyniaethus, a. hostile
Gelynol, a. hostile, adverse
Gelyst, n. sedges, flags
Gell, n. a dun hue: a. dun
Gellaig, n. pears
Gellast, n. buck-hound bitch
Gellegwydd, n. pear trees
Gellgi, n. a buck-hound
Gellhesg, n. the corn sedge
Gem, n. a gem, a jewel
Gemu, v. to set with gems
Gemydd, n. a jeweler
Gen, n. intellect; soul life; a mouth: a jaw; a chin
Genau, n. jaws, a mouth
Genedigaeth, n. nativity
Genedigol, a. native, natal
Geneth, n. a girl; a daughter
Genethaidd, a. girlish
Genethig, n. a little maid
Geneuaid, n. a chopful
Geneugoeg, n. a lizard
Geneuol. a oral, by mouth

Genfa. n. a snaffle, a bi
Geni, v. to be brought forth; to be contained
Genid, n. nativity, birth
Genill, n. offspring, issue
Genilles, n. a young nymph
Genogyl, n. the mandible
Genwair, n. angling rod
Genweiriad, n. angling
Genweiriaw, v. to angle
Ger, n. utterance; a cry: prep. by, at, near
Gerag, prep. in a direction to
Gerain, v. to squeak, to cry
Gerbron, prep. in presence of
Gerfydd, prep. in contact with
Geri, n. choler, bile, gall
Geriaidd, a. choleric, bilious
Geriawl, a. relating to bile
Gerllaw, prep. at hand, by
Germain, v. to be wailing
Gern, n. a progenitor in the fifth degree
Gerwin, a. rough, severe
Gerwinad, n. a roughening
Gerwindeb, n. roughness
Gerwino, v. to roughen
Gerwinol, a. rough; horrid
Gerwydd, prep. in presence of
Gerwynebol, a. opposite
Gerwynebu, v. to place opposite
Geryn, n. a squeaker, a drake
Geuaddoli, v. to worship falsely
Geuaddoliad, n. idolatry
Geuaddolwr, n. an idolater
Geuaw, v. to falsify, to lie
Geuawd, n. a falsifying
Geuawl, a. false, deceiving
Geubwll, n. false reason
Geudeb, n. falsehood, deceit
Geudy, n. a privy-house
Geuddadlu, v. to parologize
Geudduw, n. a false god
Geuedd, n. falsity, fallacy
Geuffydd, n. a false faith
Geulith, n. heterodoxy
Geulin, n. a chimera
Geurith, n. a phantom

Geuwedd, n. an illusion
Gewach, n. a greedy gut
Gewai, n. a lean glutton
Gewyn, n. a sinew
Gewynog, a. having sinews
Gewynol, a. relating to sinews
Gi, n. a fine fibre; a nerve
Giach, n. a snipe
Giau, n. system of the nerves
Gieuawg, a. having nerves
Gieuawl, relating to the nerves
Gid, n a she goat, a goat
Gien, n. a single nerve
Gieuedd, n. nervous system
Gieuyn, n. a nerve, a sinew
Gil, n. a yielding; a ferment
Gildiaw, v. to yield, to produce
Gilydd, n. mutual selves: pro. each other
Gin, n. a pelt; a thin skin
Gingroen, n. the toad-flax, a stinking mushroom
Giniad, n. a flaying
Ginio, v. to flay, to strip
Girad, n. mourning; a piteous
Gist, n. clay earth
Giten, n. a little she goat
Gith, n. cockle
Glafoerion, n. drivel; slaver; the foam of the mouth, spittle
Glafriad, n. a glavering
Glafru, v. to glaver, to flatter
Glai, a. glistening, smooth
Glaif, n. a crooked sword
Glain, n. that is pure, a gem; an angel; a saint: a. pure
Glân, n. a brink   side
Glân, a. pure, clear, clean; holy
Glanhad, n. a cleansing
Glanawl, a. cleansing
Glanâu, v. to purify, to cleanse
Glandeg, a. comely and fair
Glaniad, n. going ashore
Glaniaw, v. to go ashore
Glanwaith, a. clean, tidy
Glanweithiad, n. cleansing
Glanweithdra, n. cleanliness
Glanweithio, v. to make clean

Glas, n. blue; verdancy: a. blue; pale; gray
Glasawg, a. being blue or livid
Glasbaill, n. bloom of fruit
Glasdonen, n. scarlet oak
Glas iorch, n. leveret; a cub
Glasdwr, n. milk and water
Glasddydd, n. dawning day
Glasfaen n. blue stone, vitriol
Glasfaran, n. a samlet
Glasgangen, n. a grayling
Glasgoch, n. purple: a. purple
Glasgoed, n. green trees
Glasgolydd, n. the small guts
Glasgroen, n. a cuticle
Glashaid, n. a young swarm
Glasiad, n. a tingeing with blue
Glaslangc, n. a youth
Glaslannerch n. a paddock
Glasog, n. a liver; a gizzard
Glasresaw, n. half welcome
Glasrew, n. a hoar frost
Glassan, n. a greyling
Glasu, v. to make blue
Glaswelw, a. of a blue paleness
Glaswellt, n. green grass [grass
Glaswelltyn, n. a blade of green
Glaswen, n. a simper, a smirk
Glasweniad, n. a simpering
Glaswenu, v. to simper
Glaswst, n. the choloris
Glaswydd, n. green sapplings
Glaswyn, a. of a bluish white
Glaswyrdd, a. of a bluish green
Glaw, n. brightness, lucidity
Glawdd, n. lustre, splendour
Gleiad, n. dried dung, blake
Gleiaden, n. blake, a case
Gleindid, n. purity; holiness
Gleindorch, n. a string of beads
Gleinfaen, n. the alabaster
Gleiniad, n. a brightening
Gleiniadur, n. a pair of snuffers
Gleiniawu, v. to purify
Gleisiedyn, n. a salmon
Gleisiadeg, n. a salmon net
Gleision, n. clarified whey
Glendid, n. purity; fairness

Glesid, n. blueness; paleness
Glesin, n. the greensward
Glesni, n. blueness; verdancy
Gleswg, n. blueness: verdancy
Glesygen, n. a green spot
Glesyn, n. what is blue
Glew, n. a resolute man; a. persevering; brave
Glewa, v. to scrape together
Glewder, n. resolution; bravery
Glin, n. the knee
Glingam, a. knock-need
Gliniad, n. a kneeling
Glinio, v. to knee; to kneel
Gliniogai, n. cow-wheat
Glo, n. that is bright; coal
Globwll, n. a coal-pit
Gloddest, n. a carousal
Gloddestu, v. to carouse
Gloddestwr, n. a reveller
Gloen, a glower; a glow-worm
Glocn-byw, n. a butterfly
Gloes, n. a pang; a qualm
Gloesi, v. to cause a pang
Gloesiad, n. a causing a pang
Gloesineb, n. state of anguish
Gloesion, n. pangs, qualms
Gloesygiad, n. a swooning
Gloesygu, v. to faint
Gloesyndod, n. fainting state
Gloesynu, v. to swoon, to faint
Gloth, a. voluptuous; greedy
Glowr, n. a collier
Gloyn, n. a burning coal; a glow-worm
Gloyw, a. bright, transparent
Gloywdeg, a. brightly fair [ness
Gloywder, n. clearness, bright-
Gloywddu, a. of bright black
Gloywedd, n. transparency
Gloywgain, a. brightly fair
Gloywgoch, a. of bright red
Gloywi, v. to clear, to brighten
Gloywiad, n. a brightening
Gloywineb, n. lucidity
Gloywlys, n. the euphrasy
Gloywon, n. clear of liquids
Glud, n. a leader, a chief

Glwth, n. voluptuary; a couch
 a. voluptuous, sensual
Glwyd, a. of fair appearance
Glwys, a. pure; holy: fair
Glwysdeb, n. sanctitude
Glwyso, v. to sanctify
Glwysol, a. sanctified; pure
Glyd, n. glue; birdlime; a. tenacious, diligent
Glydaidd, a. of a sticky nature
Glydaw, v. to cement; to glue
Glydedd, n. viscidity
Glydiad, n. a glueing
Glydiogi, v. to make viscid
Glydiogrwydd, n. clamminess
Glydiol, a. viscous, glutinous
Glydioli, v. to make viscid
Glydrwydd, n. clamminess
Glydwydd, n. lime twigs
Glyfoer, n. drivel, slobber
Glyfoerllyd, a. apt to drivel
Glyn, n. a deep vale, a glen
Glŷn, n. adhesion, sticking: a. adherent
Glynedig, a. sticking
Glyniad, n. a clinging
Glynol, a. adhereing, sticking
Glynu, v. to stick, to cling
Glynwr, n. an adherent, stickler
Glythi, n. voluptuousness
Glythig, a. voluptuous; greedy
Glythineb, n. riotous living
Glythinebgar, a. voluptuous
Glythinebgarwch, n. voluptu-
Glythinebu, v. to revel[ousness
Glythinebwr, n. a voluptuous
Glythni, n. sensuality
Glythog, a. voluptuous
Glythol, a. voluptuous, greedy
Glythu, v. to live sensually
Glythwr, n. a gormandizer
Glythyn, n. a small couch
Glyw, n. a governer, a ruler: a. regulating, ruling
Gnawd, n. habit; custom: a. habitual, usual
Gne, n. hue, tint, complexion
Gnes, n. a flutter, a hover

Gni, n. what pervades; shock
Gnif, n. pain, anxiety; toil
Gnis, n. a brandish, a flourish
Gnisiad, n. a brandishing
Gnodawl, a. customary
Gnodi, v. to habituate,
Gnodig, a. habitual, common
Gnotâad, n. an accustoming
Gnotai, n. a token; a halo
Gnotoal, a. accustomed, usual
Go, ad. somewhat, partly
Goachol, a. somewhat puny
Gob, n. a mound, a pad
Gobaill, n. a coarse flour
Gobaillio, v. to make coarse flour
Gobaith, n. hope, expectation
Gobant, n. small dingle
Gobed, n. a cobiron
Gobeithgar, a. hopeful
Gobeithiad, n. a hoping
Gobeithio, v. to hope
Gobeithiol, a. hoping
Gobeithioldeb, n. hopefulness
Gobell, n. a pad, a saddle
Gobellu, v. to pad, to saddle
Goben, n. a penultima
Gobenol, a. penultimate
Gobenu, v. to conclude nearly
Gobenydd, n. a bolster
Gobenyddiad, n. a bracketing; bolstering
Gobenyddu, v. to bolster
Gober, n. operation, deed
Goberiad, n. an operating
Goberol, a. operating, effective
Goberu, v. to operate[dubbingly
Gobiso, v. to discharge urine
Goblyg, n. a half double
Gobr, n. recompense; fee; wages; bride
Gobriad, n. recompense
Gobrid, n. what is somewhat dear; a. somewhat dear
Gobrol, a. compensative
Gobru, v. to compensate, to fee
Gobrwy, n. reward, fee
Gobrwyad, n. a rewarding
Gobrwyaeth, n. act of feeing

| GOB | 154 | GOD |

Gobrwycdrgaeth, n. remuneration, the act of hiring
Gobrwyo, v. to reward, to remunerate; to bride
Gobrwyol, a. rewarding
Gobryn, n. dessert, merit
Gobrynol, a. meriting
Gobryniad, n. a meriting
Gobrynu, v. to meri', to deserve
Gobwyll, n. consideration
Gobwyllo, v. to consider
Gobwyllus, a. considerate
Gobwys, n. tendency to press
Gobwyso, v. to gravitate
Goganu, v. to lampoon, to sing ironically
Gochel, v. to avoid, to beware
Gocheladwy, a. avoidable
Gochelgar, a. apt to shun
Gochelgarwch, circumspection
Gocheliad, n. a shunning
Gochelog, a. avoiding, wary
Gochelyd, v. to avoid, to shun
Gochrymu, v. to crouch
Gochrynu, v. to quake a little
Gochwaeth, n. a slight taste
Gochwerw, a. somewhat bitter
Gochwilio, v. to search slightly
Gochwith, a. rather awkward
Gochwyth, n. a slight puff
God, n. incontinence; adultery
Godaer, a. slightly importunate
Godaran, n. a hollow murmur
Godarth, n. slightly vapour
Godawel, a. somewhat
Godeb, n. incontinence
Godebog, a. incontinent
Godebyg, a. slight, similar
Godech, n. a lurk, a skulk
Godechfa, n. a lurking place
Godechiad, n. a lurking about
Godechwr, n. a skulker
Godeneu, a. somewhat thin
Godew, a. somewhat thick, or fat
Godid, n. what is out of order
Godidog, a. rare; excellent
Godidogrwydd, n. excellence
Godineb, n. a dultery

Godinebiad, n. an adultering,
Godinebus: a. adulturous
Godinebu, v. to commit adultery
Godinebwr, n. an adulterer
Godlawd, a somewhat poor
Gododdi, v. to dissolve partly
Godor, n. a rupture; a let
Godori, v. interrupt; to let
Godoriant, n. interruption
Godre, n. a skirt, or edge
Godread, n. a skirting
Godref, n. lodge
Godrem, n. a glance
Godremu, v. to glance
Godrig, n. delay; an abode
Godro, n. a milking; v. to milk
Godroad, n. act of milking
Godrudd, a. slightly agitated
Godrwy, n. a wreath, a chain
Goduth, n. a jog trot
Godwrdd, n. murmur
Godwyth, n. slight elasticity
Gody, n. a shed, an outhouse
Godyrfu, v. to rumble
Goddail, n. tender leaves
Goddaith, n. a smothering fire, a burning of a wild
Goddan, n. shrubs, shrubbery
Godde, n. a design, purpose; v. to design, to intend
Goddef, n. sufferance, leave
Goddefaint, n. sufferance
Goddefgar, a. forbearing
Goddeflad, n. a suffering
Goddefiant, n. sufferance
Goddefol, a. passive
Goddefus, a. passive; forbearing
Goddeg, n. utterance, speech
Goddegiad, n. enunciation
Goddeithiad, n. a consuming
Goddeithio, v. to burn heath, &c.
Goddenu, v. to allure gently
Goddeu, n. intent, to design: v. to intend
Goddif, n. a fling: v. to fling
Goddiweddydd, n. day of doom
Goddiweddiad, n. an overtaking
Goddiweddu, v. to overtake

Goddiweddwr. n. overtaker
Goddiwes, v. to overtake
Goddiwesu, v. to come up with
Goddiwestwr, n. overtaker
Goddolawg, a. endowed
Goddoli, v. to enrich, to endow
Godduned, n. a vow; pledge
Godduw, n. a demigod
Goddwr n. an adviser
Goddyar, n. soft murmur
Goddyariad, n. a murmuring
Goddyaru, v. to murmur
Goddyfod, v. to come gradually
Goddyn, n. an axis
Goen, n. influence, bias
Goer, n. freshness: a. fresh
Gof, n. smith; metallurgist
Gofail, n. smithy
Gofal, n. care, anxiety, solicitude, charge
Gofalhad, n. becoming anxious
Gofalhau, v. to grow anxious
Gofaliad, n. a taking care
Gofalu, v. to care to mind
Gofalus, a. careful, solicitous
Gofalwr, n. a care-taker
Gofaniaeth, n. a smith's craft
Gofar, n. wrath, ire, fury
Gofaran, a. apt to be forward
Gofas, a. somewhat shallow
Gofeg, n. mind; will; affection
Gofegol, a. mental
Gofeiliant, n. solicitude
Gofer, n. a rivulet, a rill
Goferiad, n. an effusion
Goferol, a. purling, rippling
Goferu, v. to effuse slowly
Gorferwi, v. to perboil
Gofid, n. affliction, grief
Gofidiad, n. an afflicting
Gofidio, v. to afflict, to grieve
Gofidiol, a. afflixing, vexing
Gofidus, a. vexatious, grievous
Goflaen, n. a front station
Goflawd, n. mill dust
Goflodi, v. to sprinkle flour
Goflwch, n. a small box
Gofod, n. a space, a while

Gofras, a. somewhat course
Gofreg, n. frolic gambol
Gofregedd, n. frolicsomeness
Gofri, n. attribute; glory
Gofriad, n. an attribution
Gofriol, a. conferring dignity
Gofrwy, n. a spread out
Gofrwyd, n. a quirk, a maze
Gofrwysg, n. half drunk
Gofryd, n. design, purpose
Gofryn, n. a hillock
Gofrys, n. a slight haste
Gofunad, n. a vow; a wish
Gofunedu, v. to make a vow
Gofurthiach, n. slight bickering
Gofwr, n. a mound
Gofwy, n. a visit, a visitation
Gofwyo, v. to visit
Gofwyad, n. visitation
Gofwyedig, a. visited
Gofwyol, a. visiting
Gofydd, n. an artist
Gofyddeb, n. a canon: or coronical respondence
Gofyddebol, a. scientific; can-
Gofyddiad, n. a rendering scientific, or regular
Gofyddu, v. to render scientific
Gofygedd, n. a dignified state
Gofyn, n. a demand, question: v. to demand, to ask
Gofynag, n. confidence, trust
Gofynaig, n. a request
Gofynedigaeth, n. an inquiry
Gofynedigol, a. inquistorial
Gofyniad, n. an asking; question
Gofynol, a. inquisitive, asking
Gofynnod, note of interrogation
Goffrwd, n. a streamlet
Gog, n. velocity; plenty; the cuckoo
Gogaled, a. somewhat hard
Gogam, a. somewhat crooked
Gogan, n. satire, a lampoon
Goganiad, n. a lampooning
Goganol. a. lampooning
Goganu, v. to satrize, to lampoon
Goganwawd, n. irony

Gogarth, n. that is cleansing
Gogawn, n. capability; energy, plentitude: a. capable
Gogawn, v. to endue with power
Gogawr, n. a fodder
Gogel, a. somewhat concealed
Gogelu, v. to shelter [careful
Gogelus, a. apt to shun; very
Gogelyd, v. to shun, to avoid
Gogerdd, n. a burlesque
Gogern, n. a leer, a sly look
Gogi, v. to shake, to agitate
Gogil, n. small decline
Gogiliad, n. a slight recession
Gogilio, v. to recede slightly
Gogis, n. a gentle slap
Goglais, n. a tickle
Goglawd, n. a murmur, a hum
Gogledd, n. the north: a. north
Gogleddiad, a going northward
Gogleddol, a. northern
Gogleddu, v. to veer northward
Gogleddwr n. a Norman
Gogleisiad, n. a tickling
Gogleisio, v. to tickle
Goglud, n. a dependance, trust: v. to depend
Goglywed, v. to over-hear
Gognol, v. to gnaw slightly
Gogochi, v. to give a red hue
Gogof, n. a cavern, a den
Gogofawg, a. cavernous
Goganawl, a. glorious, exalted
Gogonedd, n. that is exalted glorification: a. glorious
Gogoneddu, to exalt; to glorify
Gogoneddus, a. glorious, grand
Gogoni, v. to make glorious
Gogoniant n. glory; grandeur
Gogoriad, n. foddering
Gogorio, v. to fodder
Gogr, n. a sieve, a sierce
Gograid, n. a sieveful
Gogrin, a. somewhat brittle
Gogrisbin, a. partly crinkled
Gogrych, a. partly curled
Gogrwr, n. a sifter, a siercer
Gogryddes, n. a female shifter

Gogryn, v. to sift, to bolt
Gogryniad, n. shifting, a bolting
Gogrynwr, n. a shifter
Goguddio, v. to hide partly
Gogus, n. dalliance, a toying
Gogusol, a. dallying, toying
Gogwy, a. full of motion, active
Gogwydd, n. obliquity, bent
Gogwyddedigaeth, n. an inclination, a declination
Gogwyddiad. n. an inclination
Gogwyddo, v. to incline, to lean
Gogwyddol, inclining, tending
Gogydryw, n. homogeny: a. homogenial
Gogyfaddaw, v. to threaten
Gogyfarch, a. conspicuous
Gogyfartal, a. co-equal, similar
Gogyfiad, n. equalization
Gogyfled, n. mean breadth: a. of equal breadth
Gogyfnos, n. partial twilight
Gogyfoed, a. partly coetaneous
Gogyfred, a. partly concurrent
Gogyfres, a. of uniform range
Gogyfun, a. partially united
Gogyfurdd, n. a compeer
Gogyfuwch, a of equal height
Gogyffrawd, n. slight impulse
Gogyffred, n. slight idea
Gogyhyd, a. of equal length
Gogylch, n. a circumference
Gogylchiaith, n. periphrasis
Gogymaint, of equal magnitude
Gogynnal, v. to uphold equally
Gogysgod, n. a phantom
Goheb, n. correspondence
Gohebiad, n. a corresponding
Gohebol, a. corresponding
Gohebu, to talk; to correspond
Gohebwr, n. a correspondent
Gohen, n. inclination; bias
Gohil, n. that is but half produce; a degenerate breed
Gohir, n. a linger, a delay
Gohiriad, n. a lingering; an adjournment
Gohirio, v. to delay, to adjourn

Gohiriol, a. prolonging, delaying; lingering
Gohiriwr, n. prolonger
Gohorian, v. to act sluggishly
Gohew, a. pretty, sprightly
Gohyd, n, a mean length
Goian, n. the Omnipresent
Gol, n. covering, vesture
Golaeth, n. adoration, worship
Golaith, n. death; dissolution: v. to cause disolution
Golam, n. a hop, a skip
Golas, n. pale bluish: a. bluish
Golast, n. a hoop that is put under a bee-hive
Golau, n. light: a. light
Golch, n. lie; urine; wash
Golchbren, n. wash beetle
Golchfa, n. a washing place
Golchffon, n. a battingstaff
Golchi. v. to wash, to cleanse
Golchiad, n. a washing
Golchion, n. slops; suds
Golchioni, v. to make slops
Golchwr, n. a washer
Golchydd, n. a washer
Golchwraig, n. washer-women
Gole. n. a splendour
Goleâu, v. to illumine
Golechu, v. to skulk, to lurk
Goledu, v. partly, to expand
Goleddf, n. slight obliquity
Goleddfu, v. to go a little awry
Golefain, v. to cry faintly
Goleithio,v. to cause dissolution
Goleithwch, n. state of dissolution
Goleithychu, v. to bring into a state of dissolution
Golemain, v. to hobble, to hop
Golesg, a. somewhat feeble
Goleu, n. light: a. light
Goleuâd, n. an illumination; a luminary; a light
Golëadol a. illuminative
Golëannu, v. to illumine
Goleuant, n. illumination
Goleuder, n. light; brightness

Goleuddal, n. a chandelier
Goleuddydd, n. a slpendid day
Goleuedigaeth, n. the act of enlightening
Goleuen, n. a glow-worm
Goleufawr, a. refulgent
Goleufer, n. light, splendour
Goleuferu, v. to make luminous
Goleufynag, n. explanation
Goleulawn, a. refulgent
Goleuliw, n. a light hue: a. of a light hue
Goleulosg, n. a bright burning
Goleulosgi, v. to burn brightly
Goleuni, n. light: illustration
Goleunwy, n. gaslight
Goleuo, v. to enlighten, to give light; to reveal
Goleuol, a. enlightening
Goleuwr, n. a lighter
Geleuydd, n. a lighter
Golewychu, v. to shine faintly
Golf, n. a swallow; a gulf
Golfan, n. a sparrow
Goliniaw, to push with the knee
Golith, n. a gradual training
Golithro, v. to slip gradual
Goliw, n. a faint hue
Goliwiad, n. a giving a tint
Goliwio, v. to tint faintly
Golo, n. a covering
Golöi v. to envelope; to protect
Golöad, n. an enveloping
Golochi, v. to protect partly
Golochwyd, n. a retreat
Golochwyda, v. to live secluded
Golochwydol, a. eremetical
Golöed, n. a covering
Golof, n. a covert, a shelter
Goloni, v. to cheer a little
Golosg, n. coke: a. coked
Golosged, n. char; the snuff of a candle; tinder
Golosgi, v. to char; to singe
Golosgiad, n. a charring
Goluch, n. adoration worship
Golucho, v. to adore, to worship
Golud, n. wealth, riches

Goludiad, n. a making wealthy
Goludog, a. wealthy, rich
Goludogi, v. to make wealthy
Goludd, n. an obstruction
Goluddiad, n. an obstructing
Goluddio, v. to obstruct slightly
Goluddias, n. slight obstruction
Golwch, n. adoration
Golwg, n. sight, look, view
Golwrch, n. a box
Golwst, n. an interpreter
Golwth, n. couch, sofa
Golwybr, n. a slight trace
Golwych, n. a collop
Golwytho, v. to cut chops
Golychiad, n. a worshipping
Golychu, v. to adore, to worship
Golychwyd, n. worship
Golygfa, n. scenery, scene
Golygiad, n. a looking; vision
Golygiadu, v. to superintend
Golygiannu, v. to speculate
Golygiant, n. scene
Golygol, a. perspective
Golygu, v. to behold, to view
Golygus, a. sightly, comely
Golygwr, n. speculator, overseer, intendant; an editor
Golyn, n. guard of a sword
Golyrchiad, n. a boxful
Gollwng, n. a loosing: v. to loosen, to let go
Gollyngdod, n. absolution, acquittal
Gollyngiad, n. a loosening, a letting go; remission
Gollyngol, a, loosening
Gollyngwr, n. a loosener
Gomach, n. a shank, a shin
Gommedd, n. a refusal: v. to refuse
Gommeddiad, n. a refusing
Gonaddu, v. to shave, to plane
Gonaid, n. a hop
Goneges, n. a petty errand
Gonest, a. honest
Gonestrwydd, n. honesty
Gonestu, v. to become honest

Gonofio, v. to swim partly
Gonwyf, n. liveliness
Gor, n. an extreme; an opening; a rim; a gore, a puss; a brood. Also a prefix, denoting augmentation: a. superior; high; broody: ad. greatly; above; very
Gorad, n. superior activity
Goradain, a. of great velocity
Goraddfed, a. too ripe
Goraeth, n. a tent of a wound
Goraethu, v. to tent a wound
Goraf, a. most excellent
Goraig, n. a superior source
Gorair, n. an adverb
Goralw, n. a calling out aloud
Goralw, v. to call out loudly
Gorall, n. a superior power
Goramledd, n. superabundance
Goramlu, v. to superabound
Goramlwg, a. very conspicuous
Goraniar, a. supernatural
Gorarianu, v. to silver over
Gorarw, a. extremely rough
Gorasglod, n. fine shavings
Gorasgwn, n. excrescence
Gorau, n. the superlative: a. superlative, best
Gorawen, n. transport, joy
Gorawenu, v. to be joyous
Gorawenus, a. joyous
Gorawl, a. effectual, successful
Gorbais, n. an upper coat
Gobarchu, v. to over-prize
Gorbell, a. very far
Gorben, n. pre-eminence
Gorbigrwydd, n. remorse
Gorbigo, v. to prick greatly
Gorboeth, a. intensely hot
Gorborth, n. a carrying off
Gorbwyll, n. intimation
Gorbwyllo v. to hint
Gorbwylliad, n. a hinting
Gorbwys, n. a dependence
Gorbwyso, v. to depend, to rely
Gorch, n. what encompasses
Gorchadw, v. to keep strictly

Gorchaeth, a. greatly straitened
Gorchafarwy, n. an overspreading gloom; evening
Gorchafedd, n. supremacy
Gorchafaeth, n. superiority
Gorchafu, v. to exalt, to overcome
Gorchafus, v. tending to superiority
Gorchaled, a. extremely hard
Gorchalledd, n. conceitedness
Gorcham, n. an overstride
Gorchamu, v. to overstride
Gorchan, n. canon; incantation
Gorcharfan, n. the upper jaw
Gorcharfanedd, n. palate
Gorchaw, n. descendant in the fifth degree
Gorchawn, a. towering
Gorcheidwad, n. a guardian
Gorcheifn, n. collateral relation in the seventh degree
Gorcheiniad, n. enchanter
Gorcheiniaeth, n. incantation
Gorchest, n. an enigma; a question; a feat
Gorchestiad, n. an excelling
Gorchesol, a. extraordinary
Gorchestu, v. to do a feat
Gorchfannad, n. the upper jaw
Gorchfannedd, n. the palate
Gorchfant, n. upper jaw
Gorchfygadwy, a. vincible
Gorchfygedig, a. vanquished
Gorchfygiad, n. a vanquishing
Gorchfygol, a. vanquishing
Gorchfygu, v. to vanquish
Gorchfygwr, n. a vanquisher, a subduer
Gorchoddion, n. potentates
Gorchordd, n. supreme circle
Gorchrain, a. extremely abject
Gorchroni, v. to aggregate greatly
Gorchrwm, a. extemely bowing
Gorchrynu, v. to quake much
Gorchu, v. to fence round
Gorchudd, n. an envelope, a cover, veil
Gorchuddiad, n. an enveloping
Gorchuddio, v. to envelope
Gorchuddiol, a. enveloping
Gorchwai, a. very nimble
Gorchwant, n. extreme desire
Gorchwil, n. cautious glance
Gorchwilio, v. to look cautiously
Gorchwim, n. quick motion
Gorchwimio, v. to move suddenly
Gorchwir, n. a clear truth
Gorchwith, a. clumsy
Gorchwiw, n. a sudden whirl
Gorchwasg, n. a dead sleep
Gorchwy, n. overwhelming
Gorchwyd, n. excessive vomit
Gorchwydd, n. excessive swell
Gorchwyf, n. extreme motion
Gorchwyl, n. employ, labour
Gorchwylgar, a. labourious
Gorchwyliad, n. a labouring
Gorchwyliaeth, n. a transaction
Gorchwylio, v. to labour
Gorchyfant, n. the palate
Gorchyfarwy, n. the twilight
Gorchyflym, a. very nimble
Gorchyfnai, n. a descendant in the eighth degree
Gorchyfran, n. super-proportion
Gorchyfrif, n. over-reckoning
Gorchymaint, adv. so very great
Gorchymyn, n. injunction; command: v. to command
Gorchymynedigaeth n. the act of commanding
Gorchymyngar, a. peremptory
Gorchymyniad, a commanding
Gorchythrudd, n. excess of affliction
Gordaenu, v. to overspread
Gordaliad, n. an overpaying
Gordarddu, v. to issue extremely
Gordasg, n. excessive task
Gordawel, a. very serene
Gordew, a. excessively thick
Gordirion, a. over kind
Gordoni, v. to peel the surface
Gordrethu, v. to overtax
Gordrist, a. extemely pensive
Gordroi, v. to turn excessively

Gordrosi, v. to overdrive
Gordrymâu, v. to depress much
Gordudd, n. outer covering
Gordudded, n. an overcover
Gorduddo, v. to cover over
Gordwf, n. an overgrowth
Gordwyad, n. an over-ruling
Gordwyllo, v. to deceive much
Gordwyo, v. to over-rule
Gordwyth, n. great elasticity
Gordyfu, v. to overgrow
Gordynu, v. to pull extremely
Gordywyll, a. extremely dark
Gordd, n. an impetus; a mallet; a beetle; a churn staff: a. impetuous, ardent
Gorddail, n. exterior leaves
Gorddal, Gorddaliad, n. an upholding: v. to uphold
Gordden, n. impulse; necessity
Gordderch, n. a paramour
Gordderchad, n. a wooer
Gordderchfun, n. a concubine
Gordderchiad, n. a gallanting
Gordderchol, a. wooing; adult-
Gordderchu v. to gallant [erous
Gordderchwr, n. a paramour; a wooer; an adulterer
Gorddestlu, v. to trim over-much
Gorddethol, a. very select
Gorddewis, n. nice choice
Gorddewr, a. brave excess, foolhardy
Gorddi, v. to impel; to thumb
Gorddiad, n. an impelling
Gorddial, n. extreme revenge
Gorddibed, n. an outskin
Gorddibyn, n. overhanging precipice
Gorddibyniad, n. an overhanging
Gorddibynol, a. overhanging
Gorddibynu, v. to overhang
Gorddichellu, v. to be over crafty
Gorddichlyn, a. over-diligent
Gorddichoni, v. to be more than able
Gorddifant, n. utter deletion
Gorddifanw, a. very fleeting

Gorddifwng, a. extreme firm
Gorddig, a. very irritable
Gorddigon, n. a redundance
Gorddigoni, v. to over-satiate
Gorddigor, n. prevailing passion
Gorddillyn, a. prim to excess
Gorddin, n. impulse; a. rare
Gorddinâad, n. an impelling
Gorddinâu, Gorddino, v. to impel
Gorddiniad, n. an impelling
Gorddiog, a. extremely lazy
Gorddiogi, v. to be very lazy
Gorddirwy, n. excessive fine
Gorddisgyn, n. a steep pitch
Gorddisgyniad, n. pitching over
Gorddiwedd, Gorddiweddu, v. to overtake
Gorddiwedd, n. extreme end
Gorddiwes, n. an overtaking
Gorddiwesiad, n. an overtaking
Gorddiwesu, v. to overtake
Gorddiwyd, a. over diligent
Gorddod, n. impulse: a stroke
Gorddodi, v. to place over
Gorddodo, n. a burrowing
Gorddodyn, n. a burrower
Gorddoi, a. impulsive, driving
Gorddoeth, a. over sapient
Gorddor, n. a hatch, wicket
Gorddrud, a. over daring
Gorddrws, n. a wicket; a thres-
Gorddrych, n. a similitude [hold
Gorddryn, a. terrific
Gorddu, a. of a blackish tinge
Gordduad, n. a blacking over
Gordduo, v. to black over
Gorddwfn, a. profound
Gorddwfr, n. a water brink
Gorddwy, n. impulse; violence
Gorddwyad, n. oppression
Gorddwyar, n. din of violence
Gorddwyo, v. to oppress
Gorddwyol, a. oppressive
Gorddwyn, n. mallet; a rammer
Gorddwyrain, v. to over-exalt
Gorddwyre, a. being extremely exalted
Gorddwyreain, v. to rise over

Gorddwys, a. extremely dense
Gorddyar, n. roar: a. roaring
Gorddyarad, n. a roaring
Gorddyaru, v. to make a roar
Gorddyeithr, a. over strange
Gorddyfnad, n. an habituating
Gorddyfnaid, v. to habituate
Gorddyfnder, profundity, depth
Gorddyfniad, n. what habituates
Gorddyfnu, v. to accustom, to habituate
Gorddyfod, v. to come upon
Gorddyfodi, v. to supervene
Gorddyfodiad, n. supervention; a coming upon
Gorddyfn, n. habit, custom
Gorddygai, n. what draws away, an abductor
Gorddygan, n. harmony
Gorddygiad, n. abduction
Gorddygnu, v. to overtoil
Gorddygyd, v. to superinduce
Gorddylif, n. an over-flow
Gorddylifiad, n. defluxion
Gorddylifo, v. to over flow
Gorddyn, n. a boundary
Gorddynead, n. an effusion
Gorddyneu, v. to effuse
Gorddyrchafu, v. to over-raise
Gorddysgwyl, to expect earnest-
Gorddywal, a. extremely fierce[ly
Goreb, n. a response
Gorebiad, n. a responding
Gorebu, v. to respond
Gored, n. a fishing-wear
Goredu, v. to set a wear
Gorefras, a. very plump
Goregni, n. over exertion
Goreiliad, n. a superstructing
Goreilid, n. a grievance
Goreilidiad, n. a grieving
Goreilidio, v. to aggrieve
Goreilio, v. to superstruct
Goreirian, a. extremely fair
Goreiriol, a. adverbial
Goreiste, n. a sitting aloft
Goreisteddiad, n. a presiding
Gorel, n. an aperture

Gorelu, v. to make an aperture
Gorelwain, v. to keep crying
Gorentrych, a. supercelestial
Gorenw, n. a surname
Gorenwi, v. to surname
Gorergyd, n. an over-shot
Gorerlid, v. to pursue eagerly
Gorerlyn, v. to follow eagerly
Gores, n. waste: a. open
Goresgyn, n. a coming upon; possession; conquest; a lease
Goresgyniad, n. an overcoming; a conquering
Goresgyniaeth, n. subjugation
Goresgynol, a. overcoming
Goresgynu, v. to overcome
Goresgynwr, Goresgynydd, n. an occupant; a vanquisher; a descendant in the fifth degree
Goresiad, n. a laying open
Gorest, n. a waste; a. open waste
Gorestwng, v. to yield homage
Gorestyngiad, n. liege subject
Gorestyn, n. over-extension
Goresymu, v. to talk familiarly
Goretholi, v. to select nicely
Goreu, a. best. O'r goreu very well: v. to make, to create
Goreuad, n. a bettering
Goreuaeth, n. optimism
Goreuant, n. optimacy
Goreuo, v. to make better
Goreurad, n. a troding
Goreuraid, a. done with gold
Goreuro, v. to gild
Gorewi, v. to freeze slightly
Gorewydd, n. bodily vigour
Gorewyn, n. mantling foam
Gorewynu, v. to foam over
Gorfainc, n. a supreme seat
Gorfaint, n. an oversize
Gorfalch, a. supercilious
Gorfan, a. extremely lofty
Gorfanal, n. broom-rape
Gorfanson, n. a muttering
Gorfant, n. upper mandible
Gorfantol, n. overbalance

Gorfantoli, v. to overbalance
Gorfaran, n. a grand front
Gorfas, a. extremely shallow
Gorfawr, a. extremely great
Gorfeddu, to possess overmuch
Gorfeiddio, v. to over-dare
Gorfelyn, a. very yellow
Gorferw, n. froth, scum
Gorferwi, v. to bubble
Gorfethiant, n. extreme debility
Gorfethu, v. to fail completely
Gorfin, n. the outer edge
Gorflawdd, n. extreme uproar
Gorflun, a. very tiresome
Gorfloedd, n. an outcry
Gorflwch, n. goblet, cup
Gorflwng, a. very sullen
Gorfod, n. impulse: necessity; mastery victory: v. to get superior: to necessitate, to oblige to be obliged
Gorfodaeth, n. compulsion
Gorfodedd, n. ascendency
Gorfodiad, n. a compelling
Gorfodog, a. being compelled
Gorfodogaeth, n. obligation
Gorfodogi, v. to take obligatory
Gorfodol, a. compulsive
Gorfoledd, n. triumph; gladness
Gorfoleddiad, n. a triumphing
Gorfoleddu, v. to triumph, to rejoice greatly
Gorfoleddus, a. triumphant
Gorfoli, v. to flatter
Gorfoliant, n. adulation
Gorfras, a. over gross, over fat
Gorfraint, n. superior privilege
Gorfrau, a. extremely brittle
Gorfraw, n. extreme panic
Gorfrwd, a. very ardent
Gorfryd, n. magnanimity
Gorfrydiant, n. a paroxysm
Gorfrydio, v. to overheat
Gorfrydol a. magnanimous
Gorfrys, n. great haste
Gorfuan, a. being over-quick
Gorfudd, n. supreme gain
Gorfygu, v. to vanquish

Gorfyd, n. rivalship, envy
Gorfyniad, n. emulation
Gorfynig, a. emulous, envious
Gorfynog, a. emulous, envious
Gorfynu, n. ascent, up-hill
Gorfynydd, n. an ascent
Gorfyw, a. living beyond
Gorffawd, n. extreme luck
Gorfflam, n. bright flame
Gorfflemychu, v. to flame greatly
Gorfflwch, a. extremely rife
Gorffrwd, n. a violent torrent
Gorffyniant, n. excess of prosperity
Gorffysg, n. extreme speed
Gorgoch, a. extreme red
Gorgoddi, v. to vex, to excess
Gorgred, n. implicit belief
Gorgyd, n. implicit belief
Gorgryd, n. extreme agitation
Gorguddio, v. to cover over
Gorgwyddo, v. to over fall
Gorgyfuwch, a. superior
Gorgyffraw, n. extreme agitation
Gorgyffred, n. a surmise
Gorgylch, n. an outer circle
Gorgylchynu, v. to surround
Gorhael, a. over liberal
Gorheb, n. a response
Gorhediad, n. a flying above
Gorhelaeth, a. over ample
Gorhenaint, n. extreme age
Gorhendad, n. great grandfather
Gorhendaid, great great grandfather [er
Gorhenfam, n. great grandmoth-
Gorhengaw, n. ancestor in the fifth degree [mother
Gorhennain, great great grand-
Gorhenw, n. a surname
Gorhenwi, v. to surname
Gorhesg, n. large reeds
Gorhiliog, a. very prolific
Gorhiniog, n. a lintel
Gorhirio, v. to linger much
Gorhoen, n. extreme vivacity
Gorhoeni, v. to exhilarate
Gorhoenus, a. extremely joyous

Gorhoff, a. very delectable
Gorhoffedd, n. chief delight
Gorhoffi, v. to delight extremely
Gorhofflant, n. extreme delight
Gorholi, v. to inquire overmuch, to question overmuch
Gorhoni, v. to assert overmuch
Gorhudd, n. extreme illusion
Gorhuddo, v. to overveil
Gorhun, n. excess of sleep
Gorhydru, n. over confidence
Gorhynod, a. very remarkable
Gorhynt, n. a superior course
Gori, n. brooding; suppuration: v. to brood
Goriad, n. a brooding
Gorian, v. to be querulous
Goriain, v. to keep crying out
Gorifynu, n. ascent
Gorimyn, n. a chink, a cleft
Goris, prep. inferior to below: adv. beneath, underneath
Goriselu, v. to make very low
Gorisgell, n. scum of liquor
Gorith, n. phantom, illusion
Goriw, n. gentle ascent
Gorlad, n. supreme grace
Gorlaes, a. very low or trailing
Gorlais, n. shrill tone
Gorlaith, a. extremely moist
Gorlam, n. an overskip
Gorlamu, v. to overskip
Gorlanâd, n. super-purgation
Gorlanw, n. repletion; high tide
Gorlas, n. superior blue; a. of superior blue
Gorlasar, n. blue enamel
Gorlasu, v. to give a blue hue
Gorlawen, a. extremely joyful
Gorlawn, a. over-full
Gorledu, v. to over-expand
Gorlefain, v. to cry out aloud
Gorlenwi, v. to over-fill
Gorlesu, v. to benefit extremely
Gorlewin, n. the west
Gorlidio, v. to chafe extremely
Gorlif, n. an upper current
Gorlifiant, n. a flowing over

Gorlifo, v. to flow very strongly; to flow above
Gorlithro, v. to overslip
Gorliw, n. an apparent hue
Gorliwio, v. to colour over
Gorloes, n. a murmuring sound; an organ: a murmuring
Gorloni, v. to cheer extremely
Gorlosgi, v. to over-burn
Gorlosgiad, n. an over-burning
Gorludd, n. extreme depression
Gorludded, n. extreme fatigue
Gorlwng, a. extreme indraught
Gorlwm, a. extreme bare
Gorlwybro, v. to over-trace
Gorlwyddo, v. to help on
Gorlwyno, v. to escort; to convey
Gorlwyth, n. an over-load
Gorlwytho, v. to overburden
Gorlyd, a. broody; suppurative
Gorlyfnu, v. to smooth over
Gorlyna, v. to tipple to excess
Gorlyncu, v. to gorge, to gulp, to swallow greedily
Gorllad, n. benediction
Gorlladen, n. consecrated bread
Gorllaes, a. trailing; drooping
Gorllaesu, v. to trail; to drawl
Gorllanw, n. full tide
Gorllawes, a. extremely expert
Gorllawn, a. over full, replete
Gorllechu, v. to skulk much
Gorllenwi, v. to overflow
Gorllewin, n. the ultimate; a rear; the west
Gorllewinol, a. westerly
Gorllewydd, n. the west
Gorllwyn, n. an escort
Gorllyd, a. suppurative
Gorllydd, n. an embryo
Gorllym, a. extremely sharp
Gorm, n. a plenum
Gormail, n. oppression
Gormant, n. plentitude
Gormedd, n. an over-running
Gormeillo, v. to prevail, to predominate; to over-run
Gormeisiad, n. a molester

Gormes, n. molestation
Gormesdeyrn, n. an usurping prince, an intruding tyrant
Gormesiad, n. a molesting
Gormeslyn, n. plethora
Gormesol, a. molesting, intrusive
Gormesu, v. to molest, to intrude
Gormesydd, n. a molester
Gormod, Gormodd, n. excess: a. too much
Gormodedd, n. superabundance, excess
Gormodi, v. to superabound
Gormodol, a. superabundant
Gormodoldeb, n. excess
Gormu, to intrude; to pervade
Gormwyth, n. a rheum
Gormwytho, to generate rheum
Gorne, n. superior or exterior hue; blush
Gornerth, n. superior power
Gornerthu, v. to excel in power
Gornofiad, n. swimming above
Gornofio, v. to swim above
Gornwyf, n. extreme vivacity
Gorofni, v. to fear extremely
Gorol, a. effectual, succesful
Gorolchi, v. to wash over
Gorolygu, v. to supervise
Goror, n. a confine, a border
Gorphen, n. conclusion, end: v. to conclude, to determine;
Gorphenaf, n. July [to end
Gorpheniad, n. a finishing
Gorphenol, a. concluding, finishing
Gorphwyll, n. madness; folly
Gorphwylliad, n. a distracting
Gorphwyllo, v. to grow mad
Gorphwyllus, a. irrational
Gorphwys, n. repose, rest
Gorphwysdra, n. repose
Gorphwysfa, n. a resting place
Gorphwyso, v. to repose, to rest, to take a respite
Gorphwysol, a. quiescent
Gorsaf, n. a station, a stand.
Gorsafiad, n. a stationing

Gorsafol, a. stationary [stand
Gorsafu, v. to station; to withGorsangu, v. to over-tread
Gorsedd, n. a supreme seat
Gorseddol, v. relating to session
Gorseddfainc, n. a throne
Gorseddiad, n. a presiding
Gorseddu, v. to preside
Gorseddwr, n. a president
Gorsefyll v. to take a stand
Gorsefylliad, n. a stationing
Gorsengi, v. to over-tread
Gorselu, v. to gaze steadfastly
Gorsing, Gorsin, n. a door post
Gorsylw, n. earnest regard
Gorsyllu, v. to look steadfastly
Gorsynu, v. to amaze greatly
Gort, n. a sharp spring
Gortio, v. to spring sharply
Gorth, n. what stands opposite
Gorthwasgu, v. to over-task
Gorthaw, taciturnity; patience
Gorthew, a. extremely thick
Gorthir, n. upper country
Gortho, n. an envelope; a roof
Gorthoad, n. a covering over
Gorthöi, v. to cover over
Gorthorch, n. a torque; a collar
Gorthordd, n. an exile
Gorthori, v. to cut over
Gorthoriant, n. an incision
Gorthrain, a. lavish to excess
Gorthrais, n. extreme violence
Gorthrech, n. mastery; violence
Gorthrechiad, n. a subduing
Gorthrechiant, n. domination
Gorthrechol, a. domineering
Gorthrechu, v. to master, to overcome
Gorthrechwr, n. a dominator, an oppressor
Gorthrin, n. extreme toil
Gortbröi, v. to turn over
Gorthrwch, n. a groove
Gorthrwm, a. oppressive
Gorthrychiad, n. a grooving
Gorthrymder, Gorthrymiant, n. oppression

Gorthrymiad, n. an oppressing
Gorthrymu, v. to oppress
Gorthrymus, a. oppressive
Gorthrymwr, n. an oppressor
Gorthwf, n. an overgrowth
Gorthwym, Gorthwymyn, a. overwarm
Gorthynu, v. to overstrain
Gorthywys, n. a general [to do
Goru, v. to cause, to accomplish,
Goruch, n. a supreme : a. upper adv. above, over
Goruchadeilad, n. superstructure
Goruchaf, a. most high, highest
Goruchafiaeth, n. supremacy promotion; triumph
Goruchafol, a. supereminent
Goruchafu, v. to exalt over
Goruchanian, a. supernatural
Goruchanianoldeb, n. preternaturalness [remacy
Goruchder, n. superiority; sup-
Goruchel, a. supreme, very high
Gorucheider, n. a summit
Goruchelion, n. meteors [exalt
Goruchelu, v. to render lofty, to
Goruchiad, n. heavenly body; a. planet
Goruchiant, n. supereminence
Goruchio, v. to raise supreme
Goruchiol, a. supereminent
Goruchion, n. meteors
Goruchionen, n. a meteor
Goruchlyw, n. lord paramount
Goruchragor, n. superexcellence
Goruchwyliad, n. a supervising, an overlooking [stewardship
Goruchwyliaeth, a supervision ;
Gorug, v. did, did perform, did act ; he did, he made. Imperfect tense of Goru
Gorugo, v. to accomplish
Gorugiad, n, an accomplishing
Gorun, n. surge, spray, foam
Gorurddas, n. supreme rank
Goruthro, to amaze exceedingly
Goruwch, prep. above, over
Gorwaedd, n. a loud cry
Gorwael, a. very abject
Gorwaered, n. a declivity
Gorwag, a. vain-glorious, vain
Gorwagedd, n. vain glory
Gorwall, n extreme remissness ; extreme fault
Gorwan, a. extreme weak
Gorwancu, v. to overgorge
Gorwar, a. extremely gentle
Gorwas, n. a hero, a worthy
Gorwasgu, v. to overpress
Gorwedd, n. recumbence ; v. to lie, to recline
Gorweddiad, n. a lying down
Gorweddial, n. concubinage
Gorweddol, a. recumbent
Gorwegi, n. extreme vanity
Gorwel, n. the horizon
Gorweled, v. to see over
Gorwen, a. very white
Gorwenu, v. to laugh, to grin
Gorwerthu, v. to oversell
Gorwir, a. quite true
Gorwireb, n. an hyperbole
Gorwisg, n. an outer garment
Gorwisgo, v. to clothe over
Gorwiw, a. superexcellent
Gorwlad, n. bordering country
Gorwlyb, a very wet
Gorwlychu, v. to over-drench
Gorwregus, n. a bracing girdle
Gorwy, n. a margin, a rim
Gorwych, a. very brave
Gorwydr, n. hoar frost
Gorwydd, n. a summit, a top: a courser, a steed: a. of easy progress
Gorwyddod, n. cavalry
Gorwyddfarch, managed horse
Gorwygo, v. to tear slightly
Gorwyl, n. an overlooking
Gorwyliad, n. an overlooking
Gorwylio, v. to overlook
Gorwyll, a. very gloomy
Gorwyllt, a. frantic, mad
Gorwym, n. a slight bandage
Gorwymp, a. very fair
Gorwyn, a. over-white

Gorwyr, n. a great grandson
Gorwyrain, n. of theme, praise
Gorwyres, great grand-daughter
Gorwys, n. a public summons
Gorwyth, n. very ire
Gorymboeni, v. to over-fatigue one's self
Gorymborth, n. excess of food
Gorymchwal, n. an over-spreading one's self
Gorymchwel, n. a conversion
Gorymchwylo, v. to be subverted
Gorymdaith, n. perambulation
Gorymdanu, v. to over-spread one's self
Gorymdeithio, v. to sojourn
Gorymdeithydd, n. one who travels much; a wayfaring man
Gorymddwyn, n. a bringing over
Gorymddygiad, n. abduction
GorymegFiad, n. over-exertion, an overtoiling
Gorymyl, n. great edge
Gorymyru, v. to over-pursue
Goryn, n. a pimple, a wheal
Gorynog, a. having pimples
Gorynys, n. a peninsula
Gorysgwr, n. a yoke
Gorysgwydd, n. a jutting out
Gorysu, v. to consume greatly
Goryw, n. a degenerate kind
Gorywio, v. to degenerate
Gosaig, n, a slight meal
Gosail, n. groundwork; a sole
Gosathru, v. to tread slightly
Gosbaith, a. polished, glittering
Gosbarth, n. a distinct part: prep. toward
Gosbenu, v. to particularize
Gosborthi, v. to support slightly
Gosbwyllo, v. to decide partly
Goseb, n. a handsel
Gosefyll, v. to stand slightly
Goseilad, n. a founding
Goseilio, v. to found
Gosel, n. a peep, a glance
Gosenu, v. to chide slightly
Gosgedd, n. figure, shape

Gosgeddiad, n. a shaping
Gosgeiddig, a. shapely, comely
Gosgel, n. a gloom: a. gloomy
Gosgelu, v. to half conceal
Gosgil, n. a half-retreat
Gosglwm, n. a tent fastening
Gosglymu, v. to tie slightly
Gosgo, n. obliquity, slope
Gosgoad, n. a going aside
Gogoi, v. to go aside, to avoid
Gosgordd, n. a retinue, a train
Gosgorddi, v. to form a retinue
Gosgrain, a. partly crawling
Gosgred, n. a faint belief
Gosgrynu, v. to cause quaking
Gosgudd, a. skulking, lurking
Gosgymon, n. a combustible
Goslef, n. organ of utterance; a tone, a note
Gosmeithio, v. to yield aliment
Gosod, n. a placing; a statute, an ordinance; a position; an onset [to place,
Gosod, v. to put, to set, to lay,
Gosodedigaeth, n. a proposition, an ordinance
Gosodi, v. to set, to put, to lay
Gosodiad, n. a placing; a position; an establishing; a proposition
Gosodol, a. positional statute
Gosomi, v. to partly disappoint
Goson, n. an intimation, rumour v. to intimate slightly
Gosonial, v. to be whispering
Gosori, v. to be half offended
Gosoriant, n. slight offence
Gosranu, v. to divide partly
Gosteg, n, silence, attention; a publishing; an adress. an invocation; a prelude. Gostegion priodas, bans of matrimony
Gostegiad, n. a silencing
Gostegu v. to silence, to still
Gostegwr, n. the crier of a court, who commands silence; a silencer
Gostrodyr, n. a pannel

Gostwng, n. a lowering: v. to bring down [humbled, abased
Gostyngedig, a. lowered; humble;
Gostyngeiddio, v. to become abased, to become humble
Gostyngiad, n. a lowering
Gostyngu, v. to lower, to abase
Gostyngwr, n. one who abases, inclines, lowers, or humbles
Goswydd, n. a petty office
Goswyn, n. a slight charm [port
Gosymdaith, n. provision, sup-
Gosymdeithiad, n. a provisioning
Gosymdeithio, v. to provide sustenance
Gosymerth, n. the gossamer
Gosymmaith, n. support, food
Gosymu, v. to warble
Gosymud, n. a slight move
Gosymwy, n. warbling, trilling
Gosyn, a. half amazed
Gosynio, v. to half consider
Gosyrthio v. to totter
Got, n. incontinence
Gotiar, n. a coot, a moor-hen
Gôtio, v. to commit adultery
Gotoew, n. a spur
Goth, n. repulsion; pride
Gothi, v. to scorn; to be proud, to act proudly
Gowaered, n. declivity, a slope
Gowanu, v. to divide; to gash
Gowci, n. a jackdaw
Gowel, a. transparent, clear
Gowelu, n. somewhat pale
Gowenu, v. to half smile
Gower, n. a croft, a close
Gowni, n. basting stitch
Gowregysu, v. to gird slackly
Gowrid, n. a slight blush
Gowrthodi, v. to half reject
Gowybod, v. to know partly
Gowych, a. somewhat brave
Göyfed, n. a slight nipping
Göysu, v to half consume
Gra n. frieze of cloth
Grab, n. a bluster, exuberance
Graban, n. what is clustered

Grabin, a. clasping; scrambling
Gradd, n. degree, rank, state
Graddeb, n. a climax
Graddedigaeth, n. a graduation
Graddiad, n. a graduation
Graddiannu v. to graduate
Graddiant, n. graduation
Graddineb, n. graduality
Graddio, v. to confer rank
Graddogi, v. to graduate
Graddol, a. progressive
Graddoli, v. to graduate
Grae, n. what is asperate, sharp, or rough
Graean, n. gravel, course sand
Graeanol, a. granular, gritty
Graeander, n. granulosity
Graeandde, a. granular
Gracanen, n. a grain
Graenllyd, a. gravelly, gritty
Graeanu, v. to granulate
Graen, n. asperity; grief, asperate; grievous
Graender, n. poignancy
Graenon, n. gravelly particles
Graenu, v. to make rough
Graf, n. the garlic
Grafel n. a lubber; a ruffian
Grai, n. a blight, a blast
Groiad, n. a blighting
Graid, n. sun heat; ardency, a. ardent, vehement
Grain, n. a socket; a ring
Gram, n. a sign, a symbol
Grammadeg, n. a grammar
Grammadegol, a. grammatical
Grammadegwr, a grammarian
Grammadegydd, n. a grammar-
Gran, n. the cheekbone: a. [ian precipitous, shelvy
Granwg, n. side of the face
Granygre, n. the visage
Gras, n. grace
Grawg, n. a horrid uproar
Grawn, n. berries; grain; roe of fish. Grawn Corinth, curr-
Grawnafal, pomegranate [ants
Grawnwin, n. grape wine

Grawth, n. a plunge
Grawthiad, n. a plunging
Grawys, n. a festival; lent
Gre, n. a flock, a herd; a stud
Gread, n. a herding, a flocking
Greal, n. an aggregate of elements, a code; a collection; a magazine
Grealu, to aggregate elements
Greant, n. an aggregate; a collection; a code
Greawd, n. an aggregate
Greawr, n. a flock, a herd
Greddf, n. nature; disposition
Greddfiad, n. an habituating
Greddful, a. habitual, natural
Greddfu, v. to habituate
Greff, n. a sneer; irony
Greffiad, n. a sneering
Greg, n. a cackle, a cackling
Greiad, n. a singeing
Greiau, n. what gives heat
Greiddell, a gridle, a bake-stone
Greidiad, n. the scorching of the
Greidio, to scorge, to singe [sun
Greidiol, a. scorching, blasting
Greiddyll, n. a griddle, grid-iron
Greienyn, n. a grain of gravel
Greinio, v. to form a ring
Greinyn, n. an ear-ring, a pen-
Greio, v. to singe, to blast [dant
Greiol, a. singing, blasting
Grelyn, n. a drinking-pool
Grem, n. a crash; a gnash [ing
Gremiad, a crashing; a gnash-
Gremio, v. to crash: to gnash
Gren, n. a large earthen vessel
Greolen, n. a briony plant
Gres, n. what is warm
Gresaw, n. a welcome
Gresawiad, n. a welcoming
Gresawu, v. to welcome
Gresi, n. pity compassion
Gresin, a. pitying, piteous
Gresyn, n. piteous, misery
Gresynol, a. deplorable
Gresyndod, n. pitifulness
Gresyn-gar, a. compassionate

Gresyni, n. piteousness
Gresynu, v. to commiserate
Gresynus, a. miserable, pitiful
Grêu, v. to aggregate
Grewys, n. a herd; a stud
Griddfan, n. a groan, a moan
Griff, n. the frog-spawn
Griffyll, n. frog-spawn
Grig, n. a low rustle
Grigwd, n. a rustling
Grill, n. a creak, a chirp a. creaking, chirping
Grillgnòi, v. to cranch
Grilliad, n. a creaking
Grillian, v. to keep creaking
Grilliedydd, n. a cricket
Grillio, v. to creak, to chirp
Gro, n. pebbles: n. a ridge o pebbles, formed by the sea
Groeg, n. the Greek language
Gronell, n. hard roe of fish
Gronellu, to generate roe
Gronyn, n. a grain, a particle
Gronynog, a. having grains
Gronynol, a. granular
Gronyniad, n. granulation
Gronynu, v. to granulate
Gröyn, n. a pebble
Grual, n. gruel, porridge
Grualu, v. to turn to gruel
Grud, n. grain of stone, grit
Grudd, n. cheek bone; cheek
Gruff, n. what is fierce; a griffon
Grufft, n. a griffon
Grug, n. heath, or ling
Grugiad, n. an emmet
Grugiar, n. moor-hen, grouse
Grugion, n. emmets, ants
Grugionyn, n. an emmet
Gruglwyn, n. sweet broom
Grugo, v. to gather heath
Grugog, a. having heath
Grut, n. grit; a fossil
Grutio, v. to lay on grit
Grwgach, v. to rumble
Grwgnachiad, n. a rumbling
Grwgnach, v. to grumble
Grwgnachiad, n. a grumbling

Grwgyn, n. broken rumbling
Grwng, n. a grunt; a noise
Grwm, n. a murmur; a growl
Grwn, n. a ridge in a field; a trembling noise
Grwnach, n. a grumbling
Grwnachu, v. to grumble
Grwnan, n. a hum; a purring: v. to hum, to drone
Grwniad, n. a droning
Grwys, n. wild gooseberries
Grwysed, n. a gooseberry
Grwyswydden, n. gooseberry-tree
Grwyth, n. a murmur
Grwythiad. n. a murmuring
Grwytho, v. to murmur
Gryd, n. a scream; war-hoop
Grydiau, v. to scream, to whoop
Grydiant, n. a screaming out
Grydio, v. to scream, to whoop
Grydwst, n. a murmur
Gryg, n. harshness
Gryglys, n. heath berries
Grygnant, n. harshness
Grygon, n. heath berries
Grynglad, n. a grunting
Grynglan, v. to be grunting
Gryngio, v. to grunt
Grym, n. force, energy
Grymiad, n. a making strong
Grymial, v. to mutter
Grymiala, v. to mutter
Grymialus, a. muttering
Grymian, v. to drone; to grunt
Grymiannu, v. to make potent
Grymiant, n. potency, energy
Grymio, v. to give energy
Grymus, a. powerful; nervous
Grymusder, n. potency

Gwadaeth, n. a spout, a cock
Gwadal, a. being stanch or firm
Gwadalwch, n. stanchness
Gwadiad, n. a denying
Gwadn, n. a base, a sole
Gwadnu, v. to sole,; to foot it
Gwadol, a. denying, negative
Gwadu, v. to deny; to disown
Gwadd, n. a mole
Gwaddeg, n. a spout; a scuttle
Gwaddod, n. sediment, lees
Gwaddodi, v. to cast a sedement
Gwaddodlyd, a. feculent, dreggy
Gwaddol, n. a portion; money
Gwaddoli, v, to dower
Gwae, n. woe
Gwaed, n. blood or gore
Gwaedboer, n. blood-spitting
Gwaedgi, n. a blood-hound
Gwaedglais, n. blood stripe
Gwaedgoll, n. bloodshed
Gwaediad, n. a bleeding
Gwaedled, bloody, blood-stained
Gwaedlif, n. a bloody-flux
Gwaedlin, n. an issue of blood
Gwaedlyd, a. bloody; cruel
Gwaedlydu, to stain with blood
Gwaedlys, n. blood-wort
Gwaedneu, n. a blood issue
Gwaedog, abounding with blood
Gwaedogaeth, n. sanguinity
Gwaedogen, n. a blood pudding a black pudding
Gwaedoli, v. to sanguify
Gwaedol, sanguineous of blood
Gwaedoliaeth, n. kindred by blood, consanguinity [blood
Gwaedraidd, a. running with
Gwaedrod, n. a course of blood

GWA 170 GWA

Gwäeg, n. a fibula; a clasp
Gwäegiad, n. a buckling
Gwäegu, v. to buckle; to clasp
Gwael, a. low, vile; poorly
Gwaeledd, n. vileness; misery
Gwaeleddu, v. to make wretched
Gwaelni, vileness; wretchedness
Gwaelod, n. a bottom, a base
Gwaelodi, v. to bottom
Gwaelodiad, n. a bottoming
Gwaelodion, n. bottoms
Gwaelu, v. to grow low or poor; to become faint
Gwaeddol, a. crying, shouting
Gwaeu, v. to make vile
Gwäell, gwëyll, n. a skewer, a broach; a knitting needle; a spindle. Gwäell neidr, a dragon-fly
Gwäelliad, n. a skewering
Gwäellu, v. to skewer, to broach
Gwaen, n. a meadow
Gwaeniad, n. a going headlong
Gwaened, a. headlong; furious
Gwaent, n. a full view
Gwaer, simple: rustic, clownish
Gwaered, n. a descent, a slope
Gwaeredu, v. to tend downward
Gwaes, n. a pledge
Gwaesaf, n. a pledge; a deposit a warrant; a deposition
Gwaesafiad, n. a pledging
Gwaesafu, v. to pledge; to insure
Gwaesiad, n. a giving pledge
Gwaesol, a. earnest; warranting
Gwaesu, v. to pledge
Gwaeth, a. worse
Gwaethâd, n. an impairing
Gwaethach, a. worse, more bad

Gwaew, n. pang, pain, agony, spasm; a lance
Gwaewffon, n. a javelin
Gwag, n. a void, a vacuum; a. void, empty, vacant
Gwagder, n. emptiness
Gwagedd, n. emptiness, vanity
Gwageddu, v. to act vainly
Gwagelog, a. circumspect
Gwagelu, v. to act cautiously
Gwagelyd, v. to shun, to avoid
Gwagfolach, n. vain boasting
Gwagâd, n. an emptying
Gwagâu, v. to make a void
Gwagiad, n. a making void
Gwagiaith, n. vain prattle
Gwaglais, n. a hollow voice
Gwaglwyf, n. a linden tree
Gwagoniant, n. vain glory
Gwagorchest, ostentations skill
Gwagorfoledd, n. vain triumph, or boasting
Gwagymffrost, n. swaggering
Gwagymgais, n. vain attempt
Gwang, n. greed, voracity
Gwangen, n. the shad fish
Gwangiad, n. the sewin fish
Gwahan, a. separate, distinct
Gwahanadwy, a. separable
Gwahanai, n. genitive case
Gwahanblyg, n. the diaphora
Gwahanedigaethydd, n. the genitive case
Gwahanfod, n. diversity of being
Gwahan-glwyf, n. leprosy
Gwahan-glwyfus, a. leprous
Gwahaniad, n. a separating
Gwahaniaeth, n. a separation
Gwahaniaethol, a. disjunctive

Gwahanredu, v. to distinguish
Gwahansang, n. a parenthesis
Gwahansangiad, n. interposition
Gwahansangu, v. to interpose
Gwahanu, v. to divide, to part
Gwahardd, n. a prohibition
Gwaharddedig, a. prohibited
Gwaharddiad, n. a forbidding
Gwaharddol, a. prohibitory
Gwaharddu, v. to prohibit
Gwahen, n. exhaustion
Gwaheniad, n. an exhausting
Gwahenu, to exhaust, to empty
Gwahoddedig, a. invited, or bid-
Gwahoddiad, n. invitation [den
Gwahoddi, v. to invite, to bid
Gwahoddwr, n. an inviter
Gwail, n. that is over
Gwailg, n. that turns over
Gwain, n. what serves or supports; a carriage; a sheath: a. smart, neat, brisk
Gwaint, n. what is smart or lively: a. smart, neat; brisk
Gwair, n. hay.: a. fresh, sprouting; ardent
Gwaisg, n. vigour; briskness: a. brisk, lively: ad. briskly
Gwaith, n. act, action; work: n. course, turn, time: ad. because, that, since,
Gwal. n. a couch; an inhabited region; a plat; a fallow; a rampart, a wall
Gwala, n fulness, sufficiency
Gwalabyr, n. a pathway
Gwalad, n. arrangement, order
Gwaladr, n. a ruler, a sovereign
Gwaladru, to arrange, to order

Gwalcio, v. to turn up, to cock
Gwalciog, a. turned up, cocked
Gwalch. n. that soars; a hawk; a hero
Gwalches, n. a female hawk
Gwalchiad, n. a soaring aloft
Gwalchwr, n. a falconer
Gwalchyddiaeth, n. falconry
Gwald, n. a hem; a welt
Gwaldas, n. a strengthening welt
Gwaldiad, n. a welting
Gwaldon, n. raised bank
Gwaldu, v. to welt, to hem
Gwales, n. a couch; a region
Gwalfa, n. a layer, a stratum
Gwaliad, n. a walling
Gwalio, v. to wall, to fence
Gwaling, n. a litter, a brood
Gwaltes, n. a welt of shoe
Gwalteisiad, n. a welting
Gwalteisio, v. to form a welt
Gwalwys, n. the Gauls
Gwaly, n. capacity, inside
Gwalyaw, v to make full
Gwall, n. defect, neglect
Gwallaw, v. to pour, to empty
Gwallawd, n. failure, mistake
Gwallawg, a. defective, faulty
Gwallawgair, n. error in pleading
Gwallawiad, n. a pouring out
Gwallbwyll, n. irrationality, defect of reason
Gwalldan, n. wild fire
Gwallfarn, n. faulty judgment
Gwallgof, n. distraction
Gwalgofi, v. to fail in memory
Gwalliad, n. a failing
Gwallofaint, n. defection

Gwallygus, a. defective, fallible
Gwammal, a. wavering, fickle
Gwammaldra, n. waveringness
Gwammalddyn, a flighty person
Gwammaliad, n. a wavering
Gwammalrwydd, n. fickleness
Gwammalu, v. to waver
Gwân, n. thrust, stab, prick
Gwan, a. weak, feeble; faint
Gwanâd, n. a weakening
Gwanaf, n. a layer, a row
Gwanafu, v. to place in layers
Gwanar, a. leading; forward
Gwanâu, v. to weaken
Gwanas, n. a jut; a prop; a shank; a clasp; a hook
Gwanasu, v. to prop; to clasp
Gwanawl, a. stabbing [standing
Gwanbwyll, n. a weak under-
Gwanc, a frail; a basket; vor-
Gwanclad, n. a gorging [acity
Gwanciaw, v. to gorge; to glut
Gwancus, a. voracious, greedy
Gwancusrwydd, n. voraciousness
Gwanciwr, n. a greedy devourer
Gwander, n. weakness
Gwanedig, a. divided; transfixed
Gwaneg, n. a gait; a drift; a haunch; a surge
Gwanegiad, n. a drifting
Gwanegu, v. to rise in waves
Gwanffyddiaw, v. to mistrust
Gwangalon, a. weak hearted
Gwangalondid n. timidity [ing
Gwangaloniad, n. a disheartan-
Gwangalonus, a. fainthearted
Gwangoeliaw, v. to distrust
Gwangred, n. faint belief
Gwangredu, v. to distrust
Gwanobeithiaw, v. to despond
Gwant, n. a but, or mark
Gwantan, a. fickle; wanton
Gwantiad, n. a severing
Gwantu, v. to sever; to thrust
Gwanu, v. to pierce, to thrust
Gwanwyn, n. the spring
Gwanychiad, n. a debilitating
Gwanychu, v. to debilitate

Gwang, n. greediness, voracity
Gwangen, n. the shad fish
Gwangiad, n. the suin fish
Gwâr, a. placid. tame
Gwara, n. fencing; play, game: v. to fence; to play
Gwarâad, n. a making tame
Gwaradwydd, n. a reproach
Gwaradwyddo, v. to disgrace
Gwaradwyddus, a. scandulous
Gwaradwyddwr, n. a reproacher
Gwarafun, n. restraint
Gwarafunaw, v. to begrudge
Gwarafuniad, n. a begrudging
Gwaranred, n. a guarantee
Gwaranredu, v. to guarantee
Gwarant, n. security, warrant
Gwarantawl, a. warranting
Gwarantiad, n. warranting
Gwarantu, v. to warrant
Gwarau, n. play, sport; v. to make gentle
Gwarbin, n. bow-pin of yoke
Gwarcen, n. top of the back
Gwarchad, n. a guarding
Gwarchae, n. a siege: v. to block up; to besiege
Gwarchaead, n. a besieging
Gwarchaedig, a. blocked
Gwarchadwr, n. one who guards a warden, a conservator
Gwarchan, n. an incantation
Gwarchau, v. to confine
Gwarchdwr, n. a watch-tower
Gwarched, v. to ward, to watch
Gwarcheidiol, a. conservatory: n. conservation
Gwarcheidwad, n. guardian
Gwarcheidwadaeth, n. a guardianship [trustee
Gwarcheidwadu, v. to act as a
Gwarchen, n. a surface
Gwarchglawdd, n. intrenchment
Gwarchiad, n. a covering up
Gwarchod, n. a guarding in: v. to look after
Gwarchodaeth, n. wardship
Gwarchodi, v. to ward, to watch

Gwarchodwr, n. a protector
Gward, n. a guard; a ward
Gwarder, n. placidness
Gwarddrws, n. lintel of a door
Gware, n. play, sport; a game: v. to play, to sport
Gwaread, n. playing, a gaming
Gwared, n. release, deliverance remedy; after--birth: to deliver, to redeem
Gwaredigawl, a. redemptory
Gwarediad, n. a deliverance
Gwarediant, n. deliverance
Gwaredred, n. refuge
Gwaredydd, n. a redeemer
Gwaredd, n. placidness, mildness, gentleness
Gwareddawl, a. humanizing
Gwareddogi, v. to render mild
Gwareddiad, n. a humanizing, a becoming gentle [staff
Gwarffoni, v. to trounce with a
Gwarffoniad, n. a trouncing
Gwargaled, a. stiffnecked
Gwargaledrwydd, n. stiffneckedness [born
Gwargaledu, v. to become stub-
Gwargam, a. having a stooping
Gwargemi, n. stoop in the back
Gwarged, n. a surplus; orts
Gwargrwm, a. round shouldered
Gwargrwth, a. hunch-backed
Gwargrymi, n. stoopingness
Gwargrymu, v. to stoop the back
Gwariad, n. a spending
Gwariaw, v. to expend
Gwarineb, n. gentleness
Gwariwr, n. a spender
Gwarllost, n. bar part of a yoke

Gwarth, n. a shore; reproach
Gwartha. v. to throw upon
Gwarthâad n. disparaging
Gwarthaed, n, aspersion
Gwarthaf, n. summit, surface
Gwarthaflu, v. to put on a stirrup
Gwarthafu, v. to go upon; to ride
Gwarthal, n. a thing to boot
Gwarthan, n. covert, shelter
Gwarthâu, v. to asperse
Gwarthawr, n. a quadrature
Gwarthedig. degraded, disgraced
Gwartheg, n. horned cattle
Gwarthegydd, n. a drover
Gwarther, n. a cavalier
Gwarthfa, n. the private part
Gwarthfor, n. surf of the sea
Gwarthiad, n. an aspersion
Gwarthle, n. the privities
Gwarthlef, n. calumny
Gwarthol, n. a stirrup
Gwarthrudd, n. disgrace
Gwarthruddiad, n. scandalising
Gwarthruddio, v. to scandalise, to disparage
Gwarthruddiol, a. scandalising
Gwarthu, v. to asperse
Gwarthus, a shameful
Gwarwch, n. gentleness
Gwarwg, n. a stoop, a bend
Gwarwy, n. pleasure
Gwary, n. bow of a yoke
Gwas, n. servant
Gwasaeth, n. service
Gwasan, n. a youth; a page
Gwasanaeth, v. n. service
Gwasanaethgar, a. serviceable
Gwasanaethiad, n a serving
Gwasanaethol, a. ministering

Gwasgaredd, n. the quality of being dispersed
Gwasgarfa, n. scene of scattering or dispersion
Gwasgariad, n. a scattering
Gwasgarod, n. a dispersion
Gwasgarog, a. being scattered
Gwasgarol, a. scattering
Gwasgaru, v. to scatter
Gwasgfa, n. pressure; pang
Gwasgiad, n. a pressing
Gwasgod, n. shelter, covert
Gwasgodfa, n. covert; bower
Gwasgodi, v. to shelter, to shade
Gwasgodiad, n. sheltering
Gwasgodlen, n. an awning
Gwasgodol, a. sheltering
Gwasgodwydd, n. bower, arbour
Gwasgol, a. pressing, squeezing
Gwasgrwym, n. a bandage
Gwasgu, v. to press, to squeeze
Gwasod, n. tufty, as a cow
Gwasodi, v. to be tufty
Gwasodrwydd, n. tuftiness
Gwasol, a. ministering, serving
Gwastad, n. a level, a plain: a. even, steady
Gwastadedd, n. eveness, a level
Gwastadfa, n. a level space
Gwastadfod, n. constant state
Gwastadiad, n. a levelling
Gwastadle, n. level place
Gwastadol, uniform, continued
Gwastadoldeb, n. continuity
Gwastadrwydd, n. evaness
Gwastadu, v. to make level
Gwastata, v. to be steady
Gwastatâd, n. making steady
Gwastatâu, v. to smooth; to rest, to be composed
Gwastraff, n. prodigality
Gwastraffiad, n. a squandering
Gwastraffu, v. to squander
Gwastraffwr, n. a prodigal or wasteful man
Gwastrawd, n. a groom
Gwastrin, n. servitude, toil
Gwastrodedd, n. office of a groom
Gwastrodi, v. to serve as a groom
Gwasu, v. to make as a servant
Gwatwar, n. mockery, jest: v. to mock, to deride
Gwatwaredigaeth, n. derision
Gwatwareg, n. sarcasm, irony
Gwatwargar, a. derisive, sarcatic
Gwatwargerdd, n. irony, satire
Gwatwariad, n. a mocking
Gwatwarol, a. mocking, sarcatic
Gwatwaru, v. to mock, to jest
Gwatwarus, a. mocking
Gwatwarwr, n. a mocker
Gwau, n. weaving; a knitting: v. to weave; to knit
Gwaudd, n. a daughter-in-law
Gwaun, n. a meadow, a down
Gwawch, n. a loud scream
Gwawd, n. panegyric; irony
Gwawdgar, a. fond of praise; apt to jeer
Gwawdiad, n. a panegyrising
Gwawdio, v. to jeer
Gwawdodyn, n. a metre
Gwawdus, adj. encomastic; jeering, ironical
Gwawdydd, n. a panegyrist
Gwawl, n. light, radiancy
Gwawn, n. the gossamer
Gwawr, n. the dawn; a hue
Gwawriad, n. a dawning
Gwawrio, v. to dawn
Gwb, n. a moan, a doleful cry
Gwden, n. a withe; a coil
Gwdeniad, n. a withing
Gwdenu, v. to twist a withe
Gwdd, n. what twists or turns
Gwddor, n. a wooden bridge
Gwddw, Gwddf, n. the neck
Gwddwgen, n. a neckcloth
Gwe, n. a web
Gwead, n. a weaving
Gweadur, n. weaver
Gweb, n. a visage; a phiz
Gwech, a. brave; fine, gay
Gwed, n. utterance; a saying
Gwedi, prep. after, later than: adv. after afterwards

Gwediad, n. a saying
Gwedol, a. relating to speech
Gwedresi, n. a lizard
Gwedyd, n. speaking or telling; v. to say, to speak
Gwedd, n. aspect, form; a team
Gweddaidd, orderly, appropriate
Gweddeidd-dra, n. orderliness, propriety, decency; moderation; handsomeness
Gweddeiddgar, a. orderly, decent
Gweddeiddiad, n. a making decent or becoming
Gweddi, n. supplication, prayer
Gweddïad, n. a praying
Gweddiad, n. a conforming
Gweddiant, n. conformity
Gweddig, a. seemly, decent
Gweddill, n. remnant
Gweddillio, v. to leave remnants
Gweddio, v. to pray, to supplicate
Gweddïwr, n. a supplicator, a petitioner
Gweddlys, n. the herb woad
Gweddog, a. connected, yoked
Gweddol, a. orderly; reasonable
Gweddoldeb, n. orderliness
Gweddoli, v. to render orderly
Gweddu, v. to render orderly; to yoke; to wed; to become
Gweddus, a. orderly; seemly
Gweddusdra, n. orderliness
Gweddusiad, n. making orderly
Gwedduso, v. to render orderly
Gweddw, a. fit for connection; single; widow
Gweddwad, n. a rendering single or widow
Gweddwdod, n. single state; widowhood
Gweddwi, v. to render single
Gweddyg, n. a shoe-last
Gwefl, n. a chop, a snout, a lip
Gwefliad, n. a chop-full
Gweflod, n. dash on the chops
Gweflodio, v. to dash the chops
Gweflog, a. blubber-lipped
Gwefr, n. the drug amber

Gwefraidd, the nature of amber
Gwefrol, a. of amber quality
Gwefru, v. to do with amber
Gwefus, n. the human lip
Gwefusglec, n. lip smack
Gwefusiad, n. a touching the lip
Gwefuso, v. to touch the lips
Gwefusog, a. having lips
Gwefusol, a. labial of the lip
Gweg, n. a totter, a wagging
Gwegi, n. vanity, levity
Gwegiad, n. a tottering
Gwegian, v. to keep tottering
Gwegil, n. the nape of the neck
Gwegilad, n. a turning from
Gwegilio, v. to turn the back
Gwegilsyth, a. stiffnecked
Gwegio, v. to totter, to wag
Gwegiol, a. tottering, wagging
Gweglyd, a. tottering, feeble
Gwegriad, n. a searcing, s fting
Gwegru, v. to scarce, to sift
Gwegrwr, n. a sifter
Gwegryn, n. a searcing, a sifting
Gwegryniad, n. a searcing
Gwegrynu, v. to searce, to sift
Gwengyn, n. the sewin, a fish
Gwehelyth, n. a lineage; a tribe
Gwehil, n. imperfect fruit
Gwehiliad, n. yielding of refuse
Gwehilio, v. to yield refuse
Gwehilion, n. refuse, trash
Gwehilio, v. to yield refuse
Gwehyn, n. an exhaustion
Gwehyniad, n. effusion
Gwehynol, a. effusive, pouring
Gwehynu, v. to effuse, to pour
Gweiddi, v. to cry out, to call
Gweilgi, n. torrent; ocean
Gweilging, n. a beam, a bar, a perch
Gweili, n. spare, surplusage
Gweiling, n. pale brass
Gweilw, n. a spare, a surplu
Gweilydd, n. a sparer [to serve
Gweini, v. to attend, to minister,
Gweiniad, n. a serving; a shea-
Gweiniant, a ministration (thing

Gweinid, n. attendance; service
Gweinidog, n. minister; servant
Gweinidogaeth, n. ministry, service
Gweinidogaethu, v. to minister
Gweinidoges, n. a maidservant
Gweinidogiad, n. a ministering
Gweinidogol, a. minis rant
Gweinif, n. ministration
Gweinifiad, n. one who serves
Gwein g, a. ministrant, serving
Gweinigiad, n. a ministering
Gweinigio, v. to minister
Gweinigiol, a. ministrant
Gweinio, v. to put in a sheath
Gweiniol, a. being ministrant; sheathing
Gweinydd, n. an attendant; servitor
Gweinyddes, n. female attendant
Gweinyddferch, n. a serving woman
Gweinyddiad, n. a ministering
Gweinyddiaeth, n. ministry
Gweinyddol, a. ministering
Gweirdir, n. hay land
Gweirglawdd, n. a hay-field
Gweiriad, n. a making into hay
Gweirio, v. to become hay
Gweiryn, n. a blade of hay
Gweisgwen, n. a press, a stamp
Gweisgi, a. alert, brisk, gay. Cnau gweisgi, ripe nuts
Gweisgiad, n. a rendering brisk; a slipping out
Gweisgio, v. to slip about
Gweisgion, n. husks, shells
Gweisgioni, v. to husk; to crumble
Gweisionain, n. tiny striplings
Gweitio, v. to wait
Gweithdy, n. a workhouse
Gweithfa, n. a manufactory
Gweithfuddig, a. victorious
Gweithgar, a. industrious
Gweithiad, n. a working
Gweithian, adv. now
Gweithiau, adv. sometimes

Gweithiedydd, n. an operator
Gweithio, v. to work
Gweithiol, a. working
Gweithiwr, n. a workman
Gweithle, n. a workshop
Gweithon, adv. at present, now
Gweithred, n. action, act
Gweithredai, n. an operator
Gweithrediad, n. working
Gweithrediant, n. operation
Gweithredol, a. operative, active
Gweithredu, v. to operate
Gweithredwr, n. a worker
Gwêl, n. the sight or vision
Gweladwy, a. what may be seen
Gwelameg, n. haw in the eye
Gwelchyn, n. pert little fellow
Gweled, n. vision: v. to see
Gwelediad, n. a seeing
Gwelediant, n. vision
Gweledig, a. being seen, visible
Gweledigaeth, n. a vision
Gweledydd, n. a spectator
Gweli, n. a wound; calumny
Gweliad, n. a laying open; a wounding
Gwelio, v. to lay open; to wound
Gwelw, n. a pale hue: a. pale
Gwelwad, n. a making pale
Gwelwder, n. paleness
Gwelwi, v. to grow pale
Gwelwlas, a. pale blue
Gwely, n. a bed, a couch; a plat; a tribe
Gwelyd, n. an opening; a wound
Gwelydd, n. a bed; stock of a family
Gwelyddu, v. to take respouse
Gwelyddyd, n. a repository
Gwelyf, n. a couch, or a bed
Gwelyfod, n. a lying in
Gwelyfodi, v. to lie in
Gwelyg, n. a wine press
Gwelygordd, n. a kindred
Gwelyo, v. to put in bed; to bed
Gwelyod, n. a laying-in
Gwelyog, a. bedded, having a bed; hereditary

Gwell, a. better
Gwella, v. to better, to mend
Gwellâd, n. a bettering
Gwelladwy, a. improveable
Gwellaif, n. shears, scissors
Gwellâu, v. to better, to improve
Gwellcifiad, cutting with shears
Gwelleifio, v. to cut with shears
Gwelliad, n. a bettering
Gwelliannu, to better, to mend
Gwelliant, n. amendment
Gwellig, a. improving, mending
Gwellineb, a. improvement
Gwelling, n. a benediction
Gwellt, n. grass; sward; straw
Gwelltiad, n. a turning to straw
Gwelltio, v. to turn to straw
Gwelltog, a. grassy, having straw
Gwelltorio, v. to cover with grass
Gwelltyn, n. grass blade, straw
Gwellwell, adv. better and better
Gwellyniad, n. an improving
Gwellynio, v. to improve
Gwemp, a. fair, gay or splendid
Gwempl, n. a wimple, a veil
Gwên, n. a smile, a simper
Gwen, n. a fair one, a beauty
Gwenan, n. a blister on the skin
Gwenci, n. stout, fitch, weazle
Gwendid, n. weakness, frailty
Gwendydd, n. morning star
Gwener, n. what yields bliss; Venus. Dydd Gwener, Friday
Gwenfa, n. a curd of a bridle
Gwenhwys, n. men of Gwent
Gweniaith, n. flattery
Gwenieithiad, n. a flattering
Gwenieitho, v. to flatter
Gwenie thus, a. apt to flatter
Gwenith, n. wheat
Gwenithen, n. a grain of wheat
Gwenithfaen, n. granite
Gwennol, n. a swallow; a shuttle
Gweno, n. the evening star
Gwênol, a. smiling, pleasing
Gwent, n. a fair or open region. A name for a part of Monmouthshire

Gwentas, n. a high shoe
Gwenu, v. to smile, simper
Gwenwisg, n. a surplice
Gwenwyn, n. venom, poison
Gwenwynad, n. a poisoning
Gwenwyndra, n. poisonousness; fretfulness
Gwenwynig, a. poisonous
Gwenwynllyd, a. poisonous; fretful
Gwenwyno, v. to poison
Gwenwynol, a. poisonous
Gwenyd, n. felicity; bliss
Gwenydiad, n. a making happy
Gwenyddiad, n. felecity [ing
Gwenyddol, a. felicitous; amus-
Gwenyn, n. the bees
Gwenynen, n. a single bee
Gwenynlle, n. a place for bees
Gwenynllestr, n. a beehive [bees
Gwenynog, a. abounding with
Gweol, a. relating to weaving
Gwep, n. a visage, a phiz
Gwepa, n. the visage or look
Gwepio, v. to make a long face
Gwer, n. tallow, or suet
Gwerchyr, n. a cover, a lid
Gwerchyriad, n. a covering
Gwerchyrio, v. to cover with a lid
Gwerdd, a. green, verdant
Gwerddon, n. a green spot
Gweren, n. a cake of tallow
Gwerin, n. the multitude: a. vulgar, or universal [eral
Gwerinad, n. a becoming gen
Gweriniaeth, n. democracy
Gweriniaethol, a. democratic
Gwerino, v. to spread out
Gwerinol, a. universal; vulgar
Gwerinos, n. the rabble, mob
Gwerlas, n. a green meadow
Gwerlin, n. pure, descent [alder
Gwern n. a swamp; a mead;
Gwernen, n. an alder tree
Gwerol, a. tallowy; like suet
Gwers, n. a verse, a lesson
Gwersa, v. to tattle, to gossip
Gwersig, n. a short lesson

Gwersyn, n. encampment
Gwersyllfa, n. site of a camp
Gwersylliad, n. an encamp
Gwersyllu, v. to encamp
Gwerth, n. value, price; sale
Gwerthadwy, a. salable, vend-
Gwerthefin, a. sovereign [able
Gwerthfawr, valuable precious
Gwerthfawredd, n. preciousness
Gwerthiad, n. a selling, vend-
  ing
Gwerthiant, n. price; vendition
Gwerthiog, a. precious valuable
Gwerthu, v. to sell, to traffic
Gwerthyd, n. a spindle, axis
Gwerthydaid, n. a spindle-ful
Gwerthydu, v. to put on a spin-
Gwerthyr, n. a fortification [dle
Gweru, v. to generate tallow
Gweryd, n. sward; moss
Gwerydiad, n. a swarding
Gwerydre, n. cultivated land;
  an inhabited region
Gwerydu, v. to sward; to grow
  moss; to till   [earth
Gwerydwedd, n. the face of the
Gwerydd, n. a spring; a youth
Gweryddol, a. tending to spring
Gweryddu, v. to spring; to wan-
Gweryn, n. a worm, a bot [ton
Gweryriad, n. a neighing
Gweryru, v. to neigh
Gwes, n. what is moving
Gwesgrydd, n. circumrotation
Gwesgryn, n. agitation
Gwesgrynu, to cause agitation
Gwesod, n. departure
Gwest, n. a visit
Gwesta, v. to go visiting
Gwestai, n. a visitor, a guest
Gwesteiad, n. a visiting about
Gwesteiaeth, n. act of visiting
Gwestfa, n. lodging
Gwestfil, n. a prowling animal
Gwestiad, n. a visiting
Gwestifiant, n. a visitor, a guest
Gwestle, n. a place of entertain-
  ment

Gwestledd, n. tumultuous state
Gwestliad, n. a making a riot
Gwestlog, riotous, tumultuous
Gwestlu, v. to raise a tumult
Gwestu, v. to lodge; to entertain
Gwestwng, n. a going down
Gwestyngu, v. to decline
Gwestl, n. hurly-burly, riot
Gwestr, n. a hitch, a noose
Gwesu, v. to depart, to go out
Gwesyn, n. a youth; a page
Gwesyndod, n. servility
Gwêu, v. to weave; to knit
Gweuad, n. weaving; knitting
Gweud, v. to say, to speak
Gweuol, a. weaving; knitting
Gweunblu, n. meadow-down
Gweundir, n. meadow-land
Gweurydd, n. a slave
Gwew, n. purgency; a smart
Gwewyr, n. pain, anguish
Gwewyrlys, n. anise-seed
Gwëydd, n. a weaver; loom
Gwëyddes, n. a female weaver
Gwëyddiaeth, n. weaver's trade
Gwg, n. a frown; glance
Gwi, n. a sudden emotion
Gwial, Gwiail, n. rods, twigs
Gwiala, v. to gather twigs
Gwialen, n. a rod; a perch
Gwialenaid, n. length of a rod
Gwialenffust, n. a flail-yard
Gwialenod, n. stroke of a rod
Gwialenodio, to beat with a rod
Gwialffust, n. a flail rod
Gwib, n. a serpentine course; a
  range; a drive
Gwibad, n. a ranging about
Gwiban, n. any sort of fly
Gwibed, n. flies, gnats
Gwibedyn, n. a fly
Gwiber, n. a serpent; a viper
Gwibfa, n. a wandering course
Gwibiad, n. stroller, vagrant
Gwibio, v. to rove, to gad
Gwibiol, a. erratic, wandering
Gwiblad, n. a flying about
Gwibli, n. gadding, vagrancy

Gwiblo, v. to fly or gad about
Gwiblu, n. band of vagrants
Gwibwrn, n. a whirling eddy
Gwica, v. to hawk or cry about
Gwicawr, n. a hawker
Gwiced, n. a wicket, a gate
Gwich, n. a crash; a squeak
Gwichad, n. a squeaking
Gwichell, n. creaker, squeaker
Gwichiad, Gwichiedyn, n. a periwinkle, or sea snail
Gwichian, v. to keep squeaking or squealing
Gwichydd, n. a stoat
Gwichio, v. to creak
Gwichydd, n. a stoat
Gwichyll, n. a stoat
Gwichyn, n. a stoat
Gwid, n. a quick whirl
Gwidd, a. dried, withered
Gwiddan, n. a hag; a witch
Gwiddiant, n. a withering
Gwiddon, rotted particles; mites
Gwiddoni, v. to dry rot; to breed mites
Gwiddonog, a. having mites
Gwif, n. a lever, a crow-bar
Gwifrwym, n. a fulcrum
Gwig, n. a nook, a cove
Gwigfa n. a cove, a retreat
Gwing, n. a wriggle, a wince
Gwinged, n. wriggling; wantonness
Gwingiad, n. a wriggling
Gwingo, v. to wriggle; to wince
Gwingog, Gwingol, adj. wriggling; winking
Gwingwr, n. struggler; wincer
Gwil, n. a chunning; a watch
Gwilfrai, n. a badger
Gwilff, n. an epithet for a mare
Gwilhersu, v. to romp about
Gwilhobain, v. to be gallopping
Gwiliad, n. a taking care
Gwiliadwraeth, n. a bewaring
Gwilied, v. to take care, to guard
Gwilio, v. to take care
Gwilog, a. full of starts: a mare

Gwilri, n. a wanton squeal
Gwilrin, n. a squeal of ecstacy
Gwilwst, n. an epithet for a mare
Gwill, n. strayer, vagabond
Gwilliad, n. vagrant; lurker
Gwilliades, n. female stroller
Gwin, n. wine
Gwina, v. to tipple wine
Gwinaeth, n. a vintage
Gwinaethu, v. to gather the vintage
Gwinau, a. bay, auburn
Gwinc, n. the chaffinch
Gwinegr, n. vinegar
Gwineuo, v. to turn to a bay colour
Gwingafn, n. a wine-press
Gwinien, n. a vine-tree, a vine
Gwiniolen, n. a maple-tree
Gwiniolwydd, n. maple-trees
Gwinllan, n. a vine-yard
Gwinol, a. of wine, vinous
Gwinrawn, n. vine grapes
Gwinsang, Gwinwasg, n. a wine-press
Gwinwr, Gwinydd, n. a vintner
Gwinwryf, n. a wine-press
Gwinwydd, n. vines
Gwinwydden, n. a vine
Gwipai, n. a sparrow-hawk
Gwir, n. ether; purity; truth; a. pure: right, true
Gwirawd, n. spirituous liquor
Gwiredd, n. verity, truth
Gwireddiad, n. a verifying
Gwireddol, a. veritable
Gwireddu, v. to verify
Gwirf, n. alcohol
Gwirfodd, n. good will
Gwirfoddol, a. voluntary
Gwirfoddoldeb, n. voluntariness
Gwiriad, n. a verifying
Gwiriadwy, a. verifiable
Gwiriant, n. a verification,
Gwiriedigaeth, n. verificat on
Gwiriedigaethu, v. to verify
Gwirin, a. of pure or true nature
Gwirineb, n. verity, truth
Gwirio, v. to verify, to assert

Gwiriol, a. verifying; positive
Gwirion, a. truly right; innocent; ignorant; n. innocence; ignorance
Gwirionedd, n. verity, truth
Gwirioneddiad, n. verification
Gwirioneddu, v. to verify
Gwirioneddus, a. verifying
Gwirioni, v. to become an innocent or idiot, to grow foolish
Gwirioniad, n. an innocent
Gwirodi, v. to serve spirits
Gwirodol, a. spiritous
Gwirota, v. to tipple liquors
Gwirotai, n. a dram-drinker
Gwisg, n. a garment, dress
Gwisgad, a dressing; a wearing
Gwisgiad, n. a dressing
Gwisgiadu, v. to apparel
Gwisgo, v. to dress, to put on
Gwisgogaeth, n. apparel
Gwiw, a. apt; fit, meet, worthy
Gwiwdeb, n. fitness; worthiness
Gwiwdod, n. fitness; worthiness
Gwiwell, n. a widgeon, a female [salmon
Gwiwer, n. a squirrel
Gwiwsain, n. a euphony
Gwiwydd, n. poplar trees
Gwlad, n. a country
Gwladaidd, a. country-like
Gwladeiddiad, n. rustication
Gwladeiddio, v. to rusticate
Gwladeiddrwydd, n. rusticity
Gwladgar, a. patriotic
Gwladogi, v. rusticate
Gwladol, a. of a country
Gwladwch, n. a common weal
Gwladwr, n. a countryman
Gwladwriaeth, n. a government
Gwladychiad, n. a governing
Gwladychu, v. to reign
Gwlaidd, a. mild
Gwlan, n. wool
Gwlana, v. to gather wool
Gwlanblu, n. down, hairs
Gwlanen, n. a flannel
Gwlaniach, n. downy hairs
Gwlanog, a. having wool

Gwlaw, n. rain
Gwlawiad, n. a raining
Gwlawio, v. to rain
Gwlawiog, a. of rain, rainy
Gwlawiol, a. relating to rain
Gwlawlyd, a. apt to rain, rainy
Gwledig, a. of a country
Gwledigo, v. to rusticate
Gwledwch, a. dominion
Gwledd, n. a banquet, a feast
Gwledda, v. to carouse
Gwleddiad, n. a carousing
Gwleddog, a. having a feast
Gwleddol, a. festival, festive
Gwleiddiad, n. a carousing
Gwlf, n. a channel, notch
Gwlith, n. dew
Gwlithen, n. dewsnail
Gwlithfalwen, n. a dewsnail
Gwlithiad, n. a falling of dew
Gwlitho, v. to cast a dew
Gwlithog, a. having dew, dewy
Gwlithwlaw, n. small rain
Gwlithyn, n. a dew drop
Gwlw, n. a channel, notch
Gwlib, n. liquid, moisture
Gwlyb, a. liquid, wet, moist
Gwlybâd, n. humefaction
Gwlybaniaeth, n. humidity
Gwlybân, v. to humectate
Gwlybiad, n. humectation
Gwlybu, v. to make wet
Gwlybwr, n. a liquid
Gwlybyrog, a. humid, rainy
Gwlych, n. moisture
Gwlychiad, n. a wetting
Gwlydd, n. stems of plants: a mild, tender, soft
Gwlyddâd, n. mollifying
Gwlyddâu, v. to mollify
Gwlyddiad, n. a mollifying
Gwn, n. a charger, a bowl
Gwn, v. I know
Gŵn, n. gown, loose robe
Gŵna, v. make, do, execute
Gwnedd, n. a state of toiling
Gwnelyd, v. to make, to do
Gwneuthur, v. to do, to execute

to make, to perform
Gwneuthuriad, n. a making
Gwneyd, v. to do, to perform
Gwni, n. a stitch, a sewing
Gwniad, n. a sewing
Gwniadur, n. a thimble
Gwniadydd, n. a stitcher
Gwniadyddes, n. a seamstress
Gwniedyddiaeth, n. the business of a seamstress
Gwnio, v. to sew, to stitch
Gwo, a. prefix, used for Go
Gwp, n. head and neck of a bird
Gwr, n. a man, a person, a husband
Gwra, v. to take a husband
Gwrab, n. a monkey, an ape
Gwrâch, n. a hag, an old woman, a witch
Gwrachan, n. a little creature
Gwrachanes, a little old woman
Gwrachastell, n. off board of a plough
Gwracheiddio, v. to grow haggish
Gwrachell, n. a puny dwarf
Gwrachen, n. a crabbed dwarf
Gwrachiaidd, a. like an old hag
Gwrachio, v. to become a hag, to grow decrepit
Gwradwydd, n. reproach, scandal
Gwradwyddiad, n. a scandalizing
Gwradwyddo, v. to scandalize, to disgrace
Gwradwyddus, a. scandalous
Gwradd, n. a quantity
Gwraddiad, n. an aggregation
Gwraddu, v. to aggregate, to heap [bracer
Gwrag, n. what curves off; a
Gwragen, n. a rib of a tilt, or basket [bracing
Gwrageniad, n. a ribbing; a
Gwragenu, v. to rib; to curve
Gwraich, n. a sparkle
Gwraid, n. what is ardent
Gwraidd, gwreiddion, n. a root
Gwraig, n. a woman; wife
Gwraint, n. worms in the skin; tetters

Gwrandawiad, n. a listening
Gwrandawus, n. attentive
Gwrando, n. a listening v. to listen, to hearken
Gwrau, v. to become manly
Gwrcath, n. a he cat
Gwrcatha, v. to caterwaul
Gwrcathiant n. a caterwauling
Gwrch, n. what is upon
Gwrda, n. a man of note
Gwrdäeth, n. manliness
Gwrdd, a. stout; ardent, vehement
Gwrddiad, n. a rendering ardent
Gwrddu, v. to render ardent
Gwrddyn, n. a dart; a javelin
Gwrechyn, n. a crabbed fellow
Gwregys, n. a girdle; a zone
Gwregysiad, n. a girdling
Gwregysol, a. having a girdle
Gwregysu, v. to girdle, to gird
Gwreng, n. plebian; yeoman
Gwrengaidd, a. plebian, boorish
Gwrengyn, n. a surly clown
Gwreica, n. wedding a wife: v. to take a wife
Gwreicdra, n. fondness of women, adultery
Gwreichion, n. sparks
Gwreichionen, n. a spark
Gwreichioni, v. to sparkle
Gwreichioniad, n. scintillation, a sparkling
Gwreichionog, a. full of sparks
Gwreichionol, a. sparkling
Gwreiddiad, n. a rooting [ate
Gwreiddio, v. to root, to originate
Gwreiddiog, a. having roots, rooted
Gwreiddiol, a. radical; rooted
Gwreiddioldeb, n radicalness
Gweiddrudd, n. the madder
Gwreiddyn, n. a root
Gwreigdda, n. good-woman
Gwreigen, n. a little woman
Gwreigeddos, n. gossips [ronly
Gwreigiaidd, a. female; mat-
Gwreigieiddio, v to become eff

eminate, womanish or tender
Gwreigiog, a. having a wife
Gwreigiol, a. feminine
Gwreignith, n. a little woman
Gwreindod, n. virility
Gwreinen, n. a ringworm
Gwreinyn, n. a ringworm
Gwres, n. heat, warmth
Gwresiad, n. a rendering hot
Gwresog, a. warm, fervent
Gwresogi, v. to become hot
Gwresol, a. of a heating quality
Gwresu, v. to fill with heat
Gwrferch, n. a virago
Gwrhëwerl, n. jocularity
Gwrhëwcrus, a. full of jokes
Gwrhëwg, a extremely playful
Gwrhyd, n. a fathom
Gwrhydri, n. heroism, bravery
Gwrhydu, v. to fathom
Gwriaeth, n. man's estate
Gwrial, n. a combating: v. to play the man
Gwrid, n. a blush; a flush
Gwridgoch, n. florid, ruddy
Gwridiad, n. a blushing
Gwrido, v. to blush
Gwridog, a. having a blush
Gwridogi, v. to become ruddy
Gwring, n. snap; crackle
Gwringain, to snap; to crackle
Gwringell, n. a snap; a slice
Gwringelliad, n. a snapping
Gwringellu, v. to snap; to slice
Gwriog, a. having a husband
Gwriogaeth, n. homage
Gwriogaethu, v. to do homage
Gwrith, n. what is apparent
Gwrm, n. a dusky hue, a dun
Gwrmder, n. duskiness
Gwrmlas, n. sea-green
Gwrmu, v. to make dusky
Gwrn, n. a cone; an urn; a vessel tapering upwards
Gwrnerth, n. the speedwell
Gwrol, a. manly; valiant
Gwrolaeth, n. manhood
Gwroldeb, n. manliness

Gwrolfryd, n. magnanimity
Gwrolgamp, n. a manly feat
Gwroli, v. to become manly
Gwron, n. a worthy, a hero
Gwrryw, n. a male kind
Gwrtaeth, n. what improves; manure
Gwrteithiad, n. a manuring
Gwrteithio, v. to manure
Gwrteithiol, a. meliorating
Gwrth, n. opposition, contrast prep. against, opposite to
Gwrthachos, n. contrary cause
Gwrthachwyn, n. counter complaint
Gwrthadrodd, a counter recital
Gwrthaddysg, n. heresy
Gwrthagwedd, n. counter form
Gwrthaing, n a wedge
Gwrthair, n. antiphrasis
Gwrthalw, n. a recal
Gwrthallu, n. opposing power
Gwrthamcan, n. counterproject
Gwrthanfon, n. a sending adversely
Gwrthanian, n. contrary nature
Gwrthannog, n. dehortation
Gwrthansawdd, contrary quality
Gwrtharddelw, n. counter claim
Gwrtharfod, n. counter stroke
Gwrtharwain, n. a leading back
Gwrthateb, n. replication
Gwrthattal, n. counter stop
Gwrthawel, n. adverse gale
Gwrthban, n. a blanket
Gwythbanu, v. to double mill
Gwrthben, n. counter head; rivet
Gwrthblaid, n, adverse party
Gwrthblyg, n. duplicate
Gwrthbrawf, n. refutation
Gwrthbryn, n. counter buying
Gwrthbwys, n. counterpoise
Gwrthbwyth, n. retaliation
Gwrthchwyth, n. counter blast
Gwrthdafl, n. counter throw
Gwrthdaith, n. counter march
Gwrthdal, n. counter payment

Gwrthdaro, n. a repulse
Gwrthdir, n. abutting land
Gwrthdor, n. refraction
Gwrthdrafod, n. contravention
Gwrthdramwy, n. retrogradation
Gwrthdrig, n. counter residence
Gwrthdrin, n. contravention
Gwrthdro, n. a turn back
Gwrthdroedion, n. antipodes
Gwrthwng. n. a contrary oath, a counter swearing
Gwrthdwyth, a springing back; elasticity
Gwrthdynu, v. to pull adversely
Gwrthdyst, n. counter evidence
Gwrthdywyn, reflection of light
Gwrthddadl, n. a controversy
Gwrthddadleuwr, n. a controvertist [ation
Gwrthddangos, n. contra-indic-
Gwrthddal, n. a with-holding
Gwrthddrych, n. an object
Gwrthddysg, n. a heresy
Gwrthddywedyd, v. to contradict
Gwrthddywediad, contradiction
Gwrtheb, n. an objection
Gwrthedrych, n. retrospect
Gwrthegni, n. a reaction
Gwrtheiriad, n. antiphrasis
Gwrthenwad, n. antinomasia
Gwrthergyd, n. a repulse
Gwrthern, n. a relation in the eventh degree of affinity
Gwrthfach, n. beard of a dart
Gwrthfarn, n. adverse judgment
Gwrthfechni, n. counter security
Gwrthfeiad, n. recrimination
Gwrthfin, n. a counter edge
Gwrthfodd, n. displeasure
Gwrthfrad, n. a counter plot
Gwrthfur, n. contramure
Gwrthfwriad, n. a casting back
Gwrthgas, a. perverse, forward
Gwrthgefn, n. a support
Gwrthgerdd, n. retrograde course
Gwrthgerydd, n, recrimination
Gwrthgil, n. a receding, a revolt
Gwrthgiliwr, n. a back-slider,
 a seceder, an apostate
Gwrthgis, n. retort, a rebuff
Gwrthglawdd, n. contravalatie
Gwrthgloch, n. a resoundin an echo
Gwrthgred, n. a counter beli
Gwrthgri, n. a counter clamor
Gwrthgrist, n. an antichrist
Gwrthgrych, a. cross-grained
Gwrthgur, n. a counter strok
Gwrthgwymp, n. apostacy, a fal ing away [plai
Gwrthgwyn, n. a counter com
Gwrthgyfarch, n. a rencounte
Gwrthgyfer, n. a contrast
Gwrthgyfle, n. a counter positio
Gwrthgyfnewid, n. a counte change
Gwrthgyngor, n. dehortation
Gwrthgyhudded, recriminatio
Gwrthgylch, n. a counter circl
Gwrthgynllwyn, n. a counte plot [por
Gwrthgynal, n. a counter sup
Gwrth-hawl, holion, n. counte plea
Gwrth-hoel, n. a plug; rivet
Gwrthiad, n. an opposing
Gwrthiaith, n. a contradiction
Gwrthias, n. a counter shock
Gwrthio, v. to oppose
Gwrthladd, n. resistance
Gwrthlais, n. counter sound
Gwrthlam, n. a counter step
Gwrthlef, n. a cry against
Gwrthlewyrch, n. reflected ligh
Gwrthlif, n. counter current
Gwrthlun, n. an antitype
Gwrthlys, n. repugnance
Gwrthlyw, n. a counter guide
Gwrthnaid, n. a leap backward
Gwrthnaws, n. an antipathy
Gwrthnerth, n. a counter powe
Gwrthneu, n. an objection
Gwrthnewid, n. counter change
Gwrthnod, n. a counter mark
Gwrthnysig, a. refractory
Gwrtho, v. to withstand

Gwrthod, v. to refuse, to reject : n. refusal, rejection
Gwrthodiad, n. a rejection
Gwrthol, a. adverse, contrary
Gwrtholwg, n. a retrospect
Gwrtholygu, v. to take a retrospect, to look contrarily [ion
Gwrthosod, v. to place in opposit
Gwrthosodiad, n. a placing in opposition, opposition
Gwrthran, n. a counter share
Gwrthred, n. a recurrence
Gwrthreithiad, n. antinomian
Gwrthres, n. an adverse row
Gwrthrif, n. a counter reckoning
Gwrthrimyn, n. a pair of pincers
Gwrthrith, n. reflected object
Gwrthrod, n. a hostile army; a counter-wheel
Gwrthrodiad, n. retrocession
Gwrthrodd, n. a connter gift
Gwrthrwyf, n. counter impulsion
Gwrthrwym, n. a counter bond
Gwrthryd, n. an adverse course
Gwrthryfel, n. a rebellion
Gwrthryfela, v. to rebel
Gwrthryfelgar, a. rebellious
Gwrthryfelgarwch, n. rebelliousness
Gwrthryfelwr, n. a rebel
Gwrthrym, n. contrary; energy
Gwrthryn, n. oppugnancy
Gwrthryw, n. a contrary kind
Gwrthsaf, n. opposition
Gwrthsain, n. counter sound
Gwrthsefyll, v. to withstand
Gwrthsyniad, n. counter design
Gwrthun, a. ugly, unseemly, ill-favoured
Gwrthyni n. deformity, ugliness
Gwrthwad, n. a counter denial
Gwrthwaith, n. a retroaction
Gwrthwal, n. a contramure
Gwrthwon, n. contravention
Gwrthwe, n. a lining
Gwrthwead, a counter weaving
Gwrthwediad, n. contradiction
Gwrthwedd, n. a contrast
Gwrthwenwyn, n. a counter poison; an antidote
Gwrthwyneb, n. contrariety; nausea
Gwrthwynebadwy, a. that may be opposed, resistible
Gwrthwynebiad, a. opposition, confrontation
Gwrthwynebrwydd, opposedness
Gwrthwynebu, v. to resist, to oppose; to confront
Gwrthwynebus, a. tending to turn against, disgusting
Gwrthwynebwr, n. an opposer, an adversary
Gwrthwynt; n. an adverse wind
Gwrthymchwel, n. a reverting or coming back
Gwrthymdrech, n. oppugnancy
Gwrthymdro, n. self-inversion
Gwrthymdyniad, n. a contending against
Gwrthymddangos, n. counter appearance [ence
Gwrthymddwyn, contrary infer-
Gwrtbymegniad, n. a self-exertion against [petition
Gwrthymgyrch, n. counter re-
Gwrthymladd, n. oppugnancy
Gwrthyni, n. counter energy
Gwrthysgrif, n. a rescript
Gwrwst, n. to cramp
Gwrych, n. a hedge-row; bristles
Gwrychell, n. a thicket, a brake
Gwrychiad, n. a bristling up
Gwrychu, v: to make a hedge-row; to bristle
Gwrychyn, n. hedge-row, bristle
Gŵryd, n. manliness
Gwryd, n. a chain
Gwryd, n. a wreath
Gwryddiad, n. a wreathing
Gwryddu, v. to wreath
Gwryf, n. a spring: a press
Gwryfiad, n. a pressing
Gwryfio, v. to press
Gwryfiwr, n. pressman
Gwryg, n. energy, vigour

Gwrygiad, n. invigoration
Gwrygiant, n. vigour
Gwrygio, v. to grow vigorous
Gwrygiol, a. invigorating
Gwrym, n. seam; wheal [a seam
Gwrymiad, n. the act of making
Gwrymio, v. to seam
Gwrymseirch, n. harness
Gwrys, n. ardency, violence
Gwrysedd, n. fervidity, violence
Gwrysen, n. a gooseberry
Gwrysg, n. boughs, branches
Gwrysgen, n. bough, branch
Gwrysgiad, n. a putting out boughs
Gwrysgio, v. to put out boughs
Gwrysiad, n. ardent, striving
Gwrysio, v. to strive ardently
Gwryswydden, n. gooseberry bush
Gwst, n. humour; a malady
Gwstog, a. distempered, diseased
Gwstu, v. to grow diseased
Gwth, n. a push, a thrust
Gwthgar, a. apt to push
Gwthiad, n. a pushing
Gwthio, v. to push, to thrust
Gwthiol, a. pushing, thrusting
Gwthrym, n. impulsive force
Gwthwynt, n. a squall
Gwull, n. flowerets, flowers
Gwullio, v. to bloom, to blossom
Gwy, n. fluid, liquid, water
Gwyach, n. water-fowl; grebe
Gwyal, n. a goal; the temple
Gwyalen, n. goal, mark
Gwyar, n. gore
Gwybed, n. gnats, flies
Gwybedydd, n. one who knows, a Gnostic
Gwybod, n. knowledge, science: v. to know, to perceive
Gwybodaeth, n. knowledge
Gwybodol, a. knowing
Gwybodus, a. knowing
Gwybren, n. ether; the sky
Gwybro, v. to grow subtile

Gwybrol, a. ethereal, aerial
Gwybyddiad, n. a being conscious; one who is conscious
Gwybyddiaeth, n. consciousness knowledge
Gwybyddol, a. conscious
Gwybyddu, v. to be conscious
Gwybyddus, a. acquainted
Gwych, a. gallant, brave; gaudy
Gwychder, n. gallantry, pomp
Gwychi, n. wax
Gwychlais, n. a squeaking voice
Gwychr, a. valiant, brave
Gwychu, v. to make gallant
Gwychydd, n. a hero, worthy
Gwyd, n. passion, vice
Gwydio, v. to become vicious
Gwydiol, a. vicious, wicked
Gwydn, a. tough, tenacious, viscid
Gwydnau, v. to become tough
Gwydnedd, n. toughness, tenac-
Gwydr, n. glass; green [ity
Gwydraid, n. a glass-ful
Gwydraidd, a. vitreous, glassy
Gwydrin, a. vitreous
Gwydro, v. to do with glass
Gwydrogi, v. to turn to glass
Gwydrol, a. vitreous, glassy
Gwydroli, v. to vitrify
Gwydrwr, n. a glazier
Gwydryn, n. a drinking glass
Gwydus, a. of a stubborn bent
Gwydd, presence; also cognition
Gwydd, n. trees; frame of
Gwydd, n. a goose [wood
Gwydd, a. overgrown; wild
Gwyddan, n. a sylvan, a satyr
Gwyddanes, n. a wood nymph
Gwyddbwyll, n. game of chess
Gwyddel, n. a sylvan state; a Gwyddelian, or Irishman
Gwgddeli, n. brakes, bushes
Gwyddelig, a. sylvan: savage
Gwydden, n. a standing tree
Gwydderbyn, prep. in front of
Gwyddfa, n. a tumulous, a tomb
Gwyddfaol. a. monumental

Gwyddfarch, n. an epithet for a ship
Gwyddfid, n. the woodbine
Gwyddfil, n. a wild animal
Gwyddfoch, n. wild swine
Gwyddfochyn, n. a wild boar
Gwyddgi, n. a wild dog
Gwyddhwch, n. a wild sow
Gwyddi, n. a quickset hedge
Gwyddiant, science, knowledge
Gwyddif, n. a hedging-bill
Gwydding, n. a quickset hedge
Gwyddlan, n. plantation of trees
Gwyddle, n. a woody place
Gwyddlwdn, n. a wild beast
Gwyddlwyn, n. the pimpernel
Gwyddor, n. a rudiment
Gwyddon, n. philosopher
Gwyddoni, v. to philosophize
Gwyddonol, a. philosophical
Gwyddol, a. scientific
Gwyddori, v. to form a rudiment
Gwyddorol, a. rudimental
Gwyddwal, n. a thicket
Gwyddwig, n. a woody fastness
Gwyddwydd, n. the honey suckle
Gwyf, n. what extends
Gwyfen, n. a moth, a worm
Gwyfenog, a. having moths
Gwyfo, v. to run out or fl at
Gwyfon, n. raspberries
Gwyfr, n. a wire
Gwyfyn, n. a moth, a worm
Gwyg, n. what is flaccid
Gwygbys, n. a chit-peas
Gwyglyd, flaccid ; void of energy
Gwygyl, a. flaccid ; sultry
Gwyl, n. a sight, show, festival a. modest, bashful
Gwylad, n. a beholding
Gwylaeth, n. the lettuce
Gwylan, n. a gull, a sea mew
Gwylar, n. the coral
Gwylch, n. semblance
Gwylchiad, n. a seeming
Gwylchu, v. to seem
Gwylder, n. bashfulness
Gwyled, v. to behold, to see

Gwylaed, n. bashfulness
Gwylfa, n. a watching place
Gwylfan, n. a sentry place
Gwyliad, n. vision : watching
Gwyliadur, n. a sentinel
Gwyliadwr, Gwyliwr, Gwylydd, n. a watchman
Gwyliadwraeth, n. the office or duty of a watchman ; a watch
Gwyliadwrus, a. watchful
Gwylied, Gwyllio, v. to watch
Gwyliedydd, n. a sentinel
Gwylmabsant, n. a parish wake
Gwylmabsanta, v. to keep wakes
Gwylnos, n. a wake night
Gwylnosi, v. to keep vigils
Gwylo, v. to be bashful ; to weep
Gwylog, n. the guillemot
Gwylys, n. the licorice plant
Gwyll, a. gloom, darkness
Gwyll, a. gloomy, dark, dusky
Gwylledd, n. gloom
Gwyllion, n. shades ; goblins
Gwyllt, n. a wild, wilderness
Gwyllt, n. wild, savage, rapid Dafaden, wyllt a cancer
Gwylltfil, n. a wild animal
Gwylltiad, n. a making wild
Gwylltineb, n. wildness ; rage
Gwylltio, v. to make wild ; to rage
Gwyllyn, n. culture ; aration
Gwyllyniad, n. a culturing
Gwyllynio, v. to culture
Gwyllys, n. the will ; desire
Gwyllysgar, a. willing; tractable
Gwyllysiad. n. a willing
Gywyllysio, v. to will ; to desire
Gwlylysyiol, a. willing, desirous
Gwyllysu, v. to will ; to desire
Gwymon, n. sea weed
Gwymp, a. smart, trim ; fair
Gwympedd, n. smartness
Gwyn, n. white ; what is fair : a. white ; fair ; blessed
Gwyn, n. rage, smart ; lust
Gwynad, n. a whitening
Gwynad, n. a smarting
Gwynaeth, n. felicity ; bliss

Gwynaf, n. a fretful state
Gwynafiad n. a being froward
Gwynafog, a. peevish; vicious
Gwynafu, v. to act frowardly
Gwynaint, n. the highest heaven, the empyrean
Gwynâu, v. to become white
Gwynblwm, n. white lead
Gwynder, Gwyndra, n. whiteness
Gwyndod, n. felicity, blist
Gwyndro, n. stupor; numbness
Gwyndwn, n. lay land; lay hay
Gwynddas, a. peevish, fretful
Gwynddasu, v. to act peevishly
Gwyneb, n. a face, a visage
Gwynebedd, n. superficies
Gwyneblad, n. a facing
Gwynebol, a. facing, fronting
Gwynebu, v. to face, to front
Gwynebwarth, n. shame of face, a fine so called
Gwyneg, a throb; a spasm; rheumatism
Gwynegiad, n. a throbbing
Gwynegol, a. throbbing; spasmodic
Gwynegu, v. to throb; to ache
Gwyneithiad, n. a consecrating
Gwyneithu, v. to consecrate
Gwynfryd, n. a happy mind
Gwynfyd. n. felicity, happiness
Gwynfydedig, a. blessed, happy
Gwynfydiad, n. a becoming fanatic
Gwynfydu, v. to become frantic; to become fanatic
Gwyngalch, a. being whitewashed
Gwyngalchiad, n. a whitewashing
Gwyngalchu, v. to whitewash
Gwyniad, n. a whiting, a making white; whiting, (a fish)
Gwyniaeth, n. a blessed state
Gwynias, a. of glowing heat
Gwyniasu, v. to make red hot
Gwyniedyn, n. a whiting
Gwyning, n. the sap of timber
Gwynio, v. to throb; to lust
Gwynlas, a. pale blue, whitish blue, sky-coloured
Gwynnaeth, n. flatulency
Gwynod, n. hasty pudding
Gwynog, a. passionate, full of rage
Gwynon, n. dry sticks for fuel
Gwynrew, n. numbness by cold
Gwynt, n. wind; breath
Gwynthollt, n. a wind-crack
Gwyntiad, n. ventilation
Gwyntio, v. to blow
Gwyntog, a. windy, full of wind
Gwyntyll, n. a ventilator
Gwyntylliad, n. a ventilating
Gwyntyllio, v. to ventilate
Gwynu, v. to whiten, to bleach
Gwynwg, n. whiteness
Gwynwy, n. white of egg
Gwynwydd, n. the willows
Gwynygiad, n. a glittering
Gwyr, n. pure element; ether; freshness; a green tinge: a. fresh, vigorous, verdant
Gŵyr, a. oblique, sloping
Gwyr, Gwyra, a. pure; fresh; lively
Gŵyrad, n. a making awry
Gwyraeth, n. sublimation
Gwyrain, n. barnacles! v. to sublimate
Gwyran, n. coarse rushy grass
Gwyrch, n. an overtopping
Gwyrdra, n. freshness
Gŵyrdro, n. perversion
Gŵyrdroï, v. to pervert
Gŵyrdynu, v. to draw obliquely
Gwyrdd, a. green
Gwyrddedd, n. greenness
Gwyrddfaen, n. an emerald
Gwyrddiad, n. a making green
Gwyrddlas, a. greenish blue
Gwyrddon, n. a verdant plat
Gwyrddu, v. to make green
Gwyredd, Gwyrddni, obliquity; wryness; bias
Gwyrciniad, n. sublimation
Gwyrcinio, v. to sublimate
Gwyreinig a. luxuriant; lively
Gwvrf, a. pure, fresh, not salt

Gwyrfedd, pureness, freshness
Gwyrfiad, n. a freshening
Gwyrfio, v. to freshen
Gwyrgam, a. obliquely crooked
Gwyrgamu, v. to turn awry
Gwyriaws, n. a privet
Gwyrin, a. of a fresh nature; chaste
Gwyrlen, n. a garland
Gwyrni, n. bots or wornils, maggots in cows; wryness
Gwyro, v. to swerve, to deviate
Gwyrol, a. slanting, inclining
Gwyrth, n. virtue; a miracle
Gwyrthiad, n. a giving virtue
Gwyrthio, v. to confer virtue
Gwyrthiol, virtuous; miraculous
Gwyrthioldeb, n. virtuousness miraculousness
Gwyrtos, n. ignoble persons
Gwyrydd, what is pure or chaste
Gwyryf, n. a virgin, a maid
Gwyryf, a. fresh, pure untainted
Gwyryfdod, n. virginity, chastity
Gwyryfiad, n. a making fresh
Gwyryfol, a. virginal, maiden
Gwyryfu, v. to make fresh
Gwyryng, n. maggots
Gwys, n. people, a peopled region
Gwŷs, n. a profundity: a. deep
Gwŷs, n. a summons
Gwysedig, a. being summoned
Gwysg, n. gravity; a stream: a. precipitate, headlong
Gwysgi, n. tendency to a level
Gwysgiad, n. a precipitating
Gwysgio, v. to precipitate
Gwysgiol, a. precipitant
Gwysgion, n. pottage, porridge
Gwysgiad, n. a summoning
Gwysgod, n. precipitation
Gwysigen, n. a blister, a bladder
Gwysio, v. to summon
Gwysiol, a. summoning
Gwyslythyr, n. writ of citation
Gwyso, v. to summon, to cite
Gwyst, n. what is shrunk or low

Gwystl, n. a pledge; a hostage
Gwystle, n. a pledging
Gwystledigaeth, the act of pledging
Gwystleidiaeth, n. a pledging, a mortgaging
Gwystliad, n. a pledging
Gwystlo, v. to pledge, to pawn
Gwystlwr, n. a pawner
Gwystno, v. to wither
Gwystyn, a. withered, dried
Gwyth, n. a channel; a drain; a view
Gwythad, n. irritation, chafing
Gwythaint, n. bird of wrath
Gwythen, n. a duct, a vein
Gwythenog, a. having veins
Gwythenol, a. venal, of veins
Gwythien, a vein, a blood-vessel
Gwythig, a. infuriate, wrathful
Gwythlon, a. wrathful, furious
Gwytho, v. to irritate
Gwythod, n. irritation
Gwythog, a. wrathful, angry
Gwythol, a. wrathful, raging
Gythred, n. channel of a stream
Gythreden, n. a rivulet
Gwythwr, n. an angry man
Gwyw, withered, faded; feeble
Gwywder, n. faded state
Gwywel, n. withered vegetation
Gwywiad, n. a withering
Gwywo, v. to wither, to fade
Gwywol, a tending to wither
Gybain, v. to wail, to moan
Gyda, prep. mutation of CYDA; with; in contact with
Gyferbyn, prep. over against
Gygiad, a glancing; a frowning, a looking grimly
Gygol, a. glancing; frowning
Gygu, v. to glance; to frown
Gygus, a. frowning; grim, glum
Gylf, Gylfant, a bill, or a beak
Gylfgragen, n. a scollop-shell
Gylfin, n. a bill, or beak
Gylfinbraff, n. the cross-beak
Gylfin-gam, a. hook-beaked
Gylfinhir, n. the curlew

Gylfog, a. having a beak
Gylyf, n. sickle, reaping-hook
Gyllyngdod, n. remission
Gyllyngiad, n. a loosening
Gyllyngu, v. to loosen, to relax
Gynaid, n. a cup-ful
Gynell, n. a close gown
Gynnau, adv. a little while ago
Gynog, a. wearing a gown
Gynt, adv. formely, of yore
Gynydd, n. a gunner
Gyr, n. a drive; an impulse; an onset, a drove
Gyrddu, v. to act vehemently
Gyrddwynt, n. a hurricane
Gyrfa, n. a drive, a course
Gyrfarch, n. a race-horse
Gyrferth, n. a breathing out
Gyrferthu, v. to breath out
Gyrfëydd, n. driver; racer
Gyriad, n. a driving; a racing
Gyriedydd, Gyrwr, driver, racer
Gyrn, a. imperious; supreme
Gyrod, n. a driving; impulsion
Gyrol, a. driving; impulsive
Gyrthiad, n. touching; dashing
Gyrthio, v. to touch; to push
Gyrthiol, a. coming in contact
Gyru, v. to drive, to race; to send, to convey
Gyrwynt, n. a tornado
Gyrhynt, n. a current
Gysb, n. staggers; black beetle
Gyst, a. humid, moist, damp
Gystwng, n. act of lowering
Gystyngu, v. to lower, to abase
Gyth, n. a murmur
Gythiad, n. a murmuring
Gythol, murmuring, Grumbling
Gythu, v. to murmur, to grumble

H

H A, n. scorn, disdain, hate:
ha! hey day! hey! well
Hab, n. chance, luck, fortune
Hab, interj. ha! hey'd! well!
Hac, n. cut, notch, hack
Haciad, n. a hacking
Hacio, v. to hack, to cut
Hacräd, Hacriad, n. a making ugly
Hacrâu, v. to make ugly
Hacrwydd, n. unsightliness
Hacru, v. to render unsightly
Had, n. aptness to renew; seed: a. easily yielding; pliant
Hadadfer, n. harvest season
Hadaidd, a. like seed, seedy
Haden, n. a single seed
Hadiad, n. semination
Hadlaidd, n. somewhat corrupt
Hadledd, n. rottenness, corrup-
Hadlestr, n. a seed-vessel [tion
Hadliad, n. a decaying
Hadlif, n. gonorrhœa
Hadlog, a corrupted, decayed
Hadlu, v. to decay, to corrupt
Hadlyd, a. rotten, corrupted
Hadog, a. having seed, seedy
Hadogol, a semnifical
Hadol, a. seminal, of seed
Hadolaeth, n. seminality
Hados, n. small seeds
Hadred, n. gonorrhœa
Hadu, v. to seed, to run to seed
Hadwr, n. a seedsman, a sower
Hadyd, n. seed corn
Haddef, n. a dwelling, a house
Haddefu, v. to inhabit
Haddfa, n. a dwelling, abode
Haech, n. a skirt; a hem
Haedd, n. a reach; merit
Haeddad, n. an attaining
Haeddol, Haeddiannol, a. meritorious
Haeddedigaeth, n. desert, merit
Haeddedigol, a. meritorious
Haeddel, n. a plough handle
Haeddiad, n. a meriting [it
Haeddiant, n. attainment; mer-

HAE 190 HAL

Hael, n. a liberal one : a. generous, liberal
Haelder, Haelioni, n. liberality
Haeledd, n. munificence
Haeliad, n. a becoming liberal
Haelionus, a. apt to be liberal
Haelu, v. to become liberal
Haen, n. stratum, layer
Haeniad, n. a placing in layers
Haenu, v. to put in layers
Haer, n. positively: a. positive; stubborn
Haeriad, n. a being positive
Haeriant, n. an affirmation
Haerllug, a. importunate
Haerllugo, v. to urge obstinately
Haerol, a. affirmative
Haeru, v. to affirm, to insist
Hâf, n. fulness; summer
Hafaidd, a. like summer
Hafal, a. like ; equal
Hafarch, a. listless ; restive
Hafdy, n. a summer-house
Hafiad, n. a becoming summer
Hafin, n. summer season [ous
Haflug, n. abundance: a. uber-
Hafn, n. a haven, a port, a harbour, a safe station for ships
Hafnai, n. a slattern, slut
Hafnen, n. a slattern, a trollop
Hafnol, a. slatternly, sluttish
Hafod, n. a summer dwelling ; a dairy
Hafodi, v. to reside in a summer dwelling
Hafodwr, n. a dairyman
Hafog, n. waste, havoc; a. abundant; common
Hafogi, v. to commit havoc
Hafol, a. summer; festival
Hafota, v. to pass a summer
Hafotty, n. a dairy-house
Hafr, n. a slatern ; gaot
Hafrog, a. slatternly ; a trollop
Hafren, n. a trollop, a strumpet
Hafru, v. to render sluggish
Hafu, v. to become summer
Haff, n. a snatch, a catch
Haffiad, n. a snatching
Hafio, v. to snatch, to sieze
Hagen, conj. yet, nevertheless
Hagen, ad. yet, after all, still
Hagr, a. ugly, unseemly
Hagräu, v. to make ugly; to become ugly
Hagriad, n. a rendering ugly
Hagrwch, n. ugliness
Haha, expressive of surprise
Hai, n. excitation ; haste
Hai, v. hei, quick, make haste
Haiach, n. instant, moment
Haiach, adv. instantly; almost
Haiachen, n. instant, moment
Haiachen, adv. instantaneously
Haiarn, n. iron
Haiarnddê, a. teeming with iron
Haiarnddu, n. iron black
Haiarniad, n. a doing with iron
Haiarnllyd, a. ferruginous
Haiarnol, a. of iron quality
Haiarnu, v. to do with iron
Haiarnwaith, n. ironmongery
Haiarnwedd. n. iron hue
Haiarnwr, n. ironmonger
Haib, n. superabundance
Haid, n. swarm, throng
Haidd, n. barley
Haif, n. overwhelming
Haig, n. a shoal
Haihow, interj. heigh oh! alas!
Haihwchw, interj. hallo, murder!
Hail; n. ratio ; bounty ; service
Hain, n. what spreads through
Haint, n. what is prevalent, an infection, disease, sickness. Haint y nodau, the plague
Hair, a. tedious, dilatory, long
Hais, n. what is full of points
Haith, n. aptness to reach
Hal, n. essential salt, a salt marsh
Hal, v. saline, salt; alkaline
Halaeth, n. saturation ; fulness
Haledig, a. impregnated
Halent, n. plenum : saturation
Halen, n. salt, Crwth halen, a

| HAL | 191 | HAR |

salt box, saltcellar
Halenai, n. a salt-cellar
Halenaidd, a. of a salt quality
Halenog, a. abounding in salt
Haleniad, n. a turning to salt
Halenu, v. to turn to salt
Halenwr, n. a salt merchant
Hallad, n. impregnation
Haliw, n. saliva, spittle
Haliwiad, n. salivation
Haliwio, v. to salivate
Halog, a. saturated with salt, contaminated; polluted
Halogedig, a. contaminated
Halogedigaeth, n. contamination
Halogi, v. to defile; to corrupt
Halogiad, n. a defiling
Haloglw, n. a profane oath
Halogrwydd, n. pollution
Halogwr, n. a defiler
Hallt, a. salt, saline; severe
Halltaidd, a. somewhat salt
Halltedd, n. saltness, salineness
Halltiad, n. a salting
Halltni, n. saltness
Halltol, a. of a saline tendency
Halltu, v. to salt, to make salt
Halltwr, n. salter
Ham, n. cause, circumstance
Hambwyll, n. reflection
Hambwylliad, n. consideration, reflect on
Hambwyllo, v. to consider, to reflect
Hamdden, n. leisure, respite
Hamddeniad, n. a taking respite
Hamddenol, a. being at leisure
Hamddenu, v to make respite
Han, n. what proceeds from a. produced; separated: prep. from, out of
Hanaeth, n. procedure
Hanawdd, n. derivation
Hanbwyll, n. consideration
Hanbwylliad, n. a considering
Hanbwyllo, v. to consider
Hanbwyllog, a. considerate
Handden, a. being attractive

Handdeniad, n. an attraction
Handdenol, a. attractive
Handdenu, to derive attraction
Handdyfod, v. to be, to become
Hanedig, a, derived, descended
Hanedigaeth, n. derivation
Hanes, n. relation, history
Hanesai, n. historiographer
Hanesgerdd, n. an epic poem
Hanesiad, n. a narration
Hanesiaeth, n. a narration
Hanesol, a. historical
Hanesu, v. to narrate
Haneswr, Hanesydd, a historian
Hanesyddiaeth, n. historiography; history in the abstract
Hanesyn, n. an anecdote
Hanfod, n. existence, being: v. to become existent; to proceed; to exist
Hanfodiad, n. an existing
Hanfodol, a. existent; essential
Hanfodoldeb, n. hypostasis
Hanfodoli, v. to become existent
Haniad, n. a proceeding
Hanner, n. a moiety: a. half
Hannerog, n. moiety: a half share or part; a flitch
Hannergrwn, n. a hemisphere
Hannergylch, n. a semicircle
Hanneriad, n. a halving
Hannerob, n. a flitch of bacon
Hannerog, a. having a moiety
Hannerol, a. relating to half
Hannersain, n. a semitone
Hanneru, v. to half
Hanred, parting off; recession
Hanredoli, v. to render separate
Hanredoliaeth, a separate state
Hanredu, v. to separate
Hanu, v. to proceed, to be derived
Hap, n. luck, chance, fortune
Hapiad, n. a happening
Hapio, v. to happen
Hapiol, a. happening, eventual
Hapus, a. fortunate, happy
Hapusrwydd, n. happiness
Har, n. aptness to over-top

Hardd, a. towering; handsome
Harddedd, n. handsomeness
Harddiad, n. a rendering handsome [mely
Harddiant, n. a rendering comely
Harddineb, n. handsomeness
Harddu, v. to adorn
Harddwch, n. handsomeness
Haredd, n. calmness; peace
Hariad, n. an appeasing
Hariannu, v. to render calm
Hariant, n. quietness
Harl, n. a jangling, a wrangling
Harlach n. a jangling
Harlu, v. to jangle, to wrangle
Harnais, n. harness
Harneisiad, n. a harnessing
Harneisio, v. to harness
Hatriad, n. a covering
Hatru, v. to cover, to dress
Hau, v. to strew over, to sow
Haul, n. the sun
Hauwr, n. a sower
Haw, n. what is full; an ass
Hawcaid, n. a hod-ful
Hawd, n. a whisk, a sweep
Hawdd, a. feasible, easy, facile
Hawddammawr, n. a welcome
Hawddammori, v. to welcome
Hawddammoriad, n. a welcoming
Hawddfryd, n. ease of mind
Hawddfyd, n. happiness
Hawddgar, a. amiable; lovely
Hawddgarwch, n. amiableness
Hawddineb, n. a facility, easiness
Hawes, n. a female ass
Hawg, n. fulness; perfection; space; while; an age; a hod
Hawg, ad. awhile, for sometime
Hawiad, n. a becoming full; a ripening; a becoming inactive
Hawl, n. a demand; a claim
Hawlblaid, n. a plaintiff
Hawlfainc. n. a tribunal
Hawlwr, n. a claimant
Hawn, a. eager; brisk; active
Hawni, n. eagerness; alacrity;

flue: v. to run over slightly
Hawniad, n. a doing over slightly
Hawnid, n. eagerness; briskness; liveliness
Hawnt, n. alacrity; liveliness
Hawntiad, n. an encouraging
Hawntio, v. to encourage
Hawntus, a. full of alacrity
Hawr, n. a spread
Hawriad, n. a spreading out
Hawru, v. to spread, to dilate
Haws, n. ease; more feasible
Hawsder, Hawsdra, n. feasibleness
He, n. a going: a. adventurous, daring, [dissemination
Head, n. a sowing; a scattering,
Heawd, n. a spreading; a drifting
Heb, n. a pass utterance: prep. without, void of: adv. without beside, by
Hebgor, n. a being dispensed: v. to put aside, to dispense
Hebgoradwy, a. dispensable
Hebgori, v. to dispense with
Hebgoriad, n. a dispensing with a dispensation
Hebiad, an uttering, utterance
Heblaw, prep. beside: adv. besides
Heboca, v. to hunt with a hawk
Hebog, n. a hawk, a falcon
Heboglys, n. a hawkweed
Hebogydd, n. a hawker
Hebogyddiaeth, n. hawking
Hebogyn, n, a single hawk
Hebol, a. uttering, oral
Hebraëg, n. Hebrew tongue
Hebred, n. external coarse; state of evil, or transmigration
Hebrediad, n. a traversing of the evil circle
Hebredu, v. to go in the evil circle, to transmigrate
Hwbrwng, n. a mission, a sending: v. to go on with, to send
Hebryngiad, n. a sending

Hebryngol, a. missive, sending
Hebryngu, v. to go on with
Hebryngydd, n. a conductor
Hebu, v. to utter, to speak
Heciad, n. a hopping
Hecian, v. to halt, to hop, to limp
Hecyn, n. a small notch
Hecynu, v. to make a notch
Hêd, n. a flight; also a hat
Hedeg, n. a flying: v. to fly
Hedegog, a. having flight flying, soaring; lofty; aspiring
Hedegol, a. volant, flying
Hedfan, v. to fly
Hediant, n. the act of flying
Hedin, a. flying, volant, volatile
Hediniad, n. volatilization
Hedion, n. light corn; chaff
Hedlam, n. a flying skip
Hednaid, n. a flying leap
Hedwr, Hedydd, n. one that flies; a. lark
Hedyn, n. a single seed
Hedd, n. tranquility
Heddaberth, n. peace-offering
Heddgeidwad, n. a constable, a police officer
Heddiad, n. a tranquilizing
Heddog, a. tranquil, calm
Heddswyddog, n. peace-officer
Heddu, v. to tranquilize
Heddus, a. pacific, tranquil
Hedduso, v. to make pacific
Heddwch, n. peace, quietness
Heddy, n. this day, the present day: adv. on this day
Heddychiad, n. a pacification
Heddychiadol, a. pacificatory
Heddychiadu, v. to render pacific
Heddychlon, peaceful, peaceable
Heddychlondeb, n. peacefulness
Heddychloni, v. to make peaceful
Heddychod, n. a pacification
Heddychol, a. peaceable
Heddycholdeb, n. peaceableness
Heddychu, to pacify, to appease
Heddychus, a. peaceable, pacific

Heddygu, v. to pacify, to appease
Heddyngnad, n. a justice of the peace
Hefal, n. like, similar
Hefeiliad, n. a making similar
Hefelig, a. having similitude
Hefelychiad, n. a likening
Hefelychu, v. to imitate
Hefelydd, what is like; a. equal
Hefelyddiad, n. an imitating
Hefelyddu, v. to imitate
Hefin, a. relating to summer
Hefrin, a. spreading; incompact
Hefyd, conj. in addition; also, likewise
Hefys, n. a smack, a shift
Hegab, n. a grasshopper
Hegl, n. a limb, a shank
Heglog, a. having limbs
Heiad, n. an impelling
Heibio, adv. by, beside, aside
Heidiad, n. a swarming
Heidio, v. to swarm, to throng
Heidiog, a. having swarms
Heidiol, a. swarming, flocking
Heidden, n. a grain of barley
Heiddiad, n. acquisition; merit
Heiddio, v. to obtain; to merit
Heiddiol, a. meritorious
Heiddyd, n. attainment, merit
Heigiad, n. a yielding in shoals
Heigio, v. to yield abundantly
Heigiol, a. yielding in shoals
Heilgorn, n. drinking-horn
Heiliad, a dealing, out, a serving
Heilin, a. bounteous, generous
Heilio, v. to deal out, to serve
Heilydd, n. one who serves
Hellyddiaeth, Heilyniaeth, n. the office of a waiter
Heilyn, n. a waiter
Heini, n. vivacity: a. brisk
Heiniad, n. a making active
Heiniar, n. a crop, produce
Heinif, a. lively, cheerful, brisk
Heinio, v. to pervade; to make all alive: to swarm

teeming, swarming
Heintol, a. pervasive; teeming
Heintddwyn, a. pestiferous
Heintfan, n. a plague spot
Heintfanol, a. petechial
Heintiad, a. causing contagion
Heintio, v. to cause contagion
Heintiog, a. contagious
Heintiol, a. contagious, epidemic
Heintnod, n. a pestilence
Heintnodol, a. pestilential
Heintus, a. pestilential
Heinydd, n. seat of life
Heislan, n. a hatchel, an instrument to beat flax
Heislaniad, n. a hatchelling
Heislanu, v. to hatchel flax
Heistain, n. what whets scythes
Heisyllt, n. a flax hatchel
Heisylltiad, n. a hatchelling
Heistyllu, v. to hatchel flax
Hêl, n. a holme; a dale
Hel, n. a gathering, an aggregate: v. to gather, to hunt
Hela, v. to gather, to hunt
Helaeth, a. ample, extensive
Helaethder, n. spaciousness
Helaethiad, n. amplification
Helaethiant, n. amplitude
Helaethrwydd, n. ampleness; abundance, an ample stock
Helaethu, v. to enlarge, to amplify
Helaethwr, n. an amplifier
Helbul, n. perplexity, trouble
Helbulo, v. to be full of care
Helbulus, a. full of perplexity
Helciad, n. a prying narrowly
Helcu, v. to pry carefully
Heldrin, n. business; bustle
Heledd, n. a place to make salt
Helfa, n. an aggregate; a hunt
Helffon, n. a hunting pole
Helgaeth, n. grime; soot
Helgi, n. a hunting dog
Helgig, n. venison
Helgorn, n. a hunting horn
Helgyd, v. to pry carefully

Helhynt, n. chase, course
Heli, n. brine, salt water
Heliad, n. a gathering, a collecting; a hunting: a making of brine
Heliedig, a. gathered; hunted
Helio, v. to season with brine
Helm, n. a stack, a rick
Helmiad, n. a forming a rick
Helmu, v. to form a rick
Helw, n. possesion
Helwi, v. to have possession
Helwr, Heliwr, n. a gatherer; a hunter; a venator
Helwriaeth, n. huntmanship
Hely, n. a gathering; a hunt: v. to gather; to hunt
Helyddiaeth, n. the chase
Helyg, n. willows, the salix
Helygen, n. a willow tree
Helyglys, n. a willow herb
Helynt, n. course; business
Helyntio, v. to go on a course
Helyth, n. a family stock
Hell, a. ugly, unsightly
Helltni, n. saltness, brininess
Hem, n. a hem, a border
Hemiad, n. a hemming
Hemio, v. to hem, to border
Hên, n. age, antiquity; a. old
Henad, n. a becoming old
Henadur, Henaduriad, n. elder
Henaduriaeth, n. eldership
Henaf, a. most ancient, oldest
Henafiad, a. an ancestor
Henafiaeth, n. an ancestry
Henaint, n. an old age
Hendad, n. a grandfather
Hendaid, n. a great grandfather
Hender, n. antiquity, age
Hendref, established habitation
Henddyn, n. an aged person
Heneiddiad, n. a growing old
Heneiddio, v. to grow old
Heneiddrwydd, n. agedness
Henfab, n. old bachelor
Henfam, n. grandmother
Henferch, n. an old maid

| HEN | 195 | HEU |

Henfon, n. a breeding cow
Hengof, n. an old tradition
Henllydan, n. the plantain
Hennain, a great grandmother
Heno, n. this night: adv. to night
Henoed, n. decline of age
Henu, v. to grow old or aged
Henur, n. an elder, an ancient
Henuriad, n. an elder
Henw, n. a name, appellative
Henwad, a naming, appellation
Henwadol, a. nominative
Henwedigaeth, n. nomination
Henwedigol, a. nominate
Henwi, to name, to nominate
Henwol, a. nominal titular
Henwr, n. an old man
Henwrach, n. an old woman
Heol, n. a course, a road, a street,
Heol, y gwynt, the milky way
Heolan, n. a lane, an alley
Heor, n. an anchor
Heori, v. to anchor
Hep-hun, n. a slumber
Hep-huniad, n. a slumbering
Hep-huno, v. to slumber
Hep-hynt, n. a whim, reverse
Hepiad, n. a nodding
Heplan, n. a nod; a slumber: v. to keep nodding
Hepio, v. to nod; to slumber
Heples, n. fervent, leaven
Hepwedd, n. an attribute
Her, n. a push; a challenge
Herc, n. a reach out; a jerk
Herciad, n. a reaching, a jerking
Hercian, v. to keep jerking
Herciant, n. a reaching out
Hercu, v. to reach, to fetch
Hercyn, n. a reach out; a jerk
Hergod, n. a push, a thrust
Hergwd, n. a push, a shove
Hergyd, n. a quick push
Hergydiad, n. a shoving away
Hergydio, v. to shove away
Heri, n. a jerk; a limp
Heriad, n. a defying
Herlawd, n. a tall stripling

Herlod, n. defiance, challenge
Harlodes, n. a hoiden; a damsel
Herlotyn, n. a mere stripling
Herodr, n. an ambassador
Herodraeth, n. an embassy
Hers, n. a sharp push; a flout
Hersu, n. a scouting, a flouting
Hersiad, a scouting, a flouting a packing off
Hersio, v. to scout, to pack off
Herw, n. a flight; a scouting
Herwa, v. to scout, to hurry
Herwad, n. a scouting, prowling
Herwm, n. gloss of leather
Herwr, n. a scout, a prowler
Herwriaeth, n. vagrancy
Herwth, n. the rectum
Herwydd, prep. because
Hesg, n. sedges, rushes
Hesgen, n. a sedge, a rush
Hesglif, n. a whipsaw
Hesgyn, n. a sieve, a riddle
Hesor, n. a hassock, a pad
Hesp, a. dried up, dry, barren
Hespin, n. a yearling ewe
Hespinhwch, n, a young sow
Hespwrn, n. a young sheep
Hestawr, n. two-bushel
Hestoraid, n. full of two bushels
Het, n. a hat; a garland
Hetiwr, n. a hatter
Hetys, n. a short space, instant
Heuad, n. a sowing, semination
Heuddedig, a. attained; deserved
Heuddiad, n. a reaching; a meriting
Heuddu, v. to attain; to merit
Heulen, n. a partial sunshine
Heuliad, n. a sunning
Heulladu, v. to give a sunning
Heulo, v. to shine as the sun
Heulod, n. the sun's shining
Heulog, a. sunny, sunshiny
Heulor, n. a half door
Heulorsaf, n. a solstice
Heulrod, n. a parasol; a cap
Heulwen, n. the sunshine
Heulyd, n. sunshine, sun-heat

Heuriad, n. an asserting	Hilio, v. to yield, to bring for to produce
Heuriannu, v. to vindicate	
Heuriant, n, a vindication	Hiliogaeth, n. offspring, issue
Heuro, v. to assert, to affirm	Hiliogi, v. to render prolific
Heurol, a. assertive, positive	Hilus, a. being in particles
Heusawr. n. a herdsman	Hilyn, n. a particle, emanation
Heuslan, n. the sheep-lice	Hin, n. weather; temperature
Heuso, v. to protect	Hindda, n. fair weather
Heusori, v. to tend herds	Hinio, v. to change the weather
Hew, n. a call of defiance	Hiniog, n. a door-frame; a sill
Hewcri, Hewgrach, n. pertness	Hinon, n. serene weather
Hewiad, n. a hectoring	Hinoni, v. to become serene
Hewrach, n. a squabble	Hip, n. a sudden tap
Hewydd, n. passion: zeal	Hipiad, n. a tapping, a tipping
Hewydus, a. passionate; zealous	Hipio, v. to tap, to tip
Hewydd, n. maturity	Hir, a. long; tedious; dilatory
Hewyn, n. what is mature	Hiraeth, n. longing; regret
Hi, n. a female: pron. she, her	Hiraethiad, n. a longing
Hic, n. a snap; a trick	Hiraethlon, a. full of regret
Hiced, n. a trick, cheat	Hiraethog, a. longing [ting
Hicell, n. a long handled bill	Hiraethol, a. longing; regret-
Hicio, v. to snap; to trick	Hiraethu, v. to long; to regret
Hid, a. aptness to run through	Hiraethus, a. longing; regretting
Hidl, a. distilling; shedding: n. a strainer, a colander	Hirâu, v. to lengthen
	Hirbell, a. very far, distant
Hidlaid, a. distilling, dropping: n. a distilling, a dropping	Hirbwyll, n. deliberate caution
	Hirchwedl, n. a long story
Hidlion, n. droppings	Hirder, n. length; longitude
Hidlo, v. to distil, to run	Hirdrig, a. of long tarrying
Hif, n. a skin, a surface	Hirddydd, n. a long day
Hifiad, n. the peeling of the skin	Hireinios, n. a long life
Hifio, v. to peel off the skin	Hirfod, n. a long abiding
Hifyn, n. the strip of skin	Hirfryd, a. of even mind
Hiff, n. a flake; a drift	Hirglust, a. long eared
Hiffiad, n. a flaking; a drifting	Hirglwyf, n. long-sickness
Hiffiant, n. a drift; a foam	Hirglyw, a. being long eared
Hiffio, v. to cast flakes; to drift	Hirgrwn, n. a cylinder: a. cylinderical
Hifl, n. a gush, a spirt	
Hiflaid, Hifflo, to gush, to spirt	H rgul, a. long and narrow
Hifliad, n. a spirting	Hirgwyn, n. a long complaint
Hiffyn, n. a flake; a drift	Hirgylch, n. an ellipse
Hil. n. a fragment; emanation; produce; issue; progeny	Hirhoedl, n. longevity
	Hirhoedlog, a. long-lived
Hilen, n. a bearing female	Hiriad, n. a lengthening
Hiliad, n. a producing, a generating	Hirian, n. a tall lank person
	Hiriannu, v. to prolong
Hiliant, n. issue, progeny	Hiriant, n. length, delay
Hilig, a. procreate: n. an issue	Hirio, v. to lengthen.

Hirlidio, v. to bear anger long
Hirnos, n. a long night
Hirnych, n. long affliction
Hiroddef, n. longsuffering
Hiroed, n. long waiting
Hirwlydd, n. the maidenhair
Hirtrwm, n. a fribble
Hityn, n. a ragamuffin
Hithau, pron. she also, her also
Ho, n. an exclamation; a call: interj, hallo! oh!
Hob, n. a swelling out; a swine; a measure of capacity
Hobelu, v. to hop, to hobble
Hobyn, n. a deal at cards
Hoc, n. a scythe to cut brambles
Hoced, n. a cheat, deceit, juggle
Hocedu, v. to cheat, to trick
Hocedwr, n. a cheater, one who plays tricks
Hocrell, n. a girl, a wench
Hocys, n. mallows, or althæa
Hoch, n. a hawking of phlegm
Hochi, v. to throw up phlegm
Hodi, n. wild shrubs, brakes: v to shoot, to ear
Hodiad, n. a shooting; earing
Hoddiad, n. a facilitating
Hoddio, v, to facilitate
Hoe, n. aptness; respite; rest
Hoeanu, v. to take respite
Hoed, n. delay; regret
Hoeden, n. a flirt, a coquette
Hoedl, n. duration of life
Hoedli, v. to lead a life
Hoedlog, a. having life, lived
Hoel, n. a nail, a spike
Hoelen, n. a single nail
Hoeliad, n. a nailing
Hoeliedig, a. fastened by nailing
Hoelio, v. to nail, to drive nails
Hoellwr, n. a nailer
Hoen, n. good plight; liveliness; hue, complexion
Hoeni, v. to grow blithe
Hoenus, a. blithsome, joyous
Hoenwedd, n. a blithe aspect
Hoenyn, n. a hair; a gin; a slip

Hoenynu, v. to set a springe
Hoetian, v. to suspend; to dandle
Hoeth, a. exposed, naked
Hoew, a. alert, uprightly, lively
Hoewal, n. the play of water around anything, a whirl
Hoewal, a. whirling, eddying
Hoewalu, v. to form eddies
Hoewan, a. sprightly; volatile
Hoewder, n. sprightliness
Hoewgall, a. quick witted
Hoewgred, a. of ready belief
Hoewi, v. to become sprightly
Hoewrym, a. of quick energy
Hoewserch, n. lively affection
Hof, n. what hangs or hovers
Hoflad, a. hovering, fluctuation
Hoflan, v. to hover, to fluctuate
Hofio, v. to hover, to suspend
Hoff, a. love, beloved, lovely
Hoffaidd, a. tending to be lovely
Hoffaint, n. fondness; delight; love
Hoffder, n. fondness delight
Hoffdyn, n. a cuckhold
Hoffi, v. to delight in, to love
Hog, n. a sharpening, a whet
Hogal, n. a whetstone; a strop
Hogalen, n. a whetstone
Hogen, n. a girl, a damsel
Hogenig, n. a little damsel
Hogfaen, n. a hone, whetstone
Hogi, v. to sharpen, to whet
Hogiad, n. a sharpening
Hogl, Hogldy, n. a hovel, a shed
Hoglanc, n. a stripling
Hogyn, n. a stripling, a lad
Hong, n. a hang, a dangle
Hongian. v. to hang, to dangle
Hoi, n. a call of attention
Hoiad, n. a calling attention
Hoian, v. to call attention
Hol, n. a fetch, a bringing to: v. to fetch, to go for
Holadwy, a. cognisable
Holawd, n. cognisance
Holedig, a. questioned
Holedigaeth, n. examination

Holedigol, a. interrogative
Holfainc, n. a tribunal
Holgar, a. inquisitive
Holi, v. to question, to inquire
Holiad, n. interrogation
Holiadol, a. catachetical
Holiant, n. cognisance
Holiedydd, Holwr, n. an interrogator
Holio, v. to separate
Holp, n. a holp-hole, a loop
Holl, a. all, every one
Hollallu. n. all power
Hollalluog, a. omnipotent
Hollalluogrwydd, omnipotence
Hollboeth, n. a hollocaust
Hollddoeth, a. allwise
Hollfyd, n. the universe
Hollgyfoethog, a. all-powerful, possessing all things
Hol ol, a. total, whole, entire
Holliach, a. perfectly well
Hollryw, a. omnigenous
Hollt, n. a slit, a cleft, a fissure
Hollti, v. to slit, to cleave
Holltiad, n. a slitting, a cleaving, a rifting, a spliting
Holltog, a. full of slits or rifts
Hollwybodaeth, n. omniscience
Hollwybodol, a. omniscient
Hollwybodus, a. omniscient
Hollwydd, n. omnipresence
Hollwyddol, a. omnipresent
Hollwyddoldeb, n. omnipresence
Hon, a. [feminine of Hwn] this
Hona, a. [feminine of Hwna] that
Hwnacw, a. [feminine of Hwnacw] that, at a distance
Honaid, a. evident, well-known
Honc, n. a shake, a wagging
Honcen, n. a waddling female
Honciad, n. a waggling
Honcian, v. to wagger, to stagger, to totter
Honcio, v. to shake, to wag
Honcu, v. to shake, to wag
Honedig, a. manifested, evident

Honfas, n. a chopping knife
Honffest, n. a tunic, a vest
Honi, v. to manifest; to proclaim; to object; to insist
Honiad, n. manifestation; an objecting; an insisting
Honianol, a. affirmative
Honiant, n, affirmation
Hono, a. [feminine of Hwnw] that, absent
Honof, honot, hono, honi, honom, honoch, honynt, see Ohonof
Honod, n. an affirmation
Honol, a. positive, affirmative
Honos, n. a gawky; the ling
Honsel, n. a handsel
Honw, n. what is full of motion
Honyma, [feminine] this, which is here
Honyna, [feminine] that, which is there
Hopran, n. a mill hopper
Hopranu, v. to hop in a hopper
Hor, n. rotundity; swine lice
Horen, n. a fat lazy one
Horgest n. a fat paunch
Hort, n. a reproach, calumny
Hortiad, n. a reproaching
Hortio, v. to reproach
Hortiol, a. reproaching
Horth, n. what is spread over
Horyn, n. a lazy lump
Hos, Hosan, n. a hose, a stocking
Hosanwr, n. a hosier
Hotan, n. a hood, a cap
Hotyn, n. what covers as a cap
How, interj. heigh! ho! alas
Hoyw, a. alert, sprightly, gay
Hu, n. what is apt to pervade; a. apt to pervade; bold
Huad, n. what cents; a hound
Huadgu, n. a hound dog
Huail, n. a vicegerent
Hual, n. a fetter, a gyve
Hualiad, n. a fettering
Hualog, a. having fetters
Hualu, v. to fetter, to shackle
Huan, n. Phœbus, the sun

Huano, a. harmonic; poetical
Huarwar, a. soothing; calm
Huawdl, a. eloquent
Huawdledd, n. eloquence
Hucan, n. a cob, a sea fowl
Huch, n. a thin skin, a film
Huchen, n. a film, a pellicle
Huchiad, n. a skinning over
Huchio, v. to skin over
Hûd, n. an illusion, a charm
Hudo, v. to allure, to beguile
Hudol, a. alluring, enticing
Hudedd, n. allurement
Hudiad, n. an alluring
Hudoldeb, n. illusiveness
Hudoles, n. a deceiver
Hudoli, v. to render illusive
Hudoliaeth, n. allurement
Hudoliaethu, v. to use deception
Hudwalch, n. a lure bird
Hudwg, n. a bugbear
Hudwy, n. a phantom
Hudd, n. a covert, a shade: a. dusky, dark, gloomy
Huddo, v. to cover, to shade
Huddol, a. covering, shading
Huddedig, a. covered, shaded
Huddiad, n. a covering
Huddiannu, v. to overspread
Huddiant, n. a shading over
Huddig, a. tending to be dusky
Huddwg, n. what is dusky
Huddygl, n. soot, reek
Huddyglyd, a. fuliginious, sooty
Hueng, a. encircling
Huenyd, n. what encircles
Hufen, n. what mantles; cream
Hufenaidd, a. like cream
Hufeniad, n. a forming cream
Hufenu, v. to gather cream
Hufiad, n. a mantling over
Hufio, v. to mantle over
Hufyll, a. humble, submissive
Hufylldod, a. humility
Hug, n. a loose coat or gown
Hugan, n. a loose coat
Hugwd, n. a sceptre
Hul, n. a cover, a coverlet

Huliad, n. a decking
Hulio, v. to spread over
Huliwr, n. a decker
Hulier, n. a cover, a lid
Huling, n. a coverlet, a rug
Hult, n. a dolt, a moper
Hulyn, n. a coverlet, a quilt
Hum, n. a bat, a racket
Human, n. a tennis ball
Humog, n. a bat a racket
Hûn, n. a nap, a slumber
Hun, n. one'self
Hunan, n. self
Hunanaeth, n. self; egotism
Hunananog, v. to self-excite
Hunander, n. selfishness
Hunandwyll, n. self-deception
Hunandyb, n. self-conceit
Hunandyst, n. self evidence
Hunanddoeth, a. self-wise
Hunanedd, n. selfishness [lon
Hunanfarn, n. self-condemna:
Hunanfawl, n. self-applause
Hunanfod, n. self-existence
Hunanfodd, n. self-pleasure
Hunanfudd, n. self-interest
Hunan-gar, a. selfish
Hunan-gariad, n. self-love
Hunan-gyfiawn, self-righteous
Hunanhanfod, n. self-existence
Hunanhyder, n. self confidence
Hunaniad, a becoming selfish
Hunaniaeth, n. identity
Hunanladd, n. self-murder
Hunanles, n. self-interest
Hunanol, a. relating to self
Hananoldeb, n. selfishness
Hunanrediad, n. self-motion
Hunanrith, n. self-evidence
Hunanryw, n. homogeny a homogenous
Hunansaf, n. self-standing
Hunansymud, n. self-motion
Hunanu, v. to egotise
Hunanymmod, n. self-motion
Hunanymwad, n. self-denial
Hunanysol, a. self-devouring
Hundy, n. dormitory

Hunddwyn, a. sleep-depriving
Hunedd, n. somnolence
Hunell, n. a short sleep, a nap
Hunfa, n. a dormitory
Hun-glwyf, n. a legarthy
Hunllef, n. the nightmare
Huno, v. to sleep, to slumber
Hunog, a. sleepy, drowsy
Hunyn, n. a nap, a doze
Huon, n. epithet for the Diety
Hupynt, n. a brunt; a shock; a push; a metre so called
Hur, n. wages, hire
Huren, n. a prostitute, a slut
Hurio, v. to hire
Huriwr, n. a hirer
Hurt, n. a block: a. stupid'
Hurtan, n. a blockhead
Hurtiad, n. a stupifying
Hurtio, v. to stupify
Hurtiol, a. stupefactive
Hurtyn, n. a blockhead
Hurtr, n. a boarded floor
Hurth, n. a block, a dolt
Hurthgen, n. a blockhead
Hurthiad, n. a stupifying
Hurthio, v. to stupify
Hust, n. a buzzing noise
Hustiad, n. a making a buzz
Husting, n. a buzz, a whisper
Husting, v. to buzz, to whisper
Hutan, n. an oaf; the dotterel
Hutyn, n. a stupid fellow
Hüw, n. a lullaby, a lulla
Hüysgain, a. apt to scatter
Hüysgwn, a. apt to ascend
Hüysgwr, a. aptly energetic
Hw, n. a hoot, a halloo
Hwa, v. to hoot, to halloo
Hwala, n. a halloo, a cry
Hwau, n. a hooter; an owl
Hwb, n. a push; an effort; a lift
Hwbach, n. a quick effort
Hwbiad, n. a pushing forward
Hwbian, v. to be pushing on
Hwca, what is hooked: a. hooked
Hwch, n. a push, a thrust: a sow

Hwchw, a shout, a cry, a scream
Hwd, n. a take off or away
Hwda, n. a take off, a taking: v. imper. take, accept
Hwdan, n. a reach to take
Hwdwg, n. a bugbear, a bug
Hwdwl, n. what is stark mad
Hwf, n. a hood, a cowl
Hwfan, n. a rising over
Hwfanu, v. to rise over
Hwg, n. a hook, a bend
Hwgwd, n. a dunce, a dolt
Hwhw, n. hooting of an owl
Hwi, v. to halloo
Hwin, n. what is apt to sink
Hwman, n. wavering motion
Hwn, a. this
Hwna, a. that
Hwnacw, a. that, yonder, or at a distance
Hwnt, a. outward; foreign; other, contrary
Hwnt, adv. at a distance, yonder beyond; away, aside
Hwntiau, v. to vibrate; to waggle
Hwnw, a. that; absent
Hwynyma, a. [masculine] this, which is here
Hwnyna, a. that, which is here
Hwp, n. an effort, a pull, a push
Hwpiad, n. a tugging, a pushing
Hwpio, v. to pull, to tug, to push
Hwpiol, a. tugging lugging
Hwr, n. a taking off, a taking
Hwra, v. to accept, to take
Hwrdd, n. a push, a thrust; a butt; an onset; a ram
Hwre, v. take, accept
Hwrwg, n. a lump, a hunch
Hws, n. a covering, a housing
Hwsiad, n. a putting on a cover
Hwsmon, n. a husbandman
Hwsmonaeth, husbandry, tillage
Hwstr, a. froward; morose
Hwstredd, n. frowardness
Hwswr, n. a house-wife
Hwt, n. a taking off: v. off, away
Hwta, n. a taking off, a taking

Hwtio, v. to push off; to hoot
Hwy, pron. they, them
Hwy, a. long; tedious; longer
Hwyâd, n. a lengthening
Hwyad, n. a duck
Hwyaden, n. a duck
Hwyâu, v. to lengthen
Hwyddell, n. a female salmon
Hwyedig, a. lengthened
Hwyedydd, n. a young bird
Hwyfell, n. a female salmon
Hwyl, n. a course; plight, state, or condition; a sail
Hwylbren, n. a sail yard; a mast
Hwylfa, n. a course; a lane
Hwyliad, n. a driving; a butting; a progression; a sailing
Hwylio, v. to set in course; to butt; to prepare; to sail
Hwyliog, a. having course; being under sail
Hwylus, a. orderly, prosperous
Hwyluso, v. to facilitate
Hwylusdod, n. facility
Hwyn, n. a long hair; a gin
Hwynaw, v. to lay a springe
Hwynt, pron. they, them [ves
Hwynthwy, pron. they themsel
Hwyr, n. lateness; the evening: a. slow, tedious, late
Hwyrâad, n. a growing late
Hwyrach, a. slower; later: ad. peradventure
Hwyrâu, v. to become late
Hwyrder, n. latenesss
Hwyrdrwm, a. sluggish, drowsy
Hwyrddig, a. slow to anger
Hwyrddysg, a. slow to learn
Hwyredd, n. lateness, tardiness
Hwyrfryd, a. of slow disposition
Hwyrfrydig, a. slowly disposed
Hwyrol, a. relating to evening
Hwyrweddawg, a. forbearing
Hwys, n. draught; load
Hwysaw, v. to heap together
Hwysg, n. a sweep; ravage
Hwysgaw, v. to sweep away

Hwysgiad, n. devastation
Hwyst, n. dart, glance
Hwythau, pro. they likewise
Hy, n. aptitude to proceed: a. apt; bold; audacious
Hyadlais, a. apt to resound
Hyall, a. possible, effectible
Hyalledd, n. possibility
Hyar, a. apt to resound; vocal
Hyawdledd, n. eloquence
Hyawdl, a. eloquent, fluent
Hyb, n. a getting forward; a recovery
Hyball, a. fallible, defectible
Hyballedd, n. fallibility
Hybar, a. apt to provide
Hybarch, a. reverend, revered
Hybarchedd, n. venerableness
Hybarth, a. divisible
Hybarthedd, n. divisibility
Hybawl, a recovering; saving
Hybechrwydd, n. aptness to sin
Hybell, a. far ranging; distant
Hyblad, n. a recovering
Hyblaid, n. apt to take a part
Hybleth, a. apt to weave
Hyblyg, a. easily doubted; also flexible
Hyblygedd, n. flexibility
Hyboen, a. susceptible of pain
Hyboeth, a. easily heated
Hyborth, a. easily supported
Hybrawf, a. demonstrable
Hybryn, a. easily bought
Hybu, v. to get foremost; to recover
Hybwyll, a. discreet, rational
Hybwylledd, n. deliberation
Hybwys, a. aptly pressing
Hybwysedd, n. ponderousness
Hychan, n. a little sow
Hychgryg, n. quinsy
Hychiad, n. a thrusting
Hychian, v. to grunt
Hychiaw, v. to push, to thrust
Hychig, n. little or young sow
Hychwant, a. aptly lusting
Hychwardd, a. aptly laughing

| HYCH | 202 | HYFF |

Hychwil, a. apt to pry about
Hychwyth, a. apt to blow
Hyd, n. length; continuity; while: prep. to, unto, as far as: ad. till; to the place that; while; along, ever
Hydaith, a. apt to travel
Hydal, a. apt to pay, payable
Hydardd, a. apt to break out
Hydarf, a. easily scared
Hydarth, a. aptly exhaling
Hydaw, a. apt to be silent
Hydawdd, a. apt to melt
Hydedd, n. longtitude
Hyder, n. trust, confidence
Hyderiad, n. a confiding
Hyderu, v. to rely, to confide
Hydcrus, a. confident
Hydgyllen, the brisket
Hydiad, n. a lengthening
Hydor, a. aptly breaking
Hydraeth, a. aptly reciting
Hydraidd, a. penetrable
Hydrais, a. apt to oppress
Hydranc, a. apt to perish
Hydras, a. of notable kindred
Hydraul, a. easily consumed
Hydraw, a. easily instructed
Hydred, n. longtitude
Hydredawl, a. longtitudinal
Hydref, n. autumn; October
Hydrefn, a. well-ordered [ity
Hydreiddrwydd, n. penetrabil-
Hydreigledd, a. aptness to roll
Hydrwst, a. apt to be noisy
Hydwf, a. luxuriant, thriving
Hydwyll, a. easily deceived
Hydwyth, a. elastic, nimble
Hydyn, a. tractable
Hŷdd, n. stag, deer
Hyddadl, a. disputable
Hyddail, a. apt to bear leaves
Hyddawn, a. liberal
Hyddes, n. a hind, red deer
Hyddestyl, a. apt to be nice
Hyddewis, a. aptly selecting
Hyddfref, a. rutting of deer
Hyddgant, n. stag

Hyddgen, n. skin of stag
Hyddgi, n. buck-hound
Hyddig, a. irritable, iracible
Hyddoeth, a. apt to be wise
Hyddof, a. tamable
Hyddring, a. easily climbed
Hyddrwg, a. apt to be bad
Hyddwyn, a. easily carried
Hyddysg, a. well-versed, docile
Hyddysgedd, n. aptness to learn
Hyddysgu, v. to learn quickly
Hyddysgwr, quick learner
Hyedd, n. boldness
Hyf, a. bold, paring, confident
Hyfâad, n. a becoming bold
Hyfacth, a. nourishable
Hyfagl, a. apt to entangle
Hyfai, a. culpable; faulty
Hyfarn, judicable; censorious
Hyfau, v. to become bold
Hyfawl, a. laudable
Hyfdra, n. boldness
Hyfed, a. ready for reaping
Hyfedr, a. skilful, expert
Hyfedredd, n. skilfulness
Hyferw, a. easily boiled
Hyfeth, a. fallible
Hyfoes, a. of easy manners
Hyfraw, a. being, easily awed
Hyfriw, a. apt to be broken
Hyfrwd, a. being easily heated
Hyfryd, a. cheerful, delightful
Hyfrydedd, n. delightfulness
Hyfrydu, v. to make cheerful
Hyfrydwch, n. delightfulness
Hyfrys, a. apt to be hasty
Hyfyr, n. a gelt goat
Hyff, n. a drive; a drift
Hyffagl, a. apt to flame
Hyffawd, a. aptly prospering
Hyffiad, n. a forcing on
Hyffiaw, v. to drift
Hyfflam, a. apt to flame
Hyffo, a. capable of retreating
Hyffordd, a. apt to make way
Hyfforddi, v. to direct
Hyfforddiad, n. a forwarding
Hyfforddiant, n. direction

Hyfforddus, a. dexterous
Hygael, a. obtainable
Hygant, n. community
Hygar, a. lovely, amiable
Hygardd, a. reproachable
Hygarth, a. easily cleansed out
Hygas, a. hateful
Hyged, a. liberal
Hygel, a. easily hidden
Hyglod, a. susceptible of praise
Hyglust, a. of ready ear
Hyglwyf, a. ready wounded
Hyglyw, a. audible
Hygoel, a. credible, credulous
Hygof a. easily remembered
Hygoll, a. easily lost
Hygosb, a. punishable
Hygred, a. credible
Hygryn, a. easily shaken
Hygwsg, a. easily sleeping
Hygylch, a. apt to surround
Hygyrch, a. approachable
Hyladd, a. easily cut off
Hylafar, a. ready of speech
Hylam, a. of numble step
Hylaw, a. handy, dexterous
Hylawn, a. apt to be full
Hyled, a. aptly spreading
Hylef, a. ready voice
Hyles, a. apt to benefit
Hylid, a. apt to be angry
Hylithredd, a. aptness to glide
Hylon, a. apt to be cheerful
Hylwgr, a. corruptible
Hylwydd, a. fortunate
Hylwyddo, v. to prosper
Hyll, a. gloomy; wild; ugly
Hylldra, a. ugliness
Hylldrem, n. grim aspect
Hylldremiad, n. wildly look
Hylldremwr, n. grim looker
Hylliad, n. a dismaying
Hyllu, v. to make ugly
Hyn, pron. this, this thing
Hŷn, a. elder, older, senior
Hynacw, pr. that is at a distance
Hyna, that there; that much
Hynaf, n. ancestor; elder

Hynafedd, n. seniority
Hynafiad, n. ancestor
Hynafiaeth, n. antiquity
Hynafiaethydd, n. antiquary
Hynaws, a. kind, good-natured
Hynawsedd, n. good-nature
Hynod, a. remarkable, notable
Hwnodiad, n. a making notable
Hynodiaeth, n. notable action
Hynodol, a. notable
Hynodrwydd, n. notableness
Hynoeth, a. apt to make naked
Hynt, n. course, journey, freak
Hyntiad, n. a going off abruptly
Hyny, pron. that
Hynyma, pron. this thing here
Hynyna, pron. that thing there
Hyr, n. shock, snarl
Hyran, a. aptly parted, divisible
Hyranedd, n. divisibility
Hyrdd, n. shock; a. eager
Hyrddawd, n. impulsion, push
Hyrddawl, a. impulsive
Hyrddiad, n. a pushing
Hyrddiant, n. impulsation
Hyrddu, v. to push, to impel, to butt; to make assault
Hyrddwynt, n. hurricane
Hyrddyn, n. the mullet, a fish
Hyred, a. apt to run
Hyrif, a. easily numbered
Hyrn, n. a hough, holme
Hyrwym, a. easily binding
Hyrwysg, a. of a free career
Hys, n. snarl or knarl
Hysathr, a. easily trodden
Hysbys, a. evident, manifest
Hysbysai, n. index
Hysbysiad, n. advertisement; a declaration
Hysbysrwydd, n. manifestation, notice
Hysbysu, n. to advertise, to inform, to acquaint
Hysbyswr, n. one who makes evident, advertiser
Hysgyr, n. stave; splinter
Hysiad, n. snarling, setting on

Hysian, v. to snarl, to set on
Hysigl, a. easily shaking
Hyson, apt to make noise; noisy
Hysp, a. dry, dried up; barren
Hyspu, v. to render dry
Hyspyddiad, n. an exhausting
Hyspyddu, v. to exhaust
Hytrach. a. more forward
Hytynt, n. a course, a journey
Hywad, a. deniable
Hywain, a. aptly ministering
Hywaith, a. ready at work
Hywall, a. apt to fail, fallible
Hywan, a. penetrable
Hywar, a. manageable
Hywedd, a. conformable
Hyweddiad, n. a conforming
Hyweddiant, n. tractableness
Hyweddu, v. to render tractable
Hywel, a. conspicuous, evident
Hywell, a. being remediable
Hywen, a. easily smiling
Hywerth, a. vendible, saleable
Hywir, a. apt to be true
Hywiw, a. apt to be excellent
Hywredd, n. manliness
Hywyl, a. easily perceived
Hywyn, a. aptly impassioned
Hywys, a. convenable
Hywystl, a. easily pledged

I

I prep. to; into; towards, for
,pron. I, me, for emphasis
Iâ, n. that is slippery; ice
Iach, a. sound, whole, healthy
Iachâad, n. a healing
Iachaedigaeth, the act of healing
Iachaol, a. of healing quality
Iachau, v. to cure, to heal
Iachawdwr, n. a saviour
Iachawdwriaeth, n. salvation
Iachus, a. healthy; wholesome
Iachuso, v. to render wholesome

Iachusol, of a healthy condition
Iachusrwydd, n. healthiness
Iâd, n. side of the head, pate
Iaedd, n. icy state, iciness
Iaen, n. a sheet of ice
Iain, a. icy, or very cold
Iaith, n. language, speech
Iâl, n. open space or region:
  a. clear, open, or fair
Ialain, a. of pure quality
Ialant, n. clearness, lustre
Ialedd, n. clearness, fineness
Ialen, n. a sapling; a rod
Iangedd, n. rudeness; rusticity
Iangu, v. to become rude
Iangwr, n. a rude one, a boor
Iâr, n. that stretches over; a
  shoulder; the female of birds,
  a hen
Iar, prep. from off, off, from
Iarc, n. that stretches over
Iarcw, n. that directs, a pilot
Iardy, n. a barton, a hen coop
Iarhyd, n. a shoulder-piece
Iarll, n. an earl; a lord
Iarllaeth, n. an earldom
Iarlles, n. an earl's lady
Iarth, n. a long rod; a goad
Iâs, n. what pervades; mature,
  disposition; a shock; a shiver
Iasaidd, a. of pervading tendency
Iasawl, a. apt to shock
Iasedd, n. pervading tendency
Iasiad, n. a giving a shock; pervasion
Iasu, v. to pervade with a quality
Iau, n. that is moving; the
  lungs: junior; a yoke; Jove
Dydd Iau, Thursday: a inceptive
  of progrees; junior
Iawg, n. that is keen or ardent
Iawl, n. the act of glorifying
Iawn, n. right; satisfaction; a.
  right, equitible; just; ad.
  rightly, or very
Iawnawl, a. of a right tendency
Iawnbwyll, n. right reason

Iawnder, n. rightness; equity
Iawndda, a. rightly good
Iawnedd, a. rectitude
Iawni, v. to render right
Iawniad, n. a righting
Iawnles, n. right advantage
Iawnran, n. right share
Iawnred, n. right course
Iawnryw, n. right kind
Iawnwedd, n. right aspect
Iawnymgais, n. right pursuit
Iawnysgrif, n. orthography
Ib, n. aptness to run out
Ic, n. that is pointed or accute
Ich, n. screak, squeal
Ichiad, n. a screaking
Id, n. that is drawn out; a point; pronominal agent
Idiaw, v. to acuminate
Idd, n. that is sharp: prep. to, towards; for; into
Iddas, a. pungent; subtile
Iddwf, n. St. Anthony's fire
Ië, ad. it is so; yes, yea
Iechyd, n. health, sanity
Iechydol, a. salutary, healthful
Iachawdwriaeth, n. salvation
Ieithgarwch, n. philology
Ieithiad, n. phraseology
Ieithiadur, n. grammar
Ieithio, v. to form a phrase
Ieithiog, a. having language
Ieithogi, v. to form a phrase
Ieithol, a. relating to speech
Ieithydd, n. linguist
Ieithyddiaeth, n. philology
Ieithyddu, v. to form speech
Ieithyddwr, n. linguist
Ierthi, n. driving-rod; goad
Iesin, a. radiant, glorious; fair
Iesinaw, v. to radiate; to be fair, to render fair
Iesinder, n. radiancy
Iesu, n. Jesus
Iet, n. a country gate
Ieuad, n. a joining, a yoking
Ieuaf, a. youngest
Ieuanc, n. youth; a. young

Ieuant, n. infant, youth
Ieuangaidd, a. somewhat young
Ieuenctyd, n. youth, minority
Ieugen, n. ferret
Icuo, v. to couple, to yoke
Ieuol, a. being joined or yoked
Iewin, a. clamorous, noisy
Iewidd, n. yoke collar
If, n. that is impelled or cast
Iff, n. that is forcibly ejected
Ig, n. a vexing; hickup; sob
Igiad, n. a sighing or sobbing
Igian, v. to be sobbing
Il, n. that is in motion, ferment
Iliad, n. fermentation
Iliaw, v. to ferment, to work
Ilir, n. butterfly
Ill, n. an augment, a particle: pron.their,they,used with two and three: Ill dau, ill dri
Im, n. that is extreme
Imp, n. a scion, or a shoot
Impiad, n. a germinating
Impio, v. to germinate; to graft
Impiol, a. germinating, shooting
Impog, n. osculation, or kiss
Impyn, n. a scion, a shoot
In, n. that is pervading
Indeg, n. snblimate; raving mad
Insel, n. a mark; seal, signet
Inseiliad, n. a marking; a sealing
Inseilio, v. to mark; to seal
Ing, n. a strait, a difficulty; a. straight, confined
Ingaidd, a. somewhat strait or narrow
Ingder, n. staitness
Ingol, n. tending to straiten
Io, interj. well-a-day, lack-a-day
Ioed, n. time past; ever
Iolad, n. a worshipping
Iolaeth, n. adoration, worship
Iolaethu, v. to adore
Iolawr, n. an adorer
Iolch, n. an act of devotion
Ioli, v. to praise; to worship
Ion, n. a first cause; the Lord
Ionawr, n. January

Ior, n. the eternal; the Lord
Iorn, n. a burst, a thrust
Iornad, n, a bursting through
Iorni, v. to burst through
Iorthawl, a. incessant; diligent
Iorthi, v. to be continual
Iorthyn, n. assiduity
Ir, n. that is pure; that is fresh; a. juicy; green; raw
Iraâd, n. a growing juicy
Irad, n. pungency, rage: a. pungent; grievous; rueful
Iradedd, n. grievousness
Iradrwydd, n. grievousness
Iradu, v. to render afflicting
Iradus, a. rueful, afflicting
Irai, n. a sharp point; a goad
Iraid. n. grease
Iraidd, a. juicy; sappy; fresh
Irain. a. full of juice; luxuriant
Irâu, v. to grow juicy
Irdanc, n. stupor, amazement
Irdangawl, a. stupifying, amazing. causing a stupor
Irdangiad, n. a stupifying
Irdawd, n. succulency; freshness, or rawness
Irdra, n. juiciness, freshness
Ireidiad, n. an anointing, or greasing
Ireidlyd, a. of of a greasy quality
Ireidd-dra, n. sappiness
Ireiddiad, n. a becoming juicy or fresh
Ireiddio, v. to become juicy
Ireiddlyd, a. of a juicy quality
Iriad, n. a growing fresh
Irlas, a. of a fresh verdancy
Irlasu, v. to become verdant
Irlesni, n. a fresh verdancy
Iro, v. to anoint, to grease
Irwedd, n. green appearance
Irwellt, n. fresh or green grass
Irwr, n. an anointer
Is, n. the state of going down: a. low; under; inferior: prep. below, under
Isaâd, n. a rendering low

Isaf, a. lowest
Isafiad, n. an inferior
Isathro, n. an under master
Isâu, v. to lower, to abase
Isder, n. lowness; meanness
Isel, a. low, base; humble
Iselâad, n. a making low
Iselaidd, a. low or humble
Iselâu, v. to make low
Iselder, n. lowness; humility
Iseldrem, n. a low look
Iselfryd, a. humble-minded
Iselfrydedd, n. humility
Iselgreg, a. softly rumbling
Iselgyngian, v. to make a low noise
Iseliad, n. a lowering
Iselni, n. lowness, abjectness
Iselradd, n. a low degree
Iselraith, n. a petty jury
Iselreithiwr, n. a petty juryman
Iselu, v. to abase, to depress
Isg, n. that is on the surface
Isgal, n. froth, scum
Isgell, n. broth, soup, pottage
Isgwympiedydd, n. sublapsarian
Islaw, prep. underhand, below
Islinellu, v. to underscore
Isloerawl, a. sublunary
Isod, prep. below, beneath, under: ad. in a lower place
Isradd, n. an inferior degree
Israddol, a. of an inferior degree
Isweithio, v. to underwork
Iswerth, n. an undersale
Iswerthu, v. to undersell
It. pronominal agent, it
Ith, n. a particle, a grain; corn
Iuddew, n. man of Judea, Jew
Iuddewaidd, a. judaical, jewish
Iuddewes, n. a Jewess
Iuddewiaeth, n. Judaism
Iuddewig, a. pertaining to Jews
Iw, n. that extreme
Iwbwb, n. a hollo, a cry
Iwerddon, n. Ireland, Erin
Iwin, n. a frantic one: a. outrageous frantic

Iwrch, n. a roebuck
Iwrth, prep. by, in oppossition
Iyrchaidd, a. like the roebuck
Iyrchell, n. a young roe
Iyrches, n. a roe, deer
Iyrchw, n. the roebuck

L

Lamp, n. a lamp
Laru, v. to satiate
Larwm, n. an alarm
Lassog, n. gizzard of a bird; a kidney
Lefain, n. leaven
Lefeinllyd, a. leavened
Lefeinio, v. to leaven; to inbrue; to infect
Lefiathan, n. leviathan; a water animal
Lindys, n. a caterpillar
Lol, n. noise
Lolio, v. to babble
Lôn, n. a lane; a narrow way between two hedges
Lwfer, n. a chimney
Lwfio, v. to allow
Lwlen, n. a kidney [buffer
Lwmp, n. a lump, a. box, or

LL

Lla, n. that breaks out, that is light
Llab, n. a flag; a slip; a stripe
Llabed, n. a label; a flab
Llabi, n. stripling; a looby
Llabiad, n. a slapping
Llabiaidd, a. like a looby
Llabies, n. a strapping wench
Llabio, v. to slap, to strap
Llabwst, n. a lank gawky
Llabyddio, v. to kill with stones

Llac, n. slack; quicksand: a. loose, lax, slack
Llaca, n. mire, mud, slop
Llacâad, n. a slackening
Llacâawl, a. relaxing, drooping
Llacâu, v. to slacken; to relax
Llacawd, n. a slack state
Llaciad, n. a slakening
Llaciaw, v. to slaken, to relax
Llaciawl, a. slakening
Llacrwydd, n. slackness, lavity, relaxed state
Llach, n. a ray; a slap
Llachar, a. gleaming
Llachau, n. gleams
Llachbren, n. a cudgel
Llachdwm, n, a tub
Llachffon, n. cudgel
Llachiad, n. a slapping
Llachiaw, v. to slap, to cudgel
Llachiwr, n. cudgeller
Lladaeth, n. conferring a favour
Lladawl, a. gracious
Lladin, n. the Latin language
Lladiniaeth, n. latinity
Lladiniaw, v. to latinize
Lladinydd, n. latinist
Lladmerydd, n. an interpreter, a translator
Lladrad, n. theft or stealth
Lladradaidd, a. thievish, private
Lladrata, v. to steal
Lladrataeth, n. act of thieving
Lladratiad, n. a thieving
Lladrates, Lladrones, n. female stealer
Lladratwr, n. stealer, thief
Lladron, n, thieves, robbers
Ladronaidd, a. thievish
Lladroni, v. to become thieves
Lladu, v. to confer a favour
Lladyr, n. that is without value
Lladd, n. a cut off; a killing: v. to kill, to cut off
Lladdadwy, a. that may be cut off or killed
Lladdedig, a. killed, cut off
Lladdedigaeth, n. a killing

Lladdfa, n. a slaughter
Lladdiad, n. a killing
Lladdwr, n. a killer, a slayer
Laddwriaeth, n. butchery
Llae, n. an expanse, a spread
Llaer, n. a rippling; a reflux
Llaeru, v. to ebb
Llaes, a. loose, lax, trailing low
Llaesbais, n. loose trailing coat
Llaesder, n. laxness; a trailing
Llaesiad, n. a rendering trailing, a drooping
Llaesu, v. to slacken, to trail
Llaeth, n. milk.—Llaeth enwyn, butter-milk
Llaetha, v. to collect milk
Llaethdwn, n. a lay land
Llaethedd, n. lactescene
Llaethfwyd, n. a milk diet
Llaethiad, n. turning to milk
Llaethlo, n. a suckling calf
Llaethlyd, a. milky
Llaethog, a. abounding in milk
Llaethogrwydd, n. milkiness
Llaethol, lacteal, milky
Llaethon, n. the soft roe of fish
Llaethu, v. to turn to milk
Llaethysgall, n. sow thistle
Llaf, n. that extends out
Llafan n. that bears impression
Llafanad, n. intellect, sense
Llafanawg, n. the livewort
Llafanawl, a. intellectual
Llafar, n. utterance, speech: a. vocal; loquacious
Llafarai, n. vocal, vowel
Llafarawd, n. pronunciation
Llafarawl, a. enunciative
Llafaredigaeth, n. pronunciation
Llafariad, n. pronunciation
Llafarlais, n. a clear tone
Llafaru, v. to pronounce to speak
Llafarus, a. apt to be vocal
Llafarwch, n. loquacity [ing
Llafarwedd, n. mode of speaking
Llafarwr, n. an enunciator; a speaker, a preacher
Llafas, n. the act of daring
Llafasawl, a. daring
Llafasu, v. to dare, to presume
Llafaswr, n. a presumer
Llafn, n. a blade; a flake
Llafnawr, n. blade spears
Llafnes, n. a strapping girl
Llafniad, n. a blading
Llafnu, v. to blade, to flake
Llafon, n. a lamina, a flake
Llafren, n. a large buttocked one, a squabby woman
Llafrwyn, n. the bulrushes
Llafu, v. to spread out; to breech
Llafur, n. labour; tillage
Llafuriaeth, n. a labouring
Llafurio, v. to labour, to toil
Llafurus, a. laborous, toilsome
Llafurwriaeth, n. husbandry
Llafyr, n. a spread; the breech
Llag, n. that is slack: a. slack
Llagad, n. a plash full of rushes
Llai, n. mud; raven gray: a. small; also smaller: ad. in a smaller degree
Llaib, n. a sup, or a lap
Llaid, n. clay; mire
Llaidd, n. that is mild: a mild
Llaif, n. a shear, or a shave
Llaig, n. a bubble on water
Llain, n. a blade; a long slip
Llaing, n. that closes; a clasp
Llair, n. that droops; satiety
Llais, n. a voice; a sound
Llaith, n. humid state: a. moist, pliant
Llall, n. the other: ad. other
Llam, n. stride, a step; a hap
Llamawg, a. having a stride
Llamawl, a. striding; stepping
Llamdwyad, n. a conveying
Llamdwyaw, v. to convey
Llamfa, n. stepping place
Llamfforch, n. a stile
Llamiad, n. a striding
Llamidydd, n. vaulter; porpoise
Llamidyddiaeth, n. a tumbling
Llamogan, n. a stile
Llamre, n. a skip; a bounce

Llamsach, n. a caper
Llamu, v. to stride; to step
Llamwr, n. one who strides
Llan, n. area; yard; a church
Llanastr, n. a strewed place
Llanastrawl, a. strewing
Llanastriad, n. a strewing
Llanc, n. a youth, a youngster
Llances, n. a young woman
Llancesig, n. a tiny girl
Llandref, n. a church village
Llaned, a. of a clear surface
Llanedd, n. smoothness
Llanerch, n. a clear area, a clear patch; a glade
Llanerchu, v. to lay in patches
Llant, n. an enclosed plat
Llanw, n. fulness, influx
Llanwed, n. an influx, a tide
Llar, n. that spreads, that is soft
Llariaidd, a. mild, meek, gentle
Llariain, a. full of mildness
Llarieiddiad, n. a growing mild
Llarieddio, v. to meliorate
Llarp, n. a shred, a clout
Llarpiad, n. a tearing to rags
Llarpio v. to tear, to rend
Llarpiog, a. tattered, ragged
Llaru, v. to satiate, to cloy
Llarwch, n. mildness
Llary, n. a placid one: a. placid, gentle, meek
Llaryaw, v. to render mild
Llarychu, v. to soften
Llaryedd, n. mildness, suavity
Llaryeiddio, v. to grow mild
Llas, n. incrustation; blue
Llasar, n. enamel: a. blue
Llasarn, n. a pavement: a flooring of stones
Llasarniad, n. a paving
Llasarnu, v. to pave, to floor
Llasarnwr, n. a pavier
Llasog, n. a streamer
Llast, n. a receptable, a vessel
Llaswy, n. a bluish tint
Llaswyr, n. aerial freshness
Llatai, n. a love messenger

Llatcawd, n. a shallow bowl
Llateies, n. love messenger
Llatwn, n. latten; brass
Llath, n. a rod, a staff; a yard
Llathenaid, n. a yard length
Llathen, n. a rod, a yard
Llathlud, n. seduction
Llathludo, v. to seduce
Llathr, a. glossy, glittering
Llathraid, a. glittering; polished
Llathrawl. a. glittering, glaring
Llathrciddiaw, v. to make glittering, or glossy
Llathriad, n. a glittering
Llathru, v. to make glossy, to polish, to glitter
Llathrudd, n. stupration
Llathruddaw, v. to stuprate
Llathruddiad, n. struprating
Llathryd, n. violence, a rape
Llathrydaw, n. to violate
Llathrydd, n. a polisher
Llau, v. to lay open; to slay: n. creepers, or lice
Llaw, n. a hand
Llawaeth, n. act of handing
Llawagawr, n. the culerage
Llawaid, n. a handful
Llawarwain, n. manuduction
Llawban, n. felt, felt cloth
Llawborth, n. hand feeding
Llawciad, n. a gulping
Llawciaw, v. to gulp, to gorge
Llawch, n. protection, guard
Llawchwith, a. left handed
Llawd, n. that shoots out; a lad: a. tending forward; craving, lewd
Llawdaro, n. hot-cockles
Llawdlws, a. neat-handed
Llawdr, n. trowsers, breeches
Llawdryfer, n. hand harpoon
Llawdywys, n. manuduction
Llawdd, n. pleasure, delight: a delectable, solacing
Llawddawg, a. yielding pleasure
Llawddeau, a. right handed
Llawddewiniaeth, chiromancy

Llawddu, v. to delight: to sooth
Llawegen, n. a gauntlet
Llawen, a. merry, joyful, glad
Llawenfid, n. a gladdening
Llawenâu, v. to gladden
Llawenchwedl, n. joyful news
Llawenwch, n. merriment
Llawenychawl, a. gladdening
Llawenychiad. n. a rejoicing
Llawenychu. v. to rejoice
Llawenydd, n. gladness, mirth
Llawer, n. a great many; a diversity; a great deal: a. many, much; several
Llawes, n. outskirt; a sleeve
Llawesan, n. a kind of play
Llawesgud, a. ready-handed
Llawesob, a. having outskirts
Llaweth, n. a handful, a gripe
Llawf, n. palm of the hand
Llawfaeth, a. fed by the hand
Llawfeddyg, n. surgeon
Llawfoled, n. handkerchief
Llawforwyn, n. a handmaid
Llawfrenin, n. the play of question and command
Llawfwyall, n. small hatchet
Llawffon, n. walking-stick
Llawg, n. a swallow, gulp
Llawgaead, a. close-handed
Llawgaeth, a. of restained hand
Llawgair, n. a plighted troth
Llawgallawr, n. a saucepan
Llawgelfyddyd, n. a handicraft
Llawgist, n. a hand-chest
Llawhir, a. long-handed, lavish
Llawhual, n. a manacle
Llawiad, n. a handing
Llawio, v. to hand, to handle
Llawiog, a. having hands
Llawlaw, ad. hand to hand
Llawliain, n. towel, a napkin
Llawlif, n. a hand-saw
Llawlyw, n. plough-handle
Llawn, a. full; complete
Llawnad, n. a making full
Llawnaeth, n. impletion
Llawnallu, n. plenipotence

Llawnder, n. fulness plenty
Llawndra, n. fulness; abundance, or plenty
Llawnfryd, n. full purpose
Llawnhwda, n. a nonplus
Llawnlleuad, Llawnlloer, n. a full moon
Llawnt, n. a smooth hill, lawn
Llawnwedd, n. a full form
Llawr, n. a floor; area, ground
Llawrig, n. the herb perriwinkle
Llawrodd, n. hand-gift
Llawrudd, n. a murderer: a. having a red hand
Llawruddiaeth, n. bloodshed
Llawrwydd, n. the laurel
Llawryd, n. dejection
Llawrydd, a. of unchecked hand
Llaws, a. alert, brisk
Llaw-waith, n. a manufacture
Llaw-wst, n. the chiragra
Lle, n. a place; stead, room: ad. where, at what place
Llead, n. a placing; location; a lecturing, a reading
Lleain, v. to read, to lecture
Lleawl, a. local, of a place
Lleban, n. a lank form
Llebanaidd, a. somewhat lank
Llebaneiddrwydd, n. lank ghastliness
Llebanes, n. a ghastly woman
Llebiw, n. pale yellow hue
Llecawd, n. a flagging state
Llecin, n. a second wort in brewing
Llcciad, n. a lagging, a flagging
Llech, n. a flat stone, a flag, a slate, a tablet; a skulk
Llechad, n. a flattening; a skulking
Llecheira, n. a chilblain
Llechen, n. a flag, a slate
Llechfa, n. a skulk, or a covert
Llechfaen, n. a slate stone
Llechfaen, n. a skulking place
Llechfod, n. a skulking state
Llechiad, n. a skulking down

Llechlawr, n. a flag floor
Llechog, a. flagged; skulking
Llechres, n. a pedigree-roll
Llechu, v. to skulk, to squat
Llechwedd, n. a flat aspect; side of the head; the steep or shelving of a hill
Llechweddu, v. to slope; to slant
Llechwen, n. inclining gesture
Llechwr, n. a skulker
Llechwrus, a. skulking, lurking
Lled, n. breadth, or width: a. broad, wide; broader: ad. in the mean, in part, half, partly, almost
Lledach, n. a mean descent
Lledadnabod, v to half-recognise
Lledadwy, a. expansible
Lledaddaw, v. to half-promise
Lledaddef, a. half-ripe, ripe
Lledagored, a. half-open
Lledallu, v. partly to effect
Lledammau, v. partly to suspect
Lledan, n. breadth; a flounder
Lledaniad, n. an expanding
Lledanu, v. to make broad
Lledawl, a. relating to breadth
Lledben, n. a flat head
Lledbrofi, v. partly to taste
Lledbwyll, n. a half reason
Lledchwelan, n. that is half open, or divided
Lledechwyrch, a. half-stupified
Lledewig, a. partly oosing
Lledewigwst, n. hemorrhoids
Lledfan, n. sprawl: a. sprawling
Lledfarw, a. partly, or half dead
Lledfeddw, a. half-drunk, tipsy
Lledfegin, a. half-reared, half-domesticated, or tamed
Lledfeginaw, v. to domesticate
Lledfegyn, n. domestic animal
Lledferwi, v. to parboil
Lledfryd, n. listlessness
Lledfrydig, a. apt to be listless
Lledfrydu, v. to render listless; to be half-minded

Lledfyw, a. half-alive; just dead
Lledffrom, a. somewhat peevish
Lledglaf, a. slightly diseased
Lledgloff, a. somewhat lame
Lledglywed, v. to hear partly
Lledgoel, n. a slight belief
Lledgofio, v. partly to remember
Lledhynt, n. intent, purpose
Lledjad, n. a making broad
Lledíaith, n. corrupt speech
Lledled, a. widely spreading
Lledlef, n. imperfect utterance
Lledlw, n. a vain swearing
Llednais, a. elegant, nice, neat
Llednelsrwydd, n. elegance
Lledoer, a. half cold, lukewarm
Lledofni, v. partly to fear
Lledol, n. a rearward, a rear
Lledorwedd, n. discumbency: v. partly to lie down
Lledr, n. leather
Lledrad, n. stealth, or theft
Lledradol, a. stealing, thieving
Lledrata, v. to steal, to thieve
Lledred, n. latitude; broadness
Lledriad, n. a doing with leather
Lledrith, n. illusion, disguise
Lledrithiad, n. appearing illusively
Lledrithio, v. to appear illusively
Lledrithiog, a. being half or partly visible
Lledrwr, n. a manufcturer of leather; a leatherseller
Lledryw, n, a mongrel kind: a. of degenerate kind
Lledrywiad, n. a degenerating
Lledrywiaw, v. to degenerate
Lledrywiawl, a. degenerating
Lledrywiogedd, n. degenerateness
Lledrywiogi, v. to degenerate
Lledu, v. to widen; to expand
Lledw, n. profusion; enjoyment a. profuse or abundant
Lledwad, n. a ladle
Lledwedd, n. latitude
Lledwenu, v. smiling partly

| LLED | 212 | LLEI |

Lledwg, n. a slight frown a. of a soft quality
Lledwigen, n. a creeping thing
Lledwigyn, n. a worm
Lledwiriondeb, n. half-idiotism
Lledwlyb, a. slightly wet
Lledwr, n. a spreader
Lledwydd, n. imperfect timber, or not good in kind
Lledwyllt, a. rather wild
Lledd, n. a flat, or a plain
Lleddf, a. inclining, oblique
Lleddfad, n. a drooping
Lleddfod, n. assuagement
Lleddfiad, n. a warping; a flattening; a softening
Lleddfu, v. to warp; to flatten
Lleddy, a. inclining; drooping, flat; of a mild nature
Llëen, a. literate, scholastic,
Llëen, n. literature, scholarship, erudition
Llëenawg, a. literate, having scholarship, learned
Llëenu, v. to pursue literature
Llëenydd, n. a literary man
Llëenyddawl, a. literary
Llëenyddiaeth, n. scholarship
Llef, n. a voice; a cry
Llefad, n. a crying out
Llefain, v. to cry aloud, to cry
Llefar, n. utterance, voice
Llefarwr, n. a speaker [speaking
Llefariad, n. an uttering, a
Llefaru, v. to utter, to speak
Llefawg, a. shouting, squalling
Llefeliad, n. a devising
Llefelu, v. to devise, to invent
Llefelyn, n. stye on the eye
Lleferydd, n. utterance, voice
Llefiad, n. enunciation
Llefiadawl, a. enunciate
Llefn, a. even, sleek, smooth
Llefnyn, n. a blade, a slab
Llefr, a. coward, timid, faint
Llefrin, a. of a spreading nature
Llefrith, n. sweet milk
Llefrithen, n. stye on the eye

Lleg, n. that whips round
Llegach, n. a sluggish one
Llegest, n. a gorbelly; a lobster
Llegu, v. to flag, or to lag
Llegus, a. apt to flag; sluggish
Llegynt, n. oppression
Llegyrn, n. a dwarf
Lleiad, n. diminution [smallest
Lleiaf, n. the least: a. least,
Lleian, n. a grey one; a nun
Lleianaeth, n. life of a nun
Lleiandy, n. a nunnery
Lleianu, v. to take the veil
Lleianyn, n. a wren
Lleiau, v. to diminish, to lessen
Lleibiad, n. a lapping
Lleibio, v. to lap, or to lick
Lleibiol, a. lapping, lambent
Lleibiwr, n. a lapper
Lleidfa, n. a clayey place
Lleidiogl, v. to turn clayey
Lleidiogrwydd, n. muddiness
Lleidio, v. to turn to clay
Lleidiog, a. lutulent, muddy
Lleidr, n. a thief, a stealer
Lleiddawd, n. sluggish state
Lleiddiad, n. a slayer
Lleifiad, n. a reaping
Lleifiaw, v. to cut; to reap
Lleigiaw, v. to flag; to skulk
Lleilai, a. being less and less
Lleill, n. others; the rest
Lleinell, n. a narrow slip
Lleiniad, n. a blading
Lleinio, v. to blade; to shred
Lleion, n. a dark blue marble
Lleipio, v. to lap, to lick
Lleipr, a. flaccid, flabby
Lleipraw, v. to droop, to flag
Lleipriad, n. a turning flabby
Lleiprog, n. a lamprey
Lleirwyd, n. fine for adultery
Lleisiad, n. a sounding; a tonation; a counter tide
Lleisio, v. to sound, to utter
Lleisiol, a. belonging to the voice
Lleisiwr, n. a bawler
Lleisw, n. lixivium, or dye

Lleithad, n. a turning humid
Lleithawd, n. a damping
Lleithban, n. soft roe of fish
Lleithder, n. dampness
Lleithdra, n. dampness [lution
Lleithiannu, v. to cause disso-
Lleithiant, n. a damp state
Lleithiar, a. apt to dissolve
Lleithig, n. a bench; a throne
Lleithian, n. humid weather
Lleithio, v. to moisten
Lleithlyd, a. apt to be damp
Lleithon, n. soft roe of fish
Lleithrid, n, a flash, a gleam
Llem, a. sharp, pungent
Llemain, v. to hop, or to skip
Llemidydd, bouncer; porpoise
Llemwst, n. sharp perception
Llemysien, n. sparow-hawk
Llen. n. literature, erudition
Llen, n. a veil; a curtain
Llenawg, a. literate, learned
Llenawr, n. a scholar; a clerk
Lleniad, n. a veiling over
Lleniedydd, n a veiler
Llenlath, n. a curtain rod
Lleinlian, n. sheeting, sheets
Llenoriaeth, n. literature
Llenu, v. to veil, to envelope
Llenwad, n. a filling; a flowing
Llenwi, v. to fill; to flow in
Llenwr, n. a clergyman
Lleng, n. a legion; a host
Llengawl, a. legionary
Llengcyn, n. a stripling
Llengel, n. a veil, a covering
Llengig, n. the diaphragm
Llengudd, n. a veil covering
Lleo'deb n. locality, localness
Lleoiad, n. a languing, a licking

Llerf, a subtile; sharp, acerb
Llerpyn, n. a shred, or a rag
Llerpyna, v. to shred, to tear
Llerpyniad, v. a tearing
Llerth, n. subtilty; a frenzy
Llerthiad, n. a turning frantic
Llerthu, v. to turn frantic
Lleru, v. to satiate; to be nice
Llerwyn, that is nice or delicate:
  a. nice, delicate; squeamish
Lles, n. benefit, profit, good
Llesg, n. feeble, faint; sluggish
Llesgâad, n a debilitating
Llesgâu, v. to weaken
Llesgedd, n. debility
Llesgen, n. a sluggish fit
Llesgiad, n. debilitating
Llesiad, n. a benefitting
Llesiannu, v. to make beneficial
Llesiant, n. benefit, advantage
Llesmar, n. a fainting fit
Llesmeriad, n. a swooning
Llesmerio, v. to swoon
Llesol a. advantageous
Llest, n. that heaps together
Llestair, n. let, obstruction
Llesteiriad, n an obstructing
Llesteirio, v. to obstruct
Llesteiriol, a. obstructing
Llesteiriwr, n. an obstructer
Llestr, n. a vessel; a matrix
Llestriaid, n. a vessel full; a two
  and a half bushel measure
Llestriad, n. a putting in a ves-
  sel   [vessel
Llestrwr, n. one who puts in a
Llestru, v. to put in a vessel
Llestryn, n. a small vessel
Lleswyra, v. to take airing
Llethai, a oblique; slant

Llettya, v. to lodge, to quarter
Llettyad, n. a taking lodging
Llettyaeth, n. act of lodging
Llettywr, n. a lodger
Llettywraig, n. a woman lodger
Lletwed, n. a ladle, a large spoon
Lleth, a. flabby; drooping
Llethawl, a. flattening; overlaying
Llethiad, n. a flattening; an overlaying
Llethr, n. a slope, a declivity
Llethrawd, heap of rubbish
Llethrawl, a. declivous
Lleithriad, n. a sloping down
Llethrid, n. flash, a gleam
Llethruv. to slope down
Llethu, v. to flatten, to overlay
Llethwr, n. an overlayer
Lleu, v. to explain; to lecture; to place, to lay
Lleuad, n. the moon
Lleuadawl, a. lunar, lunary
Lleuadiad, n. a lunation
Lleuawg, a. full of lice, lousy
Lleudid, n. splendor
Lleuen, n. a louse
Lleuer, n. light
Lleuerad, n. shedding of light
Lleuerawl, a. illuminating
Lleueru, v. to shine
Lleuerydd, n. a luminary
Lleufer, n. light; splendor
Lleuferu, v. to illumine
Lleuferydd, n. an illuminator
Llew, n. that devours; a lion
Llewa, v. to devour; to swallow; to take food
Llewaidd, a. leonine
Llewen, n. a point to which any thing verges; a focus
Llewenydd, n. a verging point
Llewes, n. a she lion, a lioness
Llewi, v. to swallow
Llewin, a. occident, western
Llewyg, n. a swoon, a trance
Llewygawl, a. swooning, fainting
Llewygiad, n. a fainting away

Llewygu, v. to swoon, to faint
Llewyn, n. a radiating point; the west; a gleam; the orach
Llewynu, v. to verge to a focus
Llewynydd, n. occident
Llewyrch, n. brightness, reflection of light; complexion
Llewyrchiad, n. an illuming
Llewyrchiant, n. illumination
Llewyrchu, v. to reflect light
Llewyrchus, a. lightsome
Llewyrn, n. meteor
Llewyrnu, v. to produce meteors
Lleyg, n. a layman; a yeoman
Lleyn, n. a low strip of land
Lleynlys, n. the scurvy grass
Lli, n. a flux, a flood, a stream
Lliad, n. a flooding, a streaming
Lliain, n. linen-cloth, linen; a towel; a napkin
Lliant, n. a torrent, a stream
Llias, n. a parted state
Lliasiad, n. privation
Lliaws, n. a multitude, a number: a. many, frequent, much
Llib, n. a flaccid state
Llibin, a. flaccid, limber, soft
Llibiniaw, v. to turn flaccid
Llilyn, n. a flibble
Llid, n. wrath, indignation
Llidiad, n. a raising anger
Llidiaw, v. to inflame, to enrage
Llidiog, a. wrathful; inflamed
Llidiogi, v. to become unflamed
Llidiogrwydd, n. wrathfulness
Llidus, a. wrathful
Llieingig, n. a midriff
Llieiniad, n. a putting on linen
Llieiniawg, a. wearing linen
Llieiniwr, n. a linen-draper
Llieinrwd, n. lint
Llieinwe, n. a piece of linen
Llieinwisg, n. a linen garment
Llif, n. a flood, a deluge, a saw
Llifad, n. fluxion, flowing
Llifaid, a. ground or whetted
Llifddwfr, n. a torrent
Llifedigaeth, n. grinding an edge

Llifeiriad, n. an overflowing
Llifeiriant, n. an inundation
Llifeiriaw, v. to overflow
Llifiad, n. a sawing with a saw
Llifiant, n. a defluxion, a flow
Llifio, v. to saw, to cut with a saw
Llifion, n. saw-dust; filings
Llifiwr, n. a sawyer
Llifo, v. to flow, to stream: v. to grind; to file
Llifol, a. flowing, streaming
Llifwell, n. an issue
Llifwydd, n. boards, planks
Llig, n. that shoots or glides
Llill, n. an epithet for a goat
Llillen, n. a young goat
Llimp, n. sleek or glossy
Llimprin, n. spoon meat
Llin, n. fine thread; a fibre, grain of wood; a line; a flax
Llinar, a. of a smooth nature
Llinariad, n. an assuaging
Llinaru, v. to assuage
Llindag, n. a strangle
Llindagiad, n. a strangling
Llindagu, v. to strangle
Llindagwr, n. a strangler
Llindro, n. the dodder
Llindys, n. caterpillar
Llinell, n. a line; a streak
Llinelliad, n. making lines
Llinellu, v. to draw lines
Llinen, n. a splinter; a fibre
Llinhad, n. linseed, flax-seed
Llinhesg, n. sort of reed grass
Llinon, n. grain of ash; a spear
Llinos, n. a linnet; a beauty
Llinosen, n. a little linnet
Llinwydd, n. the liverwort
Llinyn, n. a line; a string
Llinynawg, a. having strings
Llinynu, v. to line, to string
Llion, n. an aggregate of floods
Lliosbarth, a. of many parts
Lliosdroed, n. many-footed
Lliosgib, a. multicapsular
Lliosliw, a. having many colours
Llioslun, a. multiform

Lliosog, a. multitudinous
Lliosogi, v. to multiply
Lliosogrwydd, n. multitude
Lliosogwr, n. multiplier
Llipa, a. flaccid, flagging
Llipâand, n. a turning flaccid
Llipan, n. a limp or a glib one
Llipanu, v. to make glib
Llipâu, v. to grow flabby
Llipryn, n. that flags; a fribble
Lliprynrwydd, n. flabbiness
Lliprynu, v. to render flaccid
Llith, n. a lure; a bait; a mash; a lesson
Llithiad, n. an alluring; a lecturing
Llithiant, n. alectation
Llithio, v. to draw to, to attract, to entice, to lecture, to bait
Llithiogi, v. to render alluring
Llithiol, a. allective, alluring
Llithiwr, n. an allurer
Llithr, n. a glide; a slip
Llithred, n. a glide or a slip
Llithriad, n. a slipping
Llithriant, n. lubricity
Llithrig, a. sliding; slippery
Llithrigaw, v. to make slippery
Llithrigder, n. slipperiness
Llithrigiad, n. lubrification
Llithrigrwydd, n. slipperiness
Llithro, v. to glide, to slip
Llithrol, a. gliding; slipping
Llithwr, n. a lecturer
Lliw, n. a colour; a figure
Lliwadwy, a. colourable
Lliwdy, n. a dyeing-house
Lliwgar, a. of good colour
Lliwiad, n. a colouring
Lliwied, v. to stain; to reproach
Lliwio, v. to colour; to dye
Lliwiog, a. having a colour
Lliwiwr, n. a colourist, a dyer
Lliwlys, n. dying plant, woad
Lliwusrwydd, n. goodness of colour
Lliwyddiaeth, n. art of dyeing
Llo, n. a mass; a calf

Llob, n. a dolt, a blockhead
Lloc, n. a dam ; a fold
Llociad, n. a penting up
Llocio, v. to pent ; to fold
Llocust, n. a locust
Lloches, n. a refuge
Llochi, v. to harbour ; to fondle
Llochiad, n. an encourager
Llochwyd, n. a secret covert
Llod, n. a forcible utterance
Llodedd, n. a state of craving
Llodes, n. a girl, or a wench
Llodi, v. to reach out ; to crave
Llodig, a. craving ; brimming
Llodigaw, v. to be brimming
Llodigiad, n. a brimming
Llodrawg, a. having breeches
Llodri, v. to put on breeches
Llodrwr, n. a breeches-maker
Llodryn, n. a pair of breeches
Llodw, a. spirting, squirting
Llodwedd, n. a mite, a farthing
Llodwy, n. a spirt, a squirt
Llodi, v. to solace, to soothe
Lloddiad, n. a solacing
Lloegr, n. England
Lloegrwys, n. the ancient inhabitants of England
Lloer, n. the moon
Lloeran, n. a lunette
Lloerawl, a. lunar, lunary
Lloercen, n. a moon calf ; a dolt
Lloeren, n. a lunette ; a spot
Lloerenu, v. to form spots
Lloergan, n. the moonshine
Lloergant, n. orb of the moon
Lloeriad, n. a lunation
Lloerig, a. lunatic, crazy
Lloerigaw, v. to become lunatic
Lloerigen, n. a female lunatic
Lloerigyn, n. a male lunatic
Lloerni, n. moon's influence
Lloes, n. a sigh ; a pang
Lloesedd, n. languishment
Lloesi, v. to eject ; to sigh
Lloesiad, n. ejection ; a groaning
Llof, n. an excrescence

Llofelu, v. to coax, to stroke
Llofen, n. the burbot, a fish
Llofenan, n. the burbot
Llofi, v. to handle ; to bestow
Llofion, n. pickings, cullings
Llofiad, n. a handling, a giving
Lloflen, n. the palm, or grasp
Lloflenan, n. the weasel
Llofres, n. branching of the ribs
Llofrudd, n. a murderer
Llofruddiad, n. a murdering
Llofruddiaeth, n. murder
Llofruddio, v. to murder
Llofruddiog, a. murderous
Llofyn, n. a whisp ; a braid
Llofynawg, a. having a whisp
Lloffa, v. to lease, to glean
Lloffiad, n. a gleaning
Lloffwr, n. a gleaner
Lloffyn, n. bundle of gleanings
Llog, n. an augment ; a compact ; benefit ; interest ; hire
Llogail, n. a bracer, a fence ; a crib, a pen
Llogawd, n. a space parted off ; a cupboard ; a chancel
Llogawl, a. relating to interest or hire
Llogeilwydd, n. the eaves beam
Llogell, n. a partition : a closet, a drawer ; a pocket
Llogelliad, n. a pocket-full
Llogellu, v. to put up ; to pocket
Llogi, v. to covenant, to hire
Llogiad, n. a hiring, a lending
Llowgr, n. a covenanter, a hirer, a borrower
Llogwin, n. a pigmy, a dwarf
Llogwydd, n. a chancel
Llom, a. bare, naked, exposed
Llomen, n. a naked female
Llomi, v. to make bare
Llon, a. cheerful, glad, pleased
Llonaid, n. fulness, or fill
Llonaidd, a. apt to be cheerful
Llonc, n. a gulp, a swallow
Llonder, n. cheerfulness, joy

Lloni, v. to solace, to gladden	Llosgadwy, a. combustible
Lloniad, n. a gladdening	Llosgawl, a. burning, ignitive
Lloniant, n. inward pleasure	Llosged, n. that is burnt
Llonychiad, n. a giving pleasure	Llosgedig, a. scorched
Llonychu, v. to make cheerful	Llosgedd, n. state of burning
Llonydd, a. at ease, at rest, quiet	Llosgen, n. a blister
Llonyddiad, n. a quieting	Llosgfaen, n. brimstone
Llonyddol, a. tending to quiet	Llosgfal, n. a burning mountain
Llonyddu, v. to quiet	Llosgi, v. to burn; to be burning
Llonyddwch, n. quietness	Llosgiad, n. a burning
Llonyddwr, n. a tranquilizer	Llosgrach, n. scabs of itch
Llong, n. a ship	Llosgwrn, n. a tail
Llongborth, n. harbour for ships	Llosgwynt, n. a singeing blast
Llongdor, n. a shipwreck	Llosgyrnog, a. having a tail
Llongdoriad, n. shipwrecking	Llost, n. a dart; a sting; a tail
Llongddrylliad, n. shipwrecking	Llosten, n. a tail; genitals
Llongddryllio, v. to shipwreck	Llostlydan, n. spattle-tail, beaver
Llongi, v. to go on board a ship	Llostodyn, n. a metre so called
Llongiad, n. a going on board	Llu, n. a throng; a host
Llongiadaeth, n. navigation	Lluad, n. a thronging
Llongiadu, v. to navigate	Lluadu, v. to throng, to flock
Llonglwyth, n. a ship-load	Lluan, n. that glitters with light
Llongsaer, n. a shipwright	Lluanu, v. to reflect light
Llongsaerniaeth, n. the act of ship-building	Lluarth, n. an encampment
	Lluarthu, v. to form a camp
Llongwr, n. a sailo	Lluch, n. a throw; a glance a. darting, flashing
Llongwriaeth, n. seamanship	
Llongwrio, v. to work a ship	Lluched, n. a gleam; lightning
Llop, n. a buskin; a boot	Lluchedawl, a. flashing
Llopan, n. sort of shoe	Llucheden, n. a flash; a fever
Llopanu, v. to wear buskins	Lluchedenawl, a. gleaming
Llopanwr, n. a buskin-maker	Lluchedeniad, n. a gleaming
Llor, n. that bulges out; a bulb	Lluchedenu, v. to gleam
Lloriad, n. a floor-ful	Lluchediad, n. a coruscation
Llorf, n. a pillar	Lluchedyn, n. a gleam, a flash
Llorfdant, n. base string of a harp	Lluchfa, n. a drift, a throw
Lloriad, n. a laying a floor	Lluchfryd, a. of ardent passion
Llorio, v. to lay a floor	Lluchfrys, a. of ardent haste [ing
Lloriog, a. floored; groveling	Lluchiad, n. a throwing, a drift-
Llorion, n. sweepings; bottoms	Lluchiaw, v. to throw, to fling, to pelt, to drift
Llorlen, n. a floor-cloth	
Llorp, n. a side-beam; a shank	Lluchiawl, a. flinging
Llorpog, a. having a side-beam	Lluchlam, n. a darting stride
Llorwydd, n. laurel wood	Lluchochr, n. the coral
Llosg, n. a burn; heat inflammation	Lluchwayw, n. a javelin, a dart
	Lluchynt, n. a violent onset
Llosgaberth, n. burnt sacrifice	Llud, n. pure ore, wealth a. close, compact, essential
Llosgach, n. unnatural lust	

Lludlyd, a. full of ashes
Lludw, n. ashes [ashes
Lludwlyd, a. of the nature of
Lludwlys, n. the artichoke
Lludwog, a. full of ashes
Lludd, n. obstacle, let [fatigue
Lludded, n. obstruction; burden
Lluddediad, n. defatigation
Lluddedig, a. fatigued
Lluddedigaeth, n. fatigue
Lluddedu, v. to fatigue; to be weary
Lluddiad, n. an obstructing
Lluddianu, v. to form an obstacle
Lluddiant, n. a prevention
Lluddio, v. to obstruct, to let
Lluddiwr, n. a hinderer
Lluedd, n. warfare, hostility
Lluedda, v. to carry on war
Llueddawg, a. having a host
Llueddiad, n. a waging war
Llueddwr, n. one who assembles an army
Lluest, n. encampment
Lluestai, n. a campaigner
Lluestfa, n. an encampment
Lluestiad, n. an encamping
Lluestu, v. to encamp
Lluestwr, n. one who encamps
Lluestyn, n. small encampment
Llug, n. a gleam; a blotch: a. tending to appear: ad. partly, in part, half
Llugain, a. teeming with light
Llugan, n. a glare, a glitter
Lluganawl, a. tending to glitter
Lluganiad, n. a glittering
Lluganu, v. to glitter; to polish
Llugas, n. dawning of light

Llumman, n. banner, standard
Llummanu, v. to rear a standard
Llummanydd, n. a standard-bearer
Llumon, n. beacon; chimney
Llun, n. form, figure.—Dydd Llun, n. Monday
Llundain, n. London; the metropolis of Great Britain
Lluniad, n. a forming, a shaping a figuring
Lluniadawl, a. formative
Lluniadu, v. to form, to shape
Lluniaeth, n. formation; design; support; providence
Lluniaethiad, n. a formation
Lluniaethu, v. to put in form
Lluniaethwr, n. a regulator
Lluniaidd, a. shapely
Lluniannu, v. to modify
Lluniant, n. formation
Lluniedydd, n. a delineator
Lluuio, v. to form, to shape
Lluosog, a. abundant
Lluosogwr, n. a multiplier
Llur, n. a livid hue; a gloom
Llurgyn, n. a carcase, carrion
Llurguniad, n. a mangling
Llurgunio, v. to mangle
Llurguniwr, n. a mangler
Lluriad, n. a making livid
Llurs, n. razorbill
Lluryg, n. a coat of mail
Llurygaw, v. to wear a mail
Llus, n. the bilberries
Llusg, n. a draught, a drag
Llusgen, n. one that drags along
Llusgeniad, n. dragging heavily
Llusgenol, a. creeping, dragging
Llusgenu, v. to drag heavily

Lluwchio, v. to drift, to spray
Lluwchiol, a. drifting; spraying
Lluwchion, n. flying particles
Lluydd, n. warfare
Lluydda, v. to be waging in war
Lluyddiad, n. a waging war
Lluyddol, a. military, warring
Lluyddu, v. to wage war
Lluyddwf, n. a soldier
Llw, n. an oath
Llwb, n. that tends to swell
Llwch, n. dust, or powder
Llwdn, n. young of beasts
Llwfr, n. a coward
Llwf, n. a jerk; a hop; hobble
Llwg, n. that is bright; a botch; the scurvy: a. apt to break out; livid
Llwgr, n. a gall, a fret; damage
Llwm, a. bare, exposed
Llwmbren, n. a kiln spar
Llwmglwm, n. a hard knot
Llwnc, n. a gulp, a swallow; the gullet
Llwpai, n. of a sow
Llwrf, a, apt to go off; timid
Llwrw, n. direction; tendency: a. precipitant, forward: prep. toward: ad. towards
Llwrwg, n. dross, sediment
Llwry, n. that is towards; provision: a. precipitant: forward prep. towards: ad. towards, straightway
Llws, n. that shoots off; slime
Llwst, n. that parts off; a tail
Llwt, n. that is ejected
Llwtrach, n. slimy matter
Llwth, n. glibness; a gulp; greed; a glib, slippery; greedy
Llwy, n. a spoon; a spattle
Llwyaid, n. a spoonful
Llwyar, n. a spoon, a shovel
Llwyaraid, n. a shovelful
Llwyarn, n. a spattle, a trowel
Llwyaru, v. to spoon
Llwybr, n. a path or track
Llwybraidd, a. serving as a path

Llwybredd, n. passableness
Llwybreiddiaw, v. to make passable; to forward
Llwybraid, n. a making a path
Llwybro, v. to go a course
Llwybrol, a. belonging to a path
Llwybrwr, n. a wayfaring man
Llwyd, n. grey
Llwyd-ddu, n. a raven grey: a. of a greyish black [ness
Llwydedd, n. greyness, mouldi-
Llwydgoch, n. a russet colour
Llwydlas, n. a greyish blue
Llwydlasu, v. to become of a greyish blue
Llwydlys, n. mugwort [ness
Llwydni, n. greyness; mouldi-
Llwydo, v. to turn grey; to turn mouldy
Llwydrew, n. a hoarfrost
Llwydrewi, v. to cast a hoar
Llwydwyn, n. a drab colour
Llwyddiant, n. success
Llwyddiannol, a. prospering
Llwyddiannus, a. fortunate
Llwyddo, v. to prosper
Llwyddol, a. prosperous, lucky
Llwyeidio, v. to take a spoonful
Llwyf, Llwyfan, n. a form, a frame; a loft, a platform
Llwyfanen, Llwyfen, n. the elm
Llwyfo, v. to make a platform
Llwyg, n. a turn round; a mite
Llwygiad, n. a mazing
Llwygiant, a turning; a maze
Llwygo, v. to turn round; to be in a maze; to be restive
Llwygol, a. being mazed; restive
Llwyn, n. a quick turn; a quirk; the loin; a grove; a bush
Llwynhidl, n. the ribwort
Llwyniad, n. a giving a turn
Llwynin, a. apt to turn; of the
Llwyno, v. to give a motion [grove
Llwynog, a. of the grove; a fox
Llwynogaidd, a. like a fox, foxy
Llwynoges, n. a bitch fox
Llwynogwydd, n. a burgander

Llwynogyn, n. a young fox
Llwyo, v. to use a spoon
Llwyr, a. utter, quite clean
Llwyrbris, n. full purchase
Llwyrdeb, n. completeness
Llwyrdda, a. completely good
Llwyrddrwg, a. completely bad
Llwyredd, n. entireness
Lwyrles, n. universal benefit
Llwyrwad, n. complete denial
Llwyrwaith, n. complete work
Llwyrwys, n. a general summons
Llwys, a. clear, clean, pure, holy
Llwysedd, n. purity; sanctitude
Llwysiad, n. a purging, a hallowing
Llwyso, v. to clear; to sanctify
Llwysog, a. cleanly; hallowed
Llwyth, n. what is borne, a load
Llwythiad, n. a burdening, a loading
Llwytho, v. to burden, to load
Llwythog, a. burdened, loaded
Llyad, n. a licking; a lie, a slap
Llyarth, n. a gentle rise, a slope
Llych, n. what is flat; a squat, a sculk [dering
Llychiad, n. a dusting, a pow-
Llychiannu, v. to pulverise
Llychiant, n. a powdering
Llychineb, n. dustiness
Llychio, v. to reduce to dust
Llychiog, a. abounding with dust; powdery
Llychlyd, a. dusty, full of dust
Llychludo, v. to render dusty
Llychlyn, n. a gulf; brooklime
Llychol, a. squatting, cowering, sculking; flattening
Llychu, v. to squat, to cower
Llychwin, a. dusty; blotted
Llychwino, v. to make or to become dusty; to become of a dusky hue
Llychwr, n. what spreads along
Llychwyr, n. decline of light; twilight
Llychyn, n. particle of dust

Llyd, n. breadth, extent
Llydan, a. broad, wide, spacious
Llydandroed, a. broad-footed
Llydanddail, a. broad-leaved
Llydanedd, n. broadness, width
Llydaniad, n. a dilation
Llydanu, v. to expand, to dilate
Llydiad, n. an expanding
Llydn ad, n. a casting of young
Lydnig, n. a small animal
Llydnu, v. to bring forth, to foal
Llydnyn, n. a little animal
Llydu, v. to expand, to dilate
Llydw, n. abundance, enjoyment
Llydd, a. diffused, expanded
Llyddad, n. a diffusing, a pouring
Llyddo, v. to diffuse, to pour
Lluest, n. a polypus
Llyf, n. a stretch out; a licking
Llyfan, n. a string, a rope
Llyfandafod, n. tongue-tied
Llyfaniad, n. a stringing
Llyfanog, n. the liverwort
Llyfantws, n. burst-cow fly
Llyfanu, v. to string, to bind
Llyfanwst, n. a disease in cattle
Llyfas, n. a venture, an attempt
Llyfasiad, n. a venturing, a daring a presuming [presuming
Llyfasol, a. venturesome, daring,
Llyfasu, v. to venture, to attempt
Llyfeb, n. juration, swearing
Llyfedig, a. being licked, or lapped
Llyfeliad, n. a contriving; a levelling [level
Llyfelu, v. to devise, to guess; to
Llyfen, n. the loin
Llyfenol, a. relating to the loin
Llyferthiad, n. a fatiguing
Llyferthiant, n. defatigation
Llyferthin, a. exhausted, wearied
Llyferthol, a. wearisome
Llyferthus, a. wearisome, tiring
Llyfi, n. what is slimy; snivel
Llyfiad, n. a licking
Llyfio, v. to snivel
Llyfiol, a. snivelling
Llyfn, a. smooth, sleek, even, level

Llyfnâd, n. a smoothing
Llyfnâu, v. to smooth, to polish
Llyfnder, n. smoothness
Llyfniad, n. a making smooth
Llyfnu, v. to smooth, to level: to harrow
Llyfol, a. lambative, licking
Llyfr, n. what drags, the heel of a drag, n. a book
Llyfran, n. a pamphlet
Llyfrâu, v. to render timid
Llyfrder, n. cowardliness
Llyfrgell, n. a library
Llyfrith, a. eruptive, pimpled
Llyfrithen, n. a pimple; a stye
Llyfrithiad, n. an eruption
Llyfritho, to break out as a rash
Llyfrithiol a. eruptive
Llyfrol, a. relating to books
Llyfrothen, n. a gudgeon
Llyfru, v. to book
Llyfrwerthydd, n. bookseller
Llyfrwr, n. a bookman, a booker, a librarian
Llyfryn, n. a little book
Llyfu, v. to lick with the tongue
Llyffant, n. frog. Llyffant du, toad
Llyffanu, v. to hop as a frog
Llyffeth, n. a spring up; a hop
Llyffethar, n. fetlock clog
Llyffetheiriad, n. a shackling
Llyffetheirio, v. to shackle
Llyffethr, n. a fetlock-joint
Llyg, n. a mouse; a shrew
Llygad, n. eyesight, an eye
Llygadbwl, a. being dull-sighted
Llygaden, n. a glance of light
Llygadfrith, a. wall-eyed
Llygadgall, squinting outwardly
Llygadwam, a. of winking eye

Llygadog, a. having an eye
Llygadol, belonging to the eyes
Llygadronca, a. hollow-eyed
Llygadrudd, a. having a red eye
Llygadrydd, a. loose-eyed
Llygadrythiad, n. a staring
Llygadrythu, v. to stare, to gaze
Llygadwib, a. of a roving eye
Llygadwyr, a. squint-eyed
Llygaeron, n. cranberries
Llygas, n. splendour [of light
Llygeden, Llygedin, n. a glance
Llygeidiog, a. having eyes
Llygeirin, n. bogberries
Llygliw, n. a mouse colour
Llygo, v. to cast a splendour
Llygoden, n. a mouse. Llygoden ffrengig, rat
Llygol, a. brightening; livid
Llygorn, n. a lamp, a lanthorn
Llygota, to catch mice [a mouser
Llygotwr, n. a mouse catcher,
Llygrad, n. a corrupting
Llygradwy, a. corruptible
Llygredig, a. damaged, depraved, corrupted
Llygredigaeth, n. corruption
Llygredd, n. corruptness
Llygriad, n. a corrupting
Llygrol, a. corruptive, damaging
Llygroldeb, n. corruptibility
Llygru, v. to corrupt; to gall
Llygrwr, n. a corrupter, a spoiler, a depraver
Llygu, v. to break out; to spot
Llygwyn, n. the herb orach
Llynges, n. a fleet, a navy
Llyngesawr, n. an admiral
Llyngesog, a. having a fleet
Llyngesol, a. relating to a fleet

Llyman, n. a naked one
Llymant, n. a prying about
Llymanta, v. to pry about; to perform magic tricks
Llymarch, n. an oyster
Llymâu, v. to make keen, to sharpen
Llymarchen, n. an oyster
Llymder, n. keenness; sharpness; severity
Llymdost, a. acrimonious
Llymdra, n. bareness
Llymedras, n. a whetstone
Llymedd, n. keenness, sharpness; severity
Llymeidfwyd, n. spoon meat
Llymeidiad, n. a supping up
Llymeidio, v. to sup, to sip
Llymeitai, n. a bibber
Llymeitia, v. to sip
Llymeitian, v. to sip often
Llymeitio, v. to take sips
Llymeitiwr, n. one who sips continually; a tippler
Llymes, n. one who is bare
Llymgi, n. a sorry dog
Llymgoes, a. being bare-legged
Llymhun, n. a fainting fit
Llymiad, n. a making bare
Llymin, a. of sharp quality
Llyminog, a. keen, intense
Llymnoeth, a. stark naked
Llymio, v. to make bare
Llymriaid, n. sand eels
Llymrieita, v. to catch sand eels
Llymrig, a. crude, raw, harsh
Llymruwd, Llymry, n. washbrew; flummery, sour oatmeal boiled and jellied
Llymsi, a. of fickle motion
Llymu, v. to sharpen, to whet
Llymus, a. of sharp quality
Llymwas, n. a sharper
Llymwydd, n. kiln spars
Llymwst, n. a violent drive
Llymyn, n. one who is keen
Llymysten, n. a sparrow-hawk
Llymystryn, n. a lank figure

Llyn, n. a lake: a. proceeding; contagious
Llyna, v. to tiple, to booze; imper. lo there, behold
Llynan, n. a particle; a proceed
Llynawr, a. having humours
Llynciad, n. a swallowing up
Llynclyn, n. a vortex
Llyncoes, n. spavin
Llyncol, a. tending to swallow
Llyncu, v. to swallow, to gulp
Llynedd, n. the preceding year
Llyneiddio, v. to liquify
Llyn-granc, n. a wen
Llyniad, n. the forming of a pool
Llynio, v. to form a pool
Llyniog, a. having pools
Llynmeirch, n. glanders
Llynol, a. liquid: humoural
Llynori, v. to imposthumate, to form a pustule
Llynoriad, n. imposthumation
Llynorog, a. full of humours
Llynoryn, n. an abscess
Llynu, v. to spread contagion
Llynw, n. collection of liquid
Llynwyn, n. a puddle, a plash
Llynwys, n. a forming of hum-
Llyo, v. to reach out, to lick [ours
Llyol, a. lambative, licking
Llyr, n. a duct, a course, an udder; a brink, or shore
Llyre, a. gliding, streaming
Llyren, n. water-plantain
Llyryad, n. what glides
Llyryo, v. to go on the stream
Llys, n. what separates or discriminates; a slime; a court, a hall, a palace
Llysadwy a. exceptionable
Llysaidd, a court-like, courtly
Llysau, Llysiau, n. herbs, plants
Llysblant, n. step-children
Llyschwaer, n. step-sister
Llys-dad, n. a step-father
Llysdŷ, n. a court-house [to
Llysedig, a. separated; objected
Llyseiddio, v. to render courtly

Llysenw, n. a nickname
Llysenwad, n. cognomination
Llysenwi, v. to give a surname or cognomen: to nickname
Llysfab, n. a step-son; a son-in-law
Llysfam, n. step-mother; mother-in-law
Llysferch, n. step-daughter
Llysfrawd, n. brother-in-law
Llysfwyd, n. loathing of food
Llysg, n. a rod, a wand
Llysgbren, n. a billet, a stick
Llysiad, n. a setting aside, an exception; a rejection
Llysieua, v. to collect plants
Llysieuad, n. a producing plants
Llysieuedd, n. herbaceousness
Llysieuo, v. to produce plants
Llysieuol, a. producing plants
Llysieuydd, n. a herbalist
Llysieuyn, n. a herb, a plant
Llysiant, n. separation; rejection, refusal; exception
Llysiol, a. separating; rejecting
Llyslyn, n. a mucilage
Llysnaf, n. a running of snivel
Llysnafedd, n. snivel, mucus
Llysnafol, a. snivelly, mucous
Llysnafu, v. to snivel
Llysol, a. belonging to court
Llyst, n. vessel to hold liquor
Llystyn, n. recess, lodgement
Llysu, v. to part off; to loath; to reject, to refuse; to disallow
Llyswen, n. an eel. Llyswen bendoll, a lamprey
Llyswena, v. to catch eels
Llytrod, n. filth, garbage
Llytroda, v. to collect filth
Llytrodedd, n. filthiness
Llytrodiad, n. a breeding of filth
Llyth, n. what is tender: a. flat; flaccid, soft; base
Llythi, n. flounders, flatfish
Llythiad, n. a rendering flaccid
Llythien, n. a flounder, a flatfish
Llythol, a. flaccid
Llythus, a. of a flaccid tendency

Llythyn, n. a weakling
Llythyr, n. an engraved character; a letter, an epistle
Llythyraeth, n. orthography
Llythyrog, a. of letters, literary
Llythyrol, a. literal, literate
Llythyrdy, n. a post-office
Llythyredigaeth, n. a lettering, a cutting of letters
Llythyreg, n. grammar; the science of written language
Llythyregai, n. a grammatist
Llythyregol, a. grammatical
Llythyren, n. a type, a letter
Llythyreniad, n. a lettering, spelling
Llythyrenol, a. literal, literate
Llythyrenu, v. to letter, to spell
Llythyrenydd, n. type-founder
Llythyriad, n. lettering
Llythyriant, n. literature
Llythyru, v. to letter, to spell
Llythyrydd, n. letter-writer
Llythyryn, n. billet, note
Llyo, v. to lick with the tongue
Llyw, n. a ruler; a rudder
Llywaeth, n. guidance; rearing
Llywed, v. to rule, to direct
Llywedu, v. to rule, to guide
Llywedydd, n. a director; a pilot
Llywedyddes, n. a governess
Llywedyddiaeth, n. directorship; governance; pilotage
Llywel, n. the horizon
Llyweli, n. the limit of vision
Llywelu, v. to form an horizon
Llywenydd, n. western horizon
Llyweth, Llywethan, n. a muscle
Llywethog, a. muscular, brawny
Llywethol, a. musculous
Llywethu, v. to become muscular
Llywiad, n. a directing; a steering
Llywiadaeth, n. direction
Llywiadol, a. directive, steering
Llywiadu, v. to direct, to rule
Llywiadures, n. a governess
Llywiaduriaeth, n. directorship; governance

LLYW 224 MAD

Llywiaeth, n. guidance, rule
Llywiannol, a. directive
Llywiannu, v. to direct, to rule
Llywiant, n. direction, rule
Llywiawd, n. governance
Llywiawdwr, n. a governor
Llywiawdwraeth, n. governship
Llywiedigaeth, n. governance
Llywiedydd, n. a governor
Llywiedyddes, n. a governess
Llywiedyddol, a. directorial
Llywiedu, v. to act as director
Llywio, v. to rule; to steer
Llywiog, a. having guidance
Llywiol, a. guiding, directing
Llywion, n. flying particles
Llywiwr, n. a steersman
Llywodraeth, n. government
Llywodraethiad, n. a governing
Llywodraethol, a. governing
Llywodraethu, v. to govern
Llywodraethwr, n. governor, ruler
Llywy, a. of passing beauty
Llywydd, n. a director
Llywyddes, n. a female president
Llywyddiad, n. a presiding
Llywyddiaeth, n. presidency
Llywyddol, a. presidential
Llywyddu, v. to preside
Llywyn, n. the extreme of light; the west
Llywynol, a. occidental, west
Llywynydd, n. occident, west

M

MA, n. place, spot, space; state
Mab, n. a male: a boy; a son
Mabaidd, a. boyish, childlike
Maban, n. a babe, a baby
Mabanaidd, a. babyish, childish
Mabandod, n. childhood
Mabaneiddio, to become a baby
Mabanoed, n. childhood
Mabanu, v. to make as a baby
Mabddall, a. blind from birth
Mabddysg, n. infantile tuition
Mabgar, a. fond of children
Mabgath, n. a kitten
Mabgoll, n. the poppy
Mabiaeth, n. childhood; filiality
Mabiaethu, v. to treat as a child
Mabiaith, n. childish prattling
Mabin, a. juvenile, youthful
Mabineiddio, v. to make as a child
Mabinog, a. juvenile, infantine
Mablan, n. a burying place
Mabmaeth, n. a foster-son
Maboed, Mabolaeth; n. childhood, infancy
Mabol, a. like a child; filial
Maboli, v. to become as a child
Mabon, n. a youth; a hero
Mabsant, n. a patron saint
Mabsanta, v. to canonise
Mabwraig, n. a virago, a scold
Mabwys, n. adoption of a son
Mabwysiad, n. adoption
Mabwysiadol, a. relating to the adoption of a child, adoptive
Mabwysio, v. to adopt a son
Macai, n. a maggot, a grub
Maceiad, n. a maggot, a grub
Macon, n. berries
Macrell, n. a mackerel
Macswr, n. brewer
Macwy, n. a youth
Mach, n. a security, a surety, a bail
Machdaith, n. a dam, embank- [ment
Machiad, n. a making secure
Machlud, n. a setting, a going down
Machludiad, n. occultation
Machludo, v. to be obscured
Mad, n. what proceeds; a reptile; a good, a benefit
Mad, a. good, beneficial
Madalch, n. agaric, toadstool

| MAD | 225 | MAE |

Madalchu, v. to produce agaric
Madarch, n. agaric, toadstool
Madarchen, n. agaric
Madarchu, v. to produce agaric
Mad-ddall, n. a blind-worm
Madedd, n. benefit, goodness
Maden, n. a she fox, a vixen
Madfall, n. a newt, an eft
Madfelen, n. a knapweed
Madgall, n. a lizard
Madiad, n. a benefiting [teous
Madiaeth, a. beneficient, boun-
Madog, a. tending forward
Madol, a. goodly
Madraidd, a. tending to fester
Madreddiad, n. a putrefying
Madreddol, a. putrefactive
Madriad, n. a producing pus
Madrodd, n. putrid bodies
Madron, n. collection of humours
Madrondod, n. dizziness
Madronu, v. to make dizzy
Madru, v. to putrefy, to fester
Madrudd, n. the marrow [row
Madruddiad, n. forming of mar-
Madruddo, v. to form marrow
Madruddog, a. having marrow
Madruddyn, n. a vein marrow
Madrwy, n. a newt, an eft
Madryn, n. epithet for a fox
Madu, v. to render productive
Madw, a. tending to benefit
Madws, n. fulness of time
Madyn, n. epithet for a fox
Madywydd, n. the sweetgale
Madd, n. what tends to divest
Maddau, n. dismissal; pardon: v. to let go; to pardon
Maddeuad, n. a pardoning
Maddeuant, n. pardoning [given
Maddeuedig, a. dismissed; for-
Maddeugar, a. disposed to remit
Maddeuol, a. remitting, forgiving
Maddeuwr, n. forgiver, pardoner
Mae, v. is, are
Maedd, n. a buffet
Maeddgen, n. a buffet

Maeddiad, n. a buffetting
Maeddol, a. buffetting, banging
Maeddu, v. to buffet, to bang
Mael, n. gain, profit, advantage; what is worked; iron
Maela, v. to seek for profit
Maelan, n. a shop
Maelawr, Maelfa, n. a mart, a market
Maeldref, n. a market town
Maeldoll, n. the tariff
Maelera, v. to traffic, to trade
Maeleriad, n. a trafficking
Maeleriaeth, n. traffic, trade
Maelged, n. a tribute; a tax, a toll
Maelgi, n. the angel fish
Maeliad, n. a profiting, a gaining
Maeliant, n. advantage, gain
Maelier, n. a trafficker
Maelieres, n. a chap-woman
Maelierwr, n. a merchant
Maelio, v. to profit, to gain
Maelota, v. to gain by traffic
Maelotai, n. a retailer [keeper
Maelwr, n. a retailer, a shop-
Maen, n. a block of stone. Maen ched, a loadstone
Maenan, n. a cob, a soft stone
Maenawr, n. a manor district
Maendo, n. a stone covering
Maendrychiad, n. lithotomy
Maeneiddiad, n. lapidification
Maenfan, n. the beasil of a ring
Maenfedd, n. stone supelchre
Maenglawdd, n. stone quarry
Maeniad, n. a petrifying
Maenol, a. of stone, stony
Maensaer, n. stone mason
Maenu, v. to turn to stone; to stone
Maenydd, n. a lapidary [mayor
Maer, n. what tends; a steward
Maerdref, n. a dairy hamlet
Maerdy, n. a dairy house
Maeres, n. a dairy-woman
Maeron, n. a dairy farmer
Maeronaeth, n. dairy farming

Maeroni, n. dairy husbandry
Maeronwr, n. a dairy-man
Maes, n. a plain, open field
  Colli y maes, to be vanquished
Maes, adv. out, from within
Maesa, v. to turn out; to evacuate
Maesdir, n. champaign land
Maesiad, n. a taking of the field
Maesol, a. belonging to the field, champaign
Maeth, n. nurture; fosterage
Maethu, v. to get nourishment
Maethawd, n. a cherishing
Maethdad, n. a foster-father
Maethedig, a. nourished; fostered
Maethen, n. a pampered one
Maethfab, n. a foster-son
Maethfam, n. a foster-mother
Maethferch n. a foster-daughter
Maethiad, n. a nourishing
Maethiannus, a. nutrimental
Maethiant, n. nourishment
Maethid, n. nurture, feeding
Maethidiol, a. nutrimental
Maethineb, n. nourishment
Maethol, a. nurturing; fostering
Maethran, n. a mess company
Maethu, v. to nourish, to foster
Maethus, a. alimentary, nutritive
Maf, n. what is clustering
Mafon, n. raspberries
Mafonen, n. a raspberry
Mafonwydd, n. raspberry bushes
Mag, n. act of nursing, nurture
Magad, n. a brood; a multitude
Magaden, n. a nursling
Magawd, n. a nurturing
Magdan, n. a combustible, tinder, what supports fire
Magddu, n. fountain of blackness
Magfa, n. nursery
Magi, n. principle of generation
Magiad, n. a breeding, a rearing
Magiaid, n. worms, grubs
Magien, n. a worm, a glow-worm

Magiod, n. worms, grubs
Magl, n. a snare, a gin, a springe; a webb on the eye
Magledigaeth, n. entanglement; meshing
Maglen, n. a springe, a gin
Magliad, n. an entangling
Maglog, a. entangled, snared
Maglu, v. to snare, to entangle
Magodorth, n. a suppression
Magol, a. nursing, breeding
Magon, n. berries; clusters
Magu, v. to breed, to rear, to nurse
Magwriaeth, n. nourishment
Magwy, n. a cluster, a bunch
Magwyad, n. a clustering
Magwyr, n. an enclosure, a wall; a building; a house [ing
Magwyren, n. a wall of a building
Magwyriad, n. a raising of a wall
Magwyro, v. to wall; to enclose
Mai, n. field; month of May
Mai, conj. that
Maid, n. what separates or limits
Maidd, n. whey; curds and whey
Maig, n. a sudden turn
Mail, n. a bowl, a bason
Main, a. slender, fine, thin
Mainc, n. a bench, a seat
Maint, n. size, magnitude, bigness, quantity
Maip, n. turnips
Mais, n. device, contrivance
Maith, a. ample; tedious, long
Mal, a, trivial, small; light; like
Mal, conj. as if [manner as
Mal, adv. like, so; in the same
Mâl, n. what extends; what is produced; bounty; what is ground: a. ductive; smooth, [glib
Malaith, n. chilblain
Malâu, v. to make similar
Maldod, n. levity; dalliance; fondness, delight
Maldodi, v. to dally, to fondle, to act with levity

Maldodus, a. apt to dally
Maledig, a. bruised, ground
Maledd, n. dalliance; dotage
Maleithr, n. a blain; a kibe
Malen, n. what is of iron; one accustomed to violence; a shield; Bellona
Malerth, n. a chilblain
Mallad, n. a bruising, grinding
Malpai, conj. as if it were
Malu, v. to bruise, to grind. Malu ewyn, to foam
Malur, n. what is reduced small, or mouldered; a mole-hill
Maluriad, n. a mouldering
Maluriedig, a. mouldered
Malurio, v. to pound; to moulder
Maluriol, a. mouldering
Malurion, n. broken particles
Malwod, n. snails
Malwoden, n. a snail
Mall, n. want of energy; softness; a soddened state; malady; evil; blast
Mallaint, Mallawd, n. malaxation
Malldan, n. slow fire
Malldod, n. softness; wantonness; insipidity; a blast
Malldorch, n. kibe on the heel
Malldraul, n. bad digestion
Malledigaeth, n. malaxation
Malledd, n. soft state; a blasted state; wantonness
Mallgno, n. a gnawing pain
Mallgorn, n. core of a horn
Mallt, n. an evil principle
Mallu, v. to seeth; to blast
Mallus, a, sodden; blasted
Mallwaew, n. a dull pain
Mam, n. a mother, a dam. Mam gu, a grandmother
Mamaeth, n. motherhood
Mamai, n. the birth wort
Mamaidd, n. mothrly
Mamdref, n a chief town
Mamddinas, n, a metropolis
Mamedd, n. motherhood
Mameglwys, n. a mother-church

Mameiddio, to become motherly
Mamen, n. a little mother
Mames, n. mother with the first young
Mammaeth, n. a nurse
Mammeuthiad, n. a nursing
Mammeuthu, v. to nurse
Mamog, a. being a mother
Mamogaeth, n. maternity
Mamogi, v. to become a mother
Mamogiad, n. a ewe with young
Mamolrwydd, n. motherliness
Mamwch, n. maternal fondness
Mamwydd, n. a brood goose
Mamwys, n. maternity
Mamwythen, n. the cural vein
Mamychiad, n. a fondling as a mother
Mamychu, v. to fondle as a mother
Mân, n. a space, a spot, a place
Mân, a. small, little, fine, petty. Mân werthwyr, retailers
Manâd, n. a making small
Manad, n. a mass, a lump
Manaid, n. contents of a mould; a lump; a print
Manarfau, n. small arms
Manâu, v. to make small or fine
Manawd, n. a making a space, a location
Manawyd, n. staff of a banner
Manbaill, n. fine flour
Mânbeth, n. a small thing
Manblu, n. down feathers
Mandon, n. dandriff; woodroof
Mandwyn, n. scrofula, king's evil
Mandwynog, a. strumous, scrofulous
Mandwynol, a. strumatic
Manddail, n. small leaves
Manddarlun, a miniature drawing
Manddarn, n. a small piece, a little bit
Manddellt, n. fine splittings
Manddos, n. small droppings
Manddrain, n. small thorns
Manddryll, n. a small piece

Maned, n. a hand basket
Maneg, n. a gauntlet, a glove.
Menyg ellyllon, foxglove
Maneilio, v. to plat fine work
Manfrith, a finely variegated
Manfritho, v. to stripe finely
Manfriw, a. finely crumbled
Man-galed, a. of a hard grasp
Man-gan, n. fine white flour
Man-gaw, n. delicate work
Man-gawiau, n. trifles, toys
Man-geinion, n. delicate jewels
Man-gerdded, to take short steps
Man-goed, n. brushwood, shrubs
Man-gor, n. a membrane
Man-gre, n. a recess; a tangle
Manhedion, n. flying motes
Maniad, n. a placing, a spotting
Madion, n. small things s empty grains among corn
Manleidr, n. a petty thief
Manlo, n. small coals
Manllwyn, n. mutton flesh
Manod, n. small or fine snow
Manog, a. having space; spotted
Manogen, n. a speckled one
Manol, a. local; spotting; delicate; accurate, exact, minute, particular, fine
Manoli, v. to make nice
Manoliad, n. a making nice
Manolosg, n. small coal
Manon, n. paragon of beauty
Manrinion, n. trifling charms
Manro, n. small pebbles
Manswyddau, n. petty offices
Mant, n. a mandible; a mouth
Mantach, n. a toothless jaw
Mantachu, v. to expose the jaw
Mantai, n. a mumbler
Mantais, n. an advantage
Mantawl, n. a balance [tage
Manteisiad, n. a taking advan-
Manteisio, v. to take advantage
Manteisiol, a. advantageous
Mantell, n. a mantle, a cloak
Mantelliad, n. a mantling
Mantellu, v. to mantle

Mantoli, v. to turn scales
Mantoliad, n. a balancing
Manu, v. to make a space, to spot; to impress
Manus, n. husk of corn, chaff
Manw, a. of subtile quality
Manwedd, n. a subtile texture
Manweddu, v. to render fine
Manwg, n. spottedness; pimples
Manwl, a. accurate; nice; care-
Manwlaw, n. a small rain [ful
Manwy, a. fine; rare; subtile
Manwydd, n. brushwood, shrubs
Manwyedd, n. exility, fineness
Manwyn, n. the king's evil, scro-
Manwynau, n. strumæ [fula
Manwynog, a. strumous
Manwyo, v. to refine, to subtilise
Manwythi, n. capillary veins
Manyd, n. small grain of corn
Manyglawg, n. the bitter-sweet
Manyglion, n. small particles, or spots; empty grains of corn
Manyledd, n. exactness, nicety
Manyliant, n. refinement
Manylrwydd, n. exactness, minuteness [become accurate
Manylu, v. render accurate; to
Manylwch, n. accuracy, nicety
Maon, n. a people, a multitude; inhabitancy; subjects
Maowl, n. a knob on the middle of a thing; a mop
Mar, n. what is laid flat
Maran, n. a holme; a strand; a spawning salmon
Marc, n. impression, a mark
Marciad, n. a marking
Marcio, v. to mark, to observe
March, n. a horse, a stallion
Marchalan, n. elecampane
Marchasyn, n. a male ass
Marchâu, v. to ride a horse
Marchbren, n. a main beam
Marchdaran, n. a loud thunder
Marchdy, n. a stable [clap
Marchfaen, n. a horse block
Marchfiaren, n. a white brier

Marchforgrugyn, n. a large winged ant
Marchforion, n. winged ants
Marchgen, n. a horse's skin
Marchgod, n. a saddle bag
Marchiad, n. a horsing
Marchlan, n. a stable
Marchlu, n. cavalry, horse soldiers
Marchnad, n. a market, a mart
Marchnadfa, n. a market-place
Marchnadiad, n. a marketing
Marchnadol, a. of a market
Marchnadu, v. to market, to buy at market
Marchnadydd, n. a market-man
Marchnatâd, n. a marketing
Marchnatty, n. a market-house
Marchnatwr, n. a market-man
Marchocâd, n. riding a horse
Marchocâu, v. to ride a horse
Marchog, n. a knight; a jug. Haint y marchogion, or Clwyf y marchogion, the hœmorrhoids
Marchogaeth, n. horsemanship v. to ride [horsemanship
Marchogaethu, v. to practise
Marchoges, n. a riding woman; a female chevalier [soldiers
Marchoglu, n. cavalry, horse
Marchogwisg, n. riding-habit
Marchogwr, n. a rider, a horseman
Marchol, a. belonging to a horse
Marchon, n. the male ash
Marchonen, n. a male ash tree
Marchrawd, n. troop of horse
Marchredyn, n. the polypody
Marchridyll, n. a sifter, a skreen
Marchwas, n. a horseman
Marchwiail, n. saplings
Marchwraint n. tetters
Marchwreinyn, n. a tetter
Marchwriaeth, n. jockeyship
Marchwrio, v. to ride, to jockey
Marchysgall, n. Scotch thistle
Mardon, n. dead skin, scurf
Margan, n. a goddess feigned to conduct a soul on parting from the body

Marian, n. holme; a strand
Mariandir, n. holme land
Marianedd, n. a holme
Marl, n. a rich clay, marl
Marliad, n. a marling
Marm, n. dead earth; chalk
Marmor, n. chalky earth: marble
Marmoraidd, a. like marble
Marmori, v. to form marble
Marth, n. what is flat, plain, or open; sadness; what is sure
Marw, meirw, n. the dead; mortality: v. to die, to become dead a. dead, mortal, deceased
Marwâd n. a mortifying
Marwaidd, a. deadish, lifeless
Marwaol, a. mortifying, deadening
Marwâu, v. to deaden, to mortify
Marwdom, n. scurf, dandriff
Marwdy, n. an escheat by death
Marwdyst, n. a dead evidence
Marwdywarchen, n. a death clod
Marwddwfr, n. a dead water
Marwddydd, n. mortal day
Marwedd, n. a deadness
Marweiddiad, n. a deadening
Marweiddio, v. to deaden, to benumb
Marweiddiol, a. deadening [tion
Marwerydd, n. delirium, distrac-
Marwgoel, n. a death omen
Marwgwsg, n. legarthy; a dormouse
Marwhaint, n. a mortal disease
Marwhun, n. death sleep, trance
Marwlanw, n. turn of a tide, high water
Marwnad, n. death cry; elegy
Marwnadu, v. to mourn the dead
Marwol, a. deadly, mortal
Marwolâd, n. a deadening
Marwolaeth, n. death, decease; mortality
Marwolaethu, v. to put to death
Marwoldeb, n. mortality [dead
Marwolu, v. to deaden, to grow
Marwolus, a. of a dead nature

Marwor, n. burning cinders
Marworyn, n. ember
Marw-wystl, n. a mortgage
Marwydos, n. embers
Marwysgafn, n. death-bed song
Marwysgar, n. a death parting
Mas, n. a swoon; ecstacy
Masaidd, a. tending to faint
Masarn, n. the sycamore
Masarnen, n. a sycamore [ing
Masawd, n. a swooning, a faint-
Masg, n. a mesh, a net-work, lattice [netting
Masgiad, n. a reticulation, a
Masgl, n. a mesh; a pod
Masgliad, n. a reticulating; a podding
Masglog, a. reticulated; podded
Masglu, v. to reticulate; to pod
Masgnach, n. concern, business, trade [to trade
Masgnachu, v. to do business,
Masgnachwr, n. a tradesman, a dealer, a chapman
Masgol, a. reticulated, meshed
Masgu, v. to reticulate, to lattice
Masu, v. to swoon, to faint
Masw, a. fluttering; wanton; soft; languishing
Maswedd, n. languor: levity, wantonness
Masweddiad, n. a wantoning
Masweddu, v. to languish; to wanton [light
Maswy, a. wanton, sportive,
Mat, n. a mat, plaited work
Mater, n. exigency, matter
Matog, n. a mattock, a hoe
Matras, n. a mattress; a matting
Matrasu, v. to form a mattress

Maw n. what expands
Maw, a. expanding; indulgent
Mawaid, n. both hands full
Mawd, n. what is expanding
Mawl, n. worship, praise
Mawlâd, n. a praising
Mawlâu, v. to praise, to extol
Mawn, n. peat, turf
Mawn-bwll, n. a peat-pit
Mawn-dir, n. peat-land
Mawnen, n. a peat, a turf
Mawnog, n. peat-pit: a. having
Mawr, a. great, large, big [peat
Mawrâd, n. a magnifying
Mawrair, n. a boasting word
Mawrâu, v. to magnify, to enlarge
Mawrdeg, a. magnificent, grand
Mawrdra, n. greatness
Mawrdda, n. great good
Mawrddrwg, n. great evil
Mawredig, a. magnified, exalted
Mawredd, n. greatness, grandeur
Mawreddiad, n. a magnifying
Mawreddog, a. magnificent
Mawreddu, v. to magnify, to exalt
Mawreddus, adj. magnificent, grand
Mawrfaith, a. far-extending
Mawrfalch, a. greatly proud
Mawrfryd, magnanimity
Mawrfrydig, a magnanimous
Mawrfrydu, v. to grow magnanimous
Mawrfrydus, a. magnanimous
Mawriad, n. an enlarging
Mawrio, v. to magnify, to enlarge
Mawrth, n. Mars; March
Mawrwerth, n. preciousness
Mawrydi, Mawrhydi, n. majesty

Mawsiad, n. a delighting
Mawsiant, n. delectation
Me, n. an agent: pron. he, him
Mebai, n. an infant, a youth
Mebain, a. youthful, juvenile
Mebaint, n. youthfulness
Mebin, a. infantile youthful
Mebyd, n. infancy, childhood
Mebyn, n. a male infant
Mechdeyrn, n. a viceroy, a regent; a lord
Mechnïad, n. a giving surety
Mechnïaeth, n. suretyship
Mechnïaethu, v. to act as bail
Mechnïo, v. to be surety, to bail
Mechnïol, a. relating to bail
Mechnïwr, Mechnïydd, n. a surety, a bail
Mêd, n. what is extended or full
Med, prep. to the full; to, unto
Medel, n. a reaping; a reaping party
Medelwas, Medelwr, n. a reaper
Medi, n. a reaping; the month of September
Medi, v. to reap, to cut corn
Mediad, n. the act of reaping
Medr, n. skill to effect, knowledge to do
Medraeth, n. expertness, skill
Medrawd, n. accomplishment
Medredd, n. expertness, skill
Medriad, n. a being able, an effecting
Medriant, n. accomplishment
Medrol, a. accomplishing
Medroldeb, n. capability
Medroli, v. to render capable
Medru, v. to exert skill; to know how to do; to be able; to aim

Meddal, a. soft, mollient, tender
Meddalâd, n. a softening [lows
Meddalai, n. what softens; mal-
Meddalâu, v. to soften, to mollify
Meddalder, n. softness; mildness
Meddaliad, n. a softening
Meddalu, v. to soften, to mollify
Meddalwch, n. softness, mildness
Meddedig, a. possessed, enjoyed
Meddedigaeth, n. possession
Meddedigol, a. possessory
Meddf, a. soft, mild, mollient
Meddfu, v. to become mild
Meddiad, n. a possessing
Meddiannedigaeth, n. possession
Meddiannedigol, a. possessory
Meddiannol, a. possessing
Meddiannu, v. to possess, to own
Meddiannwr, Meddiannydd, n. a possessor, an owner
Meddiant, n. possession
Meddlys, n. intoxicating herbs
Meddu, v. to be able; to possess
Meddw, a. circling; drunk
Meddwad, n. an intoxicating
Meddwdod, n. drunkenness, intoxication
Meddwi, v. to intoxicate
Meddwl, m. thought, mind: v. to think, to mind; to intend
Meddwol, a. intoxicating
Meddwyn, n. a drunkard
Meddyg, n. a doctor, a physician
Meddyges, n. a doctress
Meddygfys, n. ring finger
Meddygiad, n. a doctoring
Meddygin, a. curative, medicinal
Meddyginiaeth, n. medicine
Meddyginiaethol, a. medicinal, belonging to healing

Meddylfryd, n. affection
Meddylgar, a. mindful, musing
Meddyliad, n. a thinking
Meddylio, v. to mind, to think
Mefiau, v. to pollute; to disgrace
Mefifethiant, n. a disgraceful defect [gracing
Mefliad, n. a polluting; a dis-
Meflu, v. to pollute; to disgrace
Mefus, n. strawberries
Mefusen, n. a strawberry
Meg, n. utterance, expression
Megal, n. the glow worm
Meglad, n. utterance, expression
Megidydd, n. one who nourishes
Megin, n. a pair of bellows
Megino, v. to work bellows
Megys, conj. as, so as, like as
Mehefin, n. the month of June
Mehin, n. fat, fat flesh, grease
Mehinen, n. the leaf of fat
Mehino, v. to become greasy
Mehinog, a. having grease
Meia, v. to take the field
Meiad, n. a taking the field
Meibionain, Meibionos, n. little children [a becoming bail
Meichiad, n. a becoming surety,
Meichio, v. to bail, to be bail
Meichiog, a. having surety
Meidr, n. a measure, a rule
Meio, v. to make a campaign
Meidradydd, n. a metre
Meidraeth, measurement
Meidriad, n. one who is able to effect or to accomplish
Meidro, v. to limit: to mete
Meidrol, a. limitable, comprehending [ness, capacity
Meidroldeb, n. comprehensiveness,
Meidroli, v. to bring within measure [hermit
Meidwy, n. a solitary one, a
Meidwyfod, n. a hermitage
Meidyn, n. a point; a moment
Meiddiad, n. a curdling
Meiddion, n. curds and whey
Meiddioni, v. to turn to curds

Meiddlyd, a. wheyey, curdled
Meiddlyn, n. whey drink
Meiddog, a. abounding with whey
Meifon, n. raspberries
Meigen, n. a recess, a nook
Meigiad, n. a turning suddenly; a happening
Meigrad, n. a starting suddenly
Meigro, v. to startle; to start
Meigryn, n. a startle; a vertigo
Meiliad, n. a lading with a bowl
Meiliaid, n. a bowlful
Meiliannu, v. to uphold
Meiliant, n. an upholding
Meilierydd, n. the skylark
Meilio, v. to hold up; to put in a bowl; to raise with a bowl
Meiliorn, n. transgression
Meiliorni, v. to transgress
Meilon, n. powder, flour
Meiloni, v. to reduce to powder
Meilwn, n. the small of the leg
Meilyn, n. a loop, an eye
Meilyndorch, n. a sashoon
Meillion, n. clover, trefoil
Meillionen, n. a trefoil
Meillioni, v. to yield trefoil
Meillionog, a. having trefoils
Meinâd, n. a making fine
Meinâu, v. to make fine or slender
Meincio, v. to fix benches
Meinder, n. exility, fineness
Meindwf, a. of slender growth
Mein-gan, n. a delicate fair one
Meinin, a. of stone, stony
Meinir, n. one of delicate growth
Meinoles, n. a delicate thing
Meinwar, a. delicate and gentle
Meinwedd, n. a delicate aspect
Meinwen, n. one delicately fair
Meinwyr, a. delicately chaste
Meinyn, n. a lump of stone
Meipen, n. a turnip
Meiriol, a. dissolving, thawing
Meiriolad, n. a thawing
Meirioli, v. to dissolve, to thaw
Meirion, n. a tender; a dairymaid
Meiriones, n. a dairymaid

Meirioni, n. superintendence
Meirydd, n. a steward; a mayor
Melsgyn, n. a moth
Meisiad, n. a devising
Meisio, v. to devise, to invent
Meisiol, a. devising, inventive
Meistr, n. a master, a lord
Meistres, n. a mistress
Meistrol, a. masterely, master
Meistrolaeth, n. mastery
Meistrolaethu, v. to get mastery
Meistroll, v. to sway as master
Meityn, n. a point, a space
Meithdra, n. tediousness
Meithio, v. to make tedious
Meithiw, a. extensive, tedious
Meithrin, n. nurture, nursing: v. to nourish
Meithrinfa, n. a seminary
Meithriniad, n. a nurturing
Meithrinol, a. nurturing [comb
Mêl, n. honey. Dil mêl, honey-
Mela, v. to gather honey
Melawd, n. a gathering honey
Meldardd, a. mellifluous
Melen, a. yellow; tawny
Melen-gu, n. the woad
Melenydd, n. the hawk-weed
Melfed, n. velvet; a gloss
Melfoch, n, honey swine, bears
Melgawod, n. the honey-dew
Melged, n. a tribute of honey
Melgorn, n. cell of a honey-comb
Melin, n. a mill, a grinder
Melina, v. to go to mill
Melino, v. to grind in a mill
Melinydd, n. a miller
Melog, a. having honey; n. honey-suckle
Melsugyn, n. woad, glustum
Melus, a. sweet
Meluso, v. to sweeten
Melwioges, n. a snail
Melwlith, n. the honey-dew
Melycn, n. a snail
Melyn, a. yellow
Melyndra, n. a yellowness
Melynddu, a. tawny

Melynell, n. a yellow hue
Melynfaen, n. brimstone
Melyn-goch, a. yellow red
Melyni, n. yellowness, jaundice
Melyniad, n. a making yellow
Melynlas, a. yellowish blue
Melynllwyd, a. yellowish brown
Melynllys, n. the cheesewort
Melynog, n. a mullatto; a linnet
Melynu, v. to make yellow
Melynwy, n. the yolk of an egg
Melynwyn, a. yellowish white
Melys, a. sweet
Melysder, n. sweetness [sweeten
Melysiannu, v. to dulcify, to
Melusiant, n. dulcification
Melysig, a. fond of sweets
Melysol, a. sweetening
Melysu, v. to sweeten
Melldith, n. a curse
Melldithiad, n. a malediction
Melldithio, v. to curse
Melldithiol, a. blasphemous
Melldithwr, n. a curser
Melli, Mellni, n. blight
Mellt, n. lightnings
Mellten, n. lightning
Mellteniad, n. flashing lightning
Melltenu, v. to flash lightning
Melltigaid, a. accursed, cursed
Melltigedig, a. cursed, accursed
Melltog, a. full of lightning
Mên, n. an active principle
Men, n. a wain, a cart
Menaid, n. a cart load
Menestr, n. a cup-bearer
Menestru, v. to serve, to wait
Meni, n. carting, cartage
Meniad, n. a carrying in a cart
Mensaer, n. a cartwright
Mentyn, n. a thin small lip
Menu, v. to impress
Menw, n. intellect, mind
Menwedig, a. intellectual; blessed
Menwi, v. to make intellectual
Menwin, a. intelligent
Menwol, a. intelligent [ness
Menwyd, n. intellect; blessed-

Menwydig, a. intelligent; blessed
Menwydol, a. intelligent
Menwydus, a. intelligent
Menwyn, n. talent, skill
Menyd, adv. to the place where
Menyn, n. a small spot
Menynu, v. imprint, to dot
Mer, n. what is dropped off or parted; a particle; what is still; what is received
Mêr, n. marrow
Meraidd, a. like marrow
Merch, n. a girl, a woman, a daughter
Merchaidd, a. feminine, female
Mercheta, v. to go a-wenching
Merchetwr, n, a wencher
Merchin, a. towering, rising
Merchyn, n. a little horse
Mercher, n. Mercury. Dydd Mercher, Wednesday
Merddrain, n. dog briars
Merddwfr, n. stagnant water
Mered, n. flatness, dulness
Meredig, a. flattened; stupified
Meredig, a. flat, torpid, dull
Mereiddio, v. to become marrow
Merf, a. insipid, tasteful, flat
Merfdra, n. insipidity, flatness
Merfu, v. to become insipid
Merhelyg, n. sallows
Merlad, n. a dropping down
Merin, a. dropping, trickling
Meriniad, n. a falling in drops
Merino, v. to fall in drops
Merinol, a. dropping, distilling
Merion, n. droppings, drippings
Merl, n. a little pony, a nag
Merlen, n. a little pony
Merlyn, n. a little pony
Merlys, n. a water plant
Merllyd, a. insipid, tasteless
Merllyn, n. a stagnant pool
Merog, a. having marrow
Merol, a. dropping, distilling
Merolaeth, n. flatness; mustiness
Meroli, v. to grow flat; to damp

Meroren, n. a tail, a trail
Merth, n. an exhausted state
Merthiad, n. an exhausting [out
Merthu, v. to exhaust, to wear
Merthyr, n. what is open; a martyr
Merthyraeth, n. martyrology
Merthyrdod, n. martyrdom
Merthyriad, n. a martyring
Merthyru, v. to rack; to martyr
Meru, v. to droop; to drop
Merw, a. flaccid; flat; insipid
Merwin, n. numbness, torpidity
Merwinad, n. a benumbing
Merwindod, n. numbness
Merwino, v. to benumb
Merwydd, n. mulberry trees
Merwys, n. ousel, blackbird
Merydd, n. what is sluggish; plash; sluggard; sea sedge
Meryn, n. a drop, a particle
Merys, n. a medlar tree
Meryw, n. the juniper wood
Mês, n. a portion, acorns
Mesa, v. to gather acorns
Mesen, n. a single acorn
Mesfraint, n. pannage
Mesglyn, n. a shell, a hull
Mesig, a. what may be chewed
Mesigo, v. to masticate, to chew
Mest, n. a portion of food
Mesur, n. measure; rule, metre
Mesur, Mesuro, v. to allot a share; to mete
Mesuradwy, a. measurable
Mesuredigaeth, n. measurement
Mesureg, n. mensuration
Mesuregol, a. geometrical
Mesuriad, n. a measuring
Mesuriaeth, n. mensuration
Mesuriant, n. measurement
Mesurydd, n. measurer
Mettel, n. metal; mettle
Metteliad, n. a turning to metal
Mettelu, v. to burn to metal
Mettelydd, n. a metallurgist
Mettelyddiaeth, n. mettellurgy
Mêth, n. a miss; abortion

Methadwy, a. fallible; perishable
Methdal, n. non-payment
Methedig, a. decayed; decrepit
Methedigaeth, n. failure; error
Methenw. n. a misnomer
Methiad, n. a failing, missing
Methiannu, v. to become failing
Methiannus, a. of a fallible nature
Methiant, n. failure, decay
Methineb, n. failure
Methledd, n. embarrassment
Methliad, n. an entangling
Methu, v. to fail, to miss; to decay
Methwr, n. a failer, misser
Meudwy, n. hermit
Meudwyaeth, n. hermit's life
Meudwyes, n. a hermitess
Meudwyfan, n. hermitage
Meudwyo, v. to live a hermit
Mew, n. a mew, cat's cry
Mewiad, n. a mewing
Mewian, v. to keep mewing
Mewn, prep. within, in
Mewnol, a. inward, eternal
Mewyd. n. idleness
Mewyda, v. to idle, to lounge
Mewydus, a. of an idle habit
Mi, what is identic: pron. me
Miar, n. a bramble, a briar
Miaren, n. bramble, briar
Mic. n. a hoot; a spite, pique
Micas, n. bread steeped
Miciad, n. a hooting, a spiting
Micio, v. to hoot; to spite
Mich, n. a squeal, a squeak
Michdan, v. to squeal
Midiad, n. a hemming in
Midd, n. enclosed place or pit
Middi, n. pit in a river
Mieri, n. brambles, briers
Mierinllwyn, n. bramble bush
Mig. n. a hoot; spite, malice
Migen, n. a bog; a fistulous ulcer
Miglad, n. a hooting; spitting
Mign, n. a bog, quagmire
Mignen, n. a bog, a quagmire

Migniad, n. a becoming boggy
Migus, a. hooting; malicious
Migwern, n. boggy meadow
Migwrn, n. knuckle; ankle
Migwyn, n. white moss on bogs
Migymguddio, v. hide and seek
Migyrnog. a. large knuckled
Migyrnu, v. to form a knuckle
Mil, n. an animal, a beast
Mil, n. thousand, ten hundred
Milaid, a. of an animal nature
Milaidd, a. like a beast, brutish
Milain, n. a brute; a villain: a brutish; cruel, fierce
Milast, n. a greyhound bitch
Milcerdd, n. a millepede
Mildraethawd, n. zoology
Milddail, n. a yarrow
Miled, n. a wild animal
Miledd, n. brutishness
Mileiddio, v. to brutalise
Milein-gar, a. ferocious, fierce
Mileiniad, n. a growing fierce
Mileinio, v. to grow fierce
Mileinig, a. brutish, ferocious
Milfed, a. thousandth
Milfedol, a. millesimal
Milfedran, n. thousandth part
Milfil. a. thousands of thousands
Milfiwydd. a. millennial
Milfiwyddiant, n. a millennium
Milfyd, Milfyw, n. the figwort
Milgi, n. a greyhound
Milhanes, n. zoology
Milplyg, n. thousand-fold
Milred, n. a millepede
Milrith, n. fœtus, embryo
Milrym, n. the woodsage
Milwaith, n. a thousand times
Milwr, n. a warrior
Milwraidd, a. warrior-like
Milwriad, n. a colonel
Milwriaeth, n. warfare
Milwrio, v. to carry on war
Milwrus, a. warlike, militant
Milwydd, n. the camomile
Milyn, n. a little animal
Mill, n. the vollet

Milltir, n. a mile
Millyn, n. a violet
Mîn, n. edge, brink; lip
Minau, pron. me also; I, then
Minceca, v. to pop the lips
Minedd. n. sharpness, the edge
Minfel, n. the herb yarrow
Minfelys, a. sweet-mouthed
Minfin, a. edge to edge, lip to lip
Minflys, n. daintiness of mouth
Minflysig, a. dainty-mouthed
Minfwlch, n. a hare lip
Minfylchog, a. hare-lipped
Minffug, a. of deceitful lip
Min-gam, a. wry-mouthed
Min-gamu, v. to make a grimace
Min-grach, a. scabby-mouthed
Min-gras, a. saucy-mouthed
Min-grwn, a. of a round mouth
Miniad, n. edging, sharpening
Minial, v. to move the lips
Minialedd, n. motion of the lips
Minio, v. to edge, to sharpen
Miniog, a. having an edge, edged
Mintai, n. a company
Mïod, n. fritters; manchets
Mirain, a. of fair aspect, comely
Mire, n. the aspect or visage
Mireindod, n. comeliness, beauty
Mireiniad, n. a making comely
Mireinwch, n. comeliness
Miriad, n. a rendering comely
Miriannu, v. to render comely
Miriant, n. beauty of aspect
Mis, n. catemania; a month.
 Mis yr afaeth, the honey moon
Misol, a. menstrual; monthly
Misglen, n. a muscle; kind of shell fish
Misglwyf, n. the menses
Misglwyfol, a. menstruous
Misgwaith, n. a month's space
Misyriad, n. what is a month old
Mit, n. a shallow vessel
Mo, pron. it; him, he: prep. of, concerning, more of
Moc, n. a mock, a mimic
Mociad, n. a mocking

Mocio, v. to mock, to mimic
Moch, n. swine, pigs
Mochaidd, a. like swine, hoggish
Mochi, v. to wallow as swine
Mochyn, n. a pig, a swine
Mochynaidd, a. like a hog [sure
Môd, n. a circle; a turn; enclo-
Modbren, n. a stirring stick
Modfeddu, v. to mete an inch
Modrwy, n. a ring
Modrwyfil, n. lizard; eft
Modrwyig, n. an annulet
Modrwyo, v. to form a ring
Modrwyog, a. in ringlets
Modrwyol, a. annulary; curly
Modrwywr, n. dealer in rings
Modryb, n. aunt; dame [bees
Modrydaf, n. standard; stock of
Modur, n. protector
Môdd, n. a mode, a form, a way, a means
Moddiant, n. means; form
Moddio, v. to bring to a form
Moddus, a. mannerly; decent
Moel, n. pile; conical hill
Moel, a. piled; bare; bald
Moelcen, n. a bald pate
Moelder, n. bareness, baldness
Moeldes, n. clear sunshine
Moelddwrn, n. naked fist
Moeledd, n. bareness, baldness
Moelffon, n. spatula
Moeli, v. to pile; to make bald
Moeliad, n. a making bald
Moelni, n. bareness, baldness
Moelron, n. a sea calf, a seal
Moelyn, n. a bald pated one
Moes, n. civility, behaviour
Moesaddysg, n. science of etthics
Moesog, a. mannerly, courteous
Moesol, a. ethical, moral
Moesoldeb, n. morality
Moesoli, v. to become moral
Moeth, n. delicacy, nicety
Moethen, n. a dainty one
Moethi, v. to treat nicely
Moethiad, a treating nicely
Moethineb, n. blandishment

Moethol, a. delicate, bland
Moethus, a. delicate, dainty
Moethusdra, n. blandishment
Moethyn, n. a luxurious person
Mogu, v. to stifle; to smother
Mohonof, prep. from
Moi, v. to throw out; to foal
Mol, n. a concretion; gum
Molach, n. a slight praise
Molad, n. commendation
Moladwy, a. commendable
Molaid, a. full of particles
Molawd, n. commendation
Mold, n. a mould; a knead
Moldiad, n. moulding; kneading
Moldio, v. to mould; to knead
Moled, n. a muffler, a kerchief
Moli, v. to praise, to adore
Moliannol, a. commendatory
Moliannu, v. to give praise
Moliannus, a. commendable
Moliant, n. praise, adoration
Moloch, n. tumult, uproar
Molog, a. full of humour; gummy. Y frech folog, the smallpox
Moll, n. what extends round
Molliad, n. a stretching round
Mollt, Mollwyn, n. mutton; a wether
Môn, n. what is isolated; a point
Mones, n. a sulky female
Monig, a. sulky, sullen
Monoch n. entrails, guts
Monof, pron. prep. of me
Monwent, Mynwent, n. a churchyard
Monwes, n. the bosom
Monweslad, n. a bosoming
Monwesol, a. of the bosom
Monwesu, v. to put in the bosom
Monyn, n. a sulky person
Mop, Mopren, n. a maukin; a mop
Môr, n. the sea
Mor, adv. how, so, as; how much
Mora, n. motion of the sea
Moradar, n. sea fowls
Moran, n. a whale

Morben, n. a promontory
Morbryf, n. a sea animal
Morbysg, n. sea-fish [shore
Morchwain, n. insects on the sea
Morchwydd, n. swell of the sea
Mordaith, n. a sea voyage
Mordir, n. maritime land
Mordon, n. a sea breaker
Mordrai, n. ebb of the sea
Mordwy, n. a seafaring
Mordwyaeth, n. a seafaring life
Mordwyn, n, an ant hill
Mordwyo, v. to go by sea
Mordwyol, a. seafaring; sailing
Mordwys, n. waving corn
Mordwywr, n. a mariner
Morddanadl, n. horehound
Morddarluniad, n. hydrography
Morddraenog. n. sea urchin
Morddwr, n. estuary of the sea
Morddwyd, n. the thigh
Moreryr, n. an ospray
Morfa, n. sea brink
Morfalwen, n. a sea snail
Morfan, n. sea shore strand
Morfar, n. rage of the sea
Morfarch, n. a sea horse
Morfil, n. sea animal, whale
Morfin, n. sea brink
Morflaidd, n. the base
Morfochyn, n. the grampus
Morforwyn, n. the mermaid
Morfran, n. a cormorant
Morfrwyn, n. the sea rushes
Morfuwch, n. the walrus
Morgamlas, n. an estuary
Morgant, n. a sea brink
Morgaseg, n. a sea breaker
Morgath, n. a skate, a ray
Morgelyn, n. the eringo
Morgerwyn, n. a sea gulf
Morgi, n. shark
Morgranc, n. the crab fish
Morgrug, n. hill of ants; ants
Morgrugyn, n. an ant
Morgudyn, n. the polypus
Morgyllell, n. the calamary
Morhedydd, n. a sea lark

Morhesg, n. the sea sedge	Mudanes, n. a female mute
Morhocys, n. mash mallows	Mudfa, n. a removal
Morhwch, n. a grampus	Mudiad, n. a removing
Morlad, n. a going by sea	Mudliw, n. motely colour
Morio, v. to live at sea; to sail	Mudo, v. to remove
Morionen, n, emmet, ant	Mudol, a. moving, moveable
Moriwr, n. seaman, sailor	Mudsain, n. a mute letter
Morladrad, n. a piracy	Mudw, n. what is on the move
Morlan, n. a sea brink, a beach	Mudwg, n. state of removing
Morlas, n. a sea-green colour	Mul, n. an ass, a mule : a. bashful, modest, simple
Morleidr, n. a pirate	
Morlo, n. a sea calf, a seal	Muldra, n. bashfulness
Morlwch, n. a sea spray	Mules, n. a she ass
Morlwyau, n. scurvy grass	Mulfran, n. a cormorant
Morlyffant, n. the frog fish	Mulyn, n. a little ass
Morlyswen, n. a conger eel	Mun, n. what forms; a hand
Morneidr, n. a sea snake	Munaid, n. a handful
Mordnodwydd, n. needle fish	Muned, n, epithet for a hand
Moron, n. plants with tapering roots; carrots	Muneidio, v. to give handfuls
	Munud, n. a gesture; a nod
Moronyn, n. a carrot	Munudiad, n. a making gestures
Mortais, n. a mortise	Munudio, v. to make gestures
Morwennol, n. a sea swallow	Mur, n. what is firm; a wall: a. firm, fixed, established
Morwerydd, n. the sea shore	
Morwiail, n. grass wreck	Murdd, n. a foundation
Morwiber, n. the aquatic viper	Murddyn, n. shell of a building
Morwriaeth, n. seamanship	Mugraid n. a mighty spirit
Morwyf, n. a bubble	Murio, v. to fix; to wall
Morwyn, n. a maid, a damsel	Muriwr, n. wall-builder; maker of walls
Morwynaidd, a maidenly	
Morwyndod, n. virginity	Murlysiau, n. pelitory of the wall
Morwynig, n. a little maid	Murnio, v. to hinder, to harm
Morwynol, a. of a virgin	Murniol, a. annoying, harming
Morwys, n. bubbles, bubblings	Mursen, n. a coquette; a prude
Morwysiad, n. a bubbling	Mursendod, n. coquetry
Mory, n. morrow, to morrow	Mursenu, v. to act the coquette
Moryd, n. inlet of sea water	Mursyn, n. a coxcomb, a fop
Morymdaith, n. sea voyage	Musgrell, a. hobbling, halting
Mu, n. bulk, a mass; a muid	Musgrellni, n, helplessness
Much, n. sable, gloom	Mw, n. what is upon or about
Muchiad, n. a growing sable	Mwci, n. a fog; a sprite
Muchudd, n. a jet black; jet	Mwch, a. hasty, quick, swift
Mud, n. a remove; a mew: a. making motion; mute	Mwd, n. an arch, a cieling
	Mwdran, n. washbrew; gruel
Mudadwy, a. moveable	Mwdwl, n. a stack; a cock
Mudai, n. remover, mover	Mwdd, n. an arch, a vault
Mudan, n. a mute, a dumb one	Mwg, n. smoke, fume
Mudanaeth, n. a mute state	Mwgwd, n. a blind, a mask

Mwng, n. a neck, a mane
Mwngial, v. to speak gutturally : n. a muttering
Mwl, n. a concretion, a lump
Mwlwch, Mwlwg, n. refuse, sweepings
Mwll, a. close, warm, sultry
Mwn, n. what spires up; a particle; a mine, ore
Mwnai, n. money, coin
Mwndlws, n. neck ornament
Mwn-gloddiad, n. a mining
Mwn-gloddio, v. to mine
Mwnt, n. a mound; a mount; a hundred thousand
Mwnwg, n. a neck; a swivel
Mwr, n. what tends to fall or happen
Mwrl, n. a crumbling stone
Mwrn, n. sultry weather: a. sultry, close, warm
Mwrndra, n. sultriness
Mwrno, v. to become sultry
Mwrth, n. what tends forward
Mwrthwyl, n. a hammer
Mwrthwyliad, n. a hammering
Mwrthwylio, v. to hammer
Mws, n. what shoots out; effluvia: a. of strong scent, rank
Mwsg, n. moscus, musk
Mwstardd, n mustard
Mwswg, n. moss
Mwswgl, n. moss
Mwth, a. rapid, fleet, nimble
Mwy, a. additional; more; larger: adv. more, again
Mwyâd, n. an augmenting
Mwyach, a. more; adv. more
Mwyad, increasing, augmenting
Mwyadu, v. to augment, to increase
Mwynid, n. consecrated wafers
Mwyalch, Mwyalchen, n. ousel, blackbird
Mwyar, n. acini, clustered berries
Mwyaren, n. a single berry
Mwyâu, v. to augment, to enlarge
Mwyd, n. what is soaked

Mwydion, n. soft parts; pith
Mwydioni v. to become crumby
Mwydionyn, n. crumb; pith
Mwydle, n. the fetlock
Mwydo, v. to soak, to moisten
Mwydol, a. soaking, moistening, steeping, damping
Mwyedigaeth, n. augmentation
Mwyedigo, v. to augment
Mwyeri, n. briers, brambles
Mwyfwy, adv. more and more
Mwygl, n. tepid, warm, sultry
Mwyglad, n. a growing sultry
Mwygledd, n. tepidity; sultriness
Mwyglen, n. a wanton wench
Mwygliad, n. a growing sultry
Mwyglo, v. to warm; to grow sultry
Mwyll, a. emollient, tender
Mwyn, n. enjoyment, use; sake: a. kind, gentle, mild
Mwynâd, n. an enjoying
Mwynaidd, a. tender
Mwynasu, v. to do kindness
Mwynâu, v. to enjoy, to possess
Mwynder, n. kindness
Mwyneidd-dra, n. tenderness
Mwyneiddio, v. to become kind, tender or pleasing
Mwyniant, n. enjoyment, use
Mwynlan, a. courteously fair
Mwys, n. what comprehends; what has double meaning: a pun; a hamper: five score of herrings: a. ambiguous; witty; elegant
Mwysair, n. punning word
Mwythach, n. pampered state
Mwythedd, n. emolliency, softness, blandishment
Mwythiad, n. a mollifying
Mwythig, a. puffed up, bloated
Mwytho, v. to puff; to mollify
Mwythol, a. emollient
Mwythus, a. sleek; delicate; nice
Mwythusdra, n. a pampered state
Mwythusiad, n. a pampering
My, pron. my. Inflected to FY

	240	
MYCH		MYN

Mychol, a. of rapid motion
Mychiad, n. a swineherd
Myd, n. aptitude, fluency
Mydaidd, a. like an arch, arched
Mydedd, n. archedness
Mydiad, n. cameration
Mydr, n. metre, verse
Mydraeth, n. versification
Mydriad, n. a versifying
Mydrwr, n. a versifier
Mydryddiaeth, n. versification
Mydryddu, v. to versify
Mydu, v. to arch, to vault
Mydum, n. gesture; mimicry
Mydw, n. aptitude; fluency
Mydwal, a. apt to proceed
Mydwaledd, n. fluent speech
Mydyliad, n. a stacking
Mydylu, v. to stack, to cock
Myddi, n. a hogshead
Myfi, pron. myself, I, me
Myfiaeth, n. egotism
Myfio, v. to egotise
Myfyr, n. muse, study: a. musing, pensive
Myfyrbwyll, a. of musing mind
Myfyrdod, n. contemplation
Myfyrdodol, a. contemplative
Myfyriadol, a. contemplative
Myfyrio, v. to contemplate
Myfyriol, a. contemplative
Myfyriwr, n. a contemplator, a speculator
Myg, n. solemnity, sanctitude
Mygawd, n. suffocation
Mygdarth, n. vapour, fog
Mygdarthu, v. to burn incense
Myged, n. respect, reverence: a. respected, solemn
Mygedorth, n. a funeral pile
Mygfa, n. a suffocation
Mygfaen, n. brimstone
Mygiad, n. a smoking
Myglyd, a. apt to smoke
Mygodarth, n. exhalation
Mygodfa, n. an asthma
Mygodorth, n. a flatulency
Mygol, a. fumous, smoking

Mygu, v. to smoke; to stifle
Mygyr, a. majestic, glorious
Myngog, a. having a mane
Myngen, n. the crest of a horse; a mane
Myngial, n. guttural speaking
Myngialu, v. to speak gutturally
Myharan, n. tup, a ram
Myhefin, n. month of June
Myldardd, n. what is in grains
Mylliad, n. a growing sultry
Myllu, v. grow sultry
Myllynen, n. a violet
Mym, n. what is incipient
Mympwy, n. opinion; humour
Mympwyaeth, n. opiniation
Mympwyo, to opine
Mympwyol, a. opinionative
Mymryn, n. an atom
Myn, n. will, desire, mind: n. a kid, a young goat: prep. by the will of, by
Mynach, n. a monk; a post
Mynachaeth, n. monachism
Mynachol, a. monachal, monkish
Mynaches, n. a recluse, a nun
Mynachlog, n. monastery
Mynad, n. a volition, a will
Mynag, n. a report, a recital
Mynan, n. a young kid
Mynas, n. a menace, a threat
Mynawyd, n. an awl [collar
Mynci, n. hame, part of horse
Mynechdid, n. a monastery
Myned, v. to set out, to go
Mynedfa, n. a departure
Mynediad, n. a going, departing
Mynedwy, n. running water
Mynegadwy, a. expressible
Mynegai, n. what indicates, an index
Mynegfa, n. a catalogue
Mynegfys, n. a fore finger
Mynegi, v. to express, to relate
Mynegiad, n. a declaration
Mynegiadol, a. declaratory
Mynegiaeth, n. a recital
Mynegiant, n. declaration

| MYN | 241 | NADD |

Mynegol, a. expressive, declaring; indicative
Myniad, n. a willing; a having
Myniant, n. volition; willing
Myniar, n. a snipe
Mynogaeth, n. urbanity
Mynor, n. marble
Mynori, v. to become marble
Mynta, n. a million
Myntai, n. multitude, host
Mynteio, v. to congregate
Myntumio, v. to maintain
Mynu, v. to exercise will; to attain; to seek; to will
Mynud, n. what is courteous; courteous; social
Mynudedd, n. courteousness
Mynudyn, n. deportment
Mynw, n. a person, a body
Mynwar, n. a harness collar
Mynwed, n. fellowship, society
Mynwen, n. a sepulchre
Mynwennol, a. monumental
Mynwent, n. a sepulchre; a churchyard
Mynwes, n. bosom
Mynwesol, n. of the bosom
Mynwesu, v. to bosom
Mynych, a. frequent, often
Mynychiad, n. frequenting
Mynychu, v. to frequent
Mynyd, n. a minute
Mynydd, n. a mountain
Mynyddig, a. mountainous
Mynyglog, n. the quinsy
Mynyglwisg, n. a neck-cloth
Mynyn, n. a young kid
Myr, a. essential; pure; holy: n. the sea; emmets
Myrdwyn, n. an ant-hill
Myrdd, n. infinity
Myrddiwn, n. a myriad
Myriad, n. a making pure
Myrion, n. ants, emmets
Myrionen, n. an emmet
Myrndra, n. sultriness
Myrniad, n. a growing sultry

Myrwerydd, n. sea rushes
Mysg: n. the middle, the midst
Mysgiad, n. a mixing, a blending
Mysgu, v. to mix, to mingle
Mysorig, a. yèilding a stench
Myswrn, n. an instrument
Myswynog, n. a farrow cow
Mysygan, n. a soft expression
Mysygliad, n. a gathering moss
Mysyglu, v. to gather moss
Mythdra, n. swiftness; velocity
Mythiad, n. a giving velocity
Mythl, n. infected state; canker
Mythliad, n. a cankering
Mythlu, v. to pervade; to canker
Mythu, v. to give swiftness [ant
Myw, n. what has activity; an
Mywion, n. ants
Mywionyn, n. an ant, an emmet
Mywyn, n. pith
Mywynog, a. having pith

N

NA, conj. nor, neither; than; adv. no, not; than not
Nabod, n. cognisance: v. to know, to recognise
Nac, adv. no, not
Naca, v. to make a denial
Nacâd, n. a refusal, a denial
Nacaol, a. refusing; negative
Nacâu, v. to refuse, to deny
Nâd, n. a shrill cry; clamour
Nad, adv. not, that not
Nadiad, n. a hindering
Nadu, v. to cry out, to howl
Nadd, n. what is wrought or chipped
Naddol, a. hewing, chipping
Naddiad, n. a hewing, a chipping, a cutting
Naddial, v. to keep chipping
Naddiant, n. a wrought state

Naddu, v. to hew, to chip
Nâf n. what forms; a creator
Nafiad, n. an operation
Nag, n. a negative; a denial: conj. nor, neither; than: adv. not
Nage, adv. not that, not so, no
Nagu, v. to deny; to hinder
Nai, n. a nephew
Naid, n. a refuge; a jump
Naill, a. one or other, one; conj. either, other
Nain, n. a grandmother
Nam, n. a mark, a maim, a fault; an exception
Namyn, prep. but, since, except: n. exception
Nan, adv. what
Nant, n. a ravine, a brook
Nas, adv. not; that not
Naw, a. nine
Nawd, n. nature; character: adv. effectually, easily
Nawdeg, a. ninety
Nawdd, n. refuge, protection; patronage; support
Nawf, n. a swim; the swim or wind bladder of a fish
Nawfed, a. ninth
Nawn, n. meridian, noon
Nawnol, a. meridional, noon
Nawnu, v. to uphold; to be noon, to be meridional
Naws, n. nature, disposition
Nawsaidd, a. genial; kind; soft
Nawsedd, n. temperature
Nawseiddio, v. to render genial or temperate
Nawsiad, n. a tempering, a pervading
Nawseiddiol, a. temperamental
Nawsiant, n. temperament
Nawsio, v. to temper; to pervade; to ooze
Nawsineb, n. temperament
Nawsol, a. temperate, genial
Nawsoldeb, n. temperature
Nawsoll, v. to temper; to soften

Nawswyllt, a. of wild temper
Ne, n. a state of going; a hue conj. or, otherwise, either
Nead, n. an opening to let out
Neb, n. somebody, nobody
Nebpell, adv. at no distance
Nedd, n. what turns; a dingle
Neddair, n. a grasp of the hand
Nef, n. a hollow: heaven
Nefol, a. heavenly, celestial
Nefoldeb, heavenliness
Nefolfryd, a. heavenly-minded
Nefoli v. to become heavenly
Nefoliaeth, n. heavenly state
Neges, n. errand, message
Negesa, v to go on errands; to negociate [rands, a messenger
Negesai, n. one who goes on er-
Negeseuwr, Negeswr, Negesydd, n. an errand man; a messenger
Negesiaeth, n. a commission
Negesog, a. having an errand
Negesol, a. relating to errands
Negesyddiaeth, n. business of a messenger
Neidiad n. a leaping, a jumping
Neidio, v. to leap; to throb
Neidiol, a. leaping; throbbing
Neidr, n. a snake, an adder. Gwas y neidr, the dragon-fly
Neidrllys, n. snakewort
Neifion, n. creating powers; Neptune
Neillawr, adv. at another time
Neilldu, n. other side, one side
Neillduad, n. a putting aside
Neillduaeth, n. a reservation
Neillduedd, n. separateness
Neillduol, v. to go aside; to put aside; to separate: a. separate, distinct. Cyfreithiau neilduol, by-laws
Neillduolaeth, n. discrimination
Neillduoldeb, n. discriminateness
Neillduoli, v. to render distinct
Neilliad, n. diversifying

Neisio, v. to trim up nicely
Neithio, v. to complete; to confirm
Neithior, n. completion; a marriage feast
Neithiori, v. to keep a marriage feast
Neithiwyr, n. the evening past, last night
Nemawr, n. a few in number
Nen, n. a ceiling, a canopy
Nenawr, n. upper story, garret
Nenbren, n. a roof beam
Nenfwd, n. a ceiling arch
Neniad, n. a ceiling, a vaulting
Neniar, n. a roof beam
Nenty, n. a cockloft, a garret
Nêr, n. what has self-energy; the Lord
Nerth, n. might, power
Nerthedd, n. potency, strength
Nerthfawr, a. of great power
Nerthiad, n. a strengthening
Nerthiannu, v. to make potent
Nerthiant, n. a strengthening
Nerthol, a. powerful, potent
Nerthu, v. to make powerful
Nes, n. a proximate state: a. divested of distance; nearer: adv. until, before that
Nesâd, n. approximation
Nesaol, a. approximating
Nesáu, v. to approximate
Nesefin, n. a neighbour
Nesiad, n. a drawing near
Nesiant, n. approximation
Nesnes, adv. nearer and nearer
Nesrwydd, n. nearness, proximity
Nest, n. what is compact or close
Nestig, a. compact
Nesu, v. to approximate
Neu, v. to pant; to wish or to pant for earnestly: conj. or
Neuadd, n. a hall, a large room
Neuaddol, a. belonging to a hall
Neued, n. a panting; a longing
Neufedd, n. wealth, riches
New, n. what is proceeding
Newid, n. change: v. to change, to alter
Newidiad, n. a changing
Newidiannu, to produce change
Newidiant, n. act of changing
Newidio, v. to change, to alter, to become changed
Newidiol, a. changing, mutable
Newidioldeb, n. changeableness
Newydd, n. what is new, news: a. new, novel; fresh
Newydd-dra, n. newness, novelty
Newyddiad, n. a making new
Newyddiadur, n. newspaper
Newyddol, a. of a new quality
Newyddu, v. to make new
Newyn, n. hunger; famine
Newyndra, n. a hungry state
Newyniad, n. a famishing
Newynllyd, Newynog; a. hungry, starving
Newynol a. famishing, hungry
Newynu, v. to famish, to starve
Nhw, Nhwy, pron. they, them
Nhwythau, pron. they likewise
Ni, n. a number separate; pron. we, us: adv. not
Nid, n. what is impending: adv. not
Nidr, n. impediment; delay
Nidrad, n. an entagling [plexity
Nidredd, n. entanglement; perplexity
Nidri, n. an entanglement; a perplexity
Nidro, v. to entangle
Nifer, n. a number; a host
Niferai, n. a numerator
Niferedd, n. numerousness
Niferiad, n. a numbering
Niferiaeth, n. numeration
Niferiannu, v. to enumerate
Niferog, a. numerous
Niferogi, v. to make numerous
Niferol, a. numerical, numeral
Niferu, v. to number
Niferydd, n. a numerist
Nifwl, n. a mist, a cloud
Nig, n. what is straitened
Nigiad, n. a straitening
Nigio, v. to straiten; to narrow

Nill, n. what is repeated
Nillai, n. a sickle
Ninau, pron. we also, us too
Nis, adv. not
Nith, n. what is pure: niece
Nithiad, n. a winnowing
Nithiant, n. a purifying
Nithio, v. to winnow
Nithlen, n. winnowing sheet
Niw, n. what is violent
Niwed, n. harm, damage
Niweidiad, n. a hurting; a harming
Niweidio, v. to injure, to damage, to hurt
Niweidiol, a. hurtful, noxious
Niweidioldeb, n. noxiousness
Niwl, n. a mist, a fog
Niwlen, n. a small mist, a cloud
Niwliach, n. scattered clouds
Niwliad, n. a becoming misty
Niwlio, v. to become misty
Niwliog, a. covered with mist
No, n. what stops or keeps in: adv. than
Nôd, n. a token, a mark. Haint y nodau, the plague. Hyd y nôd, even, up to the mark
Nodadwy, a. remarkable, notable
Nodedig, a. marked, noted
Noden, n. thread, yarn
Nodi, v. to mark, to note
Nodiad, n. a marking
Nodiadol, a. characteristic
Nodiadu, v. to characterise
Nodiannol, a. characteristic
Nodiannu, v. to characterise
Nodiant, n. notation, noting
Nodog, a. having a mark
Nodol, a. marked, notable

Noddiad, n. a giving refuge
Noddiant, n. protection, refuge
Noddlyd, a. juicy, full of sap
Noddlydrwydd, n. juiciness
Noddlydu, v. to become juicy
Noddwr, n. a protector
Noddyn, n. an abyss
Noe, n. a platter, a dish, a tray
Noeaid, n. a platter-full
Noeth, a. naked, bare, exposed
Noethedd, n. nakedness
Noethi, v. to make bare
Noethiad, n. a making naked
Noethiannol, a. denuding [nude
Noethiannu, v. to bare, to denude
Noethiant, n. denudation
Noethlyman, a. stark naked
Noethni, nakedness, bareness
Nof, n. what moves or flows
Nofiad, n. a swimming
Nofiadaeth, n. art of swimming
Nofiadol, a. swimming
Nofiedydd, Nofiwr, n. swimmer
Nofio, v. to swim, to cause to swim
Nog, n. a stop; restive state: conj. than
Nogio, v. to stop; to be restive
Nol, v. to fetch, to bring
Non, n. a stream, a current
Nôs, n. night. Min nôs, eve
Nosi, v. to become night
Nosiad, n. a becoming night
Nosig, n. night time, night
Nosol, a. nocturnal, nightly
Noson, n. a certain night
Noswaith, n. a certain night
Noswyl, n. evening tide
Noswyliad, n. leaving work at eve; a keeping of vigils

Nwydo, v. to have a whim or bias
Nwydol, Nwydus, a. whimsical
Nwydwyllt, a. hairbrained
Nwydd, n. essence; substance; effects. Nwyddau, goods
Nwyddo, v. to make substantial
Nwyddol, a. substantial, material (vivacity, energy, vigour
Nwyf, n. a pervading element;
Nwyfiannu, v. to cheer the spirits
Nwyfiant, n. brightness; vigour
Nwyfio, v. to enliven, to grow lively
Nwyfol, a. full of spirits; wanton
Nwyfre, n. firmament, atmosphere [ton
Nwyfus, a. full of spirits; wan-
Nwyth, n. a bent; a whim
Nwythas, n. eccentricity, oddity
Nwythus, full of whims, freaky
Nych, n. a languishing, a pining
Nycha, interj. behold, lo, see
Nychdod, n. a languishment
Nychiad, n. a languishing; a vexing, a pining
Nychlyd, a. pining; painful
Nychol, a. languishing, pining
Nychu, v. to pain; to languish
Nydwydd, n. a broach; a needle
Nydwyddes, n. a needlewoman
Nydd, n. a spin, a twist [ing
Nyddiad, n. a spinning, a twist-
Nyddol, a. spinning, twisting
Nyddu, v. to spin, to twist
Nyddwedd, n. size of yarn in spinning
Nyddwr, n. a spinner
Nyddwraig, n. a spinster
Nyf, n. snow
Nyfed, n. a pure or holy nature
Nyni, pron. we, us
Nyninau, pron. we or us likewise
Nyth, n. a nest
Nythaid, n. a nestful
Nythfa, n. a nesting place
Nythgyw, n. a nestling
Nythu, v. to nest, to nestle
Nyw, n. vivacity; vigour

O

O, n. what goes or proceeds: prep. from; of, out, of; by: conj. if: pron. it; he: interj. oh, alas
Oblegid, conj. because, for
Obry, adv. beneath, below
Ocr, Ocraeth, n. usury; profit
Ocredd, n. usuriousness
Ocri, n. usury; profit, gain
Ocriad, n. a dealing in usury
Ocru, v. to practise usury
Och, interj. oh! alas! woe!
Ochain, v. to be uttering groans
Ochan, n. a groan, a moan; woe
Ochenaid, n. a sigh
Ocheneiciad, n. a sighing
Ocheneidio, v. to sigh
Ocheneidiol, a. sighing
Ochi, v. to utter groans
Ochr, n. a side, an edge, a rim
Ochredd, n. laterality; side
Ochri, v. to side; to make a ledge
Ochriad, n. a siding; an edging, a forming a ledge
Ochrog, a. having sides
Ochrol, a. belonging to a side
Od, n. what is clear; snow: a. notable, excellent; odd: conj.
Odi, v. to snow [if
Odiad, n. a falling of snow [ity
Odiaeth, n. what is notable, rar-
Odiaethol, a. peculiar, notable
Odiaethu, v. to render notable
Odid, n. peculiarity, rarity: adv. probably; rarely [rhyme
Odli, v. to make rhyme; to
Odliad, n. a rhyming
Odlog, a. rhythmical; rhymed
Odlyd, a. niveous, or snowy
Odwlaw, n. sleet
Odyn, n. a kiln
Odynaid, n. a kilnful
Odyndy, n. a kiln-house
Odd, n. what tends out or from

| OEDD | 246 | OFA |

prep. from of, out of; by
Oddeutu, prep. on both sides; about
Oddf, n. excrescence; knob
Oddfi, v. to boss; to grow knob-
Oddfiad, n. a knobbing [bed
Oddfogi, v. to become knobbed or full of knots
Oddfyn, n. a knob, a knur
Oddi, prep. out of, from; off
Oddiacw, adv. from yonder
Oddiallan, prep. on the outside
Oddiam, prep. from round
Oddiamgylch, prep. from round
Oddiar, prep. from off; from, of, above
Oddieithr, conj. except, unless
Oddifaes, adv. from without
Oddifewn, adv. from within
Oddifry, adv. from above
Oddifyny, adv. from above
Oddigerth, prep. except; beside
Oddigylch, prep. from about
Oddihwnt, prep. from beyond
Oddilawr, adv. from below
Oddimewn, adv. from within
Oddiobry, adv. from below
Oddirhwng, prep. from between
Oddisod, adv. from below
Oddiuchod, adv. from above
Oddiwaered, adv. from below
Oddiwrth, prep. from by, from
Oddiyma, adv. hence, from this place [place
Oddiyna, adv. hence, from that
Oddiyno, adv. thence, from that place [come; set time; age
Oed, n. process of time; time to
Oedog, a. full of delay
Oedol, a. procrastinating
Oedfa, n. a set time; a meeting
Oedi, v. to set a time; to delay
Oediad, n. a delaying
Oediog, a. of long time; aged
Oedran, n. age, full age
Oedraniad, n. a growing aged
Oedranu, v. to grow aged [aged
Oedranus, a. stricken in years,

Oedwr, n. a delayer
Oedd, v. was, did exist
Oen, n. a lamb
Oenaidd, a. like a lamb
Oenan, n. a lambkin
Oenes, n. an ewe-lamb
Oenig, n. little ewe-lamb
Oenol, a. belonging to a lamb
Oenyn, n. a lambkin, a little lamb
Oer, a. cold frigid; repulsive
Oeraidd, a. somewhat cold
Oerol, a. of a cooling nature
Oerdra, n. coldness, frigidity
Oerfa, n. cool place
Oerfel, n. cold air or weather
Oergri, n. a dismal cry
Oergwymp, n. a dismal fall
Oeri, v. to cool, to chill; to become cold
Oeriad, n. a cooling, a chilling
Oerlais, n. a dismal voice
Oerlef, n. a dismal moan
Oerllyd, a. of cold quality; chilly
Oernad, n. a dismal howl
Oerni, n. coldness, chillness
Oerwaedd, n. a dismal cry
Oerwedd, n. a chilling aspect
Oerwlyb, a. cold and wet
Oerwynt, n. a cold wind
Oeryn, n. a cold person
Oes, n. an age, period of life.
Oes oesoedd, for ever and
Oes, v. there is; is there? [ever
Oesfyr, a. short-lived [live
Oesi, v. to pass through life; to
Oesiad, n. a passing through life, an existing
Oesol, a. relating to age, aged
Oesran, n. assigned period of life
Oesred, n. course of existence
Oestad, Oestadol, a. constant, constantly, always
Oethi, v. to render intense
Of, n. atoms; particles; motes
Of, a. elementary; crude; raw
Ofawd, n. a making crude; a mouldering

Ofedd, n. elementary state
Ofer, a. waste, vain, useless, idle
Ofera, v. to waste; to act idly
Oferddyn, n. a dissipated man, a spendthrift
Oferedd, n. frivolity; dissipation
Oferfost, n. a vain boasting
Ofergais, n. a fruitless attempt
Ofergoel, superstition
Oferiaith, n. useless idle talk
Oferlaeth, n. waste milk
Oferwaith, n. a useless work
Oferwas, n. a worthless chap
Oferwr, n. an idler
Oferymgais, n. an idle attempt
Oflad, n. a decomposing
Ofiannu, v. to render friable
Ofiant, n. a reducing to atoms
Oflyd, a. decomposing, jumble
Ofn, n. fear, dread, timidity
Ofnâd, an intimidation
Ofnadwy, a. terrible, frightful
Ofnâu, v. to become fearful
Ofnedig, a. intimidated, scared
Ofnedd, n. fearfulness
Ofni, v. to fear to terrify
Ofniad, n. a dreading, a fearing, intimidation
Ofnid, n. terror, dread, fear
Ofnog, a. fearful, timorous
Ofnol, a. tending to frighten
Ofnus, a. fearful, timorous
Ofnusrwydd, n. fearfulness
Ofydd, n. philosopher
Ofyddfardd, n. scientific bard
Offeiriad, n. minister, priest
Offeiriadaeth, n. a priesthood
Offeiriadol, a. priestly
Offeiriadu, v. to minister
Offer, n. implements; gear
Offeren, n. sacred service; mass
Offerena, v. to celebrate mass
Offereniad, n. a saying of mass
Offerenol, a. relating to the mass
Offerenu, v. to perform mass
Offerynol, a. instrumental
Offeiriannu, v. to act as agent
Offeru, v. to equip, to furnish

Offeryn, n. instrument, a tool
Offrwm, n. an offering, sacrifice
Offrymiad, n. a sacrificing
Offrymu, v. to sacrifice, to offer
Og, n. what is full of motion or life; youth; a harrow: a. apt to move; youthful
Ogaid, n. a stroke of a harrow
Oged, n. what stirs; a harrow
Ogedu, v. to use a harrow
Ogfaen, n. hip, fruit of briers
Ogi, v. to use the harrow
Ogiad, n. a harrowing
Ogof, n. a cave; a den
Ogofog, a. full of caves
Ongl, n. a corner, an angle
Ongli, v. to make angular
Ongliad, n. forming angles
Onglog, a. having angles
Ohonof, a pronominal preposition, from me, of me, out of me
Oi, v. to proceed; to come forward: interj. well, very well
Oiad, n. an attending; a waiting; a listening
Oian, n. a listening; a waiting
Oianu, v. to listen; to wait
Ol, n. mark, trace; track: a. hindmost. Olaf, last
Olafiad, n. a successor
Olafiaeth, n. a successorship
Olbrain, n. the herb crowfoot
Ole, n. a ravine
Olew, oil, unction
Olewwydd, n. olive trees [ing
Oliedydd, n. a pricker, in hunt-
Olion, n. leavings, refuse
Olp, n. puncture; islet-hole
Olrhain, n. a search after
Olrhead, n. a beagle
Olrheiniad, n. a tracing out
Olrheiniadwy, a. scrutable
Olrheinio, v. to scrutinise
Olrheiniwr, n. a tracer, a scrutiniser
Olwyn, n. a wheel, a trurdle
Olwynad, n. a wheeling
Olwyno, v. to wheel

Olwynog, a. having wheels
Olynol, a. following
Olysgrif, n. a postscript
Oll, a. all, whole, everyone
Ollalluog, a. almighty, omnipo[tent
Ollalluogrwydd, n. almightiness
Olldifaol, a. all-consuming
Ollddigonol, a. all-sufficient [ing
Ollddoeth, a. all-wise, all-know-
Ollgyfoethog, a. all-powerful
Olliach, n. the herb all-heal
Ollnerthedd, n. omnipotency
Ollnerthog, a. omnipotent
Ollryw, a. omnigenous
Ollwybodol a. omniscient
Om, n. what stretches round
On, n. what is superior; what is in continuity; an ash
Onc, n. what is headlong
Onco, pron. that, that there
Ond, conj. but, only; prep. except, but
Onen, n. an ash, an ash tree
Oni, Onid, adv. not? conj. if not, unless; except, until
Onidê, conj. otherwise, or else adv. if not so; is it not so?
Onis, conj. if not, unless, except: adv. not?
Onwydd, n. ash trees
Or, n. a limit; margin, brim: conj. if
Orch, n. a limit; rim
Oriad, n. a puffing, a panting
Oriadur, n. a time-piece, watch
Oriain, v. to puff, to pant: n. utterance; panting
Oriog, a. having fits, fickle
Oriol, a. belonging to the hour
Oriawr, n. time-piece, watch
Oriel, n. a porch, gallery
Orig, n. a little while; adv. now, at present
Origyn, n. a short space
Orlais, n. a time-piece, clock
Orn, n. a start; push; threat
Ornedigaeth, n. a threatening
Ornedd, n. a threatening state

Ornest, n. tilting, combat, duel
Ornestfa, n. place of combat
Ornestiad, n. a combating
Ornestu, v. to combat, to duel
Ornestwr, n. dueller
Orni, v. to start, to threaten
Oroï, v. to utter; to be uttering
Oroïan, n. a jubilation; joy: v. to shout in triumph
Os, conj. if
Osai, n. sweet juice; cyder
Osg, n. what tends out or from
Osged, n. a laver, a bason
Osgl, n. a branch; a twig
Osglen, n. a branch; a twig
Osgli, v. to branch; to shoot
Osgliad, n. a branching out
Osglod, n. a ramification
Osglog, a. branchy, branching
Osgo, n. obliquity, slope
Osgoad, n. a starting aside
Osgöedd n. obliquity; starting
Osgöi, v. to go aslant; to start
Osgoilyd, a. apt to start aside
Osgyd, n. a laver, a bason
Osiad, n. a making an essay
Osio, v. to offer to do, to essay
Ostid, n. epithet for a shield
Ostl, n. an open place; inn
Ostr, n. what is spread
Ostri, n. display, hospitality
Oswydd, n. war-horses; cavalry
Ow, n. a breathing out; a moan

P

PA, n. what is in continuity: a. what
Pab, n. a father; a pope
Pabaidd, a. papal; popish
Pabell, n. tent; tabernacle
Pabelliad, n. a fixing a tent
Pabellu, v. to pitch a tent
Pabi, n. the poppy
Pabïol, a. papaverous

Pabir, n. rushes; rush candles
Pablaidd, a. active; nervous
Pabledd, a. activity; vigour
Pabliad, n. invigoration
Pablu, v. to invigorate
Pabwyr, n. rushes
Pabwyra, v. to gather rushes
Pabwyrog, a. full of rushes
Pabwyren, n. a single rush
Pabwyryn, n. a bulrush
Pabydd, n. a papist
Pabyddol, a. papistical
Pabyddiaeth, n. popery
Pâd, n. what keeps together; what contains
Padell, n. pan
Padellaid, n. a panful
Padellan, Padellig, n. a little [pan
Padellu, v. to form a pan
Padd, n. what keeps a course
Pae, n. a constraint; a panting
Paeled, n. a spread, a plaster; a scull-cap
Paen, n. what spreads; peacock
Paenes, n. a peahen; a fine girl
Paent, n. paint; colour
Paentiad, n. a painting
Paentiedig, a. painted, coloured
Paeol, n. a pail; a pot
Paeth, n. concurrence
Paff, n. a lump; a hulk
Pafflad, n. lumping; thumping
Paffio, v. to lump; to thump
Pang, n. a convulsion; a pang
Pangiad, n. a convulsing
Pangol, a. convulsive
Pangu, v. to convulse
Paham, adv. wherefore? why?
Pai, n. what is objective
Paid, n. cessation, quiet
Paill, n. farina, flour
Pain, n. bloom; fine dust; farina
Pair, n. instrumentality; cause; a boiler, a cauldron
Pais, n. a coat; a petticoat
Paisg, n. a coating; a pod
Pâl, n. a spread; a ray; a spade
Palad, n. a radiating, a beaming, a shooting out
Paladr, n. a ray; a beam; a shaft; a stem; a stalk; axis
Paladrog, a. having a shaft
Paladriad, n. a forming a shaft
Paladru, v. to beam, to shaft; to bole
Paladrwym, n. a flail joint
Paladu, v. to beam, to radiate
Palawr, n. a delver, a digger
Paled, n. a shaft; a javelin
Paledrydd, n. a maker of darts
Paledu, v. to cast a dart
Palf, n. flat end of a shaft; a paw; a palm
Palfaid, n. a stroke of a palm
Palfaliad, n. a groping about
Palfalu, v. to grope about
Palfes, n. the shoulders of a quad-
Palfiad, n. a pawing [ruped
Palfod, n. a stroke of a paw
Palfog, a. pawed; having a palm
Paliad, n. a spreading; a delving, a digging [steep of a rock
Palis, n. a pale, a wainscot; the
Paliso, v. to pale, to wainscot
Palisog, a. paled, wainscoted
Palm, n. a spread; a flag
Palmant, n. a pavement
Palmantu, v. to lay a paving
Palmwydd, n. palm trees
Palores, n. a cough, a daw
Palu, v. to delve, to dig
Pall, n. loss of energy; a miss, a failure; nought; neglect: n. a mantle; a pavilion
Palladwy, a. fallible; perishable
Pallder, n. fallibility; failed state
Palldod, n. failure, abortiveness
Palliad, n. a failing; a neglect-
Palliant, n. failure; neglect [ing
Pallu, v. to fail; to cease
Pam, adv. wherefore, why
Pan, n. a pan, a bowl, a cup: n. down, fur; nap; fulling: adv. when, whence, since
Panan, n. what involves or works together

Panas, n. plaited straw, mat, a partition of plaited straw
Pandy, n. a fulling mill
Paned, adv. when, at which time
Paneg, n. a gut, an entrail
Panel, n. thick platting of straw; cushion of a pack saddle
Panelog, a. plaited; panelled
Panelu, v. to plait, to mat
Panfa, n. a fulling; a banging
Paniad, n. a furring; a fulling
Pannu, v. to hem in; to make a depression; to cause a panic
Pannylu, v. to cause a sinking
Pant, n. what involves; a depression, a hollow, a low place
Pantiad, n. a forming a hollow
Pantog, a. having a hollow, concavity
Pantu, v. to sink in; to dimple
Panu, v. to fur; to full; to bang
Panwaen, n. a peat moss
Panwr, n. a fuller; a banger
Panwriaeth, n. trade of a fuller
Papyr, n. paper
Papyrol, a. consisting of paper
Papyryn, n. a piece of paper
Pâr, n. state of readiness; pair
Par, n. a cause; germ; a spear
Para, v. to continue, to last
Parâd, n. continuance, duration
Parab, n. aptitude or utterance
Parabl, n. speech; discourse
Parad, n. causation, a causing
Paradwy, a. causable, effectable
Paradwyad, n. effectuation
Paradwys, n. a paradise. Cylion paradwys, Spanish flies
Paraeth, n. a causation, a cause
Paraol, a. continuing, lasting
Parâu, v. to persevere; to last
Parâus, a. constant, of long continuance
Parc, n. an enclosure; a park
Parciad, n, an enclosing
Parcio, v. to enclose, to hedge in
Parch, n. respect, reverence
Parchadwy, a. respectable

Parchedig, a. respected; reverend [respect
Parchedigaeth, n. a of showing
Parchlawn, a. respectful
Parchlonder, n. respectfulness
Parchu, v. to respect, to revere, to have regard for [able
Parchus, a. respectful; respect
Parchusedd, n. respectableness
Parddu; n. fire-black, smut
Pardduo, v. to smut, to grow smutty
Pared, n. a partition wall
Paredlys, n. pellitory of the wall
Parfaes, n. epithet for a shield
Parfyg, n. the herb henbane
Pari, n. a string, a drove, a flock
Pariad, n. a causing; a bidding
Parlas, n, a green plat of ground
Parlawr, n. a parlour
Parliant, n. interlocution
Parod, ready, prepared; prompt
Parodi, v. to make ready, to prepare
Parodiad, n. a preparing [ing
Parodol, a. preparatory, preparParodoldeb, Parodrwydd, Parodedd, n. preparedness, readiness
Parol, a. causing, creative
Parotoëdd, n. preparedness
Parotöi, v. to prepare, to get ready [paring
Parotöol, a. preparatory, preParsel, n. what is aimed at, a
Parth, n. a part; a division [butt
Parthadwy, a. discriminable
Parthed, n. a division
Parthedig, a. divided, severed
Parthedigaeth, n. discrimination
Parthedigol, a. discriminative
Parthedd. n. a divided state
Parthgymeriad, n. a participle
Parthiad, n. a dividing, a parting
Parthiannol, a. discriminative
Parthiannu, v. to discriminate
Parthiant, n. a division, a sharing [ing, dividing
Parthol, a. discriminate; part-

Parthred, n. distinction; party
Parthrediad, n. discrimination
Parthredu, v. to discriminate
Parthredus, a. discriminating
Parthu, v. to partition, to separate [to pair
Paru, v. to put in continuity;
Parwar, a. silent; calm; still
Parwyd, n. a partition
Parwyden, n. a partition, a side
Parwydo, v. to make a partition
Parwydd, n. what is cognitive of acting or causing; a verb
Parwyddiad, n. a verb
Parwyddol, a. belonging to a verb
Parydd, n. a causer, a procurator
Pas, n. an exit; a cough: hooping cough [the Passover
Pasc, n. the festival of Easter,
Pasg, n. a feeding, a flattening
Pasgedig, a. fatted, fattened
Pasgiad, n. the act of fattening
Pasiad, n. a passing
Pasio, v. to expel; to pass
Pastwn, n. a long staff, a pole
Pastynu, v. to beat with a staff
Pathawr, adv. what matters it
Pau, n. an inhabited region
Paw, n. what extends round
Pawan, n. a spreader; a peacock
Pawb, pron. every body, all persons
Pawen, n. a paw, a claw, a hoof
Paweniad, n. a using of the paw
Pawenu, v. to use the paw
Pawgen, n. a sock for a foot
Pawl, n. a pole, a stake
Pawr, n. a pasture; a grazing
Pe, n. what is causative, an agent: conj. if, though
Pebre, n. a chatter, a chat
Pebyll, n. tents, pavillions
Pebyllio, v. to pitch tents
Pebyr, n. what is uttered
Pech, n. state of inaction; sin
Pechaberth, n. a sin-offering
Pechedur, n. sinner

Pechiad, n. committing of sin
Pechod, n. sin, an evil act
Pechu, v. to commit sin, to sin
Pêd, n. what bears onward, a [foot
Ped, conj. if, though
Pedair, a. four
Pedest, n. motion of the feet
Pedestr, n. a pedestrian
Pedestrol, a. foot-travelling
Pedestru, v. to travel on foot
Pedol, n. pedal, shoe
Pedoli, v. to shoe
Pedoliad, n. a shoeing
Pedolog, a. shod, as a horse
Pedrain, n. buttock, crupper
Pedrog, a. of a square form
Pedrongl, n. quadrangle, square
Pedroglawd, n. a quadrating
Pedrogledd, n. a quadrature
Pedrongli, v. to form a square
Pedroglyn, n. a quadrate
Pedronglog, a. quadrangular
Pedror, n. a quadrangle
Pedrori, v. to quadrate, to square
Pedroriad, n. a quadrating
Pedrus, a. hesitating, dubious
Pedrusaeth, n. hesitation, doubting [tation, indecision
Pedrusdod, Pedrusder, n. hesi
Pedrusiad, n. a hesitating
Pedruso, v. to start aside; to hesitate
Pedrusol, a. hesitating, doubting
Pedrusrwydd, n. doubtfulness
Pedryad, n. a quadrating, a squaring [square
Pedryael, n. what has four skirts;
Pedrychwal, a. four ways of spreading
Pedryd, n. a square
Pedrydant, n. a quadrate state
Pedrydiad, n. a quadrating; a perfecting [pieces
Pedryfal, n. what is of four
Pedryfan, n. a quarry; a quarter
Pedryfaniad, n. a quartering
Pedryfanu, v. to quarter

between four; a pinch be-
tween the three fingers and
the thumb
Pedrylliw, n. a perfect colour
Pedrylun, n. a perfect figure
Pedryo, v. to make of four parts
Pedryoli, v. to quadrate
Pedryor, n. a quadrate [square
Pedryori, v. to quadrate, to
Pedryran, n a quadrant
Pedwar, a. four [farthing
Pedwaran, n. fourth, quartern,
Pedwarcarn, n. four hoofs: a.
 four hoofed
Pedwarcarnog, a. four-footed,
 having, four hoofs
Pedwarcarniad, n. a galloping
Pedwarcarnu, v. to gallop
Pedwardull, n. quadriform
Pedwardyblyg, n, a quadrupli-
Pedwaredd, a. fourth [cate
Pedwarlad, n. a quaternion
Pedwariant, n. a quaternity
Pedwarblyg, a. four-fold
Pedwarochrol, a. quadrilateral
Pedwartroed, n. a quadruped
Pedwartroedol, a. four-footed
Pedwerydd,a. fourth ; a quartern
Peg, n. agent of expansion ; eight
 bushel measure, a quarter
Pegaid, n. contents of a quarter
Peged, n. a quarter measure
Pegor, n. a pivot; a pert one
Pegori, v. to form a pivot or axis
Pegwn, n. a pivot, pole, or axis
Pegwr, n. a pivot or axis
Pegynol, a. belonging to an axis
Pegynu, v. to form a pivot or axis
Pei, con. if it were, if it should be
Peidiad, n. a ceasing, a desisting
Peidio, v. to cease; to leave off
Peiliad, n. a raying; a display-
 ing [radiate
Peilio, v. to spread out ; to
Peiliged, n. a tribute of flour
Peilliad, n. a bolting
Peillied, n. bolted meal, flour
Peillio, v. to bolt, to searce

Peillion, n. fine flour, powder
Peiniad, n. a yeilding of bloom
Peinio, v.to yield bloom or farina
Peiriannol, a. instrumental
Peiriannoli, v. to render causa-
 tive
Peiriannu, v. to put in a state to
 act ; to organise; to harness
Pieriant, n. instrument, tool
Peiriannwr, Peiriannydd, n.
 organizer, harnesser
Peiriwyddiad, n. a verb
Peiriennyn, n. an instrument
Peisgwyn, n. the mapple tree
Peiswyn, n. chaff
Peithas, n. a scout, a scout boat
Peithiad, n. a making clear ; a
 laying open or waste [scouting
Peithiant, n. a laying open ; a
Peithin, Peithiw, a. being open
 or plain
Peithio, v. to lay open ; to scout
Peithiog, a open, desert, waste
Peithw, a. of plain open aspect
Peithwyld, n. the slay, or the
 reeds of a loom
Peithyn, n. what is open ; open
 surface; a tile; slay of a
 loom ; a cog
Peithyndo, n. a tiled roof
Peithynen, n. sheet; page; tile
Pel, n. a moving body; a ball
Peled, n. a ball, a bullet
Peledu, v. to throw a ball
Peleidral, n. a pushing of spears
Peleidriant, n. a radiation
Peleidrio, v. to radiate [pill
Pelen, n. a little ball; bullet;
Peleniad, n. a forming a ball
Pelenu, v. to form into a ball
Pe glb, n. a racket for a ball
Pelio, v. to ray, to brandish
Pelid, n. radiancy, splendour
Pelu, v. to throw a ball: to ball
Pelyd, n. stockings without feet
Pelydr, n. a ray, a beam
Pelydriad, n. a radiating
Pelydrog, a. radiant, gleaming

Pelydru, v. to radiate, to gleam
Pelydryn, n. a ray, a beam
Pell. a distant. remote, far
Pellâd, n. removing to a distance
Pel âu, v. to put far off; to go far or dis'ant
Pellder, n. remoteness, distance
Pelldrem, n. a far view
Pelldremiant, n. a far viewing
Pellebyr, n. telegraph
Pellen, n. a round mass, ball
Pellenaidd, a. like a ball
Pellenig, a. of distant range
Pellenigrwydd, n. remoteness
Pel enu, v. to form into a ball
Pellt, what is external; surface
Pen, n. a head; a chief; an end: a. head, chief, supreme
Penadur, n. supreme, sovereign
Penaduriaeth, n. a supremacy
Penaeth, n. supremacy, a principal
Penaethu, v. to act as a chief
Penaf, a. chief, most eminent
Penagored, a. open at the top
Pensig, n. a sovereign, a chief
Penant, n. supremacy; sway
Penardd, n. projec ion of a hill
Penarth, n. a promontory
Penaur, n. the yellow hammer
Penbaladr, a. particular
Penben, adv. wi.h heads together; loggerheads
Penbleth, n. distraction of head
Penboeth, a. hot headed
Penbwl, a. blunt-headed: stupid: n. blockhead; tadpole
Penbyledd, n. blockishness
Penbyllad, n. a tadpole
Pencais, n. receiver general
Pencelrddiad, n. chief singer
Pencelsiad, n. chief collector
Pencenedl, n. cheif of a family
Pencerdd, n. master of song
Penci, n. the dog-fish
Penciwdod, n. generalissimo
Penclwm, n. knot at the end
Pencynghor, n. chief counsellor

Pencynydd, n. chief huntsman
Penchiwban, a. light-headed
Penchiwbandod, n. capriciousness [brained
Penchiwbanu, v. to become hair-
Pendant, a. express, arbitrary
Pendefig, n. nobleman
Pendefiges, n. a lady of quality
Pendefigiaeth, n. state of chieftain
Penderfyniad, n. a conclusion
Penderfynu, v. to de.ermine
Pendew, a. thick-headed; stupid
Pendist, n. piazza, colonnade
Pendodaeth, n. superiority
Pendodi, v. to render peculiar
Pendodol, a. discriminative
Pendraffolach, adv. with head over heels
Pendramwnwgl, a. headlong
Pendraphen, a. huddled; confused
Pendrawn, a. giddy headed
Pendreiglo, v. to roll the head about [head
Pendrist, a. having a drooping
Pendro, v. to vertigo; staggers
Pendröi, v. to become giddy
Pendrondod, n. giddy-headedness
Pendroni, v. to be hair-brained
Pendrwm, a. heavy headed
Pendrymu, v. to grow top-heavy
Pendwmpian, v. to be nodding
Penddar, n. vertigo; giddiness
Penddaredd, n. giddiness
Penddariad, n. a growing giddy
Penddaru, v. grow gi idy-headed
Penddifaddeu, a. indispensable
Penddiged, n. an inflamed tumour, a bile [brownwort
Penddu, n. the bird black cap;
Penddluyn, n. a botch, a bilo
Penelin, n. the elbow
Penelino, v. to elbow
Penes, n. a lady of high rank
Peneuryn, n. the yellow-hammer
Penfain, a. having a pointed head or top; copped

Penfas, a. shallow-pated; stupid
Penfeddal, a. soft-headed; simple
Penfeddw, a. giddy-headed
Penfeinio, v. to accuminate
Penfelyn, a. yellow headed
Penfoel, a. bare-headed, bald headed [fish
Penfras, a. fat-headed: the cod
Penffestin, n. helmet
Penffestr, n. head-stall; collar
Penffetur, a. headstrong
Penffluwch, a. bushy-headed
Penffrwyn, n. head-stall, muzzle
Pen-gadarn, a. strong-headed
Pen-gacad, a. closed at the top
Pen-galed, a. hard-headed; knapweed [turned; obstinate
Pen-gam, a. having the head
Pen-gamrwvdd, n. wryness of the head; perverseness, obstinacy
Pen-glog, n. a scull, a noddle
Pen-gloi, to close the end
Pen-glwm, n. knot at the end
Pen-goch, a. red-headed; n. culerage
Pen-goll, a. having the end lost
Pen-grach, a. scabby-headed
Pen-grest, a. scurfy-headed
Pen-groes, a. having the end crossed
Pen-gron, a. round-head
Pen-grwn, a. having a round head [headed
Pen-grych, a. rough or curly
Pen-gyrniad, n. round headed
Pen-guwch, n. a cap, a bonnet
Penhwntian, v. to be tottering
Penhwyad, n. the pike or jack
Peniadur, n. a principal; a top
Penial, n. a capital; a chief
Peniant, n. capitation
Penig, n. a nip, a nib, a niddle
Penlas, a. blue-headed: n. the knapweed [knee
Penlin, n. top of the knee, a
Penliniad, n. a kneeling
Penlinio, v. to kneel down

Penlöyn, n. black-cap, titmouse
Penllad, n. supreme good
Penlle, n. head-stead; numskull
Penlliain, n. a head-cloth
Penllwyd, a. grey-headed: n. a grayling [head
Penllwydi, n. greyness of the
Penllyw, n. chief leader; the stone next to a corner stone
Penllywiawdwr, n. a general
Penllywodraeth, n. supreme government
Penllywydd, n. a sovereign
Penllywyddiaeth, n. sovereignty
Pennill, n. verse, stanza
Pennilliach, n. trifling verses
Pennillio, v. to form stanzas
Pennod, n. a close; a chapter
Pennoeth, n. a bare-headed
Penod, n. conclusion, end
Penodi, v. to specify, to assign
Penodiad, n. specification
Penodol, a. particular, especial; definite, specific
Penodoli, v. to render definitive
Penol, a. capital, principal
Penon, n. a pennant, a flag
Penor, n. a headpiece; a muzzle
Penpryd, n. visage, aspect
Penre, n. a hair-lace, a fillet
Penrhaith, n. what has chief right, the chief of the law
Penrheithiant, n. sovereignty
Penrudd, a. ruddy-headed
Penrwym, n. a head-band
Penrydd, a. loose-headed; loose ended
Penryn, n. promontory, cape
Pensach, n. the mumps
Pensaer, n. chief architect
Pensag, n. the hop-plant, hops
Pensedd, n. a supreme seat
Pensel, n. a grand standard
Penswyddog, n. chief officer
Pensyfrdan, a. light-headed
Pensyfrdanod, n. craziness
Pensyfrdanu, v. to craze the head
Pentan, n. a fire back, a hob

Penteulu, n. head of a family
Pentewyn, n. a firebrand
Penteyrnedd, n. chief of princes
Pentir, n. a headland; a land
Pentref, n. a village [steward
Pentrefaeth, n. a villagery
Pentwr, n. a raised heap
Penty, n. a penthouse, a shed
Pentyriad, n. accumulation
Pentyru, v. to heap, to amass
Pentywysog, n. supreme prince
Penu, to predominate, to specify
Penwag, a. empty headed: n. a herring
Penwan, a. weak-headed
Penwendid, n. weakness of head
Penwisg, n. a head dress
Penwn, n. a banner, a standard
Penwyn, Penwen, a. white headed: n. bald buzzard
Penwyni, n. whiteness of head
Penyd, n. atonement, penance
Penydiad, n. a doing penance
Penydiol, a. atoning, expiatory
Penygen, n. a paunch, a gut
Penynad, n. a chief-justice
Penysgafn, a. light-headed
Pepra, v. to keep chattering
Pepraeth, n. chattering, babbling
Pepru, v. to chatter, to prate
Pêr, n. what pervades; sweet fruit: a. delicious, sweet, luscious
Peran, n. a pear [cious
Perarogl, n. a perfume, aroma-
Perarogledd, n. perfumery
Perarogli, v. to perfume
Peraroglus, a. odorus, fragrant
Perâu, v. to become delicious

Perchenogaeth, n. ownership
Perchenogi, v. to possess, to own
Perchi, v. to respect, to revere
Perdra, n. deliciousness, sweetness
Pereiddio, v. to dulcify [ness
Pererin, n. a pilgrim
Pererindod, n. pilgrimage
Pererinio, v. to peregrinate
Perfagl, n. the herb periwinkle
Perfedd, n. centre; entrails
Perffaith, a. perfect, complete
Perffeithrwydd, n. perfection
Perffeithiad, n. a perfecting
Perffeithio, v. to perfect
Perging, n. a screen, a settle: a. skreening, sheltering
Peri, n. a causation, a cause: v. to cause; to bid
Periad, n. a causing; a bidding
Periagur, n. a causer, a cause
Periant, n. a causation
Perig, a. extreme; perilous
Periglo, v. to make extreme; to give extreme unction
Periglor, n. a curate, a priest
Perlais, n. a melodious voice
Perloes, n. rapture, ecstacy
Perlysiau, n. aromatic herbs; grocery [berllan, a redstart
Perllan, n. an orchard. Coch y
Perllys, n. sweet herbs; parsley
Peron, n. a cause; the Lord
Peror, n. melodist, musician
Peroriad, n. a producing of melody; a playing of music
Peroriaeth, n. melody; idle talk
Perioriaethu, v. to make a melody
Peroriant, n. practice of music
Perorio, to practise music

v. to appertain, to belong
Perthynad, n. an appertaining
Perthynas, n. relation; appurtenance
Perthynasol, a. appropriate
Perthynasoli, v. to render appropriate [priate
Perthynasu, v. to render appropriate
Perthynedigaeth, appropriation
Perthynol, a. pertaining, relative
Peru, v. to cause; to effect; to bid
Perwg, n. hurdy-gurdy [ders
Perwr, n. a causer; one who orders
Perwraidd, n. liquorice root
Perwydd, n. pear-trees
Perwyl, n. occasion, purpose
Perwylus, a. eventual, incidental
Perydd, n. a causator, a causer
Peryf, n. a causer; a sovereign
Peryg, n. what is extreme
Perygl, n. danger, peril
Perygledd, n. danger
Perygliad, n. an endangering
Peryglu, v. to run into danger
Peryglus, a. dangerous, perilous
Pes, conj. if [grow fat
Pesgi, v. to feed, to fatten; to
Pesgiad, n. a feeding, a fattening
Peswch, n. a cough
Pesychiad, n. a coughing
Pesychlyd, a. troubled with cough
Pesychlys, n. the coltsfoot
Pesychu, v. to force out; to cough
Petrus, a. apt to start; hesitating
Petrusad, n. a hesitating
Petrusder, n. hesitation, doubt
Petrusen, n. a startler; partridge
Petrusi, n. startling; hesitation
Petruso, v. to startle; to hesitate
Petrusol, a. startling; hesitating
Petryael, Petryal, n. a square: a. square
Peth, n. a thing, a something; a quantity a part [pausing
Peuad, Peuant, n. a panting. a
Peuo, v. to spread out; to pant, to puff; to pause, to hesitate
Peuol, a. panting; pausing

Peuawr, a. hourly: adv. hourly
Peues, n. place of rest; a country
Peufer, a. whining; neighing
Feuferu, v. to whine; to neigh
Peunoeth, a. nocturnal, nightly
Peunos, a. nocturnal, nightly
Pi, n. state of being in, a pie
Pia, n. a pie, a magpie
Piant, n. possession, ownership
Piau, v. to own, to possess
Pib, n. a pipe; a tube; a lax
Pibellu, n. a pipe, a duct, a tube
Pibelliad, n. a piping; a forming of a pipe
Pibellog, a. having a pipe [pipe
Pibellu, v. to pipe; to form a
Pibellwr, n. pipe man, a piper
Piben, n. a pipe, a duct, a flue
Piblyd, a. apt to squirt, squirting
Piblys, n. the flixweed
Pibo, v. to pipe; to squirt
Pibol, a. piping; squirting
Pibonwy, n. icicles, sleet
Pibori, n. a piping; a budding: v. to pipe; to tud
Piborig, a. piping; budding
Pibydd, n. piper, pipe player
Pibyddiaeth, n. pipe-playing
Picell, n. a dart, a javelin
Picellai, n. a dart thrower
Picellu, v. to throw a dart
Picffon, n. a pike staff
Picfforch, n. a pitchfork
Piciad, n. a darting, a going
Picio, v. to dart, to fly suddenly
Picwd, n. the prickled dog, the hound-fish
Picyn, n. a piggin, a noggin
Picynaid, n. a piggin-full
Pid, n. a tapering point
Piff, n. puff, sudden blast
Piffio, v. to puff, to whiff
Pig, n. a point, a pike, a nip; a bill, a beak; the pip
Pigawglys, n. the spinach
Pigiain, a. sharp-pointed
Pigfan, n. mark of a point
Pigfaniad, n. a puncturing

| PIG | 257 | PLA |

Pigfanu, v. to puncture
Pigfanlad, n. accumination
Pigfeinio, v. to accuminate
Pigin, n. picking pain, stitch
Pigion, n. pickings; selections
Pigl, n. the herb hound's-tongue
Pigo, v. to prick, to pick, to peck
Pigoden, n. a pickle: a shrew
Pigog, a. pointed, full of points,
Pigoga, n. spinach [prickly
Pigwn, n. a cone; a beacon
Pigwrn, n. pinacle, spire
Pigyn, n. a stitch, a pleurisy
Pigyrnu, v. to spire, to briskle up
Pil, n. what hovers; a serjeant; a peal; a creek
Pila, n. a finch
Pilia, n. a moth, a butterfly
Pilaid, a. transient, frail; mean
Pilan, n. a sparrow-hawk
Pilc, n. what turns about
Pilcod, n. minnows
Pilcota, v. to catch minnows
Pildin, n. a gall by riding
Pilden, n. cuticle, rind; fringe
Pilenu, v. to form a cuticle
Piler, n. a pillar, a column
Pileru, v. to build upon pillars, to erect pillars
Pilg, n. a vessel of bak; a laver
Piliad, n. a paring, a peeling
Pilio, v. to peel, to pare, to strip
Pilion, n. peelings, strippings
Pilionen, n. a thin peel, a film
Pilo, n. rod of an apparitor
Pilus, a. transient, frail; mean
Pilwrn, n. a small dart
Pilyn, n. a tegument: a clout; a pillion
Pilynu, v. to put on a vesture
Pilysyn, n. a robe, a pelisse
Pill, n. a pivot; a shaft; a stem, a stock; a tong; a strong hold; a frame; a heater
Pillgorn, n. the neck joint
Pillgun, n. a plug, a stopple
Pillio, v. to shaft, to peg

Pillyn, n. a small stem; a peg
Pin, n. a pin; a stile, a pen
Pinc, n. a sprig; a finch: a. smart, brisk; gay; fine
Pincen, n. a sprig; a spray
Pincio, v. to cover with sprigs
Piniwn, n. a gable end
Pinwydd, n. pine wood
Pioden, n. magpie, pie [a jay
Piogen, n. a pie. Piogen y coed,
Pipgnau, n. chesnuts
Pipian, v. to pipe, to pule
Pipre, n. a diarrhœa, a lax
Piser, n. a jug, a pitcher
Pisg, n, a blisters, bladders, pods
Pisgen, n. a wheal; a linden
Pisgenu, v. to blister; to pod
Pisgwrn, n. a pimple, a wheal
Pisgwydd, n. linden trees
Pisgyrnu, v. to break out in pimples
Pistyll, n. spout; cataract
Pistylliad, n. a spouting out
Pistyllio, v. to spout out
Piswydd, n. the dogberry wood
Pitan, n. a teat, nipple
Pitw, a. minute, petty
Pith, n. what is granulated
Pithell, n. the fish shaid [plague
Pla, n. what breaks out; the
Plâd, n. a flat piece; a plate
Pladren, n. one who flaunts
Pladres, n. a flaunting woman
Pladur, n. a scythe
Pladuro, v. to use a scythe
Pladurwr, n. a mower [titlon
Plaid, n. a side, a party; a par-
Plan, n. a ray; a scion, a shoot
Planad, n. a shooting off: a me-
Planc, n. a plank, a board [teor
Planed, n. a shooting body; a planet
Planfa, Planigfa, n. plantation
Planiad, n. a shooting; a plant-
Planigyn, n. a plant, a shoot [ing
Planol, a. shooting; planting
Plant, n. offspring, children
Plantos, n. little children

Planu, v. to shoot off; to plant
Plâs, n. a hall, a palace
Plast, n. what is spread out
Plastr, n. a plaister, a daub
Plastriad n. a plaistering
Plau, v. to infect with a plague
Pledren, n. a bladder
Pledru, v. to stretch out
Pledryn, n. a slang, a slip
Pleiden, n. a hurdle, a wattling
Pleidgar, a. factious, partial
Pleidiad, n. a siding with; parti-
Pleidio, v. to take a part [sanship
Pleidiol, a. adherent; belonging to a party
Pleidydd, n. a partisan
Pleiniad, n. a radiation
Plent, n. a ray; a slide
Plentyn, n. a child, a baby
Plentynaidd, a. childish, babyish
Pleth, n. a plait, a braid
Plethol, a. plaiting, wreathing
Plethbin, n. a bobbin [ing
Plethiad, n. a plaiting, a braid-
Plethu, v. to plait, to wreath
Pliciad, n. a peeling off [strip
Plicio, v. to pluck, to peel, to
Plig, n. a plucking off, a peeling
Pling, n. a stripping off
Plingo, v. to flay, to strip off
Plisg, n. shells, husks, pods
Plisgo, v. to shell, to husk
Plith, n. the state of being blended [or mixed together
Plitho, v. to blend, to be blended
Ploc, Plocyn, n. a block, a plug
Plu, n. feathers, down
Pluad, n. a feathering, a fledging
Pluog, a. feathered, fledged
Plucan, n. soft feathers, down
Pludd, n. what is flexible
Pluddo, v. to render flexible
Pluen, n. a feather, a plume
Pluenu, v. to plume; to fledge
Pluf, n. plumage, feathers
Plufol, a. feathering, pluming
Plufen, n. a plume, a feather
Plufiad, n. a feathering

Pluiio, v. to plume; to deplu
Plw, n. what spreads out
Plwc, n. a space, a while; a d
Plwca, n. a spread; a plash
Plwng, n. a plunge, a splash
Plwm, n. lead [pa
Plwy, Plwyf, n. community;
Plwyfogaeth, n. parish juris tion
Plwyfogi, v. to settle in a parish
Plwyfoli, v. to render parochial
Plwyn, n. maturity; puberty [ty
Plwyno, v. to have signs of puber-
Ply, n. what is flexible or soft
Plydd, a. delicate; limber, pliant
Plyddau, v. to render pliant
Plyddo, v. to soften; to grow limber [or limber
Plyddiad, n. a rendering pliant
Plyg, n. a double, a fold
Plygain, n. early morn, dawn
Plygaint, n. dawn, day-spring
Plygeiniol, a. dawning; matin
Plygiad, n. a doubling, a folding
Plygiant, n. a duplication
Plygiedydd, n. tweezers
Plygol, a. doubling, folding
Plygu, v. to double, to fold
Plym, n. what agonises
Plymol, a. agonising, writhing
Plymen, n. plummet; flake
Plymiad, n. a leadening
Plymio, v. to leaden, to plumb
Plynu, v. to cover with lead
Po, n. what comprehends: conj. if, by how much
Pob, a. each, every
Pôb, n. a bake: a. baked
Poban, n. an oven; a roaster
Pobedig, baked, roasted, toasted
Pobi, v. to bake, to roast
Pobiant, n. a baking, a batch
Pobl, n. people
Poblach, n. low people, mob
Pobli, v. to people, to colonise
Pobliad, n. a peopling
Poblog, a. peopled, populous
Poblogaeth, n. populousness

Poblogi, v. to make populous
Pobty, n. a bakehouse
Poburies, n. a baking woman
Pobydd, n. a baker
Pobyddiaeth, n. art of baking
Podi, v. to take in, to comprehend
Poen, n. pain, torment, agony
Poenedigaeth, n. a tormenting
Poeni, v. to pain, to suffer pain
Poeniad, n. a paining, a tormenting
Poenol, a. tormenting, paining
Poenus, a. painful; toiling
Poer, n. spittle, saliva
Pocrai, n. bastard pellitory
Poeri, v. to spit, to expectorate
Poeriad, n. a spitting
Poeriant, n. a salivation
Pocrol, a. spitting, salivarous
Poeryn, n. a spitter; a sycophant
Poes, n. state of being
Poesi, v. to be existing
Poeth, a. hot, scorching, fiery
Poethder, n. hotness, heat
Poethi, v. to heat; to be heated
Pocthiad, Poethiant, n. a heating
Poethni, n. hotness, heat
Poethol, a. heating, burning
Poethwg, n. torridity, aridity: n. the razorbill
Poethwyn, n. burning passion
Polio, v. to fix a pole
Polion, n. stakes, poles
Polioni, v. to set poles
Ponar, n. a puff: a pod
Ponc, n. a hillock, a tump
Poncen, n. a small hillock
Ponciad, n. a swelling up
Poncio, v. to swell, to puff
Poncyn, n. a small hillock

Porch, n. a pig, a swine
Porchell, n. a tiny pig
Porchelliad, n. a pigging
Porchellu, v. to bring pigs
Porchellyn, n. a little pig
Porfa, n. pasture, grass
Porfâd, n. a pasturing
Porfadir, n. pasture-ground
Porfâu, v. to depasture
Porfel, n. pasture, grass
Porfelu, v. depasture
Porfelydd, n. a pasturer
Porffor, Porphor, a. purple
Pori, v. to graze, to browse
Poriad, n. a grazing, a browsing
Porianu, v. to depasture
Poriant, n. pasturage, browsing
Poriol, a. pasturing, grazing
Portreiad, n. a pattern, a sampler, a model
Porth, n. aid, help what bears; sustenance; a carriage; a ferry; a port; a gateway
Portha, v. to afford aid or help
Porthfa, n. a carrying place; a port [bear, to convey
Porthi, v. to aid, to support, to
Porthiad, n. a helping on; a bearing
Porthiadu, v. to be a support
Porthianna, v. to provide; to act as a drover
Porthianuu, v. to render support
Porthiauuus, a. having support
Porthiant, n. support, succour
Porthid, n. assistance, support
Porthladd, n. a port, a harbour
Porthle, n. a carrying place
Porthloedd, n. means of support
Porthlys, n. a porte-mote

Porthordy, n. a porter's lodge
Porthori, v. to act as porter
Porthoriaeth, n. a porter's office
Porthwy, n. assistance, support
Porthwr, n. a provider; a feeder; a porter
Porthwys, n. a ferryman
Poset, n. curdled milk, posset
Posfardd, n. a preceptive bard
Posiad, n. a questioning, a posing
Posiar, n. a fattened hen
Posio, v. to examine, to pose
Posned, n. a squat; a skillet
Post, n. a post, a pillar
Postio, v. to put up a post
Pot, n. a pot
Potel, n. a bottle; a truss
Poteliad, n. a bottling
Poteli, v. to bottle; to truss
Poten, n. a paunch; a pudding
Potenig, n. a little paunch
Potenog, a. having a paunch
Potenu, v. to form a paunch
Potes, n. a pottage, broth, soup
Potiad, n. a potting; potation
Pot, v. to pot; to pipple
Poth, n. what bulges; a boss
Pothan, n. a bump, a boss; a cub
Pothell, n. a wheal, a blister
Pothellog, a. puffy; blistered
Pothellu, v. to puff; to blister
Pothon, n. a boss; a cub
Powys, n. a state of rest
Prad, n. a gentle spread; a rub
Praff, a. ample; thick round
Praffder, n. thickness round
Praffu, v. thicken in compass
Praidd, n. a flock, a herd; booty.
Pranc, n. a frolic, a prank [prey
Prancio, v. to play a prank
Pratiad, n. a stroking, a coaxing
Pratio, v. to stroke, to coax
Praw, Prawf, profio n, n. an essay, a trial, a proof
Prawen, n. an essay; a cast in play
Prawfaen, n. a touchstone
Pre, n. the origin of a course
Pred, n. a stray; a migration

Preg, n. a greet, a greeting
Pregeth, n. a sermon
Pregethiad, n. a preaching
Pregethu, v to preach
Pregethwr, n. a preacher
Preidiad, n. a migrating
Preidio, v. to migrate
Preiddio, n. a herding; predation
Preiddio, v. to herd, to collect a herd; to predate
Preinio, v to carouse
Praethiad, a practising
Preithig, a. belonging to practice
Preithio, v. to practise
Prelad, n. a prelate
Pren, n. a tree, a timber
Prenfol, n. a wooden chest
Prenial, n, a coffer, a shrine
Prenio, v. to timber; to bar
Prenol, n. a busk of stays
Prensaer, n. a carpenter
Pres, n what is quick, sharp, or smart: haste; brushwood; fuel; anything streweed; a crib; a place of resort; brass: a. quick, hasty; sharp, over-running, frequent; present
Preseb, n. a crib, a stall
Presel, a place over-run; a brake
Preseliad, n. a yielding of brakes
Preselu, v. to be over-run of foul
Preselyn, n. a brake, a thicker
Presen, n. the present; this wife
Presenol. a. imminent; present
Presenoldeb, n. presence
Presenu, v. to make present
Present, n. a present state
Presiad, n. a hastening: a frequenting
Presol, a. imminent; quick
Prest, n. quickness, smartness
Prest, a. ready, quick; soon
Prestl, a. ready, smart fluent
Prestlaidd, a. apt to prattle
Presu, v. to hasten; to frequent
Preswyl, n. a being present or ready; a tarrying; habitation
Preswylfa, n. a place of residence

| PRE | 261 | PRO |

Preswylfod, n. a dwelling place
Preswyliad, n. a residing
Preswyliaeth, n. habitation
Preswylio, v. to fix an abode
Preswyliog, a. having resort
Preswylydd, n. an inhabitant
Pric, n. a stick; a broach
Prid, n. price, value; ransom: a. valuable, precious, dear
Pridiad, n. a setting a price
Pridiant, n. a ransoming
Pridio v, to set a price to ransom
Pridiol, a. equivalent; redeeming
Pridioldeb, n. mould, earth, soil a tile
Priddell, n. a mass of earth, a clod;
Priddell, a. consisting of masses of earth; glebous
Priddelydd, n. a tile maker
Pridden, n. an earthen vessel
Priddfaen, n. a brick; a burnt tile
Priddgalch, n. calcareous earth
Priddgist, n. potter's clay
Priddiad, n. a doing with earth
Priddin, a. of earth, earthen
Priddlestri, n. earthen ware
Priddlyd, a. mixed with earth
Priddlydu, v. to become earthy
Priddo, v. to earth; to cover with earth; to become earth
Priddol, a. of mould, of earth
Prif, a. prime, principal, chief
Prifachos, n. primary cause
Prifansawdd, n. primary quality
Prifardd, n. a primitive bard
Prifder, n. primeness; origin
Prifddinas, n. a metropolis
Prifiad, n. a thriving, a growing
Prifio, v. to thrive, to grow up
Prifies, n. a chief good
Priflys, n. a supreme court
Prifnawd, n. original habit
Prifnod, n. prime point; epoch
Prifoed, n. a primitive age
Prifran, n. primary division
Prifred, n. primary course
Prifsymudai, n. prime mover

Prifwyd, n. a chief sin
Prifysgol, n. a primary school
Priffordd, n. a high road
Prill, n. a little brook, a rill
Prin, n. what is of slight trace a. scarce, rare, scant, sparc adv. scarcely
Prinâu, v. to make or grow scarc
Prinder, n. scarcity, want
Print, n. what forms a notch,
Printiad, n. a printing [prin
Printio, v. to imprint, to print
Prinwydden, n. a scarlet oak
Priod, appropriate; fit; owned married
Priodadwy, a. marriageable
Priodas, n. marriage, a weddin
Priodasfab, n. a bridegroom
Priodasferch, n. a bride
Priodasgerdd, n. epithalamium
Priodasol, a. matrimonial
Priodedig, a. appropriated
Priodfab, n. a bridegroom
Priodferch, n. a bride
Priodi, v. to espouse, to marry
Priodiad, n. a marrying
Priodol, a. appropriate; marrie
Priodoldeb, n. appropriateness
Priodolder, n. propriety; attri bute; property; title
Priodoli, v. to appropriate
Priodoliad, n. appropriation
Priodolaeth, n. an attribute
Priodoliaethu, v. to attribute
Priodor, n. proprietor; a nativ
Priodori, v. to be a proprietor
Priodoriaeth, n. proprietorship
Prion, n. origination; imps
Prionyn, n. a little imp
Pris, n. rate, value, price
Prisiad, n. a valuation
Prisio, v. to value, to prize
Prisiedig, a. valued, appraised
Proc, n. thrust, a stab
Prociad, n. thrusting, stabbing
Procio, v. to thrust, to stab
Proest, n. a counterchange
Profadwy, a. provable, essayable

Profedig, a. proved, approved
Profedigaeth, n. a probation; a temptation
Profi, v. to prove; to taste
Profiad, n. a proving; a probation; a tasting; an essay
Profiadol, a. probationary
Profiant, n. a probation
Proffes, n. profession, vow
Proffesiad, n. a professing
Proffesu, v. to profess, to vow
Proffeswr, n. a professor
Prophwyd, n. a prophet
Prophwydo, v. to prophecy
Prophwydol, a. prophetical
Prophwydoliaeth, n. prophecy
Prudd, a. prudent; serious; sad
Pruddâu, v. to become serious
Prudd-der, n. seriousness
Prwy, n. what reaches forward; an agent
Prwys, n. tendency to protrude
Prwysg, n. what is impending or surmounting
Prwysiad n. a protruding
Prwyso, v. to protrude
Prwyst, n. what causes anxiety
Prwysti, n. anxiety, solicitude
Prwystl, a. tumultuous, bustling
Prwystlo, v. to bustle, to agitate
Pry, n. produce, food, victuals
Pryd, n. a period, a season, a time; mealtime; aspect: adv. seeing that, as it is, whilst
Pryder, n. anxiety, solicitude
Pryderiad, n. a being anxious
Pryderol, a. anxious; providen
Pryderu, v to be anxious
Pryderus, a. anxious, thoughtful
Prydfardd, n. recording bard
Prydferth, a. handsome, comely
Prydferthwch, n. comeliness
Prydferthu, v. to render comely
Prydiad, n. a delineating of nature
Prydiaith, n. poetical language
Prydio, v. to fix a season
Prydiol, a. timely, seasonable
Prydiaeth, n. milk at once
Prydlon, a. seasonable
Prydlonder, n. seasonableness
Prydnawn, n. the afternoon
Prydnawnbryd, Prydnawnfwyd, n. dinner
Prydnawn-gwaith, n. afternoon
Pryrnawnol, a. of the afternoon
Prydred, n. a chronology
Prydn, v. to delineate, to poetise
Prydus, a. comely; seasonable
Prydydd, n. poet
Prydyddes, n. a poetess
Prydyddiad, n. a poetising
Prydyddiaeth, n. poetry
Prydyddol, a. poetic, poetical
Prydyddu, v. to compose poetry
Prydd, n. what is productive: a. teeming, luxuriant
Pryddâd, n. a luxuriating
Pryddest, n. poetics; metre
Pryddestu, v. to compose metrically [vermin: a worm
Pryf, n. what is generated;
Pryfad, n. an animal; vermin
Pryfediad, v. vermination
Pryfedu, v. to breed worms
Pryfeta, v. to hunt vermin
Pryfig, a. having worms
Pryfyn, n. a worm
Pryn, n. a take; purchase; merit: a. bought, purchased [hand
Pryned, n. what takes hold; a
Prynedig, a. purchased, bought
Prynedigaeth, n. redemption
Prynol, a. purchasing, buying
Prynu, v. to take hold; to buy; to redeem [a redeemer
Prynwr, n. a buyer, a purchaser,
Prysel, n. a covert, a brake
Pryselu, v. to become braky
Prysg, n. what is over; brushwood
Prysgl, n. a copse; brushwood
Prysgliach, n. stunted trees
Prysglwyn, n. a copse
Prysgoed, n. brushwood
Prysgyll, n. a hazel copse
Prystell, n. tumult, uproar

| PRY | 263 | PWY |

Prysu, v. to form a covert or resort [ious
Prysur, a. busy, diligent ; ser-
Prysurdeb, n. assiduity ; haste
Prysuriad, n. a hastening on
Prysuro, v. to make haste
Prysurwch, n. state of haste
Puch, n. sigh; grunt [long
Pucho, v. to sigh; to pant; to
Pud, n. what tends to allure
Pul, n. what tends to straiten
Pum, n. tendency to form: a. five
Pumbys, a. five-fingered
Pumcanfed, a. five hundredth
Pumcanmil, a. five hundred thousand
Pumcant, a. five hundred
Pumdalen, n. a cinquefold
Pumdeg, a. fifty
Pummil, a. five thousand
Pumnalen, n. a cinquefold
Pumochor, n. a pentagon
Pump, a. five
Pumplyg, a. quintuple
Pumsill, a. of five syllables
Pumtant, n. a pentachord
Pumtro, a. five times or turns
Pumwaith, adv. five times
Pun, n. what is equal or even: a. equal, equivalent
Punt, n. pound, twenty shillings
Pur, n. what is pure : a. pure: adv. essentially ; very
Purad, n. a depurgation
Purdan, n. a purgatory
Purdeb, n. purity; sincerity
Puredigaeth, n. purification
Puredigol, a. purefactory
Puredd, n. purity, pureness
Pureiddio, v. to render pure
Puren, n. a sifting screen
Puriad, n. a purifying
Puriannol, a. purificative
Puriannu, v. to purify
Puriant, n. a purifying
Purion, adv. purely ; very well
Purlan, a. purely clean
Puro, v. to purify, to cleanse

Purol, a. purifying, cleansing
Puten, n. a whore, a harlot
Puteindra, n. whoredom
Puteindy, n. bawdy house
Puteinig, a. whorish, adulterous
Puteinio, v. to go a whoring
Puteiniol a. meretricious
Puteiniwr, n. a whoremonger
Pw, n. a tendency to put off
Pwca, n. a hobgoblin, a fiend
Pwci, n. a hobgoblin, a goblin
Pwd, n. a rot ; a rot in sheep
Pwdr, a. rotten, corrupt
Pwff, n. a puff, a sharp blast
Pwffio, v. to come in puffs [out
Pwg, n. what pushes or swells
Pwng, n. a cluster ; a crop
Pwngiad, n. a teeming
Pwngo, v. to teem ; to cluster
Pwngol, a. teeming; clustering
Pwl, a. blunt, obtuse ; dull
Pwll, n. a pool ; a puddle
Pwm, n. tendency to swell out
Pwmp, n. a round mass, a lump
Pwmpio, v. to thump, to bang: v. to boss, to knob
Pwmplog, a. bossed knobbed
Pwn, n. a pack; burden
Pwnc, n. point, subject
Pwniad, n. a burdening
Pwnio, v. to burden; to bang
Pwnt, n. aggregate ; a reservoir
Pwr, n. what extends ; a worm
Pwsach, n. a loud outcry
Pwt, n. any short thing
Pwtan, n. a squat female
Pwtiad, n. a butting, a poking
Pwtian, v. to keep poking
Pwtio, v. to push, to poke
Pwtwn, n. a liquor; whiskey
Pwtyn, n. a short round body
Pwy, n. a beat; a butt: adv. in advanced position: pron. who
Pwyad, n. a beating, a battering
Pwyo, v. to beat, to batter
Pwybynag, pron. whosoever
Pwyll, n. impulse; reason, sense, discretion. Gan bwyll, gently

Pwyllad, n. impulse; reason
Pwyllig, a. rational: discreet
Pwyllineb, n. rationality
Pwyllo, v. to impel; to reason; to consider
Pwyllog, a. having impulse, rational, considerate
Pwyllus, a. impulsive; rational
Pwyniad, n. a spike, a skewer
Pwynt, n. a point; plight
Pwyntel, n. a pencil; a brush
Pwyntiad, n. a pointing; a putting in good plight
Pwyntio, v. to point; to perfect; to fatten
Pwyntl, n. a pointed end
Pwys, n. state of rest; a weight; a pound weight
Pwysel, n. a bushel [ous
Pwysfawr, a. weighty, moment-
Pwysi, n. weight, heaviness
Pwysiad, a pressing; a weighing
Pwysig, a. pressing; weighty
Pwyso, v. to press, to weigh
Pwyth, n. a point; stitch; gift; at a bidding. Talu pwyth, to retaliate
Pwythiad, n. a stitching
Pwytho to thrust in; to stitch
Py, n. what is involved: a. what
Pyb, n. what is energetic
Pyblu, v. to invigorate
Pybyl, n. energy, vigour
Pybyr, n. strenuous, stout
Pybyriad, n. invigoration
Pybyru, v. to take courage
Pybyrwch, n. stoutness
Pyd, n. a pit; a snare; danger
Pydaw, Pydew, n. a quag; a spring
Pydol, a. snaring; perilous
Pydoldeb, n. dangerousness
Pydredd, n. a rottenness
Pydriad, n. a rotting
Pydru, v. to rot, to putrify
Pydd, n. a state of running out
Pyddiad, n. a running out
Pyddu, v. to run or spread out

Pyg, n. pitch, rosin of pine
Pygiad, n. a doing with pitch
Pyglian, n. a pitch plaster
Pygliw, n. a pitch colour
Pyglys, n. the wild fennel
Pygwydden, n. a pine tree
Pyngiad, n. a clustering
Pyngu, v. to teem, to cluster
Pyledd, n. bluntness; dullness
Pylgiant, n. dawn of day
Pyli, n. bluntness; dullness
Pyliad, n. a blunting
Pylor, n. dust, powder
Pyloriad, n. a powdering
Pyloru, v. to powder
Pyloryn, n. a grain of powder
Pylu, v. to blunt; to grow dull
Pylliad, n. forming of a pit
Pymtheg, n. fifteen
Pymthegfed, n. fifteenth
Pymthegnos, n. a fortnight
Pyn, n. what is in contact
Pyna, Pynag, adv. otherwise: a. soever
Pynas, n. a tribe, a nation
Pyncio, v. to note; to descant
Pynciol, a. noting; descanting
Pynfarch, n. the pack-horse; a dam
Pyniad, n. a burdening
Pynio, v. to burden, to load
Pyniol, a. burdening, loading
Pynioreg, n. a pack-saddle
Pyniori, Pynorio, v. to put on a load
Pyr, n. what spires; a fir: adv forward, toward
Pyrag, adv. wherefore, why
Pyrchwyn, n. crest of a helmet
Pyrgwyn, n. crest of a plume
Pyrdwyo, v. to point forward
Pys, n. pease, pulse
Pysen, n. a single pea, a pea
Pysg, n. a fish
Pysgodfa, n. a fishery
Pysgodlyn, n. a fishpond
Pysgodwr, n. a fisherman
Pysgodyn, n. a single fish

Pysgol, a. piscatory, of fish
Pysgota, v. to fish, to angle
Pysgydd, n. an ichthyologist
Pysgyddiaeth, n. ichthyology
Pystylad, n. restless motion
Pystyled, v. to be agog; to caper
Pystylwyn, n. a saddle crupper
Pyth, n. a period; a world: adv. ever, never
Pythefnos, n. a fortnight
Pythol, a. ever, eternal
Python, n. system of the world
Pythori, v. to be anxious
Pyw, n. a member, a limb: a. in order; complete

R

RHA, n. what forces; ertness
Rhaol, n. a forcing; impulse
Rhab, n. force; control
Rhabu, v. to control, to check
Rhac, n. what is opposite; a wrest; a spine; prep. before, from; for
Rhaca, n. a spectacle, a show
Rhacai, Rhacan, n. a rake
Rhacanad, n. a raking
Rhacanu, v. to rake
Rhaciant, n. advancement
Rhacio, v. to come forward
Rhaco, adv. yonder, there
Rhach, n. what is forced out
Rhad, n. grace, favour
Rhad, a. free, gratis; cheap
Rhadfawr, a. gracious; virtuous
Rhadferth, a. beneficent
Rhadferthwch, n. beneficence
Rhadforedd, n. graciousness
Rhadlon, a. gracious, kind
Rhadlonaeth, Rhadlondeb, n. graciousness
Rhadloni, v. to be gracious
Rhadrodd, n. free gift

Rhadu, v. to render free
Rhadwehyn, a. grace-diffusing
Rhadd, n. advance, going on
Rhae, n. constraint; battle
Rhael, n. bent, inclination
Rhaf, n. a spread, a diffusion
Rhafnwydd, n. buckthorns
Rhafol, n. service tree berries
Rhafon, n. berries growing in clusters; service tree berries
Rhafu, v. to spread, to diffuse
Rhaff, n. a rope, a cord
Rhaffan, n, a rope [rope
Rhaffio, v. to rope, to make a
Rhag, n. a front, a van; an entrance: prep before, against; from
Rhagachub, v. to get foremost
Rhagadail, n. an out-building
Rhagadrodd, n. a preface
Rhagaddasu, v. to fit before hand
Rhagaddewid, n. a previous promise
Rhagaddfed, a. precocious
Rhagafael, n. previous hold
Rhagagori, v. to open before
Rhagagweddu, v. to perform
Rhagangen, n. prior necessity
Rhagair, n. a leading word
Rhagalw, v. to call beforehand
Rhagamcan, n. a prenotion
Rhagammheu, v. to doubt before hand [ment
Rhagammod, n. previous agree-
Rhagamnaid, n. previous signal
Rhagamser, n. previous time
Rhaganfon, v. to send before
Rhagansawdd, n. prior quality
Rhagaraeth, n. prolegamena
Rhagarawd, n. exordium
Rhagarchwaeth, n. foretaste
Rhagarfaeth, n. predestination
Rhagarfaethu, v. to predestinate, to predispose
Rhagarfog, a. forearmed
Rhagarganfod, v. to foresee
Rhagargoel, n. a foretoken
Rhagarian, n. earnest money

Rhagarlwy, n. prepared food
Rhagarnawdd, n. a plough ta l
Rhagarswyd, n. previous dread
Rhagarwain, v. to lead before
Rhagarwedd, n. predisposition
Rhagarwydd, n. a prognostic
Rhagattal, n. a with-holding
Rhagateb, n. a prior answer
Rhagawd, n. a going before; a going against; opposition v. to go before; to stop
Rhagawdl, n. a leading rhyme
Rhagawl, a. opposite, opposing
Rhagbarodi, Rhagbarotöï, v. to prepare before
Rhagbenaeth, n. vicegerent
Rhagbennodi, v. to predetermine
Rhagborth, n. outer gat
Rhagbrofi, v. to foretaste
Rhagbryder, n. precaution
Rhagbrynu, v. to forestal
Rhagbwyso, v. to weigh before
Rhagchwaeth, n. a foretaste
Rhagchware, n. a prelude
Rhagchwedlu, v. to prologue
Rhagchwegr, n. grandmother-in-law [in-law
Rhagchwegrwm, n. grandfather-
Rhagchwilio, v. to search before
Rhagdal, n. frontlet, frontstall : n. payment, beforehand
Rhagdebygu, v. to presuppose
Rhagdeimlo, v. to feel before hand
Rhagder, n. advanced post
Rhagderfynu, v. to predetermine
Rhagdestun, preliminary theme
Rhagdraethawd, n. prolegomena
Rhagdrefnu, v. to preordain
Rhagdy, n. an outhouse
Rhagdyb, n. a preconceit
Rhagdyn, n. fore-draught
Rhagdyst, n. a prior witness
Rhagddangos, v. to premonstrate
Rhagddant, n. a fore-tooth [fore
Rhagddarbodi, v. to provide be-
Rhagddarlun, n. prefiguration

Rhagddarmerthu, v. to prepare before
Rhagddarn, n. a fore-piece
Rhagddarparu, to furnish before
Rhagddawn, n. a previous gift
Rhagddeall, v. to understand before
Rhagddelw, n. a prototype [fore
Rhagdderbyn, v. to receive be-
Rhagddewis, n. previous choice
Rhagddiogelu, v. to secure beforehand
Rhagddirnad, n. a presurmise
Rhagddod, n. a prefix [fix
Rhagddodi, v. to prepose, to pre-
Rhagddor, n. fore-door, wicket
Rhagddrws, n. an outer door
Rhagddryll, n. a fore piece
Rhagddychymyg, n. presupposal
Rhagddyddio, v. to antedate
Rhagddyled, n. prior debt
Rhagddywediad, n. gainsaying, con'adiction
Rhagedrych, v. to look before
Rhagenw, n. a pronoun
Rhagerchi, v. to pre-require
Rhagetholi, v. to pre-elect
Rhagfarn, n. a prejudice
Rhagfed, a. foremost, anterior
Rhagfeddiant, n. preoccupancy
Rhagfeddyliad, n. precognition
Rhagfeio, v. to blame before
Rhagflaeniad, n. a preceding
Rhagflas, n. a foretaste
Rhagfod, n. prior existence
Rhagfoddio, v. to please before-
Rhagfoel, a. bald before [hand
Rhagfraint, n. a preiogative
Rhagfur, n. a contramure
Rhagfwriad, n. a forecasting
Rhagfyfyrio, v. to premediate
Rhagfyned, v. to go before
Rhagfynegi, v. to prenunciate
Rhagfyr, n. December, the last month of the year
Rhagfyrâu, v. to foreshorten
Rhaggaer, n. advance work
Rhagganfod, v. to foresee

Rhagglod, n. former fame
Rhaggludo, v. to heap before or in front
Rhagglywed, v. to hear before
Rhaggymeriad, n. prolepsis
Rhaghanfod, n. pre-existence
Rhagholi, v. to examine before
Rhaglafar, a. prolocutory
Rhaglamu, v. to step before
Rhaglaw, n. deputy; lieutenant
Rhaglawn, n. first filling in
Rhaglefain, v. to proclaim
Rhaglewychu, v. to illumine
Rhaglith, n. a prelection
Rhagluniaeth, n. providence
Rhagluniaethol, a. providential
Rhaglunio, v. to perform; to provide
Rhaglyd, n. forecast; providence
Rhaglyw, n. a deputy governor
Rhaglywiaeth, n. prefecture
Rhagnodi, v. to mark before
Rhagnoethi, v. to make bare before
Rhagodfa, n. an ambuscade
Rhagodi, v. to get before
Rhagofal, n. a precaution
Rhagofyn, v. to bespeak
Rhagolwg, n. prospect; foresight
Rhagor, n. superiority; difference; more
Rhagorddwyn, a. excellent
Rhagorfraint, n. prerogative
Rhagori, v. to surpass
Rhagoriad, n. a surpassing
Rhagoriaeth, n. excellency; difference
Rhagorol, a. superior, excellent
Rhagoroldeb, n. excellence
Rhagosod, v. to set before
Rhagraith, n. deliberation
Rhagred, n. a prior course
Rhagrediad, n. forerunning
Rhagreithio v. to deliberate
Rhagrith, n. hypocrisy
Rhagrithio, v. to dissimulate
Rhagrithiwr, n. a dissimulator, a hypocrite

Rhagrwymo, v to bind before
Rhagrwystro, v. to preclude
Rhagrybuddiad, n. forewarning
Rhagsail, n. prior foundation
Rhagsain, n. a leading sound
Rhagsefydlu, v. to pre-establish
Rhagsylwi, v. to remark beforehand
Rhagsyllu, v. to look forward
Rhagsynied, v. to premediate
Rhagu, to get before; to oppose
Rhagwahan, n. leading division; term in prosody
Rhagwahannod, n. semicolon
Rhagwas, n. deputy servant
Rhagwedd, n, a presence
Rhagweini, v. to serve before
Rhagweled, v. to forsee
Rhagwerthu, v. to sell previously
Rhagwirio, to certify before
Rhagwisg, n. a fore-garment
Rhagwybod, v. to foreknow
Rhagwyneb, a. forthcoming: prep. in presence of
Rhagwys, n. a premonition
Rhagymadrodd, n. a preface
Rhagymddwyn, n. prolepsis
Rhagymgais, v. to attempt beforehand [self beforehand
Rhagymguddio, v. to hide one's
Rhagymlid, v. to pursue before
Rhagymrwymo, v. to bind one's self beforehand
Rhagynys, n. an adjacent isle
Rhagysgrif, n. a prescript
Rhagystafell, n. ante-chamber
Rhagystawd, n. a foremost layer
Rhagystumio v. to mould into form beforehand
Rhang, n. content; fulfilment
Rhangiad, n. a fulfilling
Rhangu, v. to fulfil; to satisfy
Rhai, n. a few: a. some
Rhaiad, n. radiation
Rhaiadr, n. a cataract
Rhraiadru, v. to spout out
Rhaiadu, v. to radiate, to ray

Rhaid, n. need, necessity: a. needful, necessity
Rhaidd, n. a ray; a spear
Rhaien, n. a ray, a skate
Rhail, n. a rail, a paddle
Rhain, n. lances, spears: a. tending forward
Rhaint, n. what is pervasive
Rhaith, n. right; law; jury
Rhal, n. character, disposition
Rhaliad, n. a characterising
Rhalu, v. to characterise
Rham, n. a rise or reach over
Rhawant, n. a token; a metaphor; a romance: a. exalting; romantic
Rhamanta, v. to use hyperbole
Rhamantol, a. romantic
Rhamiad, n. a rising over, a soaring
Rhamp, n. a running out
Rhamu, v. to rise, to soar
Rhan, n. a part, a share, a division: adv. on the part of; because
Rhanc, n. desire, craving: a content, satisfactory [ing
Rhanclad, n. a craving, a want-
Rhancu, v. to crave, to want
Rhandir, n. a region; a share-land; a district
Rhandy, n. house-room
Rhanedig, a. shared, divided
Rhanedigaeth, n. distribution
Rhanedigol, a. distributive
Rhangymeriad, n. a participle
Rhaniad, n. parting, sharing
Rhanu, v. to part, to divide
Rhasg, n. a slice, a shave
Rhasgl, n. a slicer; a draw-knife
Rhasgliad, n. a slicing, a shaving
Rhasglio, v. to use a slicer
Rhath, n. a cleared spot; a plain
Rhathell, n. a rasp, a rough file
Rhathelliad, n. a rasping
Rhathellu, v. to use a rasp
Rhathiad, n. a rubbing off
Rhau, n. a band, a chain

Rhaw, n. a shovel, a spade
Rhawaid, n. a shovel-ful
Rhawbal, n. iron edged shovel
Rhawbalar, n. a delving spade
Rhawch, n. what is extreme
Rhawd, n. a course, a rout
Rhawden, n. a footstep; a path
Rhawel, n. what is clustered
Rhawffon, n. a shovel handle
Rhawg, adv. for a long while
Rhawiad, n. a shovelling
Rhawlech, n. a slice, a shovel
Rhawn, n. coarse long hair
Rhawni, v. to grow to long hair
Rhawnyn, n. a single hair
Rhawol, n. a cluster, a bunch
Rhawr, n. a roar, a loud noise
Rhawter, n. a tumultous rout
Rhawtiad, n. a hurrying on
Rhawtio, v. to hurry on
Rhawth, n. greed: a. greedy
Rhe, n. a swift motion, a run: a. fleet, speedy: active
Rhead, n. a running; currency
Rheadu, v. to cause a running
Rheawl, a. running; current
Rheb, n. a run by, a going off
Rhebydd, n. a desolator
Rheciad, n. a hackneying
Rhecio, v. to hackney
Rhechdor, n. what breaks out or ravages
Rhed, n. a course, a race, a run
Rhedol, a. current, running
Rhedeg, n. a run: a. running; v. to run, to race
Rhedegfa, n. a race-course
Rhedegfarch, n. race-horse
Rhedegiad, n. a running, a race
Rhedegog, a. running, current
Rhedegwr, Rhedegydd, n. a runner, a racer
Rhedfa, n. a course, a run
Rhediad, n. a running
Rhediant, n. currency; a course
Rhedwas, n. a running-foot-man
Rhedweli, n. an artery
Rhedyn, n. fern

Rhedyna, v. to gather fern
Rhedyneg, n. fern brake
Rhedynen, n. a single fern
Rhedyniach, n. small straggling fern
Rhedynog, a. abounding with [fern
Rhedynos, n. small fern brake
Rhedd, n. a joint [thick
Rhef, n. a bundle: a. bundled;
Rhefedd, n. thickness about
Rhefiad, n. a thickening
Rheflog, a. blubbering, puffy
Rhefog, n. a bandage, a band
Rhefol, a. thickening; aggregating
Rhefrog, a. large bottomed
Rhefr-rwym, n. costiveness
Rhefu, v. to thicken round
Rhefr, n. the anus, the rectum
Rheffyn, n. a small rope
Rheg, n. a present; a curse
Rhegain, v. to keep muttering
Rhegen, n. a screaker; a quail
Rhegi, v. to consign; to curse
Rheglyd, a. give to cursing
Rheng, n. a row, or a rank
Rhengiad, n. setting in a row
Rheiad, n. a radiating
Rheian, n. a streak a stripe
Rheianu, v. to streak, to stripe
Rheio, v. to radiate, to gleam
Rheibes, n. a witch, a charmer
Rheibiad, n. a bewitching
Rheibiadaeth, n. witchery
Rheibiadu, v. to fascinate
Rheidiadus, a. fascinating
Rheibiaeth, n. rapacity
Rheibiant, n. a forcible possessing [ated
Rheibiedig, a. seized; fascin-
Rheibio, v. to seize, to snatch; to captivate, to bewitch
Rheibiol, a. seizing; bewitching
Rheibioldeb, n. a seized state
Rheibog, n. power of digestion
Rheibus, a. rapacious, greedy
Rheidedd, n. necessity, want

Rheidiant, n. necessity, need
Rheidio, v. to necessitate; to need
Rheidiol, a. necessary, needful
Rheidioldeb, n. necessariness
Rheidioli, v. to render needful
Rheidus, a. necessitous, needy
Rheidusni, n. neediness, need
Rheiduso, v. to render needy
Rheiddin, a. radiating; profuse
Rheiddio, v. to radiate; to dart
Rheiddyn, n. a dart, a glance
Rheiniad, n. a throwing a lance
Rheinio, v. to throw a lance
Rheitheg, n. canon of speech
Rheithfawr, a. greatly just
Rheithiad, n. a regulation
Rheithiadol, a. canonical
Rheithiadur, n. a regulator
Rheithio, v. to fix a law
Rheithiol, a. established as law
Rheithioreg, n. rhetoric
Rheithiwr, n. a juryman
Rhelyw, n. a trail; a residue, the rest
Rhem, n. what runs out
Rhemiad, n. a running out: n. a muttering [glutton
Rhemmwth, n. a gorbelly; a
Rhemp, n. an excess; frenzy: a. bewitched: crazy
Rhempiad, n. an infatuation
Rhempian, v. to snatch greedily
Rhempio, v. to run to excess
Rhen, n. the supreme, the Lord
Rhenc, n. a row, rank
Rhenciad, n. placing in a row
Rhencio, v. to place in a row
Rhent, n. an income; a rent
Rhentu, v. to get income, to
Rheol, n. a rule, an order [rent
Rheolaidd, a. orderly, regular
Rheoledigaeth, n. regulation
Rheoli, v. to order, to sway
Rheolus, a. orderly, regular
Rheolwr, n. ruler
Rhes, n. a row, a rank

Rheselu, v. to form a rack
Rhesio, v. to set in a row
Rhestog, n. plaited work; mat
Rhestr, n. array, order, rank
Rhestredigaeth, n. arrangement
Rhestriad, n. an arranging
Rhestrig, n. a row, a range
Rhestrog, a. rowed; plaited. matted
Rhestrol, a. ordinal; arrayed
Rhrestru, v. to range, to marshal
Rhesu, v. to place in a row
Rheswm, n. reason, sense
Rhesymeg, n. logic; reasoning
Rhesymiad, n. a reasoning
Rhesymol, a. rational; tolerable
Rhesymoldeb, n. rationality
Rhesymu, v. to reason, to argue
Rheth, n. a pervading quality
Rhrethren, n. a pike, a lance
Rhëu, v. to run about; to move
Rheuedd, n. activity, agility
Rhew, n. what is slippery; frost
Rhewi, v. to freeze; to be ice
Rhewiad, n. a freezing
Rhewlyd, a. freezing, frosty
Rhewyn, n. a drain, a gutter
Rhewys, a wanton, lusting
Rhi, n. what is specific; a chief
Rhiaidd, a. notable, pre-eminent
Rhial, n. an original lineage
Rhiallu, n. hundred thousand
Rhian, n. a dame, a lady
Rhianaidd, a. feminine; female
Rhianon, n. a goddess, a nymph
Rhiaint, n. a parent, a source
Rhiol, a. noble, royal
Rhib, n. a streak; a dribblet
Rhibin, n. scanty row, streak
Rhibio, v. to streak; to dribble
Rhibib, n. a reed pipe; a haut-
Rhic, n. a notch; to groove [boy
Rhicio, v. to notch; to groove
Rhiciol, a. notching; grooving
Rhid, n. a drain; semen
Rhidio, v. to drain; to secrete
Rhidyll, n. a riddle, a sieve
Rhydyllio, v. to riddle, to sift

Rhidys, n. a drain; a rill
Rhidysio, v. to flow dribbling
Rhidd, n. a centre; an obstacle
Rhiddio, v. to centre; to repel
Rhieddu, v. to act as a chief
Rhieniol, a. feminine
Rhieni, n. ancestry, parents
Rhieniaeth, n. parentage
Rhieniol, a. parental
Rhies, n. a dame, a lady
Rhif, n. what divides; number
Rhifadwy, a. numerable
Rhifedigaeth, n. numeration
Rhifedydd, Rhifiedydd, n. a numerator
Rhifedd, n. numerousness
Rhifiad, n. a numbering
Rhifiannol, a. numerary
Rhifiannu, v. to numerate
Rhifiog, a. numerous, many
Rhifnod, n. a numeral
Rhifnodol, a. numerical
Rhifnodiad, n. numeration
Rhifo, Rhifnodi, v. to numerate, to number, to count, to reckon
Rhifol, a. numeral, numerical
Rhifyddeg, n. arithmetic
Rhifyn, n. a single number
Rhifyddiaeth, n. numeration
Rhiff, n. what divides or parts
Rhifft, n. what is divided, a rift
Rhig, n. a notch, a groove; the pillory
Rhign, n. a notch, a groove
Rhignedd, n. a notched part
Rhigo, v. to notch, to groove
Rhigod, n. a pillory
Rhigol, n. a groove; trench
Rhigoliad, n. a grooving; a trenching
Rhigolydd, n. groove plane
Rhilgwm, n. a long row; rote
Rhigymu, v. to say by rote
Rhing, n. a creak, a clink
Rhingwar, n. a clamp
Rhyngyll, n. a serjeant
Rhingyllaeth, n. serjeantship
Rhil, n. an interstice

Rhill, n. a row; trench: drill
Rhilio, v. to row; to drill
Rhim, n. a rim, an edge
Rhimio, v. to rim, to edge
Rhimp, a rim, an extremity
Rhimpyn, n. an extremity; a rhyme
Rhimyn, n. a rim, an edge
Rhimynu, v. to form a rim
Rhin, n. what pervades; a channel; a virtue, a secret; a charm [quail
Rhinc, n. a creak; a gnash; a
Rhincio, v. to creak; to gnash
Rhinciol, a. creaking; clacking
Rhincyn, n. a creak, a clink, a gnash, a clack
Rhinfawr, a. greatly endowed
Rhiniad, n. an using of mystery
Rhinio, v. to endure with a virtue; to use mystery
Rhiniol, a. mysterious, secret
Rhint, n. a notch, a groove
Rhintach, a. notched, grooved
Rhinwedd, n. virtue; mystery
Rhinweddol, a. virtuous
Rhip, n. a skip, an over-skip
Rhipai, n. a hatchel
Rhipio, v. to pass or skip over
Rhis, n. what is broken into points
Rhisellt, n. a grater; a rasp
Rhisg, n. bark, rind [bark
Rhisgen, n. a dish or bowl of
Rhisgl, n. bark, coat or rind
Rhisglad, n. a barking
Rhisglo, v. to bark, to strip bark
Rhisglog, a. having bark
Rhisglyn, n. a piece of bark
Rhisgo, v. to bark, to strip of bark to peel
Rhith, n. guise, appearance, semblance, an embryo
Rhithedd, n. apparentness
Rhithiant, n. appearance
Rhithio, v. to appear, to seem
Rhithiol, a. appearing, apparent

Rhithiogi, v. to give appearance
Rhiw, n. a drift; a slope
Rho, n. what is put off; a gift
Rhoc, n. a rocking, a shake
Rhocas, n. a lad, a youth
Rhocian, v. to keep rocking
Rhocos, n. broken particles
Rhoch, n. a grunt, a groan
Rhochain, v. to keep grunting
Rhochiad, n. a grunting
Rhochi, v. to grunt, to growl
Rhôd, n. an orb; a wheel; the ecliptic
Rhodell, n. a whirl, a spindle
Rhoden, n. a switch, a whip
Rhodfa, n. a circular course
Rhodiana, v. to stroll about
Rhodianai, n. a gadding gossip
Rhodienol, a. ambulatory
Rhodio, v. to walk about
Rhodl, n. a paddle; a scull
Rhodle, n. a course, a range
Rhodli, v. to paddle, to scull
Rhodol, a. wheeling; wandering
Rhodres, n. ostentation; pomp
Rhodresgar, Rhodresol, a. ostentatious, pompous
Rhodresu, v. to swagger
Rhodreswr, n. a boaster a swaggerer
Rhodwedd, n. an orbit, a course
Rhodwydd, n. an open course
Rhodd, n. a gift, a present
Rhoddedigaeth, n. a donation
Rhoddi, v. to give, to bestow
Rhoddiannol, a. donative
Rhoddiant, n. a donation
Rhoddol, a. giving, bestowing
Rhoddwyr, n. a giver, a bestower
Rhogl, n. scent, odour, smell
Rhoi, v. to give to bestow
Rhol, n. a roll, a cylinder
Rholbren, n. a rolling-pin
Rholen, n. a roll, a roller
Rholiad, n. a rolling
Rholian, v. to be rolling about
Rholio, v. to roll or turn about

Rhon, n. a tail; a pike, a lance
Rhonc, n. a sinking
Rhonca, a. sinking [hollow
Rhoncian, v. to sink, to become
Rhonell, n. a tail; hair of a
Rhonellog, a. having a tail [tail
Rhonos, small broken particles
Rhont, n. a frisk, to gambol
Rhonta, v. to frisk, to gambol
Rhonten, n. a merry frisker
Rhontyn, n. a frisker [n. rose
Rhos, n. moist land, a moor:
Rhosb, n. a whim, a trick; a doggerel
Rhosbal, n. a doggerel rhymster
Rhosdir, n. fenny ground
Rhoslyd, a. fenny, marshy
Rhost, a. dried, browned over, roasted [roast
Rhostio, v. to brown over, to
Rhostog, n. the plover
Rhoth, a. loose; hollow
Rhu, n. a loud utterance, a roar
Rhuad, n. a roaring; loquacity
Rhuadol, a. roaring
Rhuadu, v. to make a roaring
Rhuadwy, a. roaring
Rhuch, n. a film; a husk
Rhuchion, n. husks
Rhuchioni, v. to clear of husks
Rhuchionyn, n. a husk; a film
Rhud, n. a cast or drive forward
Rhudd, a. ruddy hue, crimson: a. ruddy, crimson; callow
Rhuddain, a. crimson
Rhuddo, v. to make crimson
Rhuddog, n. the redbreast
Rhudded, n. a red streak; a path
Rhuddel, n. a ruddy hue; a glow
Rhuddeli, n. a red slave
Rhuddell, n. ruddle, red ochre to mark sheep [hue
Rhuddellen, n. one of a ruddy
Rhuddellu, v. to stain with crimson
Rhuddem, n. a ruby
Rhudden, n. a red streak [spot
Rhuddfa, Rhuddfan, n. parched

Rhuddfelyn, n. orange yellow
Rhuddgoch, a. pink red [son
Rhuddiad, n. a turning to crim-
Rhuddin, n. heart of timber
Rhuddion, n. husks
Rhuddlas, a. crimson blue
Ruddlwyd, a. russet colour
Rhuddos, n. the marigold
Rhuddwern, n. bird cherry tree
Rhuddugl, n. the radish [flush
Rhuf, n. what breaks out; a
Rhufell, n. the fish roach
Rhufon, n. a reddened one; a warrior [points
Rhug, n. what has breaks or
Rhugl, a. free, ready; fluent; rife
Rhugledd, n. quick motion,
Rhuglen, n. a drum [fluency
Rhuglgroen, n. a rattle made of dry skin with stones in it
Rhugliad, n. friction; clearance
Rhuglo, v. to clear, to smooth, to rub
Rhull, a. rife; frank; rash; hasty
Rhum, n. what projects or swells
Rhumen, n. a paunch
Rhumog, a. rotund: n. paunch
Rhumwth, n. a greedy-gut
Rhun, n. a lavish one
Rhuo, v. to roar; to talk
Rhuol, a. roaring, loquacious
Rhuor, a. roaring, blustering
Rhus, a start, a recoil; reynard
Rhuso, v. to start; t hesitate
Rhusol, a. starting: hesitating
Rhusgar, a. apt to start; restive
Rhusiad, n. a starting from
Rhuth, n. breaking out or from
Rhuthr, n. a gust, a rush, an assault, an attack; a good while
Rhuthro, v. to rush; to assault
Rhuthrol, a. rushing; assailing
Rhuthriad, n. a rushing on
Rhuwch, n. exterior coat; a rug
Rhuwchen, n. a rough coat; a
Rhwb, n. a rub, a chafe [rug
Rhwbiad, n. rubbing; friction

Rhwblo, v. to rub, to chafe
Rhwch, n. what is rough; a
Rhwchiad, n. a grunting [grunt
Rhwchial, n. a shrill grunting
Rhwchiala, v. to grunt
Rhwchiawl, a. grunting
Rhwchws, n, a ray, a skate
Rhwd, n. sediment; smut; rust
Rhwdog, a. covered with rust
Rhwf, n. what swells or puffs out
Rhwg, n. what projects; a rub
Rhwgn, n. a rub, a friction
Rhwng, n. an intermediacy
Rhwmp, n. a borer, an anger
Rhwn, what covers over
Rhwnc, n. snore; rattle
Rhwnciad n. a rattling, guggling
Rhwncian, v. to rattle, to guggle
Rhwnen, n. a single pear
Rhwnsi, n. a rough coated horse
Bhwnt, n. what covers over
Rhwnyn, n. pears
Rhws, n. cultivated region
Rhwtio, v. to corrode; to fret
Rhwtion, n. dregs
Rhwtioni, v. to produce dregs
Rhwtws n. broken parts; dregs
Rhwth, a. wide, gaping, yawing
Rhwy, n. excess, superfluity
Rhywol, a. excessive superfluity
Rhwych, n. what extends
Rhwyd, n. a net, a snare
Rhwyden, n. a small net; a caul
Rhwydiad, n. a reticulation
Rhwydo, v. to net to ensnare
Rhwydog, a. reticulated, netted
Rhwydd, a. free, easy, tolerable
Rhwyddâd, n. a making easy
Rhwyddâu, v. to facilitate
Rhwydd-deb, n. facility; success
Rhwyddineb, n easy, free state
Rhwyddoli, v. to facilitate
Rhwyddyni, v. to facilitate
Rhwyf, n. what impels; ambition; a ruler; an oar
Rhwyfadain, n. a directing fin
Rhwyfadur, n. a swayer

Rhwyfan, n. impulse; sway: v. to sway; to lead
Rhwyfaniad, n. domination
Rhwyfanu, v. to dominate
Rhwyfanus, a. imperious
Rhwyfiad, n. a swaying; a rowing
Rhwyfiant, n. domination
Rhwyfo, v. to sway; to row
Rhwyfol, a. swaying; rowing
Rhwyfolaeth, n. dictatorship
Rhwyfoldeb, n. a state of sway
Rhwyfus, apt to sway; haughty
Rhwyg, n. a rent, a rupture
Rhwygo, v. to rend, to tear
Rhwygol, a. rending; tearing
Rhwyll, n. a ring-fence; a paddock: n. an interstice, fret work; a casement
Rhwyllo, v. to form insterstices
Rhwyllog, a. fretted; cross-barred; grated
Rhwym, n. a bond, a tie: a. bound, tied, fastened
Rhwymedigaeth, n. restriction
Rhwymedigol, a. restrictive [age
Rhwymedd, n. restraint; bondRhwymiad, n. a binding, a tying
Rhwymiant, n. restriction
Rhwymo, v. to bind, to tie
Rhwymyn, n. a band: a swathe
Rhwymynu, v. to swaddle
Rhwyn, n. a wind, a twist
Rhwyno, v. to bind, to tie
Rhwyoli, v. to render excessive
Rhwys, n. vigour; wantonness; luxurance
Rhwysedd, n, vigourousness
Rhwysg, n. a carreer; sway
Rhwysglo, v. to run headlong
Rhwysglyd, a. froward, restive
Rhwysgol, a. swaying; risking
Rhwysiad, n. invigoration
Rhwysog, a. vigorous, luxuriant
Rhwysol, a. invigorating
Rhwysogi, v. to luxuriate
Rhwysoldeb, n. vigour
Rhwysoli, v. to invigorate

Rhwystredig, a. hindering
Rhwystri, n. hindrance; let
Rhwystro, to hinder, to obstruct
Rhwystrusi, n. hindrance
Rhwyth, n. what pervades: juice
Rhwytho, v, to pervade, to ooze
Rhy, n. excess, superfluity
Rhyado, v. to leave utterly
Rhyaddo, v. to promise over-
Rhyal, n. a procreation (much
Rhybarch, n. extreme regard
Rhybed, n. a clinched state
Rhybediad, n. a clinching
Rhyborthi, v. to support fully
Rhybrynu, v to purchase fully
Rhybuch, n. earnest longing
Rhybudd, n. notice warning
Rhybuddio, v. to give notice
Rhybuddiol, a. warning
Rhyburo, v. to purify fully
Rhybwyso, v. to over-weigh
Rhybwyth, n. a retort: over-play
Rhych, n. a trench, a furrow
Rhychio, Rhychu, v. to trench, to furrow
Rhychwant, n. a span length
Rhychwantu, v. to span
Rhychware, n. excess of play
Rhyd, n. a course; a ford
Rhydaf, n. an overspreading
Rhydain, n. a young deer, a fawn
Rhydalu, v. to over-pay
Rhydanu, v. to spread greatly
Rhydarf, n. excessive rout
Rhydeddu, v. to render supreme
Rhyderig, a. barren, as to breeding
Rhydgoch, a. of a russet colour
Rhydio, v. to ford, to pass
Rhydle, n. a fording place
Rhedlyd, a. apt to rust rusty
Rhydni, n. rustiness, rust
Rhydöl, v. to overspread
Rhydollt, n. sawdust
Rhydres, n. arrogance
Rhydresol a. a. supercilious
Rhydu, v. to rust, to grow rusty
Rhydwell, n. an artery

Rhydwf, n. exuberance
Rhydwng, n. an anathema
Rhydyllu, v. to perforate
Rhydyn, a. overstrained
Rhydd, n. liberty, freedom: a. at large; free; liberal
Rhyddâd, n. a liberating [much
Rhyddadlu, v. to dispute over-
Rhyddail, n. second leaves
Rhyddaol, a. loosening, freeing
Rhyddâu, v. to free, to liberate
Rhydd-did, Rhyddid, n. liberty
Rhydderchafu, v. to over exalt
Rhyddewyllys, n. freewill
Rhyddiaith, n. free language; prose [ation
Rhyddiant, n. relaxation liber-
Rhyddineb, n. freedom, facility
Rhyddogni, v. to over-supply
Rhyddonio, v. to gift greatly
Rhyddrent, n. gavelkind
Rhyerchi, v. to ask earnestly
Rhyfion, n. currants
Rhyfael, n. excessive gain
Rhyfai, n. an extreme fault
Rhyfail, n. a prepossession
Rhyfaint, n. an excess
Rhyfalu, v. to grind extremely
Rhyfanu, v. to impress
Rhyfarnu, v. to pre-judge
Rhyfawrth, n. March wind [ful
Rhyfedd, a. surprising, wonder-
Rhyfeddod, n. a surprise, a wonder [derful
Rhyfeddol, a. surprising, won-
Rhyfeddu, v. to wonder, to be surprised
Rhyfel, n. war, warfare
Rhyfela, v. to wage war, to war
Rhyfelog, a. belligerent, warring
Rhyfelgar, a. apt to war, warlike
Rhyfelu, v. to wage war, to war
Rhyferad, n. a drivelling
Rhyferthin, n. a violent gust
Rhyferthwy, n. a torent, a tempest
Rhyferwi, v. to over-boil [est
Rhyfoli, v. to praise; to flatter
Rhyforiad, n. a scrambling

Rhyfrys, n. precipitancy
Rhyfwydd, n. currant trees
Rhyfyg, n. presumption
Rhyfygol, a. presuming insolent
Rhyfygu, v. to presume
Rhyfygus, a. presumptuous
Rhyg, n. rye
Rhygaru, v. love to excess
Rhygen, n. a grain of rye
Rhyglydd, n. desert, merit
Rhyglyddiannus, a. meritorious
Rhyglyddiant, g. desert, merit
Rhyglyddu, to deserve, to merit
Rhygnol, a. tubbing; scoring
Rhygnell, n. a whipsaw
Rhygnen, n. a rasp, a file
Rhygniad, n. a rubbing; a hack-
Rhygnu, v. to rub, to hack [ing
Rhygoel, n. a superstition
Rhygoll, n an extreme loss
Rhygu, n. over-fondness
Rhygwellt, n. rye-grass
Rhygyng, n. an ambling pace
Rhygyngen, n. a rattle in the
Rhygyngu, v. to amble [throat
Rhyngad, n. intervention
Rhyngol, a. intervening
Rhyngsang, n. a diacope in
  rhetoric
Rhyngu, v. to intervene; to
  mediate. Rhyngu bodd, to
Rhylamu, v. to overstep [please
Rhylawn, a. redundant, too full
Rhyll, n. a rift, a cleft
Rhym, n. what stretches round
Rhyn, n. emotion; a shiver;
  an instant; a small quantity,
  a cape
Rhyn, a. shivering; terrible
Rhynaig, tremulous, shivering
Rhyndod, n. a shivering
Rhynedd, n. a shiveringness
Rhyni, n. agitation: shivering
Rhyniad, n. a shivering
Rhynio, v. to pervade; to have
  instinct; to agitate
Rhynion, n. shelled oats, grits
Rhynllyd, a. apt to shiver

Rhynod, n. agitation; a moment; a while; a small quantity
Rhynu, v. to shiver, to shake
Rhys, n. extreme ardency; a
  rush; a strait; a difficulty
Rhyseth, n. a putting in a
  course; a straitening
Rhysedd, n. excess, superfluity:
Rhysedda, v. to rush onward
Rhyselu, v. to look stedfastly
Rhysfa, n. a course, a rush
Rhysgiad, n. an overgrowing
Rhysio, v. to rush; to straiten
Rhysod, n. burning embers
Rhysol, rushing; over running
Rhysu, v. to rush; to entangle
Rhyswr, n. a savage; a combat-
Rhyswydd, n. privet wood [ant
Rhysyn, n. a burning ember
Rhythfol, n. a glutton
Rhythgnawd, n. bloated flesh
Rhythiad, n. a gaping, a yawn-
Rhythni, n. a gaping state [ing
Rhythu, v. to stretch out
Rhython, n. cockles
Rhyw, n. sort; sex: a. some
  adv. It is genial or natural
Rhyweled, v, to foresee
Rhywfaint, n. some quantity
Rhywfan, Rhywle, adv. somewhere [kind
Rhywiaeth, n. distinction of
Rhywiogaeth, n. a species, a
  sort, a kind
Rhywiogaethol, a. generical
Rhywiogi, v. to render or become genial
Rhywiogrwydd, n. geniality
Rhywrys, a. over ardent
Rhywun, n. somebody
Rhywynt, n. a hurricane

S

SA, n. a fixed state; a standing
Sach n. a sack

Sachaid, n. sackful, bagful	Saffwn, n. a beam, a shaft
Sachell, n. a small sack, a bag	Saffwy, n. a pike, a lance
Sachellu, v to bag; to stuff	Saffwyo, v. to use a pike
Sachliain, n. sackcloth	Sag. n. a squeeze of the chops
Sachu, v. to put in a sack	Sagied, v. to squeeze in the chops; to stifle
Sad, a. firm, steady; discreet	
Sadell, n. a dorser, a packsaddle	Sang, n. a tread; a tramble
Sadellu, v. to put on a dorser	Sangedigaeth, n act of treading
Sadio, v. to make firm [ness	Sangu, v. to tread; to tramble
Sadrwydd, n. firmness, steadi-	Sai. n. what is still or at rest
Sadwrn, n. Saturn. Dydd Sadwrn, Saturday	Saib, n. leisure; sedateness; quiet; sedate; studious
Saer, n. a wright, an artisan	Said. n. a haft; the part inserted in the hilt
Saeriad, n. a working as a wright	
Saeriant, n. architecture	Saig, n. a mess, a meal
Saeri, n. a wright's work	Sail, n. a base, a foundation
Saerniaeth, n. architecture	Saim, n. grease
Saerniaidd, a. workmanlike	Sain, n. a sound, a tone
Saernio, v. to work as a wright	Saith, a. seven
Saerniol, a. architectural	Sal. n. a pass; a plight; a cast off; ; frail; poor; ill
Saerol, mechanical, of a wright	
Saeru, v. to work as a wright	Salaidd, a. somewhat frail or ill
Saeth, n. an arrow, a dart	Salâu, v. to grow frail or ill
Saethflew, n. coarse hairs in fur	Saldra, n. frailty; poorness; illness [ugly
Saethiad, n. a shooting; ejection	
Saethol, a. shooting; ejecting	Salw, a. despicable, vile, sorry
Saethu, v. to shoot; to dart	Salwâu, v. to grow despicable
Saethydd, n. shooter, archer	Salwder, n. frailty; vileness
Saethyddiaeth, n. archery	Salwineb. n. contemptibleness
Saf, n. a fixed state; a stand	Sallt, n. an exterior state
Safadwy, a. able to stand, durable	Salltiad, n. a going out; a sallying
Safaeth, n. the act of standing	Salltring, n. snuffers [lying
Safedig, a. established, fixed	San, n. a maze: a. wary
Safedigol a. having power to stand ariness	Sanedigaeth, n. azement
	Sant, n. a saint
Safedd, n. fixed state, station-	Santaidd, a. holy
Safiad, n. a standing; stature	Santeiddiad, n. sanctifiation
Safiadol, a. stationary [stand	Santeiddio, v. to sanctify
Safle, n. a standing place, a	Santeiddiol, a. sanctified
Safn, n. a jaw, a chop	Santeiddrwydd, n. holiness
Safnaid, n. a chopful	Santes, n. a female saint
Safnol, a. relating to the jaw	Santolaeth, n. sanctitude
Safniad. n. a jawing, a mouth-	Sanu, v. to gaze, to amaze
Safnrwth, a. open jawed [ing	Sar, n. rage; insult, offence
Safol, a. standing, stationary	Sarâd, n. an insulting
Safwyr. n. savour, odour	Saraol, a. insulting, abusive
Saffr. Saffrwm, or Saffrwn, n. saffron, crocus	Saraed, n. affront, reproach
	Sarâu, v. to insult, to affront

Saraus, a. insulting, offensive
Sarausrwydd, n. offensiveness
Sarch, n. piece of harness
Sarchu, v. to cover, to harness
Sardio, v. to rebuff, to chide
Sardiol, a. rebuking, chiding
Sardd, n. what is recumbent
Sarddan, n. a creeping thing
Sarff, n. a serpent
Sarffol, a. like a serpent
Sarffwydd, n. service trees
Sarid, n. an overplus
Sarn, n. a causeway; a paving
Sarnu, v. to strew; to lay a path
Sarth, n. reptile; scorpion; hedgehog; sarcasm
Sarthu, v. to creep along
Sarug, a. surly, stern, dogged
Sarugedd, Sarugrwydd, n. surli-
Sarugo, v. to grow surly [ness
Sarugyn, n. a surly fellow
Satan, n. adversary
Sathr, n. a trampling
Sathredig, a. trodden, trampled
Sathru, v. to tread, to trample
Saw, n. what hems in; a stop
Sawch, n. a heap, a load [siege
Sawd, n. drift, plight, verge; a
Sawdio, v. to tend, to verge
Sawdl, n. a heel
Sawdrio, v. to join; to solder
Sawdwr, n. borderer; soldier
Sawdwriaeth, n. soldiership
Sawdwriol, a. soldierly
Sawdd, n. depth; a sink; a plunge; a root; power [ney
Sawell, n. a smoke hole, a chim-
Sawf, n. what stops or stands
Sawl, a. many; such
Sawyr, n. savour, taste; odour
Sawyrio, v. to savour
Sawyrus, a. savory; odorous
Se, n. what is fixed; a star: adv. as stated, to wit, so
Sead, n. a stating, a fixing
Seb, n. tendency to hem in
Sebach, a. confined, straitened; shrill

Seboni, v. to soap; to lather
Sebon, n. soap
Sebonol, a. saponaceous, soapy
Sech, a. dry, dried, parched
Sedd, n. a motionless state; a
Sedda, v. to sit habitually [seat
Seddiad, n. a seating, a sitting
Seddol, n. a sofa
Seddoldeb, n. sedentariness
Seddu, v. to seat; to be seated
Sef, a. certain, being true: conj. that is to say; namely [low
Sefnig, n. the gullet, the swal-
Sefyd, v. to stand; to stop still
Sefydledig, a. stationed, settled, established
Sefydliad, n. an establishing
Sefydlog, a. standing; stationary
Sefydlu, v. to establish, to settle
Sefydlyn, n. stagnant water
Sefyll, n. a standing, a position: v. to stand; to stop
Sefyllfa, n. a standing place
Sefyllfod, n. station, situation
Sefylliad, n. stationing [loiter
Sefyllian, v. to stand often, to
Sefylliant, n. a stationing
Sefyllio, v. to station
Sefylliog, a. apt to stand
Segan, n. a covering, a cloak
Segiad, n. an enveloping
Segru, v. to secrete, to put apart
Segur, a. untroubled; idle
Segura, v. to idle, to loiter
Segurdod, n. leisure; idleness
Seguriad, n. a taking leisure
Segurllyd, a. apt to take leisure
Seguryd, n. leisure, idleness
Sengi, v. to tread, to trample
Seibiad, n. a standing at leisure
Seibiant, n. leisure, respite
Seigen, n. a little mess, a meal
Seigio, v. to take a mess
Seigwr, n. a messer
Seilddar, n. a main beam
Seilddor, n. a threshold, a sill
Seiler, n. a basement, a cellar
Seilfaen, n. foundation stone

SEIL	SIAD
Seiliant, n. a foundation	Sêr, n. stars
Seilio, v. to lay a foundation	Serch, n. regard, or love: prep. with respect to, notwithstan- [ding
Seiliog, a. having a foundation	
Seilwaith, n. ground-work	Serchiad, n. a loving
Seilydd, n. a founder	Serchog, a. loving, amorous
Seimio, v. to grease over	Serchogi, v. to render fond
Seimiol, a. of a greasy quality	Sercholdeb, n. amorousness
Seimlyd, a. of a greasy quality	Serchu, v. to be affected; to love
Seinfawr, a. sonorous, loud	Seren, n. a star; a spangle
Seinglawr, n. sounding board	Sereniad, n. a sparkling
Seiniad, n. a sounding; accent	Serenig, n. an asterisk
Seiniant, n. a making a sound	Serenol, a. sparkling as a star
Seinio, v. to sound, to resound	Serenu, v. to sparkle
Seiniol, a. sounding; toned	Serenwyl, n. epiphany
Seintio, v. to canonise	Serf, a. whirling; dizzy, giddy
Seintiol, a. hallowed; saintly	Serfanol, a. startling; staring
Seintiolaeth, n. sanctitude	Serfanu, v. to startle; to stare
Seirch, n. equipage; harness	Serfyll, a. unsteady; shattered
Seirchio, v. to harness	Serfylliad, n. a shattering
Seirian, a. sparkling, glittering	Serig, a. starred; spangled
Seirianad, n. a sparkling	Serigl, a. studded, spangled
Seirianu, v. to sparkle	Serigliad, n. a bespangling
Seithdant, n. a heptachord	Serliw, n. starlight
Seithfed, a. seventh	Serlo, n. a star-glow; sparkling
Seithongl, n. a septangle	Serofydd, n. an astronomer
Seithug, a. futile, fruitless	Serofyddol, a. astronomical
Seithugiant, n frustration [seal	Serog, a. having stars, starry
Sel, n. espying; distant view;	Seroliaeth, n. the starry system
Selder, n. keen-sightedness	Seron, n. the starry system
Seldremio, v. to range	Seroni, v. to systemise stars
Seliad, n. an espying; perception	Seronydd, n. an astronomer
Seliant, n. a perception	Serth, n. tendency, a steep
Selsig, n. a pudding; a sausage	Serthan, n. a precipice, a cliff
Selu, v. to espy, to gaze	Serthedd, n. steepness; obscenity
Selw, n. a gaze, a beholding	Serthi, n. obscenity
Sellt, n. a limit, a border	Serthiant, n. steepness
Selltu, v. to explore, to seek	Serthol, a. precipitous; obscene
Sen, n. a stigma, a taunt	Serthu, v. to make steep; to grow steep; to grow obscenely
Senedd, n. a senate; synod	
Seneddol, a. senetorial	Serthus, a. declivious: obscene
Seneddu, v. to form a senate	Serw, a. sparkling, glittering
Seniad, n. a taunting; a chiding	Serydd, n. an astronomer
Senol, a. taunting, scoffing	Seryddiaeth, n. astronomy
Sensigl, n. a daisy	Seryddol, a. astronomical
Senu, v. to taunt; to chide	Sew, n. gravy; juice; jelly
Senw, n. a stigma; a reproach	Sewyd, n. diffusion of stars
Senyllt, n. a seneschal	Si, n. a hiss, a whiss, a buzz
Ser, n. bill, or bill-hook	Siad, n. a hissing; a buzzing

| SIAD | 279 | SIOM |

Siad, n. the top of the scull, pate
Siar, n. an articulate sound
Siarad, n. a talking, a talk
Siaradgar, a. querulous, prating, talkative
Siaradol, a. talking, speaking
Siaradus, a. talkative, talking
Siared, v. to speak, to talk
Siars, n. a charge, a command
Siaspi, n. a shoeing-horn
Sib, n. what tends to involve
Sibol, n. young onions
Sibolen, n. a young onion
Sibr, n. a sauce
Sibrad, n. a dressing with sauce
Sibro, v. to do with sauce
Sibrwd, n. soft murmur, whisper
Sibwl, n. young onions
Siclad, Siciant, n. a steeping
Siclo, v. to steep, to soak
Sicion, n. steepings, washings
Sicl, n. a shekel
Sicr, a. sure, certain
Sicrwydd, n. certainty
Sid, n. a winding, a round
Sidan, n. silk, satin
Sidana, v. to collect silk
Sidanaid, a. like silk, silky
Sidanblu, n. down feathers
Sidanen, n. what is silken
Sidanion, n. silk mercery [cer
Sidanwr, Sidanydd, n. silk-mer-
Sidell, n. a winder; a whirl; a rim of a wheel; a fly wheel
Sidellu, v. to whirl round
Sidellydd, n. a winder
Sider, n. what twirs; fringe
Sidera, v. to form twirls
Sideru, v. to twirl; to fringe

Sigl n. a shake, a stir
Siglaethan, lay of swinging
Sigledd, n. a rocking state
Siglen, n. a swing, a quag
Siglo, v. to shake, to rock
Sigo, v. to shock, to bruise
Sil, n. issue; seedling; spawn; fry; hulling of grain
Silen, n. seedling; single fry
Siliant, n. spawning; hulling of corn [led corn
Silied, n. what is produced; hul-
Silio, v. to spawn; to hull grain
Silod, n. seedlings; spawn; fry
Silodi, v. to issue seedlings
Silodyn, n. single one of a fry
Silyn, n. a seedling; a fry
Sill, Syllaf, n. a component part; a syllable
Silleb, n. a syllable
Sillebu, Silliadu, v. to spell
Silliad, n. a forming of syllables
Silliadaeth, Sillyddiaeth, n. a syllabic system
Sillio, v. to arrange parts
Sillt, n. an element; a syllable
Silltiad, n. a joining of elements
Sim, n. what is flippant or light
Simach, n. a monkey, an ape
Simdde, n. a chimney
Simer, n. levity; a frisk
Simera, v. to frisk, to dally
Simp, n. a fickle state; a flutter
Sin, n. a surface; alms
Sindal, n. fine linen, cambric
Sindw, n. scoria, cinders
Sinid, n. surface, scum
Sinidr, n. scoria, dross
Sinidro, v. to form dross

| SIOM | 280 | SUO |

Siomiant, n. disappointment
Sionc, a. brisk, nimble, sharp
Sioncedd, n. briskness
Sionci, v. to become brisk
Siplad, n. a sipping
Sipian, v. to keep sipping
Sipio, v. to draw the lips, to sip
Sipyn, n. a single sip, a sip
Sir, n. a shire, a county: n. cheer, solace, comfort
Sirion, n. cherries
Sirio, v. to cheer, to solace
Siriol, a. cheering, solacing
Sirioldeb, n. cheerfulness
Sirioli, v. to make cheerful
Sis, n. a loud sound, a whisper
Sisial, n. a whisper, a gossip
Sisiala, v. to keep whispering
Sisialu, v. to whisper, to mutter
Sitell, n. a whisk round
Sitellu, v. to whisk round
Sitio, v. to whirl, to whisk
Sitrachog, a. jagged, sheddred
Sitrachu, v. to jag, to shred
Siw, n. a hiss, a hush, a buzz
Siwen, n. the mermaid
Sob, n. a tuft, a mass
Soba, Soban, n. a small bunch
Sobr, a. temperate sober
Sobrwydd, n. sobriety, temper- [ance
Socan, n. wallower
Socyn, n. a pig; a littlle urchin
Soch, n. a sink a drain
Sodi, v. to constitute, to fix
Sodli, v. to heel, to trip the heel
Sodlog, a. having a heel
Sodol, a. tending to fix or settle
Sodwedd, n. characteristic
Soddedigaeth, n. act of sinking
Soddi, v. to sink to submerge
Soddol, a. sinking; plunging
Soddwr, n. a sinker
Soeg, grains of malt after brew- [ing, draff
Soegen, n. a swaggy female
Soegi, v. to steep; to slabber
Soeglyd, a. puffed by steeping
Sofl, n. standing studdle
Sôg, n. a wallowing, a spreading

Soga, wallowing; slovenly [ing
Sôn, n. report, rumor, mention-
Soniwr, n. mentioner, talker
Sopen, n. a mass squeezed to- [gether
Sopenu, v. to bundle
Sopiad, n. a bundling
Sor, n. a chafed state; sullenness
Sori, v. to chafe; to offend to sulk
Soriad, n. a chafing; an offend- [ing
Soriant, sulleness; offence
Sorllyd, a. apt to grow sullen
Sorod, n. dregs, dross
Sorodi, v. to yeld dregs
Sorth, a. sudden; fell; slothful
Sothach, n. refuse, dross
Su, n. what pervades; a buzz
Suad, n. a buzzing; a lulling
Sucan, n. steeping; small beer washbrew, gruel, flumm'ry
Sudd, n. what pervades; juice
Suddas, n. sinking, immersion
Suddiad, a sinking, a plunging
Suddiant, n. perversion of mois- [ture
Suddo, v. to sink in, to sink
Suddol, a. pervading; sinking
Sug, n. a suck; juice sap
Sugaethan, n. candle: poultice
Suger, n. extracted juice; cyder
Sugiad, n. a becoming juicy
Suglian, n. drawing plaister
Sugnheirint, n. a pump
Sugnbib, n. a syringe
Sugndraeth, n. quicksand
Sugnedydd, n. sucker; pump
Sugno, v. to suck, to imbibe
Sugnol, a. sucking, imbibing
Sugoli, v. to render succulent
Sugr, n. extracted juice; sugar
Sugro, v. to sugar, to sweeten
Sugrol, a. saccharine; sugary
Sul, n. what extends round; the Sun. Dydd Sul. Sunday
Sulgwyn, n. Whitsuntide
Sulw, n. observation, remark
Sum, magnitude, size; sum
Sumio, v. to deduce the size
Sumiol, a. relating to size
Suo, v. to buzz; to lull, to hush

Sur, n. an acid: a. acid; stale
Suran, n. a sour plant, sorrel
Surder, n. sourness, acidity
Surdoes, n. leaven
Surdoesi, v. to leaven
Surian, n. a cherry
Sarig, n. silk
Surni, n. sourness; staleness
Suro, v. to sour; to turn sour
Suryn, n. anything acid
Sut, n. manner, shape; plight
Sutiad, n. a shaping; a suiting
Sutio, v. to adapt; to suit
Sûwr, n. one who hushes
Sw, n. what remains; what is on
Swb, n. a pressed heap; a bun-
Swba, n. a small bundle [dle
Swbach, n. what is shrunk up
Swbachiad, n. a shrtnking up
Swbachu, v. to shrink up
Swci, n. what is soaked
Swch, sychod, n. a snout; a
  plough-share   [the snout
Swchio, v. to search without
Swd, n. manner, shape; plight
Swdd, n. frame work; a frame
Swdden, n. a beam, a raft
Swf, n. a spot, a space
Swg, n. a soak, an imbibing [ing
Swgiad, n. a soaking, a drench-
Swil, a. bashful
Swl, n. flat space; ground
Swll, n. a scene, prospect
Swllt, n. a treasure; a shilling
Swm, n. state of being together
Swmer, n. a supporter, a beam
Swmeriad, n. a propping up
Swmeru, v. to prop up
Swmio, v. to sum up
Swmwl, n. a goad
Swn, n. a noise, a sound
Swniad, n. a sounding
Swnio, v. to noise, to sound
Swp, n. pressed mass; a cluster
Swr, n. what is surly or sullen
Swrn, n. a small space; a little,
  somewhat; a fetlock

Swrth, n. what is imminent
Swrth, a. sudden; falling, fell,
  unwieldy; slothful; drowsy
Swrthlyd, a. apt to be drowsy
Swrth, n, n, a clumsy one
Swrw, a. surly sullen,; snarling
Swrwd, n. shreds; dress; frag-
Swta, what is volatile soot [ment
Swtan, n. whiting
Swtrach, n. dross, dregs
Swtrws, n. bruised mass
Swth, n. a frame; a pile
Swy. n what is on or over
Swyd, n. what extends over
Swydo, v. to intimidate
Swydd; n. employ, office, duty
  service; a suit; a shire a coun-
Swyddfa n. place of buisness [ty
Swyddog, a. having office officer
Swyddogaeth, n. office, duty
Swyddogi, v. to hold office
Swyddwr, n. an officer
Swyf, n. scum; yeast; suet [suet
Swyfedd, n. what is scummed
Swyfen, n. scum; froth, or top
Swyfi, n. scum; froth, or top
Swyfo, v. to cast a scum; to yeld
Swylo, v. to save, to put by
Swyn, n a preservative; a charm
Swyna, v. to deal in charms
Swyn-gynfaredd, n. amulet [ing
Swyniad a preserving; a charm-
Swyno, v. to preserve; to charm
Swynogol, n. an amulet a charm
Swynogli, v. to fascinate
Swynol, a. preserative; blessing
Swynwr, n. a dealer in amulets
  or charms, a magician, a wi-
Swyso, v. to give emotion [zard
Sy, n. a star; v. is, exists
Syber, a. elevated; generous,
  sober   [mindedness
Syberwyd, n. stateliness; high-
Sybyrnio, to bundle, to pack up
Sybyrnyn, n. a small bundle
Sych, n. drought: a. dry
Sichbilen, n. a dry film

Syched, n. drought, thirst
Sychedig, a. thirsty, dry
Sychedol, a. causing thirst
Sychedu, to thirst, to be thirsty
Sychiant, n. a desiccation
Sych-hin, n. dry weather
Sychu, v. to dry, to wipe dry
Sychwydd, n. dry wood, fuel
Sydyn, a. abrupt, sudden
Sydyniwydd, n. suddenness
Sydd, v. is, exists
Syfa, n. a riddle, a sieve
Syfag, n. what spreads out
Syfaldod, n. fickleness
Syflen, Syfi, n. a strawberry
Syfliad, n. a stirring
Syflyd, v. to stir, to move
Syfnol, a. of a firm quality
Syfniad, n. a making firm
Syfrdan, n. giddiness, distraction: a. giddy, stupified
Syfrdanu. v. to make giddy
Syfru, v. ro render severe
Syfyd, n. what forms a space
Syfyl, n. a tendency to move
Syg, n. a chain, a trace
Sygan, n. a whisper, a mutter
Syganol, a. whispering
Syganu, v. to whisper, to mutter
Sygn, n. a circle; a sign
Sygog, n. a shove, a move
Syl, n. surface, ground; base
Sylch, n. a furrow
Sylchdan, n. a wheel plough
Sylfan, n. foundation
Sylfaen, n. foundation stone
Sylfaenu, v. to found
Sylfaenydd, n. founder
Sylw, n. a view; remark; notice
Sylwad, n. observation; a regarding; a noticing
Sylwedd, n. substance, matter
Sylweddiad, n. a substantiation
Sylweddol, a. substantial
Sylweddoli, v. to make substantial
Sylweddoliaeth, n. materialism
Sylweddu, to make of substance
Sylwi, v. to observe, to regard

Sylwiad, n. an observing
Syll, n. a view; a gaze, a stare
Syllbeiriant, n. an optical instrument
Sylldy, n. a shop
Sylliant, n. an observation
Syllio, v. to observe; to gaze
Syllt, n. what is fair or clear
Sylltiad, n. a making clear
Syllty, n. a treasury
Syllu, v. to observe; to gaze
Syllwg, n. an open prospect
Syllwr, n. a spectator
Syllwydr, n. a spying-glass
Sym, n. what is whole
Symaeth, n. a complete state
Symerth, n. simple power
Symiant, n. comprehension
Symio, v. to comprehend
Syml, n. what is simple: a. simple
Symlad, n. a pointing; a simplifying
Symlant, n. simplicity
Symledd, n. simpleness
Symlen, n. a simple one
Symlu, v. to point; to goad
Symlyn, n. a simpleton
Symol, a. integral; middling
Symu, to render integral
Symud, v. to move
Symudadwy, a. moveable
Symudo, v. to move, to remove
Symudfa, n. a transition
Symudiad, n. a moving
Symudoldeb, n. moveableness
Symwl, n. cowslips
Symwth, a. interrupted
Symwy, a. ample, prominent
Symylen, n. a cowslip
Symyliad, n. a goading
Symylu, v. to goad
Symythu, v. to interrupt
Syn, n. feeling, preception: a. sensible; concerned; amazed
Syndod, n. concern; amazement
Synedigaeth, n. astonishment
Synedigol, a. sensitive
Syniad, n. sensation, feeling
Syniadol, a. sensitive

Syniant, n. a sentiment [dered
Syniedig, a. perceived; consi-
Synigliad, n. a stimulation
Synio, v. to feel; to be sensible
Syniol, a. sensible, perceptive
Syniolaeth, n. perceptivity
Synioldeb, n. perceptibility
Synu, v. to observe steadfastly: to be amazed
Synwr, n. a sense, meaning
Synwyreb, n. a sentence
Synwyrgar, a. sententious [sense
Synwyriad, n. a gathering of
Synwyrol, a. sensible, rational
Synwyroldeb, n. sensibleness
Sypiad n. squeezing together
Sypio, v. to squeeze together
Sypyn, n. a small bundle (stars
Syr, n. a master, a lord: sir: n.
Syrch, n. a striking against
Syrn, adv. partly, rather, half
Syrniad, n. a forming into parts
Syrth, n. a fall; chance; lot: sort; offals
Syrthfa, n. a fallen state
Syrthiant, n. a propensity
Syrthio, v. to fall, to tumble
Syrthiol. a. falling, tumbling
Syrthni, n. listlessness
Syth, n. a stiff or rigid state: a. stiff, rigid, erect
Sythder, n. stiffness; erectness
Sythi, n. what stiffens; a beam
Sythol, a. tending to stiffen
Sytholdeb, n. stiffening tendency
Sythu, v. to stiffen; to make or become erect
Syw, a. regular, trim, smart
Sywed, n. astronomy
Sywedydd. n. astronomer
Sywedyddol, a. astronomical
Sywidw, n. the titmouse
Sywino, v. to turn or use continually; to dissipate
Sywio. v. to make uniform, to put in trim
Sywydd, n. star knowledge
Sywyddol, a. astrological

Sywyddwr, n. astrologer

T

TA, n. a spread; a superior
Tab, n. a spread; a surface
Tabar, n. tabard
Tabwrdd, n. a tabour (our
Tabyrddu, v. to play on the tab-
Tacl, n. a tool; tackle
Taclu, v. to deck, to trim, to patch
Taclus, a. neat, tidy, complete
Tacluso, v. to put in trim, to smarten (derliness
Taclusder, Taclusrwydd, n. or-
Tachwedd, n. November
Tad, n. father. Tad cu, grand-
Tadaeth, n. fatherhood (father
Tadmaeth, n. foster-father
Tadogaeth, n. paternity
Tadoldeb, n. fatherliness
Tadoli, v. to become fatherly
Tadoliaeth, n. fatherhood
Tadwy. a. paternal; tuteral
Taen, n. a spreading
Taenadwy, a. expansible
Taenellu, v. to strew; to sprinkle
Taenellwr, Taenellydd, sprink-
Taenu, v. to spread (ler
Taer, n. urgent state: a. eager, ardent, urgent
Taerol, a. apt to be urgent
Taerder, n. importunity
Taeriant, Taerni, n. importunity
Taeru, v. to insist; to contend
Taethind n. a fertilising (space
Taf, n. what is spread, a flat
Tafad, n. a spreading; a dilation
Tafar, n. what spreads out
Tafarch, n. a cricket bat
Tafarn, n. a tavern, an inn
Tafarndy, n. a public-house
Tafarnwr, n. an inn-keeper
Tafarth, n. what is dilated
Tafell, n. a slice
Tafellan, n. a small slice

Tafelliad, n. a slicing
Tafellu, v. to spread; to slice
Tafian, n. a balance, scales
Taflawd, n. a roof; a loft
Tafiedigaeth, n. act of throwing
Tafledydd, n. thrower
Taflen, n. tablet
Taflenu, v. to tabulate
Taflodi, v. to interject, to cast
Taflodiad, n. an interjection
Taflodol, a. interjective
Taflrwyd, n. a casting-net
Taflu, v. to throw, to fling
Tafod, n. a tongue; a clapper
Tafodi, v. to tongue; to scold
Tafodiaith, n. action of the tongue (rote
Tafodleferydd, n. a saying by
Tafodrwym, a. tongue-tied
Tafodrydd, a. loose-tongue
Tafol, n. the dock plant
Tafolen, n. dock, dock leaf
Tafu, v. to overspread, to spread
Tâg, n. clogged state; a strangle
Tagell, n. barb; a double chin; dew-lap; a wattle
Tagellog, a. having a double chin; having wattles (chin
Tagellu, v. to form a double
Tagfa, n. a choking, a strangling
Tagfagl, n. a springe, a gin
Tagiad, n. a choking, a stifling
Tagu, v. to choke, to strangle
Tangnefedd, n. tranquillity
Tangnefeddu, v. to tranquillise
Tangnefeddus, tranquil, peaceful
Tangwystl, n. pledge of peace
Taid, n. grandfather
Tail, n. soil; manure; muck
Taioges, n. a rustic female
Taiogi, v. to become rustic
Taiogol, a. relating to a vassal
Taiogrwydd, n. boorishness
Taiogyn, n. a rude fellow
Tair, a. three
Tairth, n. ague fit
Taith, n. journey

Tâl, n. payment; a reward
Tal, n. front; a forehead; high
Taladwy, a. payable, due (tal
Talaeth, n. a frontier; a dependent territory
Talaith, n. frontlet; diadem
Talar, n. head-land in a field
Talben, n. standard value
Talcen, n. front, a forehead
Talch, n. fragment; grist
Talchu, v. to break in pieces
Taldra, n. tallness, loftiness
Talddrws, n. front door
Taledigaeth, n. remuneration, payment
Taledigol, a. remunerative
Taleithig, n. a fillet, a bandlet
Taleithiog, a. wearing a diadem
Talfa, n. pediment
Talfainc, n. a front form; a
Talfoel, a. bald-fronted (throne
Talfyr, a. short-fronted, brief
Talfyredigaeth, n. an abbreviation, an abridgement (abridge
Talfyru, v. to fore-shorten, to
Talgainc, n. brow-antler
Talgell, n. pantry, buttery
Talgrib, n. front-board of a spinning wheel (tive
Talgrwn, a. precipitate; inflec-
Talgrych, a. rough-fronted
Talgryf, a. hard-fronted, brazen
Talgrynu, v. to inflect
Taliad n. a paying; a payment
Talm, n. impression; space; while; range; small quantity
Talmu, v. to be abrupt; to impress
Talp, n. a mass, a lump, a piece
Talpen, n. a knoll, a knob
Talpentan, n. a fire-back
Talpio, v. to form lumps
Talpiog, a. in lumps, lumpy
Talu, v. to pay; to requite
Talwisg, n. a head-dress
Talwrn, n. what projects
Tall, n. a spreading out or over
Tam, Tamaid, n. morsel; while

Tamaid, n. a morsel, a bite
Tameidiad, n. a biting a bit
Tameidio, v. to take a bite
Tameidyn, n. a small bite
Tamigo, v. to nibble, to nip
Tamp, n. what is pervasive
Tamper, n. a taper, a torch
Tampog, n. a fit of passion
Tampru, v. to burn a torch
Tân, n. expansion, spread; fire
Tan, a. spreading, continuous: prep. to till, as far; under
Tanbaid, a. violent, vehement
Tanbeiriant, n. fire-engine
Tanchwa, n. fire damp
Tanchwydd, n. inflamed swelling
Tanddaerol, a. subterraneous
Tandde, n. inflamation
Tanddewiniaeth, n. pyromancy
Tanddygiad, n. seduction
Tanedigaeth, n. spreading
Tanfa, n. explosion; fire damp
Tanfflamau, v. to flame with fire
Tanffon, n. a fire-poker
Tangloddio, v. to undermine
Taniad, n. a spreading; a firing
Taniadu, v. to make a firing
Tanio, v. to fire, to put on fire, to set fire to
Tanlli, a. ignifluous; span new
Tanlliw, a. flame-coloured
Tanllwyth, n. a blazing fire
Tanllyd, a. full of fire, fiery
Taniad, n. a starting; a throbb-
Tannorth. n. substitute [ing
Tannu, v. to stretch; to throb
Tanodd, prep. under, beneath
Tanrew, n. a nipping frost
Tansangu, v. to under-tread
Tansawdd, n. submersion
Tansoddi, v. to submerge
Tant, n. stretch; start; spasm: throb. Tant telyn, harp string
Tantawr, n. a player on string music, musician [ing
Tantiad, n. a starting; a string-
Tanu, v. to expand; to spread
Tanwyd, n. a breaking out of fire

Tânwydr, n. a burning-glass
Tanwydyn, n. a meteor
Tânwydd, n. fire wood
Tanysgrifio, v. to underwrite
Tanysgrifiad, n. a subscription
Tanysgrifiwr, n. a subscriber
Tap, n. hedge; heel piece
Tapig, n. a small step or ledge
Taplas, n. a gambol; a dance
Tar, n. a shock, an impulse
Tarad, n. a pervasion; flavour
Taradr, n. a piercer, an anger
Taradru, v. to pierce, to bore
Taran, n. shock; thunder
Taranol, a. thundering
Taranon, n. the thunderer
Taranu, v. to thunder
Taranydd, a. a thunderer
Tardd, n. a breaking out, an issue, a vent, a flow, a sprout
Tarddain, v. to keep oozing
Tarddell, n. an issue; a spring
Tarddellu, v. to issue, to gush
Tardden, n. mouth of an issue
Tarddiadol, a. effusive, eruptive
Tarddiant, n. emanation
Tarddol, a. issuing, springing
Tarddu, to break out; to spring
Tarell, n. an issue: a spring
Taren, n. spot; tump
Tarenu, v. to form a tump
Tarf, n. a driving; dispersion
Tarfgryd, n. the plant feverfew
Tarfhutan, n. a scarecrow
Tarfiad, n. expulsion; scaring
Tarfu, v. to expel; to scare
Targ, n. a purcussion, a clash
Targed, n. a clasher; a target
Tariad, n. a collision; a tarrying
Tarian, n. a clasher; a shield
Tarianad, n. using of a shield
Tarianu, v. to use a shield
Tario, v. to strike; to tarry
Tarlais, n. a piercing
Tarleisiad, n. a clashing
Tarlwnc, n. an eructation
Tarlynciad, n. a belching
Tarlyncu, v. to eructate, to belch

Tarn, n. a wipe; a drying up
Tarniad, n. absorption
Taro, v. to strike; to affect
Taroden, n. a ringworm
Tarth, n. a vapour, an exhalation
Tarthain, v. to keep exhaling
Tarthog, a. having vapour
Tarthol, a. exhaling vapour
Tarthedigaeth, n. evaporation
Tarthiad, n. an evaporating
Tarthlyd, a. vaporous; foggy
Tarthu, v. to exhale [a bull
Tarw, n. what bursts through;
Tarwain, v. to gush; to flutter
Tarwedd, n. pervasion; ferment
Tarweddiad, n. fermentation
Tarweddu, v. to ferment
Tarwhaid, n. second swarm
Tas, n. what binds; a fascia
Tasel, n. sash a fringe; tassel
Taselu, v. to fringe; to tassel
Tasg, n. bond; job; task
Tasgell, n. bandlet, bunch wisk, closet, pantry
Tasgellu, v. to form a whisk
Tasgiad, n. setting a task
Tasgu, v. to job, to task; to start
Tasad, n. a combining
Taso, v. to combine; to bundle
Tau, v. to stretch out; to be still: pron. thine
Taw, n. rest, quiet, silence: a still, quiet, silent: conj. that
Tawch, n. vapour, haze, fog: a. hazy, fogy
Tawchlyd, a. hazy, sultry
Tawd, n. spreading, distension
Tawdd, n. dissolved state: a. melted, dissolved
Tawddlestr, n. a melting pot
Tawedogrwydd, n, taciturnity
Tawedwst, n. a murmuring
Tawel, a. calm, silent, quiet
Taweliad, n. a calming
Tawelu, v. to calm; to grow calm
Tawelwch, n. calmness, serenity
Tawiad, n. a growing silent
Tawl, n. a casting off, a throw,
a taking off, a cutting off
Tawlfwrdd, n. draught board
Tawlffon, n. throwing staff, sling
Tawliad, n. a casting
Tawlrym, n. projectile power
Tawlu, v. to cast off, to throw
Te, n. what is spread; tea
Tebedu, v. to render prospective
Tebyg, a similar, like, likely
Tebygol, a. likely, probable
Tebygiad, n. a likening
Tebygiaeth, n. comparison
Tebygiant, n. a similitude
Tebygoldeb, n, likeliness
Tebygoli, v. to make like
Tebygrwydd, n. likelihood
Tebygu, v. to liken, to suppose
Tecâd, n. a rendering fair
Tecâu, v. to make fair
Teclyn, n. an instrument, a tool
Tech, n. a sculk, a lurk
Techiad, n. a sculking, a lurking
Techial, v. to keep sculking
Techu, v, to sculk, to lurk
Tedu, v. to stretch, to distend
Tedd, n. a display, a row
Teddiad, n. a displaying
Teddyf, n. a socket, a hollow
Tefu, v. to spread; to become spread
Têg, a. clear, fair, beautiful
Tegan, n. a bauble; a jewel
Tegâu, v. to make fair
Tegwch, n. fairness, beauty
Tegwedd, a. of fair appearance
Tegwel, a. of fair aspect
Tegychiad, n. an embellishing
Tegychu, v. to embellish
Teng, n. what is tenacious; a
Tengl, n. a girth, a girt [tough
Tengliad, n. a tying a girth
Tenglu, v. to tie with a girth
Teilchion, n. fragments
Teilfforch, n. a dung fork
Teiliad, n. a manuring
Teilig, a. enveloping, covering
Telliwr, n. dress maker, a tailor
Teilo, v. to spread manure

| TEIL | 287 | TER |

Teilwng, a. worthy, deserving
Teilyngiad, n. a meriting
Teilyngdod, n. worthiness [safe
Teilyngu, n. to merit; to vouch-
Teimladrwydd, n. feelingness
Teimladwy, a. sensible, feeling
Teimlo, v. to feel, to be sensible
Teirthon, n. an ague fit
Teisban, n. an origin; an over-
spread, a quilt; a hassock
Teisen, n. a cake
Teisenan, n. a little cake
Teisenu, v. to form a cake
Teithdrwydded, n. a passport
Teithi, n. faculties, characteris-
tics; the catemenia
Teithiad, n. a travelling
Teithiannol, a. itinerary
Teithiannu, v. to go a journey
Teithiant, n. a journeying
Teithig, a. characteristic
Teithio, v. to travel, to journey
Teithiol, a. journeying
Teithydd, n. traveller
Tel, n. stricture; straight line;
warp: a. stretched; prompt
Têl, n. what is fair; a regulator;
a measure of capacity: a regu-
lar; compact; fair
Telaid, a. beautiful, graceful
Telan, n. a harp
Telawd, n. the act of stretching
Telc, crimpled state a shrinking
Telcu, v. to shrink, to crimp
Telchyn, n. broken piece
Teledigrwydd, n. handsomeness
Telediw, a. compact; comely
Teledrwydd, n. comeliness
Teleiddio, v. to practise mins-
Teleiddyn, n. a minstrel [trelsy
Teleinio, v. to play the harp
Teler, n. a stretcher, a frame.
Telerau, terms, conditions
Telgorn, n. a hautboy
Telgwng, n. a crimpling
Telgyngiad, n. a crimpling
Telgyngu, v. to crimple
Telgyniad, v. a rebounding

Telgynu, to rebound; to stagge
Teli, n. exactness; an art
Teliad, n. a making smooth o
exact an art
Telid, n. a compact frame
Telio, v. to make accordant
Telm, n. gimcrack; springe to
Telma, v. to play with toys
Telmiad, n. a toying; a snaring
Telmu, v. to form a toy; to snare
Telmyn, n. a little toy; a tra
Telor, n. warbler; goldfinch
Telori, v. to warble, to quaver
Telpyn, n. a little lump
Telpynu, v. to form lumps [pac
Telu. v. to strain; to make com
Telyn, n. a harp; a side of a car
Telyniad, n. a harping   [case
Telynores, n. a female harpis
Telynorio, v. to play a harp
Telynwr, n. harpist
Tellu, v. to stretch over
Tellwedd, n. oblivion; a release
Tellweddiad, n. a consigning to
oblivion; a giving a release
Tem, n. round spread or space
Temig, n. particle; portion
Teml, n. a place of sitting; a
temple
Temliad, n. a forming a seat
Temlu, v. to form a seat
Teneu, a. thin; rarified; lean
Teneuâd, n. attenuation
Teneuâu, v. to attenuate
Teneuder, n. thinness; tenuity
Tenewyn, n a flank
Tenlli, n. linsey-woolsey
Tennyn, n. cord, halter
Tent, n. what strained; a tight-
tly strained
Tepyn, n. a small ledge or step
Ter, n. aptness to pervade
Têr, n. what is clear; a clear
Terol, a. clarifiing, refining
Terc, n. a jerk, jolt
Terciad, n. a jerking, a jolting
Tercu, v. to jerk, to jolt
Terch, n. a loop, noose

| TER | 288 | TIM |

Terchu, v. to loop, to noose
Teredig, a. clarified, refined
Teredigaeth n. clarification
Teredd, n. a clarified state
Terfyn, n. extremity, limit
Terfynedigaeth n. determination
Terfynaf, n. a boundary line
Terfyn-gylch, n. a horizon
Terfyniad, n. a terminating
Terfynol, a. terminating
Terfynoldeb, n. finitness
Terfynu, v. to limit; to end
Terfysg, n. tumult
Terfysgol, a. tumultuous
Terfysgedd, n. tumultuousness
Terfysgiad, n. making a tumult
Terfysglyd, n. apt to be riotous
Terfysgu, v. to raise a tumult
Teri, v. to grow sullen, to sulk
Teriad, n. irritation
Terica, v. to irritate, to rut
Terig, a. ardent; harsh; rutting
Teriglad, n. a making ardent
Term, n. crisis; term
Termio, v. to term; to tipple
Termudo, v. to grow silent
Termudrwydd, n. taciturnity
Tern, a. ardent, vehement
Terniad, n. a moving ardent
Terogen, n. female miser
Terogi, v. to be full of avidity
Teru, y. to clear, to refine
Teru, v. to pout, to sulk
Terwyn, a. ardent, fervent
Terwynder, n. vehemency
Terwyniad, n. a growing ardent
Terwynu, v. to grow ardent
Teryddiad, n. a growing ardent
Teryg, n. what is clotted; crust
Teryliiad, n. a glancing ardently
Tes, n. sunshine, warmth, heat
Tesach, n. heat; wantonness
Tesaint, n. a teeming with heat
Tesiad, n. a dispensing of heat
Tesog, a. sunny, hot, close, sultry
Testun, n. theme, subject, text
Testuno, v. to set a theme
Teth, n. a teat, a dug, a pap

Tethan, n. a small teat
Tethog, a. having teats
Tethu, v. to grow to a teat
Teulu, n. family, tribe
Teuluaeth, n. domestic society
Teuluaidd, a. domestic, familiar
Teuluedd, n. familiarity
Teulueiddio, v. to domesticate
Teuluwriaeth, n. domestic order
Teuluyddes, n. a housewife
Tew, a. thick, fat, plump
Tewâd, n. a thickening
Tewâu, v. to thicken, to fatten
Tewder, n. thickness; fatness
Tewdws, a. thickly collected
Tewi, v. to keep silent
Tewlyd, a. apt to grow thick
Tewychiad, n. a thickening
Tewychiant, n. thickeness
Tewychu, v. to thicken
Twyn, n. a firebrand
Teyrn, n. a sovereign
Teyrnas, n. a kingdom
Teyrnasiaeth, n. a reign
Teyrnasol, a. of a kingdom;
Teyrnasu, v. to reign [regnant
Teyrnedd, n. a monarchy
Teyrn-ged, n. a tribute
Teyrnogaeth, n. a kingly office
Teyrnoldeb, n. regality
Teyrnwialen, n. a sceptre
Ti, n. what is in; what is distinct: pron. thee, thou
Tib, Tic, n. a particle, a bit
Ticiad, n. a forming particles
Ticial, v. to drain in drops
Ticyn, n. a particle, a scrap
Tid, n. a draught chain
Tidian, n. a chaining
Tidmwy, n. a tether, a tie
Tidmwyad, n. a tethering
Ting, n. a crindle; a tingle
Tingo, v. to crindle; to flinch; to tingle
Til, n. a minute particle
Tiliad, n. a very small fly
Tim, n. a little, a scrap
Timyn, n. a little bit, a scrap

Tin, n a tail, a bottom
Tinbais, n. a petticoat
Tinben, adv. tail to tail
Tinc, n. a tink, a tinkle
Tincerdd, n. the tail of a craft; a tinker
Tinciad, n. a tinking; a tinkling
Tincial, Tincian, v. to tinkle; to drain
Tincio, v. to tink, to ring
Tincion, n. last drawn milk
Tindaflu, v. to throw the tail
Tindew, a. fat-buttocked
Tindin, adv. tail to tail
Tin topio, v. to flounce
Tindraphen, adv. topsy turvy
Tindro, n. a turn of the tail
Tindroed, n. the didapper
Tindrwm, Tindrom, a. heavy-
Tinf. el, a. bare-tailed [tailed
Tin-gloff, a. hipshot [red-start
Tin-goch, a. red-tailed: n. the
Tin-grach, a. scabby-tailed
Tinlethu, v. to overlay
Tinllom, Tinllwm, Tinnoeth, a. bare-bottomed
Tino, v. to form a tail
Tinpen, n. a hassock
Tinrwth, Tinwyg, a. open-tailed
Tinsigl, n. the wagtail
Tip, n. a particle, a bit
Tipyn, n. a piece, a little bit
Tipynu, v. to part into bits
Tir, n. land, earth, ground
Tiraeth, n. a continuation
Tirdriniad, n. a dressing of land
Tirddiwyll, n. agriculture
Tirf, a. fresh, luxuriant; lively
Tirfâd, n. a freshening
Tirfâu, v. to freshen; to enrich
Tirfdra, n. freshness; richness
Tiriad, n. a making a land
Tiriadu, v. to make a landing
Tirio, v. to land; to turn the ground
Tiriog, a. having land, landed
Tiriogaeth, n. landed estate
Tiriogi, v. to possess land

Tiriol, a. terreous, earthly
Tirion, n. a familiar spot: a. pleasant, genial, lovely
Tiriondeb, n. pleasantness
Tirioni, v. to render pleasant; to become pleasant
Tirionus, pleasing, delighting
Tirionwch, n. pleasantness
Tiro, v. to extend in continuity
Tis, n. a sneeze, sternutation
Tisiad, n. act of sneezing
Tisian, Tisio, v. to sneeze, to sternutate
Titen, n. a very small fly
Titiad, n. a small fly
Titr, n. a whirl; a metre
Titw, n. a cat, in fond language
Tithau, pron. thyself, thou also
Tlawd, Tylawd, a. poor, indigent, needy
Tlodi, Tylodi, n. poverty, want
Tlos, a. pretty, fair, handsome
Tlosen, n. a pretty female
Tlws, n. a jewel: a. pretty
Tlysedd, n. prettiness, beauty
Tlysiad, n. a making pretty
Tlysu, v. to render pretty
Tlysyn, n. a pretty thing
To, n. a covering; a roof; a generation
Toad, n. a covering; a roofing
Tob, n. a summit, a top
Tobren, n. a thatcher's dibber
Tobyn, n. a summit, an apex
Toc, what is abrupt; a cap: adv. instantly, presently
Toci, n. what is cut out; a share
Tociad, n. a cutting off, a clipping
Tocio, v. to clip, to dock
Tocyn, n. a short piece; a ticket
Tocyniad, n. a ticketing
Tocynu, v. to ticket, to draw lots
Tochi, v. to soak; to grow hazy
Todi, v. to construct; to join
Todiad, n. a construction
Toddadwy, a. dissolvable, soluble
Toddaid, n. what is melting; a metre

Toddedig, a. dissolved, liquid, melting
Toddi, v. to melt, to dissolve
Toddiad, n. a dissolving, a melting
Toddiant, n. a solution, a melting
Toddion, n. meltings; drippings
Toddol, a. dissolving, melting
Töed, n. a covering; a roofing
Töedig, a. covered: roofed
Toes, n. dough, paste of bread
Toeseg, n. a kneading trough
Toesi, v. to make dough
Toesyn, n. a lump of dough
Tofi, v. to draw out in a range
Tofiad, n. a drawing in a range
Togi, v. to elongate, to extend
Toi, v. to cover over; to roof
Tolach, n. a moan: v. to moan
Tolc, n. a dent or impression by punching or striking
Tolciad, n. a driving in
Tolcio, v. to cause a sink, to dent, to crease
Tolch, Tolchen, n. a coagulated mass, a clod
Tolchenu, v. to form a clod
Tolchiad, n. a forming clods
Tolfaen, n, an omen stone
Tolgorn, n. a trump, a clarion
Toli, v. to curtail; to spare; to deal out
Toliad, n. a curtailing; sparing
Toliant, n. a privation; sparing
Tolio, v. to diminish; to spare
Tolws, n. what roars; a roarer
Toll, n. a fraction; a toll
Tollfa, n. a tolling place
Tolli, v. to take from; to toll
Tolliant, n. a toll, a custom
Tom, n. a mound; a heap of dirt; dung
Tomen, n. a mound; a dunghill
Tomi, v. to make a heap; to dung
Tomlyd, a. covered with dung
Ton, n. a surface; a sward: a peel; a skin; lay land: n. a breaker; a wave

Tôn, n. a tone, an accent; a tune
Tonc, n. a tink, a ring, a clash
Tonciad, n. a tinking, a ringing
Toncio, v. to tinkle, to ring
Tonen, n. coating; cuticle; bog
Toni, v. to form a skin; to pare
Toniad, n. a making a tone: n. a skinning, a paring
Toniar, n. a plank, a shingle: n. a breaker, a wave
Tonog, a. turbulent, boisterous; froward
T nol, a. breaking in waves
Tonyddiaeth, n. a tonation
Top, n. a top; a stopple
Topiad, n. a topping: a cresting
Topio, v. to top, to crest
Topyn, n. a top; a topple
Topynu, v. to form a top
Tor, n. a break, a rupture, a cut: n. a bulge; a belly; a boss
Toraeth, n. a produce; a store
Torbwt, n. a turbot
Torch, n. a n. a wreath a coil
Torchi, v. to wreath; to coil
Torchog, a. wreathed; coiled
Torchol, a. wreathing. coiled
Torchwr, n. a wreather, a twister; a coiler
Tordain, v. to loll, to lounge
Tordyn, a tight-bellied
Tordd, n. a murmur, a din
Torddiad, n. a raising a din
Torddu, v. to murmur, to make a din
Tored, n. what expands: a. vast
Toredwynt, n. a whirlwind
Toreithio, v. to yield increase
Toreithus, Toreithiog, a. abundant, full, teeming
Torf, n. a crowd; a troop; a host, a multitude
Torfa, n. thousand millions
Torfagl, n. the eye-bright
Torfog, a. having a host
Torfu, v. to collect a host
Torgeingl, n. a girth, a girt
Torgest, n. a hernia, a rupture

Torgestu, v. to form a hernia; to rupture [chair
Torgoch, a. red-bellied: n. a
Torgochiad, n. a char fish
Tori, v. to break, to cut, to
Toriad, n. a breaking [fracture
Toriant, n. a fraction, a fracture
Torlan, n. a broken bank
Torlla, n. a slattern, a slut
Torllwyd, Torllwydog, n. the wild tansy [womb
Torllwyth, n. the burden of a
Torm, what is stretched round
Tormach, n. a forfeit of bail
Tormaen, n. the saxifrage
Tormennu, v. to press round
Torment, n. press round; conflict
Tormiad, n. a gathering round
Tormaint, n. surrounding host
Tormu, v. to asemble round
Torog, a. having a prominence; big-bellied, applied to sows, dogs, and cats
Torogyn, n. a big-bellied one
Toron, n. plat; a decking out; a cloak
Toronaeth, n. a decking out [tle
Toroni, v. to deck out; to man-
Toronog, a. decked, mantled
Torp, n. a round mass, a lump
Torpwth, n. a short squab
Tors, n. a covering; a shelter
Torsed, n. a coverlet, a rug
Torsi, v. to cover over
Torstain, a. bulging, gorbellied
Torsyth, n. stiff-stomached
Torsythu, v. to stiffen out the belly; to swagger
Torth, n. what sustains; a loaf
Torthi, v. to cake; to settle
Torympryd, n. a breakfast
Toryn, n. a mantle, a cape
Toryniad, n. a mantling
Torynu, v. to mantle, to cloak
Tos, n. quick jerk, toss
Tosiad, n. a jerking, a tossing
Tosio, v. to jerk, to toss
Tost, a. severe, harsh, violent

Tostedd, n. severity; a strang-
Tostfrwyn, n. sea rushes [uary
Tosti, v. to rack, to torture
Tostiad, n. a torturing
Tostur, n. misery, severe plight
Tosturaol, a. commiserating
Tosturâu, v. to commiserate
Tosturi, n. compassion; pity
Tosturiaeth, n. compassion
Tosturio, v. to take pity
Tosturiol, a. compassionate
Tosturus, a. pitiful piteous
Tôwr, n. one who forms a covering, one who roofs, thatcher, tiler slater
Tra, n. an extreme, an excess; a turn: adv. and perfix, over; very; whilst
Traberwi, v. to over-boil
Trabloedd, n. great outcry
Trabludd, n. trouble; turmoil
Trabluddio, v. to trouble [led
Trabluddiol, troublous; troub-
Trach, adv. beyond, beside, at
Trachefn, adv. behind; again; afterwards
Trachoddi, v. to vex extremely
Trachuro, v. to beat extremely
Trachwant, n. cupidity; lust
Trachwanta, to desire extremely, to covet
Trachwres, n. extreme heat
Trachywed, a. very uniform
Trad, n. what spreads out
Tradilyn, v. to follow, to excess
Tradwy, n. third day to come; adv. three days hence
Tradynol, a. superhuman
Tradd, n. extreme motion
Traddiad, n. a scouring
Traddod, n. a delivery over
Traddodi, v. to deliver over
Traddodiad, n. tradition
Traddyglad, n. a transferring
Traddygyd, v. to transfer
Traed, n. feet
Traeth, n. n tract, a sand
Traethadur, n. one who treats

Traethawd, n. a treatise
Traetheg, n. a declamation
Traethell, n. a sand bank
Traethiad, n. a treating
Traethodyn, n. a kind of verse
Traethu, v. to relate; to treat
Traf, n. a strain: a stir; a scour
Trafael, extreme effort: travail
Trafaelu, v. to travel, to toil
Trafaes, n. stir, bustle; pains
Trafel, n. press; hatchel
Trafiwnc, n. a guzzle, a gulp
Traflyncu, v. to guzzle, to gulp
Trafniad, n. a ranging; a revolving
Trafnid, n. a. range; a turn a change [ness
Trafnidaeth, n. commerce, business-
Trafnidio, v. to exchange
Trafnidiol, a. commercial
Trafnig, a. mutable, declineable
Trafnoldeb, n. mutableness
Trafnu, v. to range; to revolve
Trafod, n. a stirring, bustle
Trafodaeth, n. act of stirring, a bustling, an intermeddling, a transaction
Trafodi, v. to stir; to bustle, to strive, to intermeddle
Trafodus, a. stirring, bustling
Trafolio, v. to gormandise
Trafu, v. to stir, to scour
Trafyn, a stir, a bustle, a range
Traff, n. a strewing, a scattering
Trafferth, n. business, bustle
Trafferthu, v. to bustle, to toil
Trafferthus, a. bustling [ing
Traffiad, n. a spreading, a strew-
Traffaith, a. very confused
Traffu, v. to strew, to scatter
Trag, adv. beyond, beside
Tragor, n. superabundance
Tragori, v. to transcend
Tragoriaeth, n. transcendency
Tragoroldeb, n. superexcellence
Tragoroliad, n. a transcending
Tragoruchder n. supereminence
Tragwael, a. extremely frail

Tragwerth, n. over value
Tragwiw, a. most excellent
Tragwers, n. extreme heat
Tragfyth, adv. beyond this world
Tragfythol, adv. eternally
Tragywydd, a. everlasting
Tragwyddol, a. everlasting
Tragwyddoldeb, n. eternity
Tragwyddoli, v, to eternise, t immortalise
Traha, n. presumption
Trahâu, v. to become arrogan
Trahâus, a. arrogant, haught
Trahâusder n. presumption
Trai, n. decrease; ebb tide
Traidd, n. a pierce; a strait
Traig, n. what tends over
Traigl, n. turn, revolution
Traill, n. trial, draught, turn
Trais, n. rapine ravishment
Traith, n. expression, treatis
Trallod, n. adversity, affliction
Trallodiad, n. an afflicting
Trallodol, a. afflicting, vexin
Tramgwydd, n. a downfall
Tramgwyddo, v. to tumble
Tramgwyddol, a. stumbling
Tramoli, v. to praise to exces
Tramor, a. tranmarine; foreig
Tramori, v. to pass over sea
Tramp, n. a ramble, a stray
Trampio, v. to ramble
Tramwy, n. a going about
Tramwyo, v. to go about
Tramwyol, a, traversing
Tran, n. space, stretch, distric
Tranc, n. cessation; end
Tranced, n. a cup with a handle
Trancedig, a. perished; ended
Trancell, n. a single draught
Trancol, a. perishing; ended
Trancu, v. to perish, to die
Tranial, n. field of battle
Tranoeth, adv. on the morrow
Traphlith, adv. in a confuse
Trâs, n. kindred, affinity [state
Traserch, n. dotage, fondness
Traserth, a. extremely steep

Trasg, n. what is laid together
Trasgl, n. rake
Trathyn, a. extremely tight
Traul, n. wear, cost
Traw, n. a progress; a lead; education: adv. yonder
Trawaeth, n. a circumstance
Trawdd, n. a transit; a pass
Trawddysg, n. doctrine
Trawed, n. advancement
Trawedig, a. disciplined
Trawedigaeth, n. discipline
Trawenu, v. to pass over
Trawiad, n. a surpassing; a rearing, an educating
Trawiadu, v. to educate
Trawiadur, n. an instructor
Traws, n. a traverse, a cross
Trawsamcan, n. a cross purpose
Trawsbwyth, n. cross stitch
Trawsder, n. adverseness
Trawsdeyrn, n. usurper
Trawsdoriad, n. cross-cutting
Trawsdynu, v. to pull adversely
Trawsddodi, v. to transpose
Trawsedd, n. refactoriness
Trawselfeniad, n. transubstantiation
Trawsenw, n. metonymy
Trawsfeddiant, n. usurpation
Trawsfudo, v. to emigrate
Trawsganu, v. to satirise
Trawgludo, v. to transport
Trawsglwm, n. a cross knot
Trawsglwyddo, v. to transport
Trawsiad, n. a putting across
Trawsineb, n. adverseness
Trawslath, n. transverse beam
Trawslead, n. translocation
Trawslusgo, v. to trail across
Trawsosodi, v. to transpose
Trawsrwym, n. cross band
Trawsrywiad, n. a crossing of breeds
Trawst, n. a transom, a rafter
Trawstio, v. to lay a rafter
Trawsu, v. to cross, to grow adTrawswch, n. a whisker [verse
Trawsylweddu, v. to transubstantiate
Trawsymddwyn, n. metaphor
Trawsymud, v. to transpose
Tre, n. a resort, homestead, home, hamlet, town
Trec, n. an implement, a harness
Treciad, n. a furnishing
Trecyn, n. implement, tool
Trech, a. superior; passing
Trechad, n. an overcoming
Trechedd, n. a superiority
Trechol, a. overcoming
Trechu, v. to overpower
Trechwr, n. vanquisher
Tred, n. a resort; hamlet
Tref, n. a homestead, a hamlet, a town
Trefad, n. domicile, dwelling
Trefan, n. a small hamlet
Trefedig, a. inhabited, colonised
Trefiant, n. inhabitancy
Trefig, a. homely, domestic
Treflys, n. a court leet
Trefn, n. system, order, method
Trefnau, utensils, implements
Trefnedigaeth, n. adjustment
Trefniad, n. an ordering, an arranging
Trefniant, n. system, regulation
Trefnid, n. arrangement
Trefnidaeth, management
Trefnidedd, n. economy
Trefnido, v. to manage
Trefnidol, a. economical
Trefnoldeb, n. orderliness
Trefnol, a. orderly, systematic
Trefnu, v. to order, to dispose
Trefnus, a. orderly, decent, tidy, methodical
Trefnusder, n. orderliness
Trefnydd, n. one who orders, a manager; an economist; a Methodist [Methodism
Trefnyddiaeth, n. economy;
Trefnyddio, v. to methodise
Trefol, a. relating to home
Treftad, n. patrimony

| TREF | 294 | TREW |

Treftadaeth, n. a patrimony
Treftadog, a. having patrimony
Treftadol, a. patrimonial
Treftadu, v. to form a patrimony
Trefu, v. to make a home
Trengol, a. perishing, vanishing
Trengi, v. to end, to expire
Treiad, n. a decreasing
Treidio, v. to course, to range
Treiddiad, n. a penetrating
Treiddiadwy, a. penetrable
Treiddiedig, a. penetrated
Treiddio, v. to penetrate
Treiddiol, a. penetrating
Treiddioldeb, n. penetrability
Treiddyn, n. projecting ridge
Treigiddyn, n. a wanderer
Treigled, n. revolving, rolling
Treigledig, a. being revolved, revolving
Treigledigaeth, n. revolution
Treigliad, n. a revolving, a strolling; inflection [strolling
Treigliant, n. a revolution; a
Treiglo, to turn round; to inflict
Treiglwaith, adv. once in a time
Treillio, v. to troll, to dredge
Treilliwr, n. a troller, a dredge
Treinio, v. to stray; to scatter
Treio, v. to decrease, to ebb
Treisglad, n. a clattering
Treisglo, v. to clatter
Treisaid, n. forcer: n. heifer
Treisiaeth, n. ravishment
Treisiant, n. oppression, force
Treisio, v. to force, to ravish, to oppress
Treisioldeb, n. oppressiveness
Treisiwr, Treisydd, n. a forcer, a ravisher, an oppressor
Treithio, v. to treat, to discourse
Trem, n. a sight, a look, an aspect [strument
Trembeiriant, n. optical in-
Tremiad, n. looking, a gazing
Tremiant, n. an appearance
Tremid, n. an appearance
Tremidydd, n. an observer

Tremio, v. to look, to observe
Tremiol, a. looking, observing
Tremiwr, n. a looker
Tremydiad, n. an apparition
Tremydd, n. an observer [tion
Tremyddiaeth, n. science of op-
Tremyglad, n. a contemning
Tremygu, v. to contemn
Tremygus, a. contemptuous
Tremyn, n. a look, view, glance
Tremynfa, n. watchtower
Tremyn-gar, a. observant, keen
Tremyniad, n. phantom; boar
Tremynu, v. look; to seem
Tremynydd, n. an explorer
Tren, n. force, rapidity: a. impetuous; strenuous
Treniad, n. a moving rapidly
Trenig, a. impetuous, furious
Trenllif, n. rapid torrent
Trent, n. force, rapidity
Trenu, v. to act rapidly
Trenydd, adv. two days hence, the day after to-morrow
Tres, n. toil; a whip, a trace
Tresgl, the tormentil
Tresglen, n. a thrush, a bird
Tresiad a straining, a whipping
Trest, n. what is stretched
Trestl, n. a frame; a trestle
Trestliad, n. a framing
Trestlu, v. to put on a frame; to put on a trestle; to frame
Tresu, v. to put on a trace
Treth, n. a crop, growth; a tax
Trethol, a. tributary, taxed
Trethu, v. to tax, to rate
Treulfawr, a. expensive
Treulgar, a. prodigal, profuse
Treuliad, n. a consuming
Treulio, v. to consume
Trew, n. the act of sneezing
Trewiad, n. a sneezing
Trewlwch, n. sneeze dust, snuff
Trewydd, n. push forward
Trewyn, n. a pursuasion
Trewyniad, n. a persuading
Trewynol, a. persuasive

Trewynu, v. to persuade
Tri, a. three
Triad, n. a forming into three
Triannol, a. tertian, tradic
Triannu, v. to tertiate
Triarbymtheg, a. eighteen
Triarddeg, a. thirteen
Triban, n. a triplet, metre
Tribanineth, n. triplicity
Tribanu, v. to triplicate
Tribedd, n. a tripod, a trivet
Trichannull, a. three hundred thousand
Trichant, a. three hundred
Tridant, n. a trident
Trideg, a. thirty
Tridiau, n. three days
Tridyblyg, a. threefold
Trig, n. a stay, a fixed state
Trigiad, n. a staying, a tarrying
Trigfa, n. dwelling-place
Trigfanu, v. to form a dwelling
Trigiad, n. a tarrying
Trigiannol, a. residentary
Trigiannu, v. to reside
Trigiant, n. a residence
Trigo, v. to stay; to dwell; to die
Trigol, a. tarrying; dwelling
Trin, n. management; bustle; trouble; an action, a battle: v. to meddle; to manage; to labour at; to quarrel
Trindod, n. a trinity
Trindodaeth, n. trinitarianism
Trindodol, a. trinitarian
Trindodydd, n. a trinitarian
Triniad, n. a meddling; a managing; a quarrelling
Triniaeth, n. management
Triniol, a. managing
Triniogaeth, n. management
Trioli, v. to tertiate
Trip, n. trip, slip
Tripa, n. the bowels, intestines
Tripiad, n. a tripping
Tripian, v. to keep tripping
Tripio, v. to trip, to stumble
Trist, a. pensive, sorrowful, sad

Trisâd, n. a becoming sad
Tristâu, v. to grow sorrowful
Tristlawn, a. sorrowful, rueful
Tristwch, Tristyd, n. sadness, sorrow
Trithro, a. of three turns
Trithroed, a. three-footed
Triugain, a. sixty
Triugeinfed, a. sixtieth
Tro, n. a turn; a time; a lax
Troad, n. a turning; a flexion
Troch, n. a spray; a lave
Trochfa, n. a bathing place
Trochi, v. to immerse, to dip; to plunge
Trochiad, n. an immersing
Trochion, n. splashings; suds
Trochioni, v. to raise a lather
Trochol, a. bathing, immersing
Trochwr, n. one who dips; an Anabaptist
Trochydd, n. a dipper
Trodi, v. to make a transit
Trodiad, n. a passing onward
Troddi, v. to make a transit
Troddiad, n. a transition
Troed, n. a foot
Troedfedd, n. a foot measure
Troedgall, a. club-footed
Troedgam, a. wry footed
Troediad, n. a footing; a pacing
Troedig, a. turned, converted
Troedigaeth, n. conversion
Troedio, v. to foot; to tread
Troediog, a. footed: n. footman
Troedlas, Troedlath, n. a treadle, a foot board
Troedle, n. a trodden place
Troedlen, n. a foot-board
Troedlydan, a. broad-footed
Troednoeth, a. bare footed
Troedogi, v. to fetter
Troell, n. a whirl, wheel; reel; pulley; windlass
Troellen, n. a whirl, a twirl
Troellhoel, n. a screw nail
Troelli, v. to whirl; to reel
Troelliad, n. a whirling

Tröellog, a. having a wheel
Tröellwaith, n. wheelwork
Tröellymadrodd, n. tropology
Troen, n. a twirl; a while
Troeth, n. wash; lie; urine
Troethlif, n. a diabetes
Torfa, n. turn; a tropic; glance
Torfaeg, n. a trope
Trofan, n. a tropic
Trofâu, v. to make a turn
Trofâus, a. flexuous, tortuous
Trofiad, n. a transition; a clause
Trofiant, n. a transition
Trofol, a. tending forward
Trohidl, n. a rope twister
Troi, v. turn, to revolve
Troiad, n. a turning
Trol, n. cylinder, roll; cart
Trolaidd, a. cylindrical
Trolen, n. a roundlet
Troliad, n. a rolling
Trolian, v. to roll
Trolio, v. to roll, to trundle
Trolyn, n. roller; chub
Trom, a. heavy, weighty; sad
Tron, n. a circle; throne
Troni, v. to render superior
Tiôni, to form a circumference
Tröol a. turning, revolving
Tros, n. a transverse bar: prep. over, for, instead of. Da dros ben, exceedingly good
Trosedd, n. transgression
Troseddol, a. transgressing
Troseddu, v. to transgress, to offend [gressor
Troseddwr, n. offender, trans-
Trosel, n. plaited fence
Trosenwad, n. transnomination
Trosfa, n. a turning place
Trosfynediad, n. metabasis
Trosgludo, v. to transport
Trosglwyddiad, n. a transferring; a passage, a voyage
Trosglwyddo, v. to transfer
Trosglwyddol, a. transferring
Trosi v. to turn out; to move onward; to move about

Trosedd, prep. over; beyond
Trosodd, adv. on the other side
Trosof, trosot, trosti, trosom, trosoch, trostynt, pron. prep see Tros
Trosol. n. a lever; a bar
Trosolwaew, n. lever-beam
Trosten, n. a long slender rod
Trostr, n. a slider
Trotiad, n. a trotting
Trotian, v. to keep trotting
Trotio, v. to go on a trot
Trôth, n. what tends through
Troth, prep. from side to side
Trothi, n. a passing through
Trothwy, n. a threshold
Trotiwr, n. one who trots
Trowynt, n. a whirlwind
Tru, n. an outcast state
Truan, a. wretched, miserable
Truanedd, n. wretchedness
Truanes, n. a wretched female
Truanu, v. to commiserate
Trueiniad, n. a becoming wretched; a wretched one
Trueni, n. wretchedness; pity
Truenus, a. wretched, piteous
Truenusedd, n. piteousness
Trugar, a. compassionate
Trugarâd, n. commiseration
Trugarâu, v. to commiserate
Trugaredd, n. mercy, pity
Trugareddfa, n. mercy-seat
Trugareddol, a. merciful
Trugarog, a. merciful, pitying
Trugarogrwydd, n. mercifulness
Trul, n. drilling tool
Truliad, n. a drilling
Trulio, v. to drill a hole
Trull, n. store: store of liquor
Trulliad, n. a butler
Trulliadaeth, n. butlership
Trullio, v. to draw liquor
Trum, n. a ridge, a back
Truman, n. a ridge, a cope
Trumbeithin, n. ridge tiles
Trumbren, n. a keel
Trumiad, n. a ridging; a copying

Trumicg a. ridged, coped
Trus, n. a ward, a guard
Trusi, n. what is a guard
Trusiad, n. a ward, a bulwark
Trusio, v. to ward, to guard
Truth, a. wheedling, fawning
Truhad, n. a wheedling
Truthan, n. a wheedler
Truthiad, n. a sycophant, a flatterer
Truthio, v. to weedle
Trw, n. a whirl; a pervasion: prep. through, by
Tryb, n. what is rubbed
Trwc, n. a turn; a truck
Trwca, n. a bowl, a cup
Trwcwl, n. a trundle; a truckle
Trwch, n. a cut; a section; thickness
Trwl, n. pack, cushion
Trwliad, n. a rolling up
Trwlian, v. to roll together
Trwlio, v. to bundle, to roll
Trwlyn, n. a squabby thing
Trwm, a. heavy, weighty; sad
Trwn, n. a circle
Trwnc, n. urine, lie, stale
Trwodd, adv. through
Trwpa, n. tub, hod, trollop
Trws, n. covering, dress
Trwsglyn, n. a bungler
Trwsgl, a. clumsy, bundling
Trwsiad, n. a dressing; dress
Trwsiadu, v. to clothe, to dress
Trwsiadus, a. dressed, decked
Trwsio, v. to dress, to deck
Trwst, n. noise, rustling
Trwstan, a. clumsy; unlucky
Trwstaneiddio, v. to become clumsy (n. clumsiness
Trwstaneiddwch, Trwstanwch,
Trwth, n. what tends to expand
Trwy, n. a pass through: prep. though; by means of
Trwyad, n. permeation
Trwyadl, a. alert, smart, lively
Trwyadledd, n. sprightliness
Trwyadlu, v. to act alertly
Trwyd, n. a bursting through

Trwyddad, n. a bursting through
Trwydo, v. to burst through
Trwydol, bursting, penetrating
Trwydd, n. a passing through: prep. through; by
Trwydded, n. a pass, a passport, a licence, a fare, a reception
Trwyddedog, a. having licence
Trwyddedogi, v. to give free passage
Trwyddedu, v. to pass free'y
Trwyddo, v. to pass through; to
Tewyll, n. a swivel, a ring [bore
Trwylliad, n. a swivelling
Trwyllo, v. to swivel; to troll
Trwyn, n. a point; a snout, a nozzle, a nose
Trwynswch, n. tip of the nose
Trwyo, prep. through: adv. through
Trwyogaeth, n. pervasion
Trwyogi, v. to make pervasive
Trwyth, n. a solvent; lie; decoction
Trywytho, v. to steep in lie
Trwythi, n. a menstrum; lie
Trwythiad, n. a steeping in lie
Try, n. aptness to pass through
Tryad, n. a pervasion [or over
Tryal, n. a homestead
Tryarllais, a. of stunning voice
Tryawch, n. magnetism
Tryb, n. a blended state
Trybaeddiad, n. a wallowing
Trydaeddu, v. to wallow to daub
Trybed, n. support; brand iron
Trydedd, n. a support; a trivet
Trybeddu, v. to set firmly
Trybelid, a. perspicuous, clear
Trybest, n. commotion, bustle
Trybestu, v. to bluster, to bustle
Tryboethi, v. to heat through
Tryboli, v. to huddle; to wallow
Trybylog, a. dull
Tryciad, n. a dragging, a trailing heavily
Trycio, v. to flag, to fail
Trych, n. an opening; a scope

Trycheb, n. tinesis
Trychfa, n. place that is cut
Trychfil, n. a destructive animal vermin
Trychiad, n. cutter, lopper [ted
Trychiedig a. being cut; trunca-
Trychinebus, a. disastrous
Trychion, n. cuttings
Trychionyn, a shred, cutting
Trychni, n. disaster, mishap
Trycholdeb, n. a mangled state
Trychu, v. to cut, to cut into
Trychwys, n. thorough sweat
Trychyn, n. a small cut
Trydan, n. the electric fluid
Trydaniad, n, electrifying
Trydaniaeth, n. electricity
Trydanu, v. to electrify
Trydar, n. chirp; din: v. to chirp
Trydariad, n. a chattering
Trydaru, v. to chatter; to din
Trydedd, a. third
Trydiad, n. a pervasion
Trydon, n. what pervades; agrimony, a thoroughly toned, four days hence
Trydydd, a. third
Trydd, n. what is through
Tryf, n. what is pervasive
Tryfal, n. a triangle
Tryfalu, v. to form a triangle
Tryfer, n. a harpoon, a spear
Tryferiad n. a harpooning
Tryferu, v. to harpoon
Tryfesur, n. a diameter
Tryfol, n. what is all belly
Tryfoliad, n. a gormandising
Tryfolio, v. to gormandise
Tryfrith, a thoroughly mixed swarming; teeming
Tryfrwyd, a. interweaving
Trylais, n. thorough voice
Trylef, n. thorough utterance
Tryles, n. thorough benefit
Trylifo, v. to flow through
Trylith, n. thorough training
Tryliw, n. pervading colour
Tryloes, n. pervading pang
Tryloew, a. transparent
Trylosg, n. thorough ignition
Trylwyn, a very ready or perfect
Trylyn, a, thoroughly keen
Trym, a. compact trim
Trymâd, n. a rendering heavy
Trymâu, v. to make heavy
Trymder, n. heaviness
Trymfryd, n. sadness of mind
Trwmgwsg, n. a dead sleep
Trymiad, n. a making potent
Trymlyog, a. flagging
Tryn, n. ardency, fierceness; ardent, fierce, stern
Trynaws, n. pervading quality
Trynedd, n. ardency; fierceness
Tynerth, n. thorough strength
Trynodd, n. a pervading juice
Trynwyd, n. a pervading emotion
Tryryw, n. a perfect kind
Trysain, n perfect, sound
Trysawdd, n. a cube root
Trysgledd, n. awkwardness
Trysor, n. a treasure
Trysoriad, n. a treasuring
Trysorwr, n. n. a treasurer
Trystiad, n. a blusterer
Trystiad, n. a clattering
Trystian, v. to keep clattering
Trystio, v. to bluster, to clatter, to rustle
Trythgwd, n. a satchel
Trythu, v. to swell out
Trythyll, a. voluptuous
Trythyllu, v. to follow pleasure
Trythyllwch, n. enjoyment
Tryw, n. what pervades; what is constant; a trace; truth; agrimony: a. universal; constant
Trywan, n. a thrust, a stab: a pierced, stabbed
Trywaniad, n. a transfixing
Trywanu, v. to tranfix; to stab
Trywar, a. thoroughly tame
Trywedd, n. a trace by scent
Trywel, a. perspicious
Trywiad, n. a pervading

Trywio, v. to pervade
Trywydd, n. a trace, a scent
Trywyddu, v. to trace by scent
Trywyllt, a. thoroughly wild
Trywyn, a. thoroughly happy
Trywyngar, a. conciliatory
Tu, n. side; region, part
Tua, adv. in a direction to
Tugat, prep. towards
Tuallan, adv. on the outside
Tuch, n. a grunt, a groan
Tuchan, n. a grunting: v. to grunt, to groan
Tuchaniad, n. a grunting
Tuchanllyd, a. apt to grunt
Tuchanol, a. grunting
Tuchanwr, n. grumbler, a groaner murmurer
Tud, n. a surface; a region
Tudalen n. side of a leaf; a page
Tudfach, n. a stilt
Tudlath, n. a meting rod
Tudwed, n. a sward, a sod
Tudd, n. shade; gloom; vapour
Tuddad, n. an enveloping
Tudded, n. a covering, a vesture
Tuddediad, n a habiting
Tuddedu, v. to put on a vest
Tuddo, v. to envelope
Tuedd, n. a region, a district, a coast; a tendency
Tueddiad, n. inclination
Tueddol, a. inclining, conducive
Tueddoldeb, n. inclindness
Tueddoli, v. to render partial
Tueddu, to incline, to bias
Tueddwr, n. one who inclines
Tuell, n. a covert; a cover
Tufnes, adv. on the outside

Tunad, n. a pervading
Tur, n. a reverse, a turn up
Turiad, n. a reversing
Turio, v. to reverse; to turn
Turn, n. a turn; a. round
Turnen, n. a whirl; a turning-wheel; a shaft of a wheel
Turniad, n. a turning; turnery
Turnio, v. to turn, to do turnery
Turnwr, n. a turner
Turs, n. a snout, chops
Tursyn, n. a long snout
Tus, n. what is warpped; a whisp
Tusw, n. a whisp, a bunch
Tuswad, n. a making a whisp
Tuth, n. a trot; a trudge
Tuthiad, n. a trotting
Tuthio, v. to trot; to trudge
Tw, n. a rising up; a drive; sway
Twa, v. to drive, to urge on
Twb, n. a round lump, a lid
Twba, n. a tub
Twc, n. a cut, a clip, a chip
Twca, n. a sort of knife
Twciad n, a clipping, a docking
Twcio, v. to clip, to dock
Twdd, n. n. what pokes or just out
Twddf, n, a poke; a punch
Tweg, n. a lock of hair
Twf, n. grouth; increase
Twff, n. a rise, a lift; a tuft
Twng, n. a lot, a plight, an oath
Twl, n. what is rounded; a toft
Twlc, n. a cot, a hovel, a stye
Twlch, n. a tump a knoll
Twl'en, n. a squabby female
Twlffyn, n. a squab, a chub

TWM	300	TYG

Twmpiad, n. a drooping
Twmpian, v. to drop, to nod
Twn, n. a tracture; a splint; a. fractured
Twnc, n. a deposit, a pledge
Twniad, n. a fracturing [mole
Twrch, n. a burrower; a hog; a
Twr, n. a heap, a pile; a tower
Twred, n. a pile, a turret; a tub
Twrf, n. a stir, a tumult, a turmoil, a clap, a shrink
Twriad, n. a throwing up
Twrio, v. to raise up, to heap
Twrn, n. a round, a turn
Twrnel, n. a tub, a vat
Tws, n. an extreme; an outlet
Twsel, n. a tap, a fawcet
Twt, n. what is complete: a. complete, neat, smart
Twtach, n. a hard breathing
Twti, n. an intermitted state
Twtiad, n. a making simple, unconnected, neat
Twtial, v. to intermit; to loiter
Twtio, v. to make neat
Twtnais, a. altogether neat
Twy, n. a check, a stop
Twyad, n. a checking
Twyg, n. a garment; a toga
Twygo, v. to cover, to warp
Twyll, n. deceit, fraud
Twyllad, n. a deceiving
Twylleb, n. sophistry
Twyllo, v. to deceive
Twyllodrus, a. deceitful, false
Twym, n. a heat; a flush; a. warm, hot, sultry
Twymad, n. a warming
Twymdra, n. warmness, warmth
Twymowyr, a. lukewarm
Twymnder, n. warmth
Twymniad, n. a warming
Twymnol, a. warming
Twymo, v. to warm, to heat
Twymyn, n. a heat; a fever
Twyn, n. a hillock; a bush
Twynyn, n. a tump; a bush
Twyo, v. to hem in; to check

Twyr, a. agitated; torrid [corn
Twys, n. a top, a tuft; an ear of
Twysen, n. an ear of corn [ing
Twyseniad, n. a spring; an ear-
Twysenol, a. spring; earing
Twysenu, v. to spire; to ear
Twysg, n. a mass, a quantity
Twysged, n. a mass, quantity
Twysgo, v. to amass
Twysiad, n. a tufting, a spiring
Twyth, n. elasticity; celerity
Twythad, n. a springing
Twythiad, n. a springing, a bounding
Twythiant, n. a resiliency
Twythig, a. elastic; a rising
Twytho, v. to spring, to bound
Twythus, a. tending to spring
Tŷ, n. what includes; a house
Tyaid, n. a houseful
Tyb, n. opinion, notion
Tybgar, a. opinionated
Tybiad, n. a supposing
Tybied, v. to suppose, to think
Tybio, v. to suppose, to suspect
Tybiol a. supposing, suspecting
Tybys, a. suspecting, suspicious
Tybygiad, n. an imagining
Tybygoliaeth, n. supposition
Tyciad, n. a prospering
Tyciannu, v. to cause success
Tyciannus, a. prosperous
Tyciant, n. prosperity, success
Tycio, v. to prosper
Tyciol, a. prospering
Tyd, n. what is continuous
Tydain, n. Titan, the sun
Tydi, pron. thou, thyself
Tyddfiad, n. a poking; a jutting
Tyddfu, v. to poke; to jut
Tyddiad, n. a spreading out
Tyddyn, n. a farm; a tenement
Tyfid, n. a growing, a growth
Tyfannu, v. to vegitate
Tyfiant, n. vegitation, growth
Tyfol, a. growing; vegitating
Tyfu, v. to grow, to vegetate
Tygiad, n. a prospering

| TYG | 301 | TYR |

Tygio, v. to prosper, to succeed
Tyngiad, n. a plighting; a swearing
Tyngied, n. destiny, fate, luck
Tyngiedfen, n. a destiny, fate
Tyngedfenu, v. to predestinate
Tyngediad, n. adjuration
Tyngedu, v. to adjure
Tyngiad, n. a swearing
Tyngu, v. to pledge, to swear
Tyhun, pron. thou, thyself
Tylad, n. a making smooth [ter
Tylath, n. a house beam, a raf-
Tycyn, n. a small hovel
Tylchiad, n. a forming a knoll
Tylchu, v. to form a knoll
Tyle, n. a down, a toft, a site
Tylinad, n. a kneeding
Tylino, v. to kneed dough
Tylu, n. a household
Tyledd, n. domesticity; society
Tylwyth, n. household; family
Tylwytho, v. to form a family
Tylwythog, a. having a family
Tyllgrug, n. a chink by drought
Tylliad n. a boring, perforation
Tyllog, a. having holes, perforated
Tyllu, v. to bore, to make a hole
Tymig, a. ample, full time
Tymmher, n. temperament
Tymmheriad, n. a tempering
Tymmherol, a. temperamental
Tymmheru, v. to temper
Tymmherus, a. temperate[ness
Tymmherusedd, n. temperate-
Tymmhestl, n. a tempest
Tymmhestliad, n. a storming
Tymmhestlog, a. tempestuous
Tymmhestlu, v. to storm, to boister
Tymmhestlus, a. tempestuous
Tymmhigiad, n. a prickling
Tymmor, n. season, time
Tymmoraidd, a. seasonable
Tymmori, v. to take a season
Tymmoriad, n. a fixing a season
Tymmoroldeb, n. seasonableness

Tymp, n. an enlargement; a bringing forth, a birth; a time
Tyn, n. a pull, a stretch: a tight, stretched; stubborn
Tynâd, n. a tightening
Tynâu, v. to tighten, to strain
Tynchwydd, n. a tumour
Tynder, n. tightness; rigidity
Tyndir, n. fallow land
Tyndra, n. tightness, straitness
Tyndrec, n. draught gear
Tynedigaeth, n. attraction
Tynedigol, a. attractive
Tynell, n. a barrel, a tun; a tor
Tynellaid, n. contents of a tun
Tynelliad, n. the act of filling a tun
Tynellu, v. to fill a tun
Tyner, a. tender, lenient, mild
Tyneredd, n. tenderness
Tyneriad, n. a making tender
Tyneriant, n. emollition
Tyneru, v. to make tender
Tynerus, a. of a tender nature
Tynerwch, n. tenderness
Tynfa, n. a draught, a pull
Tynfach, n. a harpoon, a grapnel
Tynfaen, n. a loadstone
Tynfarch, n. a draught horse
Tyniad, n. a pulling, draught
Tyniar, n. a bubble
Tyniedydd, n. an extractor
Tynlath, n. a draught-tree
Tyno, n. a plat, a green, a dale
Tynrwyd, n. a drag-net
Tynrwydd, n. tightness, rigidity
Tynu, v. to draw, to pull
Tyrchaidd, a. hoggish, hog-like
Tyrches, n. a splayed sow
Tyrchiad, n. a burrowing
Tyrchu, v. to burrow, to turn
Tyrchyn, n. a little hog
Tyrddain, v. to be blustering
Tyrddan, n. a blustering
Tyrddu, v. to bluster, to storm
Tyrfa, n. a multitude, a host
Tyrfain, v. to be blustering
Tyrfâu, v. to shrink together

| TYR | 302 | UCH |

Tyrfu, v. to rise up; to turn up; to contract, to skrink
Tyriad, n. a heaping, a piling
Tyru, v. to heap, to amass
Tyrwn, n. a sand bank
Tysmwy, n. a throb
Tysmwyad, n. a throbbing
Tyst, n. a witness
Tystiad, n. a witnessing
Tystiant, n. evidence
Tystio, v. to testify
Tystiol, a. testifying
Tystiolaeth, n. a testimony
Tystiolaethol, a. testimonial
Tystioliaethiad, n. a testifying
Tystiolaethu, v. to testify
Tysyn, n. a yarn-ball bottom
Tytmwy, n. a clasp, a buckle
Tyw, n. what overspreads
Tywallt, v. to pour, to spill
Tywalltiad, n. a pouring out
Tywalltol, a. pouring, shedding
Tywarch, n. sod, clod, turf
Tywarchen, n. element; sod
Tywarchiad, n. a swarding
Tywarchu, v. to form a sod
Tywas, n. a house servant
Tywel, n. a cloth, a towel
Tywell, a. dark, obscure, dusky
Tywiad, n. a spreading over
Tywio, v. to spread about
Tywod, n. sand, earth
Tywodi, v. to form sand
Tywodlyd, a. full of sand, sandy
Tywodog, a. having sand
Tywodol, a. arenacious, sandy
Tywodyn, n. a grain of sand
Tywota, v. to gather sand
Tywu, v. to spread about
Tywydd, n. the weather
Tywyll, n. dusk, gloom: a. dark, obscure, dusky
Tywylliad, n. a darkening
Tywyllod, n. obscurity
Tywyllu, v. to darken, to obscure
Tywyllwch, n. darkness
Tywyn, n. spread, ray; strand
Tywynedig, a. illumined
Tywynedigaeth, n. radiance;
Tywyniad, n. radiating, shining
Tywynol, a. radiant, shining
Tywynu, v. to radiate, to shine
Tywynwg, n. radiancy, splendour
Tywynygiad, n. illumination
Tywyngu, v. to illuminate
Tywys, n. a leading, a guidance
Tywysel, n. plug, stopple, stopper
Tywysg, n. a procession
Tywysgiad, n. a proceeding
Tywysgo, v. to proceed
Tywysiad, n. leading, conducting
Tywysog, n. a leader; a prince
Tywysogaeth, n. a principality
Tywysoges, n. a princess
Tywysogol, a. leading, guiding
Tywysydd, n. a man who leads, a leader

U

UB, n. what is high; a howl
Ubain, n. a howling: v. to howl, to moan
Uban, n. a howling, a bellowing
Uch, n. a sigh: a. being over; upper: prep. above, over: adv. above
Uchad, n. a rising over
Uchaf, a. upmost, uppermost
Uchafael, n. an ascension
Uchafed, a. being over, upper
Uchafedd, n. loftiness, height
Uchafiad, n. a rising over
Uchafiaeth, n. supremacy
Uchanian, n. a superior nature
Uchaniaeth, n. metapysics
Uchanianol, a. supernatural
Ucharn, n. the ankle
Uchder, n. height, highness
Uchediad, n. an elevating
Uchedu, v. to elevate, to soar
Uchedydd, n. a soarer; a lark
Uchedd, n. loftiness, altitude; top

| UCH | 303 | UN |

Uchel, a. high, lofty, towering
Uchelder, n. loftiness, elevation
Ucheldrem, n. a haughty look
Ucheldyb, n. high opinion
Ucheledd, n. loftiness
Uchelfa, n. a high place
Uchelfaer, n. a high constable
Uchelfal, n. the misletoe
Uchelfryd, a. high-minded
Ucheliad, n. a heightening
Ucheliant, n. elevation
Uchelraith, n. a grand jury
Uchelryw, n. a superior kind
Uchelsaf, n. a high standing
Uchelsantaeth. n a hierarchy
Uchelu, v. to make high
Uchelwr, n. a freeholder
Uchelwyl, n. a high festival
Uchelydd, n. a superior
Uchellawr, n. the misletoe
Uchenaid, n. a sigh
Uchenidiad, n. a sighing
Ucheneidio, v. to sigh
Ucher, n. gloom; evening
Ucherddo, n. evening tide
Uchergyd, n. a lofty shock
Uchelwyl, n. a vesper
Uchiad, n. a heightening
Ucho, prep. above: adv. above
Ud, n. a howl, a yell; a blast
Udfa, n. a howling, a yelling
Udgan. n. a sound of a trumpet
Udganiad, n. the act of sounding a trumpet
Udganu, v. to sound a trumpet
Udgorn, n. a trumpet
Udiad, n. a howling, a yelling
Udlef, n. a howling voice
Udo, v. to howl, to yell
Udol, a. howling, yelling
Udon, n. a solemn cry
Udoniad, n. an imprecation
Udoniaeth, n. imprecation
Udd, n. what is over; a chief
Uf, n. what is over or spread
Ufelai, n. oxygen
Ufeliar, n. what flames out
Ufelu, v. to generate fire

Ufelyddiad, n. ignition
Ufell, a. humble, obsequous
Ufudd, a. humble, obedient
Ufudd-dod, n. obedience
Ufuddgar, a. obsequous, meek
Ufuddâd, n. humiliation [ble
Ufuddâu, v. to obey, to be hum-
Ufuddoldeb, n humbleness
Uffarn, n. the ankle
Uffern, n. hell, hades
Uffernol, a. infernal, hellish
Ug, n. what is enveloping
Ugain. Ugaint, a twenty
Ugeinfed, a. twentieth
Ugeinplyg, a. twenty-fold
Ul, n. what is humid; closeness: a. damp; close, muggy
Ulai, a. hydrogen
Uliad, n. a making damp; a growing muggy
Uliar, n. a plegmatic habit
Ulo, v. to damp; to smother; to become close or muggy; to heat with dampness
Ulw, Ulwyn, n. ashes, cinders
Ull, n. what is abrupt or quick
Ullda, n. a crazy one, a fickle one, an oaf
Ulliad, n. a sudden driving
Un, n. an individual, one: a. one; identical, same
Unad, n. a making one, union
Unerbymtheg, a. sixteen
Unarddeg, a. eleven [arch; sir
Unben, Unbeniad, n. a mon-
Unbennaethol, Unbenol, a. mon-archical
Unbriodas, n. monogamy
Uncorn, n. the unicorn
Undad, a. of the same father
Undeb, n. unity; concord
Undeg, a. eleven [pleness
Under, Undod, n. unity; sim-
Undodiad, n. an unitarian
Undodiaeth, n. unitarianism
Undon, a. monotonous
Undras, a. of the same kindred
Undull, a. of the same form

Uned, n. unity; accordance
Unfaint, n. unity of size
Unfed, a. first
Unfraint, a. of equal rank
Unfryd, a. of one mind
Ungor, a. of one turn or twist
Uniad, n. a uniting
Uniaith, a. of one language
Uniant, n. unity, union
Uniawn, a. direct, straight; upright; just, perfect
Unigedd, n. loneliness [united
Unigol, a. single, singular; dis-
Unigoldeb, n. singularity
Unigrwydd, n. solitude
Unionad, n. a straightening
Uniondeb, n. rectitude
Unionder, n. straightness
Union-gred, n. orthodoxy
Union-gyrch, a. of direct course
Unioni, v. to straighten
Unionred, a. of direct course
Unionsyth, a. quite erect
Unllaw, a. single-handed
Unlle, Unman, n. one place: adv. anywhere
Unlled, a. of one breath
Unllef, a. of the same sound
Unlliw, a. of one colour
Unllygeidiog, a. monoculous
Unmodd, a. of the same mode
Unnaws, a. of the same temper
Unnerth, a. of equal power
Uno, v. to unite; to accord
Unodli, v. to agree in rhyme
Unoed, a. of the same age
Unol, a. uniting; accordant
Unoldeb, Unoliaeth, Unoliant, n. indentity, unity
Unoli, v. to become as one
Unplyg, a. of one fold
Unryw, a. of the same kind
Unsain, n. unison
Unsill, a. of one syllable
Unswydd, a. of one purpose
Untro, n. what is of one turn: a. one turn [footed
Untroed, n. one foot: a. one-

Uniu, n. one side: a. one-sided
Unwaith, a. one time: adv. once
Unwedd, a. similar: adv. alike
Ur, n. what is essential or pure
Urdd, n. sacred order; rank
Urddas, n. dignity: holy order
Urddasiad, n. dignification
Urddasog, a. having orders
Urddasol, a. sacred: dignified
Urddasu, v. to dignify; to confer orders
Urddedig, a. dignified; ordained
Urddedigaeth, n. ordination
Urddeiniad, n. dignification
Urdden, n. pure intellect
Urddiad, n. a dignifying
Urddiant, n. dignification
Urddoldeb, n. dignified state
Urddo, v. to dignify, to ordain
Urddol, a. dignified, exalted
Urddoli, v. to ordain
Urddoliad, n. ordination
Urddwisg, n. a robe of state
Us, n. what is external; chaff: a. trifling, light, frail
Usion, n. husks, chaff
Uslyd, a. full of chaff or husks
Ust, n. silence, a hush
Ustiad, n. a hushing
Ustio, v. to hush; to hiss
Uthredd, n. astonishment
Uthriad, n. an astonishing
Uthro, v. to astonish
Uthrol, a. astonishing, amazing
Uthroldeb, n. awfulness
Uwch, prep. above, over
Uwchder, n. altitude, height
Uwd, n. hasty pudding; pap
Uwdaidd, a. like hasty pudding
Uwdfys, n. nursing finger

W

WAB, n. a slap, a stroke
Wabiad, n. a slapping, a banging

| WAB | 305 | WY |

Wabio, v. to slap, to bang
Wb, n. the state of being expelled: interj. out, avaunt, ho!
Wbain, v. to keep howling
Wbwb, interj. denoting anxiety
Wch, n. expansion
Wchw, interj. denoting distress
Wedi, Wedin, adv. afterwards, then
Weithian, adv. now, at length
Weithiau, adv sometimes
Wel, conj. so, well; now
Wela, interj. look, behold, lo
Wff, n. a motion, from or out of
Wfft, n. a push off, a flight, interj. fie, for shame
Wfftio, v. to cry fie
Wi, interj. hey; heyday; oh
Wibi, the whinnying of a horse
Winc, n. the chaffinch
Wl, n. what is subtle or fine [by
Wnc, Wng, a. close, near, hard
Wo, n. a motion out; a stop [up
Wp, n. a state of being out or
Wr, n. a state of being on or at
Wrch, n. what is high or round
Wrdd, n. contact; impulse
Wrth, n. a touch, contact: prep. close to; by; with
Wrthyf, wrthyt, wrtho, wrthi, wrthym, wrthych, wrthynt, pron. prep. See WRTH
Ws, n. action; effort; ardour
Wsg, n. what separates
Wst, n. a thrust, a push; a gust
Wt, n. what is extreme or out: n light grain of corn
Wttre, n. a lane, a bye road
Wttres, n. a revel, a carousal
Wttresiad, n. a carousing
Wttresol, a. revelling, carousing
Wttresu, v. to revel, to carouse
Wth, n. what expands
Wy, n. what is produced; an egg pron. of him, of her, of it
Wybr, n flmament; sky [ia
Wybraidd, a. atmospherical, aer
Wybreiddio, v. to become as ai

Wybren, n. firmament, atmos
Wybrenol, a. firmamental [phere
Wybrgoel, n. aeromancy
Wybriad, n. what exists in air
Wybriaeth, n. aerology
Wybrliw, n. cerulean hue
Wybro, v. form air; to go into air; to soar in the air
Wybrol, a. firmamental; aerial
Wyd, v. thou art
Wyf, v. I am
Wyl, n. a flow, a gush; a wail
Wylad, n. a wailing, a weeping
Wylo, v. to wail, to weep
Wylofain, v. to keep wailing
Wylofus, a. wailing; doleful
Wyn, n. lambs
Wyneb, n. a face, a visage
Wynebiad, n. a facing
Wynebpryd, n. countenance
Wynebu, v. to face, to front
Wynos, n. lambkins
Wyr, n. a grandchild, a grandson
Wyrain, a. spreading, extending
Wyre, n. a spreading, expanse
Wy o, v. to distend, to reach out
Wys, n. an aptitude for motion
Wysg, n. a tendency forward; a bias; presence; a current; a course; a stream: adv. in a forward direction
Wyt, v. thou art
Wyth, a. eight
Wythban, a. of eight parts
Wythblyg, a. of eight folds
Wythdeg, a. eighteen (not used)
Wythdro, a. of eight turns
Wythdroed, a. having eight feet
Wythdeg, a. eighty (not used)
Wythfed, a. eighth
Wythgant, a. eight hundred
Wythnos, n. a week
Wythnosi, v. to form a week
Wythnosol, a. weekly
Wythochor, n. an octagon
Wythol, a. belonging to eight
Wythor, a. of eight borders
Wythran, a. of eight shares

| WY | 306 | YM |

Wytnryw, a. of eight kinds

Y

Y, the (preceding consonants)
, Yb, n. a state of being over, up, or out
Ybain, v. to make a howling
Ych, n. an ox: v. you are
Ychwaith, conj. neither, not so
Ychwaneg, a. more: adv. more
Ychwanegiad, n. an augmenting
Ychwanegol, a. augmentative
Ychwanegu, v. to augment
Ychwarddu, v. to cause laughter
Ychwerig, a. playful
Ychydig, n. a little, a few: a. little: adv. little
Ychydigyn, n. a very little
Yd, n. what is; being; corn: adv. it; that; doth; that it
Ydbys, n. vetches, chit-peas
Yden, n. a grain of corn
Ydfaes, n. a corn-field
Ydfran, n. a rook, a crow
Ydfwyd, n. corn food
Ydgeirch, n. wild oats
Ydgist, n. a corn bin
Ygordd, n. a corn yard
Ydi, v. it is, he is, she is, is it, is he, is she
Ydig, n. cockle
Ydlan, n. a corn-yard
Ydoedd, n. was
Ydog, a. abounding with corn
Ydwal, n. a corn garner
Ydwyf, v. am, I am, am I
Ydych, v. you are; are you
Ydym, Yin, v. we are, are we
Ydynt, v. they are; are they
Ydys, n. the calendar
Ydyw, v. is, it is, he is, she is
Ydd, a. the
Yf, n. a liquid, moisture
Yfadwy, a. drinkable
Yfed, n. a drinking; a tippling: v. to drink; to tipple [sottish
Yfedgar, a. given to tippling,
Yfgar, a. fond of drinking [ing
Yfiad, n. a drinking; an imbib-
Yfol, a. drinking; imbibing
Yfory, n. and adv. to morrow
Yff, n. tendency out or from
Yfflaw, to break; to shiver
Yfflon, shatters, shivers, pieces
Yg, n. an open or void state
Yng, n. what is close upon; a bare touch; a slight hint
Yngan, v. to intimate
Ynghyd, adv. in contact, together
Ynghylch, adv. about, round
Yl, n. what pervades or moves
Yleni, n. and adv. this year
Yll, n. what tends to part
Ylliad, n. a ripping, a dividing
Yllt, n. a rip, a rent, a parting
Yllynedd, n. and adv. last year
Yllyr, n. a mole, a wart
Ym, pref. reflects the action expressed by the word to which it is prefixed, on the actor; as LLOSGI, to burn; YMLOSGI to burn one's self; CYFIAWN-AD, justification; YMGYF-IAWNAD, self-justification. It also denotes reciprocity of action; as CYDIO, to take hold of; YMGYDIO, to take hold of each other. For the meaning of terms with this prefix, not inserted here, see the words from which they are formed: pron. my, me
Yma, adv. here, in this place
Ymachub, v. to save one's self
Ymadael, v. to forsake
Ymadferth, n. self-exertion
Ymadnabod, n. self-knowledge
Ymadnewyddu, v. to renovate one's self
Ymado, v. to forsake, to quit
Ymadrodd, n. discourse
Ymaddroddi, v. to speak, to talk
Ymadroddwr, n. a speaker

Ymafael, Ymaflyd, n. a wrestle, a struggle
Ymagori, v. to open one's self
Ymaith, adv. hence, away
Ymalw, v. to call mutually
Ymannog, n. mutual excitement, self-excitement
Ymannos, adv. night before last
Ymarbed, n. a mutual refraining; a saving one's self
Ymardderchafu, v. to uplift one's self
Ymarfer, n. practice, exercise
Ymarferiad, n. a practising
Ymarferu, v. to practise
Ymarllwys, n. self emptying
Ymaröi, v. to bear with
Ymaröus, a. long suffering
Ymarwedd, n. behaviour
Ymateb, n. a mutual answer
Ymattreg, n. a mutual pause
Ymattal, n. self-restraint
Ymbalfalu, v. to be groping
Ymballu, v. to fall into error
Ymbarotoad, n. self preparation
Ymbellâu, v. to render one's self distant
Ymbesgi, v. to fatten one's self
Ymbil, v. to implore, to crave
Ymbincio, v. to trim one's self
Ymbleidio, v. to confederate
Ymboeni, v. to pain one's self
Ymburo, v. to purify one's self
Ymbwyll, n. consideration
Ymbwys, n. a self-pressure
Ymbwyth, n. competition
Ymchwel, n. return, reverse
Ymchweliad, n. a returning
Ymchwelyd, v. to return [self
Ymchwyddo, v. to swell one's
Ymdaclu, v. to trim one's self
Ymdaenu, v. to self-expand
Ymdaeru, v. to dispute together
Ymdaith, n. journey a voyage: v. to journey, to travel
Ymdaru, v. to spread one's self
Ymdaro, v. to strike mutually; to shift for one's self
Ymdwr, n. anxious care

Ymdecâu, v. to make one's self fair or fine
Ymdeimlo, v. feel one's self
Ymdeithiad, n. a travelling
Ymderfysgu, v. to raise a tumult together [the sun
Ymdeeu, v. to bask one's self in
Ymdoddi, v. to become dissolved
Ymdrafodi, v. to bestir one's self; to strive together [self
Ymdrafferthu, v. to busy one's
Ymdrech, n. mutual struggle
Ymdreiglo, v. to roll one's self
Ymdrin, n. a mutual striving
Ymdrochi, v. to bathe one's self
Ymdröi, v. to be delaying
Ymdrabaeddu, v. to wallow, to welter [ment
Ymdryhyllwch, n. self-enjoyment
Ymdueddu, v. to self incline
Ymdwymno, v. to warm one's self [to contend together
Ymdynu, v. to pull mutually;
Ymddadwreiddio, v. to be eradicated; to self eradicate
Ymddangos, v. to appear
Ymddangosiad, n. an appearance [ment
Ymddarostwng, n. self-debasement
Ymddeffroad, n. a self-waking
Ymddial, v. to revenge, to be revenged
Ymddialydd, n. an avenger
Ymddibynu, v. to hang by or upon, to depend
Ymddianc, n. self-escape [self
Ymddidoli, v. to separate one's
Ymddienyddu, v. to make away with one's self
Ymddifad, a. forlorn, orphan
Ymddiflanu, v. to cause one's self to vanish [self of fatigue
Ymddiflino, v. to divest one's
Ymddifregru, v. to divest one's self to frailty
Ymddifwyno, v. to divest one's self of enjoyment
Ymddifyriad, n. self-diversion

Ymddiffyn, n. self-defence; v. to defend one's self [one's self
Ymddiffyniad, n. a defending
Ymddigoni, v. to self-suffice
Ymddihatru, v. to divest one's self of covering
Ymddihoeni, v. to divest one's self of vivacity
Ymddiloni, v. to divest one's self of cheerfulness [with drink
Ymddiodi, v. to supply one's self
Ymddiofalu, v. to divest one's self of care
Ymddiogeliad, n. a self-securing
Ymddiogi, v. to become lazy
Ymddiriad, n. confidence
Ymddiried, v. to confide
Ymddiserchu, v. to divest one's self of affection
Ymddwyn, n. deportment; gestation, bearing; v. to comport; to bear [one's self
Ymddychrynu, v. to frighten
Ymddychwelyd, v. to turn one's self back [one's self
Ymddyeithro, v. to estrange
Ymddyfalu, v. to imagine in one's self
Ymddygiad, n. behaviour
Ymddyrwyn, n. self-winding
Ymddyrysu, v. to self-entangle
Ymedliw, n. mutual reproach
Ymegluro, v. to self-manifest
Ymegniad, n. self-exertion
Ymegnïo, v. to exert one's self
Ymelio, v. to shave one's self
Ymelwa, v. to employ one's self in trafficking
Ymenydd, n. the brain
Ymenyn, n. butter
Ymeppilio, v. to self-produce
Ymerbyn, v. to be in opposition
Ymerlid, v. to be pursuing
Ymesmwytho, v. to make one's self easy
Ymestyn, v. to stretch one's self
Ymethol, n. self-election
Ymewino, to fasten one's nails

Ymfalchïo, v. to pride one's self
Ymfawrâu, v. to magnify one's self
Ymflino, v. to tire one's self
Ymfoddâu, Ymfoddio, v. to please or content one's self
Ymfoddloni, v. to acquiesce
Ymfrasâu, v. to fatten one's self
Ymfudwr, n. an emigrant
Ymfwynâu, v. to enjoy one's self
Ymfywâu, v. to enliven one's self
Ymffrost, n. a self-vaunting
Ymgadarnâu, v. to strengthen one's self
Ymgadw, v. to refrain, to forbear
Ymgais, n. an effort, an attempt
Ymgaledu, v. to harden one's self [self
Ymgasglu, v. to collect one's
Ymgâu, v. shut one's self
Ymgeisio, v. to make effort
Ymgeledd, n. succour, solace
Ymgeleddiad, n. a succouring
Ymgeleddu, v. to succour; to cultivate [ually
Ymgenfigeu, v. to envy mut-
Ymglodfori, v. to exalt one's self in fame
Ymglymu, v. to bind one's self
Ymglywed, v. to feel one's self
Ymgnöi, v. to keep knawing
Ymgodi, v. to raise one's self
Ymgofleidio v. to embrace mut-
Ymgomio, v. to converse [ually
Ymgrafu, v. to scratch one's self
Ymgredu, v. to b lieve mutually to pledge mutually
Ymgrino, v. to roll one's self
Ymgreuloni, v. to fill one's self with cruelty [to beware
Ymgroesi, v. to cross one's self:
Ymgrogi, v. to hang one's self
mgryfâu, v. to fortify one' self
Ymgrymiad, n. self-prostration
Ymgrymu, v. to prostrate one's Yself
Ymgusanu, v. to kiss one another mutually

Ymguddio, v. to hide one's self
Yingydio v. to lay hold mutually
Ymgyfamnodi, v. to join one's self in mutual covenant
Ymgyfarfod, v. to come together
Ymgyfartalu, v. to make one's self equal; to vie
Ymgyfarwyddo, v. to acquaint one's self [ship
Ymgyfeillach, n. mutual friend-
Ymgyfiawnâu, v. to justfy one s self [self
Ymgsfiawni, v. to complete one's
Ymgyflogi, v. to hire one's self
Ymgyflwyno, v. to consociate one's self
Yingyfodi, v. to raise one's self
Ymgyfranogi, v. to render one's self participating
Ymgyfreithio, v. to litigate mutually; to go to law
Ymgynghori, v. to consult one's self; to consult mutually
Ymgymdeithasu, v. to associate one's self
Ymgymedroli, v. to moderate one's self
Ymgymhell, v. to urge one's self; to urge mutually
Ymgymhwyso, v. to render one's self proper
Ymgymysgu, v. to mix one's self
Ymgyndynu, v. to act with mutual stubbornness
Ymgynddeiriogi, v. to madden one's self
Ymgynhenu, v. to employ one's self in wrangling
Ymgynhesu, v. to make one's self warm; to warm mutually
Ymgynhyrfu, v. to disturb one's self; to disturb mutually
Ymgynal, n. self-support
Ymgynefino, v. to accustom one's self
Ymgynulliad, n. a self-collecting, mutual self-collecting
Ymgynig, v. to offer one's self

Ymgyrchu, v. to approach mutually; to assault each other
Ymgyrhaedd, v. to reach one's self [self equal
Ymgystadlu, v. to make one's
Ymgysgodi, v. to shelter one's self; to shelter each other
Ymgysylltu, v. to conjoin one's self; to connect mutually
Ymgysuro, v. to comfort one's self; to comfort each other
Ymgyweirio, v. to put one's self in order
Ymgywilyddio, v. to shame one's self; to shame each other
Ymhaeru, v. to assert one's self
Ymhagru, v. to deform one's self
Ymhalogi, v. to defile one's self
Ymharddu, v. to adorn one's self
Ymheddychu, v. to pacify one's self to pacify each other
Ymhel, v. to be meddling
Ymhelaethu, v. to amplify one's self
Ymhell, adv. at a distance, far
Ymheneiddio, v. to make one's self seem old [tyrant
Ymherawdr, n. an emperor, a
Ymhercyd, v. to apprehend
Ymherodraeth, n. an empire
Ymherodres, n. an empress
Ymhlith, adv. amongst, amidst
Ymhoewi, v. to enliven one's
Ymhoffi, v. to take delight [self
Ymholi, v. to be questioning
Ymhoni, v. to assert one's self
Ymhwedd, n. great craving [self
Ymhyfrydu, v. to delight one's
Ymiachâu, v. to heal one's self
Ymladd, n. combat, battle: v. to fight, to combat
Ymladdiad, n. a fighting
Ymlaesu, v. to be drooping
Ymlanâu, v. to clean one's self
Ymlawenâu, v. to gladden one's self
Ymlechu, v. to secrete one's self
Ymledu, v. to expand one's self

| YM | 310 | YM |

Ymleiáu, v. to lessen one's self
Yulenwi, v. to fill one's self
Ymlid, n. a pursuit, a chase
Ymlidiad, n. a pursuing
Ymliosogi, v. to increase, to become multiplied
Ymlithro, v. to slip
Ymliw, n. reproach
Ymloni, v. to cheer one's self
Ymlonyddu, v. to appease one's self
Ymlosgi, v. to burn one's self
Ymlumo, v. to form one's self
Ymlusgo, v. to drag one's self
Ymlwybran, v. to be creeping
Ymlwytho, v. to burden one's self
Ymlygru, v. to corrupt one's self
Ymlyn, n. cohesion, adherence
Ymlyniad, n. an adherence
Ymlynu, v. to adhere together
Ymlysiad, n. a self-discarding
Ymlychu, v. to gorge one's self
Ymnabod, v. to be acquainted
Ymnacâu, v. to refuse one's self
Ymneillduad, n. self-recession
Ymnerchu, v. to strengthen one's self
Ymnesâu, v. to approach; to draw one's self near ` [self
Ymnoethi, v. to denude one's
Ymnofio, v. to swim of one's self
Ymochelyd, v. to beware
Ymofidio, v. to afflict one's self
Ymofyn, v. to be inquiring
Ymofyniad, n. an inquiring
Ymogeliad, n. an avoiding
Ymogelyd, v. beware, to avoid
Ymogoneddu, v. to glorify one's self
Ymogwyddo, v. to be inclined
Ymolchi, v. to wash one's self
Ymollwng, v. to drop one's self
Ymoralw, v. to inquire
Ymorchestu, v. to emulate [self
Ymorfoleddu, v. to exult in one's
Ymorfod, n. self conquest
Ymostwng, n. self-debasement

Ympryd, n. a fast, a fasting
Ymrafael, contention, variance
Ymrafaeliad, n. a contending
Ymrafaelio, v. to contend
Ymraint, prep. at the point of
Ymran, n. a schism, a sect
Ymranu, v. to part one's self
Ymresymu, v. to converse
Ymrithio, v. to shew one's self
Ymroddi, v. to resign one's self
Ymrolian, v. to roll one's self
Ymron, adv. nearly, almost
Ymrugio, v. to trail one's self
Ymrwygo, v. to tear one's self
Ymrwymo, v. to bind one's self
Ymryson, n. contention, dispute: v. to contend, to dispute
Ymrysonwr, n. a contender
Ymsathru, v. to tread mutually
Ymsefydlu, v. to fix one's self
Ymserchu, v. to be doating
Ymsoddi, v. to sink one's self
Ymsymud, n. self-motion
Ymunioni, v. to self-straighten
Ymwahanu, v. to seperate one's self; to be divided [self
Ymwallgofi, v. to distract one's
Ymwared, v. to deliver one's self; to avert mutually [self
Ymwarthu, v. to disgrace one's
Ymwasgaru, v. to be self-scattering; to become scattered
Ymwasgu, v. to press one's self; to press together [self even
Ymwastadâu, v. to make one's
Ymweliad, n. a visitation
Ymwellâu, v. to better one's self
Ymwerthu, v. to sell one's self
Ymwchio, v. to push one's self; to push mutually
Ymwychu, v. to adorn one's self
Ymyfed, n. a tippling
Ymyl, n. side, edge, brink
Ymylu, v. to edge, to rim
Ymyraeth, n. intermeddling
Ymyru, v. to intermeddle
Ymysgar, n. the bowels [self
Ymysgario. v. to separate one's

Ymysgwyd, v. to shake one's self
Yn, n. state of being in : prep. in, at, into ; for
Yna, adv. there, in that place ; then ; there now, lo !
Ynad, n. a judge, a justice
Ynadaeth, n. the office of a judge
Ynfer, n. an influx
Ynfyd, n. what is mad or silly : a. furious, mad ; foolish
Ynfydrwydd, n. foolishness
Ynfydu, v. to rave ; to be mad
Ynnill, n. advantage, gain : v. to gain, to win
Ynnilliad, n. a gaining
Yno, adv there, then
Ynt, v. are, they are
Yntau, pron. him also, he too
Ynte, adv. otherwise then
Ynyd, n. incipience ; shrovetide
Ynys, n. an island, an isle
Yr, n. what is opposite or off : a. the (before vowels)
Ys, n. ardency ; a consuming : v. is, hath a being, exists. Er ys dyddiau, a good while
Ysbagiad, n. a clawing
Ysbagu, v. to claw, to clutch
Ysbryd, n. a spirit, a ghost
Ysbrydiaeth, n. spirituality
Ysbrydol, a. spiritual, ghostly
Ysbrydoldeb, n. spiritualness
Ysbrydoli, v. to spiritualise
Ysbrydoliaeth, n. inspiration
Ysbyty, n. an hospital
Ysdillio, v. to plait, to fold
Ysdori, n. history, story
Ysdoriad, n. a telling a story
Ysdorïo, v. to tell a story
Ysdwriad, n. a threatening
Ysdwrio, v. to chide ; to threat
Ysdyferiad, n. distillation
Ysdyferu, v. to distil, to drop
Ysdyfnig, a. obstinate, stubborn
Ysdyfnigrwydd, n. stubbornness
Ysenyd, n. a space, a while
Ysfa, n. a consumed spot ; an itching ; a sheep walk

Ysgadan, n. herrings
Ysgadenyn, n. a herring
Ysgaen, n. a sprinkling
Ysgaeniad. n. a sprinkling
Ysgaenu, v. to sprinkle
Ysgafael, n. capture, prey
Ysgafn, n. light body ; stack
Ysgafnder, n. lightness
Ysgafnâd, n. a lightening
Ysgafnâu, v. to lighten
Ysgafniad, n. a making light
Ysgafnu, v. to make light
Ysgaffell, n. ledge, rim, brow
Ysgaffellu, v. to form a ledge
Ysgaid, n. a sprinkling
Ysgainc, n. a branch ; a skain
Ysgall, n. the thistle
Ysgallog, a. full of thistles
Ysgar, n. a share ; a divorce : v. to part, to cast off. Llythyr ysgar, a bill of divorce
Ysgarant, n. an adversary
Ysgaredig, a. separated, parted
Ysgaredigaeth, n. separation
Ysgariad, n. a separating
Ysgarlaeth, n. separation
Ysgario, v. to separate, to divorce
Ysgarlad, n. scarlet
Ysgarm, n. an outcry
Ysgarmes, n. a shouting
Ysgarth, n. an offscouring
Ysgarthiad, n. excretion
Ysgarthu, v. to purge out
Ysgatfydd, adv. perhaps, perad-
Ysgaw, n. elder wood [venture
Ysgawen, n. an elder tree
Ysgawn, n. light body : a. light
Ysgecriad, n. a bickering
Ysgecru, v. to bicker, to brawl
Ysgeler, a. atrocious
Ysgelerdra, n. atrociousness
Ysgentyn, n, a caperer, a buffoon
Ysgerbwd, n. skeleton, a carcass
Ysgeth, n. a spear, a lance
Ysgethriad, n. an iterating
Ysgethrg, v. to iterate, to repent
Ysgi, n. a cutting off ; a parer ; a hat

Ysgien, n. a slicer; a cymetar; turner's lathe; tall woman
Ysgil, n. a recess, a nook
Ysgiliad, n. a setting behind
Ysgilio, v. to set behind
Ysgin, n. a skin robe, a pellsse
Ysgip, n. a quick snatch
Ysgipiad, n. a snatching off
Ysgipio, v. to snatch away
Ysgipiol, a. snatching
Ysgiw, n. a screen, a settle; a third cousin
Ysgiwiad, n. a sheltering
Ysgiwio, n. to screen, to shelter
Ysgawring, Ysgrawling, n. glue, cement
Ysglawringo, v, to glue
Ysglem, n. a slice, a sliver
Ysglemio, v. to slice, to sliver
Ysglen, n. a sex, a kind
Ysglenol, a. sexual
Ysglent, n. a slide; a drift
Ysglyn, n. a knob, a knot
Ysglino, v. to form a knob
Ysglöen, n. a damsel, a maid
Ysglofen, n. a slip, a spray
Ysglyf, n. what seeks for prey
Ysglyfaeth, n. depredation; prey, spoil
Ysglyfaethiad, n. a depredating
Ysglyfaethu, v. to depredate, to
Ysglyfiad, n. a depredator [spoil
Ysglyfio, v. to depredate, to prey
Ysglymu, v. to form a knot [on
Ysgoad, n. a starting aside
Ysgoegyn, n. a coxcomb
Ysgog, n. motion, stir
Ysgogi, v. to wag, to stir [ing-
Ysgogiad, n. a wagging, a stirr
Ysgogyn, n. to flutterer
Ysgol, n. a school: n. a peak; a ladder: a. vehement, active
Ysgoläig, n. a scholar
Ysgoleigdod, n. scholarship
Ysgoleigiaeth, n. a schooling
Ysgoleigio, v. to school
Ysgolfaer, n. a proctor
Ysgoliad, n. a schooling

Ysgolp, n. a spar
Ysgor, n. a rampart, a bulwark
Ysgorfa, n. a place of defence
Ysgori, v. to encircle, to hem
Ysgoriad, n. an entrenching
Ysgornio, v. to scorn, slight
Ysgoth. n. a purge, a voidance
Ysgothfa, n. privy-house
Ysgrad, n. what is rigid or stiff
Ysgraell, Ysgraen, n. the sea-swallow
Ysgraf, n. what scrapes off
Ysgrafell, n. a scraper; a rasp; a currycomb
Ysgrafellu, v. to rasp, to scrape
Ysgrefiad, n. a scraping
Ysgrafu, v. to scrape, to grate
Ysgraf. n. a ferry boat, a ferry
Ysgraffiniad, n. a scarifying
Ysgraffinio, v. to scarify
Ysgrain, n. what is crawling
Ysgrawen, n. a hard crust
Ysgrech, n. a scream
Ysgrechiad, n. a shrieking
Ysgrechian, v. to keep screaming
Ysgrechio, to scream, to shriek
Ysgrechog, n. a jay
Ysgrepan, n. a wallet, a scrip
Ysgri, n. a shriek, a scream
Ysgrif, n. a notch; a writing
Ysgrifen, n. a piece of writing
Ysgrifeniad, n. a writing
Ysgrifenu, v. to write, to pen
Ysgrifenydd, n. a scribe, a writer
Ysgrifiad, n. a writing
Ysgrifo, v. to notch; to write
Ysgrifwas, n. a clerk
Ysgrogell, n. a draw-bridge
Ysgrubliad, Ysgrubl, n. a beast, a brute
Ysgrud, n. a frame; a skeleton
Ysgrwd, n. a carcase
Ysgrwth, n. a heap, a bulk
Ysgryd, n. a shiver, a shake
Ysgrydiad, n. a shivering
Ysgrythyr, n. the scripture
Ysgrythyrol, a. scriptural
Ysgub, n. a sheaf; a besom

Ysgubell, n. a whisk; a besom; a broom
Ysgubiad, n. a sweeping
Ysgubion, n. sweepings
Ysgubo, v. to whisk; to sweep
Ysgubor, n. a barn
Ysguborio, v. to put in a barn
Ysguth, n. a scud; a whisk
Ysguthan, n. a ringdove, a wood-pigeon
Ysguthell, n. a scudder
Ysguthiad, n. a scudding
Ysgw, n. guard, care; refuge
Ysgwad, n. a guarding
Ysgwaeth, n. guardianship [pity
Ysgwaetheroedd, adv. more the
Ysgwd, n. a push; a jet; a stile
Ysgwdiad, n. a pushing on
Ysgwfl, n. grapple, snatch
Ysgwthr, n. a cut out; a lop
Ysgwyd, n. a shake, a flutter: v. to shake, to flutter: n. a shield; a target
Ysgwydfa, n. a shake; a toss
Ysgwydo, v. to use a shield
Ysgwydwas, n. a shield bearer
Ysgwydd, n. a shoulder
Ysgwyddiad, n. a shouldering
Ysgwyddo, v. to shoulder
Ysgwyf, n. a sprinkle; a scum
Ysgydwad, n. an agitation
Ysgyfar, n. an ear
Ysgyfarn, n. an ear of a beast
Ysgyfarnog, n. a hare
Ysgfeinio, v. to form lungs
Ysgyfeiniog, a. pulmonary
Ysgyniad, n. an ascending
Ysgyrion, n. staves, splinters
Ysgyrioni, v. to shiver, to stave
Ysgyrnwg, n. a snarl, a grin
Ysgythriad, a lopping; a carving
Ysgythru, v. to lop; to carve
Ysiad, n. consuming
Ysiant, n. consumption
Ysig, a. fretting; corroding
Ysigdod, n. a contusion
Ysigo, v. to fret; to inflame
Ysigiad, n. a bruising

Yslac, a. distinct, loose, slack
Yslacâd, n. a slackening
Yslacio, v. to slacken
Yslaif, n. a slash
Yslapiad, n. a slapping
Yslath, n. a rod, a perch
Ysled, n. a drag, a dray
Ysledfen, n. a drag cart
Yslepan, n. a trap, a gin
Yslipan, n. glibness; burnish
Yslipaniad, n. a burnishing
Yslapanu, v. to burnish
Ysmala, a. fickle; humorous
Ysmeityn, n. a space, a while
Ysmicio, v. to blink; to ogle
Ysmot, n. a patch, a spot
Ysmwcan, n. a puff of fog
Ysmwl, n. a squab: a. squabby
Ysnid, n. a snout; a snipe
Ysniten, n. a drop at the nose
Ysnoden, n. a fillet, a lace, a band.
Ysnoden y mor, sea weeds
Ysnodeniad, n. a filleting
Ysnodenig, n. a bandlet
Ysnodenu, v. to fillet
Ysoldeb, n. a consuming state
Yspaddiad, n. an exhausting
Yspaddu, v. to exhaust
Yspaid, n. cessation; space
Yspail, n. a spoil, a prey
Yspaith, n. prospect, scene
Yspar, n. a spear, a lance
Yspardun, n. a spur
Yspardunad, n. a spurring
Ysparduno, v. to spur
Ysparth, n. separation
Ysparthiad, n. a separating
Yspeidiad, n. an intermission
Yspeiliad, n. spoliation
Yspeilio, v. to spoil
Yspeithell, n. a spectacle
Yspelwi, n. to gall, to fret
Yspennydd, n. overwhelming
Yspicell, n. a dart, a bolt
Yspicella, v. to throw a dart
Yspicelliad n. throwing of darts
Yspig, n. a spike; a spine
Yspigo, v. to spike, to prick

Yspigod, n. a spinkle; a spiggot
Yspigoglys, n. spinage
Yspil, n. a dribblet, a mite
Yspincyn, n. a finch
Yspin-glairch, n. a bridegroom
Yspinog, n. the quinsy
Ysplan, a. bright, splendid
Ysplenydd, n. splendour
Ysponc, n. a jerk; a smack
Ysponciad, n. a smacking
Ysponcio, v. to smack; to jet
Ysporion, n. refuse of fodder
Ysporthen, n, a basket, a pan-
Ysporthi, v. to support [nier
Ysporthiant, n. sustenance
Yspwng, n. light tuft; sponge
Yspwysiad, n. impression
Yspydd, n. a jut or run out
Yspyddad, n. hawthron
Yssig, a. shattered, bruised
Yssigod, n. contusion [ing
Yssigiad, n. a crushing, a bruis-
Yssigo, v. to bruise, to shatter, to crush; to quell
Ystac, n. a heap, a stack
Yspaciad, n. a stacking
Ystacio, v. to pile, to heap
Ystad, n. a state, a condition
Ystadaeth, n. statistics
Ystaen, n. stain; tin: a. stained
Ystaeniad, n. a staining; a tinning
Ystafell, n. a chamber, a room
Ystafellog, a. having a room
Ystafellu, v. to form a room
Ystafellydd, n. a chamberlain
Ystafellyddes, n. a chambermaid
Ystagiad, n. a suffocation
Ystagu, v. to suffocate, to choke
Ystang, n. a perch in measure
Ystalm, n. a good while
Ystalu, v. to form a stock
Ystalwyn, n. a stallion
Ystanc, n. a holdfast, a bracket, a wooden book. Ystanc ceffyl, a horse-block
Ystanciad, n. a bracketing
Ystancio, to stanch; to bracket

Ystarn, n. a packsaddle, a saddle
Ystarnwr, n. a saddler
Ystefaig, n. the palate
Ysteinio, v. to cause a spread
Ystel, n. what stretches out
Ystelc, n. a lurk; a loiter
Ystelciad, n. lurking; a loitering
Ystelcian, v. to lurk; to loiter
Ystelff, n. a blockhead
Ystelffu, v. to render rigid
Ysteliad, n. a straining out
Ystem, n. a base, a stem
Yster, n. what is ardent
Ysteraig, a. ardent
Ysterciad, n. a jerking out
Ystercian, v. to be jerking
Ystercio, v. to jerk out
Ysterlewyn, n. radiation
Ystern, n. what is ardent: a. of ardent tendency
Ysteru, v. to render ardent
Ystid, n. what forms a wreath
Ystido, v. to form a wreath
Ystig a. strenuous, perserving
Ystigo, v. to act strenuously
Ystle, n. a fight, a retreat
Ystlen, n. a sex, a kind
Ystlenol, a. sexual, kindred
Ystlom, n. excrement, ordure
Ystlomi, v. to void ordure
Ystlum, n. a bat, a bird
Ystlwn, n. connection, a kind
Ystlwyd, a. of a hoary hue
Ystlwyn, n. a luxuriant grove
Yslyned, n. society; kindred
Ystlyniad, n. a forming society
Ystlyniol, a. being associated
Ystlynu, v. to associate
Ystlys, n. a side, a flank
Ystlysgam, a. being lop-sided
Ystlysol, a. lateral, sided
Ystlysu, v. to go to one side
Ystod, n. a course; a layer; a swathe
Ystodi, v. to dispose a course range, layer, or swathe
Ystodiad, n. a laying of a course
Ystofen, n. a warping tray

Ys:ofi, v. to range; to warp	Ystrodur, n. the frame work of a saddle, a packsaddle
Ystoflad, n. ranging, a warping	
Ystol, n. a stool	Ystrodwm, n. a round-about
Ystola, n. scarf, a stole	Ystrwy, n. what passes through
Ystolciad, n. a butting	Ystrwyad, n. a forming a passage
Ystolcian, v. to keep butting	Ystrwyo, v. to pass through
Ystor, n. a bulk; a store, a stock; a quantity	Ystrwytho, v. to saturate
	Ystrych, n. what forms a scope
Ystoraeth, n. store, plenty [house	Ystrychu, v. to form a scope
Ystordy, n. a storehouse a ware-	Ystryd, n. a way, a street
Ystordyn, n. trigger, in bowling; a mark to jump from	Ystrym, n. a main stream or current; a channel
Ystori v. to cover with resin	Ystryw, n. a subtlety, a finesse, a stratagem, a trick
Ystorio, v. to store up	
Ystorm, n. a tempest, a storm	Ystrywgar, a. crafty, wily
Ystormus, a. tempestuous	Ystrywiad, n. a using of craft
Ystrad, n. a flat, a vale, a dale	Ystrywio, v. to use craft
Ystraff, n. what strews about	Ystrywiol, a. plotting, devising
Ystraffu, v. to strew, to waste	Ystum, n. a bend, a curve; shape fashion, gait
Ystraig, n. a buckle, a clasp	
Ystraigl, n. a turn, a detour	Ystumgar, shapely, well-formed
Ystrall, n. what is trailed; a mat	Ystumiad, n. a shaping
Ystrain, n. tribe, a crew, a breed	Ystumio, v. to form, to fashion, to bend, to turn
Ystram, n. a frame	
Ystranc, n. a trick, a while	Ystumiol, a. pliable, sinuous
Ystranciad, n. a playing of tricks	Ystun, n. what is irritating
Ystrancio v. to play tricks	Ystunad, n. an irritating [gate
Ystrancus, a. apt to play trcks	Ystuno, v. to irritate; to insti-
Ystrawu, to educate; to mature	Ystwc, n. a bucket: a shock
Ystre, n. a course, a range	Ystwff, n. a lift
Ystred, n. a village, a hamlet	Ystwffwl, n. a stock, a holdfast, a staple, the knocker of a door
Ys:ref, n. what forms a dwelling	
Ystreigio, v. to turn, to roll	Ystwng, n. a putting down
Ystreillach, n. trundling	Ystwmp, n. a stump
Ystreillio, v. to trundle [pear	Ystwr, n. a stir, a noise
Ystrem, n. what is made to ap-	Ystwrio, v. to bustle, to stir
Ystremio, v. to make to seem	Ystwy, n. a stop, a check
Ystremp, n. a dash, a stroke; a trick; a charm [witching	Ystwyad, n. a checking
	Ystwyll, n. Epiphany
Ystrempiad, n. a dashing; a be-	Ystwyo, v. to check, to restrain
Ystrempio, v. to dash; to bewitch	Ystwyr, n. what stretches out
Ystres, n. a wreath, a chain	Ystwyrain, v. to be stretching
Ystresu, v. to wreath, to chain	Ystwyriad, n. a stretching
Ystrew, n. a sneeze; a snort	Ystwyth, a. flexible, pliant
Ystrewi, to sternutate, to sneeze	Ystwythder, n. flexbility
Ystrewiad, n. a sneezing	Ystwythiad, n. a making pliant
Ystrewlwch, n. snuff	Ystwytho, v. to make flexible
Ystrewlys, n. sneeze-wort	Ystyciad, n. a bucketful

Ystycyll, n. a signal
Ystyffernach, n. utensils
Ystyffyllu, v. to stock, to log
Ystyr, n. sense, meaning
Ystyrgar, a. considerate, contemplative, meditative
Ystyriaeth, n. consideration
Ystyriaethu, v. to use consideration or reflection
Ystyried, v. to consider to reflect
Ystyrio, v. to consider, to regard
Ystyriol, a. considerate
Ystyrioldeb, n. considerateness
Ystyrmant, n. a jews-harp
Ystyw, n. a settlement
Ystywaws, n. a pair of stays
Ystywanu, v. to belabour
Ystywell, a. steady, manageable
Ystywellu, v. to make steady
Ysu, v. to hanker, to itch, to eat to corrode; to consume
Yswadan, n. a stroke, a flap
Yswail, n. what ejects
Yswellydd, n. one who casts out; a brawler
Yswain, n. an esquire, page; armour bearer
Yswatiad, n. a squatting
Yswatio, v. to squat

Yswbwb, n. a hubbub
Yswbwbio, v. to rumble
Ysweiliad, n. a brawling
Ysweilyd, n. a brawler
Ysweiniad, n. esquire, page
Yswid, n. what turns quickly
Yswidw, n. the titmouse
Yswil, a. bashful, timid
Yswilder, n. bashfulness
Yswiliad n. an abashing
Yswilio, v. to be abashed
Yswitiad, n. a chirping
Yswitian, v. to chirp, to make a small noise
Yswitio, v. to chirp, to twitter
Yswr, n. a consumer
Yswydden, n. a privet tree
Yswymbren, n. a quiver
Yswyr, n. what dawns; the east
Yswyth, n. what pervades
Yswythbysg, n. the torpedo
Yswytho, v. to pervade
Ysyn, n. a fire
Ysywaeth, adv. more the pity
Yth, n. what stretches out: pron. thee, thy
Yw, v. is, it is: n. what exists; a yew tree
Ywen, n. a yew tree

HUGHES AND SON, PRINTERS, WREXHAM.

www.ingramcontent.com/pod-product-compliance
Lightning Source LLC
Chambersburg PA
CBHW030016240426
43672CB00007B/977